Antisemitism Worl

GW01085565

THE INSTITUTE OF JEWISH AFFAIRS AND THE AMERICAN JEWISH COMMITTEE

ISBN: 0 901113 24 7
ISSN: 1350-0996

Institute of Jewish Affairs
79 Wimpole Street
London W1M 7DD
United Kingdom
Tel: 0171-935 8266 Fax: 0171-935 3252

The Institute of Jewish Affairs, established in 1941, informs policy, decision-making and action on contemporary issues of concern to Jews world-wide, by conducting and disseminating research, promoting public debate and developing new thinking.

The American Jewish Committee
The Jacob Blaustein Building
165 East 56 Street
New York, NY 10022-2746
USA
Tel: 212-751 4000 Fax: 212-751 4017

Founded in 1906, the American Jewish Committee seeks to protect the rights of Jews throughout the world; combats antisemitism and bigotry; works for the security of Israel; enhances human rights, democratic pluralism and intergroup understanding; and promotes the creative vitality of the Jewish people.

The Institute of Jewish Affairs works in an international partnership with the American Jewish Committee to enhance co-operation in research, analysis and policy-planning on issues of concern to world Jewry.

Printed by Woolnough Bookbinding Ltd.
Irthlingborough, Northamptonshire, United Kingdom

Contents

Preface

This *Report* documents antisemitism throughout the world in the year 1994. The absence of an entry on a country does not imply that antisemitism does not exist in that country. Equally, the fact that some entries are longer than others does not necessarily mean that antisemitism poses more of a problem in those countries where it is given lengthier treatment. The length of entries reflects to some extent the amount of data that were available. It is emphasized that the *Antisemitism World Report 1995* is a report on *current* antisemitism: it is not intended as a survey of the general situation of the Jewish communities of the world. Population figures, both general and Jewish, are approximations.

GENERAL EDITORS

Antony Lerman, Juliet J. Pope, Julia Schöpflin, Howard Spier

EDITORIAL CONSULTANT

David Singer

REGIONAL EDITORS

Juliet J. Pope, Julia Schöpflin, Howard Spier

RESEARCH AND EDITORIAL TEAM

Margaret Brearley, Matthew Dodd, Suzanne Gee, Nan Greifer, Bea Lewkowicz, Krystyna Sieradzka, Lena Stanley-Clamp

TECHNICAL TEAM

Michèle Brett, Jeremy Levine, Marta Magram, Jon Sacker, Pat Schotten, Catriona Sinclair, Perri Sullivan

ACKNOWLEDGEMENTS

The following individuals, organizations, institutes and publications assisted, or were consulted, in the preparation of this *Report*:

Irving Abella; Manuel Abramowicz; Joseph Alpher; Menashe Amir; Amnesty International; Anti-Defamation League, New York; Antirasistisk Senter, Oslo; Lydia Aroyo; Sydney Assor; Alicia Backal; Sonia Baevsky; Amatzia Baram; Alberto Benasuly; Ofra Bengio; Werner Bergmann; Richard Berman; Jacques Blum; Eva Bøggild; Judit Bokser-Liwerant; Peter Brod; Robert J. Brym; Michael Burleigh; Canadian Jewish Congress; Center for Democratic Renewal, Atlanta; Central Board of Jewish Communities in Greece; Centre de Recherche et de Documentation sur l'Antisémitisme, Paris; Centre de Recherche d'Information et de Documentation Antiraciste, Paris; Centre Européen Juif d'Information, Brussels; Centrum Informatie en Documentatie over Israël, the Hague; Jerome A. Chanes; Mikhail Chlenov; Lea Cohen; Commission for Racial Equality, London; Community Security Organization, Board of Deputies of British Jews; *Country Reports on Human Rights Practices for 1994*, US State Department (1995); Esther Csurka; Dokumentationsarchiv des österreichischen Widerstandes, Vienna; Jaap van Donselaar; Norma Drimmer; Amanita Dufva; *East European Jewish Affairs*; Roger Eatwell; Simon Epstein; Rainer Erb; Bernie Farber; Cathy Feldman; Leonid Finberg; Fondazione Centro di Documentazione Ebraica Contemporanea, Milan; Stephen Fruitman; Gerry Gable; Adam Garfinkle; Konstanty Gebert; Stephanie Genkin; Kristoffer Gjøtterud; Adriana Goldstaub; Gennady Gramberg; Roger Griffin; Miroslav Grinvald; Jorge A. Grünberg; Nelly Hansson; David Harris; Hadassa Hirschfeld; Institut für Demoskopie Allensbach; Inter-Parliamentary Council against Antisemitism, London; Mark Israel; Israel Government Monitoring Forum on Antisemitism; Yeshayahu Jelinek; David Kamenetzky; *Keesing's Record of World Events*; Isabel Kershner; Caroline Kerslake; Josef Klánský;

Ignacio Klich; András Kovács; Jacob Kovadloff; Stanislaw Krajewski; Martin Kramer; Ognjen Kraus; Tomáš Kraus; Douglas Krikler; Landelijk Buro Racismebestrijding, Utrecht; Ernó Lazarovits; Michael Leifer; Ronit Lentin; Katharine A. Lerman; Jeffrey Lesser; Robert M. Levine; Bea Lewkowicz; Maritza Lowinger; Ligue des droits de la personne de B'nai B'rith Canada/League of Human Rights of B'nai B'rith Canada; Bruce Maddy-Weitzmann; Victor Malka; Katie Marx; Bent Melchior; *Middle East Terrorism: Selected Group Profiles*, Yonah Alexander (1994); Richard Mitten; Monitoring des Activités Racistes et Antisémites, Brussels; David Morris; Simon Morris; Cas Mudde; Ronny Naftaniel; Nederlands-Israelitisch Kerkgenootschap; *Patterns of Prejudice*; Daniel Perdurant; Sheldon Pine; *Political Extremism and the Threat to Democracy in Europe: A Survey and Assessment of Parties, Movements and Groups*, Institute of Jewish Affairs (1994); Marcelo Pollack; The Project for the Study of Antisemitism and the Roeters Van-Lennep Database, Tel Aviv University; Harold Pupkewitz; Rachael Reeves; Relaciones Humanas B'nai B'rith Colombia; Vera Rich; José Rodríguez; Eli M. Rosenbaum; Stephen J. Roth; Ernie Salomon; Sammy Saltiel; Philip Sampson; Neal Sandberg; Robert Satloff; Savez Jevrejskih Opština Jugoslavije, Belgrade; Dieter Schonebohm; Mark Schreiber; Kirsten Schulze; *Searchlight*; Leonardo Senkman; Michael Shafir; Milton Shain; Lindsay Shanson; Peter Sherwood; Dina Sigal; Diana Silberman; Aca Singer; Henry I. Sobel; Paul Spoonley; Tim Stanley-Clamp; Swedish Committee against Antisemitism; Y. Takigawa; Suzan Nana Tarablus; Deborah Trenner; The Vidal Sassoon International Center for the Study of Anti-semitism, Hebrew University of Jerusalem; Leon Volovici; Harold M. Waller; Mike Whine; *The World in 1995*, *The Economist* (1994); Rivka Yadlin; Zentralrat der Juden in Deutschland; Židovska općina Zagreb; Oliver Zimmer; Eyal Zisser; David Zwartz.

The Institute of Jewish Affairs gratefully acknowledges the help of Jewish communal organizations and representative bodies throughout the world who reviewed entries concerning their communities; staff of the American Jewish Committee, in particular Andrew Baker, Renae Cohen, Richard Foltin, Jennifer Golub and Kenneth Stern; and many individuals who wish to remain anonymous.

Introduction

The Balance Sheet for 1994

THE MAIN POINTS

- Militant Islamic antisemitism is growing threat to Jewish security
- Neo-fascists came to power in Italy
- Serious attacks on Jews and Jewish property in Argentina, Germany, Russia, United Kingdom
- Fascism expands in cyberspace
- More countries passed laws against race-hate
- New methods to counter race-hate employed by some police authorities
- Hate on the Internet: activists fight back
- International bodies plan new initiatives to combat racism and antisemitism
- Europe:
  Pro-Islamic Welfare Party in Turkey hostile to Jews
  Antisemitic parties in coalition governments in Slovakia and Romania
  Continued instability raises fears of fascism in Russia
- North America:
  Both Canada and the USA reported rise in antisemitic incidents, but no worsening of antisemitism overall
  Nation of Islam still inciting antisemitism among African-Americans
- Middle East and North Africa:
  Antisemitism from Islamic and Islamist sources intensified
- Latin America:
  Bombing of Jewish community building in Buenos Aires resulted in heavy loss of life
- Asia:
  Response to *Schindler's List* showed potential anti-Jewish hostility

The basis of understanding trends in antisemitism throughout the world is first to examine closely the developments in each country. Only then can comparisons be drawn, and regional and global trends discerned, where there are any. Antisemitism remains stubbornly country-specific. As in past years, trends and conclusions are drawn out in the following Introduction, which is based on the data in the rest of the volume.

The yearly *Antisemitism World Report* appears for the first time as a joint publication of the Institute of Jewish Affairs and the American Jewish Committee (AJC). The AJC is well-known and highly respected for its objective and scholarly approach to the problem of contemporary antisemitism, which makes it an ideal partner in producing an authoritative survey of this kind.

GENERAL BACKGROUND

The developments reported in this volume were being played out against the background of a world economy which remains depressed, despite a degree of recovery in some of the major economies, and there is still no sense of an imminent return to prosperity in those countries which have been led to expect ever-rising standards of living. The evidence of general election results in 1994 suggests a continuing sense of dissatisfaction with mainstream partics and leaders—expressed most notably in the US mid-term elections—yet no particular readiness to regard the alternatives as that much better. The continuing crisis in the Balkans emphasized the seeming powerlessness of the international community to deal with problems of security in the post-Cold War world. Extreme nationalists must derive some degree of comfort from the way in which the will of the United Nations, NATO, the Organization on Security and Co-operation in Europe and other international bodies has been flouted. And the failure to provide any long-term solution to the problem of minorities in the region cannot inspire vulnerable minorities elsewhere with much confidence.

In general, countries which are experiencing social, political and economic dislocation, and where there is most disillusion with the political mainstream, are also the countries in which racist parties and organizations are most prominent and have made the most progress in the last year.

Belgium's deteriorating economic conditions, its financial and political scandals, and lack of understanding of the constitutional reforms have provided far-right parties with circumstances they could exploit to their advantage. In Slovakia, the confused economic and political situation made it possible for an ultra-nationalist, antisemitic party to become part of the coalition government. In Italy, the former neo-Fascist party became part of a coalition government which came to power in the wake of the scandals over political corruption involving almost all of the main parties. The Austrian election demonstrated considerable dissatisfaction with the ruling parties and the door was opened even wider to Jörg Haider's Austrian Freedom Party (FPÖ). Political and economic uncertainties in Algeria and Turkey provided a boost to Islamist parties which espouse antisemitism.

Other countries where general conditions had a direct impact on the problem of antisemitism, but which appear relatively unchanged since last year, are Russia and Romania.

RACISM AND XENOPHOBIA

With a few exceptions, there appears to be little diminution reported in the levels of racism, xenophobia, intolerance and bigotry in most of the countries covered in this year's *Report*. These attitudes are expressed most markedly in the form of opposition to perceived or imagined immigration, and to refugees and asylum-seekers, and racial attacks and harassment directed at minorities. Last year we reported on the introduction of measures to curb the numbers of foreigners entering countries in Europe and elsewhere. This year, it is clear that such measures bore fruit as asylum-seeker figures fell and more illegal immigrants were deported.

A survey of key countries makes depressing reading. In France the National Consultative Commission on Human Rights, which reports yearly, said of 1994 that racism is becoming part of everyday life in the country. Ethnic intolerance has spread throughout Italy. In the United Kingdom, police authorities estimate that there has been a 25 per cent increase in racist crimes over 1993. In Norway surveys show people, especially youth, becoming more hostile to ethnic minorities. Accurate statistics are not available in the Netherlands, but most observers agree that the number of racist incidents rose, and a new monitoring body is being set up to measure this effectively. In Belgium evidence suggests that manifestations of racism are increasing. The Hungarian minority in Romania, as well as resident foreigners in general, are targeted for abuse, and the government forcibly deported some refugees. Xenophobia, anti-ethnic expression and nationalism grew markedly in Bulgaria, mostly directed against Roma, blacks and Asians. Incitement against Roma, refugees and asylum-seekers has become a serious problem in the Czech Republic. In Switzerland, the xenophobic climate is worsening. Asian- and Arab-Australians and newer Latin American immigrants to Australia are facing increased hostility. In Uruguay, there is evidence of considerable underlying xenophobia.

In Germany and Austria, the "foreigner" issue was much less to the fore than in 1993. In Germany, this is attributed to the effect of the change in the asylum regulations which produced a 60 per cent drop in asylum-seeker applications. (Asylum regulations were also tightened in Belgium, the Netherlands, Spain, Switzerland and the UK.) In Austria it may partly be because of the special prominence of the issue in 1993 with Haider's anti-"foreigner" petition initiative and the fact that he pursued a more centrist right-wing campaign during the elections.

The tightening of immigration and asylum regulations, and public disquiet about both, was apparent not only in Europe, although most European Union (EU) governments have encouraged a more restrictive approach. Immigration was a policy concern in: Canada, where fewer immigrants will be allowed in (though refugee quotas have been increased); the USA, where there is growing concern about immigration; France, where deportations of illegal immigrants have been stepped up; Greece, where many Albanians were deported; and Argentina, where measures to counter illegal immigrants have been strengthened.

The Roma emerge as the most reviled group where relevant opinion polls were conducted, and in terms of discrimination. They face serious problems especially in Poland, Slovakia, Bulgaria, the Czech Republic and Romania.

Islamist movements in Jordan, Egypt and Algeria also turn their attention to foreign nationals and Christians.

The growing government sensitivity to immigration throughout the world is not automatically of benefit to the far right. In many cases, government action to limit immigration and asylum-seeker applications is designed partly to neutralize far-right propaganda on the issue. This is sometimes successful—as it was in Germany, where the parties which had made most capital out of the problem fared very badly in the general election—but can sometimes backfire—as it did in Austria where Haider's party increased its share of the vote despite the government's introduction of new regulations.

In the USA, the questioning of many of the programmes introduced to overcome racial inequality and discrimination and an awareness of the growing multicultural complexity of the population has produced a deepening sense of uncertainty as to the way forward for race relations in the country.

PARTIES, ORGANIZATIONS, MOVEMENTS

There has been little change in the salience of neo-fascist or neo-Nazi type groups. They remain marginal although capable of acts of terror or vandalism which earn them a prominence in the media which is out of all proportion to the threat they represent to their societies. Austria is a good example where public awareness of groups expressing racist aims remained high because of the trials of the suspected neo-Nazis and the media coverage given to two letter-bombing campaigns.

In Australia, a number of antisemitic organizations increased their public profile and level of activity; in Greece, there has been a growth in far-right activity with ultra-nationalist opinions expressed more openly; in Hungary, some of the minor extremist groups expressed antisemitism more openly; in Norway, media coverage of small neo-Nazi groupings appeared to lead to an increase in the numbers of such groupings; in Russia, there remained at least eighty ultra-nationalist parties and groups, most of them antisemitic.

Among those extremist groups and parties which have chosen to pursue their aims through the ballot box, the trend towards adopting more respectable profiles, avoiding open antisemitic statements, and distancing themselves from the extra-parliamentary groups has intensified. This intensification has created strains in some groups where members strongly object to abandoning ideological obeisance to pre-war fascist and Nazi traditions. Consequently, some groups have split with one part moving more into the main-stream and the other publicly maintaining its nostalgic approach. The Argentine MODIN party has distanced itself from anything that appears anti-Jewish in order to participate as a seemingly respectable force in the electoral process and is now the fourth largest party na-tionally. In Germany, the Republicans appeared to be adopting a more electorally respect-able stance, but lack of success in the last year led to the adoption of an election campaign which was clearly more overtly antisemitic than in previous years, when their propaganda was generally directed against "foreigners" and asylum-seekers. But this was to no avail and the party performed very badly. In Italy, the merging of the neo-Fascist Italian Social Move-ment (MSI) into the National Alliance, in order to create a "respectable" right-wing party, led militants to re-form the MSI as a party true to neo-Fascist ideals.

There is considerable evidence that whilst the leaderships of the electorally respectable far-right groups avoid open expressions of antisemitism, levels of antisemitic sentiment among their supporters and members is higher than in the population as a whole, and that protestations that their parties are not antisemitic have little basis in reality. The mask often slips, as with the Centre Democrats in the Netherlands where a councillor was heard mak-ing jokes about the gassing of 6 million Jews, and in France where Jean-Marie Le Pen ap-pointed Bruno Gollnisch, a man who has shown sympathy for Holocaust denial, to the vice-presidency of the party. There is also a level of innuendo—comments about journalists and politicians who happen to be Jewish—which sends an appropriate message to those to whom the leadership wishes to prove its credentials on Jews.

The Vlaams Blok in Belgium is an exception to the rule in that it has achieved consider-able electoral success without divesting itself of very much of its neo-Nazi baggage. In 1994, it had eighteen parliamentary representatives, and elements within the party openly express admiration for the Nazi regime and Holocaust denial.

The distinction between electorally respectable and openly neo-fascist groups and par-ties in Eastern Europe is less evident. In two countries—Romania and Slovakia—openly antisemitic parties are formally part of the coalition governments. The Slovak National Party used antisemitic slogans in its electioneering, something that was prevalent in Eastern Europe in the first years after the collapse of communism but has been largely absent in the last two years.

Figuring more prominently in this *Report*, but presaged in earlier volumes, are Islamist organizations for which antisemitism plays a significant role. From the mainly student-based Hizb al-Tahrir in the UK (which has propagated Holocaust denial in its meetings), Al-Qibla, a militant group associated with the Pan-African Congress which espouses ex-treme anti-Zionism and often antisemitism, to the Armed Islamic Group in Algeria which wants to rid the country of "Jews and Christians", the Muslim Brotherhood in Egypt whose opposition to normalization with Israel is imbued with antisemitic arguments, and Islamist groups in Jordan and Lebanon which believe in an international Jewish conspiracy to discredit Islam. The militant Islamic party creating most concern, however, is Refah in Turkey which has forty seats in the 450-seat parliament. After playing down its anti-Jewish approach early in the year, in a pre-election manifesto it referred to Jewish control of Wall Street and the world economy. Some fear that Refah has the potential to destabilize the entire Turkish state.

Perhaps the most significant development on the extra-parliamentary scene is the for-mation of militias in the USA. This was made crystal clear by the bombing of the Oklahoma federal building in April 1995 in which more than 160 people died. The militias grew rap-idly in 1994 and some were organized by people with documented links to white-supremacist and antisemitic groups. They cite the second amendment right to bear arms, and the tenth amendment which refers to the reserving of powers not delegated to the federal government "to the States . . . or to the people". They oppose the federal government which, they claim, is attacking the rights of ordinary Americans. They are heavily armed.

MAINSTREAM POLITICS

There were very few overt expressions of antisemitism in mainstream political life. Italy appears to have had more than most. In one example, the president of the cultural commission of the Italian chamber of deputies, Vittorio Sgarbi of Forza Italia, speaking at a conference, referred to the "Jewishness of the judge Colombo", a member of the panel of judges of the "clean hands" investigation, rooting out corruption in public life. In another, the campaign against Jaime Lerner's bid for governor of the state of Parana in Brazil had antisemitic elements. (Nevertheless, he was elected by a sizeable majority.) But in most countries the taboo on such expressions remains intact, if somewhat weakened.

In Eastern Europe and the former Soviet Union there is still less reluctance to make antisemitic remarks in public life, although the evidence suggests that the situation has markedly improved in the last two years as leaders have become more sensitized to the counter-productive nature of such statements. Vladimir Zhirinovsky, leader of the inappropriately named Liberal Democratic Party in Russia, made repeated anti-Jewish remarks. (Recent opinion polls show that Zhirinovsky has lost some support to the extremist Russian National Unity Party, which is led by the more virulently antisemitic Aleksandr Barkashev.) In a television interview, the former minister of information, Mikhail Poltranin, implied that there were too many Jews in the Russian media. His party, Russia's Choice, apologized on his behalf and said that his words had been taken out of context.

Antisemitism can come dangerously close to mainstream politicians in various ways and did so in 1994. In Australia, it emerged that the leader of the Liberal Party, Alexander Downer, had addressed the antisemitic Australian League of Rights in 1987 and that other mainstream politicians had spoken to far-right groups. In Canada, the Reform Party, the third largest in parliament, was plagued by revelations of neo-Nazis in its ranks, much to the public annoyance of Reform Party leaders who pledged to locate and expel such people. In France, revelations concerning President Mitterrand's role during the Vichy period, his links with René Bousquet, the former secretary-general of the Vichy police, and his claim that he was unaware of any anti-Jewish legislation—and that in any case it had been directed at "foreign Jews"—created some disquiet. In Germany, antisemitism surfaced in public life as part of a public row involving prominent members of the Party of Democratic Socialism.

MANIFESTATIONS

These include violence, cemetery desecrations, arson, graffiti, verbal abuse, harassment and the dissemination of antisemitic literature. The definitions of what constitutes an antisemitic manifestation and of the categories in which manifestations should be placed are not the same in all countries which monitor the number of incidents, so it is practically impossible to make inter-country comparisons of any value. Even figures for individual countries need careful scrutiny.

The following countries reported increases in antisemitic manifestations: Australia, Canada, France, Germany, Italy, the Netherlands and the USA. All these countries, apart from the Netherlands and Italy, reported increases in 1993; Germany and Italy reported increases in 1992. The United Kingdom total of 327 incidents was one less than in 1993. The following reported decreases in 1994: Poland, Mexico and Sweden. Sweden reported increases in 1992 and 1993. (In no other countries are there statistics available to make year-on-year comparisons.)

The most serious attack on a Jewish community in 1994 was the bombing of the AMIA building in Buenos Aires in which almost 100 people were killed. The identity of the perpetrators and their precise motives remain unknown, but the prevailing view is that the incident was related to Middle East developments and probably the work of militant Islamists or agents employed by them (see **Effects of Anti-Zionism**.)

The degree to which trends can be identified and broad conclusions can be drawn from the statistics and lists of incidents in the *Report* is uncertain. The apparently clear upward trend in some countries cannot be ignored, but the circumstances prevailing in each country must be taken into account. The rise in Germany from 656 to 935, an increase of over 40 per cent, is certainly high. Most of the increase, however, is accounted for by the growth in antisemitic propaganda material sent to Germany from countries where its production is not illegal. In addition, there is now a greater awareness of antisemitic propaganda and slander offences among the public who report them more often, and the police have devised more efficient ways of categorizing these incidents. In the United Kingdom, incidents of extreme violence (defined as a potentially life-threatening attack), 1.8 per cent of the total, were recorded for the first time since 1991. Two of these incidents were the car bombs in London, against the Israeli embassy and the offices of the Joint Israel Appeal.

Data on manifestations in Eastern Europe and the former Soviet Union have improved but there is still no systematic monitoring or compiling of statistics in any of these countries. The impression given by the data in this *Report* is that more incidents may now be occurring in Russia and Ukraine. The incidents that attract most attention are cemetery desecrations. These have occurred in Belarus, Georgia, Lithuania, Moldova, Russia (in, for example, Smolensk, St Petersburg, Krasnoyarsk, Novosibirsk, Kazan, Klintsi, Nizhny Novgorod) and Ukraine. But whether these constitute the greater part of the total of all incidents is impossible to say.

In France, both the National Consultative Commission on Human Rights and the Jewish community reported an increase in the number of antisemitic acts committed by Muslim or Arab circles, although the absolute numbers (8 in 1994 and 4 in 1993, out of 19 and 20 respectively) are small.

CULTURAL LIFE

Steven Spielberg's film *Schindler's List* has been used very effectively in many countries to educate people about the Holocaust and the ultimate consequences of bigotry and race hatred. But some countries proved unwilling to allow it to be screened, at least without some cuts. In Egypt, it was banned on grounds that it would offend public morality. In Indonesia censors wanted "sexually explicit" scenes cut. At the same time, Muslim organizations called on the government to ban the film because it was "too sympathetic to Jews". The director refused to allow the film to be censored and it was withdrawn. In Iran, the media responded to international acclaim for the film by saying "Zionism exploits the Holocaust for propaganda in different areas including the cinema." The official daily *Keyhan* referred to "the movie-making power of international Zionism, Auschwitz and the Holocaust". In Jordan, public screenings were banned on grounds of pornography. In Lebanon, the distributors withdrew the film after pre-release ads were banned. Malaysia, which has adopted strong anti-Zionist and antisemitic stands in the past, at first banned the film alleging it was propaganda for Israel and Jews. Prime Minister Mahathir rejected charges of antisemitism by insisting that he was opposed to "the conquest of Arab territories by Zionists". The intervention of Deputy Prime Minister Anwar Ibrahim reportedly led to a cabinet decision to release the film with cuts in "sexually explicit" scenes. Spielberg subsequently withdrew all his films from Malaysia. Controversy over the film in the Philippines was triggered by allegedly pornographic scenes but also revealed some antisemitic responses. Spielberg refused to release it there with the cuts proposed.

PUBLICATIONS AND MEDIA

One of the most striking facts about current antisemitism is the wide variety of media now being used by antisemites. Last year's *Report* drew attention to "electronic fascism", in particular the use of international computer networks to disseminate antisemitic material. Whilst it remains hard to assess just how widespread is the use of electronic means for racist purposes, the evidence of this year's *Report* clearly indicates that antisemitic individuals and organizations are making increasing use of all the new communication technologies. In the USA, an estimated fifty hate groups use on-line services and the Internet. Racist and antisemitic articles are readily available on the Internet, which is also used to publish lists of contacts. Bomb-making manuals have been transmitted by computer links. Internet libel can only be prosecuted on an individual basis, not by network, making it notoriously difficult because individuals can cover their tracks. Large quantities of neo-Nazi and Holocaust-denial literature have been uploaded onto the Internet; 1,500 of Germany's far-right extremists are estimated to be active on the Thule network, and the Norwegian far right was also connected to it during the year. Austrian school authorities are increasingly concerned about the circulation of computer games with Nazi and racist themes. Gary Lauck of the neo-Nazi NSDAP/AO continued to distribute *Endsieg* on computer disk and through modems to Austria, France, Germany and the Netherlands.

Besides computers, radio and public-access and cable television channels provided opportunities for neo-Nazis and antisemites to broadcast nationally and internationally. Uncensored talk-radio may provide a platform for unchallenged antisemitic remarks. Dozens of hate phone-lines purveying racist and antisemitic messages exist.

There is a vast range of antisemitic publications currently available although easier to obtain in some countries than they are in others. Consumers are spoilt for choice in Russia, where it was reported that 157 extremist publications were being published last year (a continually fluctuating figure). One of the most notorious, *Al-Quds*, which specialized in publishing material alleging a Zionist/Jewish conspiracy against Russia and the Palestinians and regularly contained lurid anti-Jewish cartoons, was closed down by the authorities in Moscow late in 1994. Another, *Zavtra*, successor to the blatantly antisemitic *Den*, was also being investigated for possible closure at the year's end.

Most antisemitic periodicals have small circulations and make no impact outside the circles of devotees who receive them. Among these publications there were few significant changes in 1994. In Argentina, the circulation of such periodicals decreased significantly in recent years. In Austria, the Styrian provincial government advertises in rightist magazines which are forums for antisemitism. The far-right press is still very active in Germany, and indicative of the increasingly ideological nature of far-right extremism are the ancient antisemitic stereotypes which have been revitalized. Among these are that Jews have rapacious sexual appetites and that they would abuse Christian children to satisfy their desires; Jews do not practise safe sex and deliberately spread the AIDS virus.

In Hungary, some antisemitic periodicals have ceased publication. Istvan Csurka's *Magyar Forum* remained the most important far-right periodical. In it he attacks Jews— financier George Soros and others. An increasing number of articles on links between the world of finance and Jews, using *The Protocols of the Elders of Zion* as an interpretative model, appeared in Italy. Though not specifically antisemitic, they play on negative stereotypes. On the left, *La lente di Marx* contained a fifty-page article on Zionist racism: Jews are bearers of a specific Jewish racism which marks their history.

In Romania, the main antisemitic publications remain those from 1990 onwards but some appeared to encounter difficulties with publication and distribution. Two additional periodicals recently appeared: one, *Invierea,* is wholly dedicated to praising the wartime fascist movement, the Iron Guard. Many of the smaller right-wing periodicals have ceased to appear in Slovakia. In South Africa, the Herstigte Nasionale Party paper *Die Afrikaner,* featured numerous antisemitic articles and Holocaust-denial material. CEDADE in Spain was one of the main producers of antisemitic publications in Europe. The far-right organization no longer exists under that name, but the publishing houses still operate and print Nazi books, some of which are exported to Latin America. In Barcelona, CEDADE published the Austrian monthly neo-Nazi magazine *Halt!* to circumvent Austrian laws. *Eidgenoss,* Switzerland's most notorious far-right, antisemitic, Holocaust-denying publication, ceased because of provisions in the new anti-racist law.

Of greater significance is where expressions of antisemitism appear in the mainstream media or are more accessible to wider and more impressionable audiences. Such occurrences are relatively rare. These can be in the form of columns by widely-read journalists in mass-circulation newspapers or readers' letters to local papers; book reviews or the appearance of antisemites on television talk shows. (This raises the question of the role of editors and producers.) In Australia, some local radio stations and press allowed the expression of antisemitic views, and references were made to the "powerful Australian Jewish lobby". Complaints were treated less than sympathetically by editors. In Austria, the most subtle expressions of antisemitism were most likely to be found in the *Neue Kronen Zeitung,* which has a readership of 1 million, especially from the pen of the columnist Richard Nimmerichter, who demonized the then minister of education, Rudolf Scholten, by alluding to his putative Jewish origins and criticized pension payments to Austrian victims of the Holocaust living in Israel.

The daily *Yomihuri Shimbun* (which has a readership of 10 million) in Japan, published an advert promoting four books that portray modern history as a series of Jewish plots to dominate the world. After protests from the Israel embassy, the Committee against Antisemitism in Japan and the AJC, the paper apologized. In the Netherlands, the satirical newspaper columnist and film-maker Theo van Gogh provoked controversy over alleged antisemitic remarks in a book review about relations between Jews and non-Jews. Claims were made on Romanian television that Jewish treatment of the Romanian armed forces was a cause of Ceaucescu's antisemitism. Anti-Jewish writings appeared in the Slovak printed media, in particular the semi-governmental *Republika* and *Zmena,* and on radio and television charging Jews with, *inter alia,* having incited the foreign press to accuse Slovaks of antisemitism. In the USA, Tony Martin, a member of African-American studies department at the élite Wellesley College, continued to promote his book *The Jewish Onslaught: Despatches from the Wellesley Battlefront,* which purportedly recounts his experiences at Wellesley since he began using the Nation of Islam's antisemitic book, *The Secret Relationship between Blacks and Jews.* The range of periodicals has not changed greatly. Antisemitic and white-supremacist groups produce radio and television programmes that are regularly broadcast. Nation of Islam leader Louis Farrakhan twice appeared as a guest on television programmes in February and stated that the media was controlled by Jews who were conspiring to destroy him.

In the Middle East and North Africa, antisemitic books and periodicals are less restrained and in most cases have official sanction. In Egypt, the portrayal of antisemitic images had receded somewhat in the wake of the Israeli-Palestinian Declaration of

Principles, but took on exaggerated dimensions in government and opposition press, and occurred in response to specific incidents like the killing of twenty-nine Muslims by a Jewish settler at a Hebron mosque. In the Gulf states, English-language programmes broadcast on state-controlled television in Saudi Arabia frequently invoked religious rhetoric to promote antisemitism. Antisemitic articles arguing that Jews undermined the revolution, and offended Islam, were published in various journals in Iran. The Iranian daily paper *Jomhuri-e Eslami* serialized an abridged version of *The Protocols*. In the Iraqi media, the USA's stand against the lifting of the embargo on Iraq was attributed to "manipulation by world Zionism and the American Jewish lobby". This notion was also vividly expressed in caricatures. In Jordan, antisemitic works in Arabic were sold by book vendors in Amman, Aqaba, Zarqa and other towns. Antisemitic themes were more common in privately-owned weekly tabloids. Antisemitic cartoons portraying Jews as ugly, hook-nosed and money-grabbing appeared regularly in the Lebanese press. In Morocco, the daily newspaper of the opposition Istiqlal Party carried a vehemently antisemitic article invoking *The Protocols*, and alleging that "Jewish evil knows no limits." In Syria, antisemitic caricatures continue to appear in the media: Jews are portrayed as deformed and as having aggressive mentalities. The Islamist media are flourishing in Turkey since the liberalization of media control, and antisemitic articles appear. Three Islamic television channels have followed suit.

Traditional antisemitic texts like *The Protocols of the Elders of Zion* and *Mein Kampf* remain widely available in Eastern Europe and the former Soviet Union, and the Middle East. Efforts to suppress *The Protocols* have only been partially successful. Numerous other publications inspired by *The Protocols* are in circulation.

RELIGION

The decline in open expressions of Christian antisemitism noted in 1993 continued. A notable exception was the publication of a popular Roman Catholic *Bible des Communautés chrétiennes*, containing notorious anti-Jewish stereotypes and reiterating the charge of deicide. Sixty thousand copies were sold in France and Belgium and 18 million copies distributed in Latin America and elsewhere. Following Jewish and Vatican protests, unsold copies are now being withdrawn.

Other problems emanating from Catholic sources include Holocaust-denial publications now in circulation in Germany among the far right produced by the publishers Pro Fide Catholica. The political crisis in Italy has led to a growth in pre-Vatican II catholicism and opposition to the historic opening to the Jews. This is expressed in publications but also in sermons. The newsletter of a small, ultra-conservative foundation in the Netherlands, Maintain Roman Catholic Life, claimed in its first issue that the greatest danger came from "Jewish freemasonry". The author referred to *The Protocols of the Elders of Zion* as leaked notes of a secret "Jewish conspiracy". In Slovakia, Catholic church spokesmen frequently praised the wartime pro-Nazi Slovak state and described its leader, Tiso, as a martyr.

Metropolitan Ioann of St Petersburg and Ladoga wrote prolifically for the Russian far-right and antisemitic press. The Russian Orthodox church formally dissociated itself from him.

The annual Women's World Day of Prayer, marked in March in most countries throughout the world, used a liturgy devoted entirely to the suffering of Palestinian women that was blatantly anti-Zionist and anti-Jewish in language and symbols. Despite protests from Jewish and Christian leaders, the liturgy was modified in only a handful of countries.

The emotive fiftieth anniversary of the Warsaw ghetto uprising evoked some hostility in church circles in Poland, but in general strengthened Christian-Jewish relations there. The Evangelical Movement for Wales distributed a leaflet using the film *Schindler's List* to urge belief in Jesus and describing Jews in the film as "selfish and aggressive".

There was concern over the stance of fundamentalist and evangelical churches in a number of countries. In Germany, the ecumenical movement has been denounced as a "plot by Jews and freemasons". Some Christian fundamentalists in New Zealand express antisemitic views, referring, for example, to "Jewish international bankers who believe that they are God's Israel but reject Christ". These ideas circulate in small communities but the preachers hold well-attended mass rallies. In the United States, the religious right gives cause for concern because of its emphasis on America as an essentially Christian nation. Explicit antisemitic statements are absent but there is a fear that oft-invoked terms like secular humanism, the media and liberals are code-words for Jews. Suspicions die hard in face of past statements by the Reverend Pat Robertson (who leads the Christian Coalition) and others. There is also concern at the links that exist between some members of the movement and known racists, antisemites and Holocaust-deniers.

Antisemitism emanating from Islamist sources and Muslim clerics was more in evidence in 1994 than in 1993. Sermons delivered in mosques in Iran, Morocco, Turkey and Pakistan made use of antisemitic imagery. The activities of the mostly student group Hizb al-Tahrir in the UK proved very worrying on some British campuses where they held meetings in which extreme anti-Jewish rhetoric was used and Holocaust denial propagated. Groups supporting Hamas (see **Effects of Anti-Zionism**) operate in a number of countries, and London serves a centre for a number of Islamist clerics, exiled from their home countries, who espouse antisemitism.

Neo-Nazi propaganda sometimes masquerades as Christian. In April, antisemitic pamphlets purporting to come from a local church were sent to hundreds of homes in North London.

The continuing controversy surrounding Professor Jan Bergman of the theological faculty at Sweden's Uppsala University, who was a witness for Ahmed Rami's defence in his 1989 trial (Rami broadcast Holocaust-denial and other antisemitic material on a radio station called Radio Islam, which ceased operating in 1992), revealed how deeply rooted are anti-Jewish attitudes in some theological circles.

HOLOCAUST DENIAL

Denial of the facts of the Holocaust plays a role in practically every organization or periodical which is either overtly or covertly antisemitic. Indeed Holocaust denial is used to mask antisemitism: its propagators claim that they are merely in the business of "historical revisionism". In fact, the link between Holocaust denial and antisemitism is usually very clear since most deniers are also active in neo-Nazi or far-right organizations and their public statements invariably reveal that hostility to Jews lies at the root of their "questioning" of the Holocaust.

There were a number of significant developments in 1994. First, in France, where it has always been thought that Holocaust denial had edged closer to the intellectual and political mainstream than anywhere else apart from Germany, there was a considerable decrease in public expressions of denial. The main reasons for this are the prominence given to the anniversary of the 1944 liberation; a fading of interest in the subject among the public; and financial difficulties facing those involved in dissemination. An additional reason is likely to be the effect of the 1990 Gayssot law which outlawed Holocaust denial. This has greatly restricted the freedom of deniers to publish and disseminate their material.

Second, a number of new books and pamphlets were published which aim to throw the facts of the Holocaust into doubt, but one text—"The Rudolf Expertise", as it has come to be known—in particular seemed to have come to prominence in denial circles. The author, Germar Rudolf, wrote the 120-page document, drawing on another recent denial text which had achieved considerable notoriety, *The Leuchter Report*, to support the defence of the Holocaust-denier Otto Ernst Remer, who is in Spain awaiting extradition to Germany. The report concludes that the gassings at Auschwitz could not have taken place. The appetite of deniers for new texts which find slightly different ways of repeating what has been said in previous texts appears insatiable. But a new document, which has the patina of a scientific report and is written by someone from a reputable research institute, might just have the chance of achieving a degree of respectability which older, infamous and discredited texts cannot do.

Third, laws against Holocaust denial in European countries appear to be having some effect, although as a result, deniers tend to try to find other means of spreading their views rather than cease their activities altogether. However, Ernst Zundel in Canada, against whom legal means were employed to end his Holocaust-denial activities, has turned Canada into a major centre for denial material. Using books, newsletters, videotapes, cable and public access television, and the Internet, his material has appeared in fifteen languages in forty countries. In the USA, the Institute for Historical Review based in California remains in the vanguard of denial activity. Its *Journal for Historical Review* is one of the main vehicles for disseminating denial material and in 1994 control of it was wrested from its founder, Willis Carto of the Liberty Lobby, by the editors who wanted to sanitize its image. In response, Carto founded his own journal.

Finally, data from new AJC-sponsored surveys in the US, Germany, Australia and Poland make it clear that Holocaust denial has had very little impact on mainstream opinion and remains essentially the preserve of hardened antisemites.

OPINION POLLS

Results of opinion polls concerning attitudes to Jews were released in 1994 in: the Czech Republic, Germany, Greece, Italy, Poland, Romania, Spain and the USA. One of the polls in Germany and one in the US, and the only poll in Poland, were conducted by the AJC which also carried out surveys of knowledge and remembrance of the Holocaust in Australia, Germany and Poland.

While the direction of the data is far from uniform, an overall pattern does emerge: hostility to Jews has remained fairly steady in recent years, or has declined; in some countries the level of antisemitism gives cause for concern, but in comparison with attitudes to other groups in the countries concerned, Jews experience less prejudice. In the Czech Republic, 19.1 per cent of respondents said they would not want a Jew as a neighbour and 31.9 per cent said they did not want a Jew as a son- or daughter-in-law, but Gypsies, Vietnamese, Russians, refugees from former Yugoslavia, Germans and Czechs repatriated from Ukraine or Kazakhstan all fared much worse. In Poland the percentages of those who did not want a Jew as a neighbour, who believed Jews behaved in a manner to provoke hostility and who thought Jews had too much influence improved by 10, 6 and 10 per cent respectively over the 1991 figures. In Spain, by contrast, a survey appeared to show increasing levels of racism among young Spaniards. Thirteen per cent said they would expel Jews from Spain (in 1986, 10 per cent). Although the change was not large, Professor Calvo Buezas, who conducted the study, considered it significant since it showed that Jews continued "to play a negative role in the collective imagination."

A major analysis of 140 scholarly studies and twenty-four national opinion polls since 1948 in the USA, sponsored by the AJC and undertaken by Tom W. Smith of the University of Chicago's National Opinion Research Center, concluded that antisemitic attitudes had decreased appreciably, and that the traditional correlates of the decline in antisemitism—higher education and wealth and lower age—continue to hold. But the study warns that antisemitic prejudices survive, albeit expressed in revamped forms.

With regard to the Holocaust, Germans were strongly knowledgeable about the facts, but were not keen on Holocaust remembrance. Poles were somewhat less knowledgeable than Germans but far keener on Holocaust remembrance. In Australia, 75 per cent had a broad understanding of what the Holocaust was.

EFFECTS OF ANTI-ZIONISM

The antisemitic effects of anti-Zionism remain generally muted as a result of developments in the Middle East peace process and the collapse of communism. However, they have become more apparent through the activities of groups opposed to the peace moves.

The starkest example of this phenomenon is probably the bombing of the AMIA building in Buenos Aires—probably, because neither the perpetrators nor their motives are known for certain. Most experts tend to assume that the terrorist act was the work of Islamic extremists attempting to undermine the Middle East peace process, perhaps carried out by agents resident in Argentina, or sub-contracted to some Argentine-based group.

Whoever was responsible, the bombing had a negative effect on the Argentine Jewish community's sense of security, and on the sense of security of other Jewish communities in the region. It raised the spectre of a possible new dynamic of anti-Jewish violence in Argentina and may have given encouragement to local antisemitic groups.

Another significant example of the effect of anti-Zionism was the response to the Hebron massacre. Those opposed to Israel and the peace process naturally made public their feelings about the incident, but in some countries that response manifested itself in antisemitic incidents—in Belgium, Denmark, France, the Netherlands, Turkey and the United Kingdom.

Antisemitism is often conflated with anti-Zionism among militant Islamic groups, Palestinian rejectionists and radical regimes opposed to the peace process. Anti-Zionist sentiment in 1994 focused on rejection of normalization between Israel and the Arab and/or Islamic worlds.

Throughout 1994, as implementation of the Israeli-Palestinian peace accord was delayed, political frustrations combined with socio-economic difficulties among Palestinians, in particular, fanned opposition to the peace process, some of which employed antisemitic innuendo.

The Arab-Israeli conflict is portrayed by Islamists as a continuation of a historical struggle between Jews and Muslims. Jews are depicted as untrustworthy, scheming and manipulative. The political success of Zionism is also attributed to the power of Jewish money, secret societies and conspiracies. Religious imagery has often been used to justify violence against Jews. Furthermore, the fact that Jews, in addition to Israelis, have been targeted for terrorist attacks outside of Israel, indicated a blurring of the distinction between Jews and Zionists.

Of the most significant Palestinian rejectionist groups, Hamas is a loosely-organized popular movement which constitutes the most serious political opposition to the Palestine Liberation Organization. The movement grew out of the Muslim Brotherhood, established in Egypt in 1928, and gained popularity in the 1970s but it was only during the *Intifada* (Palestinian uprising), from December 1987, that widespread support was mobilized through the extensive provision of welfare services, particularly in Gaza. Many Hamas activists are thought to have received training by Hizbullah following the deportation of 400 activists to Marj al-Zahour in South Lebanon in December 1992.

The covenant issued by Hamas in 1988, entitled "The Charter of Allah", asserts that Israel's expansionist plans are based on *The Protocols of the Elders of Zion*, and states that:

"The day of judgement will not come to pass until the Muslims wage war against the Jews and destroy them."

Hamas claims that *jihad* (holy war) is an obligation for all Muslims. The political rhetoric of Hamas makes it clear that Jews as well as Israelis are viewed as targets. A leaflet distributed in Gaza in April 1994 threatened to launch "a war in which Israeli blood, interests and gatherings of Jewish communities all over the world, will be legitimate targets". In one leaflet published in November 1993, Hamas quoted Imad al-Aql, the assassinated leader of Izz al-Din al-Qassam (the armed wing of Hamas) as saying: "Killing Israeli soldiers is a [form of] worship by which we get closer to God." In another leaflet issued after the killing of an Israeli settler in November 1993, Hamas stated: "We have tasted the blood and the flesh of Jews and we found it good. We promise you and Jews everywhere that we will make you suffer."

Antisemitic slogans are often combined with anti-Zionist rhetoric at meetings. For example, at a rally to mark Hamas's seventh anniversary in Gaza on 17 December, activists displayed banners proclaiming: "We count the gates of paradise with the skulls of Jews." The military wing, Izz al-Din al-Qassam, does not distinguish between Jews and Israelis in its propoganda. To cite just one example, slogans displayed at a Hamas rally in Gaza on 15 November stated: "The Qassam brigades will continue to kill Jews."

Another Palestinian rejectionist group, Islamic Jihad, has also invoked religious rhetoric to condemn steps taken by any Arab regime towards normalization of relations with Israel. Sheikh Asad Bayud al-Tamimi, leader of Islamic Jihad, criticized the January visit to Jordan of a group of American rabbis, asserting: "God curses all those who normalize relations with the Jews, for God has created a barrier between Jews and us, and the hollow peace they are talking about is but a cover for the domination of Jews over Arabs."

LEGAL MATTERS

In general, governments are making increasing use of legal remedies to combat racism and antisemitism, and some have introduced measures to improve the efficacy of existing legislation. Although in most East European and former Soviet countries anti-incitement and anti-discrimination legislation exists, its use is far more uneven and successful prosecutions are hard to obtain.

In November, the Australian government introduced a bill to make incitement to racial hatred a federal offence. It was passed in the lower house, although some of the rhetoric in the parliamentary debate gave cause for concern. The media were practically unanimous in their opposition. Changes in the prohibition law in Austria, which reduced sentences for Nazi propaganda offences, had the desired effect and made it easier to achieve successful prosecutions. In Belgium, a case has been brought to court under the anti-racist law for the first time, and a bill to outlaw Holocaust denial was passed by both houses of parliament in 1995. A bill to make an enhanced range of sentences available in hate-motivated crimes was introduced by the federal government in Canada in June and is expected to become law in 1995. In Denmark, the justice minister said it would be necessary to speed up legislation against the denial of the Holocaust and to tighten the anti-racism laws if Denmark were not to become the only West European country where the expression of Holocaust denial and racist views in public was legal. The French parliament in March amended the penal code to increase prison terms and fines for persons found guilty of discriminating on the basis of race, religion or appearance, or of desecrating grave sites of a specific ethnic, religious, national or racial group. President Göncz of Hungary introduced a bill amending the criminal code to allow more prosecutions for incitement to racial and religious hatred. But the bill was only expected to be discussed in 1995. In Italy, to improve the Mancino law relating to racial crimes, penalties were amended to allow for community service-type sentences.

The continuing problems relating to the punishment of the inciters of race hatred in Eastern Europe were highlighted in Romania where disagreement between left and right prevented the adoption of an article in the new penal code that would have prohibited fascist and communist propaganda. And although a few cases relating to racial incitement have been brought in the Czech Republic, many believe that the courts are unable to deal appropriately with hate crimes. In Russia, article 74 of the Russian penal code prohibits incitement against ethnic and racial groups, but it was ineffectively applied.

In Spain, a bill to reform the entire penal code includes a provision that, in offences motivated by racism, antisemitism or the victim's national or ethnic origin or religious beliefs, these will be considered as "aggravating circumstances" and sentences increased accordingly. Another bill proposed outlawing Holocaust denial by making a punishable offence any behaviour which could be seen as defending or disseminating ideologies which promote or support racism, or justify genocide. The bill awaited approval by the chamber of deputies and the senate in 1995. In Switzerland, a new law on incitement to race hatred and Holocaust denial was approved by a referendum after opposition by anti-immigrant and far-right groups. Dissatisfaction with the use of legislation to combat incitement in the United Kingdom led to efforts by many groups and parliamentarians of all parties to persuade the government to change it. Some minor changes were made but activists remained unsatisfied. In the USA, the Hate Crimes Sentencing Enactment Act, embodying the penalty-enhancement approach to hate crimes, was passed by the 103rd Congress in 1994. Thirty-three states and the District of Colombia have now adopted penalty enhancement hate-crime statutes. By the end of 1994 there were approximately a dozen cases pending which would test the constitutionality of state hate-crime laws, including a number based on penalty enhancement.

Among interesting cases were the following: In Denmark, the severest-ever ruling for disseminating antisemitic material was given to two elderly men: sixty and ninety days' imprisonment. A teacher and trades unionist in Tunisia was sentenced to two years' imprisonment for incitement of hatred between races, religions and peoples and eight months for publication of leaflets. The UN Working Group on Arbitrary Detention decided that Tunisian restrictions on freedom of speech in order to combat dissemination of racist ideas were compatible with international law. In Slovakia, the president of the Union of Jewish Communities, Pavel Traubner, sued for slander by the antisemitic periodical *Zmena*, countersued and won in both cases. But there was little progress in the case of Martin Savel who published *The Protocols of the Elders of Zion* in Bratislava. There have been twenty-one court hearings of this case in last three years. In the Netherlands, a court fined a company for distributing a racist and antisemitic computer game *Hate War* after deciding it discriminated against Jews, Christians and blacks.

The case of NPD leader Günther Deckert in Germany revealed a weakness in the law dealing with Holocaust denial and a new law took effect from 1 December making denial an explicit offence in a clause added to paragraph 130 of the criminal code, which deals with incitement to race hatred. The case of Alain Guyonnet in France, editor of the Holocaust-denial journal *Revision*, involved the International League against Racism and Antisemitism (LICRA) and the public prosecutor appealing against his acquittal for an article entitled "Auschwitz: 125,000 deaths". But the Paris court of appeal upheld the ruling saying that understating the number of victims of the Holocaust did not constitute a questioning of the crimes against humanity. In the Netherlands Siegfried Verbeke was banned from distributing Holocaust-denial pamphlets, and lost on appeal. He was due to appear again in March 1995 for sending the "Rudolf Expertise" Holocaust-denial text to schools and the media. His activities have raised the issue of amending legislation to make Holocaust denial a specific criminal offence. But government ministers did not see any reason to have separate prohibition included in the penal law.

The process of bringing prosecutions against suspected Nazi war criminals or of applying for their deportation continued, although in Canada, Australia and the UK, the process is very slow or has come to a complete standstill. At the end of 1994 the US justice department's Office of Special Investigations (OSI) was investigating more than 300 cases against persons suspected of Second World War crimes. A number of cases were pursued during the year. The Demjanjuk case also took its course with the OSI insisting that the revoking of his citizenship remains valid since he lied about his wartime activities, whether or not he was "Ivan the Terrible". In New Zealand, war-crimes prosecutions were rejected and one of the named suspected war criminals won a case for defamation and out-of-court costs from Television NZ. In Australia the trials process has been winding down since the closure of the special investigations unit in 1992. In Canada, the supreme court upheld the constitutionality of the war-crimes law but refused to order a new trial in the Imre Finta case. Justice Jules Deschenes, whose report on war crimes provided the basis for the enactment of the legislation, called for the use of deportation and denaturalization in order to overcome the difficulties which had emerged with the war-crimes legislation. In the UK, the Scottish war-crimes unit was closed after it was decided that there was insufficient evidence to secure a prosecution in the sole case the police were investigating.

The efficacy of using the legal system to clamp down on the far right was clearly shown in Germany where the greater readiness of the authorities to use the full power of the law during the last two years went a long way towards neutralizing the surge of violent extremist activity.

COUNTERING ANTISEMITISM

In most countries public manifestations of antisemitism remain unacceptable. When they do occur, there is ample evidence that many political leaders, members of the clergy and other opinion-formers speak out strongly in condemnation, thus setting the tone for their societies. Various East European leaders have also made attempts to apologize for the fate which befell the Jewish populations of their countries during the Nazi period, to reassure Jews and others that current manifestations of antisemitism will not be tolerated and to express regret for any impression they had given that they personally harboured antisemitic feelings. Welcome though such statements may be, it would not be unwise to consider the motives of the speakers before judging the significance of the words.

Public demonstrations against racism and antisemitism are also significant. In Argentina, 150,000 participated in a demonstration in Buenos Aires after the bombing of the AMIA building, one of the largest public demonstrations seen in Argentina in the last decade. In Denmark there were several large demonstrations against racist violence and neo-Nazis, which obliged two leading activists to leave the country. Thousands took to the streets at Easter in Germany in protest at the attack on the Lübeck synagogue. In the Netherlands and Norway, many demonstrations and campaigns took place. In Russia, an anti-fascist front was set up late in 1993 with anti-fascist committees to be set up in Moscow, St Petersburg and Russia's regions.

Action taken in schools and universities is particularly important. As a result of the opening of diplomatic relations between Israel and Jordan, the Jordanian ministry of education said it would reform social studies curriculum to minimize the emotionally charged content of schoolbooks and remove derogatory statements about Jews. The French authorities removed antisemitic Arabic textbooks from the curriculum of the French-language school in Abu Dhabi. The books, which included references to Jews as "bastards of humanity", were supplied to the school by the education ministry of the United Arab Emirates. The Joint Polish-Israeli textbook commission completed its formulation of guidelines on antisemitism in Poland during the 1930s, the Holocaust and the state of Israel. After initially accepting a Holocaust-denial advertisement from Bradley Smith of the Institute for Historical Review, the editor of Skidmore College's *Skidmore News* refused to print it and published instead a sixteen-page supplement exposing Holocaust denial. In July the AJC sent a letter about the Smith ads and a copy of the supplement to every four-year college library. The Swedish Committee against Antisemitism also intensified efforts to reach teachers and pupils, and members give lectures in schools and teachers' seminars. At an AJC meeting in Washington with the Estonian foreign minister, it was agreed that the help of Estonian Jewish scholars would be enlisted to ensure that school textbooks carried an accurate description of the Holocaust in Estonia. In Canada, the Ontario ministry published an educational booklet on Holocaust denial which was distributed to the campus editor of every university.

It is widely recognized that teaching about the Holocaust is an effective means of countering antisemitism and other forms of race hatred. Two powerful tools in this regard in 1994 were Steven Spielberg's film *Schindler's List* and the exhibition Anne Frank in the World, which was seen in St Petersburg and South Africa, among other places.

Where there is violence, harassment, intimidation and abuse, the action taken by police authorities is a crucial test of a society's will to counter racism and antisemitism. In most communities in the USA, law enforcement agencies took the lead in countering such manifestations. In Canada, three hate-crime units have been established in metropolitan areas. After a slow start, the German authorities enforced stricter policing as part of an increasingly successful campaign to clamp down on illegal extreme-right activity.

Jewish representative bodies often make representations to government and police authorities when action is needed on problems of antisemitism. International Jewish organizations like the World Jewish Congress and B'nai B'rith International also make representations to governments and intergovernmental organizations, as do major national Jewish organizations such as the AJC, the Simon Wiesenthal Center and the Board of Deputies of British Jews.

The country-by-country nature of this *Report* means that certain forms of regional or international activity, especially that devoted to countering antisemitism, racism and xenophobia, are not automatically covered in the individual entries. Here we cover some of the bodies responsible for activity of this kind in 1994 and also the role played by the government of the state of Israel.

European Union

In May, following the Italian general election in which the neo-Fascist MSI won power as part of Silvio Berlusconi's coalition, the European Parliament passed a resolution demanding that EU member states should make clear to the Italian government that it must respect democratic values. Approved by a single vote, it was seen as a warning to President Scalfaro not to allow neo-Fascist ministers into the Italian government. The resolution was criticized as interference in Italian domestic politics.

In June, at the Corfu European Council summit, a joint declaration stated: "The European Council condemns the continuing manifestations of intolerance, racism and xenophobia and affirms its determination to step up the fight against the phenomena." To this end a consultative commission was set up, to look at the continuing rise of racism and xenophobia and to make concrete proposals. The commission is chaired by Jean Kahn, then head of Crif (the representative body of French Jewry). It includes representatives from each of the member states and from the European Commission, together with two observers from the European Parliament. The commission set up three sub-committees to deal with the media, education and training, and police and justice. An interim report was produced for the European Council when it met in Essen in December, and a final report will be prepared for the Cannes European Council summit in June 1995. It is intended that the June summit will adopt an overall strategy to combat racism and xenophobia.

The justice and home affairs sector of the Council produced an interim report for the Essen summit in December. It describes the work done within the steering groups on police and customs co-operation, and on judicial co-operation. In its conclusion it states that questions of racism and xenophobia must be covered in police training. It also refers to a model for the uniform compilation of national statistics on the most significant racist and xenophobic phenomena, which was prepared for use from 1 January 1995.

The European Parliament holds an annual debate on racism and xenophobia. Following the debate in October 1994, a resolution was passed which condemned "once more, in even stronger terms, racism in all its forms, xenophobia and antisemitism and the intolerance in any form of religious discrimination". The parliament requested that a race relations directive be adopted by the European Commission, and reiterated its call for a commissioner to be given responsibility for tackling racial discrimination, xenophobia and discrimination in general.

Council of Europe

The Council of Europe is an intergovernmental organization which, among other things, works to uphold the principles of parliamentary democracy and human rights. At the Vienna summit held in October 1993, the Council adopted a Plan of Action on combating racism, xenophobia, antisemitism and intolerance. The European Commission against Racism and Intolerance was established following the summit. Its first meeting was held in March 1994 and it set up a legal working group and a working group on policies and other measures. The commission began by obtaining an overview of the situation in Europe with regard to racism and intolerance. A consultant was instructed to carry out a comparative study of legislation in force in member states in the field of combating racism and intolerance, especially anti-discriminatory measures. In addition a questionnaire was sent out to governments of member states and to a number of non-governmental organizations.

Another decision taken at the Vienna summit was to organize a youth campaign against racism, xenophobia, antisemitism and intolerance between 1994 and 1996. The campaign was launched on 10 December 1994.

In Council of Europe documents it is usual for references to racism and xenophobia to include references to antisemitism.

In March, more than 100 participants from Europe and the United States attended an international conference in Strasbourg, entitled "Europe Versus Intolerance". It was co-sponsored by the AJC, the Council of Europe and the Foundation of European Science and Culture.

In October an international symposium was held in Strasbourg, entitled "Europe against Discrimination; Vigilant for Democracy and Freedom". It was organized under the auspices of Catherine Lalumière, the secretary-general of the Council of Europe. The symposium was attended by representatives of universities, churches, trades unions, employers, sports personalities, and women's and youth organizations. The participants came from twenty-six different countries. They discussed how to strengthen the campaign against racism and intolerance in Europe and how to create a spirit of anti-racism.

In November the first "European Encounter of National Institutions for the Promotion and Protection of Human Rights" was held in Strasbourg. It was organized by the French National Consultative Commission on Human Rights together with the human rights sub-committee of the parliamentary assembly of the Council of Europe. The two main purposes of the meeting were the creation and strengthening of national institutions and combating racism, in conformity with European Council decisions, recommendations and resolutions.

Organization on Security and Co-operation in Europe (OSCE, formerly Conference on Security and Co-operation in Europe, CSCE)

The CSCE held a review conference in Budapest from 10 October to 3 December and a summit meeting of heads of states and governments from 4 to 6 December. The documents adopted by the summit included a provision to change the title from "Conference" to "Organization". The problems of antisemitism were raised during the course of the conference. In the summit declaration and decisions, references to racism and xenophobia invariably include reference to antisemitism.

The section declaration on "tolerance and non-discrimination" condemns "manifestations of intolerance, and especially aggressive nationalism, racism, chauvinism, xenophobia and antisemitism" and refers to legislation to "deter manifestations of these phenomena". This provision is significant because previous CSCE provisions in favour of anti-racist legislation were limited to legislation against incitement to violence, which could not include non-violent manifestations, such as speech.

United Nations

In March, the UN Human Rights Commission became the first UN body formally to condemn antisemitism for some decades. In its resolution on "measures to combat contemporary forms of racism, racial discrimination, xenophobia and related intolerance", the commission expressed concern about the growth of "racism, racial discrimination, antisemitism, xenophobia and related intolerance". In 1993 the commission appointed a special rapporteur on contemporary forms of racism, racial discrimination, xenophobia and related intolerance. In the resolution of March 1994 the rapporteur was specifically requested to examine incidents of antisemitism, in addition to discrimination against blacks, Arabs and Muslims, xenophobia, negrophobia and related intolerance. The resolution was sponsored by Turkey and its adoption by the Human Rights Commission was seen as a significant development in the fight against antisemitism.

Israel

The Israeli government naturally has an interest in the welfare of Jewish communities throughout the world and is deeply concerned about antisemitism. It formalized its approach to the problem by establishing a permanent forum for the monitoring of antisemitism in 1988. The Israel Government Monitoring Forum receives data on antisemitism from Israel's diplomatic missions around the world. It presents periodic reports to the prime minister and the minister of foreign affairs. It also presents summary reports to the cabinet on an annual basis. A monthly report is sent to Jewish communities, Jewish organizations and other interested parties. The forum maintains contact with a range of Jewish and academic organizations which deal with antisemitism. The information collected by the forum serves as the basis for diplomatic action on antisemitism taken by the Israeli government and its diplomatic missions. The head of the forum is the secretary to the cabinet.

In May 1993, Israel also established an inter-ministerial committee on antisemitism under the auspices of the speaker of the Knesset (parliament), Professor Shevah Weiss, which was chaired by Ovadia Eli, a member of the Knesset. This body, which meets regularly to discuss issues relating to antisemitism, belongs to the UK-based Inter-Parliamentary Council against Antisemitism led by the British MP Greville Janner.

The state of Israel has also played a key role in attempting, with other international Jewish organizations, to persuade the international community to define antisemitism as a form of racism and a violation of human rights, and in promoting research on the sources of contemporary antisemitism.

Interfaith Activity

There was also considerable interfaith activity to counter antisemitism during the year. Not all national or international Jewish or non-Jewish organizations involved in dialogue and reconciliation work can be mentioned here. The developments summarized below are intended to show the range of activity that occurred.

In February over 500 Jewish and Christian leaders from ninety-seven countries met in Jerusalem for the largest and most significant interfaith conference ever held in Israel. Speakers included Cardinal Ratzinger, Archbishop Carlo Maria Martini, the Archbishop of Canterbury and Lois Wilson, the former president of the World Council of Churches. Although the conference was convened by Rabbi David Rosen and some rabbis from the Diaspora attended, it was opposed by most leading rabbis in Israel. Nevertheless, participants regarded it as a major milestone in fostering Jewish-Christian relations at the highest level.

The Vatican-Israel accord was widely welcomed by church leaders (although it is regarded with wariness by the Orthodox churches in Israel, which are concerned over increasing Catholic influence and the question of who will influence the future jurisdiction over Jerusalem and the holy places). It was celebrated in numerous high-level Christian-Jewish receptions around the world, and was followed by the first cultural exchange agreement between Israel and the Vatican in December, to include lectures on the Holocaust and antisemitism at the Pontifical Institute.

The Pope hosted a concert in the Vatican, with the involvement of the AJC, to commemorate the Holocaust in April and launched the project of a pilgrimage in the year 2000 to Sinai (where Jewish, Christian and Muslim leaders would be invited to pray together) and Jerusalem as part of the third millennium jubilee. A book of an extended interview with the Pope, published in October to mark his sixteen years in office, included a chapter on the Jewish people and a renewed condemnation of antisemitism.

An early draft of a planned Vatican document on "Antisemitism, Shoah and the Church", commissioned in 1987 after Jewish protests against the official reception of Kurt Waldheim in the Vatican, prepared by a group of German Catholic bishops and supported by a committee of Polish bishops, was leaked at a liaison meeting in May between the Vatican's Commission for Religious Relations with Judaism and the International Jewish Commission for Inter-Religious Consultations (IJCIC). While doubtless substantially different from the eventual final document, this early draft is significant for its acknowledgement of past antisemitism, the Catholic church's passivity in the face of Nazi persecution of Jews, and the collusion of many Christians, blinded by traditional anti-Jewish teaching, in the events of the Holocaust.

Israel and Jewish leaders internationally protested against the investiture of Kurt Waldheim in July with a papal knighthood in the personal gift of the Pope; in August his wife was accorded a papal honour.

Following the publication in English of the Universal Catechism, revised in 1992 to incorporate most of the changes in Catholic teachings on Jews and Judaism since the Second Vatican Council, new initiatives on Catholic instruction on Jews and Judaism were planned in the USA, France and Poland.

In May, church leaders from sixteen European countries backed the Archbishop of Canterbury in formally denouncing racism and antisemitism. Jewish and Christian leaders in many countries denounced the Hebron massacre in February. In Switzerland Christians and Jews joined forces in June to call for a Sabbath and Sunday for Refugees, and the solidarity of Jewish and Christian leadership was regard as a contributory factor in the passage of the anti-racism law in September.

Representatives of the Lutheran church in the USA formally disowned those of Luther's writings which are anti-Jewish. The revised Roman Catholic catechism was welcomed by Jewish organizations for its stance *vis-à-vis* the Jews.

Leaders of the International Council of Christians and Jews held a conference in Warsaw for the first time and visited Belarus and Russia to explore possibilities for Christian-Jewish dialogue, especially with the Russian Orthodox church. In Britain the first ever seminar between Russian and Greek Orthodox and Jewish leaders took place.

High-level international contacts between Jews, Christians and Muslims remained warm and were further strengthened during 1994, resulting in a joint action to condemn the suffering of Bosnian Muslims and to issue a code of ethics on international business.

OVERALL ASSESSMENT

Countries where the overall antisemitic climate deteriorated are Belgium, Italy, the Netherlands and Turkey. Countries where there was an improvement overall are Hungary, Mexico and Sweden. In other countries covered in this *Report* there was either little change overall on the previous year or the data was insufficient to make an informed judgement.

The *Antisemitism World Report* first warned in 1992 of the potential threat to Jewish security posed by **antisemitism emanating from militant Islamic sources**. With hardening opposition to the peace process in the Middle East on the part of Islamist and secular Palestinian rejectionist groups, this threat has widened to become both Islamist and secular Palestinian in nature. The threat emerged in more concrete forms in 1994 with the bombing of the AMIA Jewish community building in Buenos Aires (assumed to be by militant Islamists), antisemitic incidents occurring in some communities, which appear to be inspired by events occurring in the Middle East, clearly antisemitic (and anti-foreigner) rhetoric being used by Islamist movements in Algeria, Egypt and Jordan, Islamist organizations in Western countries (such as Hizb al-Tahrir in the United Kingdom) stepping up their propaganda offensive, which includes statements calling for the death of Jews. The ideological thrust of these groups is mostly anti-Zionist, but that anti-Zionism is couched increasingly in antisemitic terms. Analysts say that antisemitic ideology is now playing a much larger part in the ideological outlook and output of Islamist clerics, a number of whom spread their message from exile in London. It must be stressed that this antisemitism emanates from only a very small part of the Islamic world and only a very small minority is actively propagating it in non-Muslim countries with sizeable Muslim communities. Nevertheless, Islamism poses a threat to certain Jewish communities, to society in general and to Muslim governments and societies for whom Islamist activity constitutes an extremely destabilizing phenomenon.

The trend towards **electronic fascism** highlighted last year appears to have gathered pace. More countries report the use of computer networks to disseminate racist and antisemitic material, maintain contact between antisemitic groups, list far-right events and activities; the setting up of telephone information lines carrying racist messages; antisemitic computer and video games (10 per cent of German young people and close to 30 per cent of Austrian young people are said to have come into contact with antisemitic computer games); public-access and cable television programmes made by Holocaust-deniers (Holocaust denial has its own newsgroup on the Internet). The new communication technologies are used by a young and impressionable audience and the far right seek to take advantage of this. Many far-right groups see the use of the Internet as the information route of the future: it is very hard to police, regulate or supervise; communication is fast and cheap; people who might otherwise be "observers" can more easily become active; the legal sanctions which apply to incitement to race hatred can be more easily avoided. Racists and antisemites do not have cyberspace to themselves, and the availability of race hate does not mean that it is automatically accessed. Moreover, there is increasing evidence of counter-activity taking place. In Canada, for example, Ken McVay monitors the Internet on a daily basis for the appearance of racist and antisemitic propaganda which he refutes using a massive "fascism and Holocaust" archive he has compiled for this very purpose. Used by a network of individuals and organizations around the world, the archive generates more than 1,000 electronic messages daily.

One of the most disturbing developments is the **electoral progress made in 1994 by the heirs of the Fascist and neo-Nazi traditions in Italy and Austria: the National Alliance (AN, formerly the MSI) and the Austrian Freedom Party (FPÖ)**. The AN was part of the ruling coalition until the fall of the Berlusconi government in December. Since then it has strengthened its position. The FPÖ (now renamed the Libertarians) won 22.6 per cent of the vote in the October 1994 general election and observers think it only a matter of time before the party joins a government. At the beginning of 1995, the AN issued a surprisingly strong condemnation of antisemitism. Haider's party has not done the same, but it has avoided open expressions of antisemitism in public. Antisemitism never figured strongly in the Italian Fascist tradition, but the signs are that, despite the protestations of AN leader Gianfranco Fini, the aggressive, unreconstructed Fascism of the past remains an integral part of the AN. As for the FPÖ, a 1995 opinion poll sponsored by the AJC shows that FPÖ supporters are much more likely to hold negative opinions about Jews than other Austrians.

It may be that both these parties have reached, or will soon reach, a point in the political civilizing process which renders their antisemitism inconsequential. Nevertheless, there can be no mechanism to ensure that this happens, and it appears that their supporters, whilst not voting for the parties specifically because those parties are antisemitic, do not recoil from the antisemitism which they know to be present. In that case, the heirs of the Fascist and Nazi traditions will have found their way into the political mainstream without abandoning what must be regarded as dangerous levels of ethnic hostility and antisemitism.

There were a **number of serious attacks on Jews and Jewish property in 1994**—in Buenos Aires, London, Lübeck and elsewhere—which highlight the vulnerability of Jewish institutions and individuals. Some countries have reported a marked increase in antisemitic incidents. In the USA, the Anti-Defamation League reported that assaults against individuals and acts of harassment increased by 11 per cent. No matter how secure Jewish communities in these place feel, such incidents exacerbate feelings of vulnerability, lead to the adoption of heightened security measures and are bound to instil fear.

But it would be wrong to conclude that such developments are necessarily part of a deteriorating antisemitic trend. In Argentina, for example, the overall incidence of antisemitic prejudice and manifestations remains sporadic. In February, the president of

Argentina's representative Jewish body, the DAIA, forecast a continuing decrease in anti-semitism. One of the two London bombs was aimed at a major Jewish communal institu-tion, yet antisemitism in the United Kingdom remains a marginal phenomenon overall. In Germany, antisemitic incidents have increased substantially, but these are mostly propa-ganda offences originating abroad. Serious problems remain, but most observers agree that the German authorities have now got a firm grip on illegal far-right activity and that the antisemitic climate is unlikely to deteriorate dramatically.

There appear therefore to be contradictory trends at work: a greater likelihood of seri-ous incidents but an increasing marginalization of antisemitism overall. But the contradic-tion can be explained. The important thing is to **distinguish between the problem of the security of Jewish institutions and the problem of antisemitism**. The serious incidents are either the work of groups acting on grievances relating to the Middle East conflict and the peace process which are marginal to the antisemitism current in the countries in which the attacks take place; or they are the work of local extremists who have a greater propen-sity to act out their beliefs in various forms of expression and who are turning to more violent methods in desperation because there is no receptive audience to their message when conveyed in non-violent ways. Indeed, the fact that the level of antisemitic incidents is not declining may well be the result of the success of most societies in keeping public expressions of antisemitism out of the mainstream, pushing determined antisemites to the margins. A certain level of antisemitic violence and terrorism may well be the price that has to be paid for the continued ostracizing of antisemitism from the mainstream.

The overall situation can be looked at regionally:

In **North America**, whilst both Canada and the USA reported a rise in antisemitic incidents, there has been no general deterioration in antisemitism. In the USA, the decline in significant forms of antisemitism continued. In Canada, antisemitism is mostly the prov-ince of isolated individuals and small hate groups. Problem areas in the USA are: the Nation of Islam and the degree to which there is receptivity to antisemitism in the African-American community (a problem which leaks across the border into Canada); the links of some within the religious right with known racists, the openness to Jewish conspiracy theo-ries and the exclusivist emphasis on America as a Christian country; and the terrorist poten-tial of the white-supremacist-militia milieu, which was already apparent to researchers contributing to this volume prior to the Oklahoma bombing.

In **Latin America**, despite the bombing of the AMIA building in Buenos Aires, anti-semitism remains a marginal problem. Communities throughout the continent increased measures to improve their security but there was no sense that the bombing would unleash a wave of antisemitism. If anything, it gave a boost to activity countering antisemitism and generated increased sympathy for Jews in the region.

In **Europe,** there continue to be some disturbing trends. The increased number of anti-semitic publications and media outlets in Turkey, together with the growing popularity of the pro-Islamic Refah Party, which has done little to hide its hostility to Jews, is of great concern. Many Jews fear for their future under a pro-Islamist regime. In Slovakia and Ro-mania, the presence in government of ultra-nationalist parties which are openly antisemitic remains a major cause of concern. Reassuring statements made by Slovak Prime Minister Vladimir Meciar and Romanian President Ion Iliescu are welcome but not sufficient. Coun-tries which profess to adhere to democratic traditions are playing a dangerous game by allowing into governing coalitions parties which want to deny civil rights to minorities. In Russia, the much-debated fears of a descent into fascism indicate the continued political instability of that country. The continued strength, with fluctuations, of the electorally "respectable" far right in Austria, Belgium, France and Italy, does not augur well for any minority groups in Europe. However, the failure of the far right in Germany to make any electoral headway during the October general election was a welcome development. The appearance of outright Holocaust denial in Eastern European countries, as opposed to the denial implied in the rehabilitation of pre-communist leaders who sympathized with or served the Nazis, is also a disturbing development.

Nevertheless, any sense that Europe was about to be engulfed by a rising tide of anti-semitism is not supported by the evidence in this volume.

In **Asia**, antisemitism hardly figures on any scale, but the reaction to *Schindler's List* in countries like Malaysia, the Philippines and Indonesia shows that there is a potential anti-Jewish hostility in some countries in the region which should not be ignored. In Japan, the spate of books blaming Japan's recession on a Jewish conspiracy has given rise to concern.

In **South Africa**, antisemitism remains of marginal significance, and the ANC's opposition to racism means that there is a more favourable climate for countering any manifestations of antisemitism than there was in the past.

In the **Middle East and North Africa**, the problem of antisemitism from Islamic and Islamist sources has undoubtedly intensified. On the one hand, there is no doubt that developments in the peace process have improved the image of Jews and Israel, and official attitudes are more favourable. On the other hand, the hardening of forces opposed to the peace process is producing an even more virulent mix of anti-Zionism and antisemitism than might normally appear.

In **Australasia**, levels of public antisemitism remain very low. A worrying development in Australia is the rhetoric indulged in by some parliamentarians which reinforces Jewish stereotypes, and the defence some parliamentarians mount after their attendance at far-right meetings is made public.

The marginal nature of the threat posed by antisemitism in most countries is partly due to the positive action taken by the wide range of forces which act to counter antisemitism: from international organizations to local interfaith groups.

Most notable in 1994 were: the developments in the legal field—the passage of new legislation in some countries, the improvement of existing legislation, and the greater use of existing legal measures; the strong public statements condemning racism and antisemitism made by world leaders; new methods being employed by police authorities in some countries to tackle hate crimes; signs that action is being taken to counter the dissemination of racism, antisemitism and Holocaust denial on the Internet; and international, but especially pan-European, initiatives to develop more effective ways of combating racism and antisemitism.

The success of *Schindler's List* as a means of educating about the Holocaust and the consequences of prejudice was a signal development in 1994. The attacks on the film by Holocaust-deniers were a sign of their desperation in the face of the impact the film has had on popular culture and awareness of the Holocaust.

The problems of an erosion of the taboo on expressions of antisemitism, as the Holocaust recedes in memory, the internationalization of contacts (both physical and in cyberspace) between organizations and individuals espousing antisemitism, the opening up of a social and political space which organizations propagating sanitized versions of racism, xenophobia and antisemitism can exploit, the increased quantities of antisemitic material circulating in various parts of the world—all remarked upon in the last two years' *Reports*—need reiterating in 1995. As does the fact that Jews are not the primary targets of racial violence, harassment, intimidation and public expressions of hatred.

On the whole, current antisemitism is expressed in less blatant forms than in the past—innuendo, Holocaust denial (which can range from "mild" questioning of the estimates of

Jews murdered to outright denial that any were killed at all), the rehabilitation of East European pre-communist leaders, computer games—and in the words of Tom W. Smith, "may therefore be more difficult to examine." The need to assess antisemitism across a range of criteria—the approach taken in the *Antisemitism World Report*—is therefore even more apparent.

Less blatant antisemitism may also be more difficult to combat in direct ways. Nevertheless, the task of monitoring, analysing and assessing must continue so that the necessary data can be provided for effective policies to be devised. And that task must be carried out as objectively and to as high a standard as possible.

Methodology

While many organizations are devoted to combating antisemitism and many individuals are engaged in researching its history and current manifestations, until the appearance of the *Antisemitism World Report 1992* there had been no internationally accepted "barometer" against which the current level of antisemitism could be measured. The year 1992 seemed therefore the right moment to attempt to create just such a "barometer" in the form of a world survey of antisemitism, country-by-country, produced as far as possible according to common criteria and categories. Following the pattern set by the major human rights monitoring organizations, the latest volume, *Antisemitism World Report 1995*, is intended to provide:

1 an internationally recognized means of monitoring the advance or decline of the phenomenon worldwide;
2 a means of judging whether government and juridical authorities are taking appropriate action to combat antisemitism in their respective countries;
3 a tool for use by organizations and Jewish representative bodies whose task it is to combat antisemitism in pressing government and juridical authorities to take action;
4 a yardstick for judging the overall democratic health particularly of those societies whose democratic institutions are at an early stage of development.

The *Antisemitism World Report 1995* is based on a wide variety of sources: specialist authors; Jewish communal organizations; monitoring organizations; research institutes; academic researchers; and the expertise and archives of the Institute of Jewish Affairs. Whenever a statement raised doubts and independent corroboration was impossible to obtain, the statement was not included.

Since one of the main purposes of this *Report* is to serve as a research-based tool for those engaged in combating antisemitism in specific countries, it was decided to structure the survey on a country-by-country basis, within regions. There are other ways of producing such a survey and some phenomena cannot be dealt with fully in a country-by-country treatment. However, overall assessments of world trends and consideration of some of the main expressions of antisemitism that transcend national boundaries and of anti-discrimination initiatives by international and pan-European organizations were included in Part I of the Introduction to this *Report*.

In regard to the question of defining antisemitism, a strictly common-sense approach has been adopted. It was found that when those who concern themselves with the phenomenon in a serious manner were asked to report on it, there was a remarkable degree of unanimity about what was being described. The only significant area where differences emerge is on the question of the relationship between anti-Zionism and antisemitism. Here, we have erred on the side of caution, including only those elements of anti-Zionism which are patently antisemitic or had antisemitic effects.

Since no single index presents a reliable way of judging the state of antisemitism, contributors to this volume were asked to organize their data in accordance with the categories listed below, which were intended to be as exhaustive as possible:

1 General and Jewish population figures
2 General political, social and economic conditions
3 Historical legacy of antisemitism
4 Prevailing racist and xenophobic climate
5 Antisemitic political parties, organizations, movements, groupings, and estimates of their numbers and influence
6 Antisemitism in mainstream political life
7 Antisemitic manifestations/incidents (violent and non-violent)
8 Antisemitism in cultural (high and popular) life
9 Antisemitism in the business/commercial world
10 Antisemitism in education
11 Social antisemitism (in sport, at the grassroots, etc.)
12 Antisemitic publications (books, newspapers, magazines, etc.) and in the electronic media (including computer networks)
13 Religious antisemitism, including Islamic fundamentalist sources
14 Denial of the Holocaust (so-called Holocaust "revisionism")
15 Manifestations of antisemitic themes deriving from anti-Zionist activities
16 Opinion polls
17 Legal matters (including prosecutions under anti-incitement and anti-discrimination legislation and cases concerning war crimes)
18 Philosemitism (both positive and negative aspects)
19 Countering antisemitism (for example, statements by non-Jewish political, religious and other leaders, educational initiatives, demonstrations, including condemnations of the general phenomena of racism and xenophobia)
20 Overall assessment (in comparison with the situation prevailing last year and with other forms of racism and discrimination, and on a scale ranging from a "marginal" to a "serious" threat to the Jewish community)

It was clear that some of these categories were overlapping and that their application might vary considerably from country to country. In addition, contributors were given the opportunity to introduce categories of their own choosing to reflect special circumstances in the countries on which they were reporting, and in some countries certain categories do not apply. However, efforts have been made to include information in the general categories wherever possible. In the text of this *Report* the category headings have been shortened and renamed for reasons of space.

The *Report* should also be seen as a contribution to the attempt to refine our techniques of assessing the significance of antisemitism and not the last word on the matter. It is hoped that, apart from fulfilling the need for an authoritative survey, the volume will also stimulate discussion about the whole problem of measuring antisemitism. Naturally, the Institute of Jewish Affairs and the American Jewish Committee welcome any comments or criticism from readers of the *Report*. Whilst every effort has been made to ensure accuracy, errors of fact may have crept in, and for these we apologize.

Americas

THE INSTITUTE OF JEWISH AFFAIRS AND THE AMERICAN JEWISH COMMITTEE

Argentina

General population: 33.1 million
Jewish population: 211,000 (more than 80 per cent in Buenos Aires, also in the province of Córdoba and the city of Rosario in the province of Santa Fe)

GENERAL BACKGROUND

Since 1989 the governing party has been the Partido Justicialista (PJ, Justicialist Party), otherwise known as the Peronists, under its leader, President Carlos Menem. On 10 April, a constituent assembly charged with the task of approving constitutional reforms was elected. The Peronists emerged as the leading party with 37.7 per cent of the vote. The Unión Cívica Radical (UCR, Radical Civic Union), formerly the principal opposition party, received 19.9 per cent of the vote, its worst performance since the return to democracy in 1983. The surprise result was the success of the left-of-centre coalition party, Frente Grande (FG, Great Front), which polled 12.5 per cent and won in the federal capital, Buenos Aires, and in Neuquén province.

The package of constitutional reforms agreed by Menem and UCR leader Raúl Alfonsín, known as the Olivos Pact, was approved by the constituent assembly in August. It included an amendment reducing the presidential term from six to four years, a clause allowing the president to stand for re-election, the elimination of the clause obliging the president to be a member of the Roman Catholic church, and the formal recognition of the rights of indigenous peoples and of their common ownership of land. In addition to the constitutional reforms, Menem announced in June the government's intention to abolish compulsory military service and to create in its stead a wholly professional armed forces.

The 18 July bombing of the Asociación Mutual Israelita Argentina (AMIA, Jewish Mutual Society of Argentina) (see **Effects of Anti-Zionism**) provided President Menem with an opportunity to proceed with the creation of the Secretariat for Security and Community Protection, a project which had previously been put on the back burner after running into opposition from legislators from both the ruling and opposition parties. Among the latter, there was real concern that such a secretariat would be used to silence legitimate government critics. Retired air force brigadier Andrés Antonietti, a man without previous experience in the intelligence community, was appointed head of the secretariat and will, in cases of emergency, have authority over the federal police, the border and river police forces, as well as the coast guard.

Economic growth continued unabated and inflation stabilized at under 4 per cent. There was strong criticism of governmental trade policy, the cost of credit and asymmetries with Brazil (with which Argentina, together with Paraguay and Uruguay, is linked in the MERCOSUR common market). The government was also finding it difficult to mobilize the support of labour because of budget cuts and a proposed reduction in employer's social security contributions. A demonstration against the effects of the free-market economic policies in July attracted some 60,000 people and was the largest since Menem came to power in 1989.

HISTORICAL LEGACY

A degree of intolerance towards Jews in Argentina had its historical roots in the Inquisition and had been inherited as part of the Spanish colonial legacy. From the beginning of mass immigration into Argentina in the nineteenth century, the country's élites did not regard the arrival of certain groups, including Jews, as particularly desirable. Nonetheless, from 1890 until 1930, unrestricted large-scale immigration was thought to be imperative for the country's development.

The arrival of large numbers of Jewish immigrants provoked disapproval from the Catholic church and other powerful sections of society. The nationalist reaction against immigration that surfaced in 1910 eventually erupted, following a general strike in January 1919, in the events of "Tragic Week", when the Argentine Patriotic League of Manuel Carles provoked a pogrom, the most serious anti-

Jewish violence ever to occur under a democratic government in Argentina's history.

The antisemitism of the Argentine élites became part of a wider xenophobia which borrowed ideas, successively, from French right-wing, Falangist, fascist and Nazi sources. During the 1930s, such influences were strongly felt in the officer corps of the armed forces and the membership of the Legion Civica, the most visible exponent of antisemitism at the time. From 1933, antisemitic activity increased, encouraged particularly by the local branch of the German Nazi Party. In 1938, an immigration decree increased discrimination against Jewish refugees. Nonetheless, during the crucial period of 1933-41, Argentina received the largest number of Jewish refugees, legal and illegal, in Latin America.

During the early 1940s, the Nationalist Liberation Alliance (ALN), a pro-Nazi group which, after the war, supported the accession to power of Juan Perón, was established. In the post-war period, Argentina became an international centre for antisemitic publications and neo-Nazi activity; but by 1953 Perón had succeeded in moving the ALN away from anti-Jewish attitudes. Argentina was a sanctuary for thousands of Nazis and former collaborators fleeing Europe, including war criminals Adolf Eichmann, Joseph Schwammberger, Walter Kutschmann and Edward Roschmann. Some of them benefited from a 1948 government amnesty for illegal entrants, which also benefited not less than 10,000 Jews.

During the 1960s, the antisemitic, Catholic, nationalist movement Tacuara succeeded in mobilizing large numbers of young people and in rocking public opinion by perpetrating frequent violent racist attacks. Of the 313 antisemitic incidents recorded world-wide in 1967, 142 occurred in Argentina (although this represented a decrease nationally, the highest number having been recorded in 1962-65).

During the military dictatorship of 1976-83, the government either encouraged or tolerated antisemitism. Jews were over-represented among the "disappeared" and the victims of torture in the clandestine centres and camps. Several hundred Jews (out of over 9,000 documented victims of state terrorism) were killed. The commission which investigated activities in the detention centres (CONADEP) revealed that Jewish prisoners received "special" treatment and that antisemitic and neo-Nazi slogans were found on the walls of the prisons.

The government of Carlos Menem has adopted an increasingly pro-Israeli, pro-Jewish and pro-US line, and has made a commitment to combat antisemitism and xenophobia.

RACISM AND XENOPHOBIA

Estimates for the size of the indigenous population in Argentina have varied from 60,000 to 150,000. The National Statistical Institute's figure for 1992 was below 100,000. The standard of living for indigenous people is considerably below average, and they suffer higher rates of illiteracy, chronic disease and unemployment.

There is considerable hostility towards immigrants from neighbouring countries, particularly "illegals" from Paraguay, Bolivia and Chile employed in Buenos Aires; there is also a degree of prejudice against Korean immigrants who are largely middle class. During 1994, there were several reported police raids against the former, which included arrests.

In January Interior Minister Carlos Ruckauf announced an intensification of border controls to counteract the arrival of illegal immigrants organized by "clandestine" groups. The decision followed an incident in which thirty Peruvian illegal immigrants had been repatriated amid allegations that members of the Peruvian guerrilla group Sendero Luminoso (Shining Path) had been involved in disturbances in the north-western province of Santiago del Estero in December 1993.

The preliminary results of a survey of attitudes conducted in September by a University of Buenos Aires academic, Mirta Lischetti, among 1,062 students of anthropology revealed an alarming degree of nationalism and racialism on the one hand, and xenophobia on the other.

Like the earlier attack on the Israeli embassy, the bombing of the AMIA building has fuelled an anti-Arab and anti-Muslim backlash. Such bigotry has been increasingly on display, especially in the media, since Carlos Menem—of Syrian Muslim descent—first won his party's nomination for the presidency in 1988.

Speculation about the possible participation of Latin Americans of Syro-Lebanese descent in both attacks partly explains the recent escalation of hostility. Since 1992, there have been discussions about the possibility of militant Shi'ite Islamic groups having built a strong base along Argentina's north-eastern border—in Brazil's Foz de Iguaçu and Paraguay's Ciudad del Este—since the Lebanese civil war of the 1970s.

PARTIES, ORGANIZATIONS, MOVEMENTS

The far-right, nationalist Movimiento por la Dignidad y la Independencia (MODIN, Movement for Dignity and Independence), founded in 1991 and headed by Aldo Rico, a cashiered lieutenant-colonel who led abortive military uprisings in 1987 and 1988, became the fourth largest party nationally in the April elections by gaining twenty seats in the constituent assembly. In October Rico was nominated as MODIN's presidential candidate for the 1995 elections. Since 1991, MODIN's leaders have distanced themselves from anything that appears anti-Jewish in order to be able to participate as a seemingly respectable force in the electoral process. But many observers believe that this respectability is only skin-deep.

Aldo Rico supported the present PJ governor of Buenos Aires province, Eduardo Duhalde, in the latter's bid to seek re-election in 1995, increasing Duhalde's share of the vote to more than 60 per cent in the October plebiscite which secured his right to seek re-election—a remarkable achievement as he had previously polled only 40 per cent of the vote.

In response to the bombing of the AMIA building in July, Aldo Rico laid the blame on Menem's pro-Western foreign policy. According to Rico, the terrorist attack was the response to Menem's alignment with the USA during the Gulf War which inflamed Middle Eastern hostility to Argentina; he condemned the president's continuing involvement with the USA elsewhere in the world. He also regretted Menem's co-operation with Mossad (the Israeli intelligence service), Interpol and the US and Spanish intelligence services in investigating the bombing.

In September a splinter group of MODIN declared that it had formed a new party called "Blue and White" Modin under the leadership of Luis Polo. At the launch of the party, Polo accused Aldo Rico of having betrayed the movement by offering to support the PJ in any second-round ballots in the 1995 elections.

Another cashiered officer, Mohamed Alí Seineldin, imprisoned for life for masterminding an abortive December 1990 military rebellion, has, according to a report in the Madrid daily *El País* of 21 June, declared his intention to contest the 1995 presidential election as leader of a "broad multi-sectoral" front against injustice, oppression and absolutism. Seineldin was previously linked to the far-right and antisemitic Movement for National Identity and Latin American Integration (MINEII), which he led from his prison cell. In April the police raided the home of Alejandro Sucksdorf, a former intelligence chief with close ties to the imprisoned Seineldin, and found an arsenal of army-issue weapons and explosives, together with a sizeable collection of antisemitic literature and photographs of Hitler.

The Partido del Nuevo Triunfo (PNT, New Triumph Party), a neo-Nazi party founded by Alejandro Biondini (originally called Alerta Nacional), and the Partido Nacionalista Constitucional (Nationalist Constitutional Party), an extreme right-wing party led by Alberto Asseff, have both suffered shrinking memberships.

Seineldin and Biondini are both members of the nationalist and antisemitic International Political Bureau of the National Socialist Workers Party of Latin America (PANTLA). PANTLA is led by Angel Dominguez Mondejar, who contributes to a number of nationalist publications and has links with the anti-Castroite group in Miami which publishes *Trinchera Nacionalista*. The group also has contacts in Peru, Ecuador and Spain.

MANIFESTATIONS

Despite genuine expressions of solidarity with the Jewish community (see **Countering Antisemitism**), the 18 July bombing of the AMIA (see **Effects of Anti-Zionism**) understandably generated fear among the Argentine population. Against the backdrop of an ensuing spate of false bomb scares—whether aimed at Buenos Aires-based Jewish institutions or individuals—several sporting events had to be postponed because of the refusal of clubs to play at Jewish facilities. The media recorded some unfortunate sentiments, such as the suggestion that Jews should move to less-populated neighbourhoods. By 23 August, however, the Argentine Sports Confederation held its weekly meeting at the Sociedad Hebraica Argentina as if to signal the absence of prejudice among the sports community.

A few other, relatively minor, incidents were reported during the year. In January, Argentina's chief rabbi, Salomón Benhamú, was assaulted in the street by four youths who reportedly shouted antisemitic abuse at him. It is not certain however that the attacker's motives were antisemitic.

In March there was an attempted armed break-in at a Jewish cemetery in the Andean city of Mendoza by a group of seven youths who were arrested after a shoot-out with police. In May the Jewish cemetery in the Buenos Aires seaside resort of Mar del Plata was desecrated for the tenth time in two years.

Late in November a bomb scare interrupted an international conference on "Discrimination and Racism in Latin America" held at the University of Buenos Aires and sponsored by, among other academic and Jewish organizations, the Argentine senate and foreign ministry. The incident did not prevent the completion of the full agenda which included papers by local and foreign specialists on a host of subjects—including prejudice against native Latin Americans, Latin Americans of African, Middle

Eastern and Asian descent, and the records of both the allied and neutral states of the Second World War towards the Jewish victims of Nazism and their tormentors—and a lively discussion on the number of war criminals who took up residence in Argentina. In a related incident in 1994, the official presentation of the published proceedings of a 1993 foreign ministry-sponsored conference on genocide was postponed because of the Universidad di Tella's concern about the safety of the proceedings.

PUBLICATIONS AND MEDIA

The principal activity of the ultra-nationalist, antisemitic groupings in Argentina is the dissemination of their ideas through journals and newspapers. Circulation figures for such publications have decreased significantly in recent years.

Nationalist groupings and the extreme right have exploited the freedom of the press achieved with the revival of democracy in 1983. At the end of 1991, fifteen ultra-nationalist publications were produced in Argentina but their number has clearly decreased in the past three years. Their distribution is at best limited to specific news-stands.

The following publications are ultra-nationalist and antisemitic. *Patria Argentina*, edited by Ibarguren, was said to be systematically circulated in army barracks and police stations. *Doctrina para el Movimiento Nacional* is one of the organs by which Seineldin disseminates his views; it apparently ceased to be available after the AMIA bombing in July. *Soberania Nacional y Pugna*, published by the priest José Gabriel del Rosario, maintains a Catholic fundamentalist line, and is available in Buenos Aires bookstalls. *El Muecin* is a militant Islamic publication. Alejandro Biondini is the editor of *El Nacionalista*, the only publication which follows a definitively national-socialist line; this journal was also reportedly unavailable after the AMIA bombing. In addition, the neo-Nazi journal *Cedade*, published in Spain, continues to be available in Argentina (see **Spain**).

The lawsuit against the rabidly antisemitic journal, *Revelaciones sobre Sociedades Secretas y Masonería*, which ceased publication in 1993, was concluded in 1994 (see **Legal Matters**).

DENIAL OF THE HOLOCAUST

In November 1993, a journal entitled *Revision* was published for the first time, under the auspices of the so-called Paul Rassinier Centre for Studies. Despite defining itself as a general interest journal, all of its published issues refer to the "fable of the six million". Spanish translations of the "classics" of Holocaust-denial, such as *El Informe Leuchter* (*The Leuchter Report*), are available in some Buenos Aires bookstalls.

EFFECTS OF ANTI-ZIONISM

On the morning of 18 July, a bomb destroyed the seven-storey building in Buenos Aires that housed the offices of, among other organizations, the AMIA and the Argentine Jewish umbrella organization, the Delegación de Asociaciones Israelitas Argentinas (DAIA, Delegation of Argentine Jewish Organizations). The death toll rose to seventy-six, and over 200 persons were wounded. Among the fatalities, twenty-seven were not Jewish. A large part of the third-floor library of the Instituto Científico Judío (IWO, Jewish Scientific Institute) was spared although important parts of its archive documenting Jewish life in Argentina were lost. Likewise spared were DAIA researchers and their photocopied archive of documents on the Nazis in Argentina (see **Legal Matters**). (This is significant in view of some initial press suggestions that the attackers may have targeted the building because of DAIA's documentation of the post-Second World War influx of Nazis into Argentina.)

Immediately following the bombing President Menem ordered all land borders, ports and airports to be sealed to prevent the escape of the perpetrators and affirmed his commitment to capture those responsible. Intelligence experts from Israel, Spain and the USA arrived in Argentina to help in the hunt for the perpetrators.

President Menem said in his earliest statements that the attack had been planned and executed by an international, foreign-based terrorist organization with local assistance. Israeli Prime Minister Yitzhak Rabin accused Iranian-supported Islamic militants and Hizbullah of responsibility for the bombing. On 20 July both Iran and Hizbullah issued statements disclaiming any responsibility (see **Iran**).

The police investigation into the bombing produced little in the way of results. Explosives experts determined that the blast was caused by a device made of ammonal manufactured in Argentina which was loaded into a van and detonated by a suicide bomber. The sale and purchase of the Renault van in which the bomb was planted were traced, and the seller of the van was arrested, together with two other Argentines employed in the garage where the van was repaired. Other Iranian, Iraqi, German, Moroccan, Lebanese and Syrian citizens detained as suspects were released. At the end of October, only one suspect remained in prison: the seller of the van.

Although the supreme court—the only

tribunal empowered to deal with foreign diplomats—considered it premature, even as late as 25 August, to take responsibility for the case, a judicial investigation had begun as early as 23 July when the federal judge in charge of the investigation, Juan José Galeano, travelled to Venezuela to hear the testimony of Manoucheh Moatamer, a "repentant" former Iranian official. Moatamer provided information on militant Islamic groups acting in Argentina, on the alleged participation of officials in the Iranian embassy, as well as on a second attack to be mounted in England. One day after Judge Galeano returned from Caracas, two bombs exploded outside Jewish targets in London (see **United Kingdom**).

The Iranian ambassador claimed that Moatamer had never been a member of its diplomatic service, and that he was an opponent of the present regime. Despite the fact that Judge Galeano was suspicious of four Iranian officials working in Buenos Aires whom Moatamer had implicated—and against whom Judge Galeano issued international arrest warrants in early August—doubts arose about the reliability of Moatamer, who was described by sources in Venezuelan intelligence as a long-time double agent who had infiltrated the Iranian intelligence services on behalf of the CIA, the US intelligence service. In addition, the involvement of the four diplomats became questionable when it was revealed that they had left Argentina between nine months and six years before the attack. In August the supreme court decided not to pursue them on the grounds of insufficient evidence, and an official apology was extended by the Argentine government to Iran. Despite calls to sever diplomatic relations with Iran, the Argentine government finally announced that it would do so only if conclusive evidence of Iranian participation in the attack emerged.

In early August, the investigation revealed that the cultural attaché at the Iranian embassy, Mohsen Rabbani, was shopping for Renault vans in Buenos Aires weeks before such a van was used in the bombing.

At the end of August, Rubén Beraja, the president of the DAIA, denounced the lack of co-ordination between the police and the intelligence service (SIDE), and criticized the investigation for failing to produce concrete results. Judge Galeano privately attributed the lack of co-ordination to the fact that SIDE vetted any information that he requested, did not execute his requests and delayed the investigation.

Serious criticism of the official investigation is also advanced in a best-selling book by Jorge Lanata, a former editor of the daily Buenos Aires opposition tabloid *Página/12*, and Joe Goldman, a correspondent for United Press International: *Cortinas de Humo: una Investigación Independiente sobre los Atentados contra la Embajada de Israel y la AMIA* (Smoke Screen: An Independent Investigation into the Attacks on the Israeli Embassy and the AMIA). The authors raise the possibility of a Syrian connection and claim that the Argentine president has a stake in the failure of the investigation since results might focus public attention on relations between some presidential aides and Monzer al-Kassar, a Marbella-based arms dealer who hails from the same Syrian town of Jabrut as Menem's forebears and his estranged wife's family. The Argentine foreign minister and the DAIA president have dismissed the idea of any direct Syrian connection with the AMIA bombing. Moreover, in November, during Menem's long-awaited first visit to Syria as president, security chief Hugo Anzorregui, a member of Menem's entourage, visited Damascus to discuss terrorism with his Syrian counterpart.

Among Lanata's earlier, unsubstantiated claims was that al-Kassar was responsible for the bombing of the Pan Am airliner over Lockerbie. Not to be dismissed out of hand, *Cortinas de Humo* deserves to be read with the utmost care, not only because it contains factual inaccuracies but also because it lends credence to the equally unsubstantiated notion that, in their quest for a Washington-brokered Syrian-Israeli peace, the US president and Israeli prime minister were prepared to turn a blind eye to the embassy and AMIA bombings. For the time being, it cannot be ruled out that, unwittingly or otherwise, Lanata and Goldman's sources have included partisan opponents of an Israeli withdrawal from the Golan Heights.

Even before the Lanata-Goldman book was published, the chief of SIDE was obliged to disclaim press reports that several intelligence officers were attempting to sabotage the course of the investigation. Two members of the opposition UCR in the chamber of deputies asked the chief of SIDE to submit all of its information concerning serious charges of obstruction made against both "Grupo Cabildo"—a group of still active, right-wing security officers who are veterans of the former military regime's "dirty war"—and his own under-secretary within SIDE; the latter was accused of having hindered the investigation of the Israeli embassy bombing.

LEGAL MATTERS

In July the Italian government requested the extradition of former SS Captain Erich Priebke to stand trial for his involvement in the massacre of 335 civilians in the Ardeatine caves near Rome in March 1944 (see **Italy**). Having lived in Bariloche under his own name since 1947, Priebke's extradition request was provoked by his appearance on a US news programme, *Prime Time Live*, broadcast on the ABC network on 5 May. According to Yaron Svoray, a former intelligence operative of the Los Angeles-based Simon Wiesenthal Center among Germany's far-right fringe groups, Priebke's identification is a consequence of the Center's earlier detection of Reinhold Kops, a one-time Nazi intelligence agent and Bariloche-based neo-Nazi publicist, whose wartime activities have yet to yield enough evidence to prompt an extradition request.

The Argentine president as well as the foreign and justice ministers stated on the record that they have no objection to deporting Priebke. The chamber of deputies' human rights commission also supported Priebke's rapid extradition. In addition, Argentina's commitment to the tracking down of other war criminals hidden in the country was emphasized by the interior minister's announcement of the establishment of a special agency charged with that task.

Nevertheless, Priebke's extradition is not expected until the completion of legal proceedings which—given that the defence strategy of Priebke's lawyers apparently hinges on such delaying tactics as a request that the Italian authorities submit, in Spanish, thousands of documents—is not imminent. Given Priebke's age and state of health, such tactics, if accepted by the judiciary, could well protect the Gestapo's former no. 2 man in Rome from being brought to justice. In the meantime, Priebke is under house arrest due to an alleged illness, a situation that has drawn fire from several quarters, the DAIA included.

A group of relatives of Italian victims of the Ardeatine massacre travelled from Rome to Bariloche, and held press conferences and other meetings with local social and educational institutions in order to publicize Priebke's crimes and to demand extradition without delay. The Italian visitors were astonished by the refusal of the local city council to issue a firm declaration repudiating Nazism.

Two other war criminals in hiding in Argentina were the subject of reports by Argentine and Brazilian journalists in May. Abraham Kipp collaborated with German SS officers after the occupation of the Netherlands, and was tried by a Dutch court which found him guilty of twenty-two murders and condemned him to death in 1949, later commuted to life imprisonment. Kipp arrived in Buenos Aires in 1949 and received Argentine citizenship in 1953. Late in 1988 the Dutch government requested his extradition but the then Alfonsín administration was replaced before the judiciary could rule against its enforcement. Despite an appeal in May from the Simon Wiesenthal Center to renew its request for Kipp's extradition, the Dutch justice ministry ruled out any further attempt due to insoluble legal problems (see **The Netherlands**).

The second war criminal exposed in Buenos Aires is the Belgian Willem Sassen, also tried and sentenced to death after the Second World War. Sassen succeeded immediately in escaping to Argentina where he found sanctuary and where he was a confidant of Adolf Eichmann. In the aftermath of Eichmann's kidnapping by Mossad, one of the theories concerning his discovery was that he had been betrayed by Sassen.

In June, the DAIA's Testimony Project—set up in 1993, under the direction of Beatriz Gurevich, to create a public archive which documents the behaviour of all sections of Argentine society *vis-à-vis* Nazi war criminals and collaborators who found sanctuary in Argentina—released a list of eighteen Nazis who escaped to Argentina and are still alive. In addition to Priebke and Kipp, the list is dominated by eleven condemned Yugoslav collaborators (former Catholic bishop of Ljubljana, Gregory Rozman; Franjo Holy; Vinko Nikolic; José Berkovic; Mirko Eterovic; Ivo Bogdan; Daniel Uvanovic; Marko Colak; Esteban Lackovic; Yakov Yovovic; and Maks Luburic). Their arrival and unhindered life in Argentina appears to have been the result of what the post-war US ambassador in Belgrade, John Cabot, has described as US-Vatican connivance to assist war criminals to leave for Argentina. Also listed were three Belgian collaborators who had been condemned to death (Pierre Adam, Lecomte (first name unknown), Andre Vandenberghe) and two other alleged war criminals (former head of the Gestapo in Portugal Erich Schroeder, and Marton Homonnay, accused of war crimes in Hungary and whose request for his extradition in 1950 was ignored in Argentina).

The lawsuit brought by Alberto de Renzis, an anti-racist activist, against Patricio Maguirre, editor-in-chief of the antisemitic journal, *Revelaciones sobre Sociedades Secretas y Masonería*, and a member of the Council for the Ecclesiastic History of the Argentine Episcopate, reached its conclusion in 1994. Despite the sudden death of Maguirre and the closing down of his review in November 1993, the judge acting in the suit agreed to prosecute the other editorial board members of the journal as well as those responsible for the Catholic church-linked Léon XIII Publishing House, which produced the sixty-three issues of the anti-Jewish journal.

COUNTERING ANTISEMITISM

On 21 July, a demonstration, attended by at least 150,000 persons, one of the largest in Argentina in the last decade, as held in Buenos Aires's central square to express revulsion at the bombing of the AMIA building. One of the slogans on display, "We are all Argentine Jews", reflected the general sense of solidarity with the Jewish community being expressed by Argentine public opinion. Addressed by leaders of the Jewish community, the rally was attended by President Menem, cabinet ministers, legislators from both the ruling and opposition parties, members of the judiciary, as well as Cardinal Antonio Quarracino, Argentina's foremost Catholic dignitary, and representatives of other religious faiths. Similar demonstrations were held simultaneously in seven other cities throughout the country; memorial services for the victims were also held in several other countries. Perhaps the most important was the multi-faith service held at the Argentine embassy in London which was officiated by Catholic and Anglican priests, three rabbis and the principal of the Muslim College.

The Argentine government immediately requested a special meeting of the United Nations Security Council which condemned the terrorist attack and extended condolences to the victims and their relatives. However, as a result of the pressure exerted by Arab countries, the fact that the target was a Jewish one was not mentioned in the official statement. Three days later, an open session of the US Congress on the attack, was attended by both the president of the DAIA and the Argentine ambassador to the USA.

As reparation, the Argentine government offered to pay the victims of the attack and their relatives over $2 million. At least eighty applications for compensation were approved and 510 applications had been filed by the end of August.

Aware of the expression of anti-Arab bigotry, as well as of the conjectures concerning Hizbullah, representatives of various Syro-Lebanese institutions in Argentina met with a leader of the DAIA to express their solidarity with the shell-shocked Jewish community. Likewise Horacio Munir Haddad, president of the Syrian Ba'ath-inspired Federación de Entidades Arabes, vigorously condemned the

bombing and denounced the press campaign of "suspicion against our community". The country's Shi'ites also condemned the attack, with Abdul Karim Paz, the leader of the Iranian-sponsored mosque in the Buenos Aires neighbourhood of Floresta, repudiating the tragedy. Paz's lamentation that in Argentina there is now "little inclination to differentiate between terrorist and Muslim groups" seems to have been taken seriously by the country's authorities: in addition to the protection awarded to Jewish institutions after the AMIA bombing, the police were reportedly taking the same precautions with regard to Muslim organizations.

On every Monday morning since early August, a group of the families of Jewish victims of both bombing attacks, together with activists of human rights organizations—who have been critical in the past both of the Argentine government's amnesties for military officers as well as the Jewish community's performance concerning the detained and "disappeared" during the "dirty war" of 1976-83 —have held a silent vigil in front of the main courthouse to demand a prompt and serious investigation. Known as Memoria Activa (Active Memory) the group initially attracted 150-300 persons to its weekly rallies and has become a significant protest movement in Buenos Aires, well-publicized by the media which repeats their call for the perpetrators of the attack to be punished. Furthermore, the relatives of victims have also written open letters to the newspapers, and organized demonstrations at the bomb site calling for those responsible to be found.

Months before the bombing, in March, the Argentine Jewish community had supported the establishment of an Argentine Council against Ethnic and Religious Discrimination, which intends to launch an information campaign on racist violence throughout Latin America.

In the Andean province of San Juan, the provincial secretary of education issued an internal circular instructing teachers of elementary and secondary schools to include in their classroom teaching the values of religious and cultural pluralism. With the backing of San Juan cultural institutions, the initiative also prompted the province's governor to request the removal from forthcoming editions of textbooks all pejorative and discriminatory references to minority groups.

ASSESSMENT

The bombing of the AMIA on 18 July was the most serious attack on a Jewish community outside of Israel since the Second World War. In terms of Argentine antisemitism, it was a vivid demonstration of a certain contradictory trend. On the one hand, the incidence of antisemitic prejudice and manifestations in the country remains sporadic, even decreasing (despite an increase in the general crime rate). Indeed, in February, the president of the DAIA issued an optimistic report forecasting a continuing decrease in antisemitism. Moreover, for the first time in the country's history, the reform of the Argentine constitution, while retaining the definition of Argentina as a Catholic country, has enfranchised non-Catholics to run for the office of head of state, thereby removing an otherwise insurmountable legal obstacle for a growing number of Jews active in Argentine politics. On the other hand the attack represented the second time in twenty-eight months that Buenos Aires was chosen as the site of international anti-Israeli or anti-Jewish terrorism.

President Carlos Menem and key members of his cabinet are aware that such attacks bring back memories of Argentina as a place where terrorism is not yet something of the past, and undermine official efforts to attract foreign investment. If for no other reason, the sincerity of their desire to get to the bottom of these attacks should not be doubted. Nevertheless, neither the three days of national mourning, the official condolences and offer of reparations, nor such other genuine expressions of solidarity as the

150,000-strong demonstration to express revulsion at the bombing has had as powerful an effect on the Argentine Jewish community as the fact that both attacks remain unresolved, thereby justifying a sense of insecurity and vulnerability.

Responsibility for the AMIA bombing has been ascribed by the Argentine, Israeli and US governments, as well as by numerous analysts (both Jewish and non-Jewish), to Islamic militants. The latter, though, may have subcontracted parts of, if not the whole of, the operation to local anti-Jewish elements— whether opposed or otherwise to the Menem administration's neo-liberal economic policies and international alignment with the USA—or to other operatives.

In the absence of solid evidence to substantiate any hypothesis, speculation on the motives and actual perpetrators of this outrage has been rife, with some claims reflecting better on their authors' political agendas than on the facts on the ground. For example, whereas the imported terrorism hypothesis can serve to divert attention from home-grown anti-Jewish elements, exclusive emphasis on the uncorroborated role of domestic antisemitic networks may be used as a distraction from the crucial fact that a Middle East-inspired operation would have been primarily an anti-Israeli, rather than an anti-Jewish, attack.

Brazil

General population: 145 million
Jewish population: 100,000 (mainly in São
Paulo, Rio de Janeiro and Porto Alegre (state of
Rio Grande do Sul))

GENERAL BACKGROUND

In October 1994 Brazil elected as president
Fernando Henrique Cardoso (Partido da Social
Democracia Brasileira, PSDB, Social Democratic Party of Brazil), a sociologist, former
senator and, as minister of the economy, architect of Brazil's most recent anti-inflationary
economic plan. This was followed in November by state and local elections in which allies of
Cardoso were elected for most key offices.
Cardoso was strongly supported by Brazil's
Jewish community.

Cardoso's predecessor was Itamar Franco,
who assumed that office following the resignation, in late December 1992, of Fernando
Collor. Collor had been democratically elected
as president in 1988 following more than
two decades of brutal military rule but his
presidency was marred by charges of corruption and impeachment proceedings against him
were about to begin when he resigned. In
December 1994 the supreme court acquitted
Collor of all charges of influence peddling but
Brazil's attorney general may now bring
embezzlement charges against him. The smooth
transition of power from Collor to Franco to
Cardoso suggests that democracy has taken
hold in Brazil.

Before July 1994 Brazil's monthly inflation
rate hovered between 30 and 50 per cent. In
July, Minister of the Economy (now President)
Cardoso implemented an anti-inflationary plan
which included the introduction of a new currency, the real, roughly pegged to the US dollar.
Since July Brazil's inflation rate has dropped to
around 2 per cent per month and the country
has received much foreign investment. There
is guarded optimism that the new economic
plan will alleviate the dire poverty in which
some 70 plus per cent of the population live—
illiteracy, for example, ranges from 11 per cent
in the urban south to 55 per cent in the poor
north-east. As president, Cardoso has promised
to continue the free-market policies of his predecessors and the modernization of the economy, although a number of important groups
(like oil workers) have gone on strike to protest the privatization of formerly state-owned
industries.

HISTORICAL LEGACY

Antisemitism has never been a major social
problem in independent Brazil because, historically, most Brazilians have had little contact
with Jews. Brazilian antisemitism is, in large
part, the creation of a tiny élite and supported
by a relatively small urban middle and upper
class.

Brazil remained a colony of Portugal into
the early nineteenth century and Brazilian culture therefore bears traces of the Inquisitorial
tradition.

Modern antisemitism in Brazil dates from
1930 when, following the Depression, a new
nationalist and nativist regime led by Getúlio
Vargas came to power. At that time nativism, of
which antisemitism was only one component,
became popular among intellectuals and the
élitist press. Groups that regularly attacked
Jews and Jewish immigration, the Society of the
Friends of Alberto Torres for example, also had
access to the corridors of power. From the mid-
1930s, the government tolerated antisemitic acts
and, during the early years of Vargas's rule, the
green shirts of the Ação Integralista Brasileira
(Integralist Party) began a virulently antisemitic
campaign that was condoned by the government. At their height, the Integralists claimed
one million members.

When Vargas created the proto-fascist
Estado Novo (New State) in late 1937, groups
like the Integralists were banned but secret anti-
Jewish immigration policies were formalized, a
situation that continued until Vargas was over-
thrown in 1945.

There is no indication of state-sponsored
antisemitism in Brazil since the end of the

Vargas regime. Since 1945 Jews have served in all areas of Brazilian political, economic and military life.

RACISM AND XENOPHOBIA

While Brazil's élite has always insisted that the country is a "racial democracy", such claims have been discredited over the last twenty years. Racial discrimination has in fact been illegal since 1951, but the poorest Brazilians are predominantly members of racial minorities, who also bear the brunt of most violence, both from the police and from criminals.

Brazilians of African descent frequently encounter discrimination when seeking employment, housing or educational opportunities. Most black Brazilians are found among the poorest sectors of society. Nearly half of the Brazilian population has some African ancestry, but blacks are hardly represented in the middle or upper echelons of government or the armed forces.

There are an estimated 250,000 indigenous peoples, who suffer from abuse, neglect and invasions of their land. Despite having a constitutional right to their traditional lands, in practice the authorities allow them only limited participation in decisions affecting their land, cultures and traditions, as well as the allocation of natural resources. In 1994 the lower house of congress passed a law to implement constitutional provisions with regard to the rights of indigenous peoples, but the senate took no action.

As Brazilians from the impoverished north-eastern part of the country have migrated southward into the large urban centres like São Paulo and Rio de Janeiro, attacks on these groups have increased. Indeed, there are some cities that have passed municipal laws (currently under review by the supreme court) that do not allow passengers to disembark from inter-city buses if they cannot prove their financial means.

São Paulo and Rio de Janeiro have recently created special police units to investigate racially-motivated crimes, although proving a racial motivation is notoriously difficult. The Jewish Federation of São Paulo will have a permanent member on the São Paulo unit's advisory board.

Brazil admits few immigrants, does not formally accept refugees for resettlement and is highly selective in granting asylum.

PARTIES, ORGANIZATIONS, MOVEMENTS

The far-right Party to Re-establish National Order (PRONA) achieved third place in the October presidential elections. It polled 7.4 per cent of the vote, compared with 0.5 per cent in

1989. While PRONA's political platform does not include antisemitism, its emphasis on a return to traditional Catholicism worries those who see modern antisemitism as being rooted in traditional Christian dogma.

There are a number of explicitly antisemitic movements currently in existence in Brazil. One is the Integralist Party (see **Historical Legacy**), revived with the return to democracy in 1988, that is based in the interior of the state of São Paulo. The new Integralist Party, however, appears to be supported by a few hundred people at most.

An avowed neo-Nazi political party is the Brazilian National Revolutionary Party (PNRB), established in 1992, which appears to have only about 200 sympathizers.

Claudio Galvão de Castro, former mayor of the city of Aparecida do Norte (380 kilometres from São Paulo), is a leader of Brazil's National Socialist Party. He has openly admitted to having pictures of Hitler in his house. It is important to note, however, that Galvão de Castro was *not* elected on a neo-Nazi platform and that the city council of the Aparecida do Norte has formally declared him *persona non grata*.

In another case, Márcio de Souza (Partido dos Trabalhadores, PT, Worker's Party), a city council member in the state of Santa Catarina, publicly denounced the White Power skinhead group. This was followed by an investigation by the state department of criminal investigations.

Brazil has a growing skinhead movement, modelled on those that currently exist in North America and Europe. A number of affiliated groups are included under the "skinhead" banner including the Skinheads, the Carecas do ABC (ABC Skinheads, named for the initials of three industrial suburbs of São Paulo), the Carecas do Suburbio (Suburban Skinheads), White Power, a grouping known as SPF and the Neo-Nazis, but it would be a mistake to assume that all such groups are ideologically linked to the principles of Nazism. Most are based in the industrial suburbs surrounding Brazil's largest cities where the economic crisis of the last half-decade has created high levels of unemployment. Over the past year the skinhead groups appear to have grown (although they may simply be more frequently noticed) but their attacks appear random rather than aimed at specific targets. This suggests that the increase in membership of skinhead groups is based on a growing predilection for thuggery rather than carefully constructed and deeply rooted bigotry. While the discourse used by neo-Nazi skinheads is frequently antisemitic, the pattern of actual attacks, when there *is* a pattern, targets migrants from Brazil's impoverished north-eastern states and those of African descent, although homosexuals and Jews have been involved as well.

MAINSTREAM POLITICS

During the campaign for governor of the state of Paraná, Jaime Lerner (Partido Democrático Trabalhista, PDT, Democratic Labour Party), former mayor of the city of Curitiba and the son of Polish Jews, was attacked for his ethnic background. The wall of a Jewish cemetery and fifteen of his campaign posters were daubed with antisemitic graffiti like "Jaime Jew", "Anti-Christ" and with the number 666. Furthermore, Vicente Goulart, an Evangelical pastor standing for the office of state representative, asked Christians not to vote for Lerner. He called Lerner anti-Christian and compared him to "other personalities in history who turned against God and ended up punished, like Lenin and Hitler". Another candidate, referring to Lerner's campaign, said that "being a Jew, Lerner should not use Nazi methods of propaganda, in which the same lie is repeated several times so as to become truth".

Several candidates, including those from other parties, defended Lerner, arguing that "this is a repetition of methods used in Germany prior to Hitler's empowerment". Rabbi Henry Sobel, senior rabbi of the Jewish congregation of São Paulo, expressed sympathy for Lerner as did Gilberto Estevão, president of the Brazilian Evangelical Centre.

The antisemitic attacks had little noticeable effect on the campaign. Lerner won the election overwhelmingly in November, garnering 45 per cent of the votes while his opponents received only 40 per cent between them (the remaining 15 per cent of the votes were invalid for various reasons).

MANIFESTATIONS

In April, in the midst of Brazil's presidential campaign, a small number of posters with a picture of Adolf Hitler and the slogan "Hitler for President" appeared in the city of Ribeirão Preto, in the state of São Paulo. They were immediately taken down and did not reappear. According to military police in the city there are no neo-Nazi groups operating in the area and two months after the posters appeared there were no clues as to who put them up.

CULTURAL LIFE

The name of Siegfried Ellwanger (see **Publications and Media**) came to the attention of the

public again after the film *Schindler's List* was released in Brazil. He orchestrated a letter-writing campaign to the newspaper *Correio do Povo* of Porto Alegre (state of Rio Grande do Sul) claiming that the film supported "the lie of the century". As always, these published statements of Holocaust denial were met with outrage by both the Jewish and non-Jewish community.

EDUCATION

In June a mock trial at the Leonardo da Vinci school in the city of Caxias do Sul, in the state of Rio Grande do Sul, absolved Hitler of having performed atrocities during the Second World War by a vote of six to four. The local community, both Jewish and non-Jewish, promptly reacted and a group made up of Eitan (the Jewish Centre for Informal Education), Curso Unificado de Caxias do Sul, the Leonardo da Vinci school, the Association of the Friends of Yad Vashem, the Caxias do Sul city council and the Zionist organization of Rio Grande do Sul jointly promoted a series of lectures and a photographic exhibition, "A Day in the Warsaw Ghetto" at the Caxias do Sul shopping mall. The students of the school that absolved Hitler visited the exhibition and attended the lectures. In a second mock trial, Hitler was condemned.

PUBLICATIONS AND MEDIA

A number of books written in the 1930s by the late Brazilian antisemite (and one-time president of the Brazilian Academy of Letters), Gustavo Barroso, have been reprinted by Editora Revisão (Revision), the publishing company of Siegfried Ellwanger (*nom de plume* "Castan"), a wealthy, sixty-eight-year-old industrialist living in the state of Rio Grande do Sul. Bearing titles like "Roosevelt Is a Jew" and "Brazil: Banker's Colony", these works were originally written as part of an anti-Jewish campaign waged by Barroso in his capacity as chief ideologue of the Integralist Party. The explicitly antisemitic nature of the books led in 1994 to their removal from bookshops under Brazil's anti-racism laws (see **Legal Matters**).

DENIAL OF THE HOLOCAUST

Literature denying the Holocaust continues to be published in Brazil, almost always privately funded by Ellwanger/Castan (see **Publications and Media**), whose publishing house, Revision, has distributed an unknown quantity of the books free of charge to politicians around Brazil. There is no indication that they have had any effect on policy. His "Holocaust: Jewish or

German?" is said to have reached its thirtieth edition (and sold 200,000 copies) but the number of copies printed is unknown. His *A Implosão da Mentira do Século* (The Collapse of the Lie of the Century, 1993) claims that the accusations of Jewish murders at the hands of the Third Reich are "Zionist lies".

In 1994 Castan offered a prize to anyone who "has lived in Brazil for twenty years and can prove that any Jew was killed in a gas chamber". A number of Jews took up the offer, but Castan refused to entertain their claims. Most Brazilians expressed outrage at the Castan prize but one newspaper, the *Diário de Petrópolis* (state of Rio de Janeiro), published an article on the prize as if it were legitimate.

Castan's books are not available in any of the major bookshop chains in Brazil but can occasionally be found in independent and second-hand bookshops. The Holocaust-denial literature, in spite of its small circulation, has been widely attacked and thus receives publicity disproportionate to its circulation.

Attempts to repress the distribution of Holocaust-denial literature in accordance with Brazil's anti-racism laws have not been actively supported by politicians and have failed under Brazil's freedom of speech and press guarantees. When Editora Revisão was removed as a member of a publisher's consortium in Rio Grande do Sul, a local judge reinstated it. Attempts to prosecute Ellwanger/Castan for defamation and injury have likewise been unsuccessful.

LEGAL MATTERS

The 1988 Brazilian constitution makes the public expression of religious or racial prejudice a crime carrying a mandatory prison sentence and no possibility of bail (Article 5, XLII). Many members of Brazil's Jewish community, however, remain cautious about using the legislation as a means of combating antisemitism since constitutional laws do not necessarily reflect social or governmental practice, and may in fact result in a growing sophistication in masking antisemitism and other forms of bigotry behind "acceptable" rhetoric. The law, however, was used in 1994 to remove explicitly antisemitic books from circulation (see **Publications and Media**).

In 1994 a law banning the use of the swastika was approved by the federal senate. Its approval was based on Article 5 of the Brazilian constitution mentioned above. Those convicted

of using a swastika are liable to be sentenced to two to five years' imprisonment.

In the state of Rio Grande do Sul a new law is under consideration that would punish any business or social institution that practises racial or sexual discrimination.

COUNTERING ANTISEMITISM

Responses to incidents of antisemitism have been rapid and widespread. The Jewish Federation of São Paulo has created a permanent commission to fight racism, and the Latin American Jewish Congress's section for inter-religious affairs has actively fought against racial hatred with support from the Brazilian National Commission for Catholic-Jewish Dialogue, an affiliate of the National Conference of Brazilian Bishops.

Following the bombing of the headquarters of the Jewish community in Buenos Aires (see **Argentina**), almost 2,000 people participated in a ceremony of solidarity with the Argentine Jewish community at the Latin American Memorial Centre in São Paulo.

ASSESSMENT

Brazil has little popular or open antisemitism. This is a result of the limited contact between a relatively small community of Jews and the mass of Brazil's impoverished urban and rural people. Jewish issues (as opposed to ones related to Israel) are kept out of the spotlight and Brazil's strong rhetoric of ethnic, cultural and racial tolerance is backed up by law, making public antisemitism a potential crime. The recent peace treaty between Israel and the Palestine Liberation Organization (PLO) has created a more positive image of the Jewish state and, by extension, Jews. The active involvement of some Jewish community leaders in popular movements to combat hunger, poverty and discrimination has been widely publicized and has presented Brazilian Jewry in a socially conscious light.

Despite the continuing growth of the small skinhead movement in Brazil and its bigoted ideological roots, it appears to be increasingly subsumed under the general category of thuggery. In fact, much of the "evidence" used to suggest that Brazil's skinhead and neo-Nazi movements are growing can as easily be interpreted as the result of better reporting techniques and an increasing unwillingness among Jews and non-Jews to let antisemitism in rhetoric or action pass without comment.

Canada

General population: 27 million
Jewish population: 356,000 (main centres:
Toronto, Montreal, Vancouver, Winnipeg,
Ottawa)

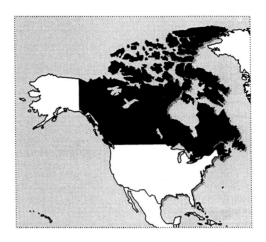

GENERAL BACKGROUND

Canada enjoyed a period of economic growth during 1994 and was among the leaders of the western nations in that category. Unemployment dropped steadily from about 12 per cent to just below 10 per cent, while interest rates moved upwards in tandem with trends in the USA. Inflation, as measured by the consumer price index, was negligible. Despite the positive signs of the gross domestic product growth rate and the decline in unemployment, there was a widespread perception that the economy had not recovered from the deep recession of the previous few years.

The Liberal Party of Prime Minister Jean Chrétien, which had taken office late in 1993, faced two major challenges, despite its large majority in the lower house of parliament. The first was the federal budget deficit, which was hovering around $40 billion, a figure that was widely regarded as unacceptably high. The government was committed to reducing it to about $25 billion by 1997, but deciding on the policies necessary to achieve that goal proved to be a daunting task. The second was the situation in Quebec, where the separatist Parti québécois (PQ) took power in the September provincial elections. The PQ had a razor-thin plurality of the popular vote but a comfortable majority of seats in the provincial legislature. It subsequently announced plans to hold a referendum on "sovereignty", which in reality would be *secession*, "sometime in 1995". The PQ's expectation was that if the referendum passed, independence would take place about a year later. At year end, most observers believed that the referendum, like its 1980 predecessor, would fail, but the volatility of the situation made it difficult to be confident about such an outcome. The Jewish community in Montreal, as well as in the rest of the country, was generally opposed to the separatist goal. Thus the success of the PQ and the possibility of secession raised the level of tension and anxiety among Quebec's Jews.

HISTORICAL LEGACY

While the first Jews came to Canada about 200 years ago, the bulk of the community is descended from twentieth-century immigrants, from Eastern Europe and Russia in the first half of the century and, more recently, from North Africa and the Middle East. The struggle for equality has been long and arduous, with public and private manifestations of antisemitism commonplace as recently as the 1930s.

The government's refusal to admit Jewish refugees from Nazism before and during the war is well documented. A book published in 1994 examined Newfoundland's refugee policy during the Nazi period, when it was a separate British colony and not part of Canada. In *Sanctuary Denied*, Gerhard Bassler documents how none of the over 5,000 refugee applicants was admitted, their requests having been blocked by vested interests in the business and professional establishments. He shows how Newfoundland had pursued a xenophobic refugee policy since the early part of the century.

Until the 1970s Montreal was the most important Jewish centre in Canada. However, the threat of Quebec separatism which emerged in the mid-1970s frightened tens of thousands of Quebec Jews, who were predominantly Anglophone, into moving to other areas, principally Ontario. Today Toronto has replaced Montreal as the home of the largest Jewish community in Canada.

During the last fifty years there has been a noticeable improvement in the status of Jews in Canadian society and the elimination of any remaining disabilities. Jewish community organizations have worked with the government to develop legislation in such fields as combating hatred against identifiable groups and prosecuting war crimes committed abroad.

RACISM AND XENOPHOBIA

Canadian hate groups and the growing skinhead movement target all the ethnic minorities that make up the multicultural fabric of society—including Jews, African Canadians, Sikhs,

Pakistanis, Chinese, Native Canadians and other groups—and show signs of increasing popularity, especially among the young, despite fluctuations in the fortunes of individual groupings.

A 1994 book by the lawyer and journalist Warren Kinsella, *Web of Hate: The Far-Right Network in Canada*, goes into extensive detail about the various extremist groups. Kinsella says that he is alarmed by the growth of the extreme right, which "definitely clings to an ideology of hate". In the book, he documents links across the Canada-USA border and identifies pro-Nazi lawyers in both countries. He shows how racists have infiltrated the armed forces, and how recruitment strategies and activities—like rallies and rock concerts—are aimed at school children, high school and university students, the unemployed and socially marginal members of society.

Racist and neo-Nazi activity in the Canadian armed forces is an area of major concern. In 1994 photographs were published of Canadian soldiers with the peace-keeping force in Somalia torturing and murdering a Somali youth; the incident was widely condemned. A film was also released which revealed widespread racist attitudes in the airborne unit, including racist treatment of black recruits. (The unit was disbanded in January 1995.)

Late in 1993, there were several incidents in which Sikhs wearing the turban required by their faith were barred from entering Royal Canadian Legion halls. Subsequently a national policy was adopted to permit Jews and Sikhs wearing religiously mandated head-coverings to be admitted, but some local branches (between 5 and 10 per cent) of the veterans' organization resisted. However, the biennial Legion convention in May in Calgary voted heavily against the executive's policy, thus leaving matters in the hands of the branches. In a related matter, a young Muslim woman in Quebec was barred from wearing the *hijab* in school.

In November citizenship and immigration minister Sergio Marchi announced a cut of 40,000 in the number of immigrants to be accepted by Canada in 1995. This marked a significant departure from the promise to maintain the annual immigration level at one per cent of the population. In addition, the new policy reverses a previous undertaking to give priority to relations of those already settled in Canada; new entrants in this category are to fall from 53 per cent to 45 per cent of the total. Instead, priority will be given to independent applicants with skills and capital. At the same time, the government increased the refugee quota by 75 per cent to a maximum of 32,000 per year.

PARTIES, ORGANIZATIONS, MOVEMENTS

Among the far-right groups, the Heritage Front continued to attract the most attention, largely because of the encounters between its leader, Wolfgang Droege, and the courts (see **Legal Matters**). Active for over twenty years in racist organizations, including the Ku Klux Klan (KKK), Droege was arrested in 1981 and jailed for two years for his role in an attempted coup in the Caribbean republic of Dominica. The group, founded in 1989 in Toronto, claims 1,800 members although a report on the Heritage Front issued in September by B'nai Brith Canada (BBC) estimated their membership at a few hundred at most. In 1994 the Front seemed to be on the wane, suffering from both financial problems and declining membership.

The Nationalist Party of Canada is a neo-Nazi group which emerged from the ashes of the Western Guard, which was itself a renamed version of the original Edmund Burke Society founded in 1967. Its leader, Don Andrews, was jailed in the mid-1970s for plotting to murder Israeli athletes in Toronto. Wolfgang Droege was formerly a member of the party and it is reported that most Heritage Front members are former Nationalist Party members. The party was virtually inactive in 1994 apart from its attempt to promote a "European Heritage Week" in October (see **Manifestations**).

The Church of the Creator is a violent and virulently racist group based in Toronto with several branches throughout Canada, and has close links to the Heritage Front. Its impact in 1994 on the active racist scene has been negligible due largely to the fact that its charismatic leader, George Burdi, has not been in the public eye since mid-1993 when he was arrested for assaulting an anti-racist activist; his trial is set for April 1995. The group publishes a clandestine newspaper, *Racial Loyalty* (although no issue has appeared since the end of 1993), and is said to engage in paramilitary training. Burdi was previously the lead singer for the neo-Nazi band RaHoWa (Race Holy War) and the founder of Resistance Records (based across the border in Detroit) which produces skinhead music CDs and tapes, organizes concerts, promotes racist bands, recruits young people and raises funds for the movement. The group has also been active in the United States.

The KKK (see **United States**) first came to Canada at the beginning of the century. It remains very small with marginal influence, primarily in Manitoba and British Columbia. The US-based Christian Identity movement (see **United States**), whose hallmark is antisemitism, has reportedly been attracting followers in Vancouver. Identity churches preach that Jews are literally the children of Satan and that the Bible permits the murder of Jews.

Aryan Nations is a white-supremacist group founded in the USA whose Canadian branch is headed by Terry Long (see **United States**).

Another white supremacist group, the Aryan Resistance Movement, is based in Mission in British Columbia.

Canadian skinhead groups tend to be anti-American, anti-black, anti-homosexual, anti-immigrant, anti-free trade, and in favour of the death penalty. Branches of the Northern Hammerskins, a racist skinhead umbrella group, have been appearing, notably in Toronto and Winnipeg, and are seemingly filling the void left by the declining fortunes of the Heritage Front and the Church of the Creator. The group, according to Bernie Farber of the Canadian Jewish Congress (CJC), is "short on philosophy and long on violence".

A racist and antisemitic group calling itself the Canadian Front has been active in Vancouver (see **Manifestations**).

The influence of the Chicago-based, antisemitic Afrocentrist organization, Nation of Islam (NOI), continued to leak over the border, fanning the flames of black-Jewish conflict. NOI rallies, particularly during the summer, attracted thousands who were addressed by both Canadian and US speakers. The organization's publication, *Final Call*, was on sale in 1994 at several sites in Toronto and Montreal.

MAINSTREAM POLITICS

The Reform Party, the third largest in the parliament, continued to face the problem of racist infiltration in its ranks. In an official statement made early in the year, the party contended that the purpose of the racist members was to "embarrass Reformers or seek publicity for their cause. These individuals are not welcome in the party and we hope they will get the message loud and clear." Despite this policy, racists continue to be attracted by the party's right-wing positions.

The party was embarrassed when a committee of a riding (constituency) association in British Columbia put out a newsletter in January containing, in its "Famous Quotes" section, a quotation from Hitler. Warren Schmidt, the Reform MP from that riding, disclaimed responsibility and expressed his disgust, even though the newsletter contained the Reform logo, the riding association's address and an article by the MP himself. He blamed an unidentified committee member.

Only a few weeks later the party expelled Armand Siksna, an ex-convict with links to neo-Nazi and racist groups who had recently joined in Calgary. The man had been involved in the KKK and in 1983 was convicted of conspiracy to murder. He was expelled two days after the *Toronto Sun* broke the story.

In September, the party learned that a Heritage Front member had joined in Toronto and expelled him as well. Max French, the man in question, asserted that three Heritage Front members were also serving on Reform riding executives in the Scarborough area near Toronto. Party leader Preston Manning reaffirmed that the party would take all necessary steps to locate and expel such people.

In August the *Toronto Sun* claimed that one of the founders of the Heritage Front, Grant Bristow, had been a paid informant for the Canadian Security Intelligence Service (CSIS) since 1989, a short time before the Front was founded. Some reports put the total payments made to him in the region of C$250,000. The *Toronto Sun* asserted that Bristow financed Heritage Front activities in various Canadian cities. Subsequent media reports claimed that Bristow had spied on prominent members of the Jewish community and passed the information to various racist and white-supremacist organizations, and that he had participated in campaigns of harassment and intimidation against various opponents of the Heritage Front. There were also suggestions that the CSIS, through Bristow, had tried to discredit the Reform Party by infiltrating it with Heritage Front members. Jewish spokespersons expressed dismay that a government agency would fund, however indirectly, the creation and maintenance of a racist group.

A subsequent 216-page report, *The Heritage Front Affair*, by the Security Intelligence Review Committee, the watchdog agency for the CSIS, was released in December. Its findings were startling: the "source" (presumably Grant Bristow, now apparently in hiding under the protection of the CSIS) had informed the CSIS of a Heritage Front assassination "hit list" containing twenty-two names, including some Jewish leaders—Bernie Farber of the CJC having been named as the Front's "most reviled enemy"—and of an organized plan for a Front member to enter the CJC offices on 26 October 1993 and "take out some people". While the CSIS had informed the police about the plan, the CJC had not been informed, a decision that Farber described as "unconscionable". The report, on the one hand, provoked criticism both for the role played by the authorities and for its "glossing over" the issue of the double role played by the "source". On the other hand, it was described by CJC president Irving Abella as "as complete and thorough a study of the racist underground as we've ever got in this country". It suggested in conclusion, less than convincingly, that Canadians owed Bristow a vote of thanks for risking his life to spy on the neo-Nazi underground, while it acknowledged that he occasionally performed his duties "overzealously". The Heritage Front denied the existence of the assassination plan. A special parliamentary sub-committee is investigating the affair.

MANIFESTATIONS

The League for Human Rights of B'nai Brith Canada's *1994 Audit of Antisemitic Incidents*, the most comprehensive source of such information, reported 290 incidents of antisemitic harassment and vandalism in 1994, which represents an increase of 11.7 per cent from 1993, and is the highest number of incidents recorded by the League in its thirteen years of documentation. The number of reported incidents of antisemitic vandalism dropped by 12.4 per cent from 1993, from 105 to 92, reflecting perhaps the reduced activity of organized neo-Nazi groups due to an increase in prosecutions and vigilance. However, the number of reported incidents of antisemitic harassment rose from 151 (in 1993) to 198, representing an increase of 31.1 per cent, the highest level of any year apart from that of the Gulf War.

Toronto was the site of half of all the reported incidents (50.3 per cent), 146 compared to 107 in 1993. The most significant rise in incidents, a 40 per cent increase, occurred in the regions of Ontario outside the cities of Toronto and Ottawa. While the number of incidents in Montreal and Winnipeg remained virtually unchanged, 55 and 16 per cent respectively, reported incidents in Ottawa dropped by 16 per cent (from 43 to 36), perhaps reflecting the establishment in the capital of the nation's first police hate crimes unit since there was a significant drop in *all* hate-motivated crime in the city.

In February and March there was a spate of bomb threats and attacks by vandals in Montreal synagogues and Jewish schools. A group of skinheads entered a Montreal yeshiva and intimidated teachers and students.

In March, in Toronto, fourteen Jewish organizations and individuals received live bullets with accompanying hate messages in the mail. Also in March, the home of a man seeking the Liberal Party's nomination in the provincial riding of Willowdale (Ontario) was daubed with antisemitic messages.

Former NOI deputy Khalid Abdul Muhammad was refused admission to Canada in April, when he was invited to speak at the University of Toronto. Denounced by Jewish community spokespersons as a "racist agitator" and a "hate monger", Muhammad nevertheless spoke to his audience via a telephone link-up to the USA. The crowd of some 300 people at a social club cheered as he denounced whites and Jews as the "enemies and the oppressors". Also in April, Minister Lynwood X, another associate of NOI leader Louis Farrakhan, delivered an anti-white diatribe to a black group in Montreal.

A new Sephardi school in a Montreal suburb was daubed with about a dozen swastikas and anti-Jewish slogans in May.

In June Tony Martin, a professor of African-American studies at the élite Wellesley College in Massachusetts, NOI supporter and author of *The Jewish Onslaught* (see **United States**), addressed a meeting of the Black Youth Congress in Toronto on the subject of "Garveyism and black-Jewish relations". Martin had caused controversy at his university when he introduced the antisemitic NOI book, *The Secret Relationship between Blacks and Jews,* in one of his courses. In his lecture Martin repeated a string of calumnies against Jews; he condemned their "control" of the media ("Nobody can slant the news like the Jews") and their purported role in the slave trade which, he claimed, was "very well documented". According to Ben Rose, a journalist who attended the meeting, it was "an uncomfortable place for a Jew to be".

In the summer a group calling itself the Canadian Front fly-posted the city centre of Victoria with swastikas, left calling cards at an East Indian restaurant, plastered a feminist bookshop with anti-abortion posters and dropped bundles of racist leaflets around the University of Victoria campus.

The neo-Nazi Nationalist Party of Canada tried to promote the week beginning 9 October as a Canada-wide "European Heritage Week" and even received a royal endorsement from a member of Queen Elizabeth's staff in London. The mayor of St Catharine's issued the appropriate proclamation but cancelled it two days later after the mayor of Toronto apprised him of the group's ideological character. Other cities that had rejected the initiative of the racist group were Victoria, Halifax and Vaughan.

A synagogue in Winnipeg Beach was vandalized with antisemitic graffiti on Halloween.

During one week in November three Jewish-owned businesses were daubed with swastikas, and swastikas were smeared on cars in a predominantly Jewish neighbourhood.

A full-size Nazi flag was prominently

displayed in the window of a motorcycle memorabilia shop on the main street of Sherbrooke, near Montreal. The unrepentant French-Canadian retailer refused to remove the flag after protests by Jewish and anti-racist groups—as well as a petition drawn up by students from a local elementary school—and claimed that the publicity had been good for business: he had sold at least six such flags.

CULTURAL LIFE

Controversy continued to surround political scientist Esther Delisle and her book, translated into English in 1993 as *The Traitor and the Jew: Anti-Semitism and the Delirium of Extremist Right-Wing Nationalism in French Canada from 1929-1939*. The book was widely attacked in Quebec intellectual circles because of its emphasis on the antisemitic attitudes of Lionel Groulx, the patron saint of modern Quebec nationalism. In a Montreal speech in April, Delisle admitted that she had touched a raw nerve by her identification of élite antisemitism, which was quite common during the 1930s. She stressed the point that the antisemitic comments cited in her book were direct quotations from the writings of Groulx and others, and that she had no personal axe to grind. Delisle was ostracized by the Quebec intelligentsia and had difficulty finding a job after her doctoral dissertation, which formed the basis of the book, was approved over the objections of two of the five members of her panel.

Writer Mordecai Richler, who had become the bane of Quebec nationalism because of his criticism of its campaign—suggesting that it had ushered in a "tribal period of great intolerance"—wrote an article for the *New York Times* in November which continued the attack but made it clear that he did not regard the current separatist movement as antisemitic. In an earlier book, he had demonstrated the integral role of antisemitism in the Quebec nationalism of the 1930s.

BUSINESS AND COMMERCE

In April an antisemitic flyer masquerading as "tax advice" was sent to accounting firms and other businesses throughout the country. The flyer criticized the Jewish faith under the pretext of helping Canadian taxpayers to get tax refunds for purchasing kosher products.

EDUCATION

Matin Yaqzan, a lecturer at the University of New Brunswick and a long-time supporter of antisemitic New Brunswick teacher and Holocaust-denier Malcolm Ross, took early retirement in January following his controversial article on date rape. He had written about Jews in the past, calling them revenge-seekers, comparing Jewish organizations to the Mafia and likening Israeli actions in Lebanon to Nazi atrocities. Shortly afterwards he wrote a letter to a Saint John newspaper to defend Ross on the grounds that his denial of the Holocaust and views about a Jewish conspiracy were "within the realm of possibility". He accused the BBC and the CJC of "bearing false witness" against Ross and whipping up hysteria.

The University of Western Ontario agreed to apologize to a group of former Arab students for official action taken in 1987 against several students and pro-Arab groups. The apology failed to note that the cause of the action was an offensive antisemitic poster that had been used to advertise a campus visit by a Palestine Liberation Organization (PLO) official. Gerda Frieberg of the CJC opposed the settlement because "it would be highly improper for university officials to apologize for condemning a poster which in our opinion should be considered antisemitic".

PUBLICATIONS AND MEDIA

Ernst Zundel, the German Holocaust-denier, continued his world-wide distribution of books, tracts and electronic broadcasts from his headquarters in Toronto (see **Denial of the Holocaust** and **Legal Matters**). After being thwarted in his attempts to spread his message on Canadian television, he looked south for outlets. One television station that agreed to carry his show, *The Voice of Freedom*, was KJLF in El Paso, Texas. The weekly programme reached as many as one million homes. Recurring themes were that the Holocaust never took place and that Auschwitz had been essentially a recreation centre. The same programme had been carried by the US satellite broadcasters Showcase America and Keystone Communications, but had subsequently been withdrawn. After intervention by local members of the clergy and educators, the El Paso station agreed to drop the programme (see **United States**).

Canada Liberty Net, a telephone hate-line (that is, a phone number that provides callers with pre-recorded racist and antisemitic messages) run by Tony McAleer was, in 1993, subject to a cease-and-desist order issued by the Canadian human rights commission, at which time it reportedly moved the service from its headquarters in Vancouver across the border to the USA where Canadian callers could continue to access it. In 1994, a human rights tribunal in British Columbia found that Canadian Liberty

Net violated the human rights act by producing telephone messages which attacked homosexuals. Liberty Net and McAleer were ordered to stop disseminating hateful phone messages.

Other hate-lines open up and close down with regularity (see **Legal Matters**). Two which were operating in 1994 but were closed down after complaints were made to the human rights commission were the Women of the Hammerskin Nations and the Rock Info Line. The Euro-Canadian Freedom Front became inactive at the end of 1994 due to the defection of its "voice" from the Heritage Front. Two apparently still in operation at the end of 1994 were White Advance and the Euro-Canadian Action Line.

Toronto radio station CIUT, which is affiliated with the University of Toronto, placed a volunteer programmer on probation for recording two interviews with members of NOI, one with Khalid Abdul Muhammad in April and one with Eric Muhammad in May (see **United States**). The latter attacked the Jews on the air: "So-called Jewish people had a prominent role in our subjugation." This was the third time in sixteen months that the station had been criticized for carrying antisemitic interviews. A retraction was broadcast daily for two weeks in June.

Racist groups in Canada have found innovative methods of communicating their messages of hate. Computer bulletin boards and the Internet, despite their utilization of telephone lines, are rapidly becoming the successors to the telephone hate-lines which have been effectively thwarted in the courts. Both the vastness of the computer "culture" and its anarchic nature make it difficult to counter with legal instruments. Computer bulletin boards allow properly trained individuals to gain access to the computer networks to read, write and disseminate electronic hate mail and messages. The Heritage Front opened a bulletin board in Toronto in December. Another bulletin board that disseminates racist propaganda and information is allegedly based in Gatineau in Quebec. Antisemitic, pro-Hamas Internet postings were reported late in the year.

The Heritage Front's monthly newspaper has, since January 1992, been *Up Front*, founded (1991) and edited by Gerry Lincoln. It is distributed to all Front members and supporters and has developed into one of the most virulently racist publications in Canada.

A Polish-language newspaper in Edmonton, *Kulisy Polonii*, published extracts from *The Protocols of the Elders of Zion* in June. The publisher claimed that he was responding to requests from readers and that he wanted to

"provide information about this book", not "make people hate Jews". Members of the Polish community took issue with the publication as well.

A catalogue featuring mugs, ashtrays, T-shirts and the like bearing racist, Nazi or antisemitic messages came to the attention of the Winnipeg police in September. It was published by a company called New Dawn Distributors, the latest venture of William Harcus, the self-proclaimed leader of the Manitoba KKK.

The *Michael Journal*, published in Quebec, regularly employs images similar to those found in *The Protocols of the Elders of Zion*. The CJC in Toronto demanded that Canada Post stop distributing the journal.

Antisemitic and racist newspapers, magazines and leaflets are published by many of the extreme right-wing organizations (see **Parties, Organizations, Movements**).

DENIAL OF THE HOLOCAUST

Canada remained a major centre of Holocaust denial due to the continuing international activities of Ernst Zundel and his Samisdat Publishing Company. In addition to books and newsletters, Zundel broadcasts and sells videotapes of himself and other Holocaust-deniers—shown regularly as paid programming or on cable access channels in the USA—and disseminates propaganda via the Internet which he transmits from the USA to avoid entanglements with Canadian law (see **United States**). His material has appeared in fifteen languages in forty countries.

Copies of the *Ball Report*, published by Ernst Zundel, were distributed widely on the University of British Columbia campus in Vancouver. The thrust of the report is John Ball's contention that the Holocaust never took place, and it uses maps and aerial photographs to present its "case". Ball had been nominated by the Social Credit party in British Columbia to run in the 1991 provincial election, but had been forced to withdraw when his ties to Zundel were made public. A history professor witnessed Ball trying to put one copy on each desk in his classroom. Over 1,700 copies were placed on car windscreens in campus parking lots.

A Holocaust-denial magazine, the *Phoenix Journal*, is published in the Parksville area, north of Victoria.

A number of neo-Nazis and Holocaust-deniers, led by Zundel and Canadian Liberty Net, attacked the film *Schindler's List* for its portrayal of the Holocaust. Liberty Net's recorded phone message described the film as "a masterpiece of propaganda". John Ball and

Doug Collins, a journalist in Vancouver, were also involved in the campaign against the film. Zundel called for a "world-wide campaign to ban *Schindler's List*". In August Holocaust-denial propaganda written by Zundel was left on cars outside a cinema showing the film in Kitchener.

British Holocaust-denier David Irving produced a videotape entitled *Search for Truth*, in which his view that the figure of six million Jews killed by the Nazis was grossly exaggerated. The British Columbia film classification board approved the video.

LEGAL MATTERS

During the year, the federal government considered new legislation to fight racism and hate crimes, a step applauded by the principal Jewish organizations. One proposed piece of legislation, known as C-41, would direct judges to consider "hate motivation" as an aggravating factor in setting sentences. The bill does not create new offences or compel stiffer sentences but would make an enhanced range of sentences available in cases of hate-motivated crimes, that is, crimes against persons singled out because of religion, colour, sexual orientation, gender, age, mental or physical disability, or nationality. The bill, introduced in June, was still mired in parliament at the year's end. It was expected to become law in 1995.

In January Wolfgang Droege appeared in the Ontario Provincial Court on charges of violating the terms of his bail by discussing the Front's activities in a radio interview. At the time of the interview Droege was planning to run for political office and as such had the right to campaign. He was acquitted on the charge, prompting the CJC to call on the Crown to appeal. The question at issue was whether or not a radio interview constituted a Heritage Front activity. The judge rejected the appeal.

In an unrelated matter, Droege signed a consent order with the Canadian human rights tribunal in which he agreed not to communicate messages which "expose a person or persons to hatred or contempt" because of race, colour etc. The order settled a case arising out of the use of a racist telephone hate-line. Another hate-line case resulted in Droege and two associates being found guilty of contempt of court in June for violating an injunction against the hate-line by setting up a second line, Equal Rights for Whites. All three were sentenced to prison terms, Droege for three months, and the Heritage Front was fined C$5,000.

In June, Droege lost his license to carry on business as a bailiff because he had omitted information about his US criminal record when applying for the license. According to Gerda Frieberg, chair of the CJC's Ontario region, "Droege is a racist agitator. He clearly has no right to be a bailiff charged with enforcing certain laws of this land."

In October, three Heritage Front members faced weapons charges after a confrontation in the Toronto apartment where one of them lived.

The James Keegstra case, which has been underway for thirteen years, continued to work its way through the courts. The former Alberta high-school teacher and mayor, who was convicted twice of promoting hatred against Jews in his classes, took his second conviction to the Alberta court of appeal. Prosecutors also appealed, arguing that the C$3,000 fine was an inadequate punishment. Keegstra's lawyer Douglas Christie, a well-known defender of such accused antisemites as Ernst Zundel and Malcolm Ross, told the court in February that the hate crimes law was unconstitutional because legal thinking had evolved since the supreme court of Canada had upheld it in 1990, and because it was too vague—an argument which was not accepted by the court. He also claimed errors by the trial judge. The appeal court handed down its judgement on the Jewish New Year, when Jewish organizations were not available for comment, overturning the guilty verdict in a 2-1 decision. The grounds cited by the court were procedural errors. The Alberta attorney-general announced that he would appeal the reversal to the supreme court. Jewish organizations praised his action. The sixty-year-old Keegstra now works as an auto mechanic.

The CJC decided to appeal a New Brunswick court of appeal decision in the case of New Brunswick teacher and Holocaust-denier, Malcolm Ross, one which might allow him to return to the classroom. In October, the supreme court agreed to hear the case, and also granted the BBC leave to intervene. The appeal court decision overturned a ruling by the provincial human rights body that removed Ross from classroom teaching. The 2-1 decision held that Ross's freedom of speech had been violated.

German-born Ernst Zundel, whose conviction for spreading Holocaust-denial literature had been reversed on appeal, applied for Canadian citizenship in 1994, thirty-six years after his arrival in Canada as a landed immigrant. Despite a 1991 conviction in Germany for neo-Nazi activities there, immigration experts believed that Zundel was eligible for Canadian citizenship. Some lawyers contended that his application could be denied only by ministerial discretion. No charges were pending against him at the time of his application.

The Alberta court of appeal agreed to hear the appeal of Mark Kreutzer, a Holocaust-denier who was convicted of assaulting a teacher in 1992 in front of a Calgary school. He had been distributing his material when confronted by a teacher who told him to leave the school property and a scuffle ensued. He was convicted for assault and was represented at trial by Douglas Christie.

In January Daniel Roussel, a neo-Nazi in Ottawa, pleaded guilty to assaulting an anti-racist activist with a chain after a skinhead rock concert in 1993. He was sentenced to forty-five days in prison and three years' probation. Two skinheads in court gave the Nazi salute.

The supreme court overturned a reversal of an Ontario skinhead's 1992 conviction by the Ontario court of appeal. It reinstated the guilty verdict against Paul Moyer for arranging in 1990 to photograph a simulated urination on Jewish graves in a Hamilton cemetery. The court unanimously found his actions to constitute defilement of human remains, a rarely used statute of the criminal code. Moyer received three years' probation.

A member of Hizbullah, (Party of God, see **Lebanon**), was deported in January because the government believed that he might engage in terrorist acts in Canada. Mohammed Hussein al-Husseini admitted membership of the group to CSIS, acknowledged that it operated in Canada, but denied that he was a terrorist. The Lebanese national entered Canada in 1991 on false documents and received refugee status. The department of immigration admitted that it had allowed Madi Ahmed Abdil Awi to enter as a refugee in 1991. Awi, wanted by French police as an Islamic Jihad terrorist, subsequently fled the country.

In June the supreme court ruled that non-Christians could not lose pay for missing work on their holy days. The case involved three Jewish teachers in a Catholic school in suburban Montreal who lost a day's pay for missing work on the Jewish day of atonement in 1985.

The issue of war crimes prosecutions remained complicated. In the case of Imre Finta, the supreme court in March upheld the constitutionality of the war crimes law, but refused to order a new trial for Finta who had been acquitted by a jury in 1990. Observers contended that the 4-3 decision would make it more difficult to secure convictions in the future. Sabina Citron of the Canadian Holocaust Remembrance Association called the decision devastating. A last-ditch effort to get the supreme court to reconsider was turned down in June by the same 4-3 margin. Subsequently the League for

Human Rights of BBC filed a petition with the Inter-American Commission on Human Rights, asking it to declare Canada in violation of international obligations to bring Nazi war criminals to justice.

Meanwhile, the case of Radislav Grujicic, accused of murder and conspiracy in connection with war-time activities in his native Yugoslavia, was stayed because of the poor physical and mental condition of the eighty-three-year-old defendant. That decision was announced in September by Justice Minister Allan Rock.

Justice Jules Deschenes, who led a commission of inquiry on war crimes, urged that the route of denaturalization and deportation be followed rather than prosecution for war crimes, in light of legal developments. Of the five cases undertaken by the war crimes unit of the justice ministry, only one, the deportation of Jacob Luitjens, succeeded (see **The Netherlands**). In August it was reported that eight cases involving possible denaturalization and deportation were under consideration by the ministry of citizenship and immigration.

New research by Quebec university graduate students Jean-François Nadeau and Gonzalo Arriaga, reported in the Montreal newspaper Le Devoir in May, indicated that prominent Quebec nationalists helped Jacques Duge, Klaus Barbie's right-hand man, and other French collaborators to settle in Quebec after the Second World War, and that Quebec historian Robert Rumilly tried to build a network of right-wing lobbyists. Others who were sheltered included Count Viktor Kayserling, Dr Georges-Benoit Montel, Dr Michel-Lucien Seigneur and Julien Labedan. Among those who helped in the process were Montreal mayor Camilien Houde, Quebec flag designer René Chaloult and Father Lionel Groulx; those still alive who signed petitions on behalf of the "refugees" are PQ politicians Denis Lazure and Dr Camille Laurin, journalist André Payette and foundation head Jean-Marc Leger.

COUNTERING ANTISEMITISM

The creation of hate crimes units in three metropolitan police services across Canada (Toronto, Winnipeg and Ottawa) has escalated the fight against racism and antisemitism. Their brief is to respond to the reporting of hate crimes, compile statistics and support the police units investigating the incidents. They are also involved in educational programmes, both for officers on the beat and for young people in schools and in the community. In addition, several metropolitan police departments, that of Montreal for example, also compile and publish hate-crime statistics.

Numerous public education campaigns to combat the spread of hatred and intolerance by racist groups were launched throughout the country. In Toronto in August large posters reading "Hate. It's taught. Stop intolerance. Stop racism. Stop the hate." have been put on bus shelters, schools and public buildings, and lectures on how hate groups recruit young people using increasingly sophisticated media have been organized. Several educational anti-hate leaflets have been produced: the BBC's League for Human Rights leaflet (*Is Your Child a Target?*) is aimed at teachers and parents; one produced by the Metropolitan Toronto Police (*Are You the Victim of a Hate Crime?*) is widely distributed in the city.

The Ontario ministry of citizenship is awarding grants for anti-racist initiatives by means of its anti-racism project funding programme. One project so funded in 1994 was an anti-racist booklet entitled *Resisting Hate*, produced by the Ontario region of the CJC and the Chinese Canadian national council. The booklet is intended as an educational tool for schools, community workers and the wider public.

Also funded by the Ontario ministry was the publication, *Holocaust Denial: Bigotry in the Guise of Scholarship*, prepared by the Simon Wiesenthal Center and the Canadian University Press, which was distributed to the campus editor of every university and college throughout Canada.

British Columbia Premier Mike Harcourt announced that his government is working to make the province free of racism and discrimination. He said: "Hate is insidious. If unchecked it will destroy the community from within." He expressed solidarity with the Jewish community's goals with regard to combating discrimination and hate propaganda. His government has also awarded grants for the production of anti-racist materials.

The federal government announced plans to establish a Canadian race relations foundation, a move applauded by Jewish groups, and condemned by the Reform Party as an extravagance. The government plans to provide a C$24 million endowment. Much of the foundation's work will be in the areas of research and policy development.

In June, the interfaith committee of the United Church of Canada repudiated the views of New Brunswick teacher and Holocaust-denier Malcolm Ross, describing them as "serious distortions of the truth". The Very Revd. Robert Smith, chair of the committee, said that he "hopes the United Church members and other Christians who have promulgated his-

toric inaccuracies will admit complicity in the persecution of the Jewish people and seek a more truthful and constructive dialogue with their Jewish neighbors".

In October, the BBC's League for Human Rights hosted a "symposium on the legal remedies for hate crimes" which was attended by more than 100 law enforcement officers, government officials, community activists, academics and prosecutors.

Ken McVay, a resident of Vancouver island, monitors the Internet on a daily basis for the appearance of antisemitic and racist propaganda, which he carefully refutes. He has compiled a massive "fascism and Holocaust archive" for use in combating the world-wide dissemination of racist propaganda and Holocaust denial on the Internet which hate crimes legislation is powerless to stop. The archive is used by a network of individuals and organizations around the world which has evolved into the Holocaust research mailing list, generating more than 1,000 electronic messages daily dealing with the development of anti-racist and anti-denial material.

Gottfried Wagner, a great-grandson of the famous composer, lectured in Montreal in March about Richard Wagner's antisemitism, and pointed out that his grandmother had been an admirer of Hitler. Because of his outspoken treatment of the racist attitudes of his forebears, Wagner has faced hostility in Germany and now resides in Italy. "I have also made the hit list of the neo-Nazi movement," stated the musicologist as he described the challenge of explaining his family's past to his own son. Wagner is active in a post-Holocaust dialogue group of Germans and Jews.

ASSESSMENT

Antisemitism in Canada continued to be a marginal phenomenon in 1994. It was represented most visibly by isolated individuals, such as Jim Keegstra, Ernst Zundel and Malcolm Ross, or by fringe groups, such as the Heritage Front and various skinhead gangs. It remains, with rare exceptions, unacceptable in mainstream society. On the other hand, it does appear regularly and requires constant vigilance to keep it in check. There is little likelihood of any serious outbreak, though the frequency of the vandalism and defacing of synagogues, cemeteries and Jewish institutions indicates that Jews remain a target of some of the nastier elements in society. Jews have found a number of allies in the struggle against racism in Canada, a fact which in itself strengthens the sense of security of the community.

There are some trends that are troubling.

One is the inability of the government and the courts to deal properly with Nazi war criminals. Despite the existence of comprehensive legislation that allows such people to be prosecuted in Canada for crimes committed in wartime Europe, the challenges of seeing cases successfully through the courts have proved to be a real dilemma. A second is the failure of the prosecution of racists, like James Keegstra, using the hate crime legislation passed in 1970. Despite multiple trials, the Crown has often been unable to prevail at the appellate level, leaving the efficacy of such prosecutions in

doubt. Third, the troubling antisemitism in the African-American community seems to be leaking across the border with disturbing frequency. As yet, there is little evidence that Louis Farrakhan's minions have been able to make significant headway among Canada's black population, but their very presence is unsettling to the Jewish community. Finally, the attacks on multiculturalism and immigration emanating primarily from the far-western provinces, though not aimed specifically at Jews, do reflect a lack of toleration of minorities that could prove dangerous in the long run.

Chile

General population: 13.5 million
Jewish population: 15,000 (mostly in Santiago)

GENERAL BACKGROUND

In December 1993 Eduardo Frei Ruíz-Tagle (Partido Demócrata Cristiano, PDC, Christian Democratic Party), the successor to President Patricio Aylwin Azócar, was elected with almost 60 per cent of the vote, an overwhelming show of support for Aylwin's coalition government. Aylwin's democratically-elected government had assumed office on 3 March 1990, ending the seventeen-year right-wing military dictatorship of General Augusto Pinochet Ugarte.

Although a constitutional reform has allowed Pinochet to remain in place as commander-in-chief of the armed forces, his influence has diminished considerably in recent years. Frei's political goal to change Pinochet's 1980 constitution to ensure a more representative form of government, dismantling some of the formal processes of direct governmental control, has so far had limited success as the balance of power in the forty-six-seat Senate is tipped—by the eight senators who are appointed by the military, i.e. Pinochet—in favour of the right-wing opposition. Nonetheless, government-military relations under Frei have been far more cordial than under Aylwin.

In September 1993, after protests from human rights groups and opposition parties, Aylwin was forced to back down on legislation which would have extended Pinochet's 1978 military amnesty law absolving the armed forces of any responsibility for the brutal violations of human rights committed between 1973 and 1978. Since the special committee appointed by Aylwin to investigate the disappearance of thousands of people produced its report, the courts have sentenced several people for atrocities committed during the military dictatorship despite some bureaucratic interference and chicanery. There are still many unresolved cases, both at the national and international level but, in an opinion poll of September 1994, only 7.4 per cent of those questioned mentioned human rights as "an important problem to be solved".

Chile's economy is widely recognized as the most successful in Latin America. In 1992, the Chilean economy grew by a spectacular 10.4 per cent but fell back to 4 per cent in 1994. In 1994, the annual rate of inflation was 9 per cent, the lowest since 1986. On the other hand, the neo-liberal economic programme has meant a severe punishment for the working class and the elderly; austerity measures, particularly between 1975 and 1981, have been particularly hard on the traditional middle class, particularly those employed in the public sector. In 1994, the rate of unemployment increased to 6.5 per cent from 4.5 per cent in 1993.

HISTORICAL LEGACY

The first Jewish immigrants in Chile at the end of the nineteenth century were from Russia and Eastern Europe. The second wave, in the 1920s, consisted mainly of Sephardi Jews from Greece and the Balkans. On the eve of, and during, the Second World War, thousands arrived from Germany, Poland and Hungary.

There is also a large number of Chileans of German origin. In the 1930s and 1940s many of them supported Germany and expressed their sympathy for Nazism in public statements and meetings, and by lobbying the government to support the Nazi-Fascist axis. On 5 September 1938 a Nazi group composed of Chileans of German origin and other ethnic backgrounds, the Movimiento Nacional Socialista de Chile under the leadership of Jorge Gonzalez von Marees, made an unsuccessful attempt to overthrow the government. Every year, on 5 September, Chilean neo-Nazis gather in the Cementerio General to remember the forceful repression of the Nazi *putsch* by the Chilean police (see **Manifestations**).

Some neo-Nazi ideologues are still active in Chile, principally Miguel Serrano, author of several antisemitic and Holocaust-denial books. Serrano, a native Chilean who was previously a member of the right-wing Partido Nacional and formerly ambassador to India, is well-known to Chileans and generally regarded as an eccentric.

Colonia Dignidad, a small German settlement in the southern town of Villa Baviera, has since the mid-1960s been accused of being a haven for ex-Nazis, and the German government has periodically insisted upon investigating its activities. During the Pinochet regime, rumours surfaced that it was also used as a centre for governmental repression of political opponents.

RACISM AND XENOPHOBIA

According to the 1992 census there are nearly one million members of the indigenous population, over 90 per cent of whom are Mapuches from southern Chile. There is widespread hostility towards indigenous peoples; as elsewhere in Latin America, the darker-skinned members of the population are generally among the most disadvantaged. A law was drafted in 1993 which recognized the ethnic diversity of the indigenous population and gave them a voice in decisions affecting their lands, cultures and traditions. However, they still participate only marginally in such decisions. About half of the indigenous population remains separated from the rest of society, largely because of historical, cultural, educational and geographical factors.

Chile assimilated a major European (mainly German) migration in the last century and a major Middle Eastern (mainly Arab) migration in the early part of this century. Smaller racial and ethnic minority groups, principally Koreans who have been migrating to Chile in increasing numbers, experience a degree of intolerance.

PARTIES, ORGANIZATIONS, MOVEMENTS

Extreme right-wing parties are almost non-existent in Chile. Those that do function are mostly ultra-nationalistic rather than overtly neo-Nazi or antisemitic.

Frente Nacionalista Patria y Libertad (Fatherland and Liberty Nationalist Front), an ultra-nationalist and anti-communist group, was founded by the lawyer Pablo Rodríguez Grez and became active in the 1970s in opposition to the newly-elected left-wing government of Salvador Allende. After the 1973 *coup*, Patria y Libertad dissolved itself voluntarily as a sign of support for the military regime, and many of its ex-members joined the DINA, the secret police. There has been speculation in recent years about attempts to revive the movement but evidence is sketchy; Rodríguez himself has denied the rumours. The group's emblem does, however, occasionally appear in graffiti in Santiago

though this may simply be the work of individual extremists.

Guardian de los Andes (Guardian of the Andes) is a neo-Nazi youth movement set up in September 1994. It currently has around twenty members who meet once a week. Its leader is Rafael Nuñez, a twenty-five-year-old philosophy student at Santiago's Catholic University, the country's most prestigious educational establishment. Nuñez has previously been linked to other neo-Nazi groups. Erwin Robertson Rodriguez, chair of the history department at the Metropolitan University, is the group's ideological mentor and a regular participant in Guardian de los Andes meetings. The group's priorities are recruitment, the indoctrination of its members and propaganda. There are currently no plans within the group to organize antisemitic acts, although this cannot be ruled out in the future. Guardian de los Andes has adopted a distinctive uniform and flag. They claim support from both Chilean and foreign neo-Nazi groups, and links with Chilean skinhead organizations.

Movimiento Nacional Revolucionario—Tercera Posicion (MNR, National Revolutionary Movement—Third Position) is another minuscule neo-Nazi youth group which is paramilitary in its paraphernalia: black uniforms and armbands bearing the group's emblem. Its leader is Marcelo Saavedra, a law student at Santiago's University of Chile.

Skinheads have recently begun to organize. Initially three young men decided to meet periodically, collect neo-Nazi literature and recruit members; they now number around sixty, all of whom are young, and they meet in the working-class Santiago district of Maipu. They claim to support Nazism, anarchism, atheism and xenophobia. Their avowed enemies are hippies, punks, drug addicts, homosexuals and Jews. Their xenophobia extends even to Chile's German community although it excludes German—and other foreign—skinheads and neo-Nazis. They support violence although they have apparently rarely used it. They claim that violent struggle will ensue if immigration increases. The skinheads believe themselves to be an army fighting to defend its principles. They are anti-democratic and show no interest at present in forming a political group as such. They apparently feel no affinity towards the traditional Chilean right. Their antisemitism is based on *The Protocols of the Elders of Zion* and is directed at the alleged "Jewish control" of Chile's media and education system. They lack a legitimate leader, the role being shared by the more long-standing members. Their clothing is standard skinhead ware (although their heads are not always shaved so as to avoid detection). They are financed mainly by means of a tattoo business. They generally attend meetings organized by Miguel Serrano (see **Historical Legacy**), Hitler's birthday commemorations and remembrance services for the 1938 Nazi *putsch*. Their potential for growth is significant, especially among disaffected working-class youth.

MANIFESTATIONS

On 5 March 1994 twelve uniformed youths waved a Chilean flag and distributed leaflets in the streets of Santiago. There were no recognizable emblems linking them to an identifiable group. The leaflets were anti-government and antisemitic in nature urging the public to read *The Protocols of the Elders of Zion*. The group, though peaceful, was arrested for organizing an unauthorized gathering. This group has never been seen before, though their behaviour suggests they are paramilitary.

Also in early March, following the massacre of Muslims by a Jewish settler in a mosque in Hebron, antisemitic graffiti appeared in the northern city of Iquique. During the second week of March, threats were reported against a cinema showing *Schindler's List* and the synagogue in Vina Del-Mar.

Four demonstrations commemorating the anniversary of the September 1938 Nazi *putsch* took place (see **Historical Legacy**). The first, on 4 September, was organized by the MNR. Forty demonstrators took part, mainly young men dressed in black uniforms and armbands. The only speaker was MNR supremo, Marcelo Saavedra. The demonstration ended with Nazi shouts and salutes.

The second, in the Cementerio General, immediately followed the MNR gathering. Survivors of the fifty-nine Nazi casualties of the *putsch* and their families took part, making a total of twenty participants.

The third, on 5 September, took place next to the plaque commemorating the fifty-nine killed. Twenty to thirty people attended.

The fourth took place in the Cementerio General. Around sixty, mainly young, working-class young men dressed in black military uniforms with swastika armbands took part. Three skinheads from the "Nazi-punk grouping of San Bernardo" also took part. The main speaker was Erwin Robertson who spoke about the need to confront enemies and use political intelligence to achieve objectives. The meeting

ended with Nazi salutes.

On 11 September, a date on which the Chilean right traditionally demonstrates their support of the 1973 *coup*, neo-Nazi youth distributed antisemitic leaflets in front of the military academy.

Throughout the year, unknown individuals have been discovered acting suspiciously in front of Jewish buildings, many of them taking photographs. Security, especially following the July bombing of the Jewish community headquarters in Argentina and the attacks on Jewish organizations in London (see **Argentina** and **United Kingdom**), has been stepped up.

PUBLICATIONS AND MEDIA

Television and press reports devoted less attention to ultra-nationalist and neo-Nazi activities than in the previous year. The demonstrations commemorating the 1938 Nazi *putsch* received very little attention this year from newspapers, magazines, television and radio; in previous years they were given more prominence that their size warranted.

Antisemitic and Holocaust-denial literature, however, such as the works of the British Holocaust-denier David Irving, *Mein Kampf* and *The Protocols of the Elders of Zion*, is readily available in many urban bookshops. Both of the latter books were on sale at this year's national book fair.

The skinhead movement has a publication called *Revista Drakkar Oi*.

ASSESSMENT

There is no significant, overt antisemitism in Chile although latent antisemitism certainly permeates most sectors of the population. This is limited to negative stereotypes of Jews and does not usually manifest itself in violence, either physical or verbal, or in any form of discrimination. For decades, Jews have been accepted members of Chile's intellectual, business and political élite. The racism in Chile is generally directed against its own indigenous population.

During 1994, propaganda activity directed against the Jewish community was in evidence, though none of it was violent. However, Jewish organizations were the target of numerous suspicious "surveillance-style" activities. Far-right groups were nonetheless active during 1994, especially at the time of the anniversary of the unsuccessful September 1938 Nazi *putsch*.

Colombia

General population: 36 million
Jewish population: 6,500 (mainly in Bogotá,
Barranquilla, Cali and Medellín)

GENERAL BACKGROUND

In the congressional elections of 13 March—in
which an estimated 72 per cent of the electorate
abstained, resulting in the lowest turnout since
1982—the two leading political parties, the Partido Liberal (PL, Liberal Party) and the Partido
Social Conservador (PSC, Social Conservative
Party), continued their traditional dominance
over Colombian politics while the presence of
the left-wing parties was sharply reduced. By
virtue of the political reforms instituted by the
1991 constitution guaranteeing political representation to previously ignored minorities, parties representing indigenous and black people
won seats in the legislature, while a number of
other groups, such as religious (Christian)
movements, also won a handful of seats.
Ernesto Samper Pizano (PL) was elected president in elections held in May-June.

In the 30 October local elections Colombians rebuffed the traditional parties and voted
non-aligned or coalition candidates to power in
30 per cent of the capital cities, including
Bogotá. This result was a response to the inca-
pacity of previous administrations to control
the high crime rate, as well as to the blatant corruption of public officials.

Colombia has endured a high level of violence for over fifty years. Conflicts between
opposing ideologies were responsible for most
of the violence in the 1940s. Gradually, leftist
guerrilla groups emerged as the principal perpetrators, until the mid-1970s when drug traffickers and paramilitary organizations funded by
powerful landowners sprang up, and both
money and the ownership of land, rather than
ideology, became the chief causal factor.
Though reduced, violence is still the result of
continual fighting between guerrilla groups,
drug traffickers, paramilitary organizations and
the security forces.

More than 15 per cent of the country is
dominated by various guerrilla groups—particularly the Fuerzas Armadas Revolucionaria
de Colombia (FARC, Revolutionary Armed
Forces of Colombia) and the Ejército de
Liberación Nacional (ELN, National Liberation Army).

The current administration, led by President Ernesto Samper Pizano (PL), has initiated
negotiations with paramilitary and guerrilla

groups, but these have as yet been only partially successful since splinter factions unwilling to negotiate are continually being formed.

Neo-liberal economic policies, including
privatization and the opening of international
markets, are now well established in the country. Unemployment decreased in 1994 by 2 per
cent, and the new administration has designed
an ambitious plan to provide employment,
housing, health and education to the impoverished population dedicating a large percentage
of the gross national product to these purposes.

HISTORICAL LEGACY

Colombia has been a Catholic stronghold since
the Spanish conquest in the sixteenth century.
A tribunal of the Inquisition was established in
the coastal city of Cartagena where Marranos
were judged and tortured. Religious antisemitism has been part of Colombian culture
since that time.

Although the upper echelons of the
Catholic Church have adoped a more positive
attitude towards Judaism since the *Nostra
Aetate* declaration of 1965, at parish level, traditional blood libels and accusations were still
commonplace, particularly amongst the less
well educated, in the 1940s and 1950s.

Jews from the Netherland Antilles were
the first to settle in the northern coastal region
of Colombia in the early seventeenth century.
The contemporary Jewish community was established with the arrival of Sephardi Jews from
North Africa and Syria after World War I, and
in the early 1930s Ashkenazi Jews came from
Eastern Europe. A relatively small group of
European Jews was able to enter the country
between 1933 and 1942.

A strong xenophobic attitude surfaced

during the 1930s and the legal immigration of foreigners was completely prohibited in 1939. While, accordingly, Colombian governments were never as influenced by Nazism as others in Latin America, antisemitic publications and articles in official newspapers were not uncommon during the 1930s and 1940s.

Antisemitic attitudes and stereotypes are apparent, particularly among the upper classes, in Colombian society. There are private clubs which do not accept Jews as members; while not openly prohibited, applications for membership by Jews are usually vetoed by board members.

RACISM AND XENOPHOBIA

There are approximately eighty distinct ethnic groups among the 800,000 indigenous Colombians. Although the constitution gives special recognition to the fundamental rights of indigenous peoples, they have frequently been the victims of violence by government security forces, paramilitary groups, narcotics traffickers and guerrillas. Most of these incidents have arisen out of land ownership conflicts.

Two million black citizens, representing about 4 per cent of the population, live primarily in the Pacific state of Choco and along the Caribbean coast. They have traditionally suffered from economic discrimination. In 1993 the Afro-Colombian Law was passed, but there has been little progress in expanding public services and private investment in Choco or other predominantly black regions.

PARTIES, ORGANIZATIONS, MOVEMENTS

The neo-Nazi and skinhead organizations which surfaced in 1990 proved to be a passing phenomenon, resulting probably from the influence of international skinhead movements and the media. There are undoubtedly still neo-Nazis among the Colombian population, but they have maintained a low profile and their numbers are insignificant.

The National Socialist Party which participated in the Bogotá city council elections three years ago disappeared from the political scene as well as from media reports.

PUBLICATIONS AND MEDIA

The publisher Editorial Solar continued to print antisemitic books and pamphlets, and sell them at low prices. Their list includes *The Protocols of the Elders of Zion, Mein Kampf* and *The Leuchter Report*, as well as several works by the Chilean neo-Nazi, Miguel Serrano (see **Chile**). Also available are Holocaust-denial materials published by the Institute of Historical Review in California (see **United States**) as well as publications of the Spanish neo-Nazi party CEDADE (see **Spain**). Antisemitic publications are sold principally in bookshops specializing in mysticism and new religious cults.

A previously unknown book, not available commercially, entitled *Adolfo Hitler, Genial Arquitecto del Tercer Reich* (Adolf Hitler, Genial Architect of the Third Reich) and written under the pseudonym of Ignaz Von Unter den Linden, was mailed in August to the Israeli embassy, the rabbi of the Sephardi community, the non-Jewish German owner of a bookshop and a German governmental institution. The author and publisher of the book are unknown as is the source of its dissemination.

DENIAL OF THE HOLOCAUST

Holocaust-denial material is available in Colombia but its volume has decreased since 1993 (see **Publications and Media**).

COUNTERING ANTISEMITISM

Steven Spielberg's film, *Schindler's List*, was a huge success and it provoked the appearance of other television programmes and books relating to the Holocaust.

The exhibition, "The World of Anne Frank", mounted in February by the Dutch government and the German cultural centre with the help of the Jewish communities in Bogotá, Cali and Medellín, was extremely successful. Visited mostly by schoolchildren in all three cities, it provided an excellent opportunity to counter Holocaust-denial myths.

ASSESSMENT

In general, Colombia is a solid democracy with a stable economy. Traditional conservative ideas—in response to modernization, the opening of international markets, the influence of the international media and the growth of multi-ethnic populations in urban centres—are giving way to more democratic and multicultural notions. Nonetheless, Colombians live in an atmosphere of chronic violence which, in terms of theft, kidnapping and assassinations, has increased significantly in the past decade.

In this context, nationalism and antisemitism are not principal concerns. Furthermore, Jews have become integrated within the fabric of society, mostly at the professional level, and are thereby able to influence public opinion against ethnic discrimination and antisemitism.

Mexico

General population: 91 million
Jewish population: 40,000 (mainly in Mexico
City)

GENERAL BACKGROUND

The centre-right Partido Revolucionario
Institucional (PRI, Institutional Revolutionary
Pary) has held power in Mexico, without inter-
ruption, for sixty-five years.

The ratification of the North American
Free Trade Agreement (NAFTA) at the end of
1993, which removed trading barriers between
Mexico, the United States and Canada, generated both rising expectations and a high degree
of uncertainty regarding its long-term effects.
This ambivalence was vividly demonstrated on
the first day of 1994, when the treaty went into
effect, by the news of an uprising in the south-
eastern state of Chiapas. The traditional gaps in
wealth distribution between peasants and landowners in the region, an unjust parcelling of the
coffee-producing land and the continuous discrimination against the indigenous population
were behind the uprising which soon reached
national dimensions in its demand for democratic and electoral reforms. Mexican society reacted in contrasting ways *vis-à-vis* the rebel
movement, the Ejército Zapatista de Liberación
Nacional (EZLN, Zapatista National Liberation Army), whose leader, known as Sub-Com-
mandant Marcos, described NAFTA as "the
death certificate for the indigenous people of
Mexico". While the most conservative sectors
called for repressive measures, progressive circles viewed the EZLN's activities sympathetically due to its popular character and its
non-institutional profile.

The weakening of the traditional pillars of
the Mexican political system brought about by
this revolutionary movement was exacerbated
by the assassination, in March, of Luis Donaldo
Colosio, the PRI presidential candidate. His
calls for democratization of the system implied
that the murder had political undertones, deriving mainly from the struggle between reformers
and "hardliners" within the PRI.

Both the assassination and the events in
Chiapas caused a flight of capital which adversely affected the economy because of
Mexico's overdependence on foreign investment. They also played a complex role in the
run-up to the presidential and legislative elections on 21 August which had a turnout of 78
per cent. A fear of change probably accounted
for the almost 50 per cent that brought the PRI

candidate, Ernesto Zedillo, to power. Nonetheless serious concern was expressed over thousands of electoral "irregularities" reported by
the Civic Alliance, an independent monitoring
group.

In September José Francisco Ruiz Massieu,
leader of the PRI majority in the newly-elected
lower house of congress (to be inaugurated in
November), was murdered. His close association with the progressive wing of the party
focused attention on the internal party conflicts
that could have been the cause of his death.

President Zedillo, who took office in December, expressed a willingness to promote a
permanent dialogue with the opposition parties
as well as to search for a negotiated solution in
Chiapas. Nevertheless, at the end of 1994, a
major economic crisis was brewing. With spe-
culative foreign investment and unrestricted
imports flooding the market, Mexico's balance
of trade showed a deficit which led to a devaluation of the peso by over 70 per cent. This provoked the closing down of hundreds of
businesses, a sharp increase in unemployment
figures and clear signs of recession.

HISTORICAL LEGACY

Antisemitism in contemporary Mexico was initially prompted by debates surrounding immigration policies during the late 1920s. Groups
such as the Anti-Chinese and Anti-Jewish National League, founded in 1930, and the Association of Honourable Traders, Industrialists
and Professionals lobbied the government to
restrict the immigration of Jews. In May 1931
250 Jewish peddlers were expelled from the
Lagunilla market and 1 June 1931 was proclaimed the "National Day of Commerce". On
that date, Mexicans protested about the Jewish
presence in commercial life.

In the 1930s, Mexico experienced outbursts of antisemitism centring on economic and racial themes. Gradually, the racial theme became dominant among right-wing groups. Among them, Mexican Revolutionary Action, founded in 1934, operated through its paramilitary units, the Golden Shirts. The antisemitic Pro-Race Committee and the Middle Class Confederation exerted pressure on the government and waged antisemitic press campaigns which reached their peak in 1938-9.

In the following decades, antisemitism was confined to fringe groups with marginal influence.

The financial crisis of 1982 and the social upheaval caused in 1985 by the earthquake in Mexico City led to the expression of anti-Jewish sentiment in the media; articles, particularly in the influential national daily *Excélsior*, accused Jewish factory owners of profiting from disaster, and of letting their workers die while saving themselves and their own property.

RACISM AND XENOPHOBIA

The indigenous population has long been the object of discriminatory treatment. The uprising in Chiapas focused attention on the demands of the indigenous peasants in that state for increased social and economic rights.

Indigenous people do not live on autonomously governed land, although some indigenous communities exercise considerable local control over economic and social issues. They remain largely outside the country's political and economic mainstream, and in many cases they have minimal participation in decisions affecting their land, cultural traditions and the allocation of natural resources.

Members of the indigenous communities who do not speak Spanish face additional problems. In criminal proceedings the law requires an interpreter to be present but the courts continue to try and sentence indigenous people without the benefit of interpreters. Knowledge of Spanish is essential for employment outside indigenous areas.

PARTIES, ORGANIZATIONS, MOVEMENTS

Throughout modern Mexico's history, with the exception of the 1930s, antisemitism has not been a central issue for political parties or movements. Nonetheless the extreme right, however marginal, has always proved to be fertile ground for the growth of antisemitic attitudes.

In 1994, there were two categories of far-right and/or neo-Nazi organizations, an "older generation" of parties—dating in a few cases from the 1930s but mostly born in response to the perceived gains of the left of the 1968 generation—and a new breed of semi-clandestine groups that have sprung up in the last decade which have formed international links with neo-Nazi groups in other Latin American countries as well as in Europe and the United States, and whose small memberships are almost exclusively composed of young, and probably middle-class, male students in their twenties or younger.

The most significant groups of the first category still active in 1994 were the LaRouche-inspired Partido Laboral Mexicano (Mexican Labour Party-LaRouche, see **United States**), Falanges Tradicionalistas Mexicanas (Mexcian Traditional Falangists), Federación Mexicana Anticomunista (Anti-Communist Mexican Federation), Movimiento Unificador de Renovación Orientadora (MURO, Unified Movement for a New Direction), Guardia Unificadora Iberoamericana (GUIA, Unified Latin American Guard) and Los Tecos, one of the most virulently anti-communist groupings in Latin America who were responsible for numerous acts of terrorism, particularly in the 1970s.

The principal organizations of the second category of groups—whose ideology includes hostility to the indigenous population and opposition to the EZLN—are Mizión Nazional (National Mission), Movimiento Nacionalista Mexicano (Mexican Nationalist Movement), Acción Radical (Radical Action), Cedade-México (see **Spain**), Vanguardia Nacionalista Joven América (Young American Nationalist Vanguard) and Amigos del Ejército (Friends of the Army).

An ideology which first appeared in Mexico in the early 1990s has since become more overt and aggressive. Dubbed as "neo-Mexicanism" its adherents promote an idealized image of Mexico's Indian past and scorn Europe's role in forging the national identity. In this context, Jews are singled out as being culpable for the acute problems which haunt the Mexican and Latin American nations. Its most vicious advocate is the relatively small Partido de las Aguilas Mexicanas (PAM, Party of the Mexican Eagles).

MANIFESTATIONS

During 1994 anti-Jewish graffiti, in particular swastikas, continued to appear in Mexico City. Throughout the year PAM supporters daubed the walls of Mexico City's cathedral with graffiti claiming that Mexican Jews controled both the politics and the finances of the country.

PUBLICATIONS AND MEDIA

The most significant channel for antisemitism is the press, whose impact on public opinion cannot be overstated.

Antisemitic publications included: *La Hoja de Combate* (Combat Newsletter), established in 1968, published by the far-right publishers Editorial Tradición (Tradition Publishers) and edited by veteran neo-Nazi Salvador Abascal; the monthly *Verdades* (Truths); the bi-monthly publication of the Mexican Labour Party-LaRouche, *Solidaridad Iberoamericana* (Latin American Solidarity); *El Picador* (The Prod); *El Inquisidor* (The Inquisitioner), the mimeographed news-sheet of Mizión Nazional; *El Caimán Volante* (The Flying Alligator), the publication of Vanguardia Nacionalista Joven América; *Unidad* (Unity), an ultra-conservative periodical published in Guadalajara and edited by long-term admirer of national socialism Alberto Martínez Pérez; *Integridad Mexicana* (Mexican Integrity), published in Mexico City; and *Réplica* (Response), the publication of Los Tecos.

Tradition Publishers also published works by the prolific antisemitic writer Salvador Borrego, including *Derrota Mundial* ("World Defeat") (1950) and "America in Danger" (1960), which are now in their thirty-eighth and eleventh editions respectively.

In contrast to previous years the mainstream media were almost devoid of anti-Jewish prejudice. Commentators maintained a positive attitude regarding the Middle East peace process. Moreover, the letters columns were generally bereft of the anti-Jewish overtones which were evident in recent years.

On the other hand, in the broadcast media several known commentators expressed antisemitic arguments, especially with regard to Mexican Jewry's legitimacy. Such was the case on 7 December when Pedro Ferriz de Con discussed the "foreign" nature of the family names of the Jewish cabinet members.

COUNTERING ANTISEMITISM

Jewish and non-Jewish contributors to Mexico's most influential newspapers—*Excélsior, El Nacional, Reforma, El Financiero* and *El Universal*—denounced antisemitism in Mexico and elsewhere. Furthermore, the public relations campaign by Tribuna Israelita, the human relations council of the Mexican Jewish community, fostered close links between opinion-makers and Mexican Jewry. The impact of these ties was reflected in the publication in Mexico's main newspapers of an open letter condemning anti-Jewish terror and antisemitism following the bombs in Buenos Aires, Panama and London (see **Argentina, Panama** and **United Kingdom**). More than 150 outstanding political, intellectual and cultural leaders signed the letter, including nine presidential candidates.

Due to the fact that Hitler's *Mein Kampf*, among a myriad of antisemitic titles, continued to circulate freely in Mexico and other Spanish-speaking countries, Tribuna Israelita appealed to the German government to enforce its copyright regarding the reprinting of the book. The book's Mexican publisher was forced to stop its circulation and refrain from publishing it further.

Congruent with his previous expressions of solidarity with the Jewish community, outgoing President Carlos Salinas de Gortari asserted, in the context of the conference of Latin American Jewish communities held in November, that "the Jewish community of Mexico is an integral part of our national family. We share a deep respect for differences. The Jewish presence contributes to diversity which enriches our homeland, enabling all of us to push jointly towards national goals."

In the framework of the cultural and political discourse prevalent nowadays in Mexico, which emphasizes pluralism and tolerance, Mexican Jewry took a more visible and assertive stance. This became evident in the unprecedented encounters between Jewish leaders and both the ruling party candidate for the presidency as well as the most important opposition candidates, who were presented for the first time ever with a specific agenda of both national and Jewish issues.

ASSESSMENT

The development of a more pluralistic approach to cultural, religious and ethnic diversity has provided a new and strong source of Jewish legitimacy. Together with the country's new international alignment, the increasingly multicultural perspective resulted in a lessening of traditional anti-foreign rhetoric. This tendency manifested itself in 1994 in, among other things, the significant number of Jews active in the Zedillo government.

In 1994 Mexico underwent some of the most radical changes in decades—in its economic, political and socio-cultural spheres—as a result of an increasingly active civil society demanding a more democratic system as well as, in many cases, because of social upheaval and violence.

The future is uncertain, with Mexico facing economic recession, and political and social instability. Nevertheless, Mexican Jewry's growing legitimacy, its new visibility and open participation in the public sphere and the emergent assertive profile of the community while lobbying for Jewish issues, seem to be irreversible.

Panama

General population: 2.5 million
Jewish population: 5,000 (mainly in Panama
City)

GENERAL BACKGROUND

The presidential, legislative and mayoral elections on 8 May returned to power the Partido Revolucionario Democrático (PRD, Revolutionary Democratic Party), which had ruled the country from the 1968 *coup d'état* by General Omar Torrijos Herrera until the US invasion in December 1989 overthrew the regime of General Manuel Antonio Noriega. Dr Ernesto Pérez Balladares was elected president although he received only 33.3 per cent of the popular vote; the remaining votes were divided amongst six other candidates all of whom opposed the PRD. Although Pérez Balladares insisted there would be no return to rule by a military regime, the nation is in a state of alert since he and his followers, despite distancing themselves from Noriega's regime, openly espouse the same policies as the previous Herrera dictatorship.

Before 1 September, when Pérez Balladares assumed office, economic conditions were stable while investors and local businessmen waited to assess the political developments. By the end of the year, however, the economy was at its weakest for three years, and the country's socio-economic problems were, if anything, worse. The gap between rich and poor was wider, and poverty, unemployment and poor health were commonplace in large sections of the population.

HISTORICAL LEGACY

Both Sephardi and Ashkenazi Jews began settling in Panama in the middle of the nineteenth century. A wave of Sephardi Jews immigrated to Panama after World War I, and a number of Ashkenazi Jews fleeing Nazi-dominated Europe arrived during the 1930s. Panamanian Jews have always been well integrated in the larger community and are engaged in all aspects of Panamanian life. Antisemitism has never been a significant problem in Panama.

RACISM AND XENOPHOBIA

There are approximately 194,000 indigenous Panamanians whose traditions and languages are protected by the constitution. In November the government created a commission to address charges that the needs of indigenous peoples had been neglected. Native Panamanians

generally endure relatively higher levels of poverty, disease, malnutrition and illiteracy than the rest of the population.

Leaders of the East Asian and South Asian communities (over 100,000 members) claim that Chinese and Indian Panamanians and others of Asian origin are treated as second-class citizens.

SPECIAL FACTOR: THE 19 JULY AIRCRAFT BOMBING

On 19 July, a local flight carrying eighteen businessmen from Colón, the largest free trade zone in the western hemisphere, to Panama City exploded in the air, killing the twenty-one people on board, twelve of whom (including four Israelis) were Jewish. After investigations conducted by Panamanian, US and other experts, pilot error and mechanical failure were both ruled out. According to a report by president-elect Pérez Balladares released on 22 July, the explosion was caused by a bomb.

There were fears that the bombing was an act of terrorism against the Jewish community —part of an international plan to derail the Middle East peace process—and linked to the bombing, just one day earlier, of the AMIA building in Buenos Aires (see **Argentina**) and the car bombs, a few days later, outside Jewish and Israeli targets in London (see **United Kingdom**).

Other reports, however—including some sources within the Panamanian Jewish community itself—thought the bombing was a drug-related attack. The *Latin American Weekly Report*, to cite just one example, reported that the bomb bore "narco-paramilitary fingerprints", referring in part to the fact that a passenger—who has been named in most media reports of the bombing—had previously been accused by the Italian authorities of gold-smuggling and ties to the Medellín drug cartel in Colombia.

Whatever its cause, the bombing was completely outside the experience of the Panamanian Jewish community, and it shattered the sense of peace and security that had for so long characterized its relations with the wider community.

COUNTERING ANTISEMITISM

Following the 19 July bombing, the Jewish community received an outpouring of support and letters of condolence, and public condemnations of the attack were issued by many institutions, national and international, Jewish and non-Jewish.

ASSESSMENT

Antisemitism has never been a major concern in Panama, and what antisemitism there is exists at the grassroots level. However, the bombing of the flight from Colón to Panama City on 19 July has left the Jewish community in a state of shock.

United States of America

General population: 260 million
Jewish population: 5.6 million (principal centres: New York, Los Angeles, Chicago, Philadelphia, Miami, Boston, Washington DC)

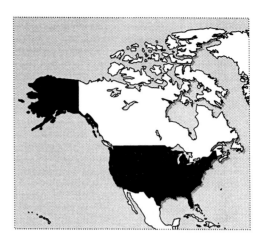

GENERAL BACKGROUND

The stunning electoral successes of the Republican Party in the November legislative and gubernatorial elections resulted in a radical change in the contours of the US Congress. The Republicans gained control of the Senate for the first time since 1986, and won a majority in the House of Representatives for the first time since 1954. They also held the governorships of 30 of the 50 states, including 7 of the 8 largest states. On the agenda for the 104th Congress was the new Speaker of the House Newt Gingrich's (Republican, Georgia) ten-point legislative programme, the so-called "Contract with America", which had provided the party with a populist conservative manifesto. Its measures included a mandatory balanced federal budget, the implementation of immediate cuts in income tax and capital gains tax, the reduction of welfare payments and legislation on term limits for elected officials.

The election result raised concern about the possibly increasing influence of the fundamentalist Christian right (see **Religion**). Well-funded and highly organized, the movement has taken control of the Republican Party in more than a dozen states, including Texas and Florida, and has made significant inroads in several others, including the large and powerful states of California and New York. According to Ralph Reed of the Christian Coalition, "forty-four of the incoming seventy-three new House members were pro-life, pro-family candidates backed by the Christian Coalition"; and according to People for the American Way, a liberal public-affairs advocacy group, 60 per cent of the 600 candidates for local, state and national offices backed by the religious right were victorious.

Noteworthy among the legislation enacted by the outgoing 103rd Congress was the omnibus crime bill passed in August which made the provision from within the USA of "material support or resources" for terrorists a new federal offence. The legislation also banned the manufacture, sale or transfer of nineteen types of semi-automatic weapons, extended the offences punishable by the death penalty and allowed for the imposition of stiffer penalties for hate crimes tried by federal courts.

HISTORICAL LEGACY

Antisemitism of a racialist bent emerged during the highly-nationalistic 1890s, when the large-scale immigration of Jews that characterized the next three decades began. The incorporation of explicit racism in American antisemitism followed the European nineteenth-century pattern, and informed "nativist" moves to restrict immigration.

One result of restrictionist trends dating back to the 1890s was the passage by the US Congress in the 1920s of national origins quotas that largely closed the doors to immigrants from Southern and Eastern Europe. These quotas meant, some years later, that the USA was unavailable as a refuge for a significant number of Jews fleeing Hitler's Europe. Another result of the "nativist" trend was the re-emergence in the early twentieth century of the Ku Klux Klan (KKK)—dormant since its first incarnation following the Civil War—which promoted antisemitism and became a potent force in a number of communities.

In the early twentieth century, antisemitic stereotypes proliferated in the popular culture of vaudeville and the stage and later in motion pictures. But two events during the early decades of the twentieth century galvanized Jewish reaction to antisemitism. In 1913 Leo Frank, a Jew, was wrongfully convicted of the murder of a young Christian woman in his factory in Atlanta, Georgia. In 1915 Frank was removed from his prison cell by a vigilante mob and lynched, a victim of rumours, slanders and calls to anti-Jewish prejudice.

In the 1920s automobile-maker Henry Ford, picking up from an American edition of

The Protocols of the Elders of Zion the libel of an international Jewish conspiracy, conducted a seven-year-long propaganda campaign through his newspaper, the *Dearborn Independent*, against what he termed the "International Jew".

The 1930s, the era of the American depression, was a time of distinct anti-Jewish bias in many areas of the social order. Economic and social antisemitism (that is, large-scale discrimination against Jews in employment, higher education and housing) combined with virulent political antisemitism resulting from the rise of Nazism in Germany and fascism in other European countries. The last major eruption of antisemitism in the USA occurred during this period, with an upsurge of ideologically-motivated and political anti-Jewish activity. The era gave rise to domestic anti-Jewish bigots, such as Father Charles Coughlin, Gerald L. K. Smith and William Dudley Pelley, leader of the Silver Shirts. It also witnessed the rise of the German-American Bund, and its leader Fritz Kuhn, and the notorious anti-Jewish speech by the aviator —and American hero—Charles A. Lindbergh to an America First Committee rally.

Especially influential was Father Coughlin, a Catholic priest whose weekly radio broadcasts with an openly antisemitic message reached millions in the 1930s. Coughlin's campaign paved the way for isolationist organizations, such as the America First Committee, to attract antisemites to their banners.

The 1940s, a period of social cohesiveness as the USA went to war against Nazism, Fascism and Japanese imperialism, saw a diminution of some forms of overt antisemitism. Nonetheless, there was continuing anti-Jewish bias in employment and housing, and in social-club and other "polite" forms of discrimination. Quotas on Jewish students also continued to exist at many major universities.

The 1950s was an era in which the Jewish communal agenda in the USA was almost synonymous with the civil rights struggle. In the years following the 1954 decision of the US Supreme Court in the case of *Brown v. Board of Education*, those who fought to preserve racial segregation caused serious social turmoil, including some scapegoating of Jews, a re-emergence of the KKK and the growth of "white citizens councils", as well as the proliferation of antisemitic fringe groups.

During the post-war years, antisemitism lost much of its ideological strength, and serious manifestations of antisemitism ceased to be a factor in the USA. There has been little political antisemitism, arguably the most virulent form of the disease, and discriminatory barriers have continued to fall in all areas of American society, including the corporate world.

Notwithstanding these trends, there have been some noteworthy manifestations of antisemitism during the past three decades. The late 1950s and 1960s witnessed—together with the McCarthyite witch-hunts—the rise and growth of radical right-wing groups advancing a theory that sometimes focused on Jews as promoters of a conspiracy to spread Communism and control the world. In 1960, during a two-month period, a swastika-daubing epidemic —643 desecrations of synagogues and other Jewish property throughout the USA—took place.

During the latter part of the 1980s, and continuing into the 1990s, the number of incidents of antisemitic vandalism and harassment rose steadily around the country. Notwithstanding these manifestations, the general diminution of most forms of antisemitism continued. Analysts suggest that there is no contradiction between the rise in the number of acts of antisemitic vandalism and the decline in anti-Jewish attitudes; those relative few who hold antisemitic views have been in recent years—a period of a general weakening of societal taboos—more likely to express these feelings in a destructive manner.

It is worth noting that in "moments of conflict" when one might expect an outburst of antisemitism—for example, the oil crises of the 1970s, the farm crisis of the 1980s and, most dramatically, the Pollard affair, which clearly invoked the question of "dual loyalty"—manifestations of antisemitism did not increase. This was clearly not the case in the USA before the Second World War, when "conflict situations" did lead to expressions of antisemitism.

One major source of anxiety in the 1990s derives from Afrocentrist antisemitism in the African-American community, and particularly the activities of the Nation of Islam (NOI). This anxiety was fuelled by two particular events. The first was the July 1991 speech of City College of New York Professor Leonard Jeffries, Jr., who claimed that Jewish conspiracies controlled, among other things, the slave trade and negative depictions of African Americans in Hollywood movies (see **Legal Matters**).

The second was the August 1991 riot in the Crown Heights area of Brooklyn set off when an African-American child was killed by an out-of-control car in a motorcade of the late Lubavicher rebbe Menachem Schneerson. A three-day riot broke out, targeting Jews and Jewish property in the neighbourhood. In the early hours of the riot, a young Australian hasidic scholar, Yankel Rosenbaum, was fatally stabbed. Lemrick Nelson, tried for

Rosenbaum's murder, was acquitted in October 1992 (see **Legal Matters**).

RACISM AND XENOPHOBIA

Virtually all the world's racial, national, ethnic, cultural and religious groupings are represented in American society. Furthermore, the ethnic complexity of the population tends increasingly to displace the hegemony of those of white European descent. According to 1990 census figures, 12.1 per cent of the population of the USA were black, 9 per cent were of Hispanic origin, 2.9 per cent were Asian Americans and 0.8 per cent were Native Americans. The 75 per cent representing those of white European descent in 1990 is expected to fall to an estimated 52.7 per cent by 2050.

Although the USA has a long democratic tradition, it also has a history of racism, and racial discrimination continues to show itself in various sectors of American society. To what degree racism contributes at present to the significant disparities that exist between white Americans and others, particularly African Americans but also Hispanic Americans, Native Americans and some groups of Asian Americans, is hotly debated by scholars, community leaders and politicians. The Arab-American community is also subject to negative stereotyping and some harassment, particularly during periods of political tension in the Middle East.

Despite the emergence of a sizeable black middle class—and highly successful black artists and sports figures—a large percentage of African Americans live in inner-city ghettos plagued by poverty, unemployment, crime, drugs, illiteracy. In 1994, almost 45 per cent of all black children lived at or beneath the poverty line. The African-American infant mortality rate was twice that of white children. Blacks accounted for an estimated 48 per cent of homeless people despite accounting for only 12 per cent of the population.

In June, the US justice department, under a mandate from the Hate Crimes Statistics Act, reported 7,684 crimes characterized as hate- or bias-motivated crimes during 1993 (the first year of reporting), with 62 per cent racially-motivated, 18 per cent motivated by religion, 12 per cent by sexual orientation and 8 per cent by "ethnicity". The figures were collected by 6,850 participating law enforcement agencies in forty-six states and the District of Columbia—regions representing a total of 56 per cent of the US population. Reporting in that first year was characterized by non-compliance by many state and local jurisdictions, as well as, in some cases, questionable numbers from those that

did report—a situation that the Federal Bureau of Investigation, the agency that collects the data, is trying to rectify for subsequent years.

According to figures from the Immigration and Naturalization Service, the largest groups of immigrants who lawfully entered the USA in 1992-93 were from Mexico, China, the Philippines, Vietnam, the former Soviet Union, the Dominican Republic and India.

Allegations of systematic deportations and violence by the border police towards undocumented Mexican immigrants have been made. There were also complaints of violence and discrimination against Mexican migrant workers.

A growing concern with immigration was manifest in the passage (by 59 to 41 per cent) of California's controversial Proposition 187 in the November elections, which will—if the provision is ever enforced (there is currently a court order against its enforcement)—prevent the state's estimated 1.6 million illegal immigrants from receiving non-emergency health care, welfare and education. The measure would also compel teachers and health professionals to inform the immigration authorities of suspected illegal immigrants or their children.

PARTIES, ORGANIZATIONS, MOVEMENTS

In terms of membership and influence, the impact of racist and antisemitic groups on the society as a whole was minimal. The most significant phenomenon to emerge in 1994 was the formation of the militias (see below). Nonetheless the white-supremacist movement as a whole has gradually expanded since the early 1980s, and has been the progenitor of occasional manifestations of violence. No single organization dominates the movement, which is composed of probably hundreds of groups of varying size and overlapping activities whose fortunes wax and wane, led by individuals who come and go. To one degree or another, however, they share the goal of creating a society dominated by white Christians in which the rights of others (particularly Jews and African Americans) are denied; many of them espouse Jewish conspiracy theories and Holocaust denial, and many are adherents of Christian Identity "churches" (see **Religion**). The number of hard-core activists in the movement has been estimated at approximately 25,000, of which roughly 60 per cent are members of the various white-supremacist sects, 20 per cent are members of the various KKK factions, 14 per cent are neo-Nazi skinheads, and 5 per cent are members of "traditional" national-socialist organizations. A much greater number of floating sympathizers attend meetings or rallies, buy literature and make donations.

The major antisemitic and white-supremacist propaganda organization in the USA is the Liberty Lobby, which was founded in 1955 by Willis A. Carto, a professed admirer of Adolf Hitler and a leading light in the Populist Party. Carto is also one of the key American figures in Holocaust denial as founder of the Institute for Historical Review and its antisemitic publishing house, Noontide Press (see **Publications and Media** and **Denial of the Holocaust**). The Lobby continues to propagate anti-Jewish bigotry and Jewish conspiracy theories in the garb of patriotism or "populism". In 1991 the Lobby launched the Populist Action Committee to support far-right candidates standing as Republicans, Democrats, Populists or independents. The organization's weekly tabloid, *Spotlight*, and its talk show, *Radio Free America*, are widely disseminated (see **Publications and Media**). In 1994 the Liberty Lobby established the Foundation to Defend the First Amendment for the purpose of suing the Anti-Defamation League (ADL) for violating the Lobby's civil rights.

Formed in 1984 under the leadership of former KKK-leader Robert Weems, the Populist Party fields candidates in local, state and federal elections. Its most famous candidate, another former KKK leader, David Duke, stood as the Populist Party's candidate in the 1988 presidential election before he entered the mainstream the following year by winning a seat in the Louisiana state congress as a Republican. The party, once the political arm of the Liberty Lobby, receives publicity and support in the Lobby's newspaper *Spotlight*. In 1994, the party split into two factions, one led by Willis Carto, the other by Don Wassall. The latter publishes a tabloid called *The Populist Observer*.

The KKK is the oldest of the contemporary racist organizations in the USA; it has enjoyed several periods of growth—after its founding in the years following the Civil War, during the 1920s, and during the 1950s and 1960s. The present incarnation, dating from the late 1970s, differs from earlier versions in that it has a younger, more media-conscious leadership, it projects a more "respectable" and less violent image, it has incorporated a Nazi-inspired antisemitism into its traditional white supremacy, and its original Protestantism has largely given way to adherence to Christian Identity beliefs (see **Religion**). The total membership of the dozens of different factions that collectively are known as the KKK is slightly over 4,000, with the ten-year decline in membership having come to a halt in 1991 and with perhaps a small upswing since 1992. After the Invisible Empire

Knights of the Ku Klux Klan, led by James W. Farrands and based in Sanford, North Carolina, was disbanded as part of the settlement of a 1993 lawsuit against them brought by the Southern Poverty Law Center, the principal KKK organization remaining in 1994 was the Knights of the Ku Klux Klan, led by Thom Robb and based in Harrison, Arkansas. Despite benefiting from the dissolution of the rival faction, Robb's group—which has attempted to appeal to a more "moderate" mainstream—has suffered defections from those who favour greater militancy.

Established in 1974 by Richard Butler, an Identity "preacher" and former Klansman, Aryan Nations acts as an umbrella organization to unite various KKK and neo-Nazi groups. Although based at a twenty-acre compound in Hayden Lake, Idaho, the group's membership is nation-wide, and in 1989 a headquarters for the South was opened in Tennessee. The group, which defines its aims as the creation of a whites-only preserve in the north-west of North America (the so-called "north-west imperative"), holds an annual "world congress" for white supremacists and neo-Nazis from the USA, Canada and Europe, where it provides instruction on urban terrorism and guerrilla warfare. The influence of the group has been declining and, in July, its congress drew about 135 people, fewer than ever; only 100 participants attended its annual youth festival to mark the anniversary of Hitler's birth in April. The organization is also active in Canada.

The Phineas Priesthood is a clandestine movement which takes its name from the Phineas legend in the Bible. It emerged in 1991 and has now reportedly replaced the recently defunct The Order, an underground network of white supremacists which formed in 1983 after two Aryan Nations leaders, Louis Beam and Robert Miles, published a small-circulation newsletter calling for a movement of "leaderless resistance" cells to carry out acts of violence and terror in order to achieve the aim of a north-western whites-only republic. In the past decade, members of The Order were responsible for—and often convicted of—numerous murders, robberies, bomb plots and other acts of terrorism. Richard Butler, Beam, Miles and seven other defendants were indicted by a federal court on charges of seditious conspiracy to overthrow the government; all ten were acquitted in Arkansas in 1988. The existence of this, or other, clandestine "revolutionary" groups may be threatened by the growth of the militias.

White Aryan Resistance (WAR) is a white supremacist organization based in San Diego and headed by former KKK leader Tom

Metzger and his son John. Metzger is best known for his half-hour television programme, *Race and Reason*, which has been broadcast on community access stations in ten states, including California, New York, Texas and Virginia. WAR espouses an ideology known as the Third Position which rejects both the capitalist West and the formerly Communist East, and claims to represent the interests of the international white working class in its "battle" against race-mixing and capitalist exploitation. Metzger also favours a loose organizational structure and "leaderless resistance". Despite being fined $12.5 million in connection with the 1988 murder of an Ethiopian immigrant, Metzger and WAR remain active. Affiliated to WAR is the Aryan Women's League, founded by Lyn Metzger, daughter of the WAR leader, which has branches in several cities.

The Christian Patriot movement unites a new breed of racists and antisemites in a loose, semi-anarchic section of the white-supremacist movement. Christian Patriots are also known as Populists, America Firsters, Identity believers or Patriots. At the time of their emergence—in the tax protest movements of the late 1970s— they mostly belonged to the Posse Comitatus (Latin for "power of the country") movement active in the 1970s and 1980s but today are affiliated to dozens of different organizations, including the Republican Party. They believe in an international Jewish banking conspiracy, that the USA should be a Christian republic— as opposed to a democracy in which the "idle and parasitic majority" have the power to subvert the "productive minority"—in which only property-owning Christians should have a voice, and that "internationalists" (usually Jews) and "aliens" are attempting to establish international socialism. In 1994 a Patriot group was developing an Idaho compound called "Almost Heaven" for settlement by like-minded whites, and Bo Gritz, a leading light in the movement and former vice-presidential candidate for David Duke on the Populist Party ticket, established the Center for Action, which publishes a newsletter.

Neo-Nazi skinheads—as opposed to anti-racist and apolitical skinheads—have menaced numerous American communities over the past nine years. Estimates of the number of hard-core neo-Nazi skinheads in 1994 range between 3,500 and 4,000 nation-wide. Violence committed by skinheads has been racist in nature, targeting African Americans, Jews and Jewish institutions, and Asian Americans, as well as homosexuals and other groups; skinhead violence has included at least twenty-two homicides since 1990, and has led to dozens of

convictions for murder, assault, arson and, most frequently, vandalism. There is no national skinhead organization, but rather loosely-linked networks of gangs with names like Northern Hammerskins, American Front, New Dawn Hammerskins, Confederate Hammerskins, American Spring, Fourth Reich, Aryan Resistance League, National Front and SS of America. Music is the unifying force of the skinhead movement; Resistance Records, founded by Canadian Church of the Creator leader George Burdi (see **Canada**), publishes skinhead rock music tapes and CDs. WAR is the "adult" organization to which neo-Nazi skinheads are most often linked, although other groups, such as the Aryan Nations, the National Alliance and, particularly in the southeast, the KKK, have attracted skinhead followers.

The National Alliance is a highly-structured hierarchical organization founded by William Pierce, author of the flagrantly pro-violence novels, *The Turner Diaries* and *Hunter*, and a follower of American Nazi Party founder George Lincoln Rockwell. The organization, based in Virginia, promotes a violent form of national socialism and calls for the extermination of non-Aryans; it has been gaining in influence, primarily among young skinheads, and recruits members in Canada and the United Kingdom. It now operates twenty-one phone message centres in fifteen states and Canada, and publishes a monthly called *National Vanguard*.

The Nationalsozialistische Deutsche Arbeiterpartei/ Auslands- und Aufbau-organisation (NSDAP/AO, German National Socialist Workers Party/Overseas Section) was founded in 1972. Headed by Gary Lauck of Lincoln, Nebraska, the NSDAP/AO has become the world's largest supplier of neo-Nazi and Holocaust-denial materials to Germany, where such propaganda is illegal, as well as to other European countries (see **Germany**). Lauck publishes his material in more than ten languages, including Russian, and disseminates it in various forms, including on computer disks and by e-mail. He also sponsors two cable television talk shows in the USA.

The bizarre pseudo-political activities of the fanatical followers of seventy-four-year-old Lyndon LaRouche—who was released from federal prison in January after serving five years of a fifteen-year prison sentence for financial irregularities—continued during 1994. Antisemitism is a mainstay of the international LaRouche network and of its rhetoric, which identifies a "hard kernel of truth" in the forgery, *The Protocols of the Elders of Zion*. In 1993 the

Supreme Court refused to hear an appeal against a ruling compelling the Federal Election Commission to provide LaRouche, a perpetual presidential candidate (even from prison), with federal funds for his 1992 campaign. In 1994, LaRouchites were actively recruiting support in various countries, especially in Russia and Eastern Europe (for active LaRouchite parties, see **Australia, Germany** and **Mexico**).

A new phenomenon in 1994 was the rapid growth of armed "militias" which are active in nearly thirty states across the country. Estimates of the number of militia members range from 10,000 to 100,000. Some—although not all—of the militias have been organized by people with documented links to white-supremacist and antisemitic groups. One of the most active is the Militia of Montana (MOM), organized by John and David Trochmann who have links to the Aryan Nations in Idaho. Militia groups cite the Second Amendment (guaranteeing the "right of the people to keep and bear arms") and the Tenth Amendment (reserving powers not delegated to the federal government "to the States . . . or to the people"). They appeal to disaffected "ordinary" Americans by talking about gun rights, the 1993 Brady Bill—legislation which outlaws nineteen types of assault rifles and ammunition clips holding over ten rounds, and mandates a waiting period for the purchase of firearms—the 1992 government shoot-out with white-supremacist Randy Weaver in Idaho, and the federal government's siege of the Branch Davidian cult in Waco, Texas in 1993 (both Weaver and the Branch Davidians were wanted for gun violations). These events, they say, prove that the federal government is encroaching on—and even attacking—the rights of ordinary Americans. Through a fog of conspiracy theories, they have attracted large groups to initial meetings. Though subsequent meetings are typically less well attended, the talk about gun control and encroaching government tends to give way to other issues, such as Jewish control of "the new world order" and other antisemitic and racist stereotypes. While the federal government is the principal target of the armed militias, wild conspiracy theories, including anti-Jewish stereotypes, drive this movement, which is growing fast and is heavily armed.

The Chicago-based Nation of Islam (NOI) was founded in 1930 by Elijah Muhammad, formerly Elijah Poole, the son of a Georgia preacher. Its espousal of black separatism made it problematic for mainstream civil rights and black organizations throughout the 1950s, 1960s and 1970s. It has long been riven by factional disputes, the most celebrated split be-ing the 1964 departure of Malcolm X who turned to orthodox Islam and was subsequently assassinated. More recently, however, under the leadership of Louis Farrakhan, the movement has become more influential in the African-American community. Estimates of the organization's size range from 10,000 to 30,000 members, with many times that number of young admirers, and NOI mosques or temples exist in 120 cities.

Antisemitic rhetoric figures largely in the movement's Afrocentrist ideology (see **Education**), as does anti-white, anti-Catholic, anti-Korean and homophobic rhetoric. An NOI book, *The Secret Relationship between Blacks and Jews* (1991), described by Henry Louis Gates, Jr., a leading African-American intellectual and professor of humanities at Harvard University, as "the bible of the new antisemitism", accuses Jews of being chiefly responsible for the slave trade, and of having exploited the civil rights movement in the USA to further their own ends. Another major theme is the insistence that the persecution suffered throughout history by blacks is worse than that suffered by the Jews under the Third Reich. The Black African Holocaust Council—headed by Eric Muhammad, an aide to Khalid Abdul Muhammad (see below)—is responsible for the distribution of *The Secret Relationship*.

In terms of the African-American community, the movement preaches black pride, self-reliance, self-defence and the importance of black economic entrepreneurship, and denounces the use of drugs and alcohol, gambling and adultery. The NOI runs numerous inner-city projects to tackle the problems of drugs, black-on-black violence and a breakdown of family patterns, including the setting up of AIDS clinics in inner-city Washington DC (which were awarded $213,000 in federal funds), and counselling programmes for drug addicts, alcoholics and street gang members. The organization operates the Muhammad University of Islam in Chicago, an elementary and secondary school run by Shelby Muhammad, whose curriculum emphasizes mathematics and science, along with religious training and discipline.

Affiliated to the NOI are private security companies NOI Security (formed in 1990 and based in Washington DC) and New Life Inc. (run by Farrakhan's son-in-law Leonard Farrakhan Muhammad and based in Chicago) which have, in the past few years, been awarded millions of dollars' worth of contracts to police and protect violent and drug-infested public housing estates in several major cities, including some under the auspices of the US department of housing and urban development. In June, for example, NOI Security signed a contract worth $2.8 million with the Baltimore housing authority to provide security at ten high-rise blocks. These contracts have drawn criticism from several quarters on the grounds that taxpayers' money should not be used to subsidize, even indirectly, a group that is unable to provide services without discrimination.

Widespread public attention to the notorious November 1993 speech by NOI deputy Khalid Abdul Muhammad at Kean College in New Jersey—in which he attacked whites, the Pope, homosexuals and especially Jews, whom he called "the bloodsuckers of the black nation"—followed the publication of a full-page advertisement by the ADL (see also **Countering Antisemitism**) in the *New York Times* on 17 January, and elsewhere. The ADL advertisement, entitled "You Decide", consisted entirely of excerpts from the Muhammad speech. Criticism of the advertisement came from several quarters on the grounds that it drew national attention to Muhammad and his remarks which otherwise would have been known to only a very few. However, the attention compelled political leaders, both black and white, to respond publicly to the speech. At a press conference on 3 February, Farrakhan "disciplined" Muhammad—a meaningless gesture since he continued speaking for the NOI around the country. Farrakhan also criticized the "tone" of Muhammad's remarks while reiterating his belief in the "truths" that Muhammad spoke. Furthermore, according to press reports of an NOI rally in late January on black-on-black violence in Harlem—which was open only to African-American males, some 10,000 of whom attended—Farrakhan characterized attempts to silence Khalid Muhammad as a "plot" by Jews and the government.

MAINSTREAM POLITICS

Weeks after appointing her in mid-December, Newt Gingrich, the speaker of the new Republican-dominated House of Representatives, was forced to dismiss his new House historian, Christina Jeffrey—an associate professor of political science at Kennesaw State College in Georgia where Gingrich himself once taught. The dismissal followed the revelation that, in 1988, she had publicly criticized a proposal to fund an educational project about the Holocaust and the Armenian genocide in the following terms: "The program gives no evidence of balance or objectivity. The Nazi point of view, however unpopular, is still a point of view and is not presented, nor is that of the Ku Klux Klan. . . . the program . . . may be

appropriate for a limited religious audience but not for wider distribution." She had reviewed the project as part of an education department panel that refused to fund the course and her comments are published in the congressional record. Denying that Gingrich knew about the incident prior to appointing Jeffrey, the speaker's spokesperson said: "As soon as [Gingrich] confirmed the facts he . . . asked for her resignation effective immediately. He still holds her in high esteem."

During a run-off mayoral election in New Orleans in March, campaign workers for candidate Donald Mintz (who is Jewish) were accused of mailing out antisemitic campaign literature slandering their own man in an effort to smear the black candidate, Marc Morial, as well as to raise funds for Mintz's campaign. Morial, a state senator and son of the city's first African-American mayor, won the election.

The aftermath of Louis Farrakhan's February press conference (see **Parties, Organizations, Movements**) produced a mixed response from African-American leaders. Congressman Major Owens, for example, continued to call on people to "reject Muhammad and Farrakhan [and instead create] a coalition of the caring majority". On the other hand the then director of the National Association for the Advancement of Colored People (NAACP), Benjamin Chavis (who had previously urged the African-American community to work with Farrakhan), said: "The NAACP is prepared to believe Minister Farrakhan's statement that he is neither antisemitic nor racist." American Jewish Committee (AJC) director David Harris criticized Chavis's "incredible" statement for overlooking not only "Minister Farrakhan's long-time ongoing promotion of bigotry" but also his own antisemitic statements during the press conference. (For example, Farrakhan praised *The Secret Relationship between Blacks and Jews*, stating that "75 per cent of the slaves owned in the South were owned by Jewish slave-holders".)

The inclusion of Farrakhan among the participants of a three-day "National African-American Leadership Summit" in Baltimore in June provoked widespread criticism, particularly from some Jewish organizations. The summit, convened by the NAACP, brought together leading members of the African-American community for the purpose of reconciling differences and planning for the future. At a press conference Chavis responded to the criticism: "Never again will we allow any external forces to dictate to the African American community who we will meet with. . . . We have locked arms and the circle will not be broken."

MANIFESTATIONS

The ADL's annual *Audit of Anti-Semitic Incidents* reported an increase in the number of such incidents in 1994. A total of 2,006 antisemitic incidents were reported during the year, 10 per cent greater than in 1993 and the highest number reported in sixteen years. Assaults against individuals and acts of harassment numbered 1,197—58 per cent of all incidents—an increase of 11 per cent; the number of incidents of property damage—vandalism of synagogues, other Jewish property and public property—totalled 863. There was an upward trend of incidents on college and university campuses as well, with 143 reported at 79 campuses, and the number of incidents perpetrated by neo-Nazi skinheads doubled. The five states in which antisemitic activity increased most markedly were New York, New Jersey, Massachusetts, California and Florida.

In the justice department's hate crimes figures for 1993 released in June (see **Racism and Xenophobia**), 18 per cent of the 7,684 incidents were defined as religiously motivated, and of those 1,189 incidents, 89 per cent were attacks on Jews; the remainder was composed of attacks on Catholics (30), Protestants (25) and Muslims (11).

In March a Lebanese-born taxi driver opened fire on a van full of Jewish students while driving across the Brooklyn Bridge in New York, of whom one, a sixteen-year-old rabbinical student of the Lubavich hasidic sect, was killed and three were wounded. Rashad Baz, the gunman, was reported, apparently in a statement by his employer (charged with aiding Baz and hindering the investigation), to have said he wanted to kill Jews in retaliation for the massacre of Muslims by a Jewish settler in a Hebron mosque four days earlier. Baz, who pleaded temporary insanity, was found guilty of second-degree murder and attempted murder in December.

A two-month spate of antisemitic vandalism in a Kansas City suburb—including spraypainting white-supremacist graffiti on two synagogues and a shopping mall, and planting a poorly-made Molotov cocktail at the local Lubavich headquarters—ended in March when police arrested three teenage boys. The police claimed that the three had no connection to skinhead or hate groups, and that they had engaged in these acts for a "lark". The symbol of the group Aryan Nations appeared in some of the graffiti. The police did not connect the teenagers to the recent dissemination of the white-supremacist paper *War Eagle* (see **Publications and Media**) in the local Jewish neighbourhood.

Also in March, in Eugene, Oregon, two skinheads were arrested in connection with a drive-by shooting of a synagogue in which two stained-glass windows were damaged. One of the perpetrators was a member of a skinhead gang in Portland called the Southeast Boot Boys.

The desecration of the Bayside Jewish cemetery in the New York borough of Queens twice in April was described as the one of the worst cases of such vandalism on record. In the first attack, which occurred between 1 and 4 April, at least fifty tombstones were overturned (one report put the figure at 200), remains were removed from coffins, bones were spread around the cemetery and four mausoleums were damaged. In the second attack, on 12 April, mausoleums were daubed with antisemitic graffiti.

A nineteen-year-old Lubavich yeshiva student was attacked with a pipe and a screwdriver by an eighteen-year-old skinhead yelling "I hate Jews! I'll kill you!" in Los Angeles in July. The student and a friend apprehended the attacker.

Jewish institutions and synagogues on Chicago's North Side were the target of vandals and arsonists. On 27-8 January four synagogues and a Hebrew school in the Jewish neighbourhood of West Rogers Park were set on fire. Thirty windows were shattered when bricks were thrown at another synagogue on 4 July, US Independence Day, and, days later, a Molotov cocktail was thrown through the basement window of another near-by synagogue, causing minor damage. The local ADL spokesperson said in July that there had been more reports of antisemitic vandalism in the area in the first six months of 1994 than in the whole of 1993. Three Palestinian Americans were charged with the January arsons.

In October the owner of a motel in North Falmouth on Cape Cod (Massachusetts) was charged with a criminal violation for her refusal to rent rooms to Jews the previous month. Wanda Szemplinski defended her right to refuse accommodation and was quoted in the local newspaper, *The Enterprise*, as saying: "If [the customer] thinks she was not rented a room because she was Jewish, then she should go to Israel where she should not have a problem."

In December, during Hanukkah (Festival of Lights), three large menorah displays were vandalized in Richmond, Virginia within a three-day period. There were no suspects.

CULTURAL LIFE

In the January issue of *Vogue* magazine, country singer Dolly Parton was quoted as saying that the idea of a television series about a country singer turning to gospel music was abandoned because "everybody's afraid to touch anything that's religious because most of the people out here [in Hollywood] are Jewish and it's a frightening thing for them to promote Christianity". After criticism, Parton apologized for the remark, which she said had been misinterpreted.

An electronic "Pinball Master" game—displaying a swastika, a tree, a tank and a telephone as images that appear as players advance from one round to another—was withdrawn from sale by Radio Shack, a nation-wide consumer outlet for electronic and audio equipment, after complaints by the ADL.

EDUCATION

Khalid Abdul Muhammad continued to lecture at college campuses across the country and to deliver his explicitly antisemitic message (see **Parties, Organizations, Movements**). Before Muhammad's speech at a rally at Howard University in Washington DC at the end of February, a student reportedly led some of the audience in antisemitic "warm-up" chants. (During one appearance at the University of California, Riverside, in May, Muhammad was shot and wounded by a former member of the NOI; the gunman was severely beaten by members of the audience, some of whom reportedly shouted, "He works for the Jews".)

Speakers at a one-day conference in April on "Documenting the Black Holocaust" at Howard University included Muhammad, Leonard Jeffries, Jr. and Tony Martin (see **Publications and Media**). At the conference, which was sponsored by the NOI-affiliated student organization, Unity Nation, and attended by some 2,000 people, comparisons of slavery with the Holocaust were a central theme, although accusations that Jews control the banks and the media, as well as being responsible for the suffering of African Americans, were also made; addressing Jews, Muhammad said: "You make me sick, always got some old crinkly, wrinkled cracker that you bring up, saying 'this is one of the Holocaust victims'. God damn it! I'm looking at a whole audience of Holocaust victims." Among the books on sale at the conference were the NOI text, *The Secret Relationship between Blacks and Jews*, Tony Martin's 1994 book, *The Jewish Onslaught* (see **Publications and Media**), Arthur Butz's Holocaust-denial "classic", *The Hoax of the Twentieth Century*, and *The Protocols of the Elders of Zion* as well as taped recordings of Muhammad's 1993 Kean College diatribe. It should be noted that many members of the Howard community, including members of the administration, students and faculty, spoke out against this antisemitic display.

At San Francisco State University in May a student mural commemorating Malcolm X, commissioned by the college and sponsored by the Pan Afrikan (*sic*) Student Union, was unveiled on campus. The mural, including Stars of David amid dollar signs, skulls and crossbones and the words "African blood", unleashed a storm of controversy on campus. Twice vandalized in the first few days of its existence—once by an African-American professor of English who tried to write "Stop Fascism" on the mural's border—the mural was eventually sandblasted after university president Robert Corrigan offered the artist the choice of removing the offensive stars or seeing the entire mural destroyed. The artist refused to remove the stars. Corrigan said: "If we were to allow the mural to remain as it is, we would be contributing to a hostile campus environment, one which says to students: 'We tolerate intolerance; we are silent in the face of bigotry.'"

All these incidents are connected by the belief of many associated with the extreme Afrocentrist school that everything which has a connection to Africa (history, people, culture etc.) is superior to everything outside Africa. In addition to claiming that blacks are biologically superior to whites and that all knowledge worth knowing originated in Africa, they reserve a special animus for the Jews, reminiscent of that of Henry Ford and Father Coughlin, whom they sometimes quote or paraphrase. They tend to believe in conspiracy theories of Jewish control of society, and blame Jews for problems in the African-American community. A common claim by Afrocentrists on campus and the NOI off campus is the inaccurate assertion of extensive Jewish participation in, and responsibility for, the slave trade. Such extreme Afrocentrism is of special concern because it combines a political group (NOI) and tenured professors working together to rewrite history —a history targeted at a new generation of African Americans—through an anti-white and antisemitic lens.

In 1994 Bradley R. Smith continued his Holocaust-denial activities aimed at the student population (see **Denial of the Holocaust**).

PUBLICATIONS AND MEDIA

Antisemitic propaganda was disseminated by means of all the various media and was, for the most part, well protected by freedom-of-speech guarantees. In terms of the printed word, many publications, including books, magazines, journals, newspapers, newsletters and pamphlets (for some which are linked to antisemitic groups, see **Parties, Organizations, Move-ments**), purveyed antisemitism. Unlike a generation ago, however, there were no antisemitic mainstream national serial publications.

Radio and public-access and cable television channels provided opportunities, protected under licensing ordinances, for white-supremacist and neo-Nazi groups to broadcast to communities around the country as well as internationally. A continuing issue in 1994 was the proliferation of uncensored "talk-radio" programmes including many that provided a forum for often-unchallenged racist and antisemitic remarks.

The dissemination of racism and antisemitism by means of the global telecommunications network has increased in recent years. Dozens of telephone hate-lines throughout the country purveyed racist and antisemitic messages and were used by almost all hate groups.

At a time when giant information empires have achieved near-total domination of the nation's media, the Internet has emerged as a "free space", an uncontrollable, unpoliceable and de-centralized zone where independent voices, however unpopular or objectionable, can speak and be heard. Anyone with access to a computer, a modem and a modest budget can send and receive messages, and read, copy and distribute documents, manifestos, essays and exposés. The number of Internet users is currently estimated at between 25 and 30 million, but the rate of growth is exponential; it reportedly grew by a staggering 1,713 per cent in 1994.

Furthermore, information in cyberspace is protected by the same freedom-of-speech guarantees—and subject to the same libel laws—as information in "real life". However, the precedent set by a federal court in 1991 which ruled that a computer network could not be sued for libel for a message it transmitted—on the grounds that it exercised no editorial control over its transmissions—means that only individual Internet users are liable for their messages, and they are notoriously difficult—impossible if they are reasonably skilled—to trace.

The California-based publishing house, Noontide Press, established by Liberty Lobby and Institute for Historical Review founder Willis Carto, continued its activities in 1994. In addition to publishing the *Journal for Historical Review* (see **Denial of the Holocaust**), Noontide Press published the "classic" texts of Holocaust-denial, such as Butz's *Hoax of the Twentieth Century* and the works of Paul Rassinier, as well as traditional antisemitica like *The Protocols of the Elders of Zion* and Henry Ford's *The International Jew*.

Tony Martin, a member of the African-American studies department at the élite Wellesley College in Massachusetts, continued to promote his 1993 book, *The Jewish On-slaught: Despatches from the Wellesley Battle-front* (published by his own Majority Press), which was also offered for sale by the NOI. The book, purportedly an account of Martin's experiences at Wellesley since he began using the NOI's *Secret Relationship between Blacks and Jews* in one of his courses, recast the entire history of black-Jewish relations as that of Jews attacking, and attempting to control, black people. (He also seemed to justify the Crown Heights murder of Yankel Rosenbaum which he described as having occurred in the "ensuing scuffles" after the "unpunished killing" of a black child, ignoring the fact that the child was killed in an automobile accident whereas Rosenbaum was stabbed solely because he was a Jew and—furthermore—only hours after the accident before any police investigation could be completed.) The president of Wellesley, Diana Chapman Walsh, sent letters to 40,000 alumnae, parents and "friends of the college" in which she criticized the book and characterized it as "offensive".

Among the more important newspapers and journals that espoused antisemitism were the following:

Spotlight (Washington DC) is a thirty-two-page weekly Liberty Lobby tabloid, founded in 1974, whose average number of subscribers approached 100,000, significantly lower than its readership a decade ago (200,000-300,000). The racist, antisemitic and Holocaust-denial articles that fill *Spotlight*'s pages are not written in the baldly crude language of KKK and neo-Nazi literature but coded in populist, anti-federal government or anti-conspiracy rhetoric.

White Patriot is a publication of Thom Robb's Knights of the Ku Klux Klan.

The Truth at Last (Georgia) is a racist, antisemitic and homophobic monthly published by long-time neo-Nazi Ed Fields, a national council member of the newly-formed America First Party.

Liberty Bell (West Virginia) is a neo-Nazi monthly published by an independent publisher.

The War Eagle is a neo-Nazi skinhead newsletter which first appeared in 1994. It was produced by veteran neo-Nazis and America First Committee members Art Jones, John McLaughlin and Roger Fountain.

The Jubilee is a bi-monthly tabloid of the Christian Identity movement (see **Religion**), published by Paul Hall in Midpines, California. It has recently been publicizing the militia movement.

Aid and Abet is a newsletter of the militia movement, published by former Arizona policeman Jack McLamb, aimed at recruiting law enforcement officers into the movement.

Taking Aim is a newsletter of the militia movement that bills itself as "the Militiaman's newsletter".

Endsieg and *The New Order* (Lincoln, Nebraska) are publications of Gary Lauck's NSDAP/AO. *The New Order* is published in English, French, German, Spanish and Hungarian, and disseminated internationally.

Final Call is the fortnightly NOI newspaper, often sold on street corners by members of the organization, whose sales records directly affect their status in the organization. Farrakhan has announced plans to build a printing plant for the paper large enough to rent space. He recently bought a Chicago "business centre" to house management and media operations as he expands into television. There are NOI bookshops selling books and tapes of NOI speeches.

The publications of Lyndon LaRouche and his followers, the *New Federalist* (formerly *New Solidarity*) and *Executive Intelligence Review*, single out prominent Jews, Jewish families and Jewish organizations for special abuse.

Antisemitic and white-supremacist groups produce radio and television programmes which are regularly broadcast. WAR leader Tom Metzger has produced more than forty-five half-hour segments of a television programme called *Race and Reason* which have been broadcast on community access stations in ten states across the country. The talk-radio programme produced by the Liberty Lobby, *Radio Free America*, is carried on more than 300 US radio stations and on short-wave to Europe, the Middle East and elsewhere. Pete Peters, a prominent Identity "preacher", hosts a weekly television show called *Truth for the Times*, as well as a radio programme that is broadcast in several American cities.

Louis Farrakhan appeared twice as a guest on television programmes in February. In an interview on the programme *Conversation with Ed Gordon*, shown on Black Entertainment Television, he stated that the media was controlled by Jews who were conspiring to destroy him, and to suppress the truth about the holocaust that African Americans had suffered which was "a hundred times worse" than that experienced by the Jews. He also appeared on *The Arsenio Hall Show*, a popular, mainstream television talk show which is syndicated to 160 stations throughout the country. Farrakhan defended the NOI text, *The Secret Relationship between Blacks and Jews*, and repeated its thesis

that Jews were heavily involved in the slave trade without being challenged or condemned during the programme or afterwards. The ADL, in an alliance with the Gay and Lesbian Community Services Center, the Catholic League for Religious and Civil Rights and the Gay and Lesbian Alliance against Defamation, protested his appearance by placing a full-page advertisement in the widely-read show business trade publication *Variety*. (The advertisement was addressed to Arsenio Hall and quoted, without comment, excerpts from Khalid Muhammad's 1993 speech at Kean College.)

The Simon Wiesenthal Center reported at the end of the year that most of the complaints it had received about racist and antisemitic messages on the Internet concerned Prodigy Services, a computer network owned by IBM and Sears, which has an estimated 2 million subscribers. In 1991 the potential use of computer networks to disseminate racist and antisemitic propaganda came to public consciousness with the revelation that Prodigy permitted subscribers to post antisemitic messages on its computer bulletin boards while disallowing responses to those messages. In response to complaints at the time, Prodigy formulated a policy that forbids "blatant expressions of hatred" on its boards (including the scanning of messages for obscenities) but, at the same time, asserted that these forms of expression were protected by free-speech guarantees. In December, a Prodigy spokesperson said that there were "more than 1.7 million notes on the board at any given time and we can't read them all". Other networks which have had similar postings are America OnLine and Compuserve. The Wiesenthal Center said that it had found more than fifty hate groups using on-line services and the Internet, and that use was increasing rapidly. Groups known to use computer bulletin board systems (BBS) include the Christian Patriots, the Liberty Lobby, WAR and the National Socialist White People's Party. A recent issue of an Institute for Historical Review newsletter stated: "The unique nature of the Internet makes this *the* information battle-ground of the future."

"Hate" articles are readily available on the Internet. An article attacking the Rothschild family in classical antisemitic terms, "Rothschild the head of the beast", was posted in October on one newsgroup. Kevin Strom, producer of a radio show for the National Alliance, reported that a review of Henry Ford's *The International Jew* entitled "The Wisdom of Henry Ford", which he posted on the Internet, was downloaded into home computers 120 times in one week.

The Internet is also used to publish lists of contacts. The Liberty Lobby sponsors a bulletin board called Logoplex BBS. The most active US bulletin board, Cyberspace Minuteman, acts as a linchpin for far-right groups throughout the USA and possibly Europe.

Bomb-making manuals have also been transmitted by computer links. The NSDAP/AO sent copies of its magazine *Endsieg*—one of which contained a do-it-yourself bomb-making recipe—on disk and by modem to Austria, Germany, France and the Netherlands.

RELIGION

The results of the November election raised concern over the increasing influence of the fundamentalist Christian movement which promotes, in addition to the issues included in the "Contract with America" (see **General Background**), the introduction of officially-sanctioned school prayer, the repeal of abortion rights and gay rights, the teaching of biblical "creationism" in schools, the banning of books, films and media programmes deemed to be anti-Christian, the elimination of multicultural curricula in schools and a diminution of the constitutionally-based distinction between church and state. What is collectively known as the "religious right" is a wide spectrum of diverse Christian evangelical and fundamentalist groups which are united in a belief that the separation of church and state mandated in the First Amendment's guarantee of freedom of religion—and its interpretation over the years in several crucial Supreme Court decisions, such as that disallowing prayer in state-funded schools and that permitting abortion—is at least in part responsible for the perceived breakdown of the nation's moral fibre. At the "moderate" end of the spectrum, evangelicals favour the weakening of governmental restrictions on the exercise of religious belief, while extremists call for the establishment of a Christian theocracy. But, to one degree or another, the movement holds that the nation has always been, and remains, an essentially Christian nation and that, in contemporary America, Christianity and its values have been sacrificed on the altar of "secular humanism" and "liberalism".

At the forefront of the movement is the Reverend Pat Robertson's Christian Coalition which claims over a million members, some 900 chapters nation-wide and a data base of over 1.8 million sympathetic voters. The grassroots influence of the Christian Coalition and many other more-or-less like-minded organizations is far-reaching: the Christian Coalition's Christian Broadcasting Network (CBN) is best known for Robertson's television programme,

The 700 Club, which reaches 59 million homes; the giant multinational corporation, Focus on the Family, founded by Dr James Dobson in 1977 and based on a forty-seven acre compound in Colorado Springs, produces daily radio programmes that are broadcast 60,000 times a week on an estimated 1,800 stations in 58 countries, and reportedly distributes more than 52 million pieces of literature and cassettes each year.

The movement has spearheaded several interventions in the mainstream political arena. One example was a campaign, backed by evangelical organizations and twenty-one senators, to throw out a set of guidelines issued in 1993 by the federal Equal Employment Opportunity Commission protecting employees from religious harassment in the workplace. What the guidelines actually accomplish, they complain, is the creation of a religion-free workplace rather than the protection of employees from harassment. A broad coalition of Jewish and Christian groups opposing the initiative testified at a Senate hearing on the subject in June saying that the removal of the guidelines would give free rein to religious intolerance in the workplace.

Within days of the November election, Newt Gingrich pledged to enact an amendment to the Constitution permitting officially-sanctioned school prayer by June 1995. While this issue, and the related issue of attempts to amend education-related legislation so as to promote school prayer, remained quiescent at the end of the year in the face of the flurry of legislation intended to enact the "Contract with America", it is expected to come to the forefront again. A coalition of religious groups has formed, ready to argue that any such school prayer enactments—including laws allowing voluntary or student-led prayers, or moments of silence—would endanger, not protect, religious liberty, and would erode the constitutionally-mandated separation between church and state.

Despite the absence of explicit antisemitic statements in the mainstream movement's rhetoric, there are suspicions that often-invoked terms such as "secular humanism", "the media" and "liberals" might in some contexts be coded references to Jews. These are suspicions that die hard in the face of some past statements by a number of the movement's notable figures—including Pat Robertson—who have been dogged for years by accusations of antisemitism. These include charges of trafficking with known racists, antisemites and Holocaust-deniers, fostering Jewish conspiracy theories, supporting Israeli and Zionist causes—which the movement as a whole does, sometimes with great enthusiasm—in order to bring about the second coming of the Christian messiah which requires the ingathering of Jews in their homeland.

In June an exposé of the movement, published by the ADL and entitled *The Religious Right: The Assault on Tolerance and Pluralism in America,* provoked considerable debate throughout the summer. An advertisement denouncing the report, signed by seventy-five Jewish conservatives, was published in the *New York Times* on 2 August, accusing it of using "marginal extremists" to portray the overall Christian conservative movement as fanatical. Critics of the book also attacked it for a lack of documentation and accusations based on innuendo and guilt by association. On the other hand, defenders of the report called it a "wake-up call", claiming that it was a sober analysis, that it did not focus on "marginal extremists" but on the movement's leading figures and organizations, and that, despite the generalized (and often long-winded) charges of shoddy scholarship, few of the book's details had been disputed.

On the extremist fringe, many members of the various white-supremacist, KKK and skinhead groups espouse the beliefs of Christian Identity. This racist pseudo-religion preaches that Jews are the children of Satan and "a race of vipers, Antichrists who have been a curse to true Israel", and that non-whites are pre-Adamic beings, created of mud before Adam, not fully human and without souls. "True Israel", according to Identity doctrine, consists of the Anglo-Saxons, descendants of the Ten Lost Tribes, who are the "chosen people". (This identification is the basis for the name "Identity".) The notion is derived from Anglo-Israelism, a doctrine that originated in Great Britain during the nineteenth century. The Identity movement runs small "churches", book and tape distribution houses, and radio ministries. One prominent Identity "preacher", Pete Peters, has led delegations of supporters to Washington to lobby against gun control and other issues.

DENIAL OF THE HOLOCAUST

Holocaust denial plays a role in virtually every antisemitic and white-supremacist organization in the USA. The vanguard of Holocaust denial however is the California-based Institute for Historical Review, founded by Willis Carto in 1979 as an offshoot of Liberty Lobby. The Institute produces a bi-monthly journal, the pseudo-academic *Journal for Historical Review*—a majority of whose editorial board members, including such well-known Holocaust-

deniers as Arthur Butz and Robert Faurisson, hold doctoral degrees—and eight newsletters per year, as well as publishing and distributing numerous books world-wide. An annual international conference hosted by the Institute draws together over 100 Holocaust deniers from around the world. In 1994 the editors of the *Journal* wrested control of the Institute from Carto as part of an effort to sanitize its image, an internal conflict which is the subject of pending litigation. The winner of the power-play is Institute director Tom Marcellus who is supported by, among others, the German-born Canadian Ernst Zundel, the French denier Robert Faurisson and the British denier David Irving.

Carto, in turn, founded a new journal dedicated to Holocaust denial called the *Barnes Review*, named after Harry Elmer Barnes, one of the "founding fathers" of Holocaust denial.

Holocaust-denial material has its own newsgroup on the Internet. The Institute of Historical Review increasingly makes use of this and other newsgroups, as well as bulletin boards, to disseminate its publications. It has stated its intention of making available everything published in the fourteen years of its quarterly *Journal of Historical Review* on the Internet. In March, well-known denier Michael A. Hoffman II and Alan R. Critchley published an article entitled "Spielberg commits fraud in film Schindler's List" on one newsgroup.

An important medium since 1991 for the dissemination of Holocaust denial among students has been the placing of advertisements in campus newspapers around the country by Bradley R. Smith, head of the so-called Committee for Open Debate on the Holocaust and media director for the Institute of Historical Review. By the end of 1994 some twenty-five college newspapers had published Smith ads, and an additional six papers had published letters or op-ed articles by Smith (see **Countering Antisemitism**). However, following exposure by university-based Jewish and other groups, the advertisements were rejected by a majority of editorial boards. Intense debate on the issues of constitutionally-protected freedom of speech and freedom of the press—generating media coverage and free publicity for Holocaust-denial materials—ensued on most campuses where the Smith advertisements were submitted. Jewish, anti-racist and other organizations pointed out that there was no First Amendment freedom-of-speech *obligation* on the part of campus newspapers to publish the advertisements. In October 1993, Smith did succeed in placing his ad in the Portland *Oregonian*, the first mainstream newspaper to carry such advertising; it was followed days later by an apology characterizing the ad as "repugnant".

Canadian Holocaust-denier Ernst Zundel, having been thwarted in his attempts to disseminate his propaganda in Canada, turned to the USA for outlets (see **Canada**). He succeeded in having his Holocaust-denial programme, *The Voice of Freedom*, aired on station KJLF in El Paso, Texas, until complaints in January from local clergymen and educators persuaded the station to cancel the programme when the contract expired, allowing seven episodes in all to be broadcast. Subsequent episodes were preceded by a disclaimer by the station and a statement that the Holocaust did in fact happen.

British Holocaust-denier David Irving made speeches around the country during 1994 (see **United Kingdom**). His fund-raising organization, the David Irving Fighting Fund, has an office in the USA (as well as in the UK, Germany and Australia).

A question in a November 1992 AJC-sponsored survey, conducted by the Roper Organization—"Does it seem possible or does it seem impossible to you that the Nazi extermination of the Jews never happened?"—which appeared to indicate widespread openness to Holocaust denial (22 per cent answered "possible" and 12 per cent "don't know") was flawed due to the presence of a double negative in the wording. A revised version of the question, eliminating the double negative—"Does it seem possible to you that the Nazi extermination of the Jews never happened, or do you feel certain that it happened?"—fielded in a follow-up Roper survey conducted for the AJC in March 1994, yielded dramatically different results: only 1 per cent considered it "possible that the Nazi extermination of the Jews never happened" and 8 per cent answered "don't know".

OPINION POLLS

Three studies released in 1994 analysed intergroup relations in the USA and provided a context for the study of antisemitism. An AJC study conducted by the Gallup Organization, *The Texture of Intergroup Relations: A National Survey*, found that, while a large majority of Americans express a strong commitment to intergroup harmony and equal rights, Americans view intergroup relations as a troubled area. According to the study, "race relations" are viewed by Americans in the most negative light, followed by "ethnic relations"; fewer Americans—although still a majority—see relations between religious groups as problematic. One in ten Americans report that they themselves have been the target of a racial, ethnic or religious slur.

A study conducted by the National Conference (formerly the National Conference of Christians and Jews), *Taking America's Pulse: The National Conference Survey on Intergroup Relations*, explored many issues in detail. With respect to prejudicial attitudes, the study found that members of minority groups are more likely than whites to agree to negative stereotypes about other minority groups. In terms of antisemitism, data revealed disturbingly high numbers in response to the "Jewish power" and "dual-loyalty" questions, both among whites and minority-group members. On the "Jewish power" question, 43 per cent of blacks and 22 per cent of whites said that Jews "have too much control over business and the media". Forty-seven per cent of blacks and 24 per cent of whites responded that Jews "are more loyal to Israel than to America".

A comprehensive analysis, *Anti-Semitism in Contemporary America*, commissioned by the AJC and written by Tom W. Smith of the University of Chicago's National Opinion Research Center, was published in June. Based on a review of more than 140 scholarly studies and the results of two dozen national opinion polls conducted since 1948, the study concluded that in the past fifty years the prevalence of antisemitic attitudes has decreased appreciably, social distance between Jews and non-Jews has narrowed and the incidence of many behavioural manifestations has ebbed. Furthermore, the traditional correlates of the decline of antisemitism—higher education and wealth, and lower age—continue to hold with respect to all groups. Nonetheless, the report cautions, antisemitic prejudices still survive. "Jews are still recognized as an ethnic and religious outgroup and are evaluated as such." The study further suggests that older and cruder forms of hatred have been revamped and modified somewhat, but not eliminated. The enmity that survives is articulated in a less blatant manner, and may therefore be more difficult to examine.

A February Time Magazine/CNN poll by Yankelovich Partners of 504 African Americans (*Time*, 28 February) found that 73 per cent were more familiar with Louis Farrakhan than with any other black leader, and two-thirds of those familiar with him viewed him favourably. Some 70 per cent of those familiar with him said he was saying things the country should hear, 62 per cent said he was good for the black community, 63 per cent said he spoke the truth and 67 per cent said he was an effective leader; more than half said he was a good role model for African-American youth, and only one-fifth

thought him antisemitic. On the question of
"power", 80 per cent thought whites had too
much power, while 28 per cent and 26 per cent
thought Jews and Catholics, respectively, had
too much power.

LEGAL MATTERS

The First Amendment of the US Constitution
guarantees both freedom of speech and the freedom of the press. The constitutional protection
of these civil liberties distinguishes the USA
from most other liberal democracies. American
political culture is more hostile to legislation
which seeks to restrict the press or the expression of beliefs and even if politicians are persuaded to pass legislation which attempts to
limit these freedoms, the federal courts are unlikely to be sympathetic and are likely to declare it unconstitutional.

However, the judiciary has never endorsed
the view that the First Amendment guarantees
are absolute. For instance, certain limitations
concerning pornography or national security,
particularly when the nation has been at war,
have been accepted by the courts. Furthermore,
judges have been prepared to distinguish between the expression of opinion, even if it is
racist or antisemitic, and "fighting words", the
advocacy of actions which are criminal. Forty-
six states, the District of Columbia and the federal government have developed a range of
legislation which is collectively known as
"hate-crimes" statutes, which cover ethnic intimidation and violence directed at a particular
racial or ethnic group. The constitutionality of
these statutes is currently under consideration,
and the first indications are that judges will
be very concerned over First Amendment
implications.

In 1992, the US Supreme Court in *RAV v.
St Paul* found a municipal statute unconstitutional on the grounds that it selectively "silenced speech on the basis of content".
However, other hate-crime laws may not have
similar constitutional flaws. In 1993 the Court
ruled in the milestone case of *Wisconsin v.
Mitchell,* that the statute was constitutionally
valid because it did not punish speech at all, but
concerned the selection of the victim of a crime
based on a suspect classification.

Those statutes based on the notion of
"penalty enhancement", which allow for an increase in the sentences of those found guilty of
selecting a victim because of race, religion, colour, disability, sexual orientation, national origin or ancestry, have received the approval of
the US Supreme Court. The Hate Crimes Sentencing Enhancement Act, embodying this approach to hate-crimes legislation, was passed by

the 103rd Congress in 1994. Moreover, thirty-
three states and the District of Columbia have
now adopted penalty-enhancement hate-crimes
statutes.

By the end of 1994, pending at various
levels in federal and state courts were approximately a dozen cases testing the constitutionality of state hate-crimes laws, including a
number based on sentence enhancement.

A legal development in 1994 that implicated the expression of antisemitism by extreme
Afrocentrists on campus concerned City College of New York Professor Leonard Jeffries, Jr.
In November, the US Supreme Court overturned an appeals court ruling that had found
that Jeffries's free speech rights had been in-
fringed when the board of the City University
of New York (which includes City College) had
first restricted Jeffries's term and then removed
him from his position as chair of the black studies department. The Supreme Court ordered
the appeals court to reconsider Jeffries's claim
in the light of another Supreme Court case concerning the disciplining of public employees. In
that case it was held that a public employer can
fire an employee if the former has a reasonable
belief that the employee's statements would
cause substantial disruption of the workplace.

In the ongoing case of the 1991 murder of
hasidic student Yankel Rosenbaum in Crown
Heights, Lemrick Nelson—acquitted of the
murder in 1992—was indicted for having violated Rosenbaum's civil rights; the indictment is
sealed pending a decision as to whether the
eighteen-year-old will be tried as an adult or a
juvenile. Meanwhile, in Brooklyn, a state grand
jury considered charges against a second suspect in the case, twenty-four-year-old Ernesto
Edwards.

The courts heard cases throughout the year
against white supremacists accused of racist and
antisemitic violence. Jonathan Preston Haynes
was sentenced to death in Chicago in May for
the murder of a plastic surgeon in 1993; at the
time of his arrest, Haynes confessed to the killing as well as to the 1987 murder of a San Francisco hair colourist, both of whom he described
as purveyors of "fake Aryan beauty". Haynes
refused counsel and used his time in court to
proclaim his neo-Nazi beliefs. In California in
August a jury found Richard Campos guilty of
two racially-motivated firebombings but was
unable to reach a verdict concerning three others, including one of a synagogue; literature of
the white-supremacist group WAR was found
in Campos's possession. In November a former
KKK member, Joseph Paul Franklin—already
serving four life sentences in an Illinois prison
for four racially-motivated killings—confessed

from his prison cell to the 1977 murder of a Jewish resident of St Louis, shot by Franklin while walking out of a synagogue; Franklin was thereafter charged with murder and faces the death penalty. An alleged neo-Nazi recruiter was indicted on illegal firearms charges in Boston in August after police confiscated a weapons arsenal and neo-Nazi literature from his home; William J. Murray, previously linked to the desecration of a Jewish cemetery in Everett, Massachusetts, faces a maximum penalty of life imprisonment.

At the end of 1994 the justice department's Office of Special Investigations (OSI) was investigating more than 300 cases against persons suspected of Second World War crimes. In April a federal judge in Milwaukee ordered the deportation of sixty-nine-year-old Croatian-born Anton Tittjung. In 1990 a federal court had revoked Tittjung's US citizenship on the grounds that he had, when entering the USA in 1952, concealed the fact that he had served as an armed guard at the Mauthausen concentration camp in Austria. Tittjung was given until the end of the month to name his destination.

In July Ferenc Koreh, an eighty-four-year-old resident of New Jersey, was stripped of his US citizenship for having lied about his wartime activities as the editor of an antisemitic and pro-Nazi newspaper in Hungary. Koreh, a retired producer and broadcaster for Radio Free Europe, was convicted of war crimes in Hungary in 1947.

After learning of the OSI's intention to launch deportation proceedings against him, seventy-year-old Peter Mueller, a retired factory worker from Colorado, voluntarily quit the USA in March for Worms in Germany. Before leaving, Mueller admitted to having served in the SS Death's Head battalion at the Natzweiller concentration camp in Alsace and its subcamp, Schorzingen, in Württemberg. Mueller acquired German citizenship in 1942 and, after emigrating to the USA in 1956, remained a German national.

Mathias Denuel, a German citizen who emigrated to the USA in 1955, quit the USA permanently for Germany in April after admitting he had served as an SS guard at the Mauthausen concentration camp, and that he had lied on his US visa application.

Denaturalization proceedings were launched against several American citizens on the grounds of having concealed their wartime activities on their naturalization applications. Chief among them was Aleksandras Lileikis, an eighty-seven-year-old retired publishing company employee from Norwood, Massachusetts, who allegedly served as chief of the Nazi-sponsored Lithuanian security police in Vilnius, and as such, according to federal prosecutors, "played a leadership role in the destruction of the Jews of Vilnius". The case has been described as "one of the most important Nazi cases brought anywhere in the world in recent history", and the first to make use of recently-released documents in Lithuanian archives.

Denaturalization proceedings were also opened against Bronislaw Hajda, a seventy-year-old former Pole now resident in Chicago who is charged with having served as an armed guard at Treblinka, and of having participated in the killing of Jewish prisoners there in July 1944 during the liquidation of the camp; Ferdinand Hammer, a seventy-three-year-old retired tool and die maker in Sterling Heights, Michigan, who allegedly served as a guard at Auschwitz and as a member of the SS Death's Head battalion; Algimantas Dailide of Brecksville, Ohio, charged with having served in the Nazi-sponsored Lithuanian security police in Vilnius; and Wiatscheslaw Rydlinskis of Bloomington, Illinois, charged with having been an SS Death's Head battalion guard at Auschwitz and Buchenwald.

The ongoing case of John Demjanjuk, a retired Cleveland auto worker, continued in 1994. Demjanjuk's legal battle began in 1981 when a Cleveland federal district court stripped him of his US citizenship for having lied about his wartime activities on his naturalization application. In 1986 he was extradited to Israel to stand trial for war crimes committed as the notorious Treblinka gas-chamber operator, "Ivan the Terrible". After he was convicted and sentenced to death in 1988, the conviction was overturned by the Israeli supreme court in July 1993 on the grounds that there was reasonable doubt that Demjanjuk was indeed the notorious "Ivan". However the court found compelling evidence that he had served as an SS guard at the Sobibor death camp as well as at the Flossenburg and Regensburg concentration camps. The extradition order was overturned in 1993 on the grounds that the OSI had withheld evidence that Demjanjuk was not "Ivan the Terrible", and Demjanjuk returned to the USA, where he now lives in seclusion in the Cleveland suburb of Seven Hills. In February, a federal appeals court in Cincinnati let stand its 1993 ruling overturning the extradition order. The OSI appealed the decision to the Supreme Court which, in October, refused to hear the case. The OSI argues that the 1981 revoking of Demjanjuk's citizenship remains valid since he lied about his wartime activities whether or not he was "Ivan the Terrible", and has asked the Cleveland district court to reaffirm its 1981 decision—paving the way for further efforts to deport Demjanjuk. Its ruling is expected in 1995.

COUNTERING ANTISEMITISM

One index of a society's response to antisemitism is the extent to which public officials and official bodies publicly reject any expression or manifestation of antisemitism. The experience in most communities in the USA was that the law-enforcement agencies, the government and so on took the lead in countering such manifestations. Local police departments were for the most part vigorous in pursuing the perpetrators of antisemitic crimes, such as acts of vandalism; and police departments in many larger cities have established "hate crimes units" whose task is to focus on the investigation of any crime in which bias or bigotry appears to be a motivating element. In this regard, the activities of church bodies are noteworthy as well. In local communities in the USA, it is often the church federation or the Catholic bishop that has taken the lead in denouncing antisemitic expression.

In 1994, to counteract the claims of the growing Christian fundamentalist movement that "there is only one set of beliefs open to people of faith", Catholic, Protestant and Jewish religious leaders established the Interfaith Alliance. One of them, Rabbi Arthur Hertzberg, said that "it is not just Jews who will suffer under the agenda being promoted by the religious right—it is anyone who may be different from the majority", and the Reverend Joan Campbell, general secretary of the National Council of Churches, said that the "radical right" represented a threat to religious freedom generally.

The AJC joined the Baptist Joint Committee and the National Council of Churches in preparing *A Shared Vision: Religious Liberty in the 21st Century*, a statement of principles demonstrating that church-state separation is an essential aspect of the protection of religious liberty. The statement was launched in July at an all-day conference at the White House addressed by Vice President Gore.

The ADL advertisement published in January which reprinted excerpts from the 1993 speech of Khalid Abdul Muhammad (see **Parties, Organizations, Movements**) rekindled a discussion within the Jewish community on tactical approaches to the countering of antisemitism. Critics of the ADL maintained that the advertisement gave Muhammad's remarks more publicity than they would otherwise have attracted. Arguments supporting the ad maintain that, in this case, the dangers arising from providing a platform, and thereby legitimacy, to

Muhammad's views were far outweighed by the possibilities for public information and education.

In January, following the ADL advertisement, several prominent African-American leaders denounced Muhammad's speech, including: the Reverend Jesse Jackson; then director of the NAACP, Benjamin Chavis; Congressional Black Caucus chair Kweisi Mfume (Democrat, Maryland); Congressmen Charles Rangel (New York) and Major Owens (Democrat, New York); New York Civil Rights Coalition head Michael Meyers; and William H. Gray, president of the United Negro College Fund. Both the Senate (unanimously on 2 February) and the House of Representatives (by a vote of 361 to 34, on 23 February) passed resolutions condemning the speech. In March, the eight-member US Commission on Civil Rights also voted unanimously to censure the speech.

The AJC organized placement of an ad in the *New York Times* of 24 February, captioned "We are Americans", in which political, religious and ethnic community leaders, including a number of African Americans, joined in repudiating the antisemitism of the leaders of the NOI.

In early February the Congressional Black Caucus—consisting of forty African-American members of the US Congress—overwhelmingly rejected the "sacred covenant" with the NOI that the Caucus chair, Congressman Mfume, had announced in September 1993. In June, after he did not attend the NAACP summit to which Farrakhan had been invited (see **Mainstream Politics**), Congressman Major Owens, an outspoken member of the Caucus, said that the crisis between the two communities had been created by a "systematic effort of the NOI to focus on Jews and target them and make them scapegoats". He criticized African-American leaders for not denouncing Farrakhan forcefully.

Numerous black-Jewish relations events were held throughout the country, including events organized jointly by synagogues and black churches, a jazz festival in Manhattan celebrating the connections between black and Jewish jazz musicians and numerous campus events. One event featuring Jewish students from Yeshiva College and African-American students from the City College of New York was held in New York in March. One participant said: "If we learn about their history and they learn about our history, you'll see that we're bonded. We both suffer."

At Skidmore College in April, the editor of the *Skidmore News* initially accepted one of Bradley Smith's antisemitic advertisements (see

Denial of the Holocaust) but, after an investigation of the issues, not only refused to print the ad but published instead a sixteen-page supplement exposing Holocaust denial. In July the AJC sent a letter about the Smith ads and a copy of this supplement to every four-year college library. Similar responses to the ad were printed in the campus newspapers at Rutgers University in New Jersey, the *Daily Targum*, and Queens College in New York, *The Quad*. The editors of those papers rejected the Smith text as an advertisement but ran it in the news or editorial columns, alongside editorial denunciation and comment by invited authors.

Appearing before Senate hearings on hate crimes, film director Steven Spielberg urged the judiciary subcommittee to push for legislation requiring every state to teach students about slavery and the Holocaust. He said that schools in only four of the fifty states were at present required to teach these events.

Spielberg's film *Schindler's List* was widely used in schools throughout the country to educate non-Jewish youth about the Holocaust, to counter incipient antisemitism, to encourage empathy between Jews and non-Jews and to dramatize the effects of intolerance. In addition, in a number of cases, young offenders convicted of acts of antisemitic vandalism were ordered to watch the film as part of their sentence.

In a speech to the French national assembly a day after the D-Day anniversary celebrations, President Clinton warned against "militant nationalism" and the "cancerous process eating away at states in the form of purposeless slaughter in Bosnia, the rise of skinheads, antisemitism and other hatreds".

The Evangelical Lutheran Church in America (the major Lutheran body in the USA with 5.2 million members) formally rejected the sixteenth-century antisemitic writings of the church's founder, Martin Luther. The declaration issued in April stated that members of the church felt a "special burden" because the Holocaust occurred "in places where the Lutheran churches were strongly represented. Grieving the complicity of our own tradition within this history of hatred, we express our urgent desire to live out our faith in Jesus Christ with love and respect for the Jewish people."

The new edition of the *Official Scrabble Player's Dictionary* printed in September removed the previously allowed terms "nigger", "spic", "dago" and "Jew" (defined as "to bargain with") after a complaint by the ADL.

ASSESSMENT

The gradual decline in significant forms of antisemitism in the USA—large-scale discrimina-

tion, political antisemitism, antisemitism of a form that would inhibit Jews from involvement in the public affairs of the body politic—continued in 1994. Studies reveal a sizeable repository of positive feelings towards Jews.

Tom W. Smith, in *Anti-Semitism in Contemporary America* (see **Opinion Polls**), indicated that "among the many intergroup conflicts and hatreds that persist in America, anti-Jewish feelings are not predominant; Jews are not the leading targets of hostility and bigotry." At the same time, Smith warned that in the USA today, "anti-Semitic prejudices still survive and anti-Semitic activities are all too common".

There has been an increase in some forms of antisemitic behaviour in recent years, notably the number of incidents of antisemitic vandalism, which, according to the ADL, increased for five years, up to 1991, declined in 1992, increased again in 1993, and again—to record numbers—in 1994. One possible explanation for the apparent contradiction between a decline in antisemitic attitudes and an increase in the number of antisemitic incidents is that, among those relatively few who profess antisemitic prejudice, there has in recent years been a greater propensity to "act out" their beliefs in various forms of expression. Clearly the erosion of traditional taboos against the expression of antisemitism and racial prejudice in general continued during 1994.

Overall, analysts suggest that, for the USA in 1994, a distinction be made between manifestations of antisemitism that do exist—that must be monitored and counteracted—and the security and well-being of the American Jewish community, which thrives due to the continuing strength of democratic institutions and constitutional protections that inhere in the society.

Nevertheless, serious questions remained in 1994. One concerns antisemitism in the African-American community, particularly among supporters of the NOI in the aftermath of the activities of Louis Farrakhan and his former deputy Khalid Abdul Muhammad in late 1993. On the one hand, the NOI, although in national terms a fringe group commanding little real economic or political power, has won the "hearts and minds" of thousands of disenfranchised, young African Americans. On the other hand, in contradistinction to many of the far-right and white-supremacist groups, the NOI is not paramilitary in character, nor does it advocate violent revolution.

Another concerns the growing power of the Christian fundamentalist movement as evidenced in the November election. There is unease among many Americans, including

Jews, over any potential "breach in the wall between church and state", a singular feature of American society that has arguably, since the nation's birth, prevented antisemitism from taking root in the same manner or to the same degree as in Europe, where it was embed- ded in the institutions—often the *formal* institutions—of power. There is also concern that the religious right's emphasis on the essential Christianity of the nation belies an exclusivist—rather than a pluralist—vision of America.

Uruguay

General population: 3.1 million
Jewish population: 23,800 (almost entirely in Montevideo)

GENERAL BACKGROUND

Political and economic developments during 1994 were influenced by the 27 November presidential and legislative elections. The widespread belief at the beginning of the year that the Partido Colorado (PC, Colorado Party) candidate, former president Julio María Sanguinetti, would almost certainly be the winner gave way to the closest race in the country's history, a three-way contest between Sanguinetti, the candidate of the left-wing coalition Frente Amplio (FA, Broad Front), Tabaré Vázquez, and Alberto Volonté, one of the candidates of the ruling Partido Nacional or Blancos (PN, National Party). The results have effectively ended the traditional two-party dominance by dividing Uruguayan politics into three blocs of almost equal strength.

On the basis of a reform programme that emphasized the economic and social importance of Uruguay's ailing industry and the role of the state as the traditional guarantor of social justice, Sanguinetti and the PC won the elections with 32.3 per cent of the votes. The PN came second (31.2 per cent) with a programme advocating the continuance of neo-liberal economic measures which had brought inflation down to an annual rate of about 40 per cent in 1994. The FA, in third place (30.6 per cent), largely profited from its successful administration of Montevideo—the left held the capital city with 44 per cent of the vote, the highest percentage ever obtained by a majority party in the city—as well as from the charismatic leader Vázquez, a former mayor of Montevideo, who managed to bring very divergent sectors of the left together behind a programme that stressed, first of all, social justice and education.

Analysts feared that the lack of a clear majority in government may lead to a potentially dangerous political stalemate, and an administration and a congress too weak to solve crucial questions such as Uruguay's role in the common market of the Southern Cone, MERCOSUR, rising unemployment, now at 10 per cent, and problems facing the country's productive enterprises. Meanwhile, the trade union movement suffered from a declining membership and strong ideological divisions.

HISTORICAL LEGACY

Uruguay has no tradition of official antisemitism. However, on several occasions during the first half of the twentieth century, government actions indicated anti-Jewish attitudes.

In January 1919, several hundred workers, many of them of Jewish origin, were arrested and charged with "subversive" activities; all of them were released within a month. By the end of the 1930s, there were several incidents of Jewish refugees from Central Europe being refused entry at the port of Montevideo.

In the early 1960s, left-wing Jews and non-Jews in Montevideo were attacked with razor blades and marked with swastikas. Those responsible were never identified.

During the military dictatorship of 1973-84, several political prisoners of Jewish origin suffered more severe torture than others, though this does not seem to have been a systematic policy of the authorities.

In December 1990, the Uruguayan public was shocked when a lone gunman attacked members of the Jewish community, leaving two dead and three severely injured. The perpetrator, a neo-fascist supporter, remains in prison under special security measures.

The 1990 and 1992 desecrations of the La Paz Jewish cemetery of Montevideo remain unresolved.

RACISM AND XENOPHOBIA

In 1994 there was no follow-up to the discussion about racism raised by the results of the opinion poll published in September 1993 in which attitudes towards the various ethnic minorities were canvassed. The ethnic groups compared were the Spanish (in the sense of the mainstream Spanish-speaking community), Italians, Blacks, "English" (Anglo-Saxons), Jews, "Rusos" (in the popular meaning of East European immigrants, including Jews) and "Turcos" (in the popular meaning of Middle Eastern immigrants, including Sephardi Jews, Armenians, Lebanese and Syrians). The groups judged most negatively were the Jews, the "Rusos" and the "Turcos". The poll revealed a considerable level of underlying xenophobia.

Blacks—who make up approximately 6 per cent of the population—fared better in the poll but in fact are scarcely represented in local, state and national government, in the liberal professions, the public sector or the civil service.

Immigration and residence legislation embody a considerable degree of tolerance. However, in 1994, intense debate about the right to political asylum followed events in August when the courts decided to extradite several Basque citizens accused of terrorist activities in Spain, and refuse their request for political asylum. The decision provoked a violent confrontation between police and demonstrators in which one man was killed.

PARTIES, ORGANIZATIONS, MOVEMENTS

The far-right Alianza Libertadora Nacionalista (ALN, National Liberator Alliance) espouses a xenophobic ideology. It boasts only a handful of members, enjoys virtually no popular support and disappeared from the public arena during the last months of the year.

MANIFESTATIONS

During 1994, the only reported incident of antisemitic activity in Uruguay was an isolated swastika daubing at a bus stop in the city of Punta del Este.

COUNTERING ANTISEMITISM

Steven Spielberg's film, *Schindler's List*, was an enormous success during its two months' showing in Montevideo, where it was seen by an estimated 50,000 people. Interviews with Emilie Schindler—a guest of honour at the opening night on 10 March—were published in the local press and broadcast on a private television channel in January and February.

In response to the bombing of the AMIA building in Buenos Aires on 18 July (see **Argentina**)—one of Uruguay's most important holidays, Constitution Day—a demonstration was held to express solidarity with the victims of the attack. About 10,000 people gathered in Montevideo's Independence Square, including the then president, Luis Alberto Lacalle, various cabinet ministers and congressional deputies, as well as the leaders of the Jewish community. Condemnation of the bombing was universal in the Uruguayan media.

In an attempt to lessen the possibility of attacks on the Jewish community in Montevideo, security measures and police vigilance have been heightened. New walls have been erected to protect Jewish communal institutions and parking has been forbidden in front of the buildings.

During 1994, Comite Central Israelita del Uruguay, the central committee of the Uruguayan Jewish community, continued to co-operate with other organizations to fight racial discrimination and antisemitism. In July and December a seminar on racism and antisemitism was organized in conjunction with Mundo Afro, the most important representative of Uruguayans of African origin.

Co-operation between both communities was also demonstrated in Jewish support for campaigns on behalf of the peoples of Rwanda and Somalia, initiated by Mundo Afro, as well as in the solidarity of the Afro-Uruguayan community after the bombings of the AMIA in Buenos Aires and of Jewish targets in London (see **United Kingdom**).

An important Holocaust memorial was unveiled in November 1994 on Montevideo's main coastal avenue, the Rambla.

ASSESSMENT

In 1994, as previously, the attitude of the government, political parties, social organizations, the civil service and the mass media remained generally positive towards Uruguay's Jewish population. Nevertheless, the terrorist attack on the headquarters of the Jewish community in Buenos Aires has led to widespread unease and a feeling that terrorism could, despite the country's liberal tradition and the low levels of antisemitism, likewise strike in Montevideo.

Asia

THE INSTITUTE OF JEWISH AFFAIRS AND THE AMERICAN JEWISH COMMITTEE

Indonesia

General population: 194.6 million
Jewish population: 30

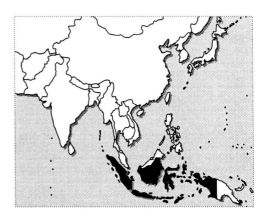

GENERAL BACKGROUND

Indonesia is ruled by President Suharto, re-elected in 1993 to his sixth five-year term. Despite pledges in 1994 to allow greater democratization, Suharto's regime has remained highly authoritarian: political life is dominated by the military and opposition is severely restricted.

Following weeks of tension Indonesian troops clashed with student demonstrators in the province of East Timor in July (see **Racism and Xenophobia**). Rioting in East Timor increased during the Asia-Pacific Economic Co-operation summit meeting in November.

Indonesia was accused by international human rights organizations, such as Human Rights Watch and Amnesty International, of major violations of human rights, including the detention and torture of political prisoners and unlawful killings of alleged criminals.

President Suharto, in his capacity as leader of the Non-Aligned Movement, met with Israeli Prime Minister Yitzhak Rabin in Jakarta in October 1993. Throughout 1994, Israelis have continued to be allowed to visit Indonesia and there is now a regular flow of Muslim pilgrimages to holy sites in Israel. Relations with Israel became a more controversial issue following the visit to Jerusalem of Abdurrahman Wahid, the head of Indonesia's largest Muslim organization, Nahdatul Ulamma (Religious Scholars), who advocated that diplomatic relations be established with Israel.

In 1994 the economy continued to expand with the gross domestic product rising by 6.5 per cent.

RACISM AND XENOPHOBIA

Indonesia, with its large Muslim majority, is relatively tolerant of racial and ethnic minorities. There is, however, underlying discrimination against ethnic Chinese, who constitute approximately 3 per cent of the population. Regulations prohibited the public display of Chinese characters but in August these regulations were relaxed to allow the use of Chinese-language materials to promote tourism.

A series of labour disputes in the Sumatran city of Medan led to a spate of anti-Chinese riots in April. Protesters attacked and looted shops and houses owned by ethnic Chinese and a Chinese factory-owner was beaten to death.

The July protests in East Timor occurred following reports that Muslim Indonesian soldiers had offended the religious sensibilities of the Christian East Timorese community by violating the sanctity of a mass.

MANIFESTATIONS

The massacre of Muslims by a Jewish settler in a mosque in Hebron on 26 February incited Muslim youths to protest outside the American embassy in Jakarta, as well as consulates in Medan and Surabaya, with posters inscribed "To Hell with You Jews" and "Jews Can't Be Trusted".

CULTURAL LIFE

Although the release of the film *Schindler's List* was initially prohibited because of the sexually explicit nature of certain scenes, controversy over the film also revealed antisemitic attitudes in Indonesia (see **Malaysia** and **Philippines**). The National Film Censorship Board indicated that the film could be shown on condition that sexually explicit scenes were cut. On 27 March the Committee for World Muslim Solidarity, which claimed to represent thousands of young Muslims, reportedly called on the government to follow Malaysia's example and ban it, because it was too sympathetic towards Jews. Hussein Umar, vice-chair of the organization, said too much sympathy for Jews would hurt the Muslim cause. Hanri Basri, chair of the Indonesian Council of Ulemas, Indonesia's highest authority on Islam, was also quoted in the daily newspaper *Pelita* as urging the government to ban *Schindler's List* for the same reason. The film was ultimately withdrawn from Indonesia when the director, Steven Spielberg, refused to allow it to be censored.

PUBLICATIONS AND MEDIA

Bookshops in Jakarta displayed such publications as "Seventy-Six Characteristics of the

Jews", "The Western and Jewish Grudge against Islam", mostly translated works from the Middle East. An antisemitic paperback entitled "The Zionist Threat against the Islamic World", which was published in Indonesia in 1991, was reissued in 1994. The author, Dr Majid Kailany, states: "The descendants of Israel kept performing evil deeds, so finally they met with the horrifying retribution of Hitler's slaughter. Allah will surely inflict even greater tortures, as was His promise . . . We are waiting for this promise to be fulfilled in the days to come."

ASSESSMENT

Most Indonesians have little knowledge of Judaism, which is often perceived as an obscure branch of Christianity. Antisemitism can be a convenient means for Islamic groups to express solidarity with Muslims world-wide.

Japan

General population: 125 million
Jewish population: 2,000 (mainly in Tokyo)

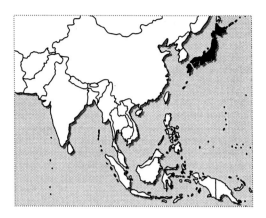

GENERAL BACKGROUND

Japan is a parliamentary democracy with an emperor as constitutional monarch. In the 1993 election to the lower house of the Diet, Japan's bicameral legislature, the Liberal Democratic Party (LDP) lost its majority for the first time since 1955. Morihiro Hosokawa, a former LDP member, became prime minister, heading a coalition of groupings which had split from the LDP. Hosokawa resigned in April 1994, and was replaced by Tsutomu Hata. When the government collapsed after only two months, Tomiichi Murayama, leader of the Social Democratic Party, became prime minister although the LDP dominated the government.

Public debate within Japan over the country's role in the Second World War intensified in 1994. Much embarrassment was caused by visits of (mainly Asian) women, who had been forced to work as sex slaves during the war, and former British prisoners-of-war seeking compensation.

The effects of international recession on the Japanese economy also drew attention to domestic concerns. A major programme of tax cuts was introduced to boost economic growth, which stood at only 0.6 per cent in 1994.

HISTORICAL LEGACY

Jews have been settling in Japan since the mid-nineteenth century. There was an early Jewish mercantile settlement in Nagasaki and Jewish communities existed in Yokohama and Kobe in 1860. The population was augmented during the next century by small numbers of refugees fleeing the Russian Revolution and Nazi Germany.

Following the Russian Revolution, *The Protocols of the Elders of Zion* was translated into Japanese and, over several decades, several books alleging a world Jewish conspiracy were published in Japan. There was a marked increase in the publication of antisemitic books in the mid-1980s, when the works of Masami Uno, a fundamentalist Christian, sold over 1 million copies and became best-sellers. Uno and a number of other "experts" claimed that an international Jewish conspiracy had led to Japan's economic difficulties. They also put forward a Holocaust-denial thesis. Although new titles continued to appear, the volume of sales of such books declined, leading many to believe that the phenomenon was a passing fad. However, a spate of antisemitic articles in weekly journals of the Japanese "yellow press", beginning in mid-1992, gave rise to fears that antisemitism would return with Japan's economic downturn.

RACISM AND XENOPHOBIA

As the Japanese seek to preserve their homogeneity through conformity to traditional cultural and societal codes, attitudes towards Jews should be viewed in the context of a more generalized suspicion of foreigners. Among the most vulnerable minorities are the Ainu, a small indigenous group of approximately 100,000 people. They live mostly in Hokkaido, and are subject to social discrimination, such as restricted access to private housing and employment. Likewise, there is widespread social prejudice against the Burakumin, whose ancestors constituted an outcast group many centuries ago.

In 1994 Japanese concern over North Korea's suspected nuclear development programme gave rise to a number of physical and verbal attacks on North Korean nationals resident in Japan, including over forty-two attacks on North Korean students.

PARTIES, ORGANIZATIONS, MOVEMENTS

There exists in Japan a tiny antisemitic party, the Chikyu Ishin-to (World Restoration Party), which is headed by Ryu Ota, the author of several antisemitic books (see **Publications and Media**). The party participated in the July 1992 parliamentary elections for the upper house and received 11,883 votes.

The Kokka Shakaishugi Domei (National Socialist Alliance) is an umbrella organization for a number of small Japanese neo-Nazi groups whose estimated total membership is 300-400. Among them is the Kokka Shakaishugi Nippon Rodoshato (Japan National Socialist Workers' Party), which published its first newsletter in July (see **Publications and Media**).

A small number of neo-Nazi activists, who aim to rid Japan of all foreigners, employ neo-Nazi slogans, salutes and symbols and are reportedly responsible for posting some flyers in and around Tokyo. The political significance of such groupings is marginal.

MAINSTREAM POLITICS

International criticism led to the withdrawal in June of a book entitled "Hitler Election Strategy: A Bible for Certain Victory in a Modern Election" by Yoshio Ogai, a public relations official of the Tokyo branch of the LDP. The book, which featured cartoons of Hitler, and excerpts from *Mein Kampf*, did not mention the Holocaust.

CULTURAL LIFE

A number of shops in Tokyo sell SS uniforms and other Nazi paraphernalia, but their clients, especially the younger ones, are not necessarily supporters of Nazi ideology. Nazi uniforms and badges, for example, are often viewed among Japanese merely as fashionable curiosities.

PUBLICATIONS AND MEDIA

Among the numerous antisemitic publications which continued to circulate in Japan in 1994 were the following: "Lucifer's Last Conspiracy" by Izumi Koishi, which explains how half of humanity will be killed by 1999 and the Japanese turned into slaves; and "The Rothschild Family: the Devil's Canon of the World Financial Clique" by Akira Kagami.

The daily *Yomiuri Shimbun*, which has the world's largest circulation of 10 million, published in October an advertisement by the Tokuma publishing company promoting four books that portray modern history as a series of Jewish plots to dominate the world. Among the titles was "Rockefeller vs. Rothschild" by Noboru Fujii, who alleged that current world events were determined by the conflicting interests of the "Zionist" British Rothschilds and the "conservative fiscal mainstream" Rockefellers. It also purported to prove that "Zionists" instigated the 1989 massacre of Chinese students in Tiananmen Square and manipulated media reports in order to discourage foreign investment in China. Following protests from the Israeli embassy, the Committee against Antisemitism in Japan and the American Jewish Committee, the newspaper apologized for carrying the advertisements and agreed to refrain from accepting similarly offensive material in the future.

Noboru Fujii repeated his antisemitic theories in a number of other publications throughout 1994. In April, he wrote a cover story for *Sapio*, a bi-monthly magazine published by Shogakukan, entitled "Why is America's influential media so intent on pursuing the Whitewater affair? Is there anything to the notion of discord between Jews and WASPs in the background?" In December Fujii published his antisemitic theories in an article entitled "The two major American and British cartels reach a *modus vivendi* and become more active in their investments to the south", which appeared in *The 21*, a monthly magazine of the PHP Institute.

Ryu Ota of Chikyu Ishin-to has published many antisemitic books, including "The Jews' Invasion of Japan: The Secret of 450 Years". He also circulates several magazines in limited numbers, such as the monthly antisemitic newsletter *Mantra*, which advertise his books. Ryu's publications were also promoted by *Compassion*, a bi-monthly journal of the Japanese League for the Abolition of Vivisection. Of little significance but also available in Japan in 1994 was *Völkischer Beobachter* (People's Observer), the newsletter of the Kokka Shakaishugi Nippon Rodoshato. The front cover of the inaugural July issue featured a photograph of Hitler and another of neo-Nazi skinheads in Germany.

DENIAL OF THE HOLOCAUST

In June, Rekishi Shusei Gakkai (Institute for Historical Review), a Japanese branch of the US-based Holocaust-denial organization, was founded with the support of its American namesake and the Liberty Lobby, the US far-right propagandist group (see **United States**). Its inaugural lecture was given by Ryu Ota of Chikyu Ishin-to and other supporters of the institute include Kokka Shakaishugi Domei, Kokka Shakaishugi Nippon Rodoshato, Sekai Senryaku Kenkyusho (Institute for World Strategy) and Hokkaido Sogo Chosakai (Hokkaido Research Associates) (see **Parties, Organizations, Movements**).

A new book which appeared in 1994, entitled *Nippon ni Shinobi-hairu Yudaya* (The Jews are Sneaking into Japan) by Ushiyama Kaichi, was published by Daiichi Kikaku Shuppan. It had attracted attention in 1993 with prominent media advertisements for a book series entitled "Strike Japan: The Last Strong Enemy". The new book denies that the Holocaust occurred and provides "historical evidence" that Japan's entire history has been a struggle between Jews and their allies in order to gain control of the country. It was issued with a yellow seal which asserted: "Prince Shotoku [an eighteenth-century political reformer] was a Jew: Is Ichiro Ohzawa [a prominent Japanese politician] a tool of the Jews? The aim of the Jews is to control Japan's politics and economy and lead to the destruction of the world."

LEGAL MATTERS

In January 1994 an American member of the Tokyo Jewish community was ordered by the Toshima small claims court to pay damages to a Japanese neo-Nazi who had been assaulted by him while parading in the street in an SS uniform.

PHILOSEMITISM

A unique brand of philosemitic literature in Japan unwittingly echoes the classical tenets of antisemitism. One prominent Japanese businessman, Den Fujita, has written six books about Jews and business, one of them entitled "The Jewish Way of Blowing a Millionaire's Bugle". He says he admires Jews and even proudly calls himself the "Jew of Ginza". Fujita, the head of the MacDonald's fast-food chain in Japan, has made it one of the country's success stories by using what he calls "Jewish business methods". Some philosemitic writers also subscribe to a theory of common descent from the ten lost tribes of Israel which seeks to co-opt the history of the Jews in order to promote notions of Japanese racial superiority.

COUNTERING ANTISEMITISM

Japan's first exhibition on the Holocaust was opened in April by the Simon Wiesenthal Center and Japan's Soka University in Tokyo's city hall. The ten-day exhibition, entitled "The Courage to Remember", included previously unpublished letters by Anne Frank, whose diary is a best-seller in Japan. It was co-sponsored by the city of Tokyo and the embassies of the US, France, the Netherlands and Israel, and attracted an estimated 85,000 visitors. The exhibition also included a display about Sugihara Chiune, dubbed "Japan's Schindler", who rescued hundreds of Jews from Nazi persecution during the Second World War.

The discovery in August of documents revealing that Chiune, acting Japanese consul in

Lithuania, had saved more than 8,000 Jews (rather than the previous estimate of 6,000) was publicized widely.

In August an *ad hoc* Committee against Antisemitism in Japan was formed. The group, which comprises about a dozen members including the president and rabbi of Tokyo's Jewish community, aims to monitor antisemitic publications in leading bookshops, underground railway kiosks and other outlets, and to use legal measures to restrict the propagation of antisemitism.

Takao Ikami, president of Nagoya Central Park and the man responsible for initiating the establishment of a park in memory of Sugihara Chiune in Yaotsu (Chiune's home town), invited Japanese-American veterans of the regiment which liberated Dachau to visit Japan. The veterans visited in September under the auspices of "The Unlikely Liberator" project, which was co-sponsored by the US-based Holocaust Oral History project, and brought with them many photographs of the liberation of Dachau which the Nagoya Central Park arranged to be exhibited throughout Japan.

David G. Goodman, a professor of Japanese literature at the University of Illinois, and Masanori Miyazawa, professor of history at Doshisha Women's College in Kyoto, published a book, entitled *Jews in the Japanese Mind: The History and Uses of a Cultural Stereotype*, which examines the paradoxical attitudes towards Jews in contemporary Japan.

In October, Beit Shalom, a Kyoto-based pro-Israeli organization, announced the establishment of a Holocaust education centre in the Hiroshima prefecture, which was due to open in June 1995.

ASSESSMENT

Although there have not been any physical attacks on Jews in Japan, concern has arisen over a spate of antisemitic books blaming a Jewish conspiracy for Japan's current economic troubles. Most of the antisemitic material published deals with a fuzzy notion of international Jewish financial power, not with the Jews living in Japan. It should also be noted that many positive books about Jews are prominently displayed in major Japanese bookshops.

Kyrgyz Republic

General population: 4.6 million
Jewish population: 4,500 (mainly in Bishkek)

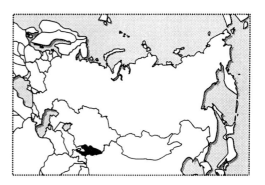

GENERAL BACKGROUND

Although the 1993 constitution defines the nation as a democratic republic, the president, Askar Akayev, continued to dominate the government. The Kyrgyz Republic, a former Soviet republic, is a very poor, mountainous country with a predominantly agricultural economy, highly dependent on trade with the other states of the former Soviet Union. In 1994 the country made significant progress in controlling inflation but industrial production and the standard of living continued to fall.

HISTORICAL LEGACY

There is no tradition of antisemitism in the Kyrgyz Republic.

PUBLICATIONS AND MEDIA

The Russian-language newspaper *Svobodniye gory*, published from February onwards a series of xenophobic articles. The paper described Jews leaving for Israel as "traitors" to their motherland, regularly wrote of "Zionist plots" and blamed the Jews for the country's problems. In an editorial Ludmila Zholmukhamedova, the newspaper's editor, claimed that she and the newspaper were victims of "Zionists". Following complaints by the Kyrgyz-Israel Friendship Society, the procurator-general took no action.

ASSESSMENT

There were no indications that antisemitism was a serious problem in the country.

Malaysia

General population: 19.2 million
Jewish population: under 10

GENERAL BACKGROUND

The prime minister, Dr Mahathir bin
Mohamad, heads the United Malays National
Organization (UMNO), the leading faction in
the governing coalition, the Barisan Nasional
(National Front). The dominant political culture of the UMNO is authoritarian and has become increasingly suffused with an Islamic
content. Constitutional amendments approved
in May by the Dewan Rakyat (House of Representatives) reduced the power of the monarchy.

Since Mahathir assumed office in 1981 economic development has accelerated, making
Malaysia a leading voice in the Third World, in
part through the Non-Aligned Movement. In
1994 the economy continued to expand, with
gross domestic product increasing by 8.4 per
cent.

In 1994 foreign and domestic policy indicated Malaysia's commitment to a moderate
form of Islam. Mahathir revealed to an UMNO
meeting on 19 June that he had corresponded
with Israeli Prime Minister Yitzhak Rabin
concerning the Middle East peace process.
Controversy surrounded the revelation that the
king's brother, Tunku Abdullah Tuanku Abdul
Rahman, and five other Malaysians had visited
Israel in July. The revelation was condemned by
several Islamic parties in Malaysia. In October,
however, the government revoked its ban on
Malaysians visiting Israel, provided they travelled "for work or religious purposes" and went
directly to Jerusalem upon arrival.

HISTORICAL LEGACY

Antisemitic sentiment in Malaysia has been
identified specifically with Prime Minister
Mahathir, whose hostile attitudes to Israel and
the Jews are viewed as a mixture of personal
prejudice and political opportunism. In his
treatise on the Malay identity, *The Malay Dilemma* (1970), Mahathir observed that "the
Jews for example are not merely hook-nosed,
but understand money instinctively . . . Jewish
stinginess and financial wizardry gained them
the commercial control of Europe and provoked an antisemitism which waxed and waned
throughout Europe through the ages."

In 1984 Malaysian authorities banned a
performance of Ernst Bloch's *Shlomo*, which is
based on Hebrew melodies, by the visiting New
York Philharmonic Orchestra. Following a

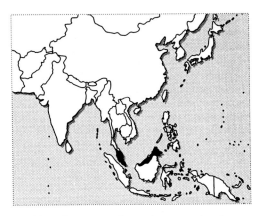

world-wide protest, the orchestra omitted Malaysia from its tour of Asia.

In 1986 Mahathir charged that Zionists and
Jews (without distinction) were attempting to
destabilize the country. He banned the *Asian
Wall Street Journal*, describing it as "Jewish-
owned", for three months and expelled two of
its resident correspondents.

In 1991 Mahathir alleged that leaders of the
Australian Jewish community were conspiring
to overthrow his government. Mustapha
Yaakub, a spokesman for an UMNO branch,
ascribed the alleged "Zionist" motive in
destabilizing Malaysia to envy of Malaysia's
achievements in the Islamic field.

RACISM AND XENOPHOBIA

The Malays (who are Muslim) comprise a bare
majority of the population. The Chinese account for 35 per cent, and Indians and other minorities about 13 per cent. By enforcing an
economic policy which ensures the political
dominance of the "Bumiputras" (ethnic
Malays) over the Chinese and Indian populations, Malaysia is distinguished by classes of
citizenship.

PARTIES, ORGANIZATIONS, MOVEMENTS

The year 1994 witnessed a government crackdown on al-Arqam, an Islamic revivalist movement led by Ashaari Mohammed, with an
estimated 100,000 sympathizers. The movement had increased its influence through a network of Muslim schools and clinics and
wide-ranging business ventures. In August the
movement was outlawed and its leaders arrested, on the grounds that they were plotting
to replace the government with an Islamist
regime.

The Parti Islam, which claims 400,000
members, and forms the government in
the state of Kelantan, opposes any dialogue
between Israel and Malaysia. It does not

distinguish between Zionists and Jews, and in 1994 continued to express both anti-Israeli and antisemitic sentiments, particularly during its "Anti-Israel Week" in four states in August.

ABIM (Moslem Youth Movement of Malaysia), a non-partisan and independent political force previously led by Anwar Ibrahim, now deputy prime minister, advocates the view that Zionism is a racist ideology leading to the supremacy of the Jewish race (see **Effects of Anti-Zionism**).

CULTURAL LIFE

The Malaysian board of film censors banned *Schindler's List*, alleging that it was propaganda designed to win support for Israel and the Jews. The board initially claimed that, since the film showed the Jewish victims as "stout-hearted" and "intelligent" while depicting the Nazis as brutal and cruel, it reflected "the virtues of a certain race only" while seeking "to tarnish the other race". Prime Minister Mahathir, who was directly responsible for decisions by the censorship board, refuted charges of antisemitism by the American Jewish Committee and other Jewish organizations in the USA and Australia, insisting that he was opposed to "the conquest of Arab territories by Zionists".

The intervention of Anwar Ibrahim reportedly led to a cabinet decision on 30 March to release the film but only on condition that certain sexually explicit scenes were cut. Steven Spielberg, the film's director, subsequently withdrew all of his films from Malaysia. Nonetheless, uncensored, inexpensive videotapes of *Schindler's List* were sold at market stalls throughout the country (see also **Indonesia** and **Philippines**).

PUBLICATIONS AND MEDIA

Antisemitic texts including *The Protocols of the Elders of Zion* continued to circulate in Malaysia in 1994.

EFFECTS OF ANTI-ZIONISM

ABIM and the Malaysian Action Front (a grouping of prominent pressure groups) have criticized Australia for having close links with Israel. ABIM's monthly newsletter, *Islamic Review*, featured an interview in April with a member of Hamas, the Palestinian Islamist group, which described their contribution to "military operations against the Jews".

ASSESSMENT

The year 1994 has been noticeable for a marked reduction in the level of anti-Zionist and antisemitic vitriol that was for so long a hallmark of Prime Minister Mahathir and the UMNO. The regime demonstrated a pragmatic shift in attitude towards Israel by recognizing the dramatic changes that have taken place in the Middle East.

Philippines

General population: 66.5 million
Jewish population: approximately10

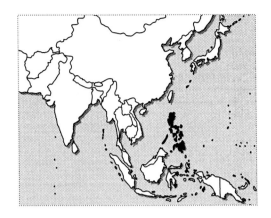

GENERAL BACKGROUND

The Republic of the Philippines is governed by President Fidel Ramos, who was elected in May 1992 following a succcessful transfer to civilian rule. In 1994 the government continued to implement a broad programme of political and economic reforms. The level of violence between the regime and the separate groups of communist and militant Islamic insurgents was reduced, partly through the widespread granting of amnesties. Nonetheless, human rights abuses continued in 1994, including extrajudicial killings, arbitrary arrests, torture and harassment of civil rights activists, suspected insurgents and their supporters.

Export-led economic growth and foreign investment contributed to economic growth, resulting in a 5 per cent rise in gross domestic product in 1994.

RACISM AND XENOPHOBIA

Muslims, who constitute 5 per cent of the population, are the largest minority group in the Philippines and have been historically alienated from the Christian majority. In 1994, militant Islamic activists were responsible for politically-motivated attacks on Christians. Members of the Abu Sayef Group attacked a bus in the Basilan province in June and killed fifteen Christians after releasing the Muslim passengers.

The US state department reported that by 1 October there were over 4,500 Vietnamese asylum-seekers in the Philippines, of whom only 1,500 had been determined to be "refugees" awaiting resettlement in third countries.

CULTURAL LIFE

As in Indonesia and Malaysia, the controversy over the film *Schindler's List* in the Philippines was initially triggered by objections to the allegedly pornographic nature of particular scenes, but also revealed some antisemitism. Following the decision of the Philippines board of censorship in February that the film could only be shown if certain scenes portraying female nudity were cut, the film's director Steven Spielberg refused to release it in the Philippines. Angry protests in the media subsequently led President Ramos to intervene and insist that the movie be shown. A former chief censor under Corazon Aquino, Manoling Morato, accused Spielberg of "attacking our moral fibre" and asserted: "If we shall allow ourselves to be cowed by an American-Jew film director, then to me this is the worst case of American imperialism" (see also **Indonesia** and **Malaysia**).

ASSESSMENT

The 1994 controversy over *Schindler's List* revealed some degree of antisemitic sentiments in the Philippines despite the absence of a substantial Jewish community.

Australasia

THE INSTITUTE OF JEWISH AFFAIRS AND THE AMERICAN JEWISH COMMITTEE

Australia

General population: 17.8 million
Jewish population: 100,000-105,000 (mainly
in Melbourne and Sydney)

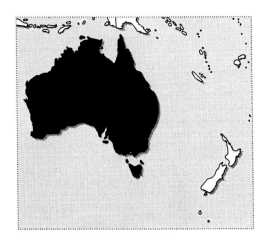

GENERAL BACKGROUND

In 1994 the federal Labor government was in
the middle of its fifth successive term, having
been in power since 1983. Until December the
government remained ahead in opinion polls
thanks largely to an improving economy and
the ongoing division within the opposition
Liberal-National coalition. In May Alexander
Downer defeated John Hewson to become the
coalition's leader. Downer's performance (after
an initial honeymoon period) failed to improve
the coalition's standing in the polls.

Economic recovery resulted in a drop in
the unemployment rate from 10.8 per cent in
1993 to 9.1 per cent in 1994. Gross domestic
product grew by 6.4 per cent and inflation remained at 2 per cent. However, the government
sought to slow economic growth by raising interest rates and was expected to increase taxa-
tion in 1995. Australia's commitment to
Asia-Pacific political and economic fora strengthened, reflecting a continuing shift in the nation's interest from Eurocentric to more
regional concerns.

HISTORICAL LEGACY

Australian Jews have experienced little or no
significant institutional or organized antisemitism; civil rights have never been restricted. This is to a large degree due to the
presence of Jews in the country since the establishment in 1788 of the British colonies,
which eventually came together as the Commonwealth of Australia. Jews have figured
prominently in Australian public life. One of
Australia's most notable military figures was
Jewish as were two of Australia's governors
general (the Australian representative of the
British monarchy).

However, according to Paul Bartrop's
Australia and the Holocaust, 1933-45 (1994),
informal restrictions, guided by a conscious
desire to minimize the number of Jews entering the country, were placed on the number
of Jewish immigrants to Australia who were
refugees from, or survivors of, Nazism.
Nevertheless, 40,000 Jewish refugees from
Europe entered Australia between 1933 and
1955.

RACISM AND XENOPHOBIA

Historically, racial and ethnic tension has centred on conflict between established populations and more recent waves of migrants,
particularly those from southern Europe and
Asia. Some hostility has remained towards
Aborigines and Torres Strait Islanders, who are
known collectively as indigenous Australians.
Successive governments have followed a multicultural policy which provides protection for
minority groups in the areas of community relations, social justice, access and equity. Despite
ethnic, cultural and racial diversity, levels of
racist vilification and harassment are generally
low.

Nevertheless, racist attitudes and practices
are a feature of everyday life for indigenous Australians. They continue to be over-
represented in rates of arrest, conviction and
imprisonment, and experience high mortality
rates, significant health problems, poor living
conditions and socio-economic disadvantages.
The Labor government has supported a process
of reconciliation between indigenous and non-
indigenous Australians founded on recent judicial recognition of Aborigine ownership of the
land prior to arrivals from Europe and in 1994
supported a new fund to enable indigenous
Australians to buy land.

High levels of racist violence are commonplace for indigenous Australians and are frequently experienced by Asian- and Arab-
Australians and more recent immigrants from
Latin America. Racist violence against non-
English-speaking Australians, like more general
anti-immigration sentiment, is fuelled by
propaganda depicting non-Anglo-Australians
as disloyal, criminal, un-Australian, and "out to
take over the country".

In response to economic growth, the government has announced that it will increase the number of residence permits to be granted next year. However, concern has recently been expressed about the rising number of South-East Asian boat people who are arriving illegally. These people have been detained by the federal government subject to determination of their refugee status.

PARTIES, ORGANIZATIONS, MOVEMENTS

In 1994 a number of antisemitic organizations increased both their public profile and their level of activity.

The largely rural-based Australian League of Rights (ALR) is the best organized and financed racist and antisemitic organization in Australia. In 1993 the ALR gained extensive media coverage during a public debate on the government's decision to deny an entry visa to British Holocaust-denier David Irving (see **United Kingdom**). It followed up its 1993 success by revealing that the then leader of the federal opposition, Alexander Downer, addressed an ALR meeting in 1987; Downer had been invited to speak by a former member of the Liberal Party's South Australian state council, Eric Isaachsen (see **Mainstream Politics**). Isaachsen claimed "The League of Rights is not racist or anti-Semitic, but Zionists who control all the money in the world are the cause of all its problems." The ALR continued to organize lectures and seminars to provide sympathizers with the information they believe is necessary to combat Zionism, Fabianism and humanism. Other rurally-based extremist groups, such as the Rural Action Movement, the AUSI Freedom Scouts and the Confederate Action Party, also demonstrated an openness to crude antisemitic myths.

The Citizens' Electoral Councils of Australia (CECs), followers of Lyndon LaRouche (see **United States**), continued their well-funded campaign against alleged Jewish conspiracies. In 1994 their targets included the Executive Council of Australian Jewry (ECAJ), the Anti-Defamation League of B'nai B'rith and anti-racist groups. Bizarre claims were made in mass mailings and in their newspaper *The Citizen* which implicated, among others, the World Jewish Congress, B'nai B'rith and the "Israeli mafia" in the massacre of Muslims by a Jewish settler at a Hebron mosque in February, which they saw as part of a conspiracy to destroy the peace process. The CECs financed a poorly attended speaking tour by Reverend James Bevel, an African-American former civil rights activist lately associated with right-wing extremists, opposing the proposed racial vilifi-

cation legislation (see **Legal Matters**).

The Australian Civil Liberties' Union (ACLU), a small organization closely linked to the ALR and aligned with the US-based Institute for Historical Review (see **United States**), continued to distribute literature, such as its twenty-first annual handbook, *Your Rights*, which denied the Holocaust and opposed any anti-racist legislation. Three small Adelaide-based groups also gained some press coverage: Australians for Free Speech organized a rally with the neo-Nazi group National Action outside South Australia's Parliament House in support of the British Holocaust denier David Irving and against the racial vilification legislation, which they characterized as the work of the so-called Zionist lobby; the Adelaide Institute briefly gained exposure in South Australia when it attempted to show a Holocaust-denial video featuring Irving on the local community television station; and the Australian Freedom Foundation (AFF), which was at one time linked to the US John Birch Society. An attempt by Irving to visit Australia was frustrated when the government refused to grant him a visa.

Small groups of neo-Nazis were active in most major Australian cities. National Action staged rallies in Melbourne and Adelaide, published a newsletter, launched a solidarity campaign with white South Africans, harassed political opponents and attempted to recruit members in South Australian educational institutions. In March five men in military clothing entered student offices at Melbourne's La Trobe University and terrorized staff and students, apparently in retaliation for student support for an anti-Nazi rally earlier that week.

Allegations were made that skinhead and other extremist groups had been involved in violent attacks on Asian students, in harassing people involved in screening Steven Spielberg's *Schindler's List* in Melbourne, and in a rampage through Adelaide's main shopping street on 26 March. The Southern Cross Hammer Skinheads advertised their presence through a sticker campaign; supporters of the US neo-Nazi group White Aryan Resistance recruited in high schools (see **United States**). While the Australian National Socialist Party distributed neo-Nazi literature in Melbourne, small rallies were held by the National Security for Defence of Australian People (NSDAP), anti-multicultural literature was distributed by the National Republican Movement and the Australian National Movement sought to re-establish itself in Perth following the release of its leaders from prison.

MAINSTREAM POLITICS

In 1994 it emerged that several coalition politicians had addressed various far-right groups in recent years. Alexander Downer defended his decision to address an ALR meeting in 1987, claiming he had been misled by the League about the nature of the seminar, that his speech had in no way been antisemitic or extreme, and that his opposition to the ALR was a matter of public record. The first poll taken after the revelation of this meeting saw a 10 per cent fall in public approval of his handling of his position as leader of the opposition. Downer received support from his party and Senator John Coulter, a former leader of the mainstream Australian Democrats.

Other politicians chose to contest portrayals of racist groups as extremist. Mike Mansfield, a Western Australian Young Liberal official, defended his two speeches at ALR meetings, claiming that the ALR consisted of "fine, upstanding people with concern for the future of Australia". Senator Nick Minchin, a Liberal federal senator and parliamentary secretary to Downer, who spoke to the AFF in September, likewise defended his decision to speak to a "Christian group" in the face of a "McCarthyist campaign" against him. Two Victorian Liberal backbenchers received reprimands from their state premier for claiming that Asian and European migrants brought violence to Australia.

Issues of race were notable by their apparent absence in the elections on 4 June in the Northern Territory, a region with a 20 per cent indigenous Australian population. However, questions of race and racism lay just below the surface and allegations were made that the ruling Country Liberal Party used the issue of prospective Aboriginal land claims to the state capital, Darwin, to exploit racial phobias among white Territorians.

Anti-Asian sentiments fuelled a political mobilization against immigration. Australians against Further Immigration (AAFI) stood in a number of by-elections, receiving some support before their links with far-right groups were exposed. In the first four months of the year, the party polled between 6.8 and 14 per cent in four different federal by-elections. In March the AAFI received endorsements from Graeme Campbell, a maverick Labor MP from Western Australia, who supported the party's anti-immigration and anti-multiculturalism stance.

MANIFESTATIONS

The ECAJ, which maintains the only comprehensive database on antisemitic incidents in Australia, received 227 reports from local monitors of incidents of violence, intimidation and vandalism in 1994. Though few of the incidents caused serious damage, this represented a 7 per cent increase on 1993 and a 29 per cent increase on the average for the previous four years. The ECAJ annual report warned of possible psychological harm, particularly if this trend reflected real increases and continued. Compared with the previous year, serious or violent incidents fell by 22 per cent; telephone intimidation and hate mail increased by 17 per cent; graffiti, posters and other vandalism rose by 18 per cent. Attacks were made on Jewish communal properties in every major city. The most serious was an arson attack at the Sydney Newtown synagogue on the fifty-fifth anniversary of Kristallnacht. Although the number of violent incidents fell, Jews were assaulted and harassed, for instance, on their way to synagogue in Melbourne and Sydney.

Telephone calls and letters containing threats and warnings of imminent attacks were received by Jewish individuals or groups in all the larger cities. At least twelve bomb threats were received. The buildings targeted included Melbourne and Queensland synagogues, Melbourne schools, meeting halls and two homes of prominent community leaders as well as the building housing a Sydney communal organization. Hate mail, including messages sent from overseas on the Internet, was also reported.

Neo-Nazi and other antisemitic graffiti were daubed on sites in Sydney, Melbourne, Canberra, Perth and Queensland. Antisemitic leaflets, posters and audio-cassettes were distributed in all the eastern states at various times during the year. In January Nazi flags were flown in public in Sydney and Brisbane. In May young Croatian supporters of the Melbourne Knights soccer team waved a flag picturing a swastika during the televised final of the National Soccer League.

CULTURAL LIFE

John Bennett of the ACLU claimed that the film *Schindler's List* was "largely a propaganda exercise and that it may incite racial hatred". David Brockshmidt, the son of a German businessman who supplied trucks to Oskar Schindler to remove Jews, claimed in a letter he distributed outside the Adelaide première of the film: "Hollywood achievers will do anything including lie, falsify historical facts and spread gross disinformation for the love of money and overblown egos".

EDUCATION

There were few reports of antisemitism in Australian schools. National Action began a recruiting campaign outside South Australian schools but was warned by the police and the state education minister not to enter school premises. The local Institute of Teachers applauded the bravery of school principals who opposed National Action, while the local Primary Schools Association emphasized the need for anti-racist education.

PUBLICATIONS AND MEDIA

None of the mainstream media in Australia could be described as antisemitic. However, the ECAJ annual report identified several questionable decisions taken by editors to allow antisemitic views to be aired on "talk" radio programmes and in letters to newspapers. Inaccurate comments about Australian Jews, the alleged Australian Jewish lobby, and, more routinely, Israel and the Jewish settlers also appeared in political commentaries in the media. On 26 March the *Border Mail* (Albury) attacked "the famous and powerful Australian Jewish lobby" for being "arrogant", "aggressive" and showing signs of "insecurity". Occasionally, complaints about these decisions were treated less than sympathetically by editors, suggesting that "inaccuracies" were not always simply the result of mistakes. The editor of the *West Australian* (circulation 235,400), in a private letter to a local Jewish community leader on 21 June, attacked his support for the racial vilification laws (see **Legal Matters**) and claimed that his "powerful lobby has had a small win against the democratic freedoms which so many migrants have been happy to embrace when they come to Australia."

During a rugby league match, shown on national television, a commentator described one player as "tough as a Jewish landlord". He made an unequivocal apology at the end of the broadcast.

In an apparent reference to arson committed as an insurance fraud, an Adelaide newspaper spoke of "Jewish lightning" affecting a non-Jewish-owned clothing business. A columnist in the South Australian *Sunday Mail* (circulation 323,600) responded to criticism by arguing that the term was widely used and amusing.

A large sector of the media serves particular ethnic communities in Australia. Letters and commentaries in the Muslim and Arab-Australian press revealed continuing antagonism towards Jews and Israel. Some of the stereotypes of Jews portrayed were particularly crude. For instance, an article in *Al-Muhamir al-Arabi* (The Arab Editor), a Sydney paper, claimed that the Jewish religion required the killing of non-Jews: "the rabbi . . . prepares the holy

unleavened bread mixed with the human blood to please the Jewish God who is thirsty for the spilling of blood." An apology and retraction were published and the newspaper closed down shortly afterwards.

Other parts of the Arab-Australian press repeated stereotypes of Jewish meanness, arrogance and aggression and depicted Zionism as a religious and national enemy of Arab Christians and Muslims. Parts of the ethnic media that serve local East European communities also occasionally gave cause for concern, with one article blaming Jewish hostility towards other nations for both the Holocaust and the "elimination by the Jews of millions of innocent victims during the famine in the USSR" ("Free Thought", 6-13 February). Several small political fringe magazines available publicly or through mail order also included antisemitic articles: *Nexus*, a New Age magazine, serialized extracts from the American writer Richard Kelly Hoskins's antisemitic book *War Cycles— Peace Cycles*; *New Dawn*, aimed at the same market, reprinted propaganda from a variety of Libyan, LaRouchite and Nation of Islam sources; and *Lock, Stock and Barrel*, a journal for the gun lobby, reviewed several antisemitic books favourably and included ads for *The Protocols of the Elders of Zion*.

RELIGION

Despite a continuing inter-faith dialogue between most religious groups, some sections of the Christian and Muslim religious communities maintained their antagonism towards Jews and Judaism. Groups such as the small "Identity" churches (see **United States**), Christian Identity Ministries, British Israel World Federation and Covenant Vision Ministries also distributed antisemitic material.

Several far-right groups attempted to use religious sensibilities to mobilize antisemitic sentiment. The Victorian-based LaRouchite publication *The Strategy* argued that the proposed legislation against racial vilification (see **Legal Matters**) was a direct attack on Christianity perpetrated by overseas rabbinic scholars and World Jewish Congress co-chair Isi Liebler: "The Hebrew crime community is working overtime to silence the voice of the Christian Church in Australia." The ALR also attacked the Talmud as undermining the Christian tenets of common law and claimed that legislation enabling the trial of war criminals was "obscene and anti-Christian".

On 4 October a spokesperson for the Muslim community claimed in two major metropolitan newspapers, the *Sydney Morning Herald* and the *West Australian*, that Jews practised female circumcision. The statement remained unretracted.

DENIAL OF THE HOLOCAUST

Holocaust denial is an important feature of antisemitism in Australia (see **Opinion Polls**). The ACLU, linked with the US-based Institute for Historical Review, sought to protect people's "right" to deny the existence of the Holocaust (see **Parties, Organizations, Movements**). The ALR claimed that Jewish leaders were intent on replacing Christianity with a religion of belief in the "Jewish Holocaust". Leaflets denying the Holocaust were distributed at screenings of *Schindler's List*. Follow-up letters to newspapers also attacked the film's producer, its Australian author and some of its supporters. A columnist in the *Weekend Australian* (circulation 313,000) who attacked Holocaust denial received a letter claiming she had been duped by the "mythology of the Holocaust".

OPINION POLLS

A poll conducted for the *Age*, a Melbourne broadsheet (circulation 230,000) reported on 7 June that Australians accepted the ideas of multiculturalism but found it difficult to cope with the consequences. Sixty-five per cent of Australians supported ethnic diversity. Young people in particular (72 per cent) felt that Australia was a better place in which to live due to the arrival of immigrants from many countries. Despite this, only 35 per cent said they respected the different lifestyle and behaviour of immigrants.

Holocaust denial is now well known in Australia. According to a poll conducted by J. Golub and R. Cohen for the American Jewish Committee, *What Do Australians Know about the Holocaust?* (1994), 70 per cent of Australians were acquainted with the phenomenon. Only 4 per cent believed it was possible that the Holocaust had never happened. Moreover, almost 75 per cent of Australians were found to have a broadly accurate understanding of the Holocaust, a similar proportion to that found in European countries. Only 12 per cent believed that Holocaust-deniers should be penalized; 81 per cent disagreed on the grounds of freedom of speech.

LEGAL MATTERS

The case against Heinrich Wagner was dropped on medical grounds at the pre-trial stage after a case to answer had been established. He was accused of having been involved in the wilful killing of 104 Jews and the murder of nineteen children in Ukraine. A report by the Common-

wealth attorney-general urged that Australia's War Crimes Act be widened to cover war crimes other than those committed in Europe during the Second World War. However, in 1992 the government closed its special investigation unit, the investigative role being transferred to the Australian federal police (AFP). Senator Minchin (see **Mainstream Politics**) attacked the three trials of alleged Nazis since 1988 as the "craziest waste of money" Australians "had ever seen".

A report tabled in the federal parliament found that war criminals had come to Australia after the Second World War and that the authorities had either been unable or unwilling to stop them. Those permitted to immigrate had included a minister of the Third Reich as well as sixteen members of a Belgrade special police unit allegedly involved in the murder of thousands of anti-Nazis during the war. In April an Australian citizen named Konrad Kalejs, accused by the United States of war crimes while a member of the Latvian auxiliary security police, was deported from the USA to Australia. The federal police chose not to investigate allegations against him. The AFP 1994 budget allocations suggested there was little intention of pursuing further war crimes allegations.

Three states have legislation outlawing racial vilification. In April the equal opportunity tribunal for New South Wales (NSW) determined that, for the purpose of the act that established the jurisdiction of the Tribunal, cases of discrimination against Jews fell within the definition of discrimination on grounds of race (*Phillips v. Aboriginal Legal Service*). For unstated reasons, NSW overhauled its legislation, increasing penalties for serious racial vilification and broadening the scope of the term "race" to include "ethno-religious" groups. NSW also became the first state to prohibit particular computer games, including one entitled "Auschwitz" which required players to force as many characters as possible into gas ovens.

In November, in response to government-initiated reports, the federal government introduced legislation to tackle racial vilification. Introducing the Racial Hatred Bill, the attorney-general said it would criminalize threats of physical violence and the destruction of property motivated by the race of the victim and provide civil protection for victims of humiliating or intimidating racist behaviour. Conduct exempted from the bill included fair statements and anything said or done reasonably and in good faith. The bill was opposed by the opposition coalition, the National Party on grounds of free speech, and by the dominant Liberal Party partner on grounds that the legislation was unnecessarily restrictive and overly broad in scope. While they favoured civil remedies, they opposed the use of criminal sanctions for this purpose.

Australia's lower house of parliament passed the bill. Some of the rhetoric employed in the debate gave cause for concern: one shadow minister and the maverick Labor MP, Graeme Campbell, attacked Jewish support for the legislation and a National MP blamed the Rothschilds for "sowing the terrible seeds that were reaped years later in the pogroms". Campbell attributed Jewish influence over the bill to "a combination of money, position, relentless lobbying and the manipulation of their victim status". The senate has not yet passed the legislation and it has not yet gained the support of the two independent Green senators who hold the balance of power.

Leading journalists conceded that the media were often insensitive to, or insufficiently informed about, ethnic communities but were virtually unanimous in their opposition to anti-vilification legislation. They argued that limitations imposed on free speech were not warranted.

COUNTERING ANTISEMITISM

Political leaders from all major parties, church leaders and others condemned racism in the context of initial bipartisan support for the racial vilification legislation. The prime minister and the deputy leader of the opposition both re-iterated their support for anti-racist legislation at the Zionist Federation biennial conference. The federal government announced its Community Relations Agenda which aimed to create a more tolerant society. The agenda prioritized work with youth, the media, police, legal professionals and local government.

Senior media commentators criticized the existence of racism, even while many opposed, on grounds of free speech, the enactment of racial vilification laws. Federal and state organizations such as the human rights and equal opportunities commissions, the anti-discrimination boards and the ethnic affairs commissions continued their work against racism, although one report by the trades union movement was critical of cuts to their budgets and the lack of a national strategy to combat racism and discrimination. In 1993-4 the commissions and boards received 458 complaints under the Commonwealth Race Discrimination Act, a 23 per cent increase on the previous year.

Some Jewish communities run services to provide speakers for non-Jewish organizations on Jewish subjects. In addition, high school teachers and Christian ministers were offered seminars on Jewish affairs. An inter-faith Christian and Jewish group held a service at the war memorial in the centre of Sydney to commemorate Kristallnacht and the Victorian council of churches published a handbook to support Christian-Jewish reconciliation. An international conference on racism and antisemitism in Melbourne in June was addressed by a broad range of Aboriginal, ethnic and religious leaders. The Melbourne-based Jewish Holocaust Museum and Research Centre marked its tenth anniversary with an address by ex-Prime Minister Bob Hawke.

Anti-racist demonstrations were held to counter National Action rallies in Adelaide and Melbourne. In Melbourne in March over 250 anti-racists (including a significant number of Jewish protesters) demonstrated outside a National Action meeting attended by twenty-five members. In Adelaide three counter-demonstrations were supported by a broad range of community, church, ethnic and Aboriginal groups, trades unions and student organizations.

David Greason, a former supporter of ALR and National Action, published his autobiography, *I was a Teenage Fascist*, in which he condemned the extreme right. The South Australian state theatre plans to produce a play based on the book aimed at young people.

ASSESSMENT

Australia remains a tolerant and open society. Its political institutions are committed to furthering a multicultural, pluralistic community. The level of public antisemitism remains low and there are well-observed public conventions against racism and antisemitism.

However, a number of ugly incidents in recent years seem to have been inspired by British, American, Arab, Christian and Islamic sources. Extremist political and religious groups have marginally raised their public profile and level of activity. They continue to propagate antisemitim and have been allowed to advocate such views without much hindrance, though this may change if the Racial Hatred Bill becomes law.

Antisemitism remains more of an "intellectual" than a "street" phenomenon, and the Jewish community has recorded a fall in the number of serious or violent incidents. However, there has been a rise in the report of antisemitic telephone calls, letters, graffiti, posters and vandalism.

The willingness of some parliamentarians to employ rhetoric that reinforces Jewish stereotypes and to defend their attendance at meetings or, in a small number of cases, actually promote the activities of extremist groups gives cause for concern. One encouraging note is the widespread censure of politicians found to have had even remote links with extremist groups. Although, in general, the media is anti-racist, isolated instances of harmful stereotypes in the mainstream and ethnic media exist.

Overall, the Jewish community does not feel threatened by antisemitism and most Jews feel secure in Australian society.

New Zealand

General population: 3.5 million
Jewish population: 5,000 (mainly in Auckland and Wellington)

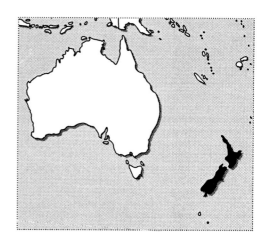

GENERAL BACKGROUND

New Zealand is experiencing substantial economic, social and political change. Current levels of unemployment are very high. There are also serious political tensions. The Labour government of 1984-90 adopted a monetarist approach to economic policy, thus confusing traditional political alliances. Green and Maori nationalists have grown in strength in the face of this political confusion and, since the 1993 election, have gained four parliamentary seats, three being held by Maoris. The next elections will be held under a new voting system (mixed member proportional) and a number of sitting members of parliament have already left the two major political parties to form their own groups.

HISTORICAL LEGACY

Unlike similar societies, such as Australia and Canada, there were no fascist groups in New Zealand in the 1930s. However, antisemitism was to be found among some owners of small farms and businesses who looked to Major C. H. Douglas and Social Credit to provide them with a scapegoat for their economic woes in the 1930s and later. This antisemitism proved relatively insignificant because Social Credit allied itself with the Labour Party, which gained power in 1935.

In the post-war period Social Credit split into two camps. One sought to retain the antisemitic arguments of Douglas; the other rejected them. By 1970 the latter had gained control of Social Credit, which by this time was a political party in its own right. The Douglasites found refuge in the Australian-based League of Rights led by Eric Butler. Butler had been involved in the Australian Social Credit movement in the 1930s and had written an antisemitic book in the late 1940s. He continues to tour New Zealand at regular intervals (see **Australia**).

The New Zealand League of Rights provides the only link with the antisemitism of the 1930s and now acts, like its Australian parent, as a pressure group. At its height in the late 1970s, its newsletter was sent to probably around 1,000 people, but currently its readers, though committed, are few.

RACISM AND XENOPHOBIA

Approximately 13 per cent of New Zealand's population claim at least one ancestor from the country's indigenous Maori or Morioni minorities. Despite a legal prohibition on discrimination, significant portions of the indigenous population remain marginally educated and economically disadvantaged.

PARTIES, ORGANIZATIONS, MOVEMENTS

There are two types of explicitly fascist groups. They first appeared in New Zealand in the 1960s and they attracted new adherents in the 1980s.

The New Zealand Nazi Party invokes the German Nazism of the 1930s and 1940s, while groups such as New Force and the Conservative Front identify with the neo-fascism of the British National Front (see **United Kingdom**). Both wish to retain links with Britain. As organizations—and there are probably less than ten such bodies active at any given time—they attract a very small membership (probably less than 200 for all groups currently active), but they have helped encourage younger New Zealanders, notably skinheads, to adopt racist and antisemitic arguments. These are expressed through graffiti, desecration of Jewish graves, pamphlets and, occasionally, threats or attacks on Jews. Attacks are rare but a cause for concern given recent incidents when skinheads or "white power" groups expressed their views publicly and violently. In 1992 the New Zealand National Front became more active in publishing and produced two magazines, *Skinhead* and *Viewpoint*.

The activities of skinheads, and especially their physical attacks on Asians and Polynesians in Christchurch, attracted considerable publicity in 1994. During the early part of the year Christchurch newspapers regularly reported attacks by skinheads, both verbal and physical, on Asian residents or visitors or teenage Polynesians especially in the city centre.

Skinheads are the most obvious and growing example of racism in New Zealand and the police have taken the step (unusual for New Zealand) of bringing charges against skinheads for the racial abuse of an Asian shop-owner. The sole previous prosecution, in 1976, involved two Nazis, one of them Colin King-Ansell, for the publication of an antisemitic pamphlet.

PUBLICATIONS AND MEDIA

Given that there has been serious concern in recent years with the antisemitism evident in some published letters to newspaper editors, 1994 provided relatively few examples of antisemitism in the print or other media. Wendy Ross, then president of the New Zealand Jewish Council, noted in late 1994 that "the media onslaught of the last ten years, including the vitriolic letters to the editors of newspapers, has all but disappeared with the [Middle East] peace process".

A television documentary entitled *Under the Carpet,* which was shown in early 1994, graphically portrayed the racism of skinheads and their commitment to neo-Nazi symbols and ideologies.

RELIGION

Fundamentalist Christianity grew considerably in the 1980s, and some representatives of the trend have expressed antisemitic sentiments. Typical is Barry Smith, a fundamentalist preacher who, in a lecture tour in 1991, said he foresaw a world government, a world church exerting "evil influences" and a cashless society based on microchips which would allow "demonic forces to track and programme people to worship the devil". Jews were said to play a major role in instituting this "new world order".

Another Christian fundamentalist, Phil Young, talks of "Jewish international bankers who believe that they are God's Israel but reject Christ". He has also commented that *The Protocols of the Elders of Zion* is the work of Talmudic Jews, "mainly rabbis", and that "Jews believe in Satan". His most recent book (1992) is entitled *Jesus Says "Go", But the Pharisees Say "No"*.

Young, a New Zealander born in the postwar period, is university-educated and runs a financial advisory service in a provincial town. His arguments echo those of the Social Credi-

tors of the 1930s and probably reflect the economic uncertainty and political changes which occurred in New Zealand in the 1980s. These arguments continue to be circulated among a relatively small fundamentalist Christian community although populist preachers, such as Barry Smith, do hold well-attended mass rallies.

DENIAL OF THE HOLOCAUST

A major event in 1993 was the declared intention of David Irving, the British Holocaust-denier, to visit Australia and New Zealand. The refusal of the Australian authorities to grant him a visa to visit that country meant that he did not, in the end, visit either country. In May 1994 the League of Rights' *New Times* published Irving's submission to the immigration department in support of an appeal for a reconsideration of his visa application. The submission outlined Irving's Holocaust-denying views and his acknowledgment that these views were contentious.

LEGAL MATTERS

In 1991 the solicitor general established a special unit on war criminals; the *Report on War Crimes Investigations* was released in December 1992. The unit had acted on seventeen names supplied by the Los Angeles-based Simon Wiesenthal Center and fourteen of these individuals had been contacted. The unit also investigated material from a variety of countries and sources. The final recommendation was that there were no grounds for bringing prosecutions against any of those identified and that it was unlikely that there would be reasons for further investigations in the future. This conclusion was a disappointment to many, including members of the Jewish community.

In May 1994 one of those named received NZ$60,000 for defamation and out-of-court costs from Television New Zealand after he had begun proceedings which sought NZ$3.25 million in damages. The matter attracted little attention and no public debate.

In the same month Dr Jan Smith, former head in South Africa of the Church of the Creator, a North American-based white supremacist and antisemitic group, migrated to New Zealand and was granted permanent residence (see **South Africa**). Anti-apartheid groups protested but no grounds for deportation were found. Immigration minister Roger Maxwell decided not to revoke Smith's residency, claiming that new immigrants should be judged by their actions, not their beliefs. Smith's entry prompted a widespread debate about permitting racists to enter the country. As a result, potential immigrants are now required as part of the application procedure to declare whether they have been members of any racist group.

The high court dismissed an appeal against the Planning Tribunal and upheld a Wellington city council abatement notice requiring a man to paint out a wall and remove from a window two swastikas about which his two neighbours had complained. The judge ruled that under the 1991 Resource Management Act the offensive nature of the swastikas adversely affected the environment and their removal impaired only very slightly the man's freedom of expression and opinion guaranteed by the 1990 Bill of Rights Act. This may prove a significant precedent.

ASSESSMENT

Antisemitism plays a minor role in New Zealand politics and life. The sole audience for such views is most likely to be found among supporters of an outdated Social Credit tradition or those displaying neo-fascist sympathies, notably skinheads. The violence of the latter is a cause for concern although the numbers involved remain relatively small. What did cause concern during 1994 was the possibility that racists and antisemites might be among those immigrating to New Zealand, particularly from South Africa. There was vocal opposition to this possibility and the government moved to identify those migrants who had been involved in racist politics in other countries.

Europe

THE INSTITUTE OF JEWISH AFFAIRS AND THE AMERICAN JEWISH COMMITTEE

Austria

General population: 7.9 million
Jewish population: 8,000 (mainly in Vienna)

GENERAL BACKGROUND

Austria is a parliamentary republic currently governed by a coalition between the Sozialdemokratische Partei Österreichs (SPÖ, Social Democratic Party) and the Österreichische Volkspartei (ÖVP, Austrian People's Party). The three opposition parties represented in parliament—the Freiheitliche Partei Österreichs (FPÖ, Austrian Freedom Party), the Grünen (Greens) and the Liberales Forum (LF, Liberal Forum)—enjoy the support of 22.6, 7.3 and 6 per cent of voters respectively, as measured by the results of the October parliamentary elections.

Politics in Austria in 1994 were dominated by two events, both of which represented major breaks with the post-war era. In June, Austrians voted by an overwhelming 66.4 per cent majority to join the European Union (EU). By October, however, the reigning euphoria among the governing parties over the EU referendum had turned to despair as they contemplated the implications of their disastrous general election results. Both parties suffered massive losses (primarily to the FPÖ), and although they formed a new coalition government, the SPÖ and ÖVP no longer commanded the two-thirds majority in parliament necessary to pass constitutional laws.

The long-term political significance of the election is uncertain. On the one hand, the FPÖ's gain of over 6 per cent since the last parliamentary elections offered signal evidence not only of the uncanny ability of the FPÖ leader, Jörg Haider, to recover the political initiative on the national and provincial level (the FPÖ also gained ground in several provincial elections in 1994 as well). It also suggested, rather more alarmingly, that increasing numbers of Austrian voters do not view Haider's open attacks on representative democracy, his official conversion of the FPÖ into a "citizens' movement" with decidedly autocratic features, or his advocacy of an Austrian "third republic" (which would grant far-ranging executive powers to the president at the expense of parliament) as obstacles to supporting him, even out of protest against the two government parties. On the other hand, the parliamentary factions of the LF and the Greens, both of which consider Haider a danger to democratic politics in Austria, were also strengthened by the elections. The performance of the leaders of their respective parliamentary groups (Madeleine Petrovic and Heide Schmidt) during the campaign indicated that articulate alternatives to the FPÖ opposition policies will be well represented in the assembly and in the media.

President Thomas Klestil, who came under fire early in the year when his wife left him because of his increasingly open affair with a presidential assistant, eventually resumed his efforts to test the limits of his constitutional authority *vis-à-vis* the chancellor and parliament. The separation of powers defined in the Austrian constitution evinces enough ambiguities to lend plausibility to Klestil's argument about the president's role in foreign affairs, though his putative claims diverge markedly from the constitutional practice of all his predecessors. The issue came to a head over Austria's representation in the Council of Europe, and pitted Chancellor Franz Vranitzky (SPÖ) against Klestil and Foreign Minister Alois Mock, both from the ÖVP. In the parliamentary debate over the constitutional changes necessary to bring Austrian law into conformity with the EU, the LF and the Greens endorsed the SPÖ view, arguing that the Austrian president, unlike the chancellor, was not subject to any parliamentary control. Klestil has recently found an ally in Haider, who has championed the constitutional prerogatives Klestil claims because he views it as a step on the way to a third republic. In the event the ÖVP and the FPÖ, voting together, blocked the attempt to specify which powers the Austrian president would exercise in connection with the EU.

This test of constitutional strength will in the end be conditioned by the constellation of political forces at any given moment. Still, given the relative weakness of the SPÖ, the interest of the president in enhancing his power, the hope of the ÖVP that in supporting the claims of the conservative president against a socialist chancellor it might strengthen its own political position, and Haider's clear interest in splitting the coalition government and perhaps thereby forcing new elections from which he hopes to benefit, this tactical alliance between the ÖVP and the FPÖ in support of the president, who has the constitutional power to appoint and dismiss governments, might set an important precedent for future co-operation.

Less severely affected than most other countries in Europe by the international recession, Austria's economy has benefited from the recent sustained economic upturn. It has continued to exceed the real growth rates of European Organization for Economic Co-operation and Development (OECD) countries, and its currency has remained one of the most stable on the continent. The unemployment rate in Austria has declined from around 7 per cent at the end of 1993, and economists predict a further drop next year. Hoping to take advantage of the favourable economic conditions to attack the deficit, the new government has adopted a series of politically unpopular cuts and caps on spending.

Though the current relatively healthy state of the economy in general should reduce the extreme social insecurity that fosters the search for extreme political solutions, the uncertain outcome of this restructuring process, combined with the new-found combativeness on the part of traditional socialists, adds one more unknown ingredient to the volatile political admixture in Austria.

For all these reasons, 1994 was an extraordinary year in Austrian politics, inaugurating a period of relative political instability and political realignment, the implications of which cannot be foreseen, but as yet offer few grounds for real alarm.

HISTORICAL LEGACY

Antisemitic prejudice in Austria historically was a mixture of beliefs and suspicions for the most part impervious to attempts to introduce sectarian "rigour". This lack of clear differentiation between racial and non-racial forms of antisemitism continued into the Austrian First Republic, whatever other real political differences might have existed among its proponents.

In the 1930s the Christian Social Party's diffuse amalgamation of religious, economic, cultural and racial prejudice, together with its reluctance to introduce discriminatory measures against Jews, was at a disadvantage against

Hitler's racial "antisemitism of reason" and the Nuremberg laws. Yet the stated objectives of these two politically disparate strands of antisemitism were not fundamentally dissimilar. In 1938 Austria was dissolved into the Third Reich, and Nazi racial policies were applied to the inhabitants of the new areas.

The Austrian Second Republic, founded in 1945, repudiated national socialism, including its racial policies. Antisemitism was re-defined officially as a relic of a hated regime, and the juridical independence of Austria, enshrined in the Moscow declaration of 1943, brought forth a corresponding explanation of the new Austria's ideological *tabula rasa*. However, the official negative connotations associated with the term "antisemitism" did not eliminate the problem of anti-Jewish prejudice after the war. Nonetheless, open public expressions of hostility towards Jews were seen to transgress, at least implicitly, recognized normative expectations of post-Auschwitz Austrian political debate, and as such were considered largely unrelated to the wider political culture.

The Waldheim affair in 1986 represented a watershed in the post-war "Jewish question" because it witnessed the willingness of a major political party (the ÖVP) to appeal to antisemitic prejudice—coded in an appropriate post-Auschwitz idiom—for political ends and indicated the potential for its success. A 1991 poll showed that even after five years of Waldheim's international isolation, a significant percentage of Austrians still held "the Jews" accountable for the Waldheim affair. The same opinion survey revealed an alarming resilience of certain anti-Jewish stereotypes in contemporary Austria. Waldheim's retirement from public office removed the principal point around which hostility towards Jews had crystallized, and while any contemporary allusion to the World Jewish Congress, Waldheim's principal critic in 1986, usually elicits a venomous response from the tabloid press and some conservative politicians, in the early 1990s, "foreigners" became the principal focus of both discursive and political intolerance.

RACISM AND XENOPHOBIA

Partly because of the public perception of the Austrian authorities' vigorous, not to say zealous, enforcement of the country's more restrictive immigration laws, partly because the numbing monotony of the pictures from war-torn Bosnia was not accompanied by a major influx of refugees, and partly because of the exigency of other issues, the "foreigner problem" did not retain quite its electoral or even discursive salience in 1994, and anti-Jewish hostility is even further removed from normal political debate.

A recent study undertaken by Werner Holzer and Rainer Münz, however, suggests that there are few reasons to doubt the potential for hostility towards immigrants that exists in present-day Austria. According to the authors, 34.2 per cent of those questioned favoured stopping totally the influx of foreigners into Austria, while a further 27.3 per cent approved of severe restrictions on immigration and were against generosity towards political refugees. Among a majority, fears of housing and job shortages translated rather directly into advocacy of a complete moratorium on immigration and the admission of refugees. Fully 66 per cent of those polled either disagreed or strongly disagreed with the statement, "The presence of foreigners is good, because in this way we [can] encounter other cultures", while over three-quarters believed or tended to believe that an increase in foreigners led to an increase in crime.

PARTIES, ORGANIZATIONS, MOVEMENTS

The only openly antisemitic parties and organizations in Austria are those on the far right. Public awareness of groups professing racialist and other national-socialist aims—primarily directed against "foreigners"—remained high in 1994, due principally to the trials of suspected neo-Nazis, and to the media coverage given to the bombing campaigns of the most violent extreme-right fringe.

The racist far right in Austria comprises not only minuscule and militant political parties, but also more diffusely organized cultural, educational and even gymnastic associations, and veterans' organizations with a pronouncedly *völkisch* character. The *Handbuch des österreichischen Rechtsextremismus* (Handbook of Austrian Right-Extremism) published in 1993, listed approximately fifty such organizations, though many of these consisted of little more than a mailing address, and memberships were frequently overlapping. The Austrian state police has estimated the hard core of neo-Nazis to be only between 300-500, though estimates of those on the periphery range up to 20,000.

Because of the trials of its leader, Gottfried Küssel, and the arrest of several activists in connection with the letter bomb campaign of December 1993, the Volkstreue Ausserparlamentarische Opposition (VAPO, Ethnically Loyal Extra-Parliamentary Opposition) has continued to attract the bulk of media attention. Although VAPO is estimated to have around 200 sympathizers, most of whom are affiliated with one or more of several "comradeships" (*Kameradschaften*), such as that in Langenlois, the arrest and imprisonment of its leadership has restricted its ability to function (see **Legal Matters**).

The Aktionsgemeinschaft für demokratische Politik (AFP, Political Action Committee for Democratic Politics), is registered as a political party, but has very few members itself. It functions as the umbrella organization of the far right and exerts a disproportionate influence within the shadowy far-right milieu in Austria by virtue of its contacts with other groups, individuals and publications on the far right both inside Austria and abroad. It publishes the *Kommentare zum Zeitgeschehen*, which is an important vehicle for the propagation of neo-Nazism and Holocaust denial. At its twenty-ninth "political academy" held in October, speakers included Robert Dürr, a former associate of the neo-Nazi paper *Sieg*, former candidate of the FPÖ in Burgenland and national chair of the extreme right-wing Notwehrgemeinschaft der Bauern (Farmers' Self-Defence Society); Rudolf Nowotny, the executive director of the Verein Dichterstein Offenhausen (Offenhausen Writers Union, see **Legal Matters**), and deputy chairman of the Wohlfahrtsvereinigung der Glasenbacher (Glasenbachers' Relief Union: Glasenbach was the prison camp set up near Salzburg in the US occupation zone in 1945, where many of the more prominent Nazis were incarcerated after the war); and Alois Wolf and Mathilde Wolf, the editors of *Kommentare zum Zeitgeschehen* and the *Wiener Beobachter*. The annual political academy of the AFP has served as the main organizational link between the extreme right and the FPÖ, offering members of the FPÖ a platform to cultivate the *völkisch* ideological affinities they share. However, Haider has abandoned his strategic opening to the extreme right and, as a consequence, has attempted to restrict or cut off too public contacts between the FPÖ and the AFP. Nonetheless, relations continue to exist between the AFP and individual FPÖ members.

The press coverage of the extreme right over the past two years, but especially in the wake of the letter bombings, has focused attention both on the programmatic congruence of issues, such as immigration, between the FPÖ under Haider's leadership and the extreme right, and on the personal contacts between FPÖ officials and extreme-right organizations at various levels. Haider has always attempted to appeal to various constituencies simultaneously, and psephological exigencies have required that his strategic opening to the political

right be tempered by the vociferous protesta-
tion of his party's commitment to constitutional legality.

With the German nationalist vote assured,
in 1994 Haider continued to pursue his strategy,
begun towards the end of 1993, of attempting to
make the FPÖ into a rallying point for conservatives of various ideological traditions. In
order to effect this shift, Haider has had all explicit references to the FPÖ's commitment to
the "German ethnic and cultural community"
eliminated from the party's recently adopted
programme, has continued to relegate German
nationalist ideologues in the party to less public
positions of influence, and has forced out some
individual FPÖ members with well-known
connections to members of VAPO. Andreas
Mölzer, for example, was forced to resign his
seat in the Austrian upper house (Bundesrat) at
Haider's insistence; indeed, Mölzer was seen as
such a political liability that the FPÖ district
organization virtually ensured that he would
not be elected to the national assembly in the
October elections. Though Haider has been
careful to reaffirm his strong German
"national[ist] convictions" where politically
appropriate, their fall from public grace has led
Mölzer and his ilk in recent months to issue dire
warnings of the impending corruption of the
FPÖ's ethnic mission. Nonetheless, Mölzer,
along with Lothar Höbelt, Haider's adviser and
front man in respectable academic circles, continue to provide ideological depth for more
intellectually ambitious FPÖ supporters. Together with Brigitte Sob, they edited "Freedom
and Responsibility", the title given to the yearbook of the Libertarian Educational Institute.

An underground terrorist organization
that has surfaced in connection with the second
wave of bombings in Austria is the Bajuwarische
Befreiungsarmee (Bavarian Liberation Army).
The Bajuwarische Befreiungsarmee was founded after the defeat of the Third Reich, and was
disbanded shortly afterwards. Bajuwar is an
archaic latinate name for Bavarians which derives from the tribal law (*Lex Bajuvariorum*);
its usage in the present context seems to validate
the ostensible racial continuity of the Teutonic
tribes in Austria against that of the Slavs. Its
aims were to bring together into a single state all
original areas settled by the Bajuwars, that is,
present-day Austria excluding Vorarlberg and
including Bavaria and South Tyrol.

Although it is important to identify the
groups and individuals who view themselves
explicitly as continuing, or reviving, the policies
and ideology of the Third Reich, and who are
prepared to use (and in some cases actually resort to) violence—and the danger which such

political violence presents should not be
minimized—such groups have become increasingly marginalized and politically irrelevant
even within the extreme-right milieu. The imprisonment of neo-Nazi leadership cadres;
Haider's unchallenged political authority in the
FPÖ; the radically xenophobic petition campaign launched and promoted by Haider's FPÖ
in 1992-3 and his recourse to anti-foreigner
themes in the EU referendum campaign; as well
as the increasingly restrictive immigration policies pursued by the government, have all combined to render the independent political
groups increasingly otiose for many individuals
who either were, or would have been, among
their activists and sympathizers.

MAINSTREAM POLITICS

All five political parties represented in the Austrian parliament explicitly oppose discrimination against Jews and national or ethnic
minorities (though the FPÖ petition initiative
in 1993 called for the ethnic segregation of
school children), and all condemn acts of political violence. Though the enormous influence of
the *Neue Kronen Zeitung* makes most mainstream politicians hesitate before criticizing
the likes of the paper's columnist Richard
Nimmerrichter, too open expressions of anti-
Jewish prejudice usually elicit at least an admo-
nition (see **Publications and Media**).

A similar commitment is sometimes found
wanting among the other parties when dealing
with expressions of ethnic prejudice directed
against foreigners or immigrants, with the notable exception of the Greens and the LF, whose
records in this respect are unimpeachable.
Arguments preaching tolerance, however, seem
to have had less effect in undermining Haider's
anti-foreigner agitation than the governing parties' emphasis on the restrictive nature of their
own immigration policies. Indeed, the government's immigration and asylum laws are so
stringent that the Austrian supreme court has
overturned certain of their provisions, and the
United Nations' high commissioner for refugees has consistently criticized the laws and
their execution. The mere perception of the
government as having the "foreigner problem"
more or less under control, of course, does little
to undermine the ethnic stereotyping of "foreigners" among those sectors of the population
most receptive to xenophobic appeals, and suggests that the potential for anti-immigrant
populism still exists.

A controversy surrounding the memorial
plaque in Wels continued in 1994. The plaque,
located in the Sigmar Chapel (Sigmarkapelle),
a public building, commemorates the SS-

Kameradschaft IV (SS-Veterans' Organization IV). Though subject to criticism from politicians from the national SPÖ (including then minister of education, Rudolf Scholten), Wels's SPÖ mayor, Karl Bregartner, saw nothing untoward about the city's honouring members of the SS, all the more—so he claimed in July—since the interior ministry had not found anything legally exceptionable about the group. Bregartner was referring to a letter he had received from Interior Minister Franz Löschnak reporting that Günther Glotz, the editor of *Die Kameradschaft*, the organization's magazine, had been acquitted the previous October of charges under the prohibition law. Glotz had been indicted because in 1989 *Die Kameradschaft* had published an article by Karl Leipert in which he wrote, among other things: "Let us think of the 100th birthday of the creator of a Reich of all Germans, that had been the dream of the best sons of all German tribes forever. Let us think of the truest of the true, who went to the heaven of the gods as martyrs of unwavering sacrifice." Leipert himself was physically incapable of standing trial, and Glotz claimed that he, the editor, had not read Leipert's "nonsense" before publication. Attention by the media was limited, and the SS commemorative plaque in Wels, it seems, will remain a source of minor political conflict for some time. In the event, the motion tabled by the Greens in the Wels municipal council to remove the plaque was defeated.

MANIFESTATIONS

Virtually without exception, pro-Nazi, anti-Jewish and anti-foreigner ideologies were linked in the publications, the slogans and the statements of those suspected, arrested or convicted for "hate crimes" (that is, crimes in which the culprits were suspected of having acted from neo-Nazi, antisemitic or xenophobic motives) in 1994. Yet the manifestations of antisemitic or xenophobic behaviour were varied in both scope and intensity. And whilst blatant Nazi propaganda and acts of vandalism and physical violence were only encountered on the far right, the range of discursive manifestations of prejudice was far wider.

According to figures supplied by the Austrian ministry of interior, there were over 600 activities which would fall under the rubric of hate crimes reported in 1994, an increase of 14 per cent over 1993. Of these, 105 incidents had been committed by members of youth gangs and, in a further 262 cases, the culprits were unknown. Evidence and neo-Nazi propaganda were seized in 120 searches carried out by the police and a total of 48 persons were arrested on

suspicion of criminal activity.

The police were able to solve 232 hate crimes altogether in 1994 and the Austrian authorities were able to register a number of arrests and successful prosecutions. In 75 cases, no charges were brought, while 61 cases ended in convictions. By the end of the year, 25 right-wing extremists, including several leading neo-Nazi figures, were either serving prison sentences or were in detention waiting trial for violations of the prohibition or other laws (see **Legal Matters**). In addition, some of the more dangerous organizations on the extreme-right fringe were dissolved outright or deprived of their legal status.

However, these very successes created new impediments for law enforcement officials. Remaining extreme-right cadres swiftly moved to reorganize themselves underground, which has made police infiltration and therefore detection and arrest more difficult. Communication between these individuals as well as the dissemination of neo-Nazi propaganda largely takes place via e-mail addresses in Germany, the Internet and other advanced communication technologies, all of which are largely beyond the reach of the Austrian police.

Thus, although there have been occasional attacks on foreigners (three in 1994) or attempted arson attacks on shelters for refugees or those seeking asylum (also three), those extreme right-wing elements engaged in political violence in Austria have preferred, in 1994 as in 1993, the more direct means of non-incendiary bombs. Most of the targets were selected for their politics, rather than their ethnicity, that is, Austrians considered too friendly towards refugees or those believed guilty of what extremists might call "racial treason". Still, linguistic minorities might have been among the intended victims of the pipe bomb planted by terrorists in August at the German-Slovenian bilingual elementary school in Klagenfurt. Police discovered the bomb at the school before it detonated, and the fact that it was found during a school holiday suggested that the intended victims were not school children. The bomb did explode a short time later while being investigated by explosive experts at the Klagenfurt airport. A police officer lost both hands as a result.

In early October, more letter bombs were discovered. Bombs had been sent to Lojze Wiesner, a Klagenfurt publisher of Slovene- and German-language authors; an information office for foreigners in Dornbirn; the personnel office of a paper products factory in Hallein; and the Wilden convent in Innsbruck, which had been housing asylum-seekers. Serious personal injury was averted only because the bombs failed to detonate due to technical deficiencies in their construction. Responsibility for these attacks was claimed by the Kampftruppe Oadilo von Bayern (Archduke Odilo of Bavaria Combat Unit) of the Salzburger Eidgenossenschaft (Salzburg Confederation) and Bajuwarische Befreiungsarmee (Bavarian Liberation Army) (see **Parties, Organizations, Movements**).

Later the same month, a letter bomb was sent to the foreign minister of the Republic of Slovenia, Lojze Peterlé, which likewise failed to detonate. The racist nature of all these crimes was clear from the letter sent to Peterlé claiming responsibility for the letter bombs and the bomb at the Klagenfurt school. In addition to precise technical details identifying the materials used in the bombs' construction, the letter contained explicit death threats against minority Slovenes as well as supporters of bilingual education: "Whoever uses the Slovene language on Austrian territory", the letter warned, "must expect to be injured or killed". Government ministers or politicians whose names suggest Slavic origin (Chancellor Vranitzky, Vice-Chancellor Busek, Green Member of Parliament Teresija Stoisits etc.), were described by the epithet *Tschuschenhauptling* (roughly equivalent to "wog chieftains"); Education Minister Rudolf Scholten was described as "evidently an Asian Jew with a German name"; and Tyrolean Provincial Governor Wendelin Weingartner was described as "dark-skinned, presumably a Gypsy". The letter from the Kampftruppe Oadilo von Bayern also claimed responsibility for the letter bombs sent the previous December, attempting thereby to exculpate Peter Binder and Franz Radl (see **Legal Matters**). The prosecutor's office in the Austrian ministry of justice, however, does not believe there to be any direct connection between the first and second series of letter bombs, at least in terms of their perpetrators.

The Einsatzgruppe zur Bekämpfung des Terrorismus (EBT, anti-terrorism task-force) was set up by the Austrian state police to investigate right-wing extremist violence. The EBT, led by Gerhard Koller, has been leading the investigations into all the bombings connected with neo-Nazis. A special commission, called "Salieri", was set up to investigate the second series of letter bombs and, by the end of the year, police had made one arrest.

While the bombings were the most alarming manifestation of racial hatred, it is important not to overlook less immediately dangerous examples of prejudice. One of the after-effects of the Waldheim affair, in particular since the change of national leadership in ÖVP,

has been a heightened sensitivity to expressions of antisemitic prejudice. However, this has been compensated for by a very high tolerance threshold for prejudiced discourse against minorities (particularly ethnic minorities) other than Jews. Given the high correlation between those who harbour anti-Jewish prejudice and those hostile towards foreigners, this circumstance offers no grounds for complacency. Indeed, the unguarded remarks of some public figures in Austria suggested that this increased sensitivity was far from uniform. In 1994, the tolerance threshold for such incidents which had become public remained relatively low in Austria, but seemed to be rising. This, however, appears to have reflected the perception of a social taboo on a form of discourse rather than the resilience of fundamentally tolerant attitudes.

Too explicit expressions of xenophobia sometimes force the FPÖ to react to the public outcry. An FPÖ lower-level municipal district (Bezirksrat) councillor, Wolfgang Fröhlich, introduced a motion into Vienna's seventh district council attributing the alleged increase in crime to the "politically instigated, high proportion of foreigners" in the city and the "multicultural bastardization of society". The motion was defeated and Fröhlich was expelled from the party.

CULTURAL LIFE

The most heated controversy concerning allegations of antisemitism in Austria came towards the end of the year, and involved some rather surprising protagonists, including Wolf Biermann, the former East German dissident whose DDR citizenship was revoked in the mid-1970s. Since the fall of the Berlin Wall, Biermann has cast scathing opprobrium on East German literary figures who had made their peace, or in some cases actively co-operated, with the Stasi (Staatssicherheit, or State Security) (see **Germany**). His hostility to the German Partei des Demokratischen Sozialismus (PDS, Party of Democratic Socialism), the successor party of the East German Sozialistische Einheitspartei Deutschlands (SED, Socialist Unity Party of Germany), and its present leaders seems visceral, and his vocabulary sometimes correspondingly caustic. On one occasion, Biermann branded Gregor Gysi, the current chair of the PDS, a criminal, and averred that he would not wish to live under laws which Gysi had passed. In the 24 November issue of *Neues Deutschland*, the paper of the PDS, Alfred Hrdlicka, the internationally renowned Austrian sculptor whose works include the memorial against war and fascism in Vienna, wrote an open letter to Biermann in which he responded (in terms of coarseness of language) at least in kind. In the view of many, however, Hrdlicka's riposte transgressed the boundaries of the tolerable, all the more remarkable coming from a professed "antifascist". The disputed passage was a direct reply to Biermann's statement about Gysi. Hrdlicka wrote: "[So] you don't want to live under laws which Gysi passes?! You should have the Nuremberg race laws on your neck, you conformist idiot!"

The Jewish journalist Henryk Broder (who was born in Poland but grew up in Germany) then published an article in the Austrian weekly *Profil* in which he quoted only the words about the Nuremberg laws, pronounced them proof of Hrdlicka's antisemitism, designated him a "left-wing Nazi", and called for his monument against war and fascism to be torn down.

The discussion surrounding the Hrdlicka controversy dominated the media for several days. Rudolf Scholten, minister of science and research in the newly-elected government, announced disciplinary action against Hrdlicka, who holds a professorship at the Vienna College of Fine Arts. Many Austrian journalists and other public figures with very different political agendas from Broder's used the occasion to boast that they had been right about the (ironically) self-styled "Euro-Stalinist" (who left the Communist Party in 1956) all along; others considered Hrdlicka's somewhat peculiar choice of polemical phrasing illustrative of an antisemitism they had either suspected for years or only recently discovered; still others attempted to explain away Hrdlicka's remarks by referring to his excessive drinking or trying to find some other basis of his diminished capacity; yet others performed a textual exegesis to show Hrdlicka's real meaning in the open letter; and some tried to make sense of the dispute by scrutinizing Biermann's and Broder's, as well as Hrdlicka's, verbal overkill.

Hrdlicka did nothing to assuage the concern of many of his former political allies; indeed, his adamant refusal to retract his initial remarks (an act which Hrdlicka himself, reasonably enough, would have considered hypocritical), combined with equally bizarre statements (for example, that Biermann, Gysi and Stefan Heym, Jewish Germans, were all "in the same racial boat") made in response to allegations of antisemitism, and his seeming inability to comprehend why people found his remarks antisemitic, have all made it difficult to evaluate the real significance of the dispute. The one certain feature is that many in the Jewish community felt a sense of profound uneasiness about the fierceness of the polemic, as well as

the equivocal resolution of the disputed issues. Should Hrdlicka actually be subject to disciplinary proceedings in 1995, the controversy will doubtless be replayed with renewed vigour.

In April, as part of the Offenhausen cultural festival, the Joseph Hiess memorial prize was awarded to Ingomar Pust, who writes regularly for *Aula* (see **Publications and Media**). Four years previously, Andreas Mölzer, at the time chief *völkisch* ideologue of the FPÖ and Haider's personal adviser, had received the prize.

PUBLICATIONS AND MEDIA

The *Deutsche Nationalzeitung*, the paper of the far-right Deutsche Volksunion (DVU, German People's Union), and the *Deutsche Wochenzeitung* were still widely circulated in Austria by their German publishers. Gerd Honsik's fugitive status in Spain enabled him to continue to distribute *Halt!* in Austria. In addition, there are a few extreme right-wing newspapers or magazines published in Austria. Among the most important are: *fakten* (Facts), published by Horst Jakob Rosenkranz; and *Kommentare zum Zeitgeschehen* (Commentaries on Contemporary Events), a publication of the AFP (see **Parties, Organizations, Movements**). These, and to a lesser extent *Aula*, the magazine of the FPÖ union of university graduates, have been instruments for expressions of antisemitic prejudice and/or attempts to challenge either the fact or the extent of the Holocaust. Nonetheless, the Styrian provincial government, through the office of Provincial Governor Josef Krainer, still advertises in rightist magazines such as *Aula*, *Lot und Waage* and *Neue Ordnung*. In response to criticism in the provincial assembly for the government's subsidy of such publications, ÖVP members insisted on the "necessary subsidy of the broadest possible spectrum of publications". The prosecutor's office in Graz has launched a preliminary inquiry to determine whether an article in the July-August issue of *Aula* denying the Holocaust violated the prohibition law (see **Legal Matters**).

Antisemitic literature of various kinds was also seized in police raids and neo-Nazi literature produced abroad continued to circulate underground. An increasing concern of Austrian school authorities has been the circulation of computer games with Nazi and racist themes.

As reported last year, the use of e-mail and computer bulletin board systems (BBS) has enabled neo-Nazis to establish an international network which remains more or less inaccessible to law enforcement agencies and has probably grown. Much of the material emanates from Gary Lauck's neo-Nazi National-sozialistische Deutsche Arbeiterpartei/Auslands- und Aufbauorganisation (NSDAP/AO, German National Socialist Workers' Party/ Overseas Section) in the United States (see **United States**). Lauck continued to distribute a magazine, *Endsieg*, on computer disk and through computer modems and BBSs to Austria, Germany, France and the Netherlands.

Jörg Haider remained unrepentant in his favourable view of certain Nazi policies. In an interview published in the *Kleine Zeitung* in February, for example, Haider restated his endorsement of the "proper employment policies of the Third Reich", a statement which in 1992 had led to his removal as provincial governor of Carinthia.

In its 1993 yearbook, published in 1994, the Richard-Wagner-Gesellschaft (RWG, Richard Wagner Society) reprinted without editorial comment an article by Nazi propaganda minister Joseph Goebbels. The yearbook also printed a leaflet of the extreme-right Junge Nationaldemokraten (Young National Democrats). Once this information came to the public's attention, the president of the RWG, Franz Ehgartner, offered to resign. A few days later, after, as he stated, "the media uproar [had] died down", Ehgartner saw no reason to carry out his offer.

While the demands of editorial self-image and the public taboo on the subject effectively excluded the appearance of primitive anti-Jewish propaganda from all Austrian national newspapers, more subtle expressions of antisemitic prejudice were most likely to be found in the conservative *Neue Kronen Zeitung*, and particularly in the columns of Richard Nimmerrichter, whose opinions reach well over 1 million readers in a country of fewer than 8 million. Attempts by Paul Grosz, the president of the Israelitische Kultusgemeinde (IKG, Austrian Jewish community organization) in Vienna, to have Richard Nimmerrichter prosecuted under the prohibition law for his trivialization of the Holocaust, have been singularly unsuccessful (see **Legal Matters**). Indeed, encouraged by the musings of sympathetic judges, Nimmerrichter's animadversion against Grosz approached the level employed against the World Jewish Congress and its leaders since 1986.

In 1994, Nimmerrichter also deployed his column to help demonize the then SPÖ minister of education, Rudolf Scholten, by alluding to his putative Jewish origins. In a column published on 21 February, for example, Nimmerrichter referred to "fellow-citizen Scholten, [who is], as the poet said, neither

Mameluke nor Christian; some are even convinced that he is not even a Scholten, but rather has another name". References to the Scholten family's earlier "Jewish" name (Pfefferkorn), ordinarily appear only in the writings of explicit racists (it appears, for example, in the letter taking responsibility for a series of bombings, and was also mentioned in a leaflet published by a previously unknown underground group called the Notwehrgemeinschaft der Sicherheitswachebeamten (Self-Defence Confraternity of Police)), which had circulated among police officers for several months before the public became aware of its existence in January 1994 (see **Legal Matters**). It was troubling enough that Nimmerrichter's carefully coded references bore such a close affinity to the brazen racialism of the Self-Defence Confraternity; what was perhaps more disturbing was that Nimmerrichter could assume that his readers would consider Scholten's Jewish family background reproachful.

Nimmerrichter also used his widely-read column to transmit distorted information about the pensions being paid to Austrian Jewish victims of the Holocaust living in Israel. In a column entitled "Remarks on a state visit", written in connection with President Thomas Klestil's visit to Israel, Nimmerrichter evinced his own understanding of historical responsibility, which stands in stark contrast to the views expressed both by Chancellor Vranitzky and President Klestil (see **Countering Antisemitism**). That during his visit, Klestil "remorsefully deplored the complicity of the Austrians in the atrocities of the Hitler regime against the Jews", was, according to Nimmerrichter, "in part rightly so, in part not rightly so". Though neither Klestil nor Vranitzky (nor anyone else for that matter) ever claimed that all Austrians had been complicit in Nazi atrocities, Nimmerrichter contrived this argument in order to rejoin that President Klestil "only represents those Austrians alive today, the overwhelming majority of whom, however, [simply] because of their age cannot have had anything to do with Hitler". Still, the principal purpose of Nimmerrichter's article was to combat the claim, also contrived, "that Austria had not done anything for its Jewish citizens who were driven out of Austria after Hitler's invasion". As evidence, Nimmerrichter cited a confidential report prepared by Austria's ambassador to Israel, Herbert Kroll, on the payments made by Austria to "persons persecuted because of their [ethnic] origin" (*abstammungsmäßig Verfolgte*).

In the sections of the report cited by Nimmerrichter, Knoll made three erroneous claims exaggerating and distorting the amounts paid to Jews and the nature of those payments. Why Nimmerrichter chose to quote from a confidential report, and not to check a single figure for its accuracy when the actual numbers were available from publicly accessible sources, is not known. But, especially at a time of cutbacks of all kinds to reduce the budget deficit, Nimmerrichter's timely reference to what he implied were overly-generous payments made by the Austrian government to Jews living abroad, seems to have edged disturbingly close to embracing the hoary cliché of Jewish parasitism.

One of the most troubling aspects of the Austrian media from the perspective of combating antisemitism and racism was the inordinately favourable attention given by Peter Michael Lingens, columnist in the liberal daily *Der Standard*, to ideas about ethnic differences in intelligence. The occasion for Lingens's foray into intelligence research was provided by the appearance of, and controversy surrounding, *The Bell Curve* by the Richard Herrnstein and Charles Murray. Citing what he believes to be neutral observations supported by the findings of science, Lingens, whose opinions sometimes bordered on parody, seemed particularly fascinated by alleged differences, such as the size of males' genitals and blacks' native abilities to dance. This series of articles was only indirectly related to the question of antisemitism (Lingens did, of course, repeat the "philosemitic" cliché about Jews' intelligence), and Lingens personally is an ardent foe of any form of antisemitism. What is potentially disturbing about Lingens's arguments, precisely because they come from the pen of a self-styled liberal writer, is that they confer legitimacy on a discourse which assumes the existence of a meaningful hierarchy of average cognitive abilities, and assumes that this hierarchy is ethnic. It is not difficult to imagine this material being adapted for antisemitic purposes.

RELIGION

In 1994, Reinhold Stecher, the bishop of the Innsbruck diocese, declared the cult of Anderle von Rinn definitively ended. The blood-libel cult was established in memory of a child, Andreas von Rinn, who according to a legend invented in the seventeenth century was the victim of a Jewish ritual murder in 1462. Though Stecher had repeatedly spoken out against the cult, and had even had a plaque erected at the Judenstein church disavowing the legend, diehard devotees of this anti-Jewish cult had continued to celebrate it. Stecher has now issued a diocesan decree, endorsed by the Vatican, pro-

hibiting all celebration of the cult and has ordered the church in Judenstein renamed as "Mariä Heimsuchung" (the Visitation of Mary). Calling belief in the legend "superstitious error", Stecher argued that ritual murder legends, such as that about Anderle, had "cost innumerable Jews their homes, property, freedom and lives". "The church", Stecher stated, has a "duty to the truth and to love", and must draw the proper consequences and recognize the intolerability of the "defamation of the Jewish religious community". Despite Stecher's decree, on 18 July, cult celebrants gathered together to commemorate Anderle, and flowers were laid against the wall of the church in Rinn, where the bones of Anderle are deposited.

Citing his role in "safeguarding human rights" during his tenure as secretary general of the UN, Donato Squicciarini, the papal nuncio to Austria, formally inducted former Austrian President Kurt Waldheim into the Ordine Piano at a ceremony held at the Vatican embassy in Vienna on 6 July. The Ordine Piano is an order of knights named directly by the Pope. Presented at the height of the summer "silly season", the Pope's award was barely noted in the Austrian press. The reactions abroad were late in coming, but uniformly critical, especially in the United States. As Robert Goldmann, the European representative of the Anti-Defamation League, stated: "One must wonder and be amazed at the judgment of those who made this award. . . . The Vatican owes the world an explanation for an award that is at least incongruous and at worst a devaluation of the work of those who genuinely labour for, and are committed to, safeguarding human rights."

LEGAL MATTERS

A range of right-wing extremist activities are punishable under Austrian criminal law. Open national-socialist activity and the public advocacy of Nazi objectives are prohibited by laws dating from 1947. Amendments to the law approved in February 1992 widened the scope of prohibited activity to include the denial of the Holocaust, or even the "crude trivialization" of Nazi genocide. At the same time, the Austrian parliament reduced the minimum sentence for convicted offences from five years to one, reasoning that the lighter minimum sentence would increase the chances of successful prosecutions. The latter amendment does indeed seem to have had the intended effect, though the long-term educational value of making the denial of the Holocaust into a criminal offence remains to be proven.

In addition to this so-called "prohibition law", the Austrian criminal code also punishes incitement to commit acts of persecution or discrimination against an individual on the basis of her or his race, religion or national origin. The same law also prohibits anyone from ridiculing members of one of the protected groups in a contemptuous fashion, or from insulting them in a manner which offends their human dignity. Though the law against incitement is often invoked to protect Jews or other minorities against physical attacks, and its latter provisions especially are used against particularly crude antisemitic indignities, this law suffers from some vagueness and elasticity of language.

In 1994, the balance of legal efforts to combat right-wing extremism was somewhat mixed. On the one hand, there were several successful prosecutions under Austrian anti-Nazi legislation.

At the same time, by the end of the year no indictments had yet been brought against suspects in the letter bomb campaign of December 1993. In press reports near the end of the year, head prosecutor Sepp Dieter Fasching was quoted as saying that he would not bring indictments against the two suspects being held, Peter Binder and Franz Radl jun., until February 1995. The case against them is based largely on circumstantial evidence plus testimony of an unnamed prosecution witness. The maximum penalty for both attempted murder and for Nazi activity is life imprisonment. All others originally arrested with Binder and Radl, including Sascha Kaspar and Alexander Wolfert, have since been released; none is under suspicion of involvement in the letter bombs, though Wolfert is being investigated for violations of the prohibition law.

The most prominent case involving right-wing extremists was the retrial of Gottfried Küssel in September. Küssel had been convicted in 1993 of violating paragraph 3g of the prohibition law and sentenced to ten years' imprisonment (the minimum sentence), but this conviction was overturned on appeal because of improper instructions given by the judge to the jury. At the new trial, Küssel was also charged under paragraph 3b, which prohibits forming a Nazi organization to undermine Austrian independence. At both trials, several witnesses, including Küssel's VAPO deputy, Hans-Jörg Schimanek jun., testified that VAPO was a loosely structured club of like-minded xenophobes without any strict hierarchy or overt political aims, and that the paramilitary training exercises were merely "fun for fun's sake".

The prosecution was able to present new evidence at the second trial, including two videos prepared by Küssel and his VAPO supporters. One recording, of a paramilitary exercise, showed Schimanek instructing thirteen-year-olds how to kill someone from behind with a knife. The other video was of the VAPO ceremony celebrating the founding of the Kameradschaft Gmund on 20 April 1991 (the 103rd anniversary of Hitler's birth). This video featured speeches by Küssel, Schimanek, Günther Reinthaler and Reinhold Kovar, among others, explaining that VAPO was building a military group to establish by violent means a German Reich reaching, in Küssel's words, "from Flensburg to Radkersburg and from Saarbrücken nearly to the Urals". This visual evidence demolished the defence's line that Küssel was a self-important dreamer with eccentric views but was not part of any serious organizational effort. This second trial ended with Küssel's conviction; however, on the basis of the new evidence, Küssel's sentence was increased to eleven years' imprisonment. Küssel has stated that he will not appeal this conviction. Upon leaving the witness stand, Schimanek and three others were arrested on suspicion of perjury; Schimanek was also being held on suspicion of violating paragraph 3b of the prohibition law. Schimanek, who is himself under investigation for neo-Nazi activity, as well as those others supected of perjury, was to be tried in 1995.

There were several other prosecutions under the anti-Nazi legislation in 1994. In one, Markus Adams, who had been involved in publishing the apologetic brochure *Die Wahrheit über die Waffen-SS* (The Truth about the Waffen-SS), was convicted of neo-Nazi activity and sentenced to one year's probation, while VAPO sympathizer Markus K, who had been recruited by convicted VAPO activists Günther Reinthaler and Jürgen Maria Lipthay, was sentenced to ten days in prison and eight months' probation.

In May, a court in Carinthia convicted Andreas Thierry and Helmut Adolf Schatzmayr of neo-Nazi activity under the prohibition law. Thierry and Schatzmayr were found guilty of having helped produce the brochure *Die Wahrheit über die Waffen-SS* and a calendar called *Alter Jahreszeitweiser* (Old [Farmer's] Almanac), both of which were held to contain prohibited neo-Nazi views. Thierry received an eighteen-month sentence, including probation, while Schatzmayr was sentenced to fifteen months' probation. Both are appealing their convictions.

On the basis of statements made by Carinthian entrepreneur Edwin Neuwirth during a visit by Russian ultra-nationalist leader Vladimir Zhirinovsky in December 1993, including one denying the existence of the gas chambers in German concentration camps, the public prosecutor's office launched a preliminary investigation in May to determine whether Neuwirth had violated provisions of the prohibition law. The investigation had not been concluded by the end of the year.

The vandalizing of the Jewish cemetery in Eisenstadt in 1992 long went unsolved. Police were given a break because of a falling out among neo-Nazi cadres. Walter Köhler had been an activist in the extreme-right milieu from the early 1990s, and had been taken into custody in 1992 shortly after the attack in October 1992, but was released four weeks later. Even prior to Küssel's arrest, Köhler—to the irritation of his VAPO comrades—presented himself as a neo-Nazi television personality (he appeared on an Austrian television news programme in May 1992). After Küssel was arrested, Köhler promoted himself as his logical successor as VAPO leader. However, Köhler was expelled from the VAPO for political free-lancing, and some of his former VAPO comrades gave evidence to the state police implicating Köhler in the desecration of the Eisenstadt cemetery. The case had not yet come to trial by the end of the year.

In December, members of the EBT investigating the letter bombs discovered two tanks and a few military vehicles stored in a barn in Lower Austria. Though most press reports emphasized the implausibility of planning a real military action with such aged attack vehicles (the tanks were Second World War vintage), during its investigation the EBT also discovered a small arsenal of arms, assorted other Nazi paraphernalia and photographs, including several picturing children with Nazi arm bands or flags. The investigations are still continuing, and the EBT has taken several people into custody, but by the end of the year no one had been indicted.

The Austrian prosecuting attorney's office decided not to file charges under the prohibition law against Reinhart Gaugg, FPÖ vice-mayor of Klagenfurt, capital city of Carinthia. Asked in an interview what he associated with the word "Nazi", Gaugg had stated "new, attractive, single-minded and imaginative [*neu, attraktiv, zielstrebig, ideenreich*]. It has nothing to do with the past." The prosecution was dropped at the insistence of the justice minister.

In August, all five members of the Wehrsportgruppe Trenck, who had been indicted on charges of having formed a paramilitary organization, were acquitted on all charges. The verdict was criticized by the IKG, Green and Liberal politicians, and by representatives of the Documentsarchiv des österreichischen

Widerstandes (Austrian Resistance Archives). The prosecutor's office announced that it would appeal against the verdict, which is allowable under Austrian law. However, to a certain degree, the acquittals reflected the weakness of the prosecution's case. The defendants were prosecuted under the law against forming paramilitary organizations, but the "arms" introduced as evidence could not actually be fired. Moreover, all five defendants played down their own involvement by implicating a fifth person who had since died.

An Austrian court sentenced Gerhard Endres, a deputy of Küssel, former youth leader of Gerd Honsik's banned Nationalistische Front (National Front) and Austrian representative of the neo-Nazi Freiheitliche Deutsche Arbeiterpartei (FAP, German Workers' Freedom Party), to two years' imprisonment for criminal neo-Nazi activity. The prosecutor's office, considering the sentence too lenient, has appealed.

It is difficult to detect any specific pattern in the Austrian courts' judgements in cases involving libel and defamation of character. Court protection of freedom of speech and the press in libel actions filed by public personalities has been erratic, at best: not infrequently, such judgements are used to suppress political debate considered legitimate in other Western democratic countries, while at other times they can be exploited to send defamatory messages against Jews. Though the decisions of the courts in 1994 were inconsistent, they seemed slightly more indulgent towards those on the political right.

For example, FPÖ leader Haider was able to enlist the courts to help restrain unfavourable political criticism. The cover of the *Handbuch des österreichischen Rechtsextremismus*, first published in 1993, featured a photomontage of what it considered the spectrum of right-wing extremism in Austria, which reached from the FPÖ to the explicit neo-Nazi right. Haider soon found a judge pliant enough to order his image concealed on all copies of the *Handbuch* in stock, and removed from the covers of all subsequent editions. This initial injunction was overturned on appeal, but was reinstated by the high court in Vienna in November. In addition, the court awarded Haider AS 1,000,000 (£59,000) in damages. The court's gag order endorsed the argument of Haider's lawyers that the cover gave the false impression that Haider was linked to the extreme right, national socialism and neo-Nazism. Readers will apparently have to be content with the written material in the book, which scrupulously details several links between Haider's FPÖ and the extreme right.

Another Austrian court, however, threw out Haider's suit against Green politician Peter Pilz. The FPÖ leader had initiated civil action against Pilz for having called Haider "the political patron and ideologist of right-wing extremist terror". The court ruled that Pilz's remark was a political opinion, which could not be the basis of a civil suit.

Perhaps the most troubling case involved Paul Grosz, head of the IKG in Vienna, and Richard Nimmerrichter, columnist for the *Neue Kronen Zeitung* (see **Publications and Media**). Nimmerrichter published a column in June 1993 in which he drew parallels between his alleged political persecution under Hitler and the ill-treatment he was ostensibly suffering at the hands of the IKG, and in particular of its president, Paul Grosz. "One who survived Hitler", Nimmerrichter wrote, "will also survive Mr Grosz". Grosz brought a civil action against Nimmerrichter for libel and defamation of character. In February, Nimmerrichter was convicted and fined AS 280,000 (£16,500), and the *Neue Kronen Zeitung* was assessed AS 50,000 (£2,900) damages. On appeal, however, although the court did not dispute the libelous nature of the statement (the damages against *Neue Kronen Zeitung* were, however, reduced to AS 45,000 (£2,650)), it did overturn the judgement against Nimmerrichter, because Grosz had not been able to prove beyond reasonable doubt that the libel was premeditated.

The problems arising out of the courts adjudicating what is ultimately a political matter were brought sharply into relief by the partisan remarks made by Helmut Schmid, presiding judge at the appeal trial. "It has become a terrible fashion", Schmid stated in announcing the court's verdict, "to call something that one doesn't like, Nazi".

Similarly, the outcome of the affair involving Walter Lüftl illustrates a problem that can arise when denial of the Holocaust is made a criminal offence: acquittals under the prohibition law that turn on legal technicalities are exploited by the far right for so-called "revisionist" political ends. In 1991, Lüftl, then head of the Austrian chamber of architects and engineers, published a thirty-six-page expert opinion entitled *Holocaust (Glaube und Fakten)* (Holocaust (Beliefs and Facts)), which concluded, among other things, that Zyklon B was "completely unsuitable as a weapon for planned genocide", and that it was "certain from an engineering [*bautechnisch*] point of view" that "the crematoria could not have processed the number of victims" that had been claimed. Selected passages of Lüftl's engineering "report" were published in *Halt!* in July

1991 and soon became a mainstay in other extreme-right Holocaust-denial publications. Without his knowledge, Lüftl's report was even made available on the Internet. After the mainstream press exposed the report in March 1992, Lüftl felt obliged to resign as president of the chamber, "in order to avoid a political discussion with false emphases".

After the prohibition law was amended to include denial of the Holocaust in 1992, the state prosecutor's office in Vienna opened a preliminary criminal investigation into Lüftl and his views. Nothing more was heard for over a year. In May 1994, Wolfgang Neugebauer, head of the Austrian Resistance Archives, wrote to Minister of Justice Nikolaus Michalek enquiring into the status of the investigation. Michalek replied that the competent prosecuting attorney's office had ceased its investigation without charges being filed owing to the fact, among other things, that Lüftl had written his "expert opinion with a clear scientific conscience". Predictably, a recent issue of *Aula*, the magazine of the FPÖ union of university graduates, triumphantly claimed that "the cessation of the investigation verifies the content of Lüftl's work and confirms that it is serious and scientific". Lüftl's rehabilitation seems to have been complete: in the elections held in September to the administrative bodies of the chamber of architects and engineers for Vienna, Lower Austria and Burgenland, the "independent list" which Lüftl headed won three seats. Lüftl again sits on a leadership body of the professional association of engineers.

In February, the administrative district of Offenhausen in Upper Austria passed a resolution—outvoting the FPÖ—ordering the extreme right-wing German-nationalist organization Verein Dichterstein Offenhausen to remove Nazi diction such as "tribal purity" (*Sippenreinheit*) and "consciousness of one's own kind" (*Artenbewußtsein*) from the steps of the Dichterstein monument in Offenhausen and to replace it by a monument commemorating a Jewish poet.

COUNTERING ANTISEMITISM

The high point of Austrian-Jewish relations in 1994 was undoubtedly President Thomas Klestil's state visit to Israel in November. Following on from the exceptionally successful visits in 1993 by Chancellor Vranitzky and Vice-Chancellor Erhard Busek, Klestil's visit took on an added symbolic dimension because his predecessor as Austrian president was Kurt Waldheim. Klestil's visit included meetings with Israeli Prime Minister Yitzhak Rabin and Foreign Minister Shimon Peres, a visit to Yad

Vashem and an address delivered to the Knesset. Though his remarks echoed themes addressed by Vranitzky in 1993 (in particular the pre-emptive ritual rejection of "collective guilt"), in certain respects they went beyond them. Historical truth, the "entire truth", Klestil stated, "is complex. The thin line that ran between perpetrators and victims at that time ran right through the people, through their families, and often enough through one and the same heart. The seed of ferment and the tragic blend of force and fascination gave rise to to the Jewish tragedy in Austria. For too long", he added, "it has inhibited a critical reappraisal of the past and proved such a burden for a frank and open dialogue of trust between our two peoples."

In the most memorable passage of the speech, Klestil remarked that "all too often we have only spoken of Austria as the first state to have lost its freedom and independence to national socialism—and far too seldom of the fact that many of the worst henchman in the Nazi dictatorship were Austrians". Rising to, and simultaneously eschewing, the expectations circulating in the Israeli press that he would apologize in the name of the Austrian people, Klestil stated bluntly that "no word of apology can ever expunge the agony of the Holocaust. On behalf of the Republic of Austria, I bow my head, with deep respect and profound emotion in front of the victims." Klestil's speech, as well as his visit as a whole, was extensively and favourably reported in the Austrian media. It is too early to know whether the promised deeds will follow the poignant words. But the conservative president, Thomas Klestil, has set the tenor and the tone for public debate about Israel and the Jews which could help counteract the disingenuous snipings of a Richard Nimmerrichter.

The schools represent one of the most important areas in which constant vigilance against racism of all sorts, including antisemitism, as well as anti-democratic ideas is required. Kurt Scholz, the president of the Vienna school board, has pursued a commendable policy designed to arrest signs of racist activities, discipline teachers who promote Holocaust-denial, and support multicultural and anti-racist initiatives in the schools. Recently honoured by the IKG for supporting the establishment of Vienna's Jewish Museum and the memorial against war and fascism, and particularly for his assistance in setting up an extensive network of Jewish schools, Scholz has shown that he is ready to act when necessary. In late autumn, for example, he suspended a teacher in a vocational school who had questioned the existence of the gas chambers in his class. In another case, Scholz has backed up a school headmistress against whom disciplinary action had been initiated by individuals on the far right, in a fairly transparent attempt to intimidate her and others.

ASSESSMENT

The proven relationship between contemporary xenophobia and anti-Jewish hostility suggests that tendencies indicating an increase in political hostility towards foreigners or of linguistic indulgence towards ideas redolent of the ideology of the Third Reich, could also have implications for Austria's Jewish community. Whether the climate of intolerance towards immigrants and qualified openness to authoritarian measures, which under certain circumstances could redound to the disadvantage of Austrian Jews, retains its potency into 1995 depends to a high degree on the ability and willingness of enough people to speak out and act against them.

Austrian politics are in a state of flux and, in 1994, Austrian voters sent very mixed signals. Party affiliations that had been a fixed feature of Austrian political life have collapsed, never to return. If as late as 1983, the two largest parties, the SPÖ and the ÖVP, could between them count on the allegiance of 90 per cent of all those eligible to vote, in the October 1994 elections, this share had dropped to 48 per cent. And if the majority of those who voted for the FPÖ do not necessarily embrace federal party leader Jörg Haider's more authoritarian political scenarios, neither do they recoil in fear of them.

The coverage given to a second series of letter bombs and the bomb at a bilingual school, as well as the trials of alleged neo-Nazis, does not seem to have led to an unequivocal conviction of the virtues of a pluralist constitutional political culture. The Austrian government has shown its resolve to combat conspicuous challenges to fundamental democratic values and grievous instances of racist violence. Yet the anti-terrorist task-force, though hard-working and more successful than its reputation suggests, is both understaffed and underfunded. More importantly, police units which combat violent far-right terror, while indispensable, cannot address the larger political questions of intolerance and racism. Here the government, in particular the SPÖ, is playing a dangerous game of chance for, as the election results seem to suggest, the social democratic interior minister's restrictive (and unconstitutional) immigration policy does not seem to have won it any votes from the FPÖ, while this very policy caused some former supporters to look to the Greens or the LF for political representation. Moreover, in as much as people perceive their present and future social situation as insecure, pious jeremiads about the dangers to representative democracy Haider poses or platitudes about inter-cultural tolerance count for precious little.

There is a general climate of insecurity in Europe, and Austria has not remained immune. Even if the commitment of the government to combating racist violence has been on the whole good, there are signs of a greater receptivity for increasingly authoritarian solutions. Yet the presence of the Greens and the LF, as well as individuals in the SPÖ and ÖVP, mean that there will continue to be articulate voices to speak out against xenophobia and threatened encroachments on democratic freedoms. Yet at the beginning of 1995, far more than at the beginning of 1994, government policies on a range of issues remain, disturbingly, a hostage to Haider's political fortunes, and largely to his political initiative.

Belarus

General population: 10.3 million
Jewish population: 34,000 (mainly in Minsk)

GENERAL BACKGROUND

Belarusian politics continued to be dominated by the dire economic condition of the country after the collapse of the Soviet Union and the widespread agricultural damage caused by the Chernobyl disaster. The Belarusian economy remained largely state-controlled.

A new constitution introducing a presidential system of government was adopted on 1 March. In July Aleksandr Lukashenko, an independent who had won over 80 per cent of the vote in a run-off presidential election, was sworn in as Belarus's first president. Lukashenko had run a populist campaign, pledging that as president he would "stop inflation, fight corruption, crush crime and restore ties with the republics of the former Soviet Union". In September Russian Prime Minister Viktor Chernomyrdin ruled out the planned monetary union with Belarus on the grounds that the economies of the two countries had diverged.

HISTORICAL LEGACY

A Jewish community was established in 1506 in the town of Pinsk in the territory now known as Belarus (formerly Byelorussia). According to the results of a census taken in 1897, Jews comprised 13.6 per cent of the population, forming the majority in the principal cities of the region. As was customary throughout the area, some Jews were enlisted by the nobility and wealthy landowners as collectors of taxes while others became innkeepers, occupations which earned them the hatred of the impoverished peasants. The early Jewish communities were exposed to further danger by Russian marauders who carried out massacres and forced conversions in some communities.

When the area fell under the control of tsarist Russia the fate of the Jews of Byelorussia became inextricably bound up with the Jewish community of Russia (see **Russia**).

In the Soviet anti-Zionist and antisemitic propaganda campaign of the late 1960s-early 1980s a number of Byelorussian propagandists, most notably Vladimir Begun, regularly published antisemitic material.

PARTIES, ORGANIZATIONS, MOVEMENTS

The year 1994 saw the development of extremist groups such as Slavyany (Slavs), Bratsva

Slavyan Rusi (Brotherhood of Slavs of Russia), Soyuz armii naroda (Union of the Army of the People), Slavyansky Sobor-Belaya Rus (Slavonic Council-White Russia) and Pravy revansh (Right Revenge). While these groups were embryonic in organization, they may be considered a potential threat to the Jewish community.

Slavyanskiye sokoly (Slavic Hawks), a youth organization led by Andrey Slobozhanin, was a paramilitary group modelled on the Russian National Unity, an organization run by the Russian ultra-nationalist Aleksandr Barkashov (see **Russia**).

The Byelorusskaya partiya svobody (Belarusian Freedom Party) was "determined to use extreme force in the name of a future free Belarus".

MANIFESTATIONS

On 11 May ninety-four tombstones in a cemetery near Gomel were desecrated. The authorities claimed the desecration was the work of drunken hooligans.

In September unattributed leaflets containing a swastika urging Belarusian youth to train in hand-to-hand combat were distributed in the centre of Minsk.

On 15 September leaflets bearing the slogan "Belarus for the Belarusians" were distributed in Minsk. The Minsk evening newspaper *Dobraga vechara* attributed them to the Belarusian Freedom Party.

On 26 October eight Jewish gravestones in Gorodok, Vitebsk region, were desecrated. The authorities blamed young hooligans.

PUBLICATIONS AND MEDIA

In September the Russian-language Minsk weekly *My i vremya* contained an interview with the Russian far-right activist Aleksandr Nevzorov. Readers were told that video-cassettes of the interview were available at the premises of *al-Quds*, the antisemitic Moscow publication (see **Russia**).

On 10 July, Belarusian Saints' Day, national television carried a film entitled "Essence" which depicted the murder in the seventeenth century of the infant St Gavril who, according to tradition, was the victim of a Jewish ritual sacrifice. Belarusian calendars for 1994 also carried a picture of Saint Gavril with a caption stating that he was murdered by Jews. A book published in Belarusian and Polish versions by Vladimir Dalya entitled "Notes on Ritual Murders" was said to be circulating in the country.

ASSESSMENT

Xenophobia in general and antisemitism in particular remained a marginal problem in Belarus. Perhaps the most serious potential threat facing Jews, in a society where Belarusian national identity is traditionally weak, was the continued existence of extremism on the fringe of the ethnic Russian section of the population.

Belgium

General population: 9.8 million
Jewish population: 35,000-40,000 (mainly in
Antwerp and Brussels, also Charleroi, Ghent
and Liège)

GENERAL BACKGROUND

In 1993, Belgium became a federal state. It is
made up of three regions (the Flemish region,
the Walloon region and Brussels), ten provinces
and three linguistic communities (French-
speaking, Flemish-speaking and German-
speaking). These three levels of government are
autonomous, with their own separate remit. It
is a complex institutional arrangement and a
great part of the population is indifferent to, or
has simply not understood the intricacies of, the
federalization of Belgium.

In 1994, the federal government was
made up of the Flemish Christelijke
Volkspartij (CVP, Christian People's Party),
the French-speaking Parti Social Chrétien
(PSC, Christian Social Party), the Flemish
Socialistische Partij (SP, Socialist Party) and
the French-speaking Parti Socialiste (PS,
Socialist Party). It was formed in March 1992
after the legislative elections held the previous November. The prime minister was Jean-
Luc Dehaene of the CVP, whose government
has been reshuffled six times. During the
year, two ministers resigned as a result of political and financial scandals.

Economic conditions have deteriorated.
The number of unemployed is estimated by
government and trade union sources as between 500,000 and 1 million. Inflation rose
slightly from 2.7 per cent in 1993 to 2.8 per
cent. Public borrowing remained high at
BFr 800,000 million and the economic targets
imposed by the Maastricht Treaty on European union have not been reached by the
present government.

Financial and political scandals, successive political setbacks for the federal government, the poor economic situation and the
general lack of understanding of the constitutional reforms have led to the creation of a
serious rift between the political establishment and the general population. There is a
growing feeling of exclusion from political
decision-making and a general hostility to
politics itself. The far-right parties have
sought to capitalize on these circumstances,
presenting themselves as the sole alternative
to a discredited system.

HISTORICAL LEGACY

Antisemitism in Belgium was most virulent in
the 1930s when the world-wide economic crisis
was at its height. At that time, the Jewish population was largely made up of foreign immigrants, exiles and political refugees. The fascist
parliamentary parties, the French-speaking Rex
party and the Vlaams Nationaal Verbond
(VNV, Flemish National Union), attacked Jews
in their election campaigns. The VNV campaigned in Antwerp with the slogan: "Antwerp
is Ours! Jews Out!" During the Nazi occupation, these parties supported the Nazi regime.
Of 25,257 Belgian Jews deported, almost all of
them to Auschwitz, only 1,205 returned.

In 1952, the first French work denying the
Holocaust, by Maurice Bardèche, was translated into Dutch by Karel Dillen, now president
of the anti-immigrant Vlaams Blok (see **Parties,
Organizations, Movements**). Antisemitic articles denouncing an alleged Jewish-communist
conspiracy were published during the Cold
War period in the Flemish Catholic daily *De
Standaard*.

In 1967, in the aftermath of the Six Day
War, antisemitism appeared in the form of left-
wing anti-Zionism. The Belgian "Euro-
revolutionary" left condoned terrorist activities
carried out in the name of Palestinian nationalism. Between 1963 and 1969, Jeune Europe
(Young Europe), a Belgian-based international
organization, maintained contacts with Syria,
Egypt, Iraq and Yassir Arafat's Fatah movement.

There was a marked increase in Holocaust-
denial activities between 1976 and 1991, with
the establishment of a publishing house, publications and foundations dedicated to Holocaust
denial.

Recent years have also seen the development of a Belgian far right, ranging from anti-immigrant political parties—the Vlaams Blok, the Front National and Agir, who have found increasing electoral success since the 1991 parliamentary elections—to more violent, neo-Nazi groupings.

RACISM AND XENOPHOBIA

Belgium has approximately 920,000 foreign residents, who constitute 9.1 per cent of the population. This figure includes around 377,000 non-Europeans (3.7 per cent), of which 145,000 are Moroccan (1.4 per cent) and 88,300 are Turkish (0.9 per cent). The number of asylum-seekers in the first nine months of 1994 was 10,800, compared to 26,900 for the whole of 1993, reflecting the tightening of Belgium's asylum laws in 1993. The majority of refugees came from the former Yugoslavia, but also from Zaire and Romania.

There is evidence to suggest that manifestations of racism are increasing. Hostels for asylum-seekers were again targets for attack in 1994. The Red Cross centre was set alight by unknown arsonists in La Louvière, and, in Morlanwelz, a house inhabited by Zairian refugees was machine-gunned in December. After the World Cup football match between Belgium and Morocco in June, there were several incidents involving far-right football supporters and young Moroccan immigrants. In Verviers, militant members of the far-right party Agir fired rifle shots at young Moroccans, one of whom was permanently maimed.

Such incidents suggest that the demagogic rhetoric directed against refugees, Moroccans and Turks by the far-right Vlaams Blok and Front National finds some resonance in parts of the population. Daniel Féret, president of the Front National, stated in an interview with the liberal daily *La Dernière Heure* in June that there were 500,000 North Africans living in Belgium—a claim which exaggerated the true figure by approximately 300,000.

Moreover, in the traditional political parties, some, claiming to provide a necessary response to the people's anxieties, have courted xenophobic sentiment. For example, representatives of the Parti Réformateur Libéral (PRL, Liberal Reform Party), the French-speaking conservative opposition party, had no difficulty comparing the immigration of Moroccans to an "invasion". A CVP member of parliament has advocated the application of the stringent measures against illegal immigrants which have been proposed in California (see **United States**).

In spite of such xenophobic sentiments, an opinion poll conducted by *Le Soir* in the week following the local elections of October 1994 showed that 49 per cent of Belgians were in favour of giving foreigners born in Belgium the right to vote in local elections. Most of this group indicated support for the green and Christian-socialist parties. Opponents were largely made up of supporters of the liberal opposition parties, the PRL and the Vlaamse Liberalen en Demokraten (VLD, Flemish Liberals and Democrats), or came from socially disadvantaged sections of society.

PARTIES, ORGANIZATIONS, MOVEMENTS

The Vlaams Blok (VB, Flemish Bloc), led by Filip Dewinter and Karel Dillen, is the most important far-right political party in Belgium and one of the most significant in the whole of Europe. It was founded in 1978, taking its ideology from the Flemish radical nationalist tradition and has succeeded in uniting the main currents in the militant populist Flemish nationalism of the right. The VB calls for the establishment of an independent Flanders (with Brussels as its capital) and campaigns for a total amnesty for Nazi collaborators. Elements within the party express open admiration for the Nazi regime and a number of former Belgian Waffen SS members and active antisemites belong to its militant wing.

The party's virulently anti-immigrant propaganda is primarily directed at Muslims from North Africa, who it portrays as the "fifth column" of an aggressive, barbaric religion intent on absorbing all others. However, the VB rejects accusations that it is racist, arguing that it does not talk in terms of the supposed superiority of races. Instead, it accuses mainstream politicians of racism for having "uprooted" immigrants from their own cultures and forced them to integrate into an "alien" society.

In addition to its anti-immigrant platform, the VB's programme advocates traditional family values, strong law-and-order policies and opposes abortion. In elections in 1994, the VB also proposed right-wing economic policies, such as privatization and increased control of trade unions, reflecting Dewinter's admiration for Thatcherism.

The VB is represented at all political levels: municipal, provincial, national (where it has 18 parliamentary representatives: 12 in the lower chamber and 6 in the senate) and European. The VB's estimates of its membership range between 7,600 and 9,000. There are more than 120 local branches.

In the June European elections, the VB received 7.8 per cent of the overall vote (12.6 per cent in Flanders and 5.5 per cent in

Brussels), and had 2 MEPs returned (compared with 1 in 1989). In the municipal elections held in October, the VB fielded 1,400 candidates throughout Flanders and in Brussels. The VB's campaign was conducted under the slogan "Order in Affairs", accompanied by a picture of a broom—a symbol used by the Walloon Nazi Léon Degrelle in the 1930s. Its most significant result was in Antwerp, where it emerged as the largest single party, with 18 seats and 28 per cent of the vote (76,877 of 274,284 votes cast). However, a coalition of other parties kept the VB out of power.

Elsewhere in Flanders, the VB's share of the vote in the October elections ranged from 5.1 per cent in Louvain to 19.7 per cent in Malines. In Brussels, the VB contested 11 of the capital's 19 communes, whereas it fielded candidates in only 7 communes in 1988. It won between 1 and 6.2 per cent of the vote and has councillors in 4 communes. The VB is now one of the main Flemish political parties in the capital, which has a French-speaking majority. In the provincial elections, which were held at the same time as the municipal elections, the VB's overall share of the vote declined from 11.9 per cent to 11.1 per cent but it more or less maintained its share in West Flanders (17.9 per cent), in East Flanders (6.6 per cent), in Limburg (9.8 per cent) and in Flemish Brabant (9.1 per cent).

In Belgium, the far-right party Agir is the VB's principal French-speaking ally, since the separatist VB has been in dispute with the Belgian-nationalist Front National for several years. The party is associated with a number of Flemish extremist organizations, such as Voorpost and Were Di (see below). At European level, the VB has contacts with the French Front national (FN, National Front), the Deutsche Liga für Volk und Heimat (DL, German League) in Germany, the Centrum-Democraten (Centre Democrats) and the Nederlands Blok (Dutch Bloc) in the Netherlands, the Eesti Rahvusliku Sõltumatuse Partei (Estonian National Independence Party) and with Croatian nationalists (see **Estonia, France, Germany** and **The Netherlands**). The party's youth organization, Vlaams Blok Jongeren (VBJ, Flemish Bloc Youth), maintains links with the French Front national de la jeunesse (National Front Youth), the Spanish Juntas Jovenes (Youth Council), the German Junge Nationaldemokraten (Young National Democrats) and the Narodny Rukh Ukrainy (People's Movement of Ukraine) (see **France, Germany, Spain** and **Ukraine**).

The Front National (FNB, National Front) is an extreme right-wing party established in 1985 with a nationalist, monarchist and anti-

immigrant outlook. It draws support from across the traditional francophone political spectrum as well as from a number of antisemitic neo-Nazi groups, including former leading members of the banned racist Parti des Forces Nouvelles (PFN, Party of the New Forces), who joined between 1989 and 1991. Although the party has not presented a specific electoral programme, has no campaigning machinery and has never held a congress since its inception in 1985, it has one member of parliament (Georges Matagne) and claims a membership of 1,000, although it is estimated to have only 100 activists.

The year 1994 was extremely successful for the FNB in electoral terms. The June European elections saw the FNB's president, Daniel Féret, become the party's first MEP with 2.9 per cent of the overall vote (7.9 per cent of the vote in Wallonia and 11.5 per cent in Brussels). Among the FNB's candidates in the election were former members of the PRL, the PFN and the Front Régional Wallon (a regionalist fringe group which had links with the VB and the French FN and was absorbed into the FNB in 1994). There was also a candidate of Italian nationality who had previously campaigned as a militant member of the Italian neo-Fascist Movimento Sociale Italiano (MSI, Italian Social Movement, see **Italy**). While the FNB has had a troubled relationship with Jean-Marie Le Pen's FN and is no longer considered a partner by the French party, it remains to be seen whether Féret and the FN MEPs will co-operate in the European Parliament for practical reasons.

In the October municipal elections, the FNB contested 17 out of the 19 communes in Brussels and had 47 councillors elected. It won significant support in Molenbeek (16.6 per cent, and 7 seats), in Anderlecht (13.2 per cent and 6 seats) and in Schaerbeek (9.6 per cent and 5 seats). Several FNB candidates in the Brussels elections emerged from former associations with the neo-Nazi and Catholic fundamentalist fringe elements of the far right. Two dissident refugees from the VB and a handful of converts from the traditional political parties, such as the PSC, the PRL and the Front Démocratique des Francophones (FDF, Democratic Front of French-Speakers—an organization devoted to the protection of the interests of the francophone population), were also on the FNB's list of candidates. The head of the FNB's list in Molenbeek was Philippe Rozenberg, a former municipal councillor for the PRL, who is of Jewish origin,

In Wallonia, the FNB contested 36 communes, compared to 4 in 1988, and won 26 seats. In Liège, it gained 5 per cent of the vote and 2 seats, in Mons, 7 per cent and 2 seats, in Charleroi 10.5 per cent and 5 seats, and in La Louvière 14.4 per cent and 6 seats. In other communes where the FNB fielded candidates, its vote ranged from 1.1 per cent in St Ode to 4.4 per cent and 1 seat in Seraing. In the provincial elections, the FNB received 5.5 per cent of the vote in Brabant-Wallon, 7.3 per cent in Hainaut, 3 per cent in Liège, 0.8 per cent in Luxembourg and 5.2 per cent in Namur, winning several seats.

Several lists presented by the FNB in Wallonia and Brussels were disqualified on grounds of electoral fraud. A Flemish candidate for the FNB in the municipal elections was found to be the author of death threats against the king, and a series of incidents after the local elections revealed the questionable backgrounds of some other FNB activists and associates.

Less than a week after the local elections, the state television channel RTBF screened a video of Daniel Leskens, a FNB councillor in Anderlecht, urinating on a Jewish grave while another man made a Nazi salute. The incident took place at a meeting of former Waffen SS members in Germany in February. Less than twenty-four hours after the broadcast, Leskens resigned his seat. Daniel Féret denied knowledge of Leskens's neo-Nazi sympathies and claimed that he would be expelled from the party. In early November, the weekly magazine *Pan* reported that Leskens was still a party member.

In Mons, it was revealed that Alfred Dartevelle, one of the FNB's two newly-elected councillors, had volunteered to fight for the Nazis on the Eastern front during the German occupation of Belgium. After the Second World War, Dartevelle had been stripped of his civil and political rights for "fighting against his country" and therefore would have been ineligible to stand for election. The mayor of Mons was seeking to have his election invalidated.

In November, Henri Laquay, one of the three newly-elected FNB councillors in the Brussels commune of Koekelberg, was found to be employed as a civil servant at the ministry of health's service for war victims. This fact was discovered by the association of former prisoners of Ravensbrück, the Nazi concentration camp, which expressed its concern to the minister of health, Jacques Santkin, that a member of a party with the FNB's views would have access to files on former political prisoners and members of the resistance. The minister announced that he would request an inquiry into whether Laquay's opinions were compatible with the position that he held.

Patrick Sessler, a former leader of the PFN who has a history of Holocaust-denial activity, was appointed as Féret's parliamentary secretary after his election to the European Parliament. In October, Sessler was elected as a municipal councillor in the Brussels commune of Schaerbeek. Sessler and Féret have on several occasions attacked Jean Gol, the president of the PRL who has Jewish origins, as a "stateless person" (*apatride*). (In the vocabulary of the antisemitic far right, this term is used specifically to describe Jews.) During the year, Sessler was instrumental in the creation of the Groupe Défense Sécurité (Security Defence Group), whose role is to provide the FNB with security, surveillance activity and "direct action". Sessler was also active in maintaining links between the FNB and extra-parliamentary neo-Nazi groups. In November 1994, Féret officially expelled Sessler from the party, ostensibly for his contacts with neo-Nazis. Sessler had also been ejected from the FNB several years previously for "neo-Nazism", but rejoined the party and became Féret's right-hand man.

Arms caches were discovered in the residences of two far-right activists in 1994. In October, the police arrested Lucien Marbaix, a former police officer who has associations with both the VB and the FNB. In the past, Marbaix was a member of the clandestine neo-Nazi group Westland New Post, which was implicated in an espionage network and two assassinations in the early 1980s. The arresting officers found a large quantity of arms, ammunition and neo-Nazi literature in Marbaix's past and present residences, together with a collection of files detailing politicians, business people, police officers and journalists as possible targets for attack.

In November, a cache of weapons was discovered at the home and office of a FNB associate, Michel Delacroix. Delacroix, a lawyer who is married to Daniel Féret's mother, has represented the interests of the FNB, Robert Faurisson, the French Holocaust-denier, and, allegedly, Jean-Marie Le Pen, the leader of the French FN. Some fifteen weapons, hundreds of rounds of ammunition and a large amount of far-right and neo-Nazi literature were discovered by the police. After his arrest, Delacroix, who is blind, claimed he was an arms collector. Other individuals close to the FNB were implicated in this affair and were also detained. Police even searched two garages which Féret had rented in 1990.

These discoveries provided evidence for the suggestion that the far right has been building parallel paramilitary structures alongside its formal political organizations.

Agir (Act), the "party of popular opposition", was founded in 1989 by dissidents in the Liège section of the PFN. The party's activities are concentrated mainly in Liège and its surrounding area in east-central Belgium. The party, led by Daniel Moreau, styles itself as a "Wallonian Front", demanding regional autonomy for Wallonia, and its leaders have been heavily influenced by New Right thinking. Several have taken part in the conferences of the French-based Groupement de Recherche et d'Etudes pour la Civilisation Européene (GRECE, Group for the Research and Study of European Civilization), a body which seeks to rehabilitate the ideology of the Third Reich (see **France**).

Estimated to have a maximum of 100 activists, the party has links with the VB, the French FN and the DL and maintains contact with neo-Nazi activists (see **France** and **Germany**). During the 1991 Gulf War, Agir's press office published anti-Zionist propaganda.

Agir is far less established than the FNB in Wallonia. In the June European elections, Agir attracted 42,917 votes, which was insufficient to gain a seat. In the October local elections, Agir, which did not field any candidates in Brussels, registered lists of candidates in thirteen communes in Wallonia. The party's results in the municipal elections ranged from 1-6.5 per cent, winning it 8 seats, 2 in its power-base of Liège. However, the party appears to have lost some momentum in Liège, since its share of the vote in the city fell from 7.2 per cent in June to 6.2 per cent in the communal elections three months later. In contrast, the FNB increased its vote in Liège over the same period. Several complaints were lodged against Agir for breaches of electoral law. The centre for equal opportunities and anti-racism was seeking to bring actions against members of Agir on the grounds that their activities violated the anti-racism legislation. By the end of the year, Agir seemed to be experiencing severe internal disputes which might affect the future direction and performance of the party.

Extra-parliamentary fringe groupings include:

The Parti Communautaire National Européen (PCN, Party of the National European Community) was founded in 1984 as a successor to Jeune Europe (Young Europe), the populist pan-European organization which existed between 1963 and 1969. Whilst officially disavowing racism, the PCN has campaigned on the slogan "American Imperialism, Zionism . . . the Common Enemy of the European Nation" and, during the June European elections, the PCN distributed leaflets warning that

Europe risked becoming an Islamic republic. Based in Charleroi and Brussels, the PCN also has branches in Paris and Budapest and has links with such revolutionary-nationalist groupings as the pan-European, anti-American European Liberation Front, Nouvelle résistance in France and the National Salvation Front in Russia (see **France** and **Russia**).

Voorpost (Outpost) was founded as a Flemish, nationalist grouping in the late 1970s around a magazine. Led by VB MP Francis Van den Inde, it is a predominantly Flemish direct-action organization, with a section in the Netherlands and a "French Flanders" chapter, and disseminates nationalist, neo-Nazi and Holocaust-denial propaganda. In August 1994, some Voorpost activists acted as stewards at a meeting of European neo-Nazis and skinheads which was part of the annual Flemish nationalist festival in Diksmuide—for many years, an established meeting place for European far-right and neo-Nazi circles.

There are also neo-Nazi skinhead groupings in both the Flemish- and French-speaking communities, which have been responsible for violent attacks on immigrants. In Wallonia, some skinhead activities were centred around the neo-Nazi grouping L'Assaut until its dissolution in September 1993. In January, two skinheads from Flanders were arrested in London during a European rally organized by Blood and Honour, the British neo-Nazi skinhead group (see **United Kingdom**).

MANIFESTATIONS

In 1994, there were no antisemitic incidents which posed a serious threat either to Jews or to Jewish property (see also **Parties, Organizations, Movements** and **Effects of Anti-Zionism**). There was some evidence of threatening or abusive behaviour directed towards Jews. For instance, a bomb threat was posted on the door of a Jewish school in Antwerp in March which claimed that bombs would be placed in the school and in the Jewish communities of New York and Miami unless $5 million was paid.

Also in Antwerp, leaflets from the US-based international neo-Nazi grouping, the Nationalsozialistische Deutsche Arbeiterpartei/Auslands- und Aufbauorganisation (NSDAP/AO, German National Socialist Workers' Party/Overseas Section), were put up on a Jewish shop proclaiming "We are back, don't buy from Jews".

BUSINESS AND COMMERCE

In 1994, there was one further development in the case of a director at Sabena, the national airline, who was accused in 1993 of holding Holocaust-denying opinions and having links with far-right and veteran Nazi circles. The president of Sabena supported the director, who was identified only as "R. A.". In October 1994, Jean-Marie Le Pen was among the guests at the wedding of Sabena's president's son in Paris.

MEDIA

The racist extreme right has a negligible press in Belgium. The VB publishes a periodical, *Vlaams Blok*, and several local newsletters. The Antwerp-based Flemish satirical weekly *'t Pallieterke* is close to the VB. Theoretical journals of a nationalist character are published in Flanders by elements in the VB and their sympathizers. These are close to the theories of the New Right, as defined for example by GRECE and Alain de Benoist in France (see **France**). The FNB produces *Le National*, a bulletin which has not been available in bookshops for over a year. Agir has no publication of its own. However, several French-language nationalist periodicals, also linked with the New Right, appear sporadically; their availability is limited and their circulation small.

A number of French far-right periodicals, such as *Minutes, L'Action française* and *Rivarol*, and the revolutionary-nationalist *Lutte du Peuple* were available in Belgian bookshops in 1994. Other publications are distributed through subscription.

DENIAL OF THE HOLOCAUST

Holocaust-denial propaganda is distributed mainly in Flanders. In 1994, the Vrij Historisch Onderzoek (VHO, Foundation for Free Historical Research) continued to direct its activities at public libraries and schools in Belgium and the Netherlands (see **The Netherlands**).

A number of Holocaust-denial articles, books and videos have, since 1988, been dispatched anonymously to individuals connected with the Université Libre de Bruxelles, a secular university. Both Robert Faurisson's *Réponse à Jean-Claude Pressac—sur le problème des chambres à gaz* (Response to Jean-Claude Pressac—On the Question of the Gas Chambers), which was published in March 1994 and distributed by the Colombes-based Revue d'Histoire Révisionniste, and Jürgen Graf's *L'Holocauste au scanner* (The Holocaust under the Scanner), produced in 1993 by the Basle-based Guideon Burg Verlag publishing house in German and subsequently in French, were distributed unsolicited during 1994. Graf's publishers are represented in Belgium by Jeanine Colson of Dworp. Colson, the wife of a former

Flemish Waffen-SS volunteer, is a long-standing Holocaust-denial activist and, along with her husband, is one of the leading members of the VHO. Colson has also been listed as an electoral candidate for the VB.

In October 1994, advertising leaflets promoting the book *La Police de la pensée contre le révisionnisme* (Thought Police against Revisionism) by right-wing lawyer Eric Delcroix, which was published in France in 1994 and distributed by the Revue d'Histoire Révisionniste, were handed out in Brussels in the vicinity of the Université Libre.

Jos Rogiers, one of the few Holocaust-denial authors in Belgium, continued to publish his periodical *Achtergronddossier* in 1994. Rogiers is a former member of the VB. Many current or past members of the VB have connections with Holocaust-denial circles and several leading figures in the FNB actively promote theories challenging or denying the facts of the Holocaust.

EFFECTS OF ANTI-ZIONISM

In early March, a public demonstration was organized in Brussels by the Anti-Imperialist League, the General Union of Students of Palestine and a private Arab radio station to protest the massacre of Muslims by a Jewish settler at a Hebron mosque in February. There were several incidents in the city centre and police stopped some of the 250 demonstrators marching on a synagogue and the hotel where Simon Wiesenthal, the Nazi war crimes investigator, was the guest of honour at a reception to mark the première of the film *Schindler's List*. According to *La Libre Belgique*, some demonstrators also painted antisemitic slogans on walls.

LEGAL MATTERS

Belgium's anti-racist legislation, enacted in 1981, was extended to include discrimination in employment and housing in 1994. The legislation has had little effect: nine out of ten cases are not brought to trial. Nevertheless, a complaint filed under the anti-racist law has been brought to the court of assizes for the first time.

In April, six neo-Nazi sympathizers were given prison sentences ranging from two to four years by a tribunal in Ghent for racist violence and for daubing racist and antisemitic graffiti.

Also in April, a royal decree prohibited the return of the ashes of Léon Degrelle, the Belgian Nazi collaborator who died in Spain at the end of March, in order to prevent his tomb becoming a place of pilgrimage.

In June, two former activists of the PFN,

later members of the VB, were prosecuted for distributing racist literature and were found guilty of belonging to a racist group by a Walloon assize court. Membership of groups which promote racial hatred is liable to imprisonment, but the higher court did not uphold an original complaint about the distribution of racist material.

In September, the VB was found to be a racist party by a Brussels tribunal in an action brought by the Flemish League of Human Rights against VB activists Koen Dillen and Johannes Carpels, the son and son-in-law of Karel Dillen. However, the court declared its own incompetence in the matter on the grounds that the facts of the case concerned alleged press offences, and that it was therefore a matter for the court of assizes. The Flemish League of Human Rights appealed against the judgement.

Also in September, a tribunal in Verviers dismissed an action brought by Agir against the organizers of "Le Vent de la Liberté", an exhibition on the Second World War and the dangers of fascism. Agir had objected to one of its tracts being displayed alongside a Nazi tract.

In October, three supporters of the Beerschot football club received prison sentences ranging from six months to two years by a tribunal in Antwerp for setting fire to a mosque in Hoboken in 1993.

Towards the end of the year, legislation to make denial of the Holocaust illegal was introduced into the federal parliament; it is due to be voted on in 1995.

COUNTERING ANTISEMITISM

Racist parties were officially condemned by the Catholic church. A number of public and private initiatives to counter the far right were also advanced, including a proposal to introduce a course in citizenship in the final year of secondary school, the screening of videos promoting tolerance on television and in cinemas, a campaign to distribute anti-fascist posters, and a proposal to ban the public financing of anti-democratic political parties.

In February, Michel Graindorge, a lawyer at the Brussels bar, deliberately overturned the statue of Edmond Picard situated in the Palace of Justice. Picard, who died in 1924, was a Belgian lawyer and senator representing the Socialist Party. He was also antisemitic, having in 1892 published attacks on Jews in a book which was re-issued by Editions de la Phalange during the Nazi occupation in 1942. Justifying his action in a letter to the king's prosecutor, Graindorge explained that his "political gesture" sought "to denounce the antisemite Picard, to raise public awareness of the rise of the far right and the disquieting increase in antisemitism". Disciplinary action against Graindorge was brought by the prosecutor's department.

A national federation of anti-racist fronts has now been established with branches in most towns and cities in Wallonia and Flanders, and a number of local councils adopted motions condemning racism and xenophobia. The Jewish community took part in demonstrations organized by the anti-racist front in Brussels. In Antwerp, the Orthodox Jewish community has supported the campaign by the anti-VB committee and its appeal, "Love thy Neighbour as thyself". Conferences and demonstrations to raise awareness of racism were held both before and after the European and municipal elections. The Jewish press has energetically exposed the antisemitic character of the far-right parties. However, in November, the monthly magazine *Contact J*, published by the Ben Gurion Circle of Brussels, provoked a heated debate within the Jewish community when it interviewed the charismatic leader of the VB, Filip Dewinter.

The revelations about the questionable backgrounds of certain FNB activists provoked press criticism of the far right. For instance, *Le Soir*, Belgium's main daily broadsheet, commented that "in the space of several weeks, three people ... have come to remind those with short or selective memories that the far right is a natural political home for the nostalgic and dishonest".

ASSESSMENT

During the 1970s, neo-fascist or neo-Nazi antisemitic propaganda was disseminated by insignificant and marginal nationalist groupings. In the 1980s, these factions of the far right (both Flemish- and French-speaking) adopted a new tactic and began to organize themselves into effective political parties. In the 1990s, the far right has established its anti-immigrant programme, and its denunciation of the traditional democratic parties is an essential part of the political and electoral landscape in Belgium. For more than ten years, racism has been growing in Belgium, both as a sociological phenomenon and in terms of the votes racist parties attract in elections. While the electoral rise of the far right has not been accompanied by serious attacks on Jews and Jewish property, the antisemitic undercurrents within the far-right parties as well as their overt racism and xenophobia are of significant concern to the Jewish community.

Bulgaria

General population: 8.9 million
Jewish population: 4,000-7,000 (mainly in Sofia and Plovdiv)

GENERAL BACKGROUND

Until 1989 a Communist-ruled country, Bulgaria is now a parliamentary republic ruled by a democratically elected government. President Zhelyu Zhelev was elected in 1992 to a five-year term in the country's first direct presidential elections. The former communist Bulgarska Sotsialisticheska Partiya (Bulgarian Socialist Party) gained an absolute majority in the legislative elections in December 1994.

The transformation of a centrally planned economy into a market-oriented system continued to be retarded by political and social resistance. In December inflation surpassed 120 per cent. Some 70 per cent of the population lived on the verge of poverty. Unemployment was over 17 per cent. Violent and organized crime and corruption continued to rise.

HISTORICAL LEGACY

There is no strong tradition of antisemitism in Bulgaria. During the Second World War, when Bulgaria was a Nazi satellite state, persecution of the Jews began with the Law for the Defence of the Nation, which was modelled on Nazi Germany's Nuremberg laws and adopted in January 1941.

About 12,000 Jews were deported from Bulgarian-occupied territories in Greece and Yugoslavia to extermination camps under German pressure and with the authorization of the Bulgarian government and King Boris III. In spring 1943 the Jews from Bulgaria proper were also ready for deportation but were rescued at the last moment under domestic and international pressure. King Boris III postponed, and later revoked, their deportation altogether.

At the time of Stalin's anti-Jewish measures in the USSR in the late 1940s and early 1950s (see **Russia**), Jews were expelled from the Bulgarian interior ministry and security services.

RACISM AND XENOPHOBIA

Xenophobia, nationalism and anti-ethnic expression grew markedly among the population at large. Roma, blacks and Asians were the most common target of racist attacks. The attacks were usually carried out by skinheads, who numbered up to 10,000 in the country as a whole. The lack of firm legislation protecting immigrants and asylum-seekers and the presence of some 15,000 illegal immigrants in the country fuelled xenophobia.

PARTIES, ORGANIZATIONS, MOVEMENTS

There was in Bulgaria a number of tiny ultra-nationalist parties and groupings. Among the former were the Bulgarska natsionalisticheska radikalna partiya (BNRP, Bulgarian National Radical Party), and the Liberalno-demokraticheska partiya (Liberal Democratic Party), a sister party to Vladimir Zhirinovsky's Liberal Democrats (see **Russia**). Among the latter were the Komitet za zashtita na natsionalnite interesi (Committee for the Defence of National Interests) and the Dvizhenie za vuzrazhdane (DV, Revivalist Movement), led by Father Gelemenov.

MANIFESTATIONS

In August, on the anniversary of Hess's death, neo-Nazis painted antisemitic slogans in a number of Bulgarian cities.

On 10 August, in an interview with the independent newspaper *Standart*, Ivan Georgiev, leader of the BNRP, claimed that the "real" surname of the Bulgarian defence minister, Valentin Aleksandrov, was Blumenfeld.

On 17 August the Israeli Russian-language paper *Vesti* reported that in Sofia neo-Nazis had beaten up three black members of the Israeli basketball team Ha-Poel. On learning that their victims were Israelis, the assailants were said to have shouted: "Isn't it enough that you're black—you're Israelis as well!"

On 6 September, the anniversary of Bulgaria's unification, DV leader Father Gelemenov demanded in Plovdiv that Jews and Roma should wear identification badges.

On 10 September, in an interview with the Bulgarian Socialist Party daily *Duma*, the MP Rumen Vodenitcharov referred to defence minister Valentin Aleksandrov as "private Blumenfeld".

PUBLICATIONS AND MEDIA

A Bulgarian version of the antisemitic book *Svetovna konspiratsiya* (The World Conspiracy) by Nikola Nikolov was reprinted for the seventh time. Said to have been written originally in English, it had, according to the publishers, also been translated into French, German, Russian, Ukrainian, Polish and Turkish and was currently being translated into Arabic, Serbo-Croat and Greek.

On sale were a further three antisemitic books by the same author—*Maskite na velichiata* (Masks of Greatness), first published in 1994, *Nov red* (New Order) and *Tainite protokoli* (The Secret Protocols), reprinted for the third time in 1994. Other antisemitic books on sale were *Satanizmat v Bulgaria* (Satanism in Bulgaria) by Iv. St Belev and *Masoni, evrei i revolyutsii* (Masons, Jews and Revolutions) by Nikola Ivanov, published in Tirnovo in 1993 by Christo Christov.

In December Christo Christov published *Uchenieto na fashisma* (The Doctrine of Fascism) by Benito Mussolini, which was immediately sold out. In a foreword, the publisher claimed that fascism was a "natural reaction" to the invasion of "world Zionism" and accused, among others, President Zhelev, the then leader of the opposition, and the US ambassador to Bulgaria of assisting "Judeo-Masonic circles" in the destruction of the Bulgarian nation.

In November the Los Angeles-based Simon Wiesenthal Center wrote to President Zhelev urging the banning of the book *Masoni, evrei i revolyutsii*. The Organization of Jews in Bulgaria "Shalom" also protested against the publication of the book.

COUNTERING ANTISEMITISM

In March President Zhelev addressed a commemoration in Paris of the rescue of Bulgarian Jews during the Second World War.

Bibliata, Israel i krayat na sveta (The Bible, Israel and the End of the World), a history of antisemitism by Todor Matchkanov sponsored by, among others, the Bulgarian First Evangelical Church and the Gospodinov family, was published in Sofia.

ASSESSMENT

During a period of considerable economic and political instability and rising xenophobia, relations between Bulgarians and Jews remained generally good. Antisemitism continued to be a marginal problem, although the continued publication of a number of antisemitic books was a matter of serious concern.

Croatia

General population: 4.9 million
Jewish population: 3,000 (mainly in Zagreb)

GENERAL BACKGROUND

Croatia is a constitutional parliamentary democracy with a powerful presidency. President
Tudjman's party, the Hrvatska Demokratska
Zajednica (Croatian Democratic Union), holds
the majority of seats in both houses of parliament. Croatia has a mixed economy in which
industry is largely state-owned and agriculture
is mainly in private hands. Inflation is low but
little progress has been made on either privatization or free market reforms.

During the year Croatia and Yugoslavia
issued a joint declaration establishing normal
relations. Croatia signed a ceasefire with the
self-declared republic of Serbian Krajina, and
the government reversed its opposition to a
renewal of the mandate in Croatia of the UN
Protection Force (UNPROFOR).

HISTORICAL LEGACY

There is no significant tradition of grassroots
antisemitism in the former Yugoslav federation.
In the 1930s and during the Second World War
antisemitism, especially of the racial variety, remained a Nazi "import" which never became
deeply rooted in Croatia. Under the pro-Nazi
Ustaša regime in the Independent State of
Croatia, many thousands of Serbs, Jews and
Roma perished in concentration camps.

In his book "Wanderings of Historical
Truth", which was published in the late 1980s
and encountered substantial criticism in the
West, President Tudjman claimed, *inter alia*,
that figures for the number of Jews who perished in the Holocaust had been exaggerated
(see **Countering Antisemitism**).

RACISM AND XENOPHOBIA

There continued to be ever-present, subtle and
sometimes open discrimination against Serbs in
such areas as the administration of justice,
employment, housing and the free exercise of
cultural rights. The Roma minority continued
to face societal discrimination.

PARTIES, ORGANIZATIONS, MOVEMENTS

On 10 April the neo-fascist Hrvatska Stranka
Prava (HSP, Croatian Party of Rights), organized a ceremony in a Zagreb hotel to mark the
fifty-second anniversary of the Independent
State of Croatia. A charter on the unification of

the HSP and the Hrvatska Demokratska
Stranka Prava (HDSP, Croatian Democratic
Party of Rights) was signed at the ceremony.

On 10 November a demonstration by the
Croatian New Right-wing Party in front of the
Jewish community building in Zagreb prompted
the country's military prosecutor to open an
invesigation into the party's activities. The leaders of the party—Mladen Schwartz, Velimir
Bujanec and others—who handed out leaflets
vilifying members of the Jewish community,
were suspected of stirring up ethnic, racial and
religious hatred, an offence which falls within
the juridiction of the military court under article 140 of the penal code. No action was taken
by the authorities.

MANIFESTATIONS

Not long after he had conferred the Order of
Prince Trpimir on Branko Lustig (see **Countering Antisemitism**), the president conferred the
same order on Ivo Rojnica, the chief of Ustaša
headquarters in Dubrovnik and author of a racist and anti-Jewish proclamation in Dubrovnik
in 1941. Rojnica, who lives in Argentina, told
the newspaper *Slobodna Dalmacija* during his
visit to Croatia that "Everything I did in 1941 I
would do again." A book of reminiscences by
Rojnica published in Zagreb in 1993 received
favourable reviews in the press of the leading
party.

On 6 May the Union of Croatian Anti-
Fascist Veterans warned, prior to the commemoration of Victory over Fascism Day, that
"anti-fascism is being marginalized while
Ustaša values are being rehabilitated". The Union stressed that since the current administration had come to power, some 3,000 anti-fascist

monuments had been destroyed and the names of 1,300 streets bearing anti-fascist names had been changed in Zagreb alone. The veterans saw the introduction of the kuna, the new official currency to replace the dinar, as part of the same trend.

On 9 May Croatia's Helsinki Human Rights Committee, also in a statement marking Victory Day, warned against the propagation of extremism and intolerance.

On 30 May the Croatian currency, the dinar, was replaced by the kuna. The move was described by Slavko Goldstein, a Zagreb Jewish activist, as "insensitive, tactless and inappropriate". It was also denounced by a number of opposition politicians as a concession to the Ustaša-oriented right wing of Tudjman's ruling party and as being harmful to Croatia's image in the West.

On 7 July the Co-ordination Committee of the Jewish Communities of Croatia stated in an open letter that there had been no response to the letter it had written in late 1993 to President Tudjman and other high officials in which it had expressed concern over what it saw as attempts to rehabilitate the Ustaša regime.

The Committee welcomed expressions of sympathy for the Jewish people, of commiseration with the victims of fascism and other antifascist statements made by President Tudjman in recent months, as well as the move to rename the Mile Budak school in Zagreb (see **Countering Antisemitism**), but it pointed out that a growing number of events in Croatian public life were causing concern and that various newspapers were fomenting national intolerance and hatred against Jews and other nations. For instance, the Committee said that on 10 April the influential Zagreb daily newspaper *Vjesnik* and various right-wing parties and groups had stated their intention of organizing public celebrations to mark the anniversary of the Independent State of Croatia and that state television had uncritically carried extensive reports of these events. The committee demanded that the public prosecutor take legal action against the *Vjesnik* for fomenting national intolerance and institute proceedings whenever and wherever similar articles appeared. It also proposed that the Croatian parliament approve legislation which would prohibit, and stipulate penalties for, the spreading of national and religious intolerance and hatred.

Nazis from across Europe have served as mercenaries in Croatia, gathering military expertise and practical experience which have been used by neo-fascist groups both in Western Europe and South Africa.

CULTURAL LIFE

In June a Belgian European Community monitor in Osijek, which was badly damaged during the 1991 war with the Serbs, said, according to a report in the *Independent* newspaper (London, 23 June), that at a screening of the film *Schindler's List* he had observed that the "audience were mostly young Croatians and they were laughing and whistling at the terrible scenes where the Jews were murdered.... I suppose they've seen so many brutal things, but this is just the same cruelty they show towards Serbs and Muslims. What kind of people behave like this?"

COUNTERING ANTISEMITISM

On 16 February it was reported that President Tudjman had written to the US-based Jewish organization B'nai B'rith that he now realized "the extent of the hurtfulness of certain portions" of his book "Wanderings of Historical Reality".

On 25 March the president attended a premiere in Zagreb of the film *Schindler's List*.

On 28 March, at a ceremony in which he conferred the Order of Prince Trpimir on Branko Lustig, a Croatian-born Jew who was a producer of *Schindler's List*, he took the opportunity to "apologize to . . . all members of the Jewish community on behalf of those who took part in the Holocaust and enforced the Nazi-fascist racist laws in the Independent State of Croatia".

In early April Croatian Jewish leaders were informed that a school in Zagreb dedicated to the Ustaša leader and war criminal Mile Budak was to have its name changed along with two streets bearing the same name.

On 8 April the day of remembrance for Croatian Jewish victims of the Holocaust was marked in front of a monument to Moses at the Mirogoj cemetery in Zagreb. The ceremony, organized by the Zagreb Jewish community, was attended by, among others, the prime minister, the parliamentary speaker and the archbishop of Zagreb. At the ceremony Croatian Jewish leader Ognjen Kraus said: "I can affirm that antisemitism in Croatia is not on the rise."

ASSESSMENT

While there were indications that the government remained concerned with toning down Croatia's chauvinistic image in the West, the rehabilitation of figures and elements associated with the pro-Nazi Independent State of Croatia in the context of the break-up of the Yugoslav federation continued to be of concern to the small Jewish community. Explicit antisemitism was not a serious problem.

Czech Republic

General population: 10.4 million
Jewish population: 3,000-8,000 (mainly in Prague)

GENERAL BACKGROUND

The Czech Republic became an independent state in 1993, following the dissolution of the Czech and Slovak Federal Republic. It is a parliamentary democracy. Prime Minister Václav Klaus and his Občanská demokratická strana (ODS, Civic Democratic Party) lead the coalition government. The country has essentially completed the political and economic reform initiated after the 1989 revolution. The 1994 inflation rate was 9.5 per cent, the unemployment rate was less than 4 per cent and gross domestic product growth was 3 per cent.

HISTORICAL LEGACY

Over 1,000 years of Jewish history in Bohemia and Moravia have witnessed periods both of prosperity and of persecution. The flourishing Jewish community under Czechoslovak president Tomáš Masaryk (1918-35), which numbered 118,000 people, was almost completely annihilated in the Holocaust. In 1952 the show trials, orchestrated by Moscow, of Rudolf Slánský and other top Communist Party officials, several of them Jewish, bore clear anti-Jewish overtones. Most survivors of the Holocaust left the country either after the Second World War or after the Soviet occupation of Czechoslovakia in 1968.

RACISM AND XENOPHOBIA

Incitement against Roma (an approximately 300,000-strong community), refugees from the Balkans and asylum-seekers from the East remained a major problem.

Particularly problematic was widespread prejudice against the Roma minority and the inability, or reluctance, of the government to counteract it. Roma live throughout the country but are concentrated in the industrial towns of northern Bohemia. They suffer from serious discrimination, particularly in employment and housing.

PARTIES, ORGANIZATIONS, MOVEMENTS

The far-right Sdruženi pro republiku-Republikánská strana Československa (SPR-RSČ, Association for the Republic-Czechoslovak Republican Party), led by Miroslav Sladek, which in the parliamentary

elections in 1992 gained 6 per cent of the votes and fourteen members of parliament, obtained in November's municipal elections only 3 per cent of the vote. Sladek's principal targets were President Václav Havel, the government, so-called German revanchism and the Roma.

In March Sladek promised to send "unsatisfied Jewish co-citizens to their Promised Land" and, in his party's weekly *Republika* (25 April), he claimed that Hitler had left Switzerland and "its Jewish banks" untouched so as to save the lives of rich Jews. He also claimed that Adolf Eichmann was a Jew.

In June Josef Krejza, a leader of the SPR-RSČ enjoying parliamentary immunity as a representative of the defunct Czechoslovak federal parliament, attacked Czech culture minister Pavel Tigrid for being of Jewish origin.

A handful of numerically unimportant but vociferous far-right and skinhead groups were active throughout the country. Their real strength was difficult to estimate on account of their often interchanging identities and overlapping membership. In various localities they were active under such names as, for example, National Fascist Community (Prague), National Confederation (Prague) and Patriotic Front (Brno) (the latter grouping was said to have contacts with Jean-Marie Le Pen's Front National).

MANIFESTATIONS

According to a survey prepared by the state attorney's office, in 1993 and the first quarter of 1994, seventy-two criminal acts with racial or ethnic motivation were committed.

In March, about 500 skinheads chanted racial and antisemitic slogans at a concert in Prague. In Teplice in the same month, a swastika was sprayed over an as yet unveiled memorial to Holocaust victims.

In April, over twenty graves at the Jewish cemetery in the Moravian town of Prerov were desecrated with anti-Jewish graffiti.

In June, participants in a meeting of Jewish youth in a Prague synagogue were taunted by skinheads.

In October, skinheads shouted anti-Jewish slogans at a concert in Brno by the pop group Shalom (none of whose members is Jewish). Some of the skinheads were taken into custody by police.

PUBLICATIONS AND MEDIA

On 11 June, in an antisemitic innuendo, the right-wing *Český deník* published a reader's letter critical of "a specific type of people with a strong adaptability who easily become domesticated in all geographical seasons . . . and who prefer political systems like that of Allende in Chile which enables them to occupy all the important posts".

On 1 November, *Český deník* published a reader's letter blaming President Havel for having condemned the genocide of the Jews but not, it was said, the genocide of his own nation under the Communist regime.

The sensationalist Prague paper *Spigl* published several examples of anti-Jewish innuendo in, *inter alia*, a series about George Soros and his relations with other financial tycoons and his alleged cooperation with Mossad.

There were several initiatives to replace the antisemitic weekly *Politika* which had been forced to disappear from the news-stands in December 1992. In Brno the monthly *Dnesek* and *Pochoden dneska* took over *Politika*'s topics and contributors.

Vladimir Sonka, a Czech émigré in France, began publication of *Vlastenecke zprávy* in an attempt to replace *Politika* with an imported paper.

About a dozen "skinzines" (low-level skinhead bulletins) appeared irregularly and in small print-runs.

In Hronov at least three issues of *Arijský boj* (Aryan Fight), calling for a world "without coloured vagabonds and Jewish types", appeared. Police in the district capital of Nachod began proceedings against one of the distributors.

Apparently prompted by commercial considerations, editions of Hitler's *Mein Kampf* appeared in bookshops, as did anonymous hate-mongering booklets based on *The Protocols of the Elders of Zion* and Henry Ford's *The International Jew*.

OPINION POLLS

An opinion survey carried out in March by the independent Prague-based Centre for Empirical Research found that, while 96 per cent of the population generally favoured freedom of expression, 36 per cent rejected the right of non-Czech ethnic minorities to observe their own customs and traditions.

Least tolerant were elderly people on both right and left extremes of the political spectrum. According to 53 per cent of respondents, the granting of Czech citizenship—and, in the view of one-third of the respondents, social security payments—ought to be dependent on the claimant's ethnic origin. As many as 62 per cent of the population favoured adopting stricter legislation for certain groups of people. While this discriminatory attitude was as high as 71 per cent among those with only basic education, it was shared by 50 per cent of those with a university education.

The targets of this discrimination were Roma (54 per cent), recidivist criminals (14 per cent), Vietnamese and refugees (6 per cent each), skinheads (4 per cent), Arabs (2 per cent) and the homeless (1 per cent).

A total of 71.9 per cent of respondents did not want as a neighbour a Gypsy, 38.2 per cent a Vietnamese, 38.2 per cent a Russian, 33.2 per cent a refugee from former Yugoslavia, 27.4 per cent a German, 19.1 per cent a Jew, 17.3 per cent a repatriate of Czech origin (whose ancestors migrated to Ukraine or Kazakhstan), and 3.5 per cent a Slovak. Those who saw no problem at all in co-existing with a Jewish neighbour numbered 49 per cent, compared with 80 per cent in relation to Slovaks, but only 8 per cent in relation to Vietnamese.

Those who did not wish to have a non-Czech son-in-law or daughter-in-law were, in the case of a Gypsy, 87.8 per cent, a Vietnamese 85.8 per cent, a Russian 61.6 per cent, a Yugoslav refugee 55.9 per cent, a Czech repatriated from Ukraine or Kazakhstan 36.5 per cent, a German 35.3 per cent, a Jew 31.9 per cent, and a Slovak 5.3 per cent.

LEGAL MATTERS

Josef Tomás, the former editor of *Politika*, protested against a January 1994 sentence of one year's suspended imprisonment. In three subsequent hearings, attended by tens of his followers, he pleaded not guilty and invoked the right of free expression. In September a Prague district court sentenced him to seven months' imprisonment. The sentence was suspended on two years' probation and a two-year ban on publishing activities.

On 20 April, Prague city court rejected an appeal by Václav Kulle, who had been given a one-year's suspended sentence by a Prague district court. Kulle had written to a Prague district mayor praising Hitler for having sent Jews to the gas chambers and threatening that the mayor (a non-Jew) would be the "first Jew" killed when, as he put it, the fascists resumed power.

In June, a Prague district court acquitted for the third time Miroslav Gabriel, publisher of a Czech translation of *The Protocols of the Elders of Zion*. The acquittal was quashed by the appeal court and Gabriel again pleaded not guilty, claiming he had published the *Protocols* for commercial reasons alone. The court accepted his argument that he had not supported any antisemitic movement because there was no movement so registered. The state attorney's appeal against this sentence has not yet been dealt with.

The shortcomings of Czech penal legislation and the inability of courts to deal appropriately with hate crimes were also manifest in proceedings against skinheads. For instance, on 2 December, the district court gave suspended short-term jail sentences to only two out of eighteen skinheads who had caused the death of a Gypsy in Pisek in September 1993.

COUNTERING ANTISEMITISM

Czech leaders, in particular President Havel, repeatedly stressed their sympathy for Jews and Jewish causes. Havel's speech at the unveiling of a Holocaust memorial in Ostrava in October was a moving tribute to Jewish victims of the Nazis and, at the same time, a most serious warning against renewed racial hatred and antisemitism.

ASSESSMENT

Whilst extremism posed no real threat to Czech political stability, the continual hostility to Roma was a major social problem. Antisemitic utterances were, as previously, mainly isolated incidents and did not represent a real threat to the small Jewish community. President Havel in particular has played an exemplary role in combating racism and antisemitism.

Denmark

General population: 5.2 million
Jewish population: 7,000

GENERAL BACKGROUND

The centre-left coalition government of Socialdemokratiet (SD, Social Democrats), Radikale Venstre (RV, Social Liberals) and Centrumdemokraterne (CD, Centre Democrats) retained power after the general election of September, having taken office following the resignation of the prime minister in 1993. However, the coalition was weakened by a fall in its share of the vote and the loss of one of its partners, Kristeligt Folkeparti (KrF, Christian People's Party), which failed to cross the 2 per cent electoral threshold. Danish politics was dominated by the problem of unemployment, the future of the welfare state and the country's place within the European Union (EU).

The Danish economy experienced strong growth in 1994. Gross domestic product grew by 4.2 per cent compared to 0.2 per cent in 1993. Inflation rose to 2 per cent from 1.2 per cent the previous year. Unemployment fell only slightly from 12.4 per cent in 1993 to 12.2 per cent.

HISTORICAL LEGACY

Denmark's reputation for being free of serious anti-Jewish prejudice is only partly true. An anti-Jewish riot in 1819 was effectively stopped by the king, who five years earlier had granted civic equality to the Jewish community.

At the turn of the century, modern political antisemitism prospered. Jewish financiers played an important economic role during this period and were subject to harsh accusations, especially during and after the First World War. Most Jewish financiers lost their money and influence in 1921-4 due to the post-war recession. Subsequently, antisemitism played only a peripheral role in public debate.

Like most other Western countries, Denmark permitted relatively few German Jews to settle in the country from 1933 onwards, although some young German Jews were admitted to study agriculture and then made their way to Palestine. Some of them were still in the country when Germany occupied Denmark in 1940. Together with more than 90 per cent of the Jewish population, they were rescued in October 1943 in a remarkable operation which took them by sea to Sweden.

After the Second World War, there was considerable sympathy for the Jews and antisemitism virtually disappeared.

The so-called Blekingegade Group (named after the Copenhagen street where the group was based) was established in 1970 by left-wing sympathizers of the Palestinian cause. The group committed several crimes, including bank robberies and the murder of a policeman. All Jews were considered potential Zionists and, consequently, enemies by the group. It established a so-called "Z-file" of Danish Jews and non-Jews said to be sympathetic to Israel. The police exposed the group in 1989 and the members received heavy prison sentences. The revelation was a shock to the Danish public and such extreme anti-Zionism must be considered exceptional.

RACISM AND XENOPHOBIA

Although there was widespread protest against the presence of neo-Nazis in the towns of Kollund and Kværs during the autumn (see **Denial of the Holocaust**), public concern about immigration continued in 1994. Moreover, opponents of refugees and asylum-seekers were more vocal than previously in media discussions concerning the ineffectiveness of Danish legislation against the public expression of Holocaust denial and racism (see **Legal Matters**).

The number of racist attacks, however, decreased. Since 1992, Danish police recorded between 200 and 300 racially-motivated crimes, 20 of which were arson attacks on refugee camps. In 1994, the total number was between 20 and 30.

PARTIES, ORGANIZATIONS, MOVEMENTS

The Danish far right encompasses an anti-immigration political party, racist organizations and overtly neo-Nazi groupings.

While the far-right populist Fremskridts-partiet (FP, Progress Party), like all parliamentary parties, does not espouse antisemitism, it has for years called for a ban on both immigration and refugees. In September's general election, the FP received 6.4 per cent of the vote and lost one of its seats. However, this was an increase from the 5.2 per cent share of the vote it secured in the November 1993 municipal elections. The party now holds 11 out of 179 parliamentary seats.

With more than 2,000 members, Den Danske Forening (DDF, The Danish Society) is the largest racist organization in Denmark. Led by Ole Hasselbalch, DDF has achieved a fairly important position in recent years as a popular voice against immigrants (primarily Muslims) and refugees, and publishes a magazine, *Danskeren*. DDF claims that it has nothing to do with neo-Nazi groups, but it has been proven that some of its members are also active in Danmarks National-Socialistiske Bevægelse (DNSB, Denmark's National Socialist Movement) and the Dansk National Front (DNF) (see below), and individual members of DDF have made anti-Jewish statements. DDF took legal action against anyone who described it as racist until two separate courts ruled that the claim that it propagated racism was justified.

Hasselbalch has met with Jean-Marie Le Pen of the French Front national and Franz Schönhuber, former leader of Die Republikaner in Germany (see **France** and **Germany**).

Many DDF public meetings have been stopped by an increasingly active anti-racist movement. At an outdoor meeting in June arranged by DDF, the principal speakers, who included Mogens Glistrup of Trivselpartiet (see below), were protected by DNSB and DNF members. The meeting ended in fighting after a group of anti-racists intervened.

Trivselpartiet (TP, Well-being Party) emerged in 1993 after a split in the FP and is led by Mogens Glistrup, a former leader of the FP. The party won two seats in the 1993 municipal elections but could not collect the 20,000 signatures necessary to register for the 1994 general election.

The Nationalpartiet Danmark (NPD, Danish National Party) also attempted to register for the general election, but failed to collect the necessary signatures. Three members of the NPD, including the party leader Kaj Wilhelmsen, who is a former member of the DNSB, stood as candidates, but none of them were elected. Wilhelmsen was convicted and fined in 1993 for making politically-motivated threats. The NPD, which demands a total ban on Third World refugees and opposes all attempts to cur-

tail Danish sovereignty, has approximately 300 members. Many former members of the disbanded Partiet de Nationale (PDN, National Party) joined the NPD following the death of PDN leader, Albert Larsen, in August.

Danmarks National-Socialistiske Bevægelse (DNSB) has between 200 and 300 members, and its leader, Jonni Hansen, claimed that his neo-Nazi group had gained many new supporters in 1994. The DNSB reprints antisemitic literature and disseminates propaganda denying the Holocaust, as well as publishing a magazine, Fædre*landet*, which is printed by the US-based Nationalsozialistische Deutsche Arbeiterpartei/Auslands- und Aufbauorganisation (NSDAP/AO, German National Socialist Workers' Party/Overseas Section, see **United States**).

Many DNSB members also belong to other far-right organizations, and the group plays a significant international role. It has links with the neo-Nazi Storm Network and Vitt Arisk Motstånd (White Aryan Resistance) in Sweden, and various German neo-Nazi groups, including Nationale Liste (see **Sweden** and **Germany**).

In September, Jonni Hansen and a group of other neo-Nazis bought a house in Greve, south of Copenhagen. This triggered off demonstrations by residents who objected to the presence of neo-Nazis in their town, as well as leading to more violent clashes between neo-Nazis and anti-racist groups. Hansen received support from both Swedish and German neo-Nazis.

During the year, a nascent racist group, Dansk National Front (DNF, Danish National Front), received a lot of media attention for having issued statements to the effect that its struggle for a "pure" Denmark could result in murder. The group is extremely violent and has members across the entire spectrum of Danish far-right organizations. It claims to have no formal membership or leadership, but does hold weekly meetings.

In June, the DNF organized a neo-Nazi concert in Høje Gladsaxe, north of Copenhagen, attended by around 300 Danish, German and Swedish skinheads. German skinheads from Brandenburg, a Berlin suburb, frequently visit Danish neo-Nazis, particularly in Birkerød, north of Copenhagen.

MANIFESTATIONS

During March, Jews in different parts of Denmark found their front doors daubed with the slogan "Juden Raus" (Jews out), with graffiti and swastikas. The graffiti were signed by a group which calls itself Fascistisk Arbejder Parti (FAB, Fascist Labour Party).

After a year of being terrorized by neo-

Nazis, a Jewish family in Copenhagen had to flee their home. The family's front door was repeatedly kicked in or spat on, and men wearing Nazi brown shirts regularly gathered outside their house.

In September, at the University of Odense, a group of academics who specialize in Jewish culture received threatening letters marked with swastikas.

PUBLICATIONS AND MEDIA

Radio Holger, a local radio station run by activists from a variety of far-right organizations, broadcast antisemitic accusations that "Jews control the media, the economy and the courts", and was subsequently charged with defamation. The station operated on a short-term licence and it seemed unlikely that this would be renewed in April 1995.

DENIAL OF THE HOLOCAUST

Thies Christophersen, the former SS overseer in Auschwitz and author of *Die Auschwitz-Lüge* (The Auschwitz Lie) was the main disseminator of Holocaust-denial propaganda in Denmark. He published a magazine called *Die Bauernschaft* and had links with the banned Gesinnungsgemeinschaft der Neuen Front (GdNF, Like-minded Association of the New Front) in Germany (see **Germany**).

In 1994, there were daily demonstrations around Christophersen's home and printing works in the southern town of Kollund. In October, he said that he could no longer tolerate the "psychological terror" of the demonstrations, and that he would return to Germany. The printing works are now thought to have been moved to Brighton in the south of England, where another Holocaust-denier, Tony Hancock, prints Christophersen's material (see **United Kingdom**). Christophersen went into hospital in December on the island of Fünen where he has a summer house. Despite risking arrest, he has reportedly been seen in Germany on several occasions.

Many people have found it unreasonable that Christophersen, a convicted Nazi with outstanding warrants in Germany, continued to be allowed to reside in Denmark despite his dissemination of Nazi hate literature throughout the world. Successive Danish ministers of justice said that Christophersen was protected by legislation concerning freedom of expression and that the law needed to be changed to stop him (see **Legal Matters**).

EFFECTS OF ANTI-ZIONISM

In March, following the massacre of Muslims by a Jewish settler in a Hebron mosque, Meyers Minde (Old-Age Home), a Jewish retirement home in Copenhagen, received a telephone call claiming that a bomb was about to explode in the building. Police searched the premises, but failed to find an explosive device.

In the same month, a Jewish football team was harassed during training by a group of young Palestinians. The Palestinians verbally abused the team and shouted that they could kill Jews, just as Jews had killed in Hebron. The Palestinians allegedly stole items of clothing from the football players, but fled the scene when the team coach threatened to call the police.

LEGAL MATTERS

The then justice minister, Erling Olsen, stated in September that it would be necessary to speed up the introduction of legislation against denial of the Holocaust and to tighten the existing anti-racism laws, if Denmark were not to become the only West European country where the expression of Holocaust denial and racist views in public was legal. German neo-Nazis have taken advantage of Denmark's liberal laws to produce literature banned in Germany. Following Olsen's statement, a proposal to reform the law on racism was introduced in parliament.

In January, the Danish high court increased from thirty to fifty days the sentence handed down to a former member of the DNSB who had been convicted of illegally carrying arms. In September, DNSB leader Jonni Hansen and another activist, Espen Rohde Kristensen, were charged with complicity in threatening violence. They had distributed the German far-right publication *Der Einblick*, which lists the details of at least 400 anti-fascists who are to be "crushed". *Der Einblick* has used Denmark as its postal address. The court case against them was pending, however, until a verdict was delivered in a case concerning the same publication in Germany (see **Germany**).

In July, a court in Lyngby gave Denmark's most severe ruling on the dissemination of antisemitic material. Two elderly men, Jørgen Arum and Guy Christensen, were sentenced to sixty and ninety days' imprisonment, respectively, for having threatened and vilified Jews, and for having encouraged "national Danes" to liquidate them.

In June, the authorities refused to investigate whether Ultima Thule, a company based in southern Denmark which distributed the antisemitic film, *The Eternal Jew*, was breaking the law.

The European court of human rights ruled in October that the conviction of Jens Olaf Jersild, a radio journalist, for "aiding and abetting the dissemination of racist remarks" was a violation of freedom of expression under article 10 of the European convention on human rights. In 1987, Jersild had been convicted by Copenhagen city court for "assisting" far-right youths to make racist remarks, after his radio station broadcast an interview he had conducted with them. The European court ruled that he had been carrying out his duties as a member of the press and that the programme did not objectively set out to propagate racist views. It ordered the reimbursement of his fine.

COUNTERING ANTISEMITISM

Fælleskomiteen for Israel (Joint Committee for Israel) held a conference in March on the prevention of the rise of antisemitism. Participants came from northern Europe, the Baltic region, Russia and Israel, and included Jewish and non-Jewish politicians and academics.

There were several large demonstrations against racist violence and neo-Nazis in 1994. In January, one fifth of the population of the town of Brande demonstrated against racism, after the demolition of a building that was to have housed refugees from former Yugoslavia.

In August, one of the leaders of the banned German Nationalistische Front, Meinolf

Schönborn, bought a house in the village of Kværs, near the home of Thies Christophersen and the German border (see **Germany**). He intended to use the house as a base for German and Danish neo-Nazis, and for printing Nazi material for his Klartext publishing house.

Schönborn's purchase sparked off daily demonstrations around the house, in which up to 2,000 local residents and protesters from all over Denmark, as well as Germany and other countries, took part. After a brief period, Schönborn abandoned his attempts to stay in Kværs, and is no longer resident in Denmark. Following Schönborn's departure, an intermediary put the house up for sale on his behalf.

ASSESSMENT

Concern about immigration has been expressed more publicly in recent years, on occasion by senior politicians. This concern has been exploited by far-right organizations. On the other hand, popular demonstrations suggest that there is active opposition to neo-Nazi and racist activities among many sections of the general public.

However, antisemitism did not appear to be a by-product of the growing anti-foreigner climate and posed a marginal threat to Danish Jewry.

Estonia

General population: 1.6 million
Jewish population: 3,000 (mainly in Tallinn)

GENERAL BACKGROUND

Estonia, a former Soviet republic which is now a parliamentary democracy, has substantially transformed the centrally planned economy it inherited into a free market system. Unemployment remains low (officially about 8 per cent).

Estonian politics continued to be dominated by relations with the country's giant neighbour Russia, the principal issues being Estonian citizenship and the withdrawal of Russian armed forces—in August, after over two years of negotiations, Russian troops withdrew from Estonia.

HISTORICAL LEGACY

The Jewish community of Estonia was founded by Jewish conscripts in the army of Tsar Nicholas 1 (1825-55). In 1922 the Jewish population numbered over 4,000.

In the 1930s, the pro-fascist group Omakaitse rapidly gained in influence, demanding curbs on Jewish commercial activities and a quota on Jewish university students.

Omakaitse units assisted the Nazi invasion in July 1941 and were active in the rounding up and slaughter of Jewish men. The Estonian so-called self-protection movement (*Selbstschutz*), acting under the supervision of the Nazis, shot Jewish men, women and children. In January 1942 the German leadership reported that 936 Jews had been killed and that Estonia was "judenfrei". The Germans also used Estonians in the running of extermination camps. The issue of Estonian complicity in the Holocaust continues to exert a negative impact on Jewish-Estonian relations to the present day.

PARTIES, ORGANIZATIONS, MOVEMENTS

The Eesti Kodanik (Estonian Civic Union), with a reported membership of 4,000, aims to weaken the position of ethnic Russians in Estonia.

The Eesti Rahvususlikliit (Estonian National Union), led by Tiit Madesson and an offshoot of the Parnu Nationalist League (also led by Madesson), advocates the creation of paramilitary units. At a meeting on 8 May near the statue of the Unknown Warrior in Tallinn, the group displayed banners containing such slogans as "Hitler Saved Europe from Bolshevism".

The Russky sobor Estonii (Russian Council of Estonia), led by Aleksey Zybin, continued to function. Its founding congress in April 1993, which received a message of support from Vladimir Zhirinovsky, declared its aim to be the uniting of the Slavs of Estonia; Boris Yeltsin was accused of treachery and Jews were declared Russia's principal enemies.

The Liberal Demokraatiik Partei (Liberal Democratic Party), a sister party of Zhirinovsky's Russian Liberal Democrats led by Petr Rozhok, continued its activities.

Rozhok has engaged in antisemitic activities since 1989. In March 1989, at a Tallinn meeting of the Russian ultra-nationalist Interdvizhenie (Intermovement), Rozhok called for the use of violence as a means to political ends. In May 1990 he was a leader of a violent attempt to take over the seat of government at Toompea Castle in Tallinn. In early 1993 he began to identify himself as the Baltic representative of Zhirinovsky's Liberal Democrats. In an interview with *Sillamaesky vestnik* in January 1994 Rozhok called on retired and reserve Soviet military officers to form para-military units to fight the Estonian authorities. The above incident resulted in criminal charges, requiring him to remain at his place of residence in Tallinn. In September in Narva Rozhok was removed from a Tallinn-Moscow train in violation of the order. During a search of his home a number of antisemitic pamphlets and other materials were found. In the summer Rozhok outlined to a meeting of Estonian far-right activists alleged Jewish plans to attain power via economic and commercial means.

MANIFESTATIONS

In February antisemitic graffiti were found in a telephone kiosk near a Jewish school on Narva shosse in Tallinn. In the same month graffiti on a wall in Tallinn enjoining Jews to treat non-Jews badly was alleged to be a quote from Jewish religious writings, while Aleksandr Dusman, vice-chairman of the Jewish Cultural Club in Kokhtlya-Yarve (north-western Estonia), received a threatening letter from the local branch of the Russian extremist organization Pamyat.

On 9 July a rally of 20th SS Division veterans in Sinimaed (north-east Estonia), commemorating a battle against the Red Army, was condemned by the Russian foreign ministry as "mocking the memory of millions of people of different nationalities who died at the hands of the Nazis and their accomplices". The Estonian government rejected the charge that the veterans had collaborated in Nazi war crimes and said they had fought solely for Estonian independence and against Bolshevism.

In August the centrist Russian-language newspaper *Estonia* carried a photograph showing anti-Jewish graffiti in a telephone kiosk in Tallinn.

In October it was reported that a kiosk in the premises of the Russian embassy in Tallinn was selling antisemitic publications including *The Protocols of the Elders of Zion* and the Russian newspaper *Rossiyanin*.

PUBLICATIONS AND MEDIA

On 17 August the ultra-nationalist weekly *Eesti* carried an article by Yuri Lina, an Estonian émigré in Sweden, claiming that *The Protocols of the Elders of Zion* was authentic and demanding the removal of Estonian restrictions on its publication.

COUNTERING ANTISEMITISM

On 31 August Prime Minister Laar attended the unveiling of a memorial to Jews massacred by the Nazis at Klooga. He expressed regret that Estonians had taken part in "both red terrorism and brown terrorism" and added: "Today we can be sure that in the new Estonia a repetition of this tragedy would be impossible."

On 2 September, writing in *Rakhva Häael* in connection with the Klooga unveiling, Major-General Aleksandr Einselm, commander-in-chief of the Estonian defence force, said: "It is known that under the SS leadership Estonians too took part in the criminal activity of genocide. We cannot possibly call them 'freedom fighters'. Quite the contrary: they too are murderers and traitors to the Estonian people."

On 4 October at a meeting in Washington with the American Jewish Committee, Estonian Foreign Minister Juri Luik agreed that the help of Estonian Jewish scholars would be enlisted to ensure that school textbooks provided an accurate description of the Holocaust in the country. The Estonian ambassador to the United States, Toomas Hendrik Ilves, suggested that a travelling exhibition of the work of Louis Kahn, an American architect of Estonian Jewish extraction, should be displayed in Estonia to strengthen ties between the two peoples.

ASSESSMENT

Estonian politics appeared to be fairly stable and there were few organized xenophobic activities. While antisemitism was not a serious issue for the country's small Jewish community, the activities of Russian extremists, together with the sensitive issue of Estonian complicity in the Holocaust, continued to give cause for concern.

Finland

General population: 5 million
Jewish population: 1,000 (mainly in Helsinki and Turku)

GENERAL BACKGROUND

In 1994, Finland was governed by a coalition of the Keskustapuolue (KESK, Centre Party), the Kansallinen Kokoomus (KOK, National Coalition Party), the Suomen Kristillinen Liitto (SKL, Finnish Christian League) and the Svenska Folkspartiet (SFP, Swedish People's Party), which had been in power since April 1991.

Presidential elections were held in January and February and were won by the candidate of the Suomen Sosialidemokraattinen Puolue (SDP, Finnish Social Democratic Party), Martti Ahtisaari. In October, Finland's membership of the European Union (EU) was approved by 57 per cent of the voters in a referendum, and the country was due to join the EU in January 1995.

Attention was also focused on efforts to reduce unemployment. In October, unemployment stood at 18 per cent compared to 21 per cent at the end of 1993. The country was emerging from a deep recession with a growth rate of 2.5 per cent in 1994.

HISTORICAL LEGACY

Jews were granted full civil rights in 1918. Antisemitism appeared among extreme-right circles in the 1920s and 1930s mainly in written form, but there was no serious threat to Finnish Jewry. During the Second World War, despite Finland's status as a Nazi ally, no anti-Jewish legislation was enacted and Jews fought in the national army.

Minor threats have been made against the Jewish community at times of crisis in the Middle East, although Finland's pro-Arab orientation since the 1967 Six Day War in itself has not affected Jews domestically. Many Jews are involved in Finnish public life and their Jewishness has not been an issue.

In 1975, antisemitic writings were published and distributed in Turku by Pekka Siitoin and Antti Sipilä. Among these publications were *The Protocols of the Elders of Zion*, the first part of the book *Miksi juutalainen menestyy* (Why Does the Jew Succeed?) and *Nationalisti pasuuna* (The Nationalist Horn) (see **Publications and Media**). In 1977, the city

court of Turku fined Pekka Siitoin and Antti Sipilä for incitement to ethnic hatred and ordered the publications to be confiscated and the print blocks to be destroyed.

PARTIES, ORGANIZATIONS, MOVEMENTS

There are no overt antisemitic parties as such but three registered groups and other small groupings have displayed antisemitic attitudes. They are not generally known to the public and their influence is marginal.

Nova Hierosolyma (New Jerusalem) was established in 1987 and claims to be a religious organization. During the 1991 Gulf War, its chairman, Erkki Kivilohkare, wrote to newspapers in support of Iraq's invasion of Kuwait, attacking Israel and Jews. Following complaints by Jews and non-Jews, newspapers ceased publishing his material. The organization has not been active since and its membership is estimated to be in single figures.

Kansallinen Radikaalipuolue (KR, National Radical Party), which was known as the Organization of the National Unity before April 1991, was founded in 1985. It has imported ideas from other countries in Europe, where intolerance towards foreigners and asylum-seekers (although in Finland there have been relatively few of the latter) has been a feature of the resurgence of the far right.

Tapio Linna, the leader of the organization, claimed a membership of 170 in 1993, but the organization has gained little publicity. In January 1993, Linna, as editor of the organization's paper, was fined for incitement to ethnic hatred and infringement of the freedom of religion. In a 1993 newspaper interview, Linna accused Jews of being responsible for communism and modern art, which, he believed people were deceived into following by propaganda and brainwashing. The group apparently maintained a low public profile in 1994.

There are some anti-immigrant groups which support racial purity slogans. In July 1991, a Skullhead-Skinhead movement was founded in Helsinki. Mark Parland, the editor of *Skullhead-Skinhead*, the group's magazine, wrote newspaper articles condemning Nazi crimes and was expelled from the group, apparently as a result.

In the southern town of Lahti, a group called Lahden Arjalainen Germaaniveljeskunta (LAG, Aryan German Brotherhood Community of Lahti) was found in 1992 to be disseminating neo-Nazi propaganda in school neighbourhoods. The group's members were thought to be imitating other such groups in Germany. Väinö Kuisma, the group's leader, appeared on an hour-long television documentary in October. He argued against giving development aid to Third World countries, expressed his contempt for refugees and stressed the need for "racial purity". He was shown distributing leaflets to young people on the streets of Lahti and Helsinki. Kuisma claimed the group's membership to be 500, but the documentary showed only a handful of people attending his public meetings. According to the security police, fewer than ten people had paid a membership fee in 1993.

In August, Väinö Kuisma registered his organization under a new name: Isänmaallinen Oikeisto (IO, Patriotic Right). Kuisma expressed his willingness to participate in the general election of March 1995. Finnish law prohibits the registration of neo-Nazi groups.

In 1993, Väinö Kuisma and Pekka Siitoin from Naantali, founded the Kansallinen Liittoneuvosto (KL, National League Council) as an umbrella organization for far-right activists, but only the LAG joined. In the summer, Väinö Kuisma claimed that he wanted to move away from Siitoin and neo-Nazi politics, in order to register the IO as a political party.

There is also a tiny neo-Nazi grouping in Oulu, centred around Michael Aalto, which disseminates neo-Nazi propaganda.

In addition, there are far-right groups which support claims to a "Greater Finland", but officially reject antisemitic attitudes.

Launched in July 1993 in Seinäjoki, the Isänmaallinen Kansallis Liitto (IKL, Patriotic National Union) imitates the flag and uniforms of the fascist Isänmaallinen Kansanliike (Patriotic Nationalist Movement), which was active in the 1930s and dissolved in 1944. IKL's leader,

Matti Järviharju, a KOK member of the Kauhajoki town council, believes that patriotism does not depend on ethnic origin and that Nazi doctrines do not fit modern society. However, the IKL calls for an end to immigration and the launch was attended by about 200 black-shirted supporters. In 1993, the IKL's publication *Ajan suunta* (The Direction of the Era) published a map of Finland including lands annexed by Soviet Union but it strives to separate the group from the neo-Nazism and racism of other far-right nationalist organizations. Järviharju claimed in 1993 that the IKL had 500 members, although others estimate membership to be much smaller. The organization intended to take part in the general election of March 1995.

Mika Treuhardt, the leader of the Suomen Kansan Järjestö (Finland's People's Organization) claimed in 1993 that 350 people had contacted the group and denied that the patriotic group had any neo-Nazi sympathies. The security police estimate its membership at less than fifty.

MANIFESTATIONS

In 1994, there were a few sporadic daubings of swastikas and other anti-Jewish graffiti on Jewish-owned property and public buildings.

PUBLICATIONS AND MEDIA

Pekka Siitoin from Naantali, Tapio Linna, leader of KR, and Mark Parland in Helsinki are the primary producers of antisemitic literature.

During 1991-2, the KR published five editions of its paper *Uusi Suunta* (New Direction), with a print-run of about 500 each time. The paper carried antisemitic articles, apparently translated from material published by neo-Nazi sources in Central Europe. In 1991, the Jewish community asked the ministry of justice to investigate the matter (see **Legal Matters**).

In Turku in January, Pekka Siitoin, the head of the KL, published the third part of his book series *Miksi juutalainen menestyy* (Why Does the Jew Succeed?), apparently translated from French. The second part was published in 1993. In March, Mark Parland published the first issue of a magazine *Sinivalkoinen maa* (Blue-White Country), which contained racist and antisemitic articles. In December, he appeared on a television talk show "Talking Heads", where he promoted the idea of "racial purity" and spoke against foreigners and mixed marriages.

Pekka Siitoin also produces *Rautaristi* (Iron Cross), a pamphlet which contains advertisements for Nazi memorabilia.

LEGAL MATTERS

The Finnish criminal code prohibits incitement to ethnic hatred. Publication of *The Protocols of the Elders of Zion* was banned by a court decision in Turku in 1977. There are no specific laws regarding antisemitism.

Following a request by the Finnish Jewish community, the ministry of justice decided in 1992 to prosecute those responsible for the *Uusi Suunta* and to confiscate its print blocks (see **Publications and Media**). The Helsinki city court reached its verdict in January 1993 and fined the leader of KR, Tapio Linna, for incitement to ethnic discrimination and infringing the freedom of religion.

ASSESSMENT

Concern over the incidence of racist violence in Europe was expressed in the Finnish media.

However, Finland's democratic culture is well developed and solid, and the few far-right groups are not seen as a threat. There were no serious incidents in 1994, following the desecrations and prosecutions of 1992 and 1993. The incidents that did occur were isolated and few, and the police took them seriously. The security police monitor the development of the far-right groups in Finland, which are little known and have marginal influence. Economic crisis, unemployment and the issue of asylum-seekers, especially during the last few years, have stirred up intolerance towards immigrants and minorities. Nonetheless, people generally view the future with considerable optimism. The life of the Jewish community, like that of society in general, has remained stable.

France

General population: 57.9 million
Jewish population: 600,000

GENERAL BACKGROUND

In 1994, France continued to be governed by a right-wing coalition of the Gaullist Rassemblement pour la république (RPR, Rally for the Republic) and the centre-right Union pour la démocratie française (UDF, Union for French Democracy) which resoundingly defeated the ruling Parti socialiste (PS, Socialist Party) in the March 1993 general election. Michel Rocard, the leader of the PS, was replaced by Henri Emmanuelli after the party's poor showing in the June 1994 European elections (see below).

During 1994, public confidence was shaken by a number of financial scandals involving high-ranking politicians and leading industrialists. Three government ministers subsequently resigned their posts and, in December, the national assembly and senate approved a series of measures to control corruption in public life.

The RPR performed strongly in the cantonal elections in March, gaining 10 additional seats to win a total of 382, but the other mainstream parties suffered losses: the PS won 532 seats (a loss of 8), the UDF won 446 (a loss of 69) and the Parti communiste français (PCF, French Communist Party) won 145 (a loss of 8).

Protest votes were evident in elections to the European Parliament in June when the UDF-RPR list won 25.6 per cent of the vote, while the PS secured only 14.4 per cent. The newly-formed independent list of the anti-European conservative nationalist Philippe de Villiers won 12.3 per cent; the pro-European Energie Radicale (Radical Energy) list, headed by the former PS minister Bernard Tapie, won just over 12 per cent; and the far-right Front national won 10.5 per cent (see **Parties, Organizations, Movements**).

France's economic performance in 1994 continued to be affected by the European recession, with a rise in unemployment to over 12.5 per cent of the population in November (11.7 per cent in 1993). Despite the government's commitment to a "strong franc" policy, a climate of instability prevailed. A survey published in February by the Centre for the Study of Incomes and Costs concluded that half of the active population was in a situation of "economic and social fragility".

The trial of Paul Touvier heightened public debate over the role of the Vichy regime as did the controversy over President Mitterrand's wartime past (see **Mainstream Politics** and **Legal Matters**).

HISTORICAL LEGACY

The first Jews settled in what is now France during Roman times. Following the first crusades, their situation deteriorated: religious antisemitism and the royal desire to appropriate the wealth of the Jews led to a series of expulsions. With the integration of new lands into the realm, France "acquired" Jews together with its new territories (for example, Alsace and Lorraine). In the sixteenth century, Marranos (covert Jews) from Spain and Portugal found shelter in France.

While some called for the emancipation of the Jews, a trend within the eighteenth-century Enlightenment initiated a non-Christian tradition of antisemitism, making the Jews the symbol of the obscurantism and fanaticism of religion and equating them with financial power.

At the time of the French Revolution, the Jewish minority was highly stratified: the small group of former Marranos enjoyed a high level of culture and wealth and, being well integrated, increasingly resented the special status and limitations imposed on them. However, most of French Jewry, in the eastern part of the country, was very poor and subject to a virulent popular antisemitism. In 1791-2, French Jews were emancipated.

The nineteenth century brought new trends in antisemitism: the identification of the Jews with the harshness of industrial society;

xenophobia towards Jews coming from abroad (mainly Germany and, at the end of the century, the Russian empire); and the distrust of assimilated Jews. A new conservative nationalism developed, drawing on the ideas of race-science and "Aryan" mythology. In 1886, Edouard Drumont published *La France juive*, the first antisemitic "bestseller" in France, which raised the myth of the Jew to the status of an ideology.

The Dreyfus affair—the trial, conviction and subsequent exoneration of a Jewish captain falsely accused of spying for Germany in 1894—took place at a time of intense antisemitic agitation and seriously affected the position of assimilated French Jews. But it also led to the mobilization of forces committed to human rights, creating a polarization of opinion according to a pattern that was valid at least until the Second World War and perhaps even 1967.

The 1930s saw a wave of antisemitism nourished by the mass immigration of Jews from the East at a time of economic crisis, by the fears aroused by the rise of a Socialist government (led by a Jew) in 1936, and by Nazi propaganda.

The wartime Vichy government introduced anti-Jewish legislation and helped its administration to identify and arrest Jews. Some 74,000 Jews who were deported from France died in the concentration camps. After the war, the far right was reduced to tiny groups. In 1954, however, a wave of antisemitism marked the appointment of Pierre Mendès-France, a Jew, as prime minister. A new phase in antisemitism began in 1967: some felt that de Gaulle's remark in November 1967—that the Jews were "an élite people, sure of itself and domineering"—opened the gates to a new antisemitism. What is indisputable is that Israel's victory in the Six Day War and the subsequent anti-Zionist propaganda created a feeling of unease in the 1970s and 1980s.

In the past decade, attention has been focused on the advance of the Front national (FN, National Front), the growth of Holocaust denial and, in the last two years, concern has grown over communal tensions, particularly in suburban areas, between Jews and a tiny, but active, minority of militant Islamic youths of North-African origin.

RACISM AND XENOPHOBIA

The 1994 report of the Commission consultative nationale des Droits de l'Homme (CCNDH, National Consultative Commission on Human Rights), based on figures supplied by the interior ministry, highlighted the fact that racism was becoming part of everyday life in France. Although, the number of incidents of racist violence decreased from 38 in 1993 to 34 in 1994, there was one killing—the murder of a young man of North-African origin in August—in addition to 27 injuries. Racist incidents were particularly prevalent in the Paris area, the region of Provence-Alpes-Côte d'Azur (Marseilles and the South) and, to a lesser degree, Lorraine and Rhône-Alpes (Lyons). Arson attacks were targeted at mosques or Islamic prayer centres in Bonifacio, Creil, Nantes, Castelnaudary, Metz and Orange; a small incendiary device was found at an Islamic cultural centre in Rennes.

An opinion poll conducted for the CCNDH found that 77 per cent considered North Africans to be the principal victims of racism and 67 per cent thought that those of North-African origin born in France were also victims. Only 47 per cent, however, expressed sympathy for North Africans and 42 per cent indicated antipathy towards them. In contrast, 71 per cent expressed sympathy with (South-East) Asian immigrants and only 17 per cent antipathy.

Concerning measures to combat racism, 57 per cent considered the tighter control of clandestine immigration to be a solution. This option was ranked second, behind the banning of neo-Nazi groups but ahead of educational initiatives (54 per cent) and steps to help the integration of immigrants (29 per cent).

During 1994, governmental policies on immigration and policing contributed to a climate of uncertainty among foreign and immigrant communities. In February, foreign nationals from thirteen countries (Afghanistan, Armenia, Azerbaydzhan, Georgia, Iran, Iraq, Jordan, North Korea, Lebanon, Libya, Sudan, Syria and Yemen), as well as Palestinians, were ordered to obtain exit visas before leaving France. The action was reportedly aimed at curbing the illegal entry of immigrants who had acquired documents belonging to foreigners resident in France.

Relations between the police and minority groups were damaged by a series of violent confrontations in the crisis-ridden suburbs, which are home to sizeable immigrant populations. These incidents tended to follow large-scale intervention by the police to stop petty crime, and led to clashes in Rouen in January, Lyons and Toulon in April, Evreux in May and Manosque (Haute Provence) in December. In November, a further confrontation followed police interruption of a party in Amiens, being held by teenagers of *harki* origin (Algerians with French citizenship who supported France during the war of independence).

France's involvement in the political crisis in Algeria put further strains on domestic race relations. Following the assassinations of French officials in Algeria in August, arbitrary identity checks by police were increased in areas with sizeable immigrant populations, particularly those with black or North-African residents. Interior Minister Charles Pasqua also conducted a high-profile campaign to uncover militant Islamic networks. In December, the regulations were tightened for Algerians seeking to enter or to remain in France. While the authorities claimed that some Muslim community organizations were acting as fronts for terrorist activity, concern was expressed about the fanning of anti-Islamic sentiment.

The relationship between the secular French state and religious minorities remained problematic. Public debate continued over the 1989 decision by the highest administrative court that the wearing of head scarves by female Muslim students could violate a law prohibiting proselytizing in schools. On 20 September, the education minister, François Bayrou, issued a directive prohibiting the wearing of "ostentatious political and religious symbols" in schools. On 30 September, hundreds of pupils at a school in Goussainville, north of Paris, protested when four young Muslim women were banned from the school for wearing scarves. By the end of 1994, some seventy-nine young women had been excluded from state schools for refusing to remove their veils in school. As the authorities sought to enforce the secularist principles in schools, a degree of radicalization was evident within the Muslim community with increasing numbers of young Muslim women refusing to participate in physical education or biology classes for religious reasons.

This polarization of the authorities and religious groups is not restricted to the Muslim community: Jewish pupils' participation in Saturday classes is becoming an issue within the Jewish community. An administrative tribunal in Nice rejected the appeal of a Jewish pupil in post-secondary education who claimed that the principal of his school had acted unfairly in punishing him after he refused to sign a guarantee that he would attend classes on Saturday mornings. Invoking the principle of secularism in state schools, the tribunal stipulated that religious observance should not affect educational activities. The pupil subsequently appealed to the highest administrative court.

General hostility to the display of communal differences was evident in the answers to a question in the CCNDH poll concerning the wearing of veils by Muslim women. Only 8 per cent found it "natural" that young Muslim

women should be allowed to cover their heads in school, compared to 39 per cent in a previous poll published in the weekly *La Vie* in 1989; 89 per cent did not find it "natural" (53 per cent in 1989).

PARTIES, ORGANIZATIONS, MOVEMENTS

The leading far-right party in France, the Front national (FN, National Front), continued to denounce immigration and the European Union (EU) in 1994, but refrained from public expressions of antisemitism. The FN retained its position as one of Europe's most influential far-right parties, but faced competition from the conservative anti-EU movement of Philippe de Villiers and from the hardline immigration and law-and-order policies of Interior Minister Charles Pasqua.

The nomination by FN leader, Jean-Marie Le Pen, of Bruno Gollnisch, a professor of Japanese at the University of Lyons III, who has shown some sympathy for Holocaust-denial views, to the vice-presidency of the party, fanned internal tensions between the populist wing of the party embodied by Gollnisch and the technocratic faction of the party's deputy leader, Bruno Mégret.

The FN was further weakened in 1994 by a series of resignations, including that of Jacques Peyrat, the leading FN activist in Nice, who left the party in August after refusing to comply with conditions imposed by the party's central office. Prior to his resignation, Peyrat stood as the FN candidate in a parliamentary by-election in Nice in March, winning 43.5 per cent of the vote in the second round but losing to the city's RPR mayor, Jean-Paul Barety, who presented himself as an all-party anti-FN candidate and won 56.5 per cent. Two other FN representatives on the municipal council in Nice, Michel Moulin and Adrienne Franchi, subsequently resigned from the party in order to join Peyrat's new far-right movement, the Entente républicaine de Nice (Republican Alliance of Nice), in preparation for his bid for the mayoralty in 1995.

The FN contested 95 per cent of the cantonal seats which were up for election in March. Benefiting from a relatively low turn-out of 40.4 per cent, the party increased its overall share of the vote from 5.4 per cent in 1988 (the last time those particular seats were contested) to 9.8 per cent and performed particularly well in the Paris and Ile-de-France region, such as in the district of Seine-Saint-Denis, where it gained 18.3 per cent.

FN candidates reached the second round in 93 cantonal ballots, as opposed to only 13 in 1988. In Canisy (Manche) and Dreux-Ouest, the FN candidates were re-elected, and in Toulon-Six, the successful FN candidate benefited from the support of other right-wing groupings. In Mulhouse-Nord (Upper Rhine), however, the RPR called on voters to support the PS candidate in the second round. The FN candidacy of Philippe Poitrineau, a magistrate, in Cognin provoked criticism from the Syndicat de la magistrature (Bar Association).

In the June elections to the European Parliament, the FN saw its share of the vote drop from 12 per cent in 1989 to 10.5 per cent, but nevertheless won an extra seat, bringing its total to eleven. However, the loss of seats by Die Republikaner in Germany meant that the FN-led faction of far-right MEPs in the European Parliament, the Groupe technique de la droite européenne (DR, Technical Group of the European Right), no longer had sufficient members to qualify as an officially-funded grouping.

The annual demonstration organized by the FN in Paris to mark the festival of Joan of Arc in May was attended by 10,000 activists (5,000 according to the police). The theme of the demonstration was opposition to the Maastricht treaty on European union. At the annual Bleu-Blanc-Rouge (Blue, White, Red) festival on 18 September, attended by 5,000-10,000 far-right activists, Le Pen announced his candidacy for the 1995 presidential elections and his plan to establish a sixth republic with a new constitution that would enshrine the principle of proportional representation. (A change to the first-past-the-post electoral system meant that the FN failed to win any seats in the national assembly in the 1993 legislative elections, despite winning 12.5 per cent of the vote.) He also stated that he "had never believed that Marshall Pétain [the head of the Vichy regime] had been a traitor". Le Pen subsequently declared that his presidential campaign theme would be the struggle against corruption. In October, some 200 FN supporters joined Le Pen to show support for the death penalty.

The FN continued to promote the Front national de la jeunesse (FNJ, National Youth Front) and Renouveau étudiant (RE, Student Renewal), its youth and student affiliates. In 1994, RE joined with the extremist Union et défense des étudiants d'Assas (UDEA, Union for the Defence of Assas Students) to form the Collectif nationaliste étudiant (National Student Collective) in order to contest university elections, but lost all four of its seats and is no longer represented.

There were numerous extreme-right movements active in France in 1994, but their influence on public opinion remained negligible. No precise membership figures were available but in most cases they did not exceed a few hundred.

The main neo-Nazi organization in France, the Parti nationaliste français et européen (PNFE, French and European Nationalist Party) remained active in 1994 but experienced a split at the beginning of the year when its treasurer, Marc Nicoud, withdrew party funds and leading activist Michel Faci was expelled. Despite the merger in 1993 with the Faisceaux nationalistes européens (European Nationalist Fascists), membership of the PNFE reportedly fell to less than 100.

The PNFE leader, Claude Cornilleau, continued to promote the organization as the main French neo-Nazi contact with Gary Lauck's Nationalsozialistische Deutsche Arbeiterpartei/ Auslands- und Aufbauorganisation (NSDAP/ AO, German National Socialist Workers' Party/Overseas Section) in the US (see **United States**). Cornilleau has made regular appearances at the annual rally of the British National Party (see **United Kingdom**).

Three members of L'Oeuvre française (OF, French Work), the ultra-nationalist, antisemitic organization founded in 1968, were arrested at the end of 1993 in connection with a planned attack on Patrick Gaubert, the government official with responsibility for anti-racism. OF's publication, *Jeune Nation*, continued to appear in 1994.

In July, a split within the Alliance Populaire (Popular Alliance), itself a splinter group of the FNJ, led to the formation of a new far-right group called the Alliance Nationale (National Alliance).

Among revolutionary nationalists, or "third positionists", Nouvelle résistance (New Resistance), led by Christian Bouchet, is strongly anti-American (it has campaigned against MacDonalds and EuroDisney). In 1994, it hosted an international meeting of third positionists which provided further evidence of the so-called "red-brown" coalitions (the making of common cause between neo-fascists and hardline communists) developing in France. Speakers were invited from various far-right organizations and publications including: Third Way, *Scorpion* and *Perspective* from the UK; *Orion* from Italy; *Tribuna de Europa* from Spain; *Vouloir* from Belgium; and *Elementi* from Russia (see **Italy** and **Russia**). Nouvelle résistance defines itself as a "European nationalist" organization and has pledged support to the Corsican and Basque separatist movements. Pro-Arab, it has links with George Habash's Popular Front for the Liberation of Palestine and the UK-based Islamic Council for the Defence of Europe.

Nouvelle Droite (New Right) intellectual organizations, such as the Groupement de recherche et d'études pour la civilisation européenne (GRECE, Group for the Research and Study of European Civilization), maintained a relatively low profile in 1994. *Krisis*, the publication of Alain de Benoist, a former leading member of GRECE, did not appear in 1994. In recent years, de Benoist has pursued a "red-brown" strategy, promoting dialogue between the anti-liberal, anti-American far left and far right.

Skinheads continued their activities in 1994 and, according to the CCNDH, were responsible for just over a third of the violent racist incidents, compared to almost a half in 1993. However, although the number of incidents of skinhead violence decreased, those that did occur were of an increased severity. In August, a young man of North-African origin was attacked by skinheads in Le Havre and four skinheads were arrested after a tear-gas attack on Turkish immigrants in Saverne (Alsace) in November.

Contact continued between the FN's youth and student affiliates, the FNJ and RE, and smaller ultra-nationalist and skinhead groups. Jeunesses nationalistes révolutionnaires (JNR, Nationalist Revolutionary Youth), a skinhead group led by Serge Ayoub, participated in the FN-organized Joan of Arc Festival. Also represented at the march were the FNJ, RE, and UDEA, which was formerly a branch of the Groupe-Union-Défense (GUD, Union Defence Group) at the law faculty of the University of Paris II. The UDEA is far-right group, close to the ideology of the FN, but employing direct-action tactics.

On 8 May, hundreds of far-right activists defied a police ban in order to stage a rally in Paris to protest "fifty years of American imperialism". The rally brought together the UDEA, FNJ, RE and JNR. Following violent clashes with the police, 107 far-right activists were arrested. One of the demonstrators, Sébastien Deyzieu, who had been associated with OF, fell off a roof while escaping from the police and died the following day. In protest at his death, sixty members of GUD/UDEA raided a popular radio station, held two presenters hostage and remained on air long enough to broadcast racist slogans.

A loose network, known as the Comité du 9 mai (Committee of 9 May), was set up in the offices of the FN by the FNJ, GUD/UDEA, JNR, RE and OF. It organized a rally on 16 May which attracted approximately 600 activists, including some thirty FN regional councillors from the Ile-de-France. During this demonstration,

several members of the JNR were arrested, Serge Ayoub amongst them. Darklord, the shop belonging to Ayoub, which served as a meeting-place for skinheads, was subsequently closed down by the authorities.

The GUD/UDEA was responsible for violence on the Saint Hippolyte campus of the University of Paris in mid-December in which two students were injured.

MAINSTREAM POLITICS

There were no antisemitic references made by mainstream political parties or politicians in 1994. However, the public debate over French policies during the Vichy period was heightened by the publication in September of Pierre Péan's book, *Une jeunesse française: François Mitterrand 1934-47* (A French youth: François Mitterrand 1934-47), with which the president had co-operated, which revealed that he had been more supportive of Pétain's ideology during his employment as a civil servant in the Vichy regime than was previously thought and confirmed his links with René Bousquet, the former secretary-general of the Vichy police who was being prosecuted for crimes against humanity until his assassination in 1993. During a television interview on 12 September, Mitterrand claimed that he had been unaware of the Vichy regime's anti-Jewish laws and that, in any case, they had been directed against "foreign Jews". He acknowledged in the interview that he had intervened personally in order to delay the prosecution of alleged former collaborators in the interests of national reconciliation.

The disclosures of the book and the television interview did not provoke the degree of controversy that might have been expected, probably due to the poor state of the president's health, and Mitterrand found an unusual ally in the press close to the FN which supported him whole-heartedly. However, the disclosures contributed to a degree of uneasiness concerning Mitterrand's participation in the various celebrations and commemorations marking the fiftieth anniversary of the liberation of France.

In May, the mayors of two Normandy villages were present at the D-Day commemorations of Waffen SS veterans. The mayor of the village of Maizet subsequently apologized but the mayor of Esquay explained that such ceremonies had taken place frequently since 1984.

MANIFESTATIONS

Antisemitic activity in France is recorded by the CCNDH, which, using figures supplied by the interior ministry, counts only those incidents that were the subject of an official complaint or police report. In addition, the Jewish community's Centre de recherche et de documentation sur l'antisémitisme (CRDA, Centre for the Research and Documentation of Antisemitism) records all incidents brought to its attention although its monitoring work is concentrated primarily in the Paris region. As in previous years, there was some disparity between the figures for antisemitic manifestations quoted in the CCNDH's report and those of the Jewish community. Nevertheless, both sets of statistics indicated a rise in the number of antisemitic acts committed by Muslim or Arab circles and showed that the level of antisemitic activity emanating from the far right had remained constant.

According to the CCNDH's report, there were 143 antisemitic acts in 1994, in contrast to 164 in 1993 and 109 in 1992. These figures were compiled according to a modified set of criteria which place more emphasis on judicial inquiries to establish the motive of attacks. According to the CRDA, there were 159 "hostile acts" against Jews in the Paris region alone, an increase from 135 in 1993 and 105 in 1992. The majority of "hostile acts" involved propaganda, including the daubing of graffiti and the dissemination of antisemitic mailings.

The CCNDH reported 19 acts of violence against Jews in 1994, of which 8 were attributed to Muslim or Arab circles and 11 to the far right. In contrast, of the 20 violent acts recorded in 1993, 4 were attributed to Muslims or Arabs and 16 to the far right. The Jewish community recorded 36 acts of violence in the Paris region alone in 1994, compared to 24 in 1993 and 14 in 1992. The main reason for such a discrepancy between the two sources is probably their different methods of recording incidents.

According to the CCNDH, the geographical distribution of antisemitic incidents was uneven. Four areas were particularly affected: the Paris and Ile-de-France region accounted for over half of the cases of threatening behaviour, with 74 incidents and 9 cases of violent acts (63 and 8 in 1993); Provence-Alpes-Côte d'Azur, where there were 19 incidents of threatening behaviour and 3 acts of violence (9 and 2 in 1993); the Rhône-Alpes region, with 9 examples of threatening behaviour and 5 incidents of violence (16 and 1 in 1993); and Lorraine, where 11 threats were recorded but no violent acts (13 and 3 in 1993).

A wave of antisemitic incidents in February and March, including stone-throwing, telephone threats and daubings, was considered to have occurred in response to the massacre of Muslims by a Jewish settler in a Hebron

mosque (see **Effects of Anti-Zionism**). There was a second peak of antisemitic activity in the autumn around the time of the Jewish high holidays.

Most attacks were targeted at Jewish property. For instance, the community centre and synagogue in Garges-les-Gonesses was vandalized and broken into at least seven times during the year. Antisemitic slogans were also daubed on synagogues in Altkirch and Wasselone.

The phenomenon of cemetery desecration, both Jewish and Christian, continued in 1994, reflecting a trend that has been on the rise since the widely-publicized 1990 desecration of a Jewish cemetery in Carpentras in the south of the country. Most of the 1994 desecrations of Jewish cemeteries took place in Alsace-Lorraine. In March, the Jewish cemetery at Moyeuvre-Grande was vandalized. Two groups of teenagers were arrested in April following the desecration of two other Jewish cemeteries in Alsace-Lorraine: in Struth, fifteen headstones were broken and forty monuments overturned, and in Merzwiller, twelve headstones were broken. Police investigations suggested that the young vandals were not necessarily motivated by antisemitism. Over 100 headstones were overturned at the cemetery in Fegersheim, near Strasbourg, in August. The cemetery at Champigny in suburban Paris was also desecrated during 1994.

The memorial on the site of the former Drancy camp outside Paris, where Jews were rounded up before deportation during the Nazi occupation, was vandalized on 20 October, three days before a ceremony to commemorate the anniversary of the last convoy of 200 children. Vandals twice desecrated plaques commemorating the killing of seven Jews ordered by Paul Touvier in Rillieux-la-Pape (see **Legal Matters**). In May, the plaque was smashed and Interior Minister Charles Pasqua subsequently unveiled three new plaques on 28 June, but these were daubed with swastikas and antisemitic graffiti in July.

In January, a leaflet featuring antisemitic cartoons and the slogan "L'Argent=le sang des Juifs" (Money=The Blood of Jews), was sent to at least thirty Jewish organizations in Paris by the GUD/UDEA. In the same month, the coincidence of a public lecture on the Holocaust with a gathering of far-right activists at the Sorbonne led to verbal abuse and scuffles.

In April, a Jewish shopkeeper in Villeurbanne, outside Lyons, was assaulted by far-right activists who left stickers bearing the name of the neo-Nazi NSDAP/AO.

Insults and stones were thrown at Jews attending synagogues in Bobigny in March,

September and October, in Pantin in November and in Noisy le-Sec in December.

EDUCATION

Some controversy arose at the University of Nantes when students sitting a psychopathology examination were asked to provide clinical and sociological answers to the question: "Pour quelles raisons à votre avis, les juifs de divers pays, et dans leur majorité, ont accueilli la déportation en 1939 et 1942 comme un fait inéluctable?" (For what reasons, in your opinion, did the majority of Jews of different countries regard deportation in 1939 and 1942 as inevitable?). The exam was cancelled and the teacher who set the question was reprimanded.

While not necessarily indicative of antisemitism, there was some unease concerning the vote (for a second time) by the University of Humanities in Strasbourg against being named after Marc Bloch, a renowned historian who was arrested and shot by the Gestapo as a partisan in June 1944. An anonymous leaflet circulated before the vote questioned whether "it was really appropriate that, today, a university located on the Rhine should name itself after a man who was tortured and murdered by the German occupiers . . . this is almost a provocation."

GRASSROOTS

A member of the Cercle de l'union, a private club in Lyons with 400 members, resigned in March, in protest at its systematic refusal to accept applications from Jewish candidates.

PUBLICATIONS AND MEDIA

According to Les Droites nationales et radicales en France, a book by Jean-Yves Camus and René Monzat which was published in 1992, there were approximately 87 periodicals expressing FN views, 72 Catholic fundamentalist publications, 5 denying the Holocaust, 18 of the neo-Nazi trend, 17 Nouvelle Droite, 7 defending the memory of Marshall Pétain, 23 Maurassian (far-right royalist), 14 revolutionary-nationalist and 5 skinhead magazines. Many of these antisemitic periodicals have only local circulations and/or are published irregularly.

While these figures referred to the early 1990s, the number of periodicals available is not thought to have changed dramatically since then. However, there were a few significant changes to the range of antisemitic publications in 1994. Two Maurassian journals, Réaction and Vu de France, ceased publication and the satirical monthly, Pas d'panique à bord, went out

of circulation in June but was re-launched in November.

National-Hebdo, which has close links with the FN, celebrated its 500th edition in February. A new editorial team led by Martin Peltier included François Brigneau, Jean Mabire and Dr Perenna. Présent, a Catholic fundamentalist daily which supports the FN, celebrated its 3,000th issue in 1994. In October it launched a new supplement aimed at younger readers, called Présent Jeunesse. FN deputy leader Bruno Mégret financed a new far-right daily through his Carnix network which was regarded as a rival to Présent. It first appeared in October, initially called Le Peuple, but was subsequently renamed Le Français.

Also new in 1994 was a publishing company named Première Ligne, whose editor-in-chief, Christian Durante, was previously associated with La Lettre de Magazine Hebdo.

Two new skinhead fanzines, Terreur d'élite and Vaincre, appeared in 1994. These viciously racist and antisemitic publications included articles by members of the American neo-Nazi group, The Order (see **United States**).

A second-hand book stall in Paris was found to be selling a copy of Mein Kampf inscribed by Hitler as well as other publications prohibited by the legislation against Holocaust denial. The neo-Nazi text, Les Damnés de la terre (The Damned of the Earth) by Alexis Arette, a FN regional councillor and director of L'Action rurale de France (Rural Action of France), was seized in police raids in Paris.

The centenary of the birth of the antisemitic writer Louis-Ferdinand Céline was marked by several far-right organizations. The journal, Bulletin célinien, edited by Marc Laudelout, organized a commemorative meeting in Paris in April.

During the annual Bleu-Blanc-Rouge festival in Paris in September, several far-right publications glorifying Marshall Pétain were displayed as well as a number of antisemitic pamphlets, including Les Beaux draps (The Beautiful Sheets) and Bagatelles pour un massacre (Bagatelles for a Massacre) by Céline, Refaire la France (Remaking France) by Jacques Doriot, Hitler et moi (Hitler and I) by Abel Bonnard, Les mémoires d'un fasciste (Memoirs of a Fascist) by Lucien Rebatet, and a commemorative album dedicated to the veteran Belgian Nazi who died in 1994, Léon Degrelle et la légion de Wallonie, 1941-45 (Léon Degrelle and the Walloon Legion, 1941-45).

RELIGION

A permanent strain of antisemitism emanates from the Catholic fundamentalist movement through the circulation of the works of the late Monsignor Lefebvre, the pre-Vatican II arch-traditionalist. However, these elements maintained a low profile in 1994.

The only manifestation of religious antisemitism within the Christian churches during the year was the dissemination of 100,000 copies of the French version of the *Bible des communautés chrétiennes* (Bible of Christian Communities), published by the Madrid-based International Catholic Bible Society in 1994 (see **Spain**). A number of Jewish groups complained that this "popular language" translation, by French missionaries Bernard and Louis Herrault, included many antisemitic references and the controversy looked set to continue into 1995.

Islamist groups (more commonly known as Islamic fundamentalists) also regularly display a hatred of Jews of a kind which goes beyond political anti-Zionism or anti-Israel activity and which must legitimately be described as antisemitism. While the lack of primary sources available in French make it difficult to obtain a clear picture of the situation, there are developments which suggest the spread of Islamist propaganda.

A number of welfare associations have emerged in urban areas with a sizeable concentration of immigrant populations of North-African origin where the social and economic problems of integration, housing, employment and drugs are prevalent. Such associations are organized largely by committed Islamists and one effect has been to promote a growing attraction towards ultra-orthodox Islamic practice and belief, no doubt in response to the misery of deprivation.

There are also a number of cells in the country which support the Algerian Front islamique du salut (FIS, Islamic Salvation Front) and the Groupe islamique armé (GIA, Armed Islamic Group) (see **Algeria**), as well as Hamas, the Palestinian Islamic resistance movement. While some police raids on such cells during the year led to the discovery of weapons and plans for terrorist attacks, the activities of the Algerian groups are primarily directed at French, rather than Jewish or Israeli, targets because of the government's support for the Algerian regime with which they are in conflict, as was evident in the hijacking of an Air France plane in Algeria on 24 December. Nevertheless, there were antisemitic incidents during the year emanating from Islamist sources (see **Effects of Anti-Zionism**).

It is important to emphasize the fact that, while there are clear reasons for disquiet about future developments, it would be wrong to suppose that the Muslim community in general is

influenced by fundamentalist rhetoric. Islamism offers some individuals a way of responding to a crisis of a more or less personal kind. Moreover, some of the measures adopted by the interior ministry to counter Islamist extremism have affected Muslims in general and may have fanned anti-Muslim prejudice, despite the facts that few Islamist supporters actually resort to terrorism and Islamists represent a minority of the Muslim community, albeit a vocal and growing one (see **Racism and Xenophobia**).

DENIAL OF THE HOLOCAUST

The year 1994 saw a significant decrease in public expressions of Holocaust denial although they continued to appear among far-right publications. This decline has been attributed by some commentators to three factors: the financial difficulties of the groups involved in the dissemination of Holocaust-denial material, a decreasing public interest in the subject and the dominance of commemorations of France's liberation in 1944, although the latter provided some far-right elements with the opportunity to comment on the Holocaust.

Commenting on the trial of Paul Touvier, many far-right publications questioned the facts of the Holocaust and the role of the Vichy regime in persecuting Jews (see **Legal Matters**). The Maurassian weekly, *Rivarol*, continued to promote the work of French Holocaust-denier Robert Faurisson.

Jean-Dominique Larrieu, alias Bertrand Leforestier or André Chelain, distributed a booklet entitled *Revue d'histoire non-conformiste* (Nonconformist Historical Review), which contained the works of veteran Nazi, Léon Degrelle. The booklet attempted to circumvent the law prohibiting Holocaust denial by carrying a "disclaimer" inviting readers to differentiate "between truth and lies" (see also **Legal Matters**).

L'Holocauste au scanner (The Holocaust under the Scanner), a work by the Swiss Holocaust-denier, Jürgen Graf, which is dedicated to Robert Faurisson, was sent to approximately thirty deputies and several Jewish organizations in July (see **Switzerland**).

Frustrated by the restrictions placed on the publication of Holocaust-denial propaganda by the Gayssot law of 1990, some Holocaust-deniers have attempted to organize a defence through associations, such as Mémoire et Histoire, which is presided over by Phillipe Costa, who was president of the Association nationale des internés victimes de la loi Gayssot (ANIV, National Association for the Prisoners and Victims of the Gayssot Law) until it was banned (see also **Legal Matters**).

EFFECTS OF ANTI-ZIONISM

There was an upsurge in antisemitic incidents in February and March following the massacre of Muslims by a Jewish settler at a Hebron mosque. Several threatening telephone calls were made to Jewish institutions in Paris, Lyons and Marseilles. Stones were thrown at Jews leaving synagogues in Paris at Epinay-sur-Seine, La Courneuve, Levallois-Perret and Garges-les-Gonesses, and in the Lyons suburb of Les Minguettes. Molotov cocktails, bricks or stones were thrown at several synagogues, including those in Aulnay-sous-Bois and Villiers-Le-Bel in Paris, and Vénissieux and Vaulx-en-Velin in Lyons. Bullets were fired at the ORT school in Marseilles. In most of these cases, the perpetrators were not found but, in Argenteuil and Villiers-Le-Bel, young men of North-African origin were arrested. The synagogue and community centre of Sarcelles was sprayed with the slogan "Juifs, Palestine vaincra" (Jews, Palestine will triumph). Graffiti showing a Star of David dripping with blood and slogans calling for revenge after the Hebron massacre were daubed on shops in the Paris suburb of La Défense in March. A group of French youths of North-African origin were subsequently arrested. Also in March, a Jewish child wearing a skull-cap was attacked by six North-African youths in Marseilles.

Anti-Zionist and antisemitic graffiti were also sprayed on several shops owned by Jews in La Défense in April. Stones were thrown at the synagogue in Créteil in July by youths of North-African origin.

In November, Islamist graffiti, including some bearing the name of the FIS, were daubed in Arabic and French at the community centre and synagogue in Garges-les-Gonesses in Paris, where ten rooms were ransacked and the holy ark was damaged.

In December, a serious incident was averted in Lyons when a car packed with explosives was found outside a small synagogue. Islamist extremists were suspected to be behind the attempted attack.

Police operations led to the discovery of weapons and plans for terrorist attacks on Israeli targets within France. Police raids in Paris and Calais in April led to the detention of ninety-five suspected Islamist activists belonging to the GIA. Police also arrested Islamists in southern France who were planning a joint operation with the Palestinian Islamist group, Hamas (Islamic Resistance Movement), against Jewish targets in Spain (see **Spain**).

OPINION POLLS

Three 1994 polls gave an insight into French opinion on issues of Jewish concern.

Attitudes towards the role of the Vichy regime and the trial of Paul Touvier (see **Legal Matters**) were revealed by a survey, conducted in March by the Harris organization for *Globe* magazine amongst 1,002 adults. Thirty-three per cent of respondents believed it was "useless to try former Nazi collaborators or members of the Vichy militia" for crimes committed during the Second World War; 54 per cent considered that the Vichy regime had acted in concert with the Nazis; 19 per cent thought that Vichy had tried to limit the number of victims; and 27 per cent abstained from answering. According to another survey, carried out in April by CSA for the Catholic daily *La Croix* amongst 1,003 people, 52 per cent of practising Catholics did not believe that Touvier should have been tried.

A Sofres poll for *Le Monde* on attitudes to the ideas of Jean-Marie Le Pen, showed that 79 per cent disagreed with Le Pen, compared to 65 per cent in 1991; 73 per cent considered him a "danger to democracy" (66 per cent in 1993); 87 per cent considered the FN to be "racist"; 86 per cent "sectarian" and 86 per cent "unable to govern".

LEGAL MATTERS

Paul Touvier, former director of the Vichy Milice, the pro-Nazi militia, in Lyons was found guilty of crimes against humanity and sentenced on 20 April to life imprisonment. He was prosecuted for ordering the executions on 29 June 1944 of seven Jewish hostages at Rillieux-la-Pape in reprisal for the murder by the French resistance of the Vichy propaganda minister, Phillipe Henriot.

The Touvier trial was the first time that a French citizen was prosecuted for crimes against humanity, a charge introduced into the legal code in 1974, which is not covered by a statute of limitations. The trial highlighted the role of the Catholic church, which had helped to hide Touvier for over four decades. Touvier had been sentenced to death twice for war crimes in 1946 and 1947 but had managed to evade arrest. In 1972, at the behest of church officials, he was pardoned by President Pompidou. Following a public outcry, he went into hiding again until he was discovered in a priory near Nice in 1989 and charged with crimes against humanity.

However, the Touvier trial was not the trial of French collaboration that some hoped it might be. In part, this was because the court defined crimes against humanity as those committed in the service of a totalitarian regime, thus obliging most of the lawyers involved in the case to stress the linkage between the Milice and the Gestapo rather than its specific role in

France. Moreover, Touvier was a middle-ranking official who used the occupation as an opportunity to express his personal sadism and antisemitism. As a mere member of the Milice, Touvier could not become the central figure in a symbolic trial of Vichy France, its responsibilities and its legacy.

Nevertheless, the Touvier trial increased public pressure for Maurice Papon to stand trial for crimes against humanity. The eighty-three-year-old Papon is accused of sending 1,690 Jews, including 223 children, to concentration camps while he was a civil servant in Bordeaux. After the war, he became chief of police under Charles de Gaulle and subsequently budget minister under Giscard d'Estaing.

The Bordeaux court of appeal ruled in June to postpone a libel case brought by Maurice Papon against the lawyer, Gerard Boulanger, author of *Maurice Papon: un bureaucrate français* (Maurice Papon: A French Bureaucrat).

In 1994, the file concerning former Nazi, Alois Brunner, who was believed to be hiding in Syria, was passed to the public prosecutor. A warrant for Brunner's arrest for ordering the deportation of French Jews in 1943 and 1944 was issued in 1988.

In March, parliament amended the penal code to increase prison terms and fines for persons found guilty of discriminating on the basis of race, origin, religion or appearance, or of desecrating grave sites of a specific ethnic, religious, national or racial group. The amendments also make organizations, as well as individuals, liable to charges of discrimination and broaden the definition of crimes against humanity.

Some legal action was also taken against the far-right press. In April, Camille-Claire Galic (a pseudonym for Marie-Luce Wacquez), the director of the far-right publication, *Rivarol*, and Françoise Pichard, known as Chard, were fined Fr15,000 for an antisemitic caricature published in November 1992. However, the cartoonist, Aramis, was not prosecuted for defamation for publishing a caricature which portrayed former Prime Minister Laurent Fabius, who has Jewish origins, as a vampire on the cover of *Minute* in November 1992.

There were several prosecutions for Holocaust denial. Jean-Dominique Larrieu, former director of the far-right book shop Ogmios (which is now closed), was fined Fr30,000 in March for Holocaust denial after publishing *Non-lieu pour Paul Touvier* (No Case against Paul Touvier) under a pseudonym, André Chelain. Larrieu was also ordered to pay Fr2,000 damages to four organizations of former deportees.

Jean-Luc Lundi, the owner of the Ulysses book shop in Bordeaux, was convicted in July of selling Holocaust-denial materials, such as the *Revue d'Histoire Révisionniste* and *Annales d'Histoire Révisionniste*. Lundi was sentenced to six months in prison plus a six-month suspended sentence and fined Fr20,000.

However, in two other cases, prosecutions for Holocaust denial were reversed or unsuccessful. A Paris court of appeal ruled in January that the former ANIV president, Phillipe Costa, prosecuted for distributing leaflets promoting the writings of Robert Faurisson in Nancy, Metz and Fontainebleau, had been the victim of a mistrial.

In March, Alain Guyonnet, editor of the Holocaust-denial journal, *Revision*, was acquitted of "denial of crimes against humanity". Guyonnet, who had previously been convicted of Holocaust denial and incitement to racial hatred, had published an article entitled "Auschwitz: 125,000 deaths". The public prosecution, together with the Ligue internationale contre racisme et antisémitisme (LICRA, International League Against Racism and Antisemitism) appealed against the ruling. On 15 September, the Paris court of appeal upheld the judgement, and ruled that understating the number of victims of the Holocaust did not constitute a questioning of the crimes against humanity.

The sale of neo-Nazi publications by post was prohibited in July when an order was issued against Société européenne de distributions Cornilleau et Cie, the company owned by PNFE leader Claude Cornilleau.

A court in Poitiers sentenced Laurent Jacquillard to three months' imprisonment and fined him Fr4,000 for carrying a weapon and wearing the uniform of a criminal organization, after he was arrested wearing the uniform of the Waffen SS in August 1993.

In January, Serge Ayoub of the JNR and three others were given suspended prison sentences and fined Fr120,000 for an attack on North Africans at a football match in 1990. Marc Georges, an FN candidate in legislative and district elections, was sentenced in April to eighteen months' imprisonment for violent offences, after he was found guilty of being an accomplice to the shooting of three young men whilst fly-posting.

COUNTERING ANTISEMITISM

As in previous years, most attempts to mobilize opinion concerned racism and xenophobia in general, rather than antisemitism, due to the fact that such phenomena were much more visible than specifically antisemitic manifestations.

There were also a number of anti-FN protests and demonstrations against the laws on immigration, citizenship and identity controls which were introduced by Interior Minister Charles Pasqua in 1993.

On 5 January, there were several rallies against the new immigration, citizenship and identity controls: 15,000 and 20,000 people demonstrated in Paris, 2,000 in Rouen and 1,000 in Lyons. On 6 February, 12,000-15,000 people in Paris protested the Pasqua laws.

In March, 200 people attended a demonstration, organized by the socialists, communists and greens, in favour of changing the name of Rue Alexis Carrel (Alexis Carrel Street), on the grounds that Carrel had espoused eugenic theories in the 1930s. Their protest was unsuccessful.

In April, President Mitterrand opened a museum in Izieu near Lyons to commemorate the deportation of forty-four Jewish children to concentration camps. In November, as part of the commemorations of the fiftieth anniversary of the liberation of Strasbourg, the president inaugurated a memorial on the site of the city's former synagogue, which was burned down in September 1940. Following a series of attacks by vandals in July, Interior Minister Pasqua unveiled three new plaques to commemorate the seven Jews murdered on the orders of Paul Touvier in Rillieux-la-Pape.

The Union des étudiants juifs de France (Union of Jewish Students of France) held a small protest outside the home of Maurice Papon on 15 July in Paris, the day before the national day of commemoration for the crimes of Vichy, to demand the rapid processing of Papon's file (see **Legal Matters**).

In February, a protest against a FN meeting to be addressed by Bruno Gollnisch in Rennes led to scuffles. In April, 150 demonstrated against Jean-Marie Le Pen in Caens. In October, Jean-Paul Barety, the mayor of Nice and a RPR MP, refused to allow the FN use of the congress hall in Nice. Some 150 anti-racist demonstrators delayed Le Pen's departure from the French island of Réunion in December.

France removed antisemitic Arabic textbooks from the curriculum of the French-language school in Abu Dhabi. The books, which included references to Jews as "bastards of humanity", were supplied to the school by the education ministry of the United Arab Emirates (see **Gulf States**).

The mayor of Drancy, Maurice Niles, and other local officials condemned the October attack on the memorial to the former concentration camp at Drancy.

The centenary of the Dreyfus affair was marked by the publication of several articles recalling the events (see **Historical Legacy**). A statue located near the site of the prison in which Dreyfus was first incarcerated was unveiled in October after a six-year search for a suitable location. Defence Minister François Léotard dismissed Paul Gaujac, a retired colonel and head of the Service historique de l'armée de terre, the military historical archives, for casting doubt on the innocence of Alfred Dreyfus in an article published in February. Gaujac described Dreyfus's innocence as "the thesis generally accepted by historians".

ASSESSMENT

In a climate of domestic socio-economic instability, with much public attention focused on international events in Algeria, Bosnia and Rwanda, antisemitism was not considered a central issue of French life in 1994, particularly when compared to racism and xenophobia. As reports of a growing mood of racism on France's streets increased, the North-African immigrant population was the main focus of hostility.

A large and significant constituency for the far right remained despite the internal disputes of the Front national in 1994, a fact underlined by the success of the new political group centred around Philippe de Villiers. Preparations for Le Pen's presidential candidacy in 1995 offered an opportunity for the FN to reassemble its forces.

The absence of a major antisemitic incident of the kind seen in previous years kept antisemitism off the political agenda. However, the revelations of the extent of President Mitterrand's involvement with the Vichy regime and the trial of Paul Touvier both served as uneasy reminders of the legacy of antisemitism in France.

There was no decline in the number of antisemitic attacks perpetrated by the far right and a worrying trend was the growing number of incidents, mostly near synagogues, involving young men of North-African Muslim origin. This suggested that community relations within France could be influenced by developments in the Middle East, such as the Hebron massacre, and by the rising appeal of Islamism amongst unemployed and marginalized groups in the suburban ghettos.

Georgia

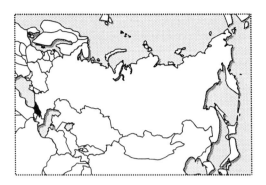

General population: 5.5 million
Jewish population: 13,000 (mainly in Tbilisi)

GENERAL BACKGROUND

Georgia is a former Soviet republic. Following multi-party parliamentary elections in 1992, Eduard Shevardnadze became head of state. Internal conflicts and the disruption of trade links with the other republics of the former Soviet Union have left Georgia's economy in ruins. The government's anti-crime campaign reduced much of the random violent crime in Tbilisi, the capital. However, corruption on the part of law enforcement officials and police brutality were pervasive.

HISTORICAL LEGACY

Jews settled in what is now Georgia in biblical times. There is no tradition of antisemitism: on the contrary, Georgian-Jewish relations have traditionally been very good.

MANIFESTATIONS

The desecration of gravestones in a Jewish cemetery in the Ortachala district of Tbilisi on 30 January was condemned by Eduard Shevardnadze as "barbaric" and "alien to the many centuries of the history of Jewish-Georgian relations". He announced that the cabinet would assist the implementation of a project for the maintenance and protection of Jewish monuments in Georgia.

ASSESSMENT

In a period of considerable political instability, relations between Georgians and the small Jewish population remained good. The desecration of the Jewish cemetery in Tbilisi in January does not appear to have been part of any pattern of antisemitic agitation.

Germany

General population: 80.6 million
Jewish population: 60,000-70,000 (including
20,000-30,000 outside the community,
amongst them immigrants from the former Soviet Union and Israeli citizens)

GENERAL BACKGROUND

Political life in Germany in 1994 was shaped by
continuous electioneering: nine state (*Land*)
elections, the general election, elections to the
European Parliament and several local elections. In eight of the nine state elections, voters
re-elected the ruling parties. The general
election in October was again won by the
ruling parliamentary coalition—the Christlich
Demokratische Union (CDU, Christian Democratic Union), the Christlich Soziale Union
(CSU, Christian Social Union, the Bavarian sister party of the CDU) and the Freie
Demokratische Partei (FDP, Free Democratic
Party) which won 34.2 per cent, 7.3 per cent and
6.9 per cent of the vote respectively, despite
heavy losses. The Sozialdemokratische Partei
Deutschlands (SPD, German Social Democratic Party) won 36.4 per cent of the vote and
was able to reinforce its stronghold in the
Länder and thus in the German Bundesrat (federal council, the upper chamber of parliament).
   The Partei des Demokratischen Sozialismus (PDS, Party of Democratic Socialism),
the successor party to the communist
Sozialistische Einheitspartei Deutschlands (SED,
Socialist Unity Party of Germany), addressed
the dissatisfaction of many East Germans regarding their social and economic situation,
with the result that it became the third most influential party in the new states, establishing itself, with 16-19 per cent of the vote, firmly on
the national political stage. It even gained seats
in parliament with 4.4 per cent of the vote, since
it was able to win four direct mandates in East
Berlin.
   Amongst the losers in the elections (parties
that were unable to clear the 5 per cent barrier), apart from the far-right parties—
Die Republikaner (REP, The Republicans),
Deutsche Volksunion (DVU, German People's
Union) and Nationaldemokratische Partei
Deutschlands (NPD, German National Democratic Party) (see **Parties, Organizations,
Movements**)—was the FDP. It only just managed to secure seats in the Bundestag (federal
parliament) with a loss of 4.1 per cent on 1990.
Earlier predictions that the REP would cross
the 5 per cent threshold proved unfounded.

   In May, Roman Herzog, the former president of the supreme court and the CDU/CSU
candidate for federal president, was elected to
the post succeeding Richard von Weizsäcker.
The CDU had previously withdrawn its first
candidate, Steffen Heitmann, following serious
public controversy surrounding his declaration
that he did not believe that Germany had "a
special role until the end of history . . . for the
organized death of millions of Jews". In interviews with the press, Herzog expressed the
view that "Germany must always be ready to
draw conclusions from the hideousness of the
[Nazi] extermination of Jews and other minorities". Herzog further called on Germany's judicial system to "deal head on" with the far right
and said he had little use for nationalism.
   The economy began to recover after the
first months of the year. Gross national product
increased by 2.8 per cent, although the cost of
necessary structural modernization was still being felt. The inflation rate in 1994 was 2.8 per
cent, down from 4.1 per cent in 1993. However,
unemployment remained high at 8.2 per cent in
western Germany and 15.6 per cent in the East
(the overall rate being 9.6 per cent).

HISTORICAL LEGACY

Modern German antisemitism developed in the
last quarter of the nineteenth century, but it
built on a long tradition of "Jew hatred" in
Christian Europe and could claim theological
sanction in the writings of Martin Luther,
whose emphasis on a scripturally-based faith in
Jesus Christ had led him to demonize Jews and
Judaism in a series of aggressive polemics. The
term "antisemitism" was first coined by the
German publicist Wilhelm Marr in 1879 and its

rapid adoption reflected widespread recognition of the emergence of a new, more ideological and active hostility towards Jews after the unification of Germany. Antisemitism in Germany prior to the First World War involved a rejection of Jewish emancipation, liberalism and modernism, and was closely connected to the growth of German nationalism and racism. Economic insecurities attendant upon the rapid industrialization of Germany further encouraged the formation of antisemitic political parties and organizations which served to radicalize mainstream German conservatism and to promote the respectability of antisemitic views in official circles.

The conservative élites of the German Kaiserreich were antisemitic as a matter of course and were highly suspicious of the Weimar Republic. These élites did not accept their responsibility for Germany's defeat in the First World War, but explained it as an act of "Jewish betrayal". In addition, they saw the November revolution of 1918 as a "Jewish conspiracy". Thus, from the inception in 1919 of the Weimar Republic, conservative forces in Germany denounced and opposed it as a "Jewish republic".

Influential people within the political and economic élites offered no resistance to the plethora of *völkisch*, militaristic and anti-democratic movements which found Germany's domestic problems and the world economic crisis of the 1920s and 1930s to be a favourable environment. In 1933, Hitler's Nationalsozialistische Deutsche Arbeiterpartei (NSDAP, German National Socialist Workers' Party) was seen to offer a solution to Germany's economic and political crisis. Some did not take the radical antisemitic programme of the NSDAP seriously, while others sympathized with a fundamental "solution to the Jewish question".

Immediately after seizing power, the National-Socialist government began to put its antisemitic programme into effect. German Jews were discriminated against in stages: their exclusion from public service and the boycott of Jewish businesses limited their economic existence; with the 1935 Nuremberg laws, they lost their civil rights. Increasingly restrictive legislation drove them into social isolation or emigration. With the November 1938 pogrom (Kristallnacht), the public use of force was added to legislative discrimination.

The first murders of Polish Jews occurred after the German occupation of Poland. From February 1940, Jews were deported from reich territory to occupied Poland where the Jewish population was ghettoized. Before the start of the Russian campaign, *Einsatzgruppen* were formed which, from the summer of 1941, began the systematic murder of Jews. From the autumn of 1941, this programme of murder was carried out through gassing facilities especially created for the purpose in death camps. The Wannsee Conference of January 1941 served to co-ordinate the eradication of European Jewry. By 1945, 6 million Jews had been killed.

Following the defeat of the Third Reich, the Allies tried to eliminate racism and antisemitism in the Federal Republic of Germany (BDR or West Germany). The new-found democratic parties took up and pursued this policy. Since 1960, anti-Jewish incitement has been a criminal offence. In 1985, denial of the Holocaust was also criminalized. Today, antisemitism in what was West Germany exists both as personal prejudice (as shown by opinion polls) and in an organized form on the political far right.

In the former German Democratic Republic (DDR or East Germany), racism and antisemitism were seen as having been "stamped out" by the introduction of socialism. Following a brief period of "political cleansing", responsibility for the crimes of the Third Reich was placed on the BDR. Despite the policy of anti-fascism, far-right and antisemitic groups began to appear in the early 1980s. The fall of the Berlin Wall in November 1989 and the subsequent freedom of reporting brought the existence of right-wing extremism in the GDR to world attention.

Party bans and the arrest of leading neo-Nazis and activists largely denied far-right extremists a public forum, so that the development of a more significant, violent far-right scene in the new *Länder* was hindered. Contrary to their own assertions, the far-right West German parties—the REP, DVU and NPD—did not succeed in winning sufficient members and officials in the new *Länder* and accordingly, with local exceptions, far-right party campaigns among the wider public were unsuccessful.

RACISM AND XENOPHOBIA

Since the new asylum law came into effect in July 1993, the number of applications (127,210) for political asylum declined sharply (by 60 per cent) compared to 1993 (322,599) and the issue of "foreigners" lost much of its impact. Instead, the social causes of the violence and extremism amongst young people became a public issue. In view of the number of elections in 1994, the proposed new German citizenship regulations, which raised the possibility of introducing dual nationality, and the question of immigration laws were not properly discussed. They were only partially re-addressed towards the end of the year when half-hearted consideration was given to the idea of granting citizenship to children born in Germany to non-German parents (children would then decide at eighteen whether to take German citizenship or that of their parents).

The number of racially-motivated offences also remained high in 1994 with 1,336 reported incidents, but the nature of the offences has changed. In 1994, no murders were committed (despite seven attempted murders). There were 262 arson attacks in 1993; but only 85 up until 30 November 1994; and the number of physical attacks declined from 760 to 488 by the end of November. The profile of the offenders has essentially remained the same, yet they are on average somewhat older and are more likely to be members of extreme right-wing organizations.

One of the worst racist incidents in 1994 was the assault by 100 neo-Nazis on black African students in Magdeburg in May. The neo-Nazis shouted "Germany for the Germans" and stampeded through the streets of the town, smashing shop windows, chasing the students into a cafe and beating them with iron rods.

Careful analysis of the violence must take into account the fact that, since 1993, there have been a number of cases where people have made false allegations about being victims of far-right or racist attacks. Some of these cases received a great deal of publicity, for example, that of a disabled young woman who in January 1994 cut swastikas into her face, and a Ghanaian who in September was involved in a train accident which he falsely claimed to be the consequence of a skinhead attack. The far-right press used these incidents to claim that racist violence in general was a fabrication on the part of the victims or the press.

In September, twenty Hamburg policemen were suspended from duty and a legal investigation began. They were accused of having caused bodily harm motivated by racism and xenophobia. As a result of this investigation, Hamburg's SPD minister of the interior, Werner Hackmann, resigned. The reasons he gave for his resignation were the increasing number of police attacks against foreigners and the links between some members of the police and far-right organizations.

PARTIES, ORGANIZATIONS, MOVEMENTS

In 1994, the far-right organizations and their numbers did not change significantly, although there was a slight decline from 1993. In 1993, the Bundesamt für Verfassungsschutz (BfV, Federal Office for the Protection of the Consti-

tution) counted, excluding the REP, 81 far-right extremist organizations with 42,100 members (multiple memberships were not taken into account), including 6,200 violent far-right extremists, some of them skinheads, operating in loosely-organized groups at regional and local levels; other estimates put the number of far-right activists as high as 67,000. The BfV's figures showed little change over 1992. Of the 81 organizations, 27 were neo-Nazi groups.

The main far-right political parties—the REP, DVU and NPD—tend to avoid public expressions of antisemitism but opinion polls indicate that members and supporters of such parties are far more likely to be antisemitic than other voters.

In the REP, the largest far-right party, antisemitism mostly occurs in the form of innuendo. There is talk, for example, of "shaking off the responsibility for the consequences of Nazism", of rejecting "Jewish criticism"; there are allegations that the government is "kowtowing" to the Jewish "lobby" and references to the Zentralrat der Juden in Deutschland (ZJD, Central Council of Jews in Germany) as "the fifth occupying force".

At a party convention in Passau, Franz Schönhuber, the then REP chair, attacked Ignatz Bubis, president of the ZJD, for being "the self-appointed guardian of public morals". When, following the arson attack on a synagogue in Lübeck on 25 March, Bubis blamed the extreme right for having committed "spiritual arson", Schönhuber (at a Bavarian party rally in Erding on 26 March) branded Bubis "one of the worst public agitators in Germany". He went on to say that people like Bubis were the main cause of antisemitism.

In August 1994, Schönhuber met Gerhard Frey, chair of the DVU, and they jointly declared that their parties had formed a "right-wing defence force" against what they termed the "leftist popular front". The announcement of an alliance between the two parties was interpreted as an attempt to increase the political impact of the far right in the run-up to the October general election, in view of the 5 per cent threshold required to win parliamentary seats. The move prompted Manfred Kanther, the interior minister, to order tighter surveillance of REP activities in order to determine whether or not the party should be reclassified as "hostile to the constitution". (The party had already been classified as a far-right organization in December 1992, ensuring that its activities would be monitored by the federal authorities.) The decision to join forces with the DVU reportedly was taken independently by Schönhuber and provoked criticism within the party as some activists feared that a *rapprochement* with the DVU could alienate many middle-class REP voters who would take exception to the DVU's more overtly racist ideology.

Subsequently, on 1 October, the national party dismissed Schönhuber from his position as party chair. Schönhuber appealed successfully against this decision in the courts but did not put himself forward as a candidate when a new leader was chosen on 17-18 December. Schönhuber's successor, the thirty-nine-year-old doctor and lawyer Rolf Schlierer, party chair in the *Land* parliament of Baden-Württemberg, follows a line similar to that of Jörg Haider in Austria (see **Austria**). His deputy, the veterinarian Rudolph Krause from Thüringen, represents the more extreme wing of the party.

In Germany's federal elections on 16 October, the REP received 1.9 per cent of the vote, a decrease from the 2.1 per cent it won in the 1990 elections, and failed once again to cross the 5 per cent electoral threshold necessary for parliamentary representation. In state elections held on the same day, the REP won 1.3 per cent in Thuringen and 1 per cent in Mecklenburg-West Pommern , both in eastern Germany, and 1.4 per cent of the vote in Saarland. In local elections held in Nordrhein-Westphalen, the REP took only 0.6 per cent of the vote, a drop from the 2.3 per cent it received in 1989.

These were the latest in a series of major electoral upsets for the REP in 1994. In the June European elections, the REP lost all six of its seats in the European Parliament after its vote fell from 7.1 per cent in 1989 to 3.9 per cent. In September, the party failed to win any seats in the state elections of Bavaria, the region long considered its power base. Its vote dropped to 3.9 per cent, down from 4.9 per cent in the previous state elections and well below its peak of 5.4 per cent in the Bavarian local elections of 1990. The REP's share of the vote in Bavaria in the federal elections fell further to 2.8 per cent. Even in Baden-Württemberg, where the party received its highest percentage of votes in the federal elections, its share of 3.1 per cent was less than a third of the amount it won in the state elections there in 1992.

The membership of the REP decreased from 23,000 in 1993 to about 17,000, largely because middle-class members did not want to back Schönhuber's radical line. The clearly negative political and media response to the REP was one of the reasons for the party's unexpectedly poor performance in the elections. The election campaign in 1994 was clearly more overtly antisemitic than in previous years, when REP propaganda was generally directed against "foreigners" and asylum-seekers. The REP's image was also damaged by the fact that party members were actively involved in racist offences and that one branch did not expel its members despite conclusive evidence to that effect.

With the enactment of the new immigration law and the fear of losing a political platform, far-right parties tried to incorporate environmental issues into their agendas. Schönhuber, for example, proclaimed that "we are the real leaders of our environment".

The NPD asserts that it adheres to the constitution, although, like the REP, it is classified as a far-right organization by the BfV and is therefore subject to federal monitoring. It expresses hostility to foreigners and its leader, Günther Deckert, has been prosecuted for denying the Holocaust and incitement to racial hatred (see **Legal Matters**). In the June European elections, the NPD received 0.2 per cent of the vote.

The DVU, led by Gerhard Frey, is also subject to federal monitoring. Frey has close links with antisemites and Holocaust-deniers. The party's publications show relentless hostility to the German Jewish population and often publish articles with Holocaust-denial themes.

The Deutsche Liga für Volk and Heimat (DL, German League for People and Homeland), created out of a split in the REP in 1991, is ideologically close to the NPD and places a particular emphasis on the collective identity of the German people. DL candidates stood in local and state elections in the early 1990s. Classified as a far-right party by the BfV, the DL acts as a "respectable" shelter for members of banned extreme-right groupings.

In addition to the REP and the NPD, other far-right parties to field candidates in the June European elections were Solidarität (Solidarity), a LaRouchite grouping (see **United States**), which received 0.1 per cent, and the Ökologische Demokratische Partei (Democratic Ecology Party), which won 0.8 per cent. The Bund für Freie Bürger (BFB, League of Free Citizens), which received a 1.1 per cent share, is a far-right conservative party founded in January by Manfred Brunner, a former FDP member and senior civil servant in the European Commission, and received the support of the Austrian far-right leader Jörg Haider. The BFB campaigned on a platform opposed to the Maastricht treaty on European union; Brunner declared: "Europe can be no substitute for Fatherland."

The most significant extreme-right organizations include:
The Nationale Offensive (NO, National

Offensive) (see **Poland**), led by Michael Swierczeck, was founded in July 1990 by former members of the Freiheitliche Deutsche Arbeiterpartei (see below) and banned in December 1992, though it remains largely intact. The NO, which has approximately 140 members or sympathizers, is based in Baden-Württemberg, Bavaria, Berlin-Brandenburg and Saxony. It campaigns against liberal democratic institutions and foreigners and is openly antisemitic and anti-Zionist.

The Nationalistische Front (NF, Nationalist Front), founded in 1985, was led by Meinolf Schönborn until his removal in May 1993. Schönborn subsequently sought to transfer his operation to Denmark to run a printing house but members of the Danish public protested successfully to prevent Schönborn's move (see **Denmark**). Based in Bremen, Berlin and Bielefeld, some of the NF's estimated 500 members or sympathizers have been responsible for attacks on asylum-seekers and foreigners. The NF has propagated antisemitism and organized celebrations of the anniversary of Hitler's birth. The discovery of NF "commandos" (*Einsatzkommandos*), trained for action against foreigners, political opponents and state institutions in favour of a *völkisch* Germany and in possession of weapons and explosives, led to the subsequent banning of the NF in 1992; the group nonetheless remains largely intact through its successor organization, the Direkte Aktion Mitteldeutschland (DAM, Central German Direct Action).

The Deutsche Alternative (DA, German Alternative), led by former DVU and NPD activist Frank Hübner, was founded in Bremen in May 1989 and banned in December 1992. The DA was best organized in the new *Länder* and its strongest grouping was in Cottbus with 100 members. With a programme paralleling that of the NSDAP in the 1920s, it has been particularly outspoken against liberal democratic institutions and foreigners. DA activists have been involved in attacks on foreigners and have targeted school pupils as potential members.

The Freiheitliche Deutsche Arbeiterpartei (FAP, German Workers' Freedom Party), led by Friedhelm Busse, was founded in 1979. Unlike other neo-Nazi groups, it is registered as a political party but, unlike other parties, it makes references to Nazism, although these are restricted to its journals. Its programme, "German Socialism for the 1990s", outlines themes of nationalism, xenophobia, anti-pluralism, *völkisch* community, neutrality from the Western alliance, privileges for German workers and national unity. The FAP's main activities have been daubing graffiti, and distributing posters

and leaflets. Members and sympathizers, whose numbers are estimated at approximately 200-1,500, engage in arson attacks and assaults on foreigners, political opponents and their property. In September 1993, the federal interior ministry moved to ban the FAP (see **Legal Matters**).

The small Hamburg-based Nationale Liste (NL, National List), founded in 1989 and led by Christian Worch (see **Legal Matters**), is an organization linked to the much larger, banned Gesinnungsgemeinschaft der Neuen Front (GdNF, Like-Minded Association of the New Front), also led by Worch, which describes itself as the revolutionary wing of neo-Nazism. Worch was the prime mover in the "anti-antifa[scist]" campaign initiated late in 1993 with the publication of a European-wide "hit list" of anti-fascist activists called *Der Einblick*.

Also linked to the GdNF is the Hilfsgemeinschaft für nationale politische Gefangene und deren Angehörige (HNG, Support Organization for National Political Prisoners and their Relatives), led by Ursula Müller and Christian Malcoci. Founded in 1979, the HNG provides advice and support for imprisoned far-right militants and attempts to mobilize amongst younger prisoners.

The US-based neo-Nazi organization, the Nationalsozialistische Deutsche Arbeiterpartei/ Auslands- und Aufbauorganisation (NSDAP/ AO, German National Socialist Workers' Party/Overseas Section), led by Gary Lauck, is also active in Germany (see **United States**). The NSDAP/AO's principal activity is the production and dissemination of neo-Nazi and antisemitic literature in several languages throughout Europe and North America and it has taken advantage of developments in information technology, including computer software and international computer networks, such as the Internet, to spread its propaganda (see **Publications and Media**).

In November, the neo-Nazi Wiking Jugend (WJ, Viking Youth), with 400 members, was banned and its assets were seized (see **Legal Matters**). The WJ was established in 1952 to introduce young people to neo-Nazi ideology, in the mould of the Hitler Jugend (Hitler Youth), and to "train" them in paramilitary exercises.

German far-right and neo-Nazi organizations continued to consolidate their international contacts, particularly with extremist organizations in Eastern Europe. At the beginning of the year, Vladimir Zhirinovsky, the leader of the Liberal Democratic Party of Russia, was invited on separate occasions to demonstrations by the DVU, NPD and DL but was refused an entry visa by the German government (see **Russia**).

As in 1993 some neo-Nazi organizations planned to hold a march in August to commemorate the seventh anniversary of the death of Hitler's deputy, Rudolph Hess. But, in contrast to last year, the German authorities prevented the planned rallies (see **Countering Antisemitism**). As a result, about 100 right-wing extremists went to Luxembourg, where they waved Nazi flags and threw stones at the German embassy. They were subsequently arrested and escorted to the German border where they were handed over to the German authorities.

MAINSTREAM POLITICS

Antisemitism surfaced in mainstream politics as part of a public row involving prominent PDS members of Jewish origin: the PDS leader, Gregor Gysi, and the writer and PDS member of parliament Stefan Heym.

In November, after the PDS took its seats in parliament, the songwriter Wolf Biermann, exiled from the GDR in the 1970s, fiercely attacked Gysi, calling him a "criminal", and adding that he was a "Stasi informer through and through". He also described Heym as a "rebellious coward" and a "hypocrite" who was "climbing into the political bed alongside Gysi" out of vanity. The Austrian sculptor, Alfred Hrdlicka, on the far left of the political spectrum, took this attack as an opportunity to criticise Biermann strongly in the PDS organ *Neues Deutschland*. Amongst other things, he said: "So you don't want to live under laws which Gysi passes?—You should have the Nuremberg race laws on your neck, you conformist idiot!" (see **Austria**).

Reacting to this statement, the journalist Henryk M. Broder described Hrdlicka indirectly as a "left-wing Nazi...who only remains an anti-fascist as long as he does not feel provoked by a Jew". As a result of Broder's article, the subject was widely debated in newspaper feature columns until the end of the year. The focus of the media discussion was whether this remark by Hrdlicka, well-known as an outspoken artist, should be accepted as an expression of artistic anarchy or whether, as a result, his memorial against war and fascism in Vienna should be removed. According to Biermann, the PDS, and Heym and Gysi in particular, perceive themselves to be the new persecuted Jews in the federal republic, falling victim to similar injustices as the German Jews after 1933. Heym, accordingly, interpreted the political attacks directed against his PDS candidacy during the election campaign as assaults against the

"Jew Heym". To prove the anti-Jewish nature of these verbal assaults, Heym claimed that Ignatz Bubis had warned him that "he knows the risk for a Jew who dares to put himself on the public stage in Germany. It is life-threatening." Bubis, however, denied having ever spoken to Heym and said that Heym invented the statement. Bubis also accused Heym and Gysi, among other things, of suddenly using their Jewishness for political gain—something, furthermore, that had not been their concern while they were citizens of the DDR.

MANIFESTATIONS

According to the BfV, incidents of far-right violence decreased from 2,232 in 1993 to 1,489 in 1994 (1992: 2,639; 1991: 1,488) (All 1994 BFV figures quoted are interim.). The figure included no murders. The number of general far-right incidents also decreased from 10,561 in 1993 to 7,952 in 1994. Instead of large-scale rioting, night attacks involving fewer offenders commenced; and instead of high-risk violent acts, a trend towards so-called "propaganda offences", committed anonymously, emerged (1991: 2,401; 1992: 5,045; 1993: 8,329; 1994: 4,709 until 30 November). This downward trend could also be seen in the membership figures of extreme right-wing organizations and in the votes cast for extreme right-wing parties.

However, the number of antisemitic incidents has gone up since 1992. There was an increase in violent antisemitic incidents—from 72 in 1993 to 96 in 1994—as well as in the total number of antisemitic incidents, which rose from 656 in 1993 to 935 in 1994. At a conference of Jewish organizations and German authorities in Königswinter at the end of May, Interior Minister Manfred Kanther declared that "far-right extremists are increasingly fomenting antisemitism". Kanther said that the trend of antisemitic crimes was continuing to rise and he estimated the number of openly antisemitic activists to be "around 8,000".

This increase in the number of general antisemitic offences can partly be attributed to the greater awareness of the public, who are now reporting offences of this nature more often, and to the improved categorizing of these incidents by the police authorities. This increase is also partly due to the fact that, during the election campaigns, posters of the PDS, in particular those of its leading candidates Gregor Gysi and Stefan Heym, were daubed with antisemitic slogans and symbols. A further reason for the increase is the greater amount of antisemitic propaganda disseminated in Germany from abroad, although the total figure includes prosecutions in different *Länder* of the same antisemitic material.

Sixty-five cases of Jewish cemetery desecrations and attacks on synagogues, Jewish communal institutions and memorials were recorded (67 in 1993), including the arson attack on the Lübeck synagogue, where five people were asleep on the first floor. This was the worst attack on a synagogue since the end of the Third Reich and it prompted nation-wide indignation and angry protests. Whilst previous attacks on asylum-seekers' hostels and the homes of Turks triggered other attacks, no such offences followed the Lübeck incident (see also **Legal Matters**).

The desecration of the memorial at the former Buchenwald concentration camp (near Weimar) on 23 July also produced an international outcry. Twenty-three youths, most of whom had been drinking heavily, committed numerous violent offences when a concert by the skinhead band Oithanasie (Euthanasia) was cancelled at short notice. They went on to destroy exhibits at the memorial site and threatened to burn an employee. The scandal surrounding this case lay principally in the misconduct of the police who were watching the group but failed to intervene and eventually lost track of them. When the police finally arrived at Buchenwald, they interrogated the group and released all but one. It was only some time after the incident had taken place that the youths were arrested by the police (see **Legal Matters**).

Seven German soldiers who belong to the élite Guard of Honour were investigated for having shouted "Foreigners Out" and "Gas the Jews" and for having beaten up a German passenger on a bus in Siegburg, where the soldiers were stationed. This incident highlighted some of the issues which were discussed in a study by the sociological institute of the Bundeswehr (the German armed forces) in 1993 in which warnings of the growing influence of the far right were given. The survey found that at least 6 per cent of people in the sixteen-to-eighteen age group characterized themselves as extreme right-wing and that 75 per cent of that group wanted to join the Bundeswehr.

CULTURAL LIFE

After the attack in Lübeck, Ignatz Bubis blamed the "changed right-wing climate" for the wave of far-right violence, and he referred to the intellectual influences responsible for this changed climate. These included, among others, the historian Ernst Nolte, whose claim that the Holocaust was merely a "copy" of murderous policies followed by Stalin helped trigger the *Historikerstreit* (the historians' debate) in the mid-1980s, and the author Botho Strauss, because of his essay published in June 1993 in *Der Spiegel* entitled "Anschwellender Bocksgesang" (Swelling song of the ram).

Both responded publicly to these claims. Whilst Nolte branded Bubis "the forerunner of an unconstitutional curtailment of freedom of intellectual expression in Germany" in the *Tagesspiegel* of 6 May 1994, Strauss, supported even by some of his critics, vehemently denied any connection with the antisemitic cause and neo-Nazi offences. Anyone who did make this connection, he said in a brief response in *Der Spiegel* in April, is "either an idiot, a barbarian or a political informer".

Bubis subsequently toned down his criticism. According to Bubis, Strauss is not of the same persuasion as such ultra-right thinkers as Ernst Nolte, who has continued to make provocative and scandalous statements since the *Historikerstreit*, blurring the boundaries between social science, politics and agitation. He has also criticized criminal prosecution of the "Auschwitz Lüge" (the Auschwitz lie, or Holocaust denial) as a threat to intellectual freedom in Germany. Nolte, who proposed that so-called "revisionism" should be raised to the rank of a serious social science, argued that the law was directed principally against the "radical revisionists" and implied that they could potentially make a serious contribution towards comprehending the "truth". Nolte was criticized harshly by colleagues and journalists for this, and the former chair of the historian's association, Christian Meyer, accused him of intellectual dishonesty and obsession.

GRASSROOTS

After protests in both countries, a football match planned for 20 April, the date of Hitler's birth, between England and Germany in Berlin, was cancelled by the British and German football associations, to allay fears that neo-Nazis and hooligans would use the occasion for propagandist activities and that there might be serious racist and antisemitic riots. This decision was criticized by some who viewed the cancellation of the match as a victory for the far right, drawing political attention to a date that had not been significant for the last forty years.

PUBLICATIONS AND MEDIA

The far right publishes a number of weeklies and other periodicals, some appearing irregularly, which contain antisemitic comment and innuendo. These periodicals include:

Deutsche Nationalzeitung, the weekly publication of the DVU, which was established in 1950. With a self-declared circulation of 130,000, it is the most widespread publication of the German far right, although independent sources estimate a circulation of 63,000. *Deutsche Stimme*, which claims a circulation of 250,000 (independent sources estimate approximately 10,000), is the monthly journal of the NPD. *Deutsche Rundschau*, which claims a circulation of 50,000, is the monthly journal of the DL. Founded in 1951, the theoretical journal *Nation und Europa* appears monthly with a circulation of 10,000. It is associated with the NPD and the DL.

Junge Freiheit (Potsdam), published weekly since January 1994, propagates the ideas of the "conservative revolution" of the interwar period. Its target audience is the authoritarian right and the conservative end of the political spectrum; it has a circulation of about 20,000. *Deutscher Jahresweiser*, a quarterly with a circulation of several thousand, is edited by the neo-Nazi lawyer Manfred Roeder. *Klartext*, which appears irregularly, is the journal of the NF. *Code*, a monthly publication with an estimated circulation of several thousand, has links with *New American View* and *Spotlight* (see **United States**). *Elemente*, which appears twice a year, is produced by Thule-Seminar, a racist think-tank. *Der Scheinwerfer* appears monthly with an estimated circulation of 1,000. *Der Schulungsbrief* is a neo-Nazi monthly with a circulation of 100.

It is indicative of the increasingly ideological nature of far-right extremism that, along with the violent desecrations of cemeteries and memorials, ancient antisemitic stereotypes are now being revitalized. Among these is the accusation that Jews have a rapacious sexual appetite and that, in order to gratify their desire, they would even abuse Christian children. The *Deutsche Nationalzeitung* of 16 December accused the prominent Green politician Daniel Cohn-Bendit of masturbating with children when he worked in a nursery at the beginning of the 1970s. In the same vein is the antisemitic claim that Jews do not practise safe sex and deliberately spread the AIDS virus.

The far-right sub-culture which has developed among skinheads, and which propagates militant xenophobia and antisemitism, remains active. Such ideas are spread mainly through magazines, concerts, records and computer games. There are also between 80 and 100 skinhead magazines, usually poorly produced, at least 30 of which spread a brutalized version of racism and antisemitism. In the multifarious skinhead music scene, there are also numerous records which contain antisemitic texts. Although the police have clamped down on skinhead bands, it has not been possible to prevent completely the dissemination of such texts

by the authors and publishers. This kind of music is imported from the United Kingdom and printed matter has come from Switzerland and the US.

Large quantities of neo-Nazi and Holocaust-denial literature have been up-loaded (inputted) on to the Internet, the international computer network. The computer magazine *Chip* estimated that about 1,500 of Germany's far-right extremists were active on the "Thule" computer network. This network consists of at least a dozen bulletin boards in several other countries and derives its name from the small élite 1920s movement considered to be the Nazi vanguard. According to counter-intelligence sources, passwords, such as *Germania* or *Endsieg* (final victory), have enabled neo-Nazis to access details of forthcoming events and lists of far-right contacts. Names of anti-fascist activists, code-named *Zecken* (ticks), as well as "undesirable" judges and journalists can also be obtained. Code-names such as *schöne Mädchen* (beautiful girls) have been used to refer to the police. Computer disks, some originating from the neo-Nazi NSDAP/AO in the US, provide detailed bomb-making instructions and such texts as the Holocaust-denying *Leuchter Report* have been circulated on the Internet (see **United States**).

Federal officials and law officers in Baden-Württemberg, Bavaria, and North Rhine-Westphalia, where the Thule bulletin boards are located, face difficulties in gathering firm evidence for prosecution because members of the network post messages and announcements either under pseudonyms or anonymously.

To avoid confiscation, neo-Nazis have resorted to having their publications printed abroad (in Poland, Lithuania, Spain and the UK).

As well as interpreting events on a *völkisch* basis, other themes, such as the impact of immigration on the environment are also given racist interpretations in far-right literature. The ideology of a particularly "German" way of life has led to a resurgence of a neo-heathenism on the basis of the Wotan cult, a Germanic pagan religion which opposes Christian-Jewish universalism.

Electoral failure in 1994 led to a slight drop in the numbers of far-right publications. The greater readiness to bring criminal prosecutions made the authors of these far-right publications much more careful not to go beyond the limits of what is legally permissible. For example, instead of referring to "Jewish world power", or the "Zionist Occupation Government" (ZOG), the more neutral "influential anti-German lobby" was used.

In a review of Steven Spielberg's film, *Schindler's List*, in the national daily *Die Welt*, Will Tremper recalled a 1943 speech by Heinrich Himmler in which he warned SS officers against "incorrect" behaviour, and went on to say: "In Spielberg's film, there is no such hesitation. Young Polish soldiers in SS uniforms storm through the street of the Krakow Ghetto . . . and brutally shoot everything that moves, preferably helpless women and children. Just imagine, at that exact moment, standing by the cameras and spurring on the extras with shouts of 'Action! Action!'—it's repulsive." He went on to note that survivors have "here and there rather dramatized their time of suffering in Krakow".

RELIGION

Certain Christian fundamentalist and evangelical church groups continued to spread antisemitism. The ecumenical movement in particular, in which various faiths co-operate, is denounced as a plot masterminded by Jews and freemasons. Publications produced by the publishers Pro Fide Catholica in 1990 and 1992, which propagated Holocaust denial, are now in circulation among far-right groups.

DENIAL OF THE HOLOCAUST

The *Leuchter Report* and similar Holocaust-denial texts and videos continued to be disseminated. At the end of the year, the Tübingen-based publishing house Grabert Verlag, known for producing Holocaust-denial material, published a collection of essays by practically all the well-known Holocaust-deniers, entitled *Grundlagen zur Zeitgeschichte. Ein Handbuch über Strittige Fragen des 20. Jahrhunderts* (Foundations of Contemporary History. A Reader on Controversial Questions of the Twentieth Century).

Wherever the state prosecutor is able to find those who produce Holocaust-denial material, charges are brought. This year, a number of prominent far-right activists were sentenced for incitement to racial hatred and insulting the memory of the dead (for example, the national chair of the NPD, Günther Deckert, and the neo-Nazi activist Bela Ewald Althans) (see **Legal Matters**).

The proceedings against wrongful dismissal, lodged by Germar Rudolf (the author of a pseudo-scientific Holocaust-denial text— the *Gutachten über die Bilding und Nachweisbarkeit von Cyanidverbindungen in den "Gaskammern" von Auschwitz* (Expert Report on the Formation and Detection of Cyanide Compounds in the "Gas Chambers" of Auschwitz)—which has become known as

the "Rudolf Expertise", written to support the defence of the Holocaust-denier Otto Ernst Remer) against the Max Planck Institute of Solid State Physics, ended with a settlement (see **Legal Matters**).

EFFECTS OF ANTI-ZIONISM

In far-right circles, the term "Zionism" continues to be a code word for Jewish world domination. This far-right antisemitism pinpoints the US as the centre of Jewish power and is therefore also anti-American. Thus anti-Zionism has become the ideological basis for a "liberation nationalism" of the European far right which fights against the "Zionist-American one-world government" and attacks the "Zionist Occupation Government".

Undertones of antisemitic anti-Zionism have also been present on the political left. Henryk Broder's book *Der ewige Antisemit* (The Eternal Antisemite) provided many examples of the hidden antisemitic agenda of the political left, an agenda which became, for example, apparent during the Gulf War.

Attention should be drawn here to an anti-Zionist phenomenon hitherto hardly acknowledged in Germany. Germany has a sizeable population of Arabs, Palestinians and Turks, most of whom are Muslim. A small number of Islamist groups (more commonly known as Islamic fundamentalists) and secular Marxist Palestinian groups are active within the Muslim population; the BfV counted fourteen extreme Islamist groups in 1994 with 21,200 members or sympathizers (1 per cent of the Muslim community). Among some members of these groups, politically-motivated anti-Zionism is often intermingled with antisemitic attitudes, expressed for example in the spread of conspiracy myths through the Turkish press, through attacks on Jewish institutions (the "Old Synagogue" Museum in Essen was singled out for attack following the massacre of Muslims by a Jewish settler at a Hebron mosque in February), and through slanderous letters to Jewish community representatives. In Berlin, some Palestinian children reportedly applauded the shooting of Jews when their class went to see the film *Schindler's List*. At the opening of the new mosque in Mannheim, copies of *Mein Kampf* in Turkish were available for sale. Developments in the Middle East conflict have an impact in Germany, and Arabic anti-Zionism and German antisemitism could forge a dangerous alliance.

The close link between the Jewish community, Israel, and the Middle East conflict was also clearly visible when "very concrete evidence" emerged in September that the

Palestinian Abu Nidal group was seeking to attack "Jewish targets" and to kill Ignatz Bubis, the president of the ZJD. Security was then stepped up at Jewish communal institutions.

OPINION POLLS

A survey of the attitudes of a representative sample of the German population towards Jews and other minorities was conducted by the Emnid Institute in January 1994 for the American Jewish Committee (AJC). In this study, some of the questions raised in a 1990 AJC poll were addressed. Out of 1,434 people questioned, nearly a third believed that Jews had too much influence on world events, almost 40 per cent said Jews were exploiting the Holocaust for their own purposes, 28 per cent would disapprove if a party nominated a Jew as its candidate for president of Germany, and 22 per cent would prefer not to have Jews as neighbours. Commenting on these findings, Ignatz Bubis pointed out that "though antisemitism does not appear to be increasing, it shows its face more often these days".

While 8 per cent of Germans said that Jews "behave in a manner which provokes hostility towards them in our country", 40 per cent felt that way about Gypsies, 22 per cent about Turks, 20 per cent about Poles and 18 per cent about Arabs. Attitudes towards Africans (11 per cent) and Vietnamese (9 per cent) resembled those towards Jews.

In the AJC/Emnid poll, Germans emerge as well-informed about the Holocaust, in comparison with other countries. When asked in an open-ended format "As far as you know, what does the term 'the Holocaust' refer to?", 87 per cent were able to answer with some degree of accuracy. With regard to Holocaust remembrance, 52 per cent of Germans considered it "correct" and 34 per cent "incorrect" that "today, in the aftermath of German unification, we should not talk so much about the Holocaust, but should rather draw a line under the past"; 14 per cent did not know. Questioned about the proposal to establish a national Holocaust memorial museum in Germany, 37 per cent "approved" and 37 per cent "disapproved"; 26 per cent did not know. Willingness to commemorate the Holocaust was more common amongst eastern Germans (52 per cent) than western Germans (33 per cent).

The Allensbach Institute of Opinion Research, based on a previously unpublished study, reported that the percentage of people clearly prejudiced against Jews was at a postwar low of 15 per cent. Eight per cent of the population were considered to be vehemently antisemitic. The Allensbach Institute has been

analysing antisemitism since 1949, when every third German was found to be distinctly anti-Jewish. The present survey found that older Germans were more inclined towards antisemitism than younger ones. But compared with other ethnic groups, Jews experienced less prejudice.

Another opinion poll, conducted by the FORSA Institute, showed that two out of three Germans questioned believed that it was a positive thing that Germany lost the Second World War and that Nazi thinking was "wrong and bad".

LEGAL MATTERS

Seven of the most militant neo-Nazi organizations were banned by the interior ministry in 1992; in November 1994, a further organization, the Wiking Jugend was banned and its assets were seized.

The FAP protested the interior ministry's prohibition order against it within the period allowed by the constitutional court, and, by the end of 1994, the matter had not been resolved.

The proceedings against wrongful dismissal, lodged by Germar Rudolf (the author of the Holocaust-denying "Rudolf Expertise", written to support the defence of the Holocaust-denier Otto Ernst Remer) against the Max Planck Institute of Solid State Physics, ended with a settlement. Rudolf's contract of employment was dissolved by mutual agreement and made retrospective to the time of the dismissal, which, after assessment by the court, was deemed correct. Today Rudolf is unemployed. The octogenarian Remer, who had been sentenced to twenty-two months' imprisonment in 1993 for his denial of the Holocaust, evaded justice by fleeing to Spain. The Spanish government endorsed the petition for extradition, but the Spanish high court has to ensure that the offence of Holocaust denial is also punishable according to Spanish law. Until a decision is reached, Remer remains under house arrest at his villa in Malaga (see **Spain**).

In February, British Holocaust-denier David Irving was sentenced to three months' imprisonment *in absentia* for contempt of court in a row with a German publisher (see **United Kingdom**).

In the case of Fred Leuchter, accused by the Mannheim state court of Holocaust denial, who failed to make an appearance at his trial in September, the public prosecutor doubted whether the American authorities would grant extradition.

During the legal proceedings which followed the arson attack on the memorials in Sachsenhausen in September 1992, the supreme court reversed the acquittal issued by the Potsdam district court at the end of August and referred the case against the two young suspects to a different youth court for retrial.

By the beginning of September, the first offenders in the July incident at Buchenwald had been sentenced. The public prosecutor investigated four police officers who were suspected of failing to make an arrest on duty. Disciplinary action was taken against eleven others.

In the case of the attack on the Lübeck synagogue, a special branch of the police apprehended four young men aged between twenty and twenty-five, three of whom admitted responsibility for the crime. They belonged to the Lübeck skinhead milieu. It could not be proved, however, that they were members of an organized extreme-right movement or that they had been incited by a third party. The trial began in November. The defendants were charged with arson and the attempted murder of five people.

In November 1992, the Mannheim district court sentenced NPD chair Günther Deckert to one year's imprisonment and a DM10,000 fine for incitement to racial hatred. At a hearing in March 1994, the German supreme court lifted the sentence because the original grounds for Deckert's conviction for incitement—arranging a public Holocaust denial meeting—were not included in the provisions of article 130 of the German criminal code, under which Deckert was prosecuted. The supreme court ordered a retrial to clarify how far the accused engaged in incitement or identified himself with Nazi ideology. This decision was widely, but incorrectly, seen as recognizing the validity of Holocaust denial in Germany. The ruling was attacked in many quarters ("a perversion of legal thinking" *Die Zeit* said on 25 March). Holocaust denial on its own could only be prosecuted (until December 1994) under article 185 of the criminal code on "insult".

Deckert was convicted of incitement once again by the Mannheim lower district court on 22 June and given a one-year suspended sentence with probation. The grounds for the sentence, published in August, caused a legal uproar. The three judges sympathized with Deckert's "legitimate interest . . . in opposing the claims held against Germany because of the Holocaust even after nearly half a century". The suspended sentence was justified because, according to the judges, the case dealt with a man "of strong character, a person aware of responsibility with clear principles".

The German government regretted the sentence. Chancellor Kohl denounced it, and its justification by the judges, as a disgrace, whilst

the justice minister, Sabine Leutheusser-Schnarrenberger, described the decision as a "slap in the face of all Holocaust victims".

The chair of the German confederation of judges—a professional body which does not often comment on individual cases—expressed his anger about the sentence because the grounds cited appeared to negate the values enshrined in the constitution. Following this severe attack on the court's ruling, the judges involved took sick leave.

The judges were also widely accused of perverting the course of justice. Judge Orlet, who had drawn up the grounds of the sentence, continued to defend them as proper and correct in an interview, and accused the critics of lack of objectivity. In the autumn, the return of the judges to office was accompanied by protests. The independence of the judiciary, guaranteed by law, meant that no disciplinary action could be taken against them. To remedy this, at the beginning of December, the SPD put forward a motion in the state court of Baden-Württemberg to make possible the prosecution of judges who violate the constitution (a two-thirds majority would be required). No decision has yet been reached on this motion.

The state prosecutor's office once again lodged an appeal. On 15 December, the supreme court quashed the Mannheim sentence for a second time and referred the case to the state court of Karlsruhe for retrial. The supreme court dismissed the mitigation grounds cited in the Mannheim trial as an affront to objective law: "Anyone who shuts their eyes to historical truth and who refuses to acknowledge it does not deserve mitigation." This decision was welcomed publicly as a long-overdue clarification of the position.

The legal proceedings and debates surrounding the Deckert case prompted discussion about a change in the German criminal code. The new law was finally passed in the Bundestag in September and took effect from 1 December. Added to paragraph 130 was the following clause through which denial of the Holocaust was made an explicit criminal offence: "a prison sentence of up to five years or a fine will be imposed on the offender who, in public or in an assembly, approves, denies or trivializes an act committed under the rule of national socialism described in paragraph 220 [Genocide] in a way designed to disrupt public order."

In February, two skinheads and a Polish bar owner were jailed for between eight and fourteen years for kicking and burning a man to death in a Wuppertal pub in 1992 because they thought that he was Jewish. Judge Rolf Watty handed out the sentences after finding them guilty of murder and inflicting bodily harm. He said that "as long as there are Germans in whose names Jews were mistreated and killed in concentration camps and gas chambers, we must take it upon ourselves to be especially watchful against right-wing extremist developments".

In November, the NL leader Christian Worch was sentenced to two years' imprisonment for continuing the activities of the banned Aktionsfront Nationaler Sozialisten under the guise of the GdNF, which is considered to be its successor organization. In the grounds for the sentence, Worch was described as a notorious neo-Nazi who posed a danger to society.

One of Germany's most infamous neo-Nazis, Bela Ewald Althans, went on trial in September for making documentary videos that glorified Adolf Hitler, insulted Jews and intended to introduce young people to fascism. The twenty-eight-year-old Althans had planned to set up an operation for the rental of "history videos". For years Althans has been illegally copying and distributing antisemitic films produced during the Nazi era. Althans is the main figure in the documentary *Beruf Neo-Nazi* (Profession: Neo-Nazi) whose makers and distributors intended to expose neo-Nazis and received funding from several *Länder* for this purpose. Critics of the film said that young neo-Nazis could be encouraged by it through the lack of commentary. In October, a court in Berlin decided that the film could no longer be shown publicly.

COUNTERING ANTISEMITISM

The effects of stricter policing and legal prosecutions against militant far-right and xenophobic offences were evident in 1994; in the first three months over 4,163 cases were investigated and many of them ended in a court sentence. The banning policy removed nearly every opportunity from the far-right organizations to congregate on a large scale and to promote themselves in parades; for example, thirty reported demonstrations planned by neo-Nazi activists in commemoration of Rudolf Hess were banned, gatherings of neo-Nazis broken up, and those involved taken into police custody. A hard core of FAP and NO members travelled to neighbouring Luxembourg in order to protest to the German embassy against what they considered to be the repression of freedom of speech in Germany (see **Parties, Organizations, Movements**). Many election events were banned on the grounds that they could incite counter demonstrations and thus cause public affray. The banning policy, together with countless raids and house searches, which led in

turn to further arrests, and the confiscation of weapons and banned propaganda material, deprived the neo-Nazis of their public forum, thereby lessening their appeal to potential sympathizers. This success has been very labour intensive since the use of electronic communication systems (computer mail boxes, mobile phones) by far-right groups impedes effective surveillance (see **Publications and Media**). In addition, the official banning of organizations and propaganda material pose a constitutional dilemma since it can been seen as an attempt to limit the political rights of freedom of speech and assembly. The far right uses the "freedom of speech" argument to justify its "campaign of national resistance" with the motto: "where a right becomes a wrong, resistance becomes a duty".

Against the background of xenophobic attacks, leading politicians and representatives of the churches and other institutions used official occasions for remembrance and civic receptions as an opportunity to speak out against far-right extremism and antisemitism. President Herzog stressed in a speech in Israel that "nothing should cloak remembrance of the Holocaust" and that "any call for a final break with what occurred in the past should be silenced in the face of the sheer historical magnitude of this crime: indeed, we Germans have a responsibility to keep the memory of our darkest historical chapter alive and to make our younger generations aware of what Germans were, and human beings are, capable of doing." Federal Interior Minister Manfred Kanther also pledged to step up the fight against antisemitism. In May, he said that "we must do more against those crimes motivated by antisemitism" which had been steadily on the rise in Germany since 1992.

For the first time, the German army remembered Jews who were killed in the First World War. On the national day of mourning, the general inspector of the armed forces, Klaus Neumann, laid a wreath in their honour in Berlin-Weissensee.

Ten days after the arson attack on the Lübeck synagogue, tens of thousands of Germans (the organizers' estimate was 50,000) took part in Easter marches against racism and antisemitism in Berlin, Frankfurt, and Cologne.

In response to the arson attack on the Lübeck synagogue, the Youth Union (the youth organization of the CDU) nominated Michel Friedman, member of the ZJD and a local politician in Frankfurt, for election to the party's general assembly. At the CDU party conference in November, he received 610 of the 919 votes, thereby securing a seat on the board.

Some excesses emerged on the fringes of

this protest movement. Militant anti-fascist groups violently attacked people or establishments who they defined as "fascist". One example was the arson attack on a printing firm in Weimar, where the young conservative weekly paper *Junge Freiheit* (Young Freedom) was printed. Because of the damage caused, which ran into millions of deutschmarks, the printers discontinued their contract with the paper. Journalists and politicians of various political persuasions protested against this severe infringement of the freedom of the press.

The city of Berlin allocated DM16 million for the construction of the Central Holocaust Memorial to the Murdered Jews of Europe. This memorial project has fuelled the ongoing debate over how Germany should deal with its Nazi past. A 1,000-strong group of prominent German politicians, academics and writers has called for a Holocaust museum, arguing that a memorial alone does not do justice to the victims of the Holocaust and that it is crucial to build a Holocaust museum in Berlin, similar to those in Washington DC and Los Angeles. The critics of the museum project warned about an "overdose" of Holocaust remembrance and pointed out that a new museum would detract from, and compete with, other existing monuments and exhibitions.

The continued interest in the history of German Jews was apparent in the amount of research being conducted and the wealth of books and exhibitions on the subject. In the last year or so, Jewish studies were given a considerable boost in Germany with the foundation of the Moses Mendelssohn Centre for European Jewish Studies at the University of Potsdam.

ASSESSMENT

Since 1991, Germany has experienced an upsurge of racism and antisemitic violence in some states; far-right parties have been able to achieve some degree of electoral success; and neo-Nazi organizations have seen an increase in their membership figures. The bitter debate about restricting the right to asylum, which went on during 1991 and 1992 amidst a generally xenophobic climate, provided the far-right racist and anti-Jewish press with a set of circumstances they could exploit to their own advantage. The end of 1992 marked the beginning of a new trend. Mass anti-racist civil protests, bans on far-right-wing organizations, vigorous criminal prosecutions against violent offenders and a more restrictive version of the right to asylum were evidence that the political system was responding more actively.

As a result, the number of general far-right incidents has dropped sharply, with violent incidents falling by approximately 30 per cent over 1993. Antisemitic incidents are up, however, increasing by over 40 per cent on 1993, which means that they are a much larger proportion of the total than last year. This is certainly a worrying development by any standards but there are specific mitigating circumstances—such as the fact that the increase is mostly due to the import of antisemitic propaganda from other countries—and it would be wrong to read too much into these figures.

The collapse of the far-right vote in the general election was encouraging. They may recover but it shows that there is nothing inevitable about their progress and that the German political system is able to cope with the problem of extremists.

The controversy over the Deckert Holocaust denial judgement highlights a number of points about current attitudes to antisemitism. First, it shows a new determination on the part of the authorities not only to deal severely with public expressions of antisemitism but also to ensure that judges are not allowed to get away with decisions which fly in the face of common sense. Second, it shows that some in Germany have not come to terms with the meaning of the Nazi period and never will.

Antisemitism remains a troubling phenomenon for German society, but in spite of the rise in incidents, the overall situation has not deteriorated, and indeed, there are signs of improvement in some areas.

Greece

General population: 10 million
Jewish population: 5,000 (mainly in Athens and Thessaloniki)

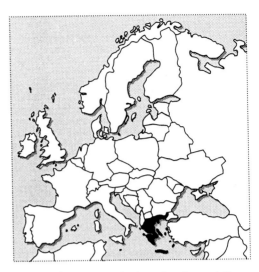

GENERAL BACKGROUND

The Panellinion Sosialistikon Kinema (PASOK, Panhellenic Socialist Movement) returned to power following a general election in October 1993, replacing Nea Demokratia (ND, New Democracy). Its leader, Andreas Papandreou, became prime minister. PASOK retained control of most municipal councils following local elections in October 1994. In the European elections of June 1994, both main parties saw their vote fall from the levels of the parliamentary elections. Politiki Anixi (POLA, Political Spring), a new nationalist mainstream party founded by former Foreign Minister Antonis Samaras in 1993, gained 8.5 per cent of the vote in the European elections.

Greece is one of the poorest countries in the European Union (EU) in terms of gross national product per capita. In 1994, growth was 0.7 per cent, up from 0.5 per cent the previous year. Inflation fell to 11 per cent from 14.1 per cent. Unemployment in 1994 increased slightly from 9.5 per cent to 10.1 per cent.

Greece is engaged in an ongoing controversy over the former Yugoslav republic of Macedonia (FYROM). While most EU states have formally recognized Macedonia, Greece has refused to do so, arguing that no other country has the right to use the same name as Greece's northern province. Greece did not attend any political or sporting event at which a delegation was permitted to use the title "Macedonia", rather than the name "FYROM", or allowed to display its "Sun of Vergina" flag, which Greece claims as one of its national symbols. In consequence, Greece was the only European country which did not attend the Holocaust commemoration ceremony in Auschwitz in January 1995.

HISTORICAL LEGACY

Jews have lived in Greece since at least the third century BCE. When Greece became part of the Ottoman Empire in the fifteenth century, many Jews fleeing the Inquisition in Spain and Portugal settled in the Balkan peninsula. Thessaloniki became home to the largest Jewish population in the region.

During the Greek struggle for independence in the nineteenth century, relations between Christian Orthodox Greeks and Jews deteriorated considerably, the Jews being known for their support of the Ottoman Empire.

In 1931, in the atmosphere of fierce economic competition between Jews and refugees from Asia Minor, who were settled in Greece after the population exchange with Turkey in 1923, the Jewish neighbourhood of Kampel in Thessaloniki was burned down. The perpetrators were never found, although they were suspected of belonging to the fascist Ethniko Enosis Ellas (EEE, National Union of Greece).

Following the Nazi invasion of Greece in 1941, 65,000 Jews—85 per cent of the Greek Jewish population—were deported to concentration camps. Protests against deportations by Greek intellectual and religious leaders were in vain. However, on Zakynthos, the local Orthodox metropolitan and the mayor protected the island's 275 Jews, who all survived the Holocaust.

Since the Second World War, antisemitism has not been apparent in any institutionalized form. Nevertheless, unofficial antisemitism has appeared in several contexts, including the Arab-Israeli conflict. While anti-Zionist attitudes do not necessarily stem from antisemitic sentiments, in specific circumstances the two phenomena may be closely related. Greece was the only European country which voted against the UN partition plan in 1947 and has traditionally maintained close ties with the Arab states. When the socialist PASOK party came to power in 1981 and the Lebanon war broke out in the following year, criticism of Israel grew dramatically. Some far-right political groups called for a boycott of Greek Jewish shops. The *Intifada* and the presence of many Palestinian and Arab students in Greece have contributed to the persistence of strong anti-Israeli sentiments; public opinion often identifies Greek Jews with Israel. Nonetheless, political and commercial links between Greece and Israel have become stronger in recent years.

Antisemitism has figured in anti-Jewish theological discourse, in the context of popular antisemitic folkloric stereotypes about Jews and, more recently, in the context of far-right organizations which have sought to extend their influence among high school students.

In 1992, the quincentenary of Jewish life in the northern region of Macedonia was commemorated by a number of public ceremonies, principally in Thessaloniki. However, one press report depicted this as an attempt to undermine the "Greekness" of Macedonia. Criticism was directed at a medal, issued by the Jewish community in Thessaloniki, depicting a menorah on one side and the star of ancient Macedonia on the other.

RACISM AND XENOPHOBIA

In recent years, immigrants have been widely blamed for rising crime rates. Some saw the Greek authorities' deportation of large numbers of "illegal alien" Albanians as a response to public opinion on this issue. Following allegations that illegal immigrants numbered 700,000, or 7 per cent of the population, Stelios Papathemelis, the minister for public order, described them as "parasites". Official statistics put the number of foreigners at 230,000, of whom one-third was illegal. As a result, Papathemelis called for curbs on illegal immigration.

There is no official monitoring of racist activities in Greece.

PARTIES, ORGANIZATIONS, MOVEMENTS

The far right as a whole remained fragmented in 1994, and no far-right political party received more than 1 per cent in the European elections. However, there has been a growth in the activity of the far right and, whilst its xenophobic and ultra-nationalist opinions are in no way mainstream, they are expressed far more frequently than before.

The following are currently active far-right groups which hold antisemitic views. All are small and none has parliamentary representation:

Enieo Etnekistiko Kinima (ENEK, United Nationalist Movement) was founded in 1979. It maintains a bookshop and publishing house in Athens called Nea Thessis (New Position) which circulates a Greek version of *The Protocols of the Elders of Zion* that is distributed, for example, by some of the monasteries

in the semi-autonomous "theocratic region" of Mount Athos.

Laikos Syndesmos/Chrissi Avgi (Popular League/Golden Daybreak), founded in 1981, is led by, among others, Nikolas Michaloloakos. It publishes the monthly magazine *Chrissi Avgi* (Golden Daybreak) and a weekly newspaper of the same name. Antisemitism forms part of its xenophobic and ultra-nationalist agenda and it maintains close connections with foreign far-right organizations, including Pamyat in Russia, CEDADE in Spain, the Front national in France and the AWB in South Africa (see **France, South Africa, Spain** and **Russia**). In 1994, this very active neo-Nazi organization opened ten new offices throughout Greece. The number of active members of Laikos Syndesmos/Chrissi Avgi is estimated at 800, while the number of supporters is approximately 2,000-3,000. The rise in support in 1994 has been attributed to the organization's weekly publication, the opening of its new offices and its participation in the June European elections, in which it received 0.11 per cent of the vote (7,264 votes).

Ethniko Metopo (National Front), founded in 1987, is led by, among others, M. Konstas. It publishes the magazine *Metopo* (Front).

MAINSTREAM POLITICS

Antisemitism is rare in mainstream Greek politics. However, there was some controversy over the question of religious identity in 1993, after the Greek parliament overwhelmingly rejected a government amendment to make the listing of religion on national identity cards optional rather than obligatory. The amendment, which was endorsed by the Jewish and Catholic minorities as well as a few dissenting deputies, was denounced by the Greek Orthodox church, to which approximately 98 per cent of the population belongs.

While no other EU country issues identity cards which list religious affiliations, the obligatory listing was supported by a cross-parliamentary coalition of right-wingers, socialists and communists on the grounds that Orthodoxy was an integral part of Greece's identity. The Central Board of Jewish Communities in Greece (KIS), which opposes the inclusion of a religion category, considered challenging the regulation in the Greek high court and the international court of justice in the Hague. Representations about the identity cards were made to the Greek government by Jewish leaders from other countries. The controversy remained unresolved in 1994 and no new identity cards were issued.

MANIFESTATIONS

Whilst there were no reports of graffiti on synagogues or Jewish-owned property in 1994, antisemitic daubings were still common. In January, graffiti signed by Chrissi Avgi was found on houses and two primary schools in Volos, central Greece. In Chalkis in Eubea, in the same month, antisemitic graffiti was daubed on the walls of a high school. The slogan "Forest of Jewish Victims of Nazism" was painted in black letters in March in a suburb of Volos. Antisemitic references to Greece's new identity cards appeared in graffiti in Athens in June.

GRASSROOTS

Covert discrimination and anti-Jewish remarks in the army have repeatedly been reported by Jewish soldiers. On the popular level, Jews are often perceived in stereotypical terms as wealthy, stingy, omnipotent and omnipresent.

PUBLICATIONS AND MEDIA

All the following antisemitic or anti-Zionist publications (anti-Zionism in Greece often displays antisemitic attitudes) have low print-runs, and mainly circulate in religious and army circles.

Stochos (Target) is a far-right weekly paper published by Ghiorgos Kapsalis with a circulation of 5,500-10,000. It publishes articles denying the Holocaust and has launched a campaign against the erection of Jewish monuments in Greece. It argues that Jews have no right to put up monuments because, in Greece, only monuments for Greeks should be erected. In July 1993, Kapsalis was sentenced to five months' imprisonment for publishing an article which called for the destruction of Jewish monuments. Until recently, *Stochos* also published a "Questionnaire for the Jews" which implied that Greek Jews were spying for Israel and that their real allegiance was to Israel and not to Greece. *Stochos* has been the subject of several successful complaints by the KIS, and the paper has been obliged to print a number of apologies. However, this has failed to deter it from continuing to publish such articles. In 1994, *Stochos* serialized *The Protocols of the Elders of Zion*.

Chrissi Avgi (Golden Daybreak) is the title of both a monthly magazine and weekly newspaper published by Laikos Syndesmos.

Other antisemitic and anti-Zionist publications include: the dailies *Avriani* (Tomorrow's Press), a mainstream socialist paper owned by the brother of a PASOK MP, and *Elephteri Ora* (Free Time); the weekly *Nei Anthropi* (New Man), which has the same editor (Grigoris Mihalopouloshas) as *Elephteri Ora*; *Christin aniki* (Christian) and *Nea Tassis* (New Position), which appear irregularly; and the monthly *Antidoto* (Antidote).

Agathangelos (Archangel) is another unofficial ecclesiastical publication, edited by a group of monks on Mount Athos.

Publishers who produce antisemitic books with a para-psychological religious focus include Sichroni Enimerosi (Modern Update) and Orthodox Typos (Orthodox Press). Their publications are available in some large bookshops. In them, Jews are portrayed as the embodiment of the Antichrist. In reference to the proposal to include a computerized bar code on the new EU identity cards, some publications have alleged the Jews have introduced this new form of identification in order to control the world.

Editions of *The Protocols of the Elders of Zion* are widely available in Greece, even in many mainstream bookshops. Specialist bookshops in central Athens have been found to stock Nazi literature.

Certain private television channels have provided a forum for antisemitic opinions. Tile-Tora (Tele-Now), whose logo is the Sun of Vergina, one of the Greek national symbols, is owned by Grigoris Mihalopouloshas, the editor of *Elephteri Ora* and *Nei Anthropi* and has been broadcasting for three years in Athens. It has a regular programme presented by Kostas Plevris, author of a book denying the Holocaust (see **Denial of the Holocaust**). Plevris has denounced Jews and questioned their loyalty to Greece. In 1994, Tile-Tora broadcast a programme presented by Maria Douraki, a former singer who holds extreme religious views and who refers to Jews as the Antichrist.

Vasselis Levendis, owner and presenter of Channel 67, has made comments about the supposed power, dark influence and disloyalty of Greece's Jews. Levendis is the leader of a tiny political party Enosis Kendroon (EK, Centrist Union), which presents itself as an alternative to the two main parties. Although antisemitism is not part of the EK's platform, through its television channel it has given airtime to those holding antisemitic views, including some Greek Orthodox priests.

RELIGION

The Christian Orthodox church plays a very important role in the self-perception of the Greek state and the vast majority of the country's citizens belong to this church. Primary teachers in state schools must be Christian Orthodox.

Although the Orthodox church has never adopted an overtly antisemitic stance, its strong endorsement of the obligatory listing of religion in identity cards caused concern amongst the Jewish community. Moreover, some members of the clergy have played a considerable role in shaping a negative image of Jews. The most common religious allegations concern the murder of Jesus Christ. The ancient custom of burning a Judas puppet at Easter, which is still practised in a few villages, reinforces this image.

The monastery at Esfigmenou on Mount Athos is particularly known for the fact that antisemitic material is distributed within the monastery and to pilgrims.

However, anti-Judaism expressed by Orthodox circles is often a function of internal struggles within the clergy and the church's general struggle with other religions.

DENIAL OF THE HOLOCAUST

Six or seven publications on this subject have appeared in Greece, including Greek versions of Robert Faurisson's "Is the Diary of Anne Frank Genuine?" and Richard Harwood's "Myth or Holocaust?", which have been published by the Elepheri Skepsis (Free Thought) publishing house. While most are translations, the book *O Mythos* (The Myth) was written by the Greek author Kostas Plevris. Holocaust-denial references frequently appear in articles published by *Stochos* and *Chrissi Avgi*.

OPINION POLLS

In April, an opinion poll on Greek attitudes to minorities and foreigners was commissioned by an organization monitoring adherence to the Helsinki treaty on human rights. According to the results, 57 per cent of Greeks harboured negative feelings towards Jews and 15 per cent, positive feelings. Turks (89 per cent), Albanians (76 per cent) and the Muslim community of Western Thrace (62 per cent) were all disliked more than the Jews. Other minorities received a lower percentage. Initially, the results of the poll were only published in the left-wing newspaper, *Avgi*. In January 1995, however, the popular magazine "Seven Days TV" published the results as its main feature. The organization which commissioned the poll said that the results proved that racism and xenophobia were a problem in Greece, despite official assertions to the contrary.

COUNTERING ANTISEMITISM

The Holocaust and the history of Greek Jewry have not received much attention from Greek educational institutions or the media, although a short entry about the Holocaust now appears in official school textbooks. In 1994, as in the previous year, there was a notable increase in public interest in the Holocaust. This was reflected in the positive response given to Steven Spielberg's film *Schindler's List*, in the number of television interviews conducted with Greek Jews and in the publication of articles and research about Jews. In March, a Thessalonikan newspaper published a special supplement entitled "Thessaloniki-Auschwitz". The Jewish community of Thessaloniki organized a special event in May to honour the non-Jewish Greeks who helped Jews during the German occupation which received wide media coverage. In September, the city of Ioanina erected a monument in its town centre to commemorate Ioanian Jews who had been deported.

As part of the EU "Year against Racism and Antisemitism", Yorgos Papandreou, the minister of education and religion, set up a committee to organize a series of events on racism and antisemitism due to take place over the next three years. The committee included representatives from the Jewish organization, Descendants of Holocaust Survivors.

In 1994, the KIS began to monitor the levels of antisemitism in Greek high schools.

In July, a visit by a fundraising party for the Italian far-right Alleanza Nazionale (National Alliance) was met by 200 mainly left-wing protesters at the port of Piraeus.

ASSESSMENT

In 1994, antisemitism did not pose a direct threat to the Jewish community in Greece. Greek Jewry and the history of Greek Jews received more coverage in the media than in previous years. The increase in organized neo-Nazi vandalism witnessed in 1993 was not repeated.

However, an opinion poll carried out in April suggested that over half of the Greek population "disliked" Jews.

Antisemitism in Greece can be used as part of an anti-European discourse, as it was in the debate over listing religious affiliation on new identity cards. The rise of nationalism in the Balkans, the ongoing controversy over recognition of the former Yugoslav republic of Macedonia and the expulsion of illegal Albanian immigrants following tensions between Greece and Albania, all contributed to an atmosphere in which far-right organizations and publications could gain wider support.

The potential success of the far right was reduced by the ability of mainstream political parties to mobilize around nationalist issues and respond to political pressure to reinforce Greece's Christian-Orthodox identity over its European identity.

Hungary

General population:10.5 million
Jewish population:100,000 (mainly in Budapest)

GENERAL BACKGROUND
The May general election swept away the centre-right coalition which had governed the country since the end of Communist rule and returned the reform communists, now known as the Magyar Szocialista Párt (Hungarian Socialist Party) and led by Gyula Horn. They accepted the burden of governing only in coalition with the liberal Szabat Demokrata Szövetség (Alliance of Free Democrats).

The election result did not change the situation in regard to the economy. The currency was repeatedly devalued. Estimates for 1995 were 20 per cent inflation, an increase in unemployment by some 200,000 persons and large price increases for basic utilities. The budgetary deficit was over Ft300 billion (about US $3 billion).

Furthermore, people perceived in the new government many autocratic "reflexes" from the Communist era as well as a failure to eradicate the corruption which had become endemic in the privatization process.

HISTORICAL LEGACY
Following the emancipation of the Jews in 1867, antisemitism became a serious issue only after the First World War (although a well-known blood libel case occurred in 1882). In 1920 Hungary adopted the so-called *numerus clausus* law which restricted the admission of Jews to universities. In addition, the inter-war Horthy regime was characterized by social antisemitism as well as the *de facto* exclusion of Jews from certain positions in the civil service, law, medicine and similar areas. Nevertheless, until the early 1940s Hungary was widely perceived as something of a haven for Jews.

Following Hitler's rise to power, and particularly after the Anschluss, Hungary adopted a series of anti-Jewish laws as well as a forced labour service for Jewish men (in which 25,000-40,000 perished). Antisemitic agitation was rife. The Nazi invasion of Hungary in March 1944 led to the destruction of much of Hungarian Jewry: close to 600,000 people were exterminated, with considerable collaboration by the Hungarian authorities.

After the Second World War there were several minor pogroms. Following the assumption of power by the Communists in 1948, anti-Zionist agitation became a regular feature in the press, although it was generally milder than in the neighbouring Soviet satellite states.

RACISM AND XENOPHOBIA
Such ethnic discrimination as existed in Hungary in 1994 was directed principally against the Roma, asylum-seekers from Eastern Europe and foreign, mainly African and Asian, students.

PARTIES, ORGANIZATIONS, MOVEMENTS
In a departure from the previous position, a number of minor groups openly expressed their antisemitic ideology.

One such group was the Világnemzeti Népuralmista Párt (VNP, World National Popular Rule Party), headed by Albert Szabó, a Hungarian who returned from Australia in 1993. The VNP, registered in October 1993, describes itself as a "Hungarist" party—the name of the Arrow Cross party which played such a shameful role in the Holocaust. Its role model is the Arrow Cross leader Ferenc Szálasi, who was executed as a war criminal. The party advocates a new *numerus clausus* against Jews and other minorities, denies the Holocaust and attacks so-called Jewish influence in the media.

In January the authorities began an investigation into two VNP leaders on the grounds that they had organized an unconstitutional association and had engaged in incitement to ethnic hatred. In May the party was banned by a court decision.

In April Albert Szabó and István Györkös, a far-right activist previously convicted of incitement and given a suspended sentence, were arrested. They were released in July. As far as can be ascertained, no criminal proceedings were instituted against them.

A smaller, openly antisemitic group was the Szálasi Gárda (Szálasi Guard), whose teenage leader calls himself Mengele.

Organizationally amorphous but more dangerous were the skinheads. According to a statement in July by the deputy director of the Office for National Security, they had 4,000 followers throughout the country. The skinheads had close connections with, or supported, the various other antisemitic groupings.

There were two far-right political parties— István Csurka's Magyar Igazság és Elet Pártja (Party of Hungarian Justice and Life) and Izabella B. Király's Magyar Erdek Párt (Party of Hungarian Interest), which is particularly close to skinheads. The May general election showed that both had little popular backing: they received 1.6 and 0.6 per cent of the votes respectively and remained without parliamentary representation. Király, expelled from the Magyar Demokrata Fórum (Hungarian Democratic Forum) in 1993 on account of her extremist views, is, generally, no longer taken seriously.

The case of Csurka is different. Although he had lost considerable prestige he retained a party machinery and the journal *Magyar Fórum* and is an able publicist. His connection with József Torgyán, the leader of the Függitlen Kisgazda Párt (FKP, Independent Smallholders), provided him with a political base, although there is a difference in their outlook: Torgyán is an extreme nationalist and, possibly, a xenophobe but neither *völkisch* nor antisemitic. Csurka's party denied that it was antisemitic but statements Csurka made (see **Publications and Media**) contradicted this assertion.

The municipal election in December slightly changed the picture which emerged from the May general election. Csurka's party, jointly with the FKP, gained seats in several locations, including seven (out of sixty-six) in Budapest. It must be emphasized that Csurka's success in the municipal election was due only to his alliance with the FKP.

PUBLICATIONS AND MEDIA

The monthly *Hunnia* continued to publish material offensive to Jews but, in a concrete case, the journal's editor and one of its columnists were acquitted of "incitement" (see **Legal Matters**).

The daily *Pesti Hirlap*, which was close to the Antall-Boross governments and contained much material hostile to Jews, ceased publica-

tion for financial reasons. The other pro-MDF daily, *Új Magyarország*, continued to appear but its influence was considerably diminished and its tone different, apparently a realization that antisemitism was not proving an attractive proposition.

However, a new weekly, *Új Demokrata*, joined the ranks of ultra-right publications. Furthermore, the *Pest Megyei Hirlap* contained many antisemitic articles, most of them by András Sándor. On 10 March, in an article entitled "Who should rule Hungary", Sándor said that the Magyars "may, if they behave well, remain as shoeshine boys, waiters or car-washers and even get a tip in the country of Iván Petö, Gyoergy Konrád and Miklós Haraszti, and in particular the [Hungarian-born] philanthropist George Soros". Petö is chairman of the Alliance of Free Democrats, Konrád Hungary's leading writer, and Haraszti a former Alliance of Free Democrats member of parliament; all four mentioned are Jews. On 21 May Sándor wrote that not only Bolshevism but also Zionism too had identical roots with fascism: a Jewish fascism now existed. The Pest *Megyei Hirlap* has since ceased publication.

The most important journal of the far right remained Csurka's weekly *Magyar Fórum*, although even this publication received far less attention than before the May election. Csurka regularly attacked George Soros, "a stooge of the Rothschild Anglo-American bank complex", Iván Berend, the Jewish former head of the Hungarian Academy of Sciences and former leading Communist Party member who is now a professor in the USA, and other prominent Jewish personalities. He also claimed that the late premier Antall had, on a visit to the USA in 1989, been given instructions by the World Jewish Congress to exclude right-wingers from his government and for this reason a genuine "change of the system" had never taken place in Hungary.

At the same time, Csurka insisted that "the antisemitism of the pubs [i.e. crude antisemitism] must not be allowed to spread like weeds" and declared himself willing to accept Jews as "partners" provided, as he put it, they gave up their accusations of collective Hungarian guilt, ceased making capital out of past suffering and dissociated themselves from the extremists among them.

As a throwback to the 1993 "Landeszmann affair", in which Chief Rabbi George Landeszmann had made negative remarks about the Jewish-Hungarian relationship, a volume containing documentation relating to the incident was published with an introduction which trivialized the antisemitic manifestations and accused Jews of "hysteria".

MANIFESTATIONS

The year began with a number of bomb scares and threats to synagogues, including the main one on Dohány Street, and various other Jewish targets. There were also several incidents in which skinheads assaulted individual Jews. These occurrences compelled the Jewish community to make a public appeal in January for assistance in curbing such manifestations.

The Jewish community also publicly protested against the appearance of neo-Nazis and skinheads at the commemoration on 23 October of the anniversary of the 1956 Hungarian uprising.

In the May election campaign the Hungarian Interest Party used posters bearing a Nazi-type caricature of a Jew. The police did not institute proceedings.

RELIGION

In January the editor of the (defunct) newspaper of the Dominican order in Hungary participated in a meeting of the VNP. The head of the order subsequently declared that "the Arrow Cross movement also had positive features" and that the Jews were themselves partly responsible for the spread of antisemitism. The Hungarian Bishops' Collegium swiftly dissociated the church from these remarks and the head of the order publicly apologized.

LEGAL MATTERS

On account of the restrictive interpretation by the courts of the provisions of the criminal code concerning incitement to hatred and violence on racial or religious grounds, immediately prior to the general election President Göncz took the unusual step of introducing a bill of his own amending the criminal code. However, by the end of the year his bill was not yet on the agenda and was expected to be discussed in spring 1995.

On 20 September an appeal by the state prosecutor against the acquittal in October of Ferenc Kúnszabó, editor of the journal *Hunnia*, and János Fodor, a contributor to the journal, on charges of incitement to ethnic hatred, was rejected by the supreme court.

The dissolution of the VNP was referred to above. However, in regard to other complaints about antisemitic manifestations the authorities were slow, or unwilling, to take action.

Although the two parties which formed the new government coalition declared they wished to fulfil Hungary's obligations in regard to compensation of victims of Nazism, little progress was made. The anti-Jewish author Áron Mónus collected signatures for a petition opposing special compensation for Jews.

COUNTERING ANTISEMITISM

Most condemnations of antisemitism were linked to the fiftieth anniversary of the Holocaust in Hungary, the commemoration of which made a deep impression on the Hungarian public. Throughout the year various conferences and exhibitions commemorated the event.

Perhaps the most important event in the life of Hungarian Jewry in 1994 was the forthright condemnation by the new government of antisemitism and its expressions of apology concerning the Holocaust.

In July, in one of the first acts of his administration, Prime Minister Gyula Horn sent the following message to a Jewish memorial gathering: "Fifty years' historical experience should be sufficient time for Hungarians to look at themselves bravely and honestly. . . . The exclusion, even persecution, of the Jews did not begin on 19 March 1944 with the invasion of German troops. We cannot forget the killings by terror commandos [in the "White Terror" after World War One following the overthrow of Hungary's brief Communist government], the *numerus clausus* law [of 1920] and the disgraceful anti-Jewish laws [of 1938-43]. Our historic burden is to apologize to Jewry for the 600,000 people exterminated and the tens of thousands of Jewish compatriots deported."

This statement was reiterated forcefully by Foreign Minister László Kovács at a meeting with the World Jewish Congress leadership in New York in October.

On 19 July at the opening of a Holocaust exhibition in Budapest, Minister of Culture Gábor Fodor said: "For the Hungarian government and its cultural policy there is not—and shall not be—any 'Jewish question'"; constitutional guarantees for freedom of expression could not excuse antisemitism, "which has no place in a cultured society"; and the extreme right and the antisemites "should not expect anything but that the constitutional order will be maintained with the utmost severity".

On 15 October, the anniversary of the Arrow Cross's coming to power (thus heralding the deportation of the Jews from the Hungarian countryside), Cardinal László Paskai, primate of Hungary, issued a pastoral letter to be read in all churches in which he declared that "the extermination of hundreds of thousands solely on account of their origin is the greatest shame on our century . . . a flagrant sin which burdens our history, our communities and—beyond commemoration—calls for the obligation of propitiation".

In November the Catholic Bishops Conference and the Ecumenical Council of the Churches in Hungary issued a similar declaration.

ASSESSMENT

In the May general election Hungarians decisively rejected extremism. Antisemitism diminished both as a political force and even as a subject for daily discussion in the press. Hungarian Jews attained what they most needed—benign neglect. Moreover, the fact that 1994 was the fiftieth anniversary of the Holocaust in Hungary led to a number of highly sympathetic expressions towards Jews.

Ireland

General population: 3.5 million
Jewish population: 1,580

GENERAL BACKGROUND

Until November, Ireland was governed by a Fianna Fail-Labour coalition, which had been in power since January 1993 under the premiership of Albert Reynolds. In November, a deep political crisis was brought about by the attorney general's delay in extraditing to Northern Ireland a Catholic priest found guilty of child abuse. The crisis led to the withdrawal of the Labour ministers from the cabinet and the resignation of the prime minister. In December, a new coalition government was formed of Fine Gael, the Labour Party and the Democratic Left, with John Bruton, the Fine Gael leader, as prime minister.

As a result of the December 1993 British-Irish Downing Street Declaration on Northern Ireland, Sinn Fein, the political wing of the Irish Republican Army (IRA), announced a cease-fire in August 1994. This was followed by a cease-fire by the Loyalist paramilitaries. All Irish political parties, except the Northern Irish Unionists, took part in the Forum for Peace and Reconciliation in Dublin, which had its first meeting in October. Preliminary talks between British government officials and Sinn Fein began in December.

The Irish economy remained relatively stable, with inflation at 2.5 per cent (1.5 per cent in 1993) and low interest rates. Unemployment, whilst remaining high, decreased in 1994 to around 15 per cent (16.9 per cent in 1993).

HISTORICAL LEGACY

Jews have lived in Ireland since the seventeenth century, but the majority came to Ireland in the 1880s. By the early twentieth century, the Jewish community numbered some 4,000 people. Many have since emigrated to Britain, Israel and the United States.

In 1904, in Limerick, Father John Creagh, a priest of the Redemptorist order, incited the local population against "blood-sucking" Jewish money-lenders and travelling peddlers. His sermons brought about a two-year trade boycott of Jewish businesses which was accompanied by intimidation, abuse, harassment and beatings (although there were no fatalities) and resulted in the almost total departure of the 150-strong Limerick Jewish community.

This issue has resurfaced three times in the past thirty years, when various individuals

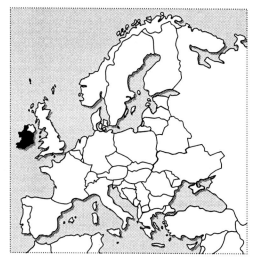

sought to justify it *a posteriori*. In 1965, a correspondence resulted from a television programme on the incident. In 1970, there was further controversy after the then lord mayor of Limerick, Stephen Coughlan, declared his support for Father Creagh's "defending the impoverished Limerick population against the exploitative Jews". The issue flared up again in 1984, with the Jews being defended mainly by left-wing politicians. Only in 1990 did Limerick seek to make amends by restoring the city's Jewish cemetery.

In the Republican movement, Arthur Griffith, the founder of Sinn Fein, wrote many antisemitic articles in the nationalist paper, *The United Irishman*, at the turn of the century. In 1943, Oliver J. Flanagan, a member of the Dáil (parliament) for the Fine Gael party, proposed that the parliament "rout the Jews out of this country". None of his fellow Dáil members protested.

Attempts to settle Jewish refugees in neutral Ireland during the Second World War met with consistent government opposition. There is no wartime evidence that the prime minister, Eamon de Valera, who was primarily concerned with Irish territorial integrity, condemned of German atrocities. In January 1939, de Valera, in a recorded discussion with Eduard Hempel, the German minister to Eire, agreed that Nazi procedures against the Jews "must primarily be explained by the behaviour of the Jews after the [1914-1918] war". Historian Dermot Keogh pointed out that the high "number of visa refusals by the department of justice had tragic consequences. The Irish must live with that guilt." In 1991, a claim by writer and former Labour cabinet minister, Conor Cruise O'Brien that Ireland's 4,000 Jews would have been handed over to the Nazis had Germany won the war, was the subject of much controversy.

With no race relations legislation enacted until 1989, the National Socialist Irish Workers' Party (NSIWP) was active in distributing Nazi literature which was illegal elsewhere in Europe. The NSIWP also printed its own publications, including business-type cards with Holocaust-denial, Nazi, antisemitic and anti-Traveller slogans, a monthly magazine and pamphlets. The NSIWP may have been responsible for a series of attacks on a Jewish butcher shop in Dublin in 1986. The party has not been heard of since and there is no evidence of the existence of any other extreme right-wing groups.

RACISM AND XENOPHOBIA

In 1994, debates about refugees and asylum-seekers became more public as a refugee bill reached the committee stage in the Dáil. According to official figures, there were 393 asylum applications awaiting decision—the majority made in 1994. In the last three years, four people were recognized as refugees under the terms of the 1951 UN convention relating to the status of refugees. A further fifteen were granted permission to remain in Ireland on humanitarian grounds. According to unofficial estimates, there were 5,000 economic and political refugees without access to such facilities as free legal aid or guidance on welfare rights. The only body working with refugees is the voluntarily-run and funded Irish Refugee Trust.

In December, the minister for the environment launched a report, entitled *Still No Place To Go*, which revealed the poor provision of properly-serviced accommodation for Travellers in Dublin during 1993-4. At the launch, the minister commented that "too little has been done to tackle the 'Ku Klux Klan'-type attacks against Travellers in various parts of Ireland".

MANIFESTATIONS

The Gardai (Irish police) received no reports of manifestations of racial hatred. In April, over thirty tombstones at the Progressive Jewish cemetery in the Dublin suburb of Rathfarnham were vandalized during the Easter holiday. Dáil member Ben Briscoe, who is Jewish, denounced the attack, saying it was proof that "fascism did exist in Ireland". No graffiti was found in the cemetery and similar attacks on the Catholic Glasnevin and Mount Jerome cemeteries took place at the same time. The Gardai believe the attack was the work of "mindless vandals" and no perpetrators had been found by the end of 1994.

LEGAL MATTERS

There were no prosecutions under the 1989 Prohibition of Incitement to Hatred Act in 1994.

A paper proposing equal status legislation in non-employment areas was published by the minister for equality and law reform in November. The proposed legislation would prohibit discrimination on account of religion, colour, race, nationality and national or ethnic origin, including membership of the travelling community (and also gender, marital or parental status, sexual orientation and disability). It would make discrimination unlawful in the workplace, in education, and in the provision of goods, facilities and services.

OPINION POLLS

The autumn 1994 issue of *The Jewish Voice: Dublin's Alternative Jewish Press* published a survey of opinions within the Jewish community. Only 14 per cent of the respondents thought "racism was a problem in Dublin", while 24 per cent thought "antisemitism was on the rise in Ireland". Only 10 per cent have been "affected by antisemitism in the last five years", but 48 per cent did not think "the police do enough in these circumstances" or that "Irish law protects Jews from racism".

ASSESSMENT

During 1994, racial discrimination, particularly in relation to Irish Travellers, was discussed more openly in Ireland. Some felt that the country was becoming a more pluralistic society. There was one case of a vandalization of a Jewish cemetery in April, but the general feeling was that the motive was not antisemitic. Overt antisemitism is minimal in comparison with other European countries and poses little threat to the Jewish community.

Italy

General population: 57 million
Jewish population: 32,000 (mainly in Rome
and Milan)

GENERAL BACKGROUND

The upheavals in Italian political life continued
to be dominant in 1994. The collapse of the two
parties—the Partito della Democrazia Cristiana
(DC, Christian Democrat Party) and the
Partito Socialista Italiana (PSI, Italian Socialist
Party)—which had governed the country since
the Second World War was confirmed by the
general election of 27-28 March. Their demise
was attributable to a very serious economic and
social crisis, the 1992 *Tangentopoli* (Bribesville)
corruption scandal, mismanagement of public
services and the change in the balance of international alliances since the end of the Cold War.

The March general election was the first to
be conducted under a predominantly first-past-
the-post system for the chamber of deputies
and by proportional representation for the senate. The elections were won by a right-wing
coalition of Silvio Berlusconi's Forza Italia (FI,
Go Italy!), the federalist Lega Nord (LN,
Northern League), led by Umberto Bossi, and
the neo-fascist-led Alleanza Nazionale (AN,
National Alliance, see **Parties, Organizations,
Movements**) of Gianfranco Fini. The coalition
in turn was made up of two alliances: the Polo
della Libertà (Freedom Alliance) of FI and the
LN in the north (the AN contested this region
on its own) and the Polo del Buon Governo
(Good Government Alliance) of FI, the AN
and the tiny Centro Cristiana Democratico
(CCD, Christian Democratic Centre), led by
Pierferdinando Casini, in central and southern
Italy.

The right-wing coalition won an absolute
majority in the chamber of deputies (366 out of
630 seats) and emerged as the largest single
grouping in the senate (156 out of 315 seats). FI
won 21 per cent of the vote, a remarkable result
for a party which was only formed shortly before the election campaign; the AN won 13.5
per cent, becoming the first Fascist-influenced
party to form part of the governing coalition of
a democratic European state since the Second
World War; and the LN won 8.4 per cent.

Berlusconi became prime minister in May
and FI repeated its success in the June elections
to the European Parliament, winning 30.6 per
cent of the vote, but fared less well in administrative elections in Sardinia and Sicily that month,
losing out to the AN and the centre-left parties.

Berlusconi and his governing coalition
were the subjects of strong criticism concerning
the way in which they were exercising power
and the degree of respect they appeared to show
for the democratic process. Berlusconi was also
criticized for the attacks by him or his government on the judiciary (which was also investigating allegations of corruption in his business
empire), the presidency of the republic, the
state bank, the three state television networks
(managed under the supervision of parliament),
and for his indecision in resolving the conflicts
of interest which resulted from his position as
prime minister and his proprietorship of many
large multinational companies, particularly the
three largest private television networks.

At the end of December, the government
fell after the LN left the coalition and President
Scalfaro entrusted the former treasury minister,
Lamberto Dini, with the task of forming a new
government, made up of non-elected experts
with no previous involvement in politics.

In the economic arena, Italy's gross national product grew by 2.1 per cent and the
weakness of the lira led to a 9 per cent rise in
exports. Inflation continued its gradual decline
to below 4 per cent from 4.5 per cent in 1993.
However, the unemployment rate grew to approximately 12 per cent nationally (over 20 per
cent in the south), from over 10 per cent in
1993. The public sector deficit remained one of
the highest in the European Union (EU) and
proposed measures to reduce it were the cause
of much political debate during 1994 and the
issue is likely to remain significant in 1995.

HISTORICAL LEGACY

Jews have lived continuously in the Italian
peninsula for over 2,000 years. Their treatment

has differed according to the areas in which they have lived. Times of relative tolerance and fruitful growth have alternated with times of serious anti-Jewish prejudice.

From the middle of the sixteenth century onwards, the attitude of the Popes towards the Jews became more ambiguous. This attitude culminated in 1555 with the issuance of the Bull *Cum nimis absurdum* by Pope Paul IV, which marked the beginning of a harsh policy towards Jews living in the Papal state, with the closing of the ghettos, the exclusion of Jews from many cities and villages, and forced baptisms.

Since the unification of Italy in 1861, Jews have had full civil and political rights.

The Fascist era (1922-45) may be divided into three periods: up to 1938, the regime was indifferent to the Jewish problem; in 1938, anti-Jewish legislation deprived Jews of their rights; and in 1943-5, the collaboration of the authorities of the Repubblica Sociale Italiana (Italian Social Republic) with the Nazi occupation led to the deportation of 8,566 Jews from Italy and Italian territories in the Aegean basin.

The 1970s saw a return to anti-Jewish prejudice both among the general population and in the political arena. This was traced to the influence of the far right, and to the moderate left and the far left as a by-product of anti-Zionism. The most violent antisemitic action was the attack by international terrorists on the Rome synagogue in October 1982 in which a child was killed and thirty-six people were injured.

RACISM AND XENOPHOBIA

According to data from the ministry of internal affairs, there were 900,000 foreigners legally present in Italy at the end of 1994. Of these, 84 per cent originated from countries outside the EU, 10 per cent came from Morocco, the rest from former Yugoslavia, the Philippines and Tunisia, as well as small numbers of immigrants from Senegal, Egypt and Albania. Almost half reside in northern Italy, a third in the central region (predominantly in Rome), and the rest in the south and the islands. There was a 7 per cent drop in applications on 1993 which was due to the difference between the 60,000 new requests and the cancellation of earlier requests, which had expired or had been duplicated, after review.

According to the Catholic charity Caritas Italiana, there are an estimated 300,000-400,000 immigrants without leave to remain in the country. The majority of these are resident in the south and in the islands and are often seasonal agricultural workers or family members of immigrants. Approximately 100,000 are unemployed.

Notwithstanding this relatively small number of foreigners, little more than 2 per cent of the population, for some years intolerance has spread throughout Italy, particularly in certain regions and cities. There is a degree of xenophobia which is reinforced by the perception that there are "too many" immigrants, they take away jobs and make use of public facilities (schools, hospitals) which would otherwise be available to native-born Italians.

Extreme manifestations of such xenophobic attitudes are seen in violent attacks on immigrants, especially against those from African countries, particularly Morocco, and from Albania. There were no official statistics for violent racist incidents in 1994 but a study was published on the subject by the sociologist Luigi Manconi, who is also a senator for the Federazione Nazionale per Le Liste Verdi (National Federation for the Green List), which drew on 19 newspapers, 4 weekly publications and 5 press agencies. Manconi's survey found 126 acts of reported violence: 17 in northern Italy, 97 in central Italy (84 in Rome and the surrounding area) and 12 in the south. Criminologists estimate that, in general, only one in four acts of violence are reported in the media or to the police but, for immigrants, who are or who feel barely protected either socially or legally, the rate of reporting is lower.

According to Manconi, a more realistic estimate of the true figure for violent incidents would be at least double the number reported. The perpetrators tend to be young Italian men, usually from those sections of the population who perceive themselves to be most threatened by foreign immigration.

According to an inquiry carried out for the Triveneto association of religious information, amongst a sample of 5,446 adolescents aged between fourteen and nineteen, 12 per cent of young people, the vast majority of whom had little schooling and came from economically disadvantaged homes, openly declared their intolerance of foreigners.

PARTIES, ORGANIZATIONS, MOVEMENTS

The neo-fascist Movimento Sociale Italiano-Destra Nazionale (MSI-DN, Italian Social Movement-National Right), which is modelled on Mussolini's political movement and led by Gianfranco Fini, does not espouse antisemitism and party leaders have condemned Mussolini's antisemitic racial laws as an "error" and a "horror". Nevertheless, its anti-immigrant platform panders to the xenophobic elements amongst its supporters and its electoral success in 1994 makes it the most significant organization in the far-right milieu.

During the year, Fini continued his efforts to re-orient the MSI as a "respectable" right-wing party. At the end of 1993, the MSI eschewed the most blatant symbols of Fascism and regrouped as the AN, incorporating members of the defunct DC.

In February 1994, the neo-Fascists' status as political pariahs ended when the AN/MSI joined FI and the LN in a pact for the March general election. The credibility given to the AN/MSI by the pact was particularly notable south of Rome where the AN/MSI-FI alliance emerged as the largest political grouping. Southern Italy has traditionally been an economically deprived region, subject to the political patronage of generations of post-war governments. Although the MSI had always received its greatest support in the conservative south, in the elections, the AN/MSI built upon its bedrock of nostalgic voters and won the support of the working and lower-middle classes, who were unable to vote for the defunct DC and unwilling to support the left.

In the March general election, the AN/MSI won over 5 million votes (13.5 per cent), gaining 105 out of the 366 seats won by the right in the 630-member chamber of deputies and 43 out of the 156 seats won by the right in the 315-member senate.

On 10 May, three former MSI activists—Giuseppe Tatarella, Adriana Poli Bortone and Altero Matteoli—were appointed to the Italian cabinet as minister for telecommunications and one of two deputy prime ministers, minister of agriculture and minister for the environment respectively. Two other AN deputies, Domenico Fisichella and Publio Fiori, joined the cabinet as minister of cultural heritage and minister of transport respectively. Ten AN/MSI deputies were appointed as junior ministers. Although he was explicitly excluded from the government, Fini hailed the appointment of the three neo-Fascist ministers as signalling an end to the "ideological ostracism of the right".

In the June European elections, the AN/MSI won 12.5 per cent of the vote and received eleven seats. Although this was less than the 13.5 per cent share it received in the general election, the results represented a significant improvement on the 6 per cent and four seats won by the MSI in 1989.

In the administrative elections of 26 June, at which the mayoralties of twenty cities were contested, the AN/MSI suffered a slight fall in popularity and only in Rieti (Lazio) did it obtain a higher percentage (25.7 per cent) than the March national average.

In municipal elections held on 20 November and 4 December, the AN/MSI received 12.1 per cent of the vote after the second round. Polls were held in 242 municipalities and involved only 5 per cent of electors. AN/MSI-supported candidates won in seven municipalities, including the provincial capital of Pescara, where the party gained 20 per cent of the vote.

Despite the apparent willingness of voters to accept the AN/MSI's respectability, doubts remained over the party's commitment to the democratic process. Fini praised Mussolini on a number of occasions (for example, his description of the Fascist leader as the "greatest statesman of the century" immediately after the general election) and declared that the Fascist period was one which had been "overcome" but was not to be "repudiated".

At the end of April, AN/MSI deputy Mirko Tremaglia emphasized Italy's historic claim to Istria and Dalmatia, currently part of Slovenia and Croatia, and declared that Italy should tear up the treaty of Osimo, signed with the former Yugoslavia in 1975, which settled the border between Italy and Slovenia. The return of these territories has always been an official neo-Fascist policy but was treated as a joke while the MSI was in the political wilderness. In May, AN/MSI deputies attempted to lift the prohibition of the Fascist party, although the bill was subsequently withdrawn. Prior to the June European elections, AN/MSI candidate Piero Buscaroli suggested that homosexuals should be placed in concentration camps.

Moreover, elements nostalgic for the past, who regard Fini's "modernization" attempts as a "betrayal" of the MSI's Fascist roots, remained influential in the party organization. Among these are the former MSI leader, Pino Rauti MEP, and the head of the party's federation in Rome, Teodoro Buontempo MP. The latter, in contrast to the moderate leadership of the party, participated in the celebration of the anniversary of the "march on Rome" (28 October 1922) at the tomb of Mussolini. Approximately 3,000 people, among them many skinheads, attended this ceremony.

On 25-29 January 1995, the MSI was formally dissolved and absorbed into the AN. The radical and nostalgic wing of the MSI, led by Pino Rauti, refused to accept the dissolution of the MSI and is in the process of establishing a party which adheres to traditional Fascism. At its dissolution, the MSI had 8,412 branches with 210,000 members and, in addition to its seats in the national and European parliaments, held 44 mayoralties and 750 town council chairs, with 2,600 town councillors, 176 provincial councillors and 45 regional councillors. Prior to the merger, the AN had 1,750 branches and 40,000 members.

It remains to be seen whether the transformation of the MSI into the AN represents a genuine move towards democracy and whether Fini will achieve his ambition to lead a right-wing party in a presidential republic.

On the extreme-right fringe, there are numerous organizations whose platforms are not expressly antisemitic but whose ideology includes anti-Jewish themes, frequently associated with racism. A common theme amongst the various extreme-right movements is anti-Jewishness and the struggle against mondialism (*mondialismo*), a global conspiracy theory which propounds that world "powers"—including Jews, Zionists and freemasons—seek the creation of a unified, consumerist society inhabited by a single, multi-ethnic race.

As in 1993, one of the issues which divided far-right organizations and groupings was the role envisaged for Muslim immigrants in Italy. Some openly xenophobic and racist groupings and individuals favour a "pure-race" Europe. Others advocate a Eurasian-Islamic alliance, in the belief that Islam is the instrument to combat the materialistic, consumerist and multiracial culture of the potential mondialist society. For the latter, the cultural input of Islam would be necessary and Muslim immigration into Italy would have revolutionary potential.

The numerous organizations of the extreme-right fringe present a confusing picture, although their influence on public opinion remained minimal. They have reduced or ostensibly suspended their activities since the passing of the 1993 Mancino law against racial, ethnic or religious discrimination. A number of police operations, judicial inquiries and trials led to the closure of the headquarters of some groupings and the restriction of movement of their leaders. However, while the organizations have been formally suspended, their members still pursue their activities unofficially.

This applies, for example, to the skinheads, 250 of whom took part in a demonstration in Vicenza (Veneto region) in May, after the appointment of three neo-Fascist ministers to the cabinet. Thirty young MSI members and the regional secretary of the Fronte della Gioventù (Youth Front), the MSI's youth movement, also participated in the demonstration, which had been authorized by the local police authority. Teodoro Buontempo hailed the events in Vicenza as "a memorable demonstration" adding that "one cannot prevent belief in ideals".

Also in May, the secretary of an AN/MSI branch declared that skinheads and Maurizio Boccacci, the leader of the Movimento Politico Occidentale (MPO, Western Political Movement) whose headquarters were closed under the Mancino law, were welcome in his branch.

Rome, the traditional stronghold of the MSI, is also where numerous extreme-right organizations were founded in the 1970s. During the early 1990s, a number of small extreme-right groups also emerged in the city, such as the Fronte Italiano di Liberazione (Italian Liberation Front), the Gruppo Nazifascista (Nazi-Fascist Group), the Gruppo Antisemitico Nazionale (National Antisemitic Group), Meridiano Zero (Zero Meridian) and the MPO. Their headquarters were shut down in 1993 by law, but the groups continued to operate, for example, through acts of aggression against left-wing centres and participation in demonstrations against Gypsies. MPO sympathizers claimed responsibility for the majority of xenophobic and antisemitic manifestations in Rome.

The Fronte Nazionale (FN, National Front), a racist organization founded by Franco Freda in Milan in 1991, was also closed. In an interview a few days before his arrest, the FN's co-ordinator, Cesare Ferri, criticized children of "mixed parentage" and expressed the opinion that Jews should return to their "home", that is, Israel.

Other small far-right groupings, which are less overtly neo-Nazi, continued to operate unhindered by the new law. These include the Comunità Politica di Avanguardia (CPA, Political Community of the Avant-garde), whose headquarters are in Trapani and has support groups in Pescara, Modena, Perugia, and in a further six cities in the regions of Puglia, Tuscany, Lombardy, Veneto and Sardinia. Its logo is a Celtic cross and it is closely connected with the *Avanguardia* magazine in which it publishes its views (see **Publications and Media**). Popular nationalist, anti-capitalist and against international finance (often code-words for Jews), one of its objectives is the fight against the "New World Order hegemonized by the international Zionist plutocracy", which it considers to be controlled by the "mondialism of Jewish-masonic high finance".

MAINSTREAM POLITICS

While in the past such statements had been fairly rare, in 1994 six major cases were recorded of members of parties who entered the government in March and made statements which contained prejudiced opinions about Jews.

The strongest view was expressed in January by Nicola Cucullo, the newly-elected MSI mayor of the small city of Chieti. According to the newspaper *Sette* (a supplement of *Il Corriere della Sera*), Cucullo declared that Hitler had been the cleverest man in the world, but that the Germans had been mistaken and should have fried all of the Jews.

During the March electoral campaign, the film-director Pasquale Squitieri, an AN candidate, declared on a private television station in southern Italy that a coup was being prepared against Berlusconi and that one only had to read *The Protocols of the Elders of Zion* to understand how it was being done. Squitieri went on to suggest that those at Botteghe Oscure, the headquarters of the former communist Partito Democratico della Sinistra (PDS, Democratic Party of the Left), must have studied *The Protocols* thoroughly, since the book had originated in Russia in 1890.

In August, the CCD minister of employment, Clemente Mastella, seeking to explain the collapse of the lira in the currency markets, declared to the press that perhaps the presence of AN/MSI in the government had worried the New York "Jewish lobby", and that it was necessary to explain to the "great Jewish financiers" that Fini was continually moving the party away from the nostalgic right.

The other cases involved members of parliament or of the government. In May, after the skinhead demonstration in Vicenza, the AN/MSI under-secretary of defence, Ugo Lo Porto, alluded to the fact that the skinheads might have been manipulated in some way by Mossad (the Israeli secret service).

In June, Alessandra Mussolini, the AN MP and granddaughter of the dictator, declared in an interview that the US film industry was dominated by the American left, which is Jewish. She added that fortunately it was not imbued with communism, like the Italian left, but was nonetheless Jewish.

Also in June, Vittorio Sgarbi, the FI president of the cultural commission of the chamber of deputies, made a comment in the course of a conference held in Rome to celebrate the philosopher Julius Evola, the proponent of "spiritual racism" during the Fascist era. During the conference, Sgarbi referred to the "Jewishness of the judge Colombo", a member of the panel of judges handling the "clean hands" anti-corruption investigation, for whom the "real manoeuvres of the investigation would be carried out in the impenetrable places of the chosen race".

There were also four or five cases, in which AN/MSI representatives, both during the March election campaign and while the AN/MSI was a member of the coalition government, publicly expressed opinions with clear anti-Jewish overtones.

MANIFESTATIONS

The number of antisemitic manifestations reported in 1994 was similar to previous years:

slightly over 100 incidents. A geographical analysis shows a greater density of reported incidents in the central and northern regions: almost half occurred either in Milan or Rome, reflecting perhaps that these cities are home to the two largest Jewish communities in Italy as well as the organizations that most efficiently monitor antisemitic incidents. Furthermore, Rome is the base for a number of extreme-right groupings whose sympathizers carry out small-scale actions.

Thirty per cent of the 100 or so reported incidents in 1994 consisted of verbal or written antisemitic insults: of these, 20 per cent were instances of antisemitic graffiti. Just under 20 per cent of the total involved threats directed at Jewish individuals or institutions, including three cases of violence or property damage, four cases of antisemitic graffiti or letters, and nine cases of antisemitic insults directly addressed to Jews.

Of the two cases which involved physical violence, the most serious occurred in Assisi (Umbria) in August, when a Jewish woman was insulted and assaulted in the street by three youths who scratched her face with a razor-blade, and threatened to do it again on a future occasion if she did not leave Assisi. The second case involved a young Jewish boy who, while playing on a recreation ground near Milan's Jewish school, was attacked by three teenage youths wearing Celtic crosses around their necks who first asked the boy if he was Jewish.

Although the number of reported incidents has not varied in recent years, some minor but significant trends were more evident and indicated a degree of more widespread anti-Jewish prejudice. For example, one growing trend is the public expression of opinions with clear anti-Jewish overtones by members of political parties which entered the government in March (see **Mainstream Politics**). Another, even more frequent occurrence among the reported incidents (about 10 per cent), was the inscription of antisemitic phrases on a variety of "ordinary" documents, such as in the visitors' book at an exhibition, on a form for ordering a book, a restaurant menu and some L5,000 and L10,000 notes.

The cultural and ideological backgrounds of reported incidents were often those of the extreme and Catholic right or of fundamentalist Catholicism. Also represented were examples of "generic antisemitism", which did not appear to come from any specific ideological milieu.

The themes most often invoked concerned the Holocaust and the supposed power of the "Jewish lobby", particularly in the financial world. Antisemitism was also expressed by football supporters, the term "Jew" being used as an insult, to signify a supporter or a team which should be "exterminated" (see **Grassroots**).

CULTURAL LIFE

Political events in 1994 contributed to the erosion of some cultural and political taboos on the right. Writers who were ideologues of the right and of Fascism, and had previously been ignored by the majority of Italians, were no longer demonized. Such rehabilitation was mostly on account of the intellectual merits of their work but it resulted in the reprinting of some antisemitic pamphlets.

Recently, Leon Bloy, author of the antisemitic book entitled *Dagli ebrei la salvezza* (Salvation From Jews), and Ernst von Salomon, another antisemitic writer, were published by major publishing houses. There were also conferences and radio broadcasts on the French antisemitic writer Louis-Ferdinand Céline and the Italian race theorist Julius Evola. Books by Drieu La Rochelle and Ernst Junger are expected in 1995. Bloy also republished works without antisemitic content by the same authors. These works, now clearly no longer contentious, were previously disregarded because they were by writers who had also produced virulently antisemitic works, like Céline and Evola.

EDUCATION

A few photocopied pages of an unknown text, which alleged an international Jewish conspiracy and that Jews were an instrument of Satan to destroy the Catholic church, were distributed by a teacher during an English-language course for adults.

GRASSROOTS

The MPO is reported to have some influence amongst the supporters of Rome's two football teams. There is also evidence of support for neo-Nazism amongst the supporters of football clubs in many other Italian cities. Moreover, the word "Jew" has become an insult used by some football fans who are not necessarily supportive of neo-Nazism.

PUBLICATIONS AND MEDIA

The range of periodicals in 1994 which contained antisemitic articles was similar to that of last year, with an increase in Catholic fundamentalist publications (see **Religion**). There was an increase in the number of articles in small publications on links between the world of finance and Jews, often with fanciful and strained attributions. The publications of the extreme right placed particular emphasis on their "discovery" of a *Protocols*-type Jewish conspiracy. Apart from these journals, which are distributed in very limited circles, the incidents of anti-Jewish prejudice in national, daily or periodical publications in 1994 were negligible.

The left-wing magazine *La lente di Marx* included in its October issue a fifty-page supplement devoted to a "reflection on Zionist racism". Refuting the assumption that Jews take pleasure in a "positive myth" that leads to "a taboo for which the Jew is an untouchable god" for the left, the magazine attempted to demonstrate that Jews, by means of a kind of "warlike and military Jewish psychosis", are bearers of a specific Jewish racism which marks their history, from biblical times to the birth of Zionism and the Arab-Israeli conflict. Historical writings and diverse theories, taken out of context, were bound together by brief editorial comment to support this idea.

The MSI daily *Il Secolo d'Italia* published an article in June, which referred to Gad Lerner, the deputy editor of the mainstream *La Stampa,* who is Jewish, as the "former rabble-rouser, who for years has powdered his predatory nose with knowing touches of democratic make-up". Also in June, *Il Secolo d'Italia* alluded to the "orchestrated manoeuvre against Italy and the appointment of ministers of the Alleanza Nazionale" and went on to claim that the "socialist businessman Berge . . . is no doubt a supporter of this campaign. One suspects that Berge sympathizes with the weekly publication of the left *Globe Hebdo* and the Jewish lobby of the left headed by the former [French] Prime Minister Fabius."

Avanguardia, the monthly of the CPA, was founded twelve years ago as a review for MSI militants. Edited by Leonardo Fonte, it is registered in Trapani (Sicily) with three regional editorial offices and has a circulation of approximately 2,000. During 1994, it experienced financial difficulties due to a lack of donations and to a reduction in sales and subscriptions.

Avanguardia's editorial line is anti-mondialist, Holocaust-denying, anti-Zionist and antisemitic. It supports the establishment of a Eurasian-Islamic alliance and highlights Iran as its only political ally in the struggle against mondialism and anti-Zionism. Articles about, or casual references to, Jews are commonplace in every issue and range from analysis of the reasons for Hitler's antisemitism and the anti-Jewish theories advanced by Julius Evola, to the reprinting of extracts of out-of-print antisemitic books. Also rife are references to the "clear evidence of Jewish mondialist power" in the Italian state just as in the West, which has a culture strongly linked to Judaism, freemasonry and Zionism.

The monthly *Orion* was founded in 1984 and is published by the Milan-based Società Editrice Barbarossa, which shares its address with the Italian branch of the Front Europeo di Liberazione (European Liberation Front), a third-positionist organization which supports a "red-brown" alliance between ultra-nationalists and hardline communists. Edited by Marco Battarra, *Orion*'s circulation, which grew in 1994, is estimated at 2,000 copies, distributed in about thirty Italian cities. Like *Avanguardia*, *Orion* also sympathizes with Islamic fundamentalism. It campaigns for a Eurasian-Islamic alliance to counter imperialism, mondialism and Zionism and never fails to refer to "international Jewish propaganda" and the supposed "Jewish lobbies". It claims the right to re-evaluate the "true or alleged" Holocaust, publishing various Holocaust-denial articles, including criticism of the film *Schindler's List*.

In July, the author of an article about an attack in Iran the previous month, asserted that it had been proved beyond doubt that the incident was the work of "the great Satan", that is, "American-Zionist imperialism which inspires conspiracies and infests the world with bombs".

L'Uomo Libero, published quarterly by the Milan-based Edizioni l'Uomo Libero, was founded in 1980. Edited by Piero Sella, the journal is anti-Zionist and anti-mondialist. Many members of its editorial board have been affected by the Mancino law. In 1994, only the January issue portrayed Jews negatively and even then the references were minimal.

Aurora, the "monthly of combative political action", was founded in 1987 and is distributed free. Edited by Luigi Costa, it has eight regional editorial offices through which it maintains contact with groups holding similar positions. Ideologically, it claims its origins in national socialism, Fascism and the 1943-5 Salò Republic.

In 1994, *Aurora* encountered financial difficulties which occasionally prevented its publication. It is nationalistic, anti-mondialist and pro-Islam. Some 1994 articles included references to the Jews' long-standing involvement in usury, and espionage by Jewish Americans who sold plans of the atomic bomb to the Soviet Union. It also published favourable reviews of Holocaust-denial books or works which purported to show the "insidiousness" of the Talmud. In March, one book review presented evidence of the supposed "historical foundation" of the myth of Jewish ritual murder.

In June, *Aurora* declared that it did not want to hear any more "old stories" of the "Jewish-masonic conspiracy", which it considered to be the "trash" of the extreme right, and that it wished to oppose only "the racist and Zionist policies of the state of Israel and its ally, the United States". Since then, the journal has made only sporadic and limited mention of Jews and Israel.

The US-based neo-Nazi organization, the Nationalsozialistische Deutsche Arbeiterpartei/ Auslands- und Aufbauorganisation (NDSAP/ AO, German National Socialist Workers' Party/Overseas Section) irregularly publishes the *Bollettino Novità NS della NSDAP/AO* (NS Newsletter of the NSDAP/AO), although it is thought that the Italian edition is produced outside the country. Issue "no. 7" appeared during 1994 and featured advertisements for stickers bearing swastikas and the words "Jews out", available from the NSDAP/AO in Lincoln, Nebraska (see **United States**). It also included an article denouncing the 1993 Mancino law which, it claimed, was issued by the "pro-Zionist minister Mancino" following "opportunist requests by the Roman Jewish community to destroy the liberty of the skinheads".

A series of magazines and audio-visual cassettes on *Nazismo Esoterico. Mito, sacro e occulto* (Esoteric Nazism. Myth, Sacred and Occult) was produced during 1994 by Marco Dolcetta of Hobby & Work Italiana Editrice Cinisello Balsamo in Milan. The seventh of twelve planned editions appeared in December and was available for sale at news-stands. This series, the first of which was entitled "Léon Degrelle, il cattolicesimo nel nazionalsocialismo" (Léon Degrelle, Catholicism in National Socialism) and the seventh "Le ragioni mistiche dell'antisemitismo. Dai progrom ai *Protocolli dei Savi Anziani di Sion*" (The Mystic Reasons for Antisemitism. From the programme of *The Protocols of the Elders of Zion*), reproduces various racist and antisemitic texts and opinions from the Nazi period without any editorial criticism. In the seventh edition, *The Protocols* are presented by the respected French academic Pierre-André Taguieff, who puts them in a historical context. But it also includes Claudio Mutti (editor of an edition of *The Protocols* for Edizioni di Ar in 1976, who runs a far-right publishing house), who demonstrates at great length similarities also in the Talmud and the Bible.

Approximately fifty books published in previous years remained in circulation, sold mainly by subscription through specialist bookshops or militant groups. The majority originated from far-right publishing houses, such as the Parma-based Edizioni all'Insegna del Veltro, run by Claudio Mutti, Franco Freda's Edizioni di Ar, based in Padua and Salerno, La Sfinge, La Sentinella d'Italia in Monfalcone (near Trieste), and Edizioni l'Uomo Libero. The authors ranged from Julius Evola and Hitler to contemporary antisemitic writers, such as the Russian far-right ideologue Igor Shafarevich and the Italian Holocaust-denier Carlo Mattogno.

In 1994, remaindered copies of Hitler's *Mein Kampf*, published in Varese without any critical commentary, continued to be available in some bookshops. Another edition of *Mein Kampf*, published by La Sentinella d'Italia, was available in several bookshops in the Prato area (near Florence).

RELIGION

The socio-political crisis in Italy has encouraged the re-emergence of pre-Vatican II ideas and proposed solutions to the evils afflicting the country, which may be attributed to Jews. Among the numerous small organizations on the fundamentalist Catholic fringes, modern consumerism and materialism are considered to have caused the disintegration of morals and the church is criticized for having sacrificed traditional Catholic values for modernity through its policies following the Second Vatican Council. These fringe groups cite the Trent Council (1542) and the teachings of Saint Pius V and are marginal in the church.

In this context, there is opposition to the Catholic church's "concession" to the Jews which is alleged to have allowed the chuch to become controlled by Jews and freemasons. Ancient antisemitic myths and stereotypes, such as accusations of deicide and ritual murder, are being resuscitated. Articles on these themes appeared in the fundamentalist Catholic press.

The weekly *Sodalitium*, which has a broad cultural ambit, is published by the Mater Boni Consilii di Verrua Savoia Institute, whose editor-in-chief is Don Francesco Ricossa. The bias of the journal is Catholic fundamentalist, similar to the arch-traditionalist views of Monsignor Lefebvre, but more critical of the Roman Catholic church and the Second Vatican Council and it strongly opposes the church's opening towards the Jews. However, the journal has a small circulation and little influence within the Catholic church.

Issues published in 1994 included: a long article highly critical of the Second Vatican Council, of Cardinal Bea and Pope John XXIII; an article on "Jewish-masonic infiltration" of the church; a review of a book by Emmanuel

Ratier entitled *Mystères et secrets du B'nai B'rith. La plus importante organisation Juive internationale* (Mysteries and Secrets of B'nai Brith. The Most Important International Jewish Organization); and an article by Don Curzio Nitoglia on Marranos (covert Jews) whose "clandestine activity provides proof of so much that one reads in books . . . as if they were legends or exaggerations, like the mystery of blood or ritual murder, transmitted orally from father to son, and carried out in the secrecy of basements".

The fortnightly Catholic fundamentalist *Si Si, No, No* was established in 1974. Edited by a priest, Emmanuel de Taveau, the journal is published in Rome and distributed amongst Roman Catholic clergy. It has printed a number of anti-Jewish articles in the past, and in April, criticized the openness of some Catholic prelates towards Jews because "the accusation of deicide must remain extant".

The monthly *Identità*, published by the Identità di Milan co-operative, employed Irene Pivetti as its political editor until March. (Pivetti, a LN MP and Lefebvrist who was elected speaker of the chamber of deputies after the March general election, suggested in parliament in 1993 that "Jewish masonry" had played a role in the compilation of the *Antisemitism World Report 1993*.) *Identità* was not published between March and October, when it reappeared under the editorship of Giulio Ferrari.

In the November issue, in an article by Solaro Della Margherita entitled "Younger brother. Catholicism, Judaism and loss of identity", the author criticized the Second Vatican Council and found the present Pope's positive gestures towards Judaism "surprising" because he thought deicide and traditional Catholic doctrine would constitute an insurmountable obstacle to an alliance between church and synagogue. It appears that by the end of 1994, *Identità* had ceased publication.

Several pamphlets of twenty-thirty pages were reproduced and distributed by the San Giorgio di Ferrara Cultural Centre. These pamphlets, which depicted Jews according to eighteenth-century Catholic tradition, included *Il complotto della sinagoga* (The Conspiracy of the Synagogue) by Don I. A. Santangelo, published in 1985, which summarizes the theories of *The Protocols of the Elders of Zion*; *Il popolo deicida* (The Deicidal People) and *I vignaioli perfidi* (The Treacherous Vinedressers) by Don Giorgio Maffei, both on the subject of deicide for which, he alleges, even Jews alive today are considered culpable; *L'omicidio rituale praticato dai giudei* (The Ritual Murder Practised by the Jews) by Don Curzio Nitoglia, which was extracted from an article published in *Sodalitium* in 1992.

In December, *Nichita Roncalli, controvita di un Papa* (Nichita Roncalli, Counterlife of a Pope), a book by F. Bellegrandi, was presented to the Vatican. The book claimed that Popes John XXIII and Paul VI caused the Catholic church to abandon its age-old attitudes by affirming the Second Vatican Council in accordance with the plan made by "clandestine forces", that is, communism, freemasonry, Judaism and Protestantism.

There are reports that these subjects are often addressed in church sermons, such as those of one friar in Chiesa who, in his Christmas sermon in Bologna, repeated the accusation that the Jews killed Jesus Christ. Another incident involved a mass celebrated by Don Curzio Nitoglia of the Mater Boni Consilii Institute, the institute which publishes *Sodalitium* and which also runs a training seminary for priests. In January, Don Nitoglia celebrated mass at the MSI office in Via Acca Larenzia in Rome, which is one of the MSI branches closest to the extreme-right skinheads. During the sermon, he declared, among other things, that communism is the offspring of Judaism and that: "we are right to defend ourselves and to defend the true Catholic church against communism and the masonic and Jewish lobbies."

A small Rome-based organization, Militia Christi, distributed a leaflet in January, at the bottom of which was a Vandean Cross (a heart covered by a cross). The text established the difference between antisemitism and anti-Zionism, and recorded the merits of the church in the defence of the Jews. It went on to make accusations against several "Jewish" banks for having financed national socialism and the "Zionist government" for "conducting its own affairs against all other peoples and being ready to take possession of the whole world".

DENIAL OF THE HOLOCAUST

In 1994, two Holocaust-denial works in Italian were added to those already in circulation. The first, *Auschwitz: fine di una leggenda. Considerazioni storico-tecniche sul libro di Jean-Claude Pressac* (Auschwitz: The End of a Legend. Historical-Technical Considerations on the Book by Jean-Claude Pressac), is by Carlo Mattogno, the author of a number of Holocaust-denial works, and published by Edizioni di Ar.

The second, *Dallo sfruttamento nei lager allo sfruttamento dei lager. Una messa a punto marxista sulla questione del revisionismo storico* (From the Exploitation in the Camps to the Exploitation of the Camps. A Marxist Update

on the Question of Revisionist History), comes from the opposite end of the political spectrum. Produced by the Genoa-based Graphos publishing house, the work is a translation of an article published in France in 1979 on "La Guerre sociale" (The social war) which denies the existence of the gas chambers, radically reappraises the number of those murdered in the Holocaust and cites wartime conditions as the cause of those deaths that did occur. The Graphos publishing house and Cesare Saletta, one of the translators, have been responsible for other Holocaust-denial publications in previous years.

Orion and *Avanguardia* continued to publish a number of references to Holocaust-denial, including cartoons and book reviews.

Special screenings of the film *Schindler's List* were organized for secondary school pupils in many Italian cities. In Genoa, Siena and Lodi, some pupils shouted insults and noisily applauded some scenes of violence against Jews.

At a school in Torino, where *Schindler's List* was screened during school hours, the film was described reportedly as "inopportune" and "misinformative" in that it apparently showed only a part of the tragedy without the context of the full complex picture.

OPINION POLLS

In 1994 there was very little research conducted and that which was done was of very limited scope. The first poll was conducted among a sample of 1,015 adults by the Instituto Studi sulla Pubblica Opinione on daily minor conflicts. One question concerned the potential nuisance the interviewee might experience in having a Jew as a neighbour. Of the interviewees, only 1.8 per cent replied "yes, a great nuisance" and only 1.9 per cent replied "yes, quite a nuisance". These replies were more accentuated among older interviewees, those with a low level of education and residents of southern Italy and the islands.

Another poll was conducted among a sample of 1,000 people by the Federazione Italiana Psicologi in December on the image of Jews. According to 20 per cent of those interviewed, Jews were mean; 15 per cent thought that they had hooked noses and low foreheads; 43.6 per cent considered Jews to be guilty of the crucifixion of Jesus Christ; and 23.7 per cent were sure of the existence of dangerous and powerful Jewish lobbies.

In February, a questionnaire on the subject of antisemitism was distributed by some teachers in a secondary school in Savona to 700 students. Among the various replies, 80 per cent declared their belief in the existence of antisemitism; 65 per cent thought that something should be done to combat it; 37 per cent thought that the Jews were somewhat to blame for it; and 34 per cent considered Jews to be a "race".

LEGAL MATTERS

In order to improve the 1993 Mancino law against racial, ethnic or religious discrimination, the justice ministry issued a decree which set rules to determine non-fiscal or custodial penalties for activities which contravened the anti-discrimination legislation. Therefore, those found guilty of non-violent offences under the Mancino legislation can be sentenced to restore and maintain property defaced by graffiti, emblems or symbols, or to work for social welfare organizations and community service projects.

In 1994, various judicial inquiries were carried out and a number of trials commenced regarding far-right extremists. In the Veneto region in May, two inquiries took place: one in Vicenza, following the demonstration of skinheads on 14 May, and one in Verona where seventy neo-Nazis were accused of inciting racial hatred and reconstituting the Fascist party. FN founder Franco Freda was also sent for trial on charges relating to the reconstitution of the Fascist party. In the areas surrounding Verona, Padova and Treviso, some ten people, and a sophisticated network of circles, meeting places and shops specializing in neo-Nazi gadgetry were all under investigation.

In November in Milan, sixty-three far-right extremists—including skinheads, football supporters and members of the Front della Gioventù—were sent for trial (due to take place in April 1995) on charges of having violated the Mancino law.

In January, a far-right extremist was sentenced to four months' imprisonment after he was found guilty of affixing yellow stickers emblazoned with a Star of David and the words "Zionists: Get Out of Italy" on the shutters of twenty-five Jewish-owned shops in Rome in November 1992.

In April, a tribunal in Monza (near Milan) sentenced the headmaster of a secondary school who in 1993 had berated a (non-Jewish) boy who arrived fifteen minutes late for school with the words: "Jew, impostor, thief. . . . You come from a family which has given you a Jewish education." The prefect imposed a fine of L1 million and awarded damages of L5 million not so much for using the term "Jew", which he considered to be a commonplace if tasteless insult, but for using the term in a school.

COUNTERING ANTISEMITISM

While anti-Jewish prejudices have become more prevalent in Italy in recent years, the "rejection" of antisemitism still predominates and declarations against antisemitism tend to include affirmations of a commitment to democracy.

There was a plethora of articles in the mainstream media which forcefully denounced antisemitic incidents and strongly condemned the phenomenon in general.

In the speeches of Pope John Paul II and of some bishops, in particular, Cardinal Maria Martini of Milan, there were condemnations of both past and present antisemitism.

In June, Prime Minister Silvio Berlusconi, highlighting the action taken by the government to seek the extradition from Argentina of Nazi Erich Priebke who is accused of war crimes (see **Argentina**), stated that this action was "dictated by the repudiation, profoundly rooted in Italy, of antisemitism".

At the January 1995 AN/MSI congress, an AN motion was approved with a "specific, definitive and final condemnation of every form of antisemitism and anti-Jewish sentiment, even when camouflaged by the propagandist cloak of anti-Zionism". The AN further stated its solidarity with the *Nostra Aetate* declaration of the Second Vatican Council, which repudiated Jewish responsibility for the death of Jesus. Lastly, it stated that it considered the racial laws which were issued during the Fascist era to be "a shame which will burn forever in the conscience of men and of Italians".

ASSESSMENT

In 1994, the demonstrations of antisemitism increased compared to the previous year and returned to levels witnessed in 1992.

As in 1993, it was not considered unreasonable to use antisemitic stereotypes in personal discussions and the use of the term "Jew" as an insult by young neo-Fascists and football supporters, noted in recent years, was becoming more common.

Another worrying development in 1993 was the claim by the extreme right that the open declaration of antisemitic prejudices constituted part of its right to freedom of expression. This attitude continued to prevail in 1994 and may not be merely the preserve of the extreme right. Moreover, the allegations by mainstream politicians of Jewish conspiracies behind the instability of the lira and the anti-corruption investigation suggested a willingness to blame Jews for Italy's political and economic crisis.

Also prevalent in 1994 was the tendency

to re-interpret the last seventy years of Italian history, to re-evaluate fascism and the Italian Social Republic and to give equal emphasis to the ideals on which fascism itself was based. The rehabilitation of authors whose works included antisemitic writings is a further example of this.

In the political arena, the grave economic, social and institutional crisis which Italy continued to experience in 1994 brought profound party political changes.

The neo-Fascist MSI's significant electoral breakthrough is a direct result of the party's exclusion from the corrupt political mainstream rather than an endorsement of its Fascist ideals. Indeed, its regrouping as the "respectable" AN and eschewal of obvious Fascist symbols

suggest that the party leadership is aware of the electoral unpalatability of overt neo-Fascism. Despite this, differences between the MSI's militant and modernizing wings were apparent during 1994 and nostalgic elements were still influential in the party organization. It remains to be seen whether those elements will support the hard-liners who broke away in January 1995 and leave Fini free to pursue his re-orientation of the party as a conservative right-wing force. However, Fini still has to prove to many electors that the AN has a genuine commitment to democracy. Nevertheless, should Prime Minister Dini's non-elected administration fall in 1995, the AN could emerge as a key power-broker in the formation of a new government.

Latvia

General population: 2.7 million
Jewish population: 15,000 (mainly in Riga)

GENERAL BACKGROUND

Latvia, a former Soviet republic, is a parliamentary democracy. Traditionally dominated by agriculture and forestry-based industries, Latvia's varied economy is increasingly oriented towards the service sector. In 1994 unemployment was around 8 per cent and annual inflation around 25 per cent and falling.

In June the Latvian parliament overwhelmingly approved a bill restricting the awarding of Latvian citizenship. The bill was based on quota arrangements which were expected to mean the refusal of citizenship to between 300,000 and 500,000 people, many of them ethnic Russians.

HISTORICAL LEGACY

Jews settled in Livonia and Kurland, the central and western regions of Latvia, in the sixteenth century. At the beginning of the twentieth century there was a Jewish population of 200,000 in these areas but expulsions and emigration contributed to cutting that number by half.

Latvia became an independent republic in 1918 and Jews, along with other minorities, were granted broad educational and cultural autonomy. The liberal regime was short-lived. In May 1934 Latvia became a pro-Nazi totalitarian state.

During the Nazi occupation of the country, over 80,000 Jews were murdered with the collaboration of Latvian police units. A number of Latvians joined special killing units operating under the instructions of the Nazis. The major unit of this kind was the Arajs Commando which operated around Riga.

PARTIES, GROUPS, ORGANIZATIONS

The ultra-nationalist Latvijas Nacionalas Neatkavibus Kustiba (LNNK, National Independence Movement of Latvia) receives financial support from émigré Latvians in the West, notably Joachim Siegerist. Siegerist has formed the party For Latvia, together with Odysee Kostanda, the former leader of the LNNK. For Latvia is the only political party in Latvia which restricts membership to Latvian citizens. In 1994 Siegerist announced that he would stand as a candidate in the 1995 Latvian presidential election.

The Tevzemel un Brivibal (TB, Fatherland and Freedom Party) was formed in 1992 from radical-nationalist elements of the Popular Front which led the campaign for independence from the former Soviet Union. In July 1993 it formed a bloc with the LNNK in its anti-Russian stance.

The youth organization Mazpulki (referring to a pre-war fascist group) is modelled on the Hitler Youth.

The Dvizhene za natsionalnuyu nezavisimost Latvii (DNNL, Movement for National Independence of Latvia) is a Russian ultra-nationalist group.

MANIFESTATIONS

In February the presentation by President Ulmanis of history books to two schools provoked protests from Jewish circles. The books, published by the Latvian ministry of education and written by Adolf Shild, a pre-war fascist leader and Nazi collaborator, praised the Nazi occupation. The president's press secretary, Anta Busa, told the popular newspaper *Dienna*: "It would be better if the Jews could finally leave us alone. We have trembled and knelt before them long enough. It should stop once and for all." President Ulmanis assured Latvian Jewish leaders that antisemitism existed neither in state institutions nor in society in general: the cause of anti-Jewish incidents were errors or bad manners. He accepted the resignation of Anta Busa because she had "committed a number of inaccuracies".

In March DNNL supporters picketed the parliament building and chanted antisemitic slogans at the Jewish deputies Edvins Inkens and Egils Levits.

On 20 March an article in the ultra-nationalist weekly *Pavalstnieks* stated: "The villains who recently painted the swastikas [on Jewish gravestones] were probably paid by the kikes themselves so that the incident could be blown up as a world-shattering sensation."

In June it was reported that as part of a series depicting the history of Latvian aviation, the Latvian post office had published a stamped envelope showing an aircraft with swastika markings. The London-based *Briva Latvia*, 21-8 November, quoted a Latvian MP as claiming that the swastika was an old Latvian symbol purloined by Hitler.

In June Mikhail Gleizer, a photographer of Jewish origins with the liberal newspaper *SM Sevodnya*, was attacked outside the parliament building.

On 18 August on the first day of the newly elected parliament, ultra-nationalist deputies heckled Jewish parliamentarian Rut Maryash.

PUBLICATIONS AND MEDIA

In its 15 April issue *Lauku Avize* published a letter which referred to "the intensive propaganda of the kikes".

The newspaper *Yaunais Laike*, which has been attacked in the Latvian press for its alleged racism, reprinted in its September issue (no. 16) an interview with the US rock group, Das Reich. In the interview, which originally appeared in the North American publication *Resistance,* the group was said to have described the Holocaust as "one more example of the Yids spreading snivelling lies" and the Holocaust museum in Washington as the museum of "holoillusion", adding: "As our song says, 'Let bombs rain down on it'."

On 25 November *Nakts*, a sensationalist daily, reported an interview with Brunis Rubess, a board member of the Bank of Latvia, who was quoted as saying: "Traders are generally regarded as scoundrels. Our problem is that too many of our traders are kikes, Gypsies, Russians and Chechens. All people without honour."

COUNTERING ANTISEMITISM

On a visit to Israel in February the Latvian prime minister, Vladis Birkavs, said: "There is a fable in the world that Latvians hate Jews. This is not true. The time has come to stop doubting the honesty of our relationship with Israel and the Jewish people." He claimed the government had done a great deal to remind Latvians about the wartime atrocities carried out by the Nazis and their Latvian collaborators and said that the topic would be included in schoolbooks in 1995.

On 14 June President Ulmanis told a world Jewish cultural congress in Riga that Latvia extended cultural autonomy to all ethnic minorities, including Jews.

On 14 October Riga city council announced its intention of banning several Russian newspapers including the hard-right *Zavtra, Sovetskaya Rossiya* and *Russky sobor.*

In October Premier Maris Gailis announced the government's intention to set up an independent organization to promote human rights which would be accessible to all Latvia's residents and follow recommendations from the United Nations Development Programme.

ASSESSMENT

The major problem facing the small Jewish community is, in the context of Latvian post-communist nationalism, the country's slow coming-to-terms with the part played by Nazi collaborators in the Holocaust. There is also some evidence of extremism among the sizeable Russian population.

Lithuania

General population: 3.8 million
Jewish population: 6,000 (mainly in Vilnius)

GENERAL BACKGROUND

Lithuania, a parliamentary democracy, regained its independence in 1991. In elections in 1992 the Lietuvos Democratine Darbo Partija (Lithuanian Democratic Labour Party), the successor to the Communist Party of Lithuania, won a majority of parliamentary seats and formed the government.

Since independence from the former Soviet Union, Lithuania has made steady progress in developing a market economy. Over 40 per cent of state property has been privatized. Lithuania slashed its annual inflation rate to 70 per cent, a 400 per cent reduction over the previous year. Although living conditions for the general population remain harsh, both the economy and the general political situation are stable.

HISTORICAL LEGACY

Jews have lived in what is now Lithuania since the fourteenth century. By the seventeenth century Vilno (Vilnius) was renowned as a centre of Jewish learning. In 1881-2, when the country formed part of the tsarist Russian empire, pogroms persuaded many Jews to emigrate.

During the period of Lithuanian independence a variety of antisemitic organizations were active, among them Verslas, Jaunoji Lietuva and Voldemarists (Iron Wolf), which took power following a coup in 1926.

When in October 1939 the Lithuanian army retook Vilnius from the Poles, anti-Jewish pogroms were carried out with the approval of the new government. Approximately 200 Jews were injured.

The Soviets occupied Lithuania in June 1940. Among underground organizations opposing them was the pro-Nazi Lithuanian Active Front.

When the Nazis occupied the country in 1941 many Lithuanians assisted them in the extermination of Jews. Over 200,000 Lithuanian Jews died in the Holocaust.

MANIFESTATIONS

On 20 April, Hitler's birth date, posters announcing a football match between the Lithuanian and Israeli Olympic teams were defaced with swastikas. At the match itself a small group of skinheads chanted anti-Jewish slogans.

Jewish leaders called on officials to provide better police protection for Jewish cemeteries in Kaunas, Vilnius and Kalvaria which had been increasingly subject to vandalism. Kaunas officials established an *ad hoc* committee, including police and Jewish community representatives, to look for ways to improve security at the cemeteries and said they would increase funding for the upkeep and protection of the cemeteries.

PUBLICATIONS AND MEDIA

The book *Walka z żydo-masonami o wiarę i Polskę* (The Struggle against Judeo-Masons for Faith and for Poland) by the Polish antisemite Bolesław Tejkowski (see **Poland**) was published by the Vilnius publishing house ZSA Proyektservisas. The Organization of Catholic Poles in Lithuania ordered 1,500 copies. In June it was reported that the ministry of justice's press department had warned the publishing house that it was in danger of losing its printing licence.

Towards the end of the year, the Jewish community became apprehensive regarding antisemitic articles in a leading independent newspaper and sent an open letter to the president asking that he condemn the articles. Jewish representatives noted that the president had met them to discuss the issues raised in the letter, but by the end of the year he had not publicly condemned the articles in question.

COUNTERING ANTISEMITISM

In a television address on 22 September Lithuanian Prime Minister Adolfas Šleževičius urged citizens to accept responsibility for the wartime genocide against Lithuanian Jews. He said that at least 200,000 Lithuanian Jews, out of a pre-war population of some 240,000, had been killed and that "hundreds of Lithuanians [had taken] direct part in this genocide". He added that the Lithuanian government had assumed "responsibility for prosecuting those who participated in murder".

ASSESSMENT

There appeared to be little organized extremist activity in Lithuania. Antisemitism remained a minor problem. The acknowledgment by the Lithuanian prime minister of the complicity of some Lithuanians in the Holocaust on Lithuanian soil did much to assuage a very sensitive issue.

Moldova

General population: 4.4 million
Jewish population: 40,000 (mainly in Chichinau (Kishinev))

GENERAL BACKGROUND

Moldova, independent from the former Soviet Union since 1991, adopted in the summer a new constitution establishing the country as a "presidential parliamentary republic". In February parliamentary elections resulted in gains for the country's largest political party, the Agrarian Democratic Party, and losses for the pro-Romanian opposition. Moldova made considerable progress in economic reform in 1994. The country remained divided, with mostly Slavic separatists still controlling the Transdniestr region ("capital" Tiraspol). In October the Moldovan and Russian prime ministers signed an agreement providing for the withdrawal within three years of the Russian 14th army stationed in Moldova.

HISTORICAL LEGACY

Jews settled in the area now known as Moldova in the eighteenth century. In the nineteenth century, under Russian rule, Jews first experienced restrictions on residence and expulsions.

The Kishinev pogrom of April 1903, which received world-wide notoriety, resulted in the massacre of some fifty Jews. In October that year a further pogrom killed nineteen Jews.

During the Second World War most of Moldova was under Romanian control. A massacre carried out by Romanian gendarmes and Germans in and around Kishinev in 1941 claimed 53,000 Jewish victims. Jews from Moldova and from German-occupied areas were deported to labour camps in Transnistria, where the overwhelming majority perished.

PARTIES, ORGANIZATIONS, MOVEMENTS

In the separatist Transdniestr region there was marginal support for the extremist Front natsionalnogo spaseniya (National Salvation Front) (see **Russia**) and Russkaya pesnya (Russian Song).

MANIFESTATIONS

In March the old Jewish cemetery in Chichinau (Kishinev) was vandalized. Sixty-four monuments were smashed or defaced. There were bullet marks on some of the headstones.

In late April leaflets calling on "kikes" and Russians to quit Moldova or face retribution were put into letterboxes of flats in Chichinau. A Jewish family received a similar message in a bottle thrown through their window.

In September it was reported that the Jewish journalist Lev Rosenburg had been beaten up in Tiraspol outside a theatre hosting a festival of Slavic and Russian Orthodox films. Among the audience were delegations of Russian ultra-nationalists and Serbs. The attack came in the wake of a rally in which "international Zionists" were attacked.

The Russian-language newspaper *Vecherny Kishinev* reported that a Jewish couple leaving the country for Israel had been beaten up on a bus.

In the Transdniestr region, Jewish leaders complained about antisemitic statements made during official celebrations of the separatist "republic" by an alleged Serbian nun, who made strongly nationalistic speeches.

PUBLICATIONS AND MEDIA

Mein Kampf and a number of Russian-language antisemitic newspapers and leaflets were on sale in kiosks in the Transdniestr region.

ASSESSMENT

In Moldova, a country heavily influenced by its Romanian and Slavic neighbours, anti-Jewish sentiment was not a serious problem. It remained confined for the most part to the secessionist Transdniestr region, where marginal sympathy for the Russian far right was expressed.

The Netherlands

General population: 15.3 million
Jewish population: 25,000-30,000 (mainly in Amsterdam)

GENERAL BACKGROUND

The Netherlands is governed by a coalition of the socialist Partij van de Arbeid (PvdA, Labour Party), led by Prime Minister Wim Kok, the liberal Volkspartij voor Vrijheid en Democratie (VVD, People's Party for Freedom and Democracy) and the liberal Democraten 66 (D66, Democrats 66) which came to power in August following elections to the lower chamber of parliament in May. The centre-right Christen Democratisch Appel (CDA, Christian Democratic Appeal) was excluded from government for the first time since the introduction of universal suffrage in 1917.

The main issues in the parliamentary election campaign were reform of the welfare system and the CDA's dominance of Dutch politics. The election results reflected voter disillusionment with the traditional political parties and a marked decline in support for the PvdA and the CDA. The VVD and the D66 made major gains and two pensioners' parties also won seats, reflecting public discontent with a CDA proposal to freeze pensions for four years in a country where nearly half the electorate is aged over fifty.

Declining support for the PvdA and the CDA was also reflected in the June European elections, with both parties' share of the vote falling while the VVD's and the D66's share increased.

In 1994, the economy appeared to be recovering from the effects of the Europe-wide recession with growth rising to 1.8 per cent (after falling by 0.2 per cent in 1993) and unemployment falling to 7.5 per cent (8.3 per cent in 1993); inflation, however, increased slightly to 2.9 per cent (2 per cent in 1993).

RACISM AND XENOPHOBIA

In 1994, the treatment of ethnic minorities, immigrants and asylum-seekers was the subject of much debate.

The Netherlands has a traditionally liberal policy towards asylum-seekers and its procedures take into account conditions in the applicant's country of origin. Applicants who fail to meet the criteria for political asylum are given leave to remain, without refugee status, if they are likely to be endangered by conditions in their countries of origin. Although tighter asylum regulations came into force at the beginning of January, the number of asylum-seekers increased in 1994 to approximately 55,000 (compared to nearly 40,000 in 1993).

While the far-right parties crudely exploited the notion that immigrants were the main beneficiaries of the country's welfare provisions, there was some recognition of public sensitivities about immigration by mainstream parties and the issue featured in the parliamentary election campaign. For instance, Ruud Lubbers, CDA prime minister until May, declared that "immigrants cannot merely expect to be looked after, they are going to have to go out and look for work". The VVD suggested plans to ban schooling in the Netherlands for the children of illegal immigrants and a VVD parliamentarian questioned the ability of the country's Muslim community to assimilate. In December, following the introduction of similar legislation in Germany in 1993, the lower chamber of parliament passed legislation restricting the granting of asylum to applicants from "safe" countries of origin and those who arrive via a "safe third country" where asylum would have been possible.

There was evidence that levels of racist violence, threats and harassment rose in 1994 although there were no official statistics available for the year. The government's concern that the system of counting racist and antisemitic incidents needs to be improved prompted it to give funds for this purpose to the Landelijk Buro Racismebestrijding (LBR, National Bureau against Racial Discrimination). The LBR, which is in the process of setting up a national register of racist incidents, did not record the total number of complaints of racial discrimination in 1994 but believed that there was an increase on the 2,840 complaints registered by local anti-discrimination bureaux in 1993. Experts in racism and right-wing extremism at the University of Leiden, who issued a survey in 1994 recording 352 racist and/or far-right violent incidents in 1993, estimate, on the basis of data available for some areas extrapolated to the whole country, that there were approximately 1,200-1,500 incidents of racist violence and threats in 1994.

At least three mosques were the targets of racially-motivated attacks in 1994—in Stadskanaal in February, in Meeden in July and in Delfzijl in August. In the Delfzijl incident, swastikas were carved into the walls of the Yunus Emre mosque and slogans, such as "I love Adolf Hitler" and "Rudolf Hess", were daubed.

Given such indications of a rising level of racist violence and an increasing willingness of electors to vote for far-right parties (see **Parties, Organizations, Movements**), the government sought to raise awareness of racism and xenophobia through publicity campaigns and legislative initiatives. For example, evidence that the main immigrant communities—from Surinam, the Dutch Antilles, Aruba, Turkey and Morocco—suffer disproportionately high levels of unemployment prompted the government to work with employers' groups and trades unions to address this problem. At the beginning of July, a law came into force requiring employers with more than thirty-five employees to register with the local chambers of commerce the number of their employees who choose to identify themselves as members of a non-Dutch ethnic group. Employers must also submit confidential plans for affirmative action, including recruitment targets and strategies. However, the law attracted considerable criticism on the grounds that its provisions recalled the registration requirements imposed during the Nazi occupation and that the measures would not actually improve the situation of immigrant communities but, rather, would serve to stigmatize them.

HISTORICAL LEGACY

A Jewish community is known to have existed in what is now the kingdom of the Netherlands since the Middle Ages and was, at times, subject to persecution and expulsion from various provinces.

In the early seventeenth century, the community was swelled by the arrival of descendants of Sephardi Jews who had fled the Spanish Inquisition. While the community was free to practise Judaism, Jews were restricted to certain trades because they were excluded from the existing guilds until the granting of emancipation in 1796.

In the 1930s, several national-socialist parties emerged, some more antisemitic than others. During the Nazi occupation of 1940-45, contrary to the perception outside the country, social antisemitism increased sharply. In the early post-war years, anti-Jewish sentiment continued in certain circles, despite the fact that some 100,000 of the Netherlands' 140,000 Jews had perished in the Holocaust. Though social antisemitism has by no means completely disappeared, it remains publicly unacceptable.

PARTIES, ORGANIZATIONS, MOVEMENTS

There are no overtly antisemitic parties in the Netherlands. The far-right parties—the Centrum-Democraten (CD, Centre Democrats) and the more radical Centrumpartij '86 (CP'86, Centre Party '86)—direct their propaganda at immigrants from Mediterranean countries and the Third World. While the CD and CP'86 eschew antisemitic remarks and their party programmes do not contain antisemitic slogans, individual party activists do not always follow suit (see below).

The CD, which was founded in 1984 by party leader Hans Janmaat, has sought to capitalize on the effects of recession, unemployment and welfare cuts and claims that foreigners are the main beneficiaries of welfare provision. During 1994, the party campaigned on the slogan "Full is Full" and its election manifesto proposed labour camps for asylum-seekers and the repatriation of unemployed immigrants.

The CP'86, led by Henk Ruitenberg, competes with the CD for the anti-immigrant vote. The party, which campaigns on the slogan "Our Own People First", is the subject of an ongoing investigation by the ministry of justice. The CP'86 has links with the far-right Nationaldemokratische Partei Deutschlands in Germany and several South African far-right parties, particularly the Boerestaatpartij; party members have contacts with the Vlaams Blok (VB, Flemish Bloc) in Belgium and the British skinhead group Blood and Honour (see **Belgium**, **Germany** and **United Kingdom**).

The Nederlands Blok (NB, Dutch Bloc) is a CD splinter grouping, modelled on the Belgian Vlaams Blok, which campaigns primarily in Utrecht. The NB is led by Wim Vreeswijk, a former CD activist who joined the party in 1993.

In March, the far-right parties made significant gains in the municipal elections. The CD won 77 out of a total 2,442 council seats, an increase of 66 on the previous elections in 1990.

The CP'86 won 9 seats, an increase of 5. The CD and CP'86 contested 51 municipalities and won representation for the first time on 34 local councils. The NB, which contested the elections only in Utrecht, won a single seat.

The far-right parties performed particularly well in the four largest cities. In Amsterdam, the CD received 7.9 per cent of the vote (4.4 per cent in 1990) and the CP'86 won 1.8 per cent (down from 2.4 per cent). Thus, the total far-right share in the city was higher than that of the CDA. While the CP'86 lost the seat it held on the city council, the CD doubled the number of its council seats to 4. In the Hague, the CD won 9.2 per cent of the vote (4.3 per cent in 1990) and doubled its seats to 4. The CP'86 received 2.7 per cent of the vote (up from 2.1 per cent) and retained its only seat. In Utrecht, the CD increased its seats from 1 to 3 with 6.4 per cent of the vote (up from 3.9 per cent). The CP'86 did not win any seats but gained 1.7 per cent of the vote (up from 1.1 per cent). The NB won 2.1 per cent of the vote and one seat. In Rotterdam, the CD gained a 10.2 per cent share and won 4 seats, bringing its total to 5. The CP'86 retained its seat and won a 3.5 per cent share (3.3 per cent in 1990).

The potential impact of the eighty-seven far-right councillors became apparent after the elections since the municipality law requires council committees to have a balanced political representation. Therefore, far-right councillors legally were entitled to be admitted to all committees, even those dealing with discrimination and security, in most local authorities. Nevertheless, in Amsterdam, councillors from the mainstream parties voted to exclude the far-right parties from committees after a CD councillor claimed that there was a link between the city's "new" citizens and AIDS. However, in many municipalities, far-right councillors frequently failed to turn up for meetings or did not take their seats.

The relative success of the far-right parties in the municipal elections raised fears that they would make significant gains in the general election on 3 May. In the event, the CD received 2.5 per cent of the vote, increasing its representation in the 150-member lower chamber to 3, up 2 from the single seat won by Hans Janmaat with 0.9 per cent in 1989. The CP'86 managed to win only 0.4 per cent of the vote, which was insufficient to gain a seat.

The CD received only half the number of votes in May in almost all of the municipalities where it fielded candidates in March. Its vote remained stable only in the southern province of Limburg. The national elections showed a geographical shift in far-right support from the west to the south and, to some extent, from the urban centres to smaller communities. Traditionally, CD and CP'86 strongholds lay in the cities of the urbanized western part of the country. The local elections saw the CD extend its support to cities in the south, in the provinces of Limburg, Zeeland and Noord Brabant. In the national elections, the CD retained its strength in the southern cities and towns but its vote dropped in the west, although support in the four largest cities held up relatively well, with the party winning 6.5 per cent in Rotterdam, 5.1 per cent in the Hague, 4.2 per cent in Utrecht and 3.7 per cent in Amsterdam.

That far-right support did not hold up in the national elections can be explained by a number of reasons. In the local elections, some electors probably voted for the far right to protest their disillusionment with the established parties but may have opted not to "waste" votes on a far-right protest party at the national level. Also, with a turn-out of 78.6 per cent, an unprecedented low for Dutch national elections, voters who had supported the far right in March may have voiced their protest in May by staying at home. Moreover, with twenty-five parties standing at the national elections, it is also likely that the protest vote may have been split amongst the numerous other small parties.

The considerable negative publicity devoted to the CD after the March elections, particularly in the final days prior to the May poll, may also have affected its electoral performance. Media exposés by several journalists who infiltrated the CD revealed not only the party's racism but also the violent and criminal tendencies of some of its members. Yge Graman, a prominent CD member and newly-elected Amsterdam councillor, was filmed (by a hidden camera) boasting that he had fire-bombed refugee support centres, killing several Surinamese immigrants (see **Legal Matters**). The same film also showed CD members in Amsterdam expressing their desire to draft a programme as influential as *Mein Kampf*. Also fimed by a hidden camera was Richard Van der Plas, a CD councillor in Purmerend, while making jokes about the gassing of 6 million Jews; he was also convicted of insurance fraud and possession of firearms in April (see **Legal Matters**). The CD suspended both Graman and Van der Plas just before the May elections.

The far-right party leaders themselves were not immune from controversy. Willem (Wim) Beaux, the CP'86 deputy leader, was convicted for possession of racist pamphlets just before the national elections. Comments made by Janmaat following the death of a PvdA minister caused several CD members to resign or refuse to take their council seats and Janmaat was found guilty of incitement to racial hatred, although his conviction was announced the day after the elections (see **Legal Matters**).

The CD was the only Dutch far-right party to contest the European elections. Fears that the party would win its first Euro-seat were allayed when it received only 1 per cent of the vote, although its share was slightly higher in the four largest cities—3.1 per cent in Rotterdam, 2.1 per cent in the Hague and Amsterdam, and 1.6 per cent in Utrecht. One factor which may have contributed to the CD's unexpectedly poor performance was the unprecedentedly low turnout of 35.6 per cent.

The end of the year saw the CD beset by internecine disputes, in part due to Janmaat's reported authoritarian behaviour. Six of its seats remained unoccupied because candidates had withdrawn or were elected in more than one municipality, and twenty-one other councillors, mainly in Utrecht and Limburg, left the party for CD splinter parties, the NB and the Burgerpartij Nederland.

The CP'86 reportedly was also beset by factional infighting between a militant wing, led by Rotterdam councillor Martijn Freling, who advocates the repatriation of non-white Dutch citizens, and the veteran party leaders, who want the party to maintain a more "moderate" approach in order to avoid the risk of being banned by the government. The CP'86 also had some problems holding its annual conference. Originally scheduled for 5 November in the Hague, the meeting was banned because of a student demonstration against education cuts on the same day. Postponed to 19 November in Zoetermeer, the conference was again banned because the local mayor wanted to avoid disruption of the annual visit of St Nicholas, the Dutch Santa Claus. Delegates travelled to Lisse instead, until they were forced to abandon their meeting by anti-racist demonstrators.

The Aktiefront Nationaler Socialisten (ANS, Action Front of National Socialists), founded in 1983, is the Dutch counterpart of the banned German Gesinnungsgemeinschaft der Neuen Front (see **Germany**). The ANS, led by Eite Homann, is estimated to have between twenty-five and fifty members and has been responsible for attacks on foreigners, squatters and homosexuals and engages in "propaganda actions"—daubing walls and posting neo-Nazi stickers.

On 16 July, the ANS organized a protest against the banning of several German neo-Nazi groups in Venlo, near the German border. Approximately sixty neo-Nazis, including some from Belgium and Germany, attended.

The police made one arrest and confiscated neo-Nazi banners and propaganda material. The police had prevented the demonstration from taking place in Nijmegen, where an Allied war cemetery was vandalized in 1993, and arrested several people, including Homann.

On 26 November, the ANS was involved in organizing a demonstration in Zevenaar on the Dutch-German border against the prohibition of the expression of Nazi ideas. Approximately fifty neo-Nazis attended the protest and twenty were arrested for shouting racist slogans. A dozen members of the German neo-Nazi Freiheitliche Deutsche Arbeiterpartei (FAP, German Workers' Freedom Party) were prevented from crossing the border (see **Germany**).

The US-based international neo-Nazi grouping, the Nationalsozialistische Deutsche Arbeiterpartei/Auslands- und Aufbauorganisation (NSDAP/AO, German National Socialist Workers' Party/Overseas Section), operates through the ANS in the Netherlands (see **United States**). Supporters have distributed its antisemitic and racist publications, including stickers, leaflets glorifying Hitler, pamphlets preaching the supremacy of the "white race", and have sent threatening letters to Jewish organizations.

MANIFESTATIONS

Three synagogues were attacked in 1994—probably the first time that synagogues have been targeted in the Netherlands. Two of the attacks occurred in February, after the massacre of Muslims in a Hebron mosque by a Jewish settler (see **Effects of anti-Zionism**).

The third attack occurred on 5 May, the Dutch Liberation Day, when an attempt was made to set fire to the Jewish cultural centre in Amsterdam, which houses a synagogue and the offices of the Nederlands-Israelitisch Kerkgenootschap (Organization of Dutch Jewish Communities) and the Jewish Community of Amsterdam, the two largest Dutch Jewish organizations. No one claimed responsibility and the perpetrators have yet to be found.

In August, an Israeli man in Oostzaan was attacked by a group of teenagers with swastika tattoos who shouted neo-Nazi slogans. A Turkish immigrant who tried to intervene was also set upon.

In September, swastikas were daubed on a monument to Dutch victims of the Sachsenhausen concentration camp in Vught on the day it was unveiled. The day after the incident, several hundred schoolchildren demonstrated against the vandalization.

Several Jewish organizations received

antisemitic telephone calls during the year: some of the callers threatened to "send some more Jews to Auschwitz". Jewish organizations also received antisemitic hate mail. For instance, a letter addressed to the Centrum Informatie en Documentatie over Israël (CIDI, Centre for Information and Documentation on Israel) accused Jews of being "dirty, stinking rats . . . not much better than foreigners".

Between February and June, a Jewish family in Amsterdam was harassed by antisemitic telephone calls. Although the telephone service was able to trace the perpetrator, it refused to release his or her name because its regulations stipulate that a harasser's identity can be revealed only if three offensive calls are made within a three-week period. Therefore, no complaint could be brought whilst the perpetrator's identity remained unknown. Despite appeals by the police, the telephone company adhered to its regulations but sent a formal warning to the harasser.

In a summons used in proceedings against an Israeli family, a member of the family was referred to as "the other nose" by an Amsterdam police officer. The CIDI asked the acting mayor of Amsterdam to take disciplinary action against the officer on the grounds that the reference showed evidence of racial prejudice. The Amsterdam police apologized and the acting mayor confirmed that the remarks were insulting but did not pursue the matter since the police had already reacted.

A prominent member of the Jewish community received two packages at home from a Jewish organization abroad containing suspicious metal objects. A bomb disposal unit discovered that the packages contained metal car parts and further investigations pointed to the likelihood that the objects had been placed in the packages in the Netherlands before they were sent on to the recipient.

In 1994, the CIDI received five reports of local problems, three of which concerned neighbours' arguments with antisemitic overtones. The two other incidents concerned swastika graffiti but it was not clear if these were aimed at specific targets. The CIDI also received nine reports of verbal antisemitic incidents. Five of these were arguments with neighbours and had antisemitic overtones. In two of these cases, it was not clear if it was specifically aimed at a Jewish person. At least five Jewish families discovered antisemitic letters or pamphlets in their letterboxes.

In December, the police arrested a forty-four-year old Dutch man in the German city of Aachen who for the last year had been bombarding Jewish citizens and organizations in the Netherlands, Belgium and Germany with racist and antisemitic material. The man, who had for years been living in a small village in the Heinsberg region, confessed that he had obtained the addresses of his victims through advertisements and articles in various magazines dealing with Jewish artists and organizations.

GRASSROOTS

Antisemitic and racist behaviour during football matches, particularly those involving the clubs of Utrecht, Feyenoord (in Rotterdam) and Ajax (in Amsterdam), remained an issue in 1994 and there was some suggestion in the media that far-right groups have tried to gain a foothold in football supporters' associations in recent years. Antisemitic chants and taunts were directed at Ajax because it is considered to be a "Jewish" team by rival supporters since players and management have previously included members with Jewish origins. Some (non-Jewish) Ajax supporters encourage this perception and wave Israeli flags, wear scarves featuring Stars of David and inscribe the word "Jew" on their jackets (see **Legal Matters**).

After a number of black players with Ajax and Feyenoord received threatening letters, the Professional Football Supporters' Federation established in January 1995 a working group called Supporters against Discrimination and Racism, in which the ministry of social affairs, the Royal Dutch Football Association (KNVB) and the municipality of Amsterdam also participated. The new group intends to regulate the distribution of information, stickers and advertisements. Supporters will be encouraged to write letters to the media to counter-balance the amount of publicity received by far-right groups. This project was launched after a similar initiative by the KNVB in 1993 was not successful.

A Jewish member of a sports club was insulted by a fellow member to the effect that Jews were always seeking to make a profit out of everything. The Jewish man brought the incident to the attention of the board of the club. The chair condemned the remarks and commented that, although he had never noticed any form of antisemitism in the club, he would make every effort to ensure that no such incident would happen again.

PUBLICATIONS AND MEDIA

In January, CD leader Hans Janmaat, in an interview published in the weekly magazine *Elsevier*, appeared to make antisemitic insinuations about the Jewish origins of the minister of justice and was quoted as saying that Jews should not hold public office because they roam "like nomads". He also said that only third-generation (or more) immigrants should hold office and called for the resignation of the Hungarian-born agriculture minister and a PvdA parliamentarian with Greek origins. In the same interview, Janmaat stated that he would never make antisemitic remarks "since you don't win voters in Holland with antisemitism". The LBR filed a penal complaint against Janmaat after these comments.

Janmaat protested that *Elsevier* had misrepresented him and, when the magazine published the entire text of the interview in a subsequent issue, it became clear that he had not made antisemitic remarks although his xenophobic comments were reported correctly.

Theo van Gogh, a satirical newspaper columnist and film-maker, provoked controversy over alleged antisemitic remarks made in a review of a book about relations between Jews and non-Jews in the Netherlands by Eveline Gans, a Jewish author. Van Gogh suggested in the student newspaper *Folio* that the author's sexual fantasies were probably about Dr Mengele.

In the last few years, van Gogh has been the subject of a number of legal actions concerning allegations of antisemitism in his writings. In one case, he was found guilty by the high court, while he was acquitted in another. Opinions are divided concerning van Gogh's comments: some view them as antisemitic while others, citing freedom of expression, consider them to be tasteless but acceptable.

A pamphlet entitled "What a World. The Secret of Lawlessness and God's Restoration Plan", published by the Dutch Israeli Book Fund, was sent to Jewish organizations during the year. The publication claimed that, since the beginning of the Christian era, Jews have been trying to destroy Christianity. It also advanced notions of racial purity and cited the far-right slogan "Our Own People First". The issue was apparently the fifty-fourth edition of the pamphlet, which claimed to be in its thirteenth year of publication.

A Dutch television programme, "SS in Spain", interviewed Auke Pattist (also known as Elko Patist), a former SS lieutenant now resident in Spain who is accused of war crimes. Pattist, who was born in Utrecht but settled in Spain in 1951, denied that he tortured and murdered dozens of people while he was a member of the Black Tulip organization in the Dutch region of Veld in November 1944. Pattist stated: "I have never participated in any hunts of Jews. I have nothing against these people. There are good ones and there are bad ones, like any

social or ethnic group. What I do not agree with is their desire for separation, to be different, marrying only each other and not integrating with others whom they live with. They feel national pride because they consider themselves to be the chosen people, and have maintained this for 2,000 years. But I think they as individuals should integrate with the societies in which they live. Not to do this provokes rejections as has happened with the Gypsies in Spain." The Dutch government sought Pattist's extradition ten years ago, but the Spanish authorities turned down the request (see **Spain**).

RELIGION

Copies of *Evangelist*, an anti-Jewish newsletter previously known as *Evan*, were distributed by Jenny Goeree-Manschot during the year. The twenty-ninth issue, entitled "Are We Helping Hitler Back in the Saddle?", had the words "Christianity is superior. Judaism and Islam are false religions!" emblazoned on its cover. In 1985, a judge forbade Jenny Goeree and her then husband to distribute publications which contained such material.

Katholieke Stemmen (Catholic Voices), the newsletter of a small ultra-conservative Roman Catholic foundation Maintain Roman Catholic Life, claimed in its first issue of 1994 that the greatest danger came from "Jewish freemasonry". The author, former missionary H. Hendrikx from Heusden, referred to *The Protocols of the Elders of Zion* as leaked notes of a secret "Jewish conspiracy".

DENIAL OF THE HOLOCAUST

The main source of Holocaust-denial material in the Netherlands is the Antwerp-based Vrij Historisch Onderzoek (VHO, Institute for Free Historical Research, see **Belgium**). Leading VHO activist Siegfried Verbeke remained the subject of legal action in 1994 after copies of the "Rudolf Expertise", which Verbeke had translated into Flemish, were sent to schools and the media in October (see **Legal Matters**). The "Rudolf Expertise", which employs pseudo-scientific methods to deny the existence of the gas chambers and frequently cites the pseudo-scientific Holocaust-denying *Leuchter Report*, was prepared as part of veteran German Nazi Otto Ernst Remer's defence in his 1992 trial for denying the Holocaust, and has become a standard text in neo-Nazi and Holocaust-denial circles in Europe and the United States (see **Germany**). The justice of the peace of the Hague confiscated 2,000 copies of the "Rudolf Expertise" at the end of November after house searches in Belgium.

EFFECTS OF ANTI-ZIONISM

On 27 February, shortly after the massacre of Muslims in a Hebron mosque by a Jewish settler, a Molotov cocktail was thrown at the synagogue of the Liberal Jewish community of Amsterdam, causing some damage to its roof. Arabic slogans and the word "Hamas" (in Latin script) were daubed on a wall of the building. Also on 27 February, stones were thrown at a synagogue in Rotterdam.

LEGAL MATTERS

In March, a court in Assen handed down a suspended sentence involving a fine of fl 15,000 on the Amicomp company of Koekange, which imported 6,000 copies of a racist and antisemitic computer game entitled "Hate War" in 1993. The game depicted Hitler, swastikas and the words "Raus, Juden, Raus" (Out, Jews, Out) and involved the shooting of black and Jewish figures. The court considered the game to be insulting to Jews, Christians and blacks but suspended the imposition of the fine because the diskettes had been confiscated before they were distributed.

On 27 April, Richard Van der Plas, the CD councillor who was filmed making jokes about the gassing of 6 million Jews by a hidden camera, was sentenced to three months in prison for falsely reporting incidents of car theft and being in possession of a firearm (see **Parties, Organizations, Movements**). The public prosecutor of Alkmaar had tried since 1990 to have Van der Plas convicted for possession of firearms and neo-Nazi and discriminatory propaganda material, membership of the neo-Nazi ANS, and for incitement to racial hatred against ethnic minorities. In December, the Alkmaar court fined him Fl 1,000 and handed down a two-week suspended prison sentence for distributing a racist pamphlet in 1991.

In September, Yge Graman was sentenced to six years' imprisonment by an Amsterdam court after he boasted to a hidden camera of his involvement in arson attacks against ethnic minorities. The court found Graman guilty of attempted murder by setting fire to a drug rehabilitation centre in 1979. He was also accused of possessing a firearm and membership of a criminal organization.

Willem Beaux, the CP'86 deputy leader, was arrested in February, together with five other CP'86 members while they were campaigning in the municipal elections, for being in possession of racist pamphlets featuring the slogan "Our Own People First". The court in Amsterdam sentenced him on appeal in May, just before the parliamentary elections, to a three-week prison term, suspended for two years, and fined him Fl 1,000. The court in Zwolle had sentenced him earlier to a one-year suspended sentence and fined him Fl 1,000. The public prosecutor in Amsterdam has for some time been investigating the racist nature of CP'86 material.

The day after the May elections, Hans Janmaat, the CD leader, was fined Fl 6,000 for incitement to racial hatred and discrimination.

In November 1992, the Hague district court banned the Belgian Holocaust-denier Siegfried Verbeke from distributing Holocaust-denial pamphlets in the Netherlands after the CIDI, the Anne Frank Stichting and the LBR filed a civil suit against him. Verbeke appealed and, in June 1994, the Hague higher district court upheld the prohibition on pain of a Fl 10,000 fine for every breach.

Verbeke is due to appear before a court again in March 1995, having been charged, on the basis of the anti-racist legislation, with the distribution of Holocaust-denial pamphlets in 1992, with insulting language during an earlier trial and with sending copies of the "Rudolf Expertise" to schools and the media in October 1994.

Verbeke's activities have raised the issue of amending the country's legislation to make Holocaust denial a specific criminal offence. Three members of parliament (two from the opposition and one from the government) put down written questions to the ministers of justice and foreign affairs, asking if they were prepared to consider special, complementary legislation to combat Holocaust denial. They referred to the European Parliament resolution of November 1994 which condemned racism, xenophobia and antisemitism, and called for the criminalization of Holocaust denial within the European Union (EU) and the adjustment of the anti-racism laws of EU member states to include Holocaust denial.

In their answer, the ministers agreed that the distribution of the "Rudolf Expertise" should be prevented by the courts. For the time being, however, they did not see any reason for a separate prohibition of Holocaust denial to be included in penal law. The minister of justice agreed that the "Rudolf Expertise" falsified history in an unacceptable way, was an insult to war victims and could encourage a repetition of the Nazi period. However, together with the public prosecutor, the minister believed that the whole issue was a matter for the criminal courts.

A fine of Fl 1,000 was imposed on a journalist who used the headline "Let's demolish those Jew kids" in a 1993 article about football violence which appeared in the freely distrib-uted *De Stedendriehoek* (West Holland Conur-bation). The attorney general in Apeldoorn was of the opinion that "a journalist cannot write anything he pleases just for a good headline". Ironically, the aim of the article was actually to warn against football hooliganism anticipated at a forthcoming match between Go Ahead Eagles and Ajax (see **Grassroots**).

There were developments in the cases of two Dutch war criminals. In March, the deputy justice minister informed parliament that Jacob Luitjens would be released in March 1995. Luitjens was a member of the Landwacht, a local police force established by the Nazis to round up Jews and resistance fighters. He was convicted of war crimes in 1948 and sentenced to life imprisonment *in absentia*. In 1992, he was deported from Canada, where he had been living since 1961, and imprisoned on his arrival in the Netherlands. The reasons given by the authorities for commuting seventy-four-year-old Luitjens's life sentence were his age and the reduction of sentences in similar cases.

In May, an Argentine television pro-gramme reported that the Dutch Nazi collabo-rator Abraham Kipp was living in Buenos Aires (see **Argentina**). Kipp, an SS member who handed over Jews and resistance fighters to the Nazi occupying forces, was sentenced to death for war crimes (later commuted to life impris-onment) after the Second World War but fled the Netherlands in 1949. The Dutch govern-ment's request for Kipp's extradition was re-jected in 1989 after he was discovered in Argentina in 1988. In August, Paul Brilman, the public prosecutor who represents the Dutch government in war crimes extradition cases, admitted on Dutch television that there were insoluble legal problems involved in Kipp's case which would probably make his extradition impossible.

COUNTERING ANTISEMITISM

Awareness of the dangers of racism and xeno-phobia, together with concern at the apparent rise in support for the far-right parties, was shown by the number of demonstrations and campaigns organized at both local and national levels in 1994.

In January, an open letter was sent to the chief candidates of all the political parties by twenty social institutions including trades unions, the Raad van Kerken (Council of Churches) and the Nederlands Centrum Buitenlanders (Dutch Centre for Foreigners). They requested that the candidates take care during election campaigns not to give the im-pression that immigrants and refugees were the cause of social problems facing the Nether-lands.

Also in January, the CIDI organized a round-table discussion on the dangers of neo-Nazism—the first time that the issue had been discussed openly in the Jewish community.

In February, the Foundation Nederland Bekent Kleur (Holland Shows Its Hand) launched a campaign entitled "I Vote and I Vote for Colour" with the aim of persuading electors not to vote for the far-right parties. On 26 March, the foundation organized the annual demonstration against racism in the Hague, in which approximately 10,000 people participated.

In March, the Christelijk Nederlands Vakverbond (CNV, Christian Trades Union) voted to suspend members who were active in far-right political parties after four CNV mem-bers put themselves forward as candidates for the CD and the CP'86 in the municipal elec-tions. The CNV decision followed a similar vote by the Federatie van Nederlandse Vakbewegingen (FNV, Dutch Federation of Trades Unions), the largest trades union organi-zation, in 1993.

In April, prior to the national elections, the Magenta Foundation arranged for an "anti-racist train" to travel across the country carrying well-known personalities. The train stopped in 246 municipalities, where pamphlets requesting people not to vote for the far-right parties were distributed.

After the May elections, PvdA leader Wim Kok described the rise of the far right as a "black page in Dutch history" and said: "We must stop this poisonous campaign of hatred towards foreigners by the right-wing extremists in our country."

Trainee police officers demonstrated against racism and fascism in the Hague with the support of the police unions. In May, civil servants from twenty-three municipalities es-tablished a national network of local govern-ment officers against racism (known as "Later") to combat racism and discrimination in the workplace and refused to work for far-right councillors.

In November, the Aric Information Centre in Rotterdam distributed matchboxes and post-cards with a picture of a swastika going up in flames. 200,000 postcards were printed and some 15,000 matchboxes were sold.

The installation of the eighty-seven far-right councillors, also in November, was marked by some demonstrations. In Arnhem, the protests turned violent and, in four other municipalities, noisy demonstrators were re-moved from the council chambers.

ASSESSMENT

Reports of antisemitic incidents increased in 1994 compared to 1993 and synagogues were attacked for the first time. However, according to experts on racism and far-right extremism, estimated figures for violent attacks on, and threats against, visible ethnic minorities rose by 350-400 per cent compared to 1993, suggesting that immigrants remained the principal targets of far-right violence.

Despite the Netherlands' reputation as a country tolerant of foreigners, anti-immigrant parties remained a feature of the Dutch political landscape in 1994. After the far right made significant gains in the municipal elections in March, there was some unease that increasing numbers of voters were prepared to support its anti-immigrant platform. However, while the size of the far right's municipal gains was unexpected, some electors probably voted for the parties to protest their disillusionment with mainstream politicians and the far right performed more modestly in the parliamentary and European elections. Moreover, revelations about the racist and criminal backgrounds of some far-right activists and the parties' internecine disputes certainly weakened their appeal.

By the end of the year, it appeared that the electoral threat posed by the far-right parties was a marginal one. Nevertheless, their anti-immigrant policies have had some impact in prompting a debate within the mainstream parties about ethnic minorities and how to treat them. While some parliamentarians made statements which could be viewed as pandering to xenophobic sentiment, the government was in the process of formulating policies for the better integration of immigrants.

Although a strong taboo on extremist opinions and their violent expression remained —as seen in the protests and demonstrations against racism, antisemitism and the far right as well as in the willingness of the Dutch judiciary to prosecute breaches of the anti-racism legislation—the increase in antisemitic and racist incidents was a cause for concern in 1994.

Norway

General population: 4.3 million
Jewish population: 1,000 (mainly in Oslo)

GENERAL BACKGROUND

In 1994, Norway continued to be governed by Det norske Arbeiderparti (DNA, The Norwegian Labour Party), which marginally increased its share of the vote in the September 1993 general election. In 1994, the country's economy performed relatively well in comparison to neighbouring countries, largely as a result of its oil revenue. Inflation fell to 1.4 per cent (2.3 per cent in 1993) and gross domestic product grew by 3.8 per cent.

Political life was dominated by the debate over Norway's proposed membership of the European Union (EU). On 28 November, Norway's EU membership was rejected by 52.2 per cent of the electorate in a referendum.

HISTORICAL LEGACY

Antisemitism and scientific racism had proponents in Norway since the beginning of the century, including John Alfred Mjoen, Eivind Saxlund and Mikal Sylten. Their writings did not go unchallenged and, in a few cases, were the subject of court cases. In the 1930s, the National Union Party led by Vidkun Quisling and other minor political groups advocated Nazi ideas and participated in Hitler's actions against the Jews. The left-wing press and two non-socialist newspapers took a clear stand against Nazism and antisemitism. Most of the press sharply condemned the events of Kristallnacht and attacks on Jewish property in Oslo, but the government was reluctant to receive refugees from Germany.

When Germany invaded Norway on 9 April 1940, the country's Jewish population numbered 1,800. Under Nazi occupation, persecution of the Jews began in 1941 and Quisling was elevated to the role of minister president in February 1942. In October 1942, Jewish property was confiscated and several hundred Jews were arrested. On 10 November 1942, the joint leadership of the Norwegian church and other Christian organizations wrote to Quisling protesting against these measures. On 26 November 1942, 530 Jews were deported to the Nazi extermination camps. Altogether, 760 Jews were deported from Norway and only twenty-four survived. About 930 Jews fled to Sweden and some sixty remained in hiding in Norway. After the war, the Norwegian government extended a special invitation to Jews who had sur-

vived the camps to settle in the country.

After a spate of swastika-daubing in early 1960, measures were introduced to combat antisemitism. For example, the ministry of church and education instructed schools to keep a close watch on anti-Jewish teachers. In 1963, parliament approved legislation outlawing actions or expressions offensive to a minority faith or ethnic group; in 1970, the legislation was amended and strengthened. The law has rarely been applied. In 1977, a teacher was given a 120-day suspended sentence for making antisemitic statements in two Oslo newspapers.

In 1975, an antisemitic group called the National People's Party attempted unsuccessfully to enter mainstream political life. In 1985, it blew up a mosque in Oslo and sprayed Nazi slogans on the synagogue. The party apparently disbanded in 1991.

RACISM AND XENOPHOBIA

Several surveys have shown that the Norwegian majority, particularly Norwegian youth, is becoming more hostile towards ethnic minorities. In one survey, a third of the young people questioned stated that Norwegians were "better human beings" than immigrants. However, during 1994, more than 200 Kosova Albanian refugees were sheltered in forty-one churches in an attempt to prevent them from being deported. The first such "church asylums" occurred in February 1993, when more than 140 churches gave sanctuary to refugees after the government decided to return them to Kosova in former Yugoslavia. As a result, more than 746 refugees were granted permission to stay, and others continued their appeals against deportation.

During 1994, the debate continued as to whether current restrictions on non-Nordic immigration, in effect since 1975, are racially motivated and whether immigrant minority groups, such as Pakistanis, Vietnamese, Turks and Africans, are accorded equal rights under the law, despite the fact that there is legal protection for the rights of all minorities. Prior to the immigration of the 1970s, the main minority groups were the Sami and a tiny Finnish population in the north-east of Norway.

PARTIES, ORGANIZATIONS, MOVEMENTS

The Norwegian far right encompasses racist parties seeking electoral representation as well as a skinhead culture, which emulates its neo-Nazi counterparts elsewhere in Europe. A 1994 report, entitled *The Far Right in Norway 1994*, by the Antirasistisk Senter (Anti-Racism Centre) in Oslo noted an increase in the activities of the militant groups while anti-immigrant parties concentrated their efforts on campaigning against Norway's EU membership during 1994.

The most significant anti-immigrant party is the Fremskrittspartiet (FRP, Progress Party), which now holds 10 seats in the 165-member parliament, but prior to the 1993 general election held 22 seats. The FRP's year-long internal struggle between racist and more moderate factions was resolved in 1994 when most of the moderates opposing leader Carl Hagen left the party. After their departure, Hagen committed the FRP to a strongly anti-immigration platform and local branches distributed racist propaganda in many parts of the country. The FRP split raised questions about the party's electoral prospects, given that several parties are competing for the anti-immigrant vote and that Norway's tightening of immigration controls is thought to have contributed to the FRP's losses at the 1993 elections.

Fedrelandspartiet (FLP, Fatherland Party), led by Harald Trefall and Bjarne Dahl, is an anti-immigration party which received 0.5 per cent of the vote in the 1993 parliamentary elections and has two representatives on local councils. At the end of October, the FLP's annual meeting was attended by about thirty participants, including Øyvind Mossing of Norge Mot Innvandring (see below) and Jan Høegh of Folkebevegelsen Mot Innvandring (see below). A proposal was adopted to co-operate with Stopp Innvandringen (see below). The FLP is the only racist party to have formed a youth section, the Fedrelandspartiets Ungdom (FLPU, Fatherland Party Youth), led by Arnljot Moseng.

The FLP's leaders took part in several television talk shows during 1994 and Trefall participated in a school debate in Heimdal, where he was met by angry protesters who emptied a bucket of glue and a sack of feathers over his head.

Stopp Innvandringen (SI, Stop Immigration) is led by Jack Erik Kjuus. In 1993, SI fielded candidates in only four counties and received 0.1 per cent of the vote. In March in preparation for the 1995 local elections, Kjuus and Bjarne Dahl of the FLP signed a co-operation agreement and announced the formation of their new Felleslisten Mot Fremmedinnvandring (United List against Alien Immigration). It is likely that the FLP and the SI will participate in the 1995 local elections in all nineteen counties.

The Norges Patriotiske Enhetsparti (NPE, National Patriotic Unity Party), led by army lieutenant Knut Westland, is inspired by Quisling's wartime National Unity Party. During 1994, the NPE, which aims to restore a "pure and white Norway", was still trying to collect the 5,000 signatures necessary to register as a party.

Norge Mot Innvandring (NMI, Norway against Immigration), founded in 1991 by Arne Myrdal, has been the driving force behind far-right activities in recent years. The NMI's primary activity is keeping files on immigrants and "traitors" (anti-racists and left-wingers) but Myrdal has also been involved in arranging public meetings against immigration and working with the FLP in order to set up electoral lists, as well as writing racist leaflets and letters to the press.

Myrdal spent the first part of 1994 in jail for attacking an anti-racism protest. On his release, he invited Vladimir Zhirinovsky of the Liberal Democratic Party of Russia to Norway because they "had the same view on Pakistanis, Negroes and other trash that has invaded our country". Myrdal subsequently ceased his activities, apparently due to ill health. He was succeeded as leader of the NMI by Øyvind Mossing, who apparently appeals to a younger generation of Norwegian racists and who has links to several key neo-Nazi organizers.

In September, the NMI held an open-air meeting in the town of Brumunddal, where Mossing and Arild Elvsveen, a local leader who was jailed for three months in 1993 for attacking anti-racists and the police, addressed fewer than fifteen spectators. Some skinheads were stopped by the police on their way to the town.

The racist pressure group Folkebevegelsen Mot Innvandring (FMI, People's Movement against Immigration) was founded in 1987 and was led by Arne Myrdal until 1991, when he established the NMI. The split marked a dramatic decrease in the FMI's activities. However, members of the group may well work with the

FLP in the 1995 local election campaign, as they did in the 1993 national elections.

Den Norske Forening (The Norwegian Society), led by Aksel Breian, was active in consolidating links with other racist groups in Denmark and Sweden in 1993, but maintained a low profile during 1994.

Regarding the militant fringe, the Antirasistisk Senter reported an increase in the activities of neo-Nazi groups in 1994, whose numbers and impact nonetheless remained minimal. Although such groups were evident mainly in southern parts of Norway, the following general pattern was apparent: media coverage following a racist incident attracted the attention of racist groups outside the area, which made contact with local militants who organized a new group, which in turn received publicity in the local media, attracting more members and raising the likelihood of further attacks on immigrants and anti-racists.

During the year, there were a number of incidents of threats, harassment and serious attacks on anti-racist activists, including journalists, local officials and politicians, throughout the country, suggesting that Norwegian neo-Nazis had expanded their operations to include so-called "anti-antifa[scist]" activities.

The most serious incident occurred on 22 August, when a bomb was thrown at an anti-racist centre in Oslo called the Blitz-house. The bomb hit a fence surrounding the centre and no one was hurt. More than 1,000 people marched through Oslo to protest the attack, which was also denounced across the political spectrum. In October, it was revealed that the Blitz-house had been infiltrated by a woman who stole an internal telephone directory, which led to an increase in neo-Nazi threats against, and harassment of, anti-racist activists.

The Drammen-based Boot Boys are the veterans of the Norwegian neo-Nazi scene, but now appear to serve more as role models than as an active force. The neo-Nazi group Zorn 88 (8 refers to H, the eighth letter of the German alphabet; 88 stands for "Heil Hitler") maintained a low profile during 1994. Two closely-linked groups, Hvit Arisk Motstand (HAM, White Aryan Resistance) and Birkebeinerne, which co-operate in the areas of Gjøvik and Brumunddal, were linked to the Swedish neo-Nazi Vitt Ariskt Motstånd (VAM, White Aryan Resistance, see **Sweden**). Other groups active in 1994 included Nasjonalistisk Ungdom (Nationalist Youth) and the Viking group in Oslo, which attracted members as young as thirteen; Ariske Brødre (Aryan Brothers) in Tønsberg; Varg in Sørumsand; VOR in Risør; and Djerv in Trondheim.

The umbrella body for the various skinhead organizations is Norsk Ungdom (Norwegian Youth), which was established in 1992. Its main activity was the publication of *Ung Front*, but skinheads with connections to Norsk Ungdom were also involved in a number of confrontations with anti-racists in 1994. In November, two neo-Nazis were beaten up in Oslo at an anti-racist concert. Two weeks later, nearly seventy neo-Nazis, wearing uniforms and shouting racist abuse and "Sieg Heil", marched through the streets of Hønefoss, north of Oslo. The police prevented another forty from entering the town and intervened in the march after one participant attacked a spectator.

MANIFESTATIONS

The self-declared antisemite, Ola Misvær, distributed antisemitic and Holocaust-denial material. In a letter of 20 December to the Swedish Antisemitic Committee he expressed his wish to establish a similar committee of Norwegian antisemites.

PUBLICATIONS AND MEDIA

Michael Knutsen is a central figure of the far right in Norway and his monthly magazine, *Norsk Blad/Fritt Forum*, remained the most professional of all the far-right publications. Nine issues appeared in 1994 whose contents ranged from the history of Norwegian psychology to instructive articles on computers, but were dominated by articles on anti-racists, giving details of names and organizations.

The magazine re-organized its ownership through the creation of a foundation which brought in more funds and a tighter structure. Its telephone information line continued to operate for a second year, disseminating weekly news about far-right activities. Knutsen also published a bi-weekly newsletter, *Rapport*.

Knutsen was also behind the establishment of a mail order company, Nord Effektor, to sell Swedish "Viking rock", neo-Nazi publications and other such items, and a video distribution company, Nordfilm, which produced one title —the annual meeting of the FLP in October— which was sold through *Fritt Forum*. A publishing company was also set up, but no titles have yet appeared.

There were also several minor fanzines circulating on an irregular basis.

The community radio station Radio Bergen has been broadcasting racial hatred for a number of years despite several complaints to the police. The editor, Ivar Garberg, was succeeded by his son during the year and Garberg senior continued as a talk-show host.

The Oslo-based community radio station

Nite Rocket has played a crucial role in the rise of the far right in the Oslo region. The station plays "Nazi-rock" and its studio is used as a meeting place for neo-Nazis. In January, 2,000 anti-racists marched to the radio station to express their contempt for its views and broadcasts. In September, the station held a memorial for the British neo-Nazi Blood and Honour leader Ian Stuart Donaldson, who died in 1993, which was attended by over fifty neo-Nazis (see **United Kingdom**). Local residents gathered in the street to prevent a march from taking place and there were some scuffles between the protesters and the neo-Nazis, who shouted "ZOG [Zionist Occupation Government] swine" and "Jewish whores" at passers-by.

During the year, the FLP sponsored the establishment of a computer bulletin board system (BBS), Nasjonal Allianse BBS, which was operated by the leader of FLPU, Arnljot Moseng. The bulletin board files included FLP propaganda and articles from *Fritt Forum* and several discussion groups were set up. Moseng admitted to the press that he was establishing links with the German neo-Nazi Thule network in order to exchange regular reports (see **Germany**). When the BBS was exposed in the national newspaper *Aftenposten*, Moseng closed down the operation.

RELIGION

Wiggo Wilhelmsen, the leader of a charismatic Christian congregation in the city of Tønsberg, had been teaching *The Protocols of the Elders of Zion* as fact. In October 1993, Norwegian radio broadcast a discussion on *The Protocols*, in which Wilhelmsen stated that he had been confused and withdrew everything he had said about it. The programme was retransmitted in January 1994.

DENIAL OF THE HOLOCAUST

Alfred Olsen is the foremost Holocaust-denial propagandist in Norway and is responsible for privately publishing a Norwegian version of *The Protocols of the Elders of Zion*. He leads an organization called the Folkets Motstandsbeveglse (People's Resistance Movement), which claims to be a Christian alternative to Marxism and freemasonry and seeks to combat "racist Zionist violation". During the year, Olsen published a booklet entitled "The Racist, Zionist Mafia in Norway", in which he urged comrades to unite to face the "Zionist plot" (see also **Legal Matters**).

In October, the daily *Dagbladet* published an article by Hans Fredrik Dahl, a professor of media at the University of Oslo. In the article, Dahl questioned the outlawing of Holocaust denial in Germany and France, and claimed that the laws constituted a threat to freedom of expression. He argued that since there is a "debate" about the number of victims at Auschwitz, it could not be illegal to claim that no Jews were gassed. In December, *Dagbladet* published a strong rebuttal of Dahl's article, written by the psychiatrist and Holocaust survivor, Professor Emeritus Leo Eitinger.

LEGAL MATTERS

In 1992, a member of parliament and the Nansen Committee (the Norwegian Committee against Antisemitism) asked the director of public prosecutions to investigate whether Alfred Olsen's antisemitic activities constituted sufficient violation of the law to merit prosecution. In 1994, the director general of public prosecutions decided that they did not merit prosecution but the Nansen Committee intends to pursue the matter.

COUNTERING ANTISEMITISM

In September, the Norwegian Association against Antisemitism arranged a one-day seminar in Oslo on antisemitism.

Inge Lønning, professor of theology at the University of Oslo, was asked to give an independent evaluation of the Jan Bergman case and the faculty of theology at the University of Uppsala (see **Sweden**). He strongly condemned the antisemitism of Professor Bergman's statements and writings in connection with the trial of Swedish Holocaust-denier Ahmed Rami and the continuing defence of Bergman by the Uppsala faculty.

The large numbers of participants in demonstrations against racism, antisemitism and neo-Nazism in recent years indicate that a considerable proportion of the Norwegian population actively rejects these ideologies.

ASSESSMENT

Despite the increase in the activities of small neo-Nazi groups in 1994, antisemitism remained a marginal phenomenon in Norway which posed little threat to the Jewish community, particularly when compared to racist sentiment against asylum-seekers and immigrants. However, the targeting of anti-racist activists by neo-Nazis was a worrying development.

Poland

General population: 38.5 million
Jewish population: 5,000-15,000 (about half
in Warsaw)

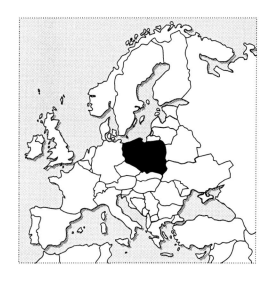

GENERAL BACKGROUND

Five years after the fall of Communism, Poland
is a parliamentary democracy. The government,
composed of a coalition of the Sojusz Lewicy
Demokratycznej (SLD, Democratic Left Alliance), a successor to the former Communist
Party, and the Polskie Stronnictwo Ludowe
(PSL, Polish Peasant Party), enjoys a comfortable majority in both houses of parliament.

In 1994 Poland's market economy registered 4.5 per cent growth. While unemployment had declined relative to previous years, it
still stood at 16 per cent. The annual inflation
rate for 1994 was 30 per cent.

On 30 July-1 August a series of ceremonies
commemorated the fiftieth anniversary of the
Warsaw uprising against Nazi occupation.

In September the last Russian soldiers officially left Polish soil after a presence there span-
ning half a century.

HISTORICAL LEGACY

Today's Jewish community is a tiny remnant of
an ancient community which became established in the Middle Ages. On the eve of the
Second World War it numbered 3.5 million.

Until the seventeenth century the situation
of the Jews in Poland was, on balance, better
than in most countries of Europe but with the
decline of the Rzeczpospolita (Polish
Commonwealth) it deteriorated. With the
emergence of modern Polish nationalism, antisemitism became incorporated into the platform of the National Democracy movement
(Endecja).

During the Second Republic (1918-39)
Jews encountered hostility from wide sections
of the population and a significant proportion
of the Polish social and political establishment,
and public opinion found in the Jewish mercantile community a scapegoat for economic difficulties. During the Holocaust the Jews felt that
they went to their deaths in the face of the
indifference, and in some cases hostility, of the
general population.

Post-war hopes of a more amicable Polish-
Jewish relationship were thwarted first by the
grassroots antisemitism of the immediate post-
war period, which reached its apogee in the
Kielce pogrom of 1946, and then by Commu-
nist-inspired antisemitism, which culminated in

the "anti-Zionist" campaign of 1968. During
the 1980s and, in particular, during the height of
the martial law period (1982-4) an antisemitic
propaganda campaign, which had the covert
blessing of the authorities, was conducted.
Following the overthrow of Communism antisemitism was given new impetus with "Jewish
communists", from Marx onwards, cited by extremist nationalist groupings as the cause of all
Poland's ills.

The episcopal letter issued on the twenty-
fifth anniversary of *Nostra Aetate* and read in
the churches on 20 January 1991 was said by the
New York Times to represent "the most unequivocal stand [on antisemitism] ever taken by
the Polish Church".

RACISM AND XENOPHOBIA

According to the leaders of the Roma community, the Roma faced disproportionately high
unemployment and were more negatively affected by the current economic changes and reforms than were ethnic Poles.

PARTIES, ORGANIZATIONS, MOVEMENTS

On the eve of the 1993 parliamentary elections,
there were in Poland over 200 registered political parties. In late 1994 discussions over possible mergers in preparation for the 1995
presidential elections were much in evidence.
Most of the parties, including far-right groupings, were tiny and the introduction in 1993 of a
threshold of 5 per cent of the vote for individual
parties (8 per cent for electoral blocs) to gain
representation in parliament effectively barred
them from mainstream political life.

All ultra-nationalist groupings claim links
with the pre-war Endecja (National Democracy

movement) and the legacy of its leader, Roman Dmowski, a legacy which includes antisemitism and anti-Germanism.

Polska Wspólnota Narodowa-Polskie Stronnictwo Narodowe (PWN-PSN, Polish National Community-Polish National Party) is one of the most extreme far-right organizations. Its leader, Bolesław Tejkowski, was a Communist Party official in the 1950s. He took part in the 1968 "anti-Zionist" campaign as a witness for the prosecution in trials of student dissidents. Shortly afterwards he founded the far-right party Światowid. Later he became a lecturer in the Polish army's Military Technical Academy. The party promotes "traditional values" but opposes the Vatican and the church hierarchy. It maintains that the number of Jewish victims of the Holocaust has been grossly exaggerated and that most of Poland's Jews survived, are still living in Poland under different names, and are to be found in high state and church offices. The PWN-PSN claims some 20,000 members. In its activities, such as demonstrations, it mobilizes skinheads. But it lost some support in 1994, particularly among young people, who defected mainly to the Polski Front Narodowy (PFN, Polish National Front) of Janusz Bryczkowski. The PWN-PSN has branches in several Polish cities and boasts contacts with, among others, France's Front national. In October Warsaw's regional court found Tejkowski guilty of charges including slandering the supreme authorities of Poland, the Jews and the Pope and of inciting ethnic strife. He was given a one-year prison sentence suspended for two years. The party fielded candidates in the 1993 parliamentary election: it received about 15,000 votes and failed to win any seats.

The Stronnictwo Narodowe "Senioralne" (SNSe, "Senioral" National Party) claims 4,000 members. It is led by Maciej Giertych, son of the late Endek leader Jędrzej Giertych. The party has a strong clerical slant. In 1986-90 Giertych was deputy chairman of the Polish Primate's Social Council. The party's activities are evidently protected by the conservative wing of the church, although official church support has recently been soft-pedalled. The party's organ, *Od Nova*, edited by Andrzej Fedorowicz, is hostile to all Poland's minorities, including the Jews. The SNSe fielded candidates in the 1991 and 1993 parliamentary elections but won no seats.

The Stronnictwo Narodowe "Szczerbiec" (SNSz, National Party "Szczerbiec") was founded in 1989. The party's leaders are Marian Barański and Jan Majewski. There are no data on membership, though it is believed to be one of the larger ultra-nationalist parties. Its affiliated organizations—Komitet Pamięci Ofiar Stalinizmu w Polsce (KPOSP, Memorial Committee for the Victims of Stalinism in Poland), the Komitet Ścigania Zbrodni i Bezprawia na Narodzie Polskim (KSZBNP, Committee to Prosecute Crimes against the Polish Nation), and the Roman Dmowski National Association—are tiny. The party has a strong skinhead component. Its organ, *Głos Narodu*, is edited by J. Majewski, Mirosław Skorupka and Józef Janowski.

The Stronnictwo Narodowe "Ojczyzna" (SNO, National Party "Fatherland") claims 3,500 members. Its leaders are the lawyer and economist Bogusław Rybicki and the translator and journalist Bogusław Jeznach. Its press organ is *Ojczyzna*. During the 1993 election campaign Rybicki attempted to prevent the name "Fatherland" from being used by a right-wing electoral bloc: "Since homosexuals, masons and Jews cannot hide themselves behind national or Christian slogans, they are hiding behind the slogan 'Fatherland'." In April the party formed an alliance for the presidential elections with the Katolicki Blok Wspierania Rzeczpospolitej (KBWR, Catholic Bloc for the Support of the Republic), which is led by Jan Paszkiewicz, the Stowarzyszenie Słowian Polskich (SSP, Association of Polish Slavs), led by Józef Czachora, the Polskie Stronnictwo Ludowe "Solidarność" (PSLS, Polish Peasant Party "Solidarity"), which has about about 13,000 members and whose leader is Janusz Ostrowski, and defectors from Tejkowski's PWN-PSN. The new party retained the name Stronnictwo Narodowe "Ojczyzna", with Rybicki as its leader.

The Stronnictwo Narodowo-Demokratyczne (SND, National Democratic Party), was founded in 1991 by circles close to the Instytut Historyczny im. Romana Dmowskiego (Roman Dmowski Historical Institute) and the Stronnictwo Narodowe na Obczyźnie (SNnO, National Party Abroad). The SND is headed by Jan Zamoyski, a scion of the Polish nobility and has around 1,000 members. It is a moderate right-wing party. Ideologically it is closest to the Zjednoczenie Chrześcijańsko-Narodowe (ZChN, Christian National Union). It differs from most nationalist parties in that it regards the democratic traditions of the early Endecja as better suited to Poland's contemporary needs. It is critical of what it sees as the ideological shallowness of most other national parties, distances itself from the extremism of the ultra-nationalist parties and avoids overtly antisemitic propaganda. Zamoyski was the only candidate for the senate in the 1991 elections to win a seat on a nationalist (and tacitly antisemitic) platform. He lost his seat in the September 1993 elections.

In 1989 local overtly fascist and racist "national front" groupings began to emerge in Poland. In March 1991 the Narodowy Front Polski (NFP, National Front of Poland) was registered. The NFP is based in the Gdańsk-Sopot-Gdynia conurbation. Its other main centres are the cities of Katowice, Kraków, Bytom, Białystok, Lublin and Szczecin. Its leaders, Wojciech Podjacki and Wojciech Bela, are in their twenties and most of its 2,000 members are in their late teens or early twenties, many of them unemployed. The party views the nation as a community of race and culture and the August 1989-September 1993 governments as agents of Western finance, which is allegedly dominated by Jews and Germans. Its organ, *Szaniec*, is edited by Marcin Jastrzębski and Andrzej Wojciechowski. The party claims it is anti-Jewish to the same extent that it is anti-German, anti-Lithuanian and anti-Ukrainian. In the 1993 parliamentary election it obtained 565 votes.

Another "national front" grouping, the Polski Front Narodowy (PFN, Polish National Front), was registered in January 1994. The PFN is headed by Janusz Bryczkowski, a shady businessman involved in trade with Russia. In 1990-1 Bryczkowski was the leader of the centrist Polska Partia Zielonych (PPZ, Polish Green Party). In December 1991, following criticism of the PPZ leadership for, among other things, infiltration of party cells by former communist activists, he ceased to be its leader. He then became a leading member of the militant Związek Zawodowy Rolników "Samoobrona" (ZZRSO, Self-Defence Farmers' Trade Union), which was registered in January 1992, and deputy leader of the Przymierze Samoobrona (PSO, Self-Defence Alliance), founded in June 1992 by the union's leadership. In both organizations he was responsible for paramilitary structures. He quit the ZZRSO after it was routed in the 1993 parliamentary elections and formed his own party, the Front Narodowy "Samoobrona" (FNSO, Self-Defence National Front), which changed its name to Polski Front Narodowy (PFN, Polish National Front) at its congress in March 1994, and founded the paramilitary youth section Legion Polski (Polish Legion), whose members, mostly skinheads, dress in Nazi-style uniforms. The PFN claims 700 members. It seeks allies in Moscow, opposes the "forces of corruption" which, it claims, include the police, and seeks to "defend" Poland against foreign capital and national minorities. In 1994

Bryczowski also hosted a visit to Poland by Vladimir Zhirinovsky (see **Russia**).

Akcja Narodowa (AN, National Action), established in 1992 and led by Marian Jeżak, is affiliated to the KSZBNP. The AN, whose avowed purpose is to fight "Judeo-Masons", maintains that there are 233 Jews in the 460-seat lower chamber of the Polish parliament.

The Narodowe Odrodzenie Polski (NOP, National Revival of Poland), which is sometimes referred to as Narodowe Ocalenie Polski (National Salvation of Poland), regards itself as the successor to the pre-war Obóz Narodowo-Radykalny (ONR, National Radical Camp), an avowedly fascist offspring of the Endecja.

The Aryjski Front Przetrwania (AFP, Aryan Survival Front) is believed to maintain contacts with the German neo-fascist Nationale Offensive, led by Günther Boschütz (see **Germany**). Activists of the Nationale Offensive, which was declared illegal in Germany, have operated in Poland since 1992 and have been particularly active in Opole province. In late 1992 all such activists, including Boschütz, were deported from Poland. In October Boschütz was arrested in Opole province and charged with having crossed the frontier illegally.

Mention should also be made of nationalist youth organizations such as Młodzież Wszechpolska (MW, All-Polish Youth), which had 1,500 members in 1993. The MW, a pre-war organization which resumed its activities in 1989, issues the bulletin *Bastion*. It enjoys the support of the Zjednoczenie Chrześcijańsko-Narodowe (ZChN, Christian National Union), whose claimed membership is 6,000. A fundamentalist Christian group, it has been, since the 1993 election, an extra-parliamentary party.

Special interest groups which occasionally take an antisemitic line include the ZZRSO (leader Andrzej Lepper). The movement demands the cancellation, or at least recycling, of all peasants' debts. In 1993 it waged an election campaign which blamed the peasants' economic ills on "Judeo-Communism". On 11 November (the anniversary of the restoration of Polish statehood in 1918) the ZZRSO and four other organizations set up the Narodowe Forum Patriotyczne 11 Listopada (11 November National Patriotic Forum), aimed, according to Lepper, at promoting patriotism and a feeling of responsibility for Poland and striving to expand the state's welfare policy. The other four members of the Forum are the Zjednoczenie Patriotyczne Grunwald (Grunwald Patriotic Association), the KPOSP, the Partia Sprawiedliwości Społecznej (PSS, Social Justice Party) and the Powszechna Partia Słowian i Narodów Sprzymierzonych (PPSNS, Universal Party of Slavs and Allied Nations), which is based in Gdańsk-Oliwa and was registered in November 1990.

The Solidarity trade union movement includes a number of ultra-nationalists and antisemites some of whom hold positions of authority at the workplace level. Antisemitic slogans have occasionally appeared at Solidarity-sponsored events. Interviewed in *Wprost* in June, the head of the Mazowsze branch, stressed that if Solidarity were to become a truly "professional" trade union, this "generation of militants", among whom he named Zygmunt Wrzodak from the Warsaw Engineering Works "Ursus", must depart.

Kornel Morawiecki's Partia Wolności (PW, Freedom Party), which was established in Wrocław as an offshoot of the mainstream "Solidarność" Trade Union in 1982 and until 1990 was known as Solidarność Walcząca (SW, Fighting Solidarity), and the splinter faction Niezależny Samorządny Związek Zawodowy "Solidarność '80" (NSZZ S '80, Independent Self-Governing Trade Union "Solidarity '80"), which was founded in 1990 by Marian Jurczyk and has a membership of about 145,000, have not so far formally renounced their antisemitic stance, though it has been less in evidence in recent pronouncements. The PW's influence is concentrated in working-class centres such as the cities of Łódź and Szczecin, the region of Silesia and the steelworks of Nowa Huta and Warsaw.

Niezależne Zrzeszenie Studentów (NZS, Independent Students' Association), founded in 1980 as a student equivalent of the Solidarity movement and banned in 1982-9, was originally established as a democratic alternative to the official Socialist Polish Students' Association and as such has always been right-of-centre and pro-Catholic. In its early days it tended to take a philosemitic line, staging illegal demonstrations against the March 1968 campaign and cleaning up disused Jewish cemeteries. But in 1989 antisemitic slogans demanding the NZS's legal reinstatement began to appear at rallies. The organization's then leaders claimed these slogans were secret police provocations. In early summer 1993 activists from the Warsaw University branch of the NZS undoubtedly took part in anti-Wałęsa and anti-government demonstrations which had antisemitic overtones. There seem to have been no overt manifestations of antisemitism within the NZS in 1994, while in January the organization took part in a picket outside the foreign ministry demanding that the Russian extremist Vladimir Zhirinovsky be denied entry to Poland.

Poland's skinhead movement consists of perhaps several thousand individuals. They frequently provide bodyguards at meetings of ultra-nationalist groups and commit acts of violence on behalf of militant organizations. In 1994 many skinheads reportedly transferred their allegiance from Tejkowski's to Bryczkowski's organization. According to the police, the skinheads are the most dangerous of the extremists. Their strongholds are Nowa Huta, Łódź, Katowice, Wrocław, Poznań, Częstochowa and Legnica.

At the other end of the political spectrum, antisemitism is to be found among former hardliners of the Communist Party who played a militant role in the antisemitic policies in the late 1960s. Many of them, including Grunwald supporters, have emerged in Partia "X". The party's leader, Stanisław Tymiński, emigrated from Poland to Canada in 1959; he returned in 1990 to run for the presidency and gained the second largest number of votes. His second-in-command is Józef Kossecki, a former Grunwald activist and an antisemitic propagandist under the Communist regime. Partia "X" spokespersons have frequently resorted to antisemitic propaganda.

A splinter group broke away from Partia "X" in December 1991 and registered in January 1992 as Partia Pracy (PP, Labour Party) under Józef Ciuruś. A further group split off from Partia "X" in January 1992 and founded Partia "X"-Frakcja Polska (Party "X"-Polish Faction) under Zdzisław Zaleski, the author of several antisemitic tracts.

Partia "X" claims over 5,000 members and has an organ named *Listy X*. It has a youth group, Organizacja Orła Białego (Organization of the White Eagle). Partia "X" had three members in the 1991-3 parliament but in mid-1992 they ceased to function as a parliamentary group. In the 1993 parliamentary elections Partia "X" ran 315 candidates in over fifty electoral districts but gained no seats.

As for the mainstream parties which form the present coalition government, Polskie Stronnictwo Ludowe (PSL, Polish Peasant Party), whose membership is about 200,000, tolerates an antisemitic culture within its ranks, though the leadership is careful that this should not be expressed publicly. There are also antisemitic tendencies among members of the parties which form the SLD, though these sentiments are not expressed publicly.

MANIFESTATIONS

No violent antisemitic incidents were reported in 1994.

The Jewish cemetery in Warsaw's Okopowa Street, seriously damaged in 1993, was again a target of vandalism in January 1994. The office was damaged and glass on the notice boards smashed. Antisemitic graffiti were sprayed.

In March there were street scuffles in Wrocław between skinhead supporters of Tejkowski's PWN-PSN and anti-racist demonstrators. Over twenty people were arrested.

On 27 May a demonstration of approximately 15,000 people organized by Solidarity took place in Warsaw. The slogans included anti-Jewish ones.

On a visit to the Ursus tractor factory in Warsaw, veteran Solidarity activists Jacek Kuroń and Maciej Jankowski were barracked by supporters of Wrzodak, who, *inter alia*, described Kuroń as a "Jew and a traitor". (Kuroń, currently the Sejm Commissioner for National Minorities, is, in fact, not Jewish.)

The fiftieth anniversary of the Warsaw uprising in August was marked by a fierce debate on Polish-Jewish relations during the Second World War. In an article in *Gazeta Wyborcza* entitled "Poles and Jews: Black pages in the history of the Warsaw uprising", Michał Cichy discussed anti-Jewish prejudice among the civilian population and the underground Home Army as well as providing many examples of assistance to Jews. Although some 1,000 Jews took part in the uprising, it is estimated that from twenty-five to 100 Jews were murdered during this period by criminal elements, mostly members of the far-right National Armed Forces. *Gazeta Wyborcza* received numerous protests claiming that Cichy had revived the old Stalinist propaganda against the Home Army. *Gazeta Wyborcza* editor Adam Michnik (himself of Jewish descent) praised the article. A number of eminent scholars and writers supported Michnik's view.

PUBLICATIONS AND MEDIA

A number of antisemitic papers continued to appear. Among the most virulent were the news-sheet *Najjaśniejsza Rzeczpospolita*, whose editor, Andrzej Reymann, maintains that Poland is becoming progressively Judaized, with many ministerial posts, at least 20 per cent of the seats in parliament, hundreds of posts in the judiciary and thousands of senior civil service posts being filled by Jews. *Najwyższy Czas*, published twice a week by Janusz Korwin-Mikke's liberal-conservative Unia Polityki Realnej (UPR, Union of Real Politics, membership 3,000), likewise raised the bogey of a "Jewish lobby" of prominent politicians and journalists of allegedly Jewish origin, though those named had little, if any, connection with Jewish community life in Poland.

In October the television programme "Who was Bolesław Piasecki?" gave rise to many protests. Piasecki, founder of the pre-war National-Radical Camp and the Falangist movement in Poland, was imprisoned by the Russians as a well-known fascist. In 1945 he re-emerged in Warsaw as a *persona grata* of the Communist regime in Poland. He is believed to have co-operated with the Russian secret service and in 1955 founded the PAX movement, a pro-Communist movement of lay Catholics. In the late 1950s Piasecki's son was murdered. The perpetrators were never found and the programme concluded that the boy had been murdered by Jews in reprisal for his father's approval of anti-Jewish violence in the 1930s.

The Warsaw publishing house Fulman published anti-Jewish books including works by Jean-Marie Le Pen (see **France**) and Father Michał Poradowski's *Talmud czy Biblia? Gdzie są "korzenie" Chrześcijaństwa w judaizmie czy mozaizmie w Talmudzie czy w Biblii?* (Talmud or Bible: Where Are the "Roots" of Christianity —In Judaism or Mosaism, in the Talmud or the Bible?).

In September it emerged that the Intergraf printing works in Sopot and the Warmex printing works in Gdańsk had for several months been printing leaflets and posters for the far-right Nationale Demokratische Partei Deutschlands (see **Germany**). The directors of both plants claimed this was a purely commercial contract.

RELIGION

Much remained to be done, particularly on the parish level, in the sphere of implementing the episcopal letter issued on the twenty-fifth anniversary of *Nostra Aetate* and read in the churches on 20 January 1991 (see **Historical Legacy**).

OPINION POLLS

In a public opinion survey for the American Jewish Committee (AJC), the Warsaw-based Demoskop conducted 1,145 face-to-face interviews between 29 December 1994 and 5 January 1995.

It showed that the vast majority of Poles were strongly in favour of keeping the memory of the Holocaust alive. Thus, 85 per cent felt that "we should keep the remembrance of the extermination of the Jews strong even after the passage of time", as against 10 per cent who said that "50 years after the end of World War II, it is time to put the memory of the Nazi extermination of the Jews behind us". A comparison with the corresponding figures for Poles in a survey carried out for the AJC in 1991—81 per cent as against 13 per cent—showed little movement in this trend.

Poles displayed strong factual knowledge about some aspects of the Holocaust but were far less knowledgeable about other aspects. Thus, 91 per cent of respondents identified Auschwitz, Dachau and Treblinka as concentration camps, and 74 per cent cited the yellow star or a variant as the symbol Jews were forced to wear during the Second World War.

At the same time, only 34 per cent chose "6 million" as the appropriate number of Jews killed by the Nazis during the Second World War, while 38 per cent chose much lower figures, and 22 per cent responded "don't know".

When asked what percentage of Polish Jews were killed by the Nazis during the Second World War only 13 per cent of Polish respondents correctly answered "80+ per cent". While 48 per cent replied "don't know" to the question, "What does the term 'the Holocaust' refer to?", this reflected lack of usage of the English term "Holocaust" in Poland. In fact, 99 per cent of respondents were aware of the Nazi extermination of the Jews.

In answer to the question, "In your view, who was the main victim of the Nazis during the Second World War?", 28 per cent answered "Jews", 26 per cent "Poles" and 28 per cent "Jews and Poles". Asked directly, "Which group suffered more from Nazi persecution during the Second World War: Poles or Jews?", 40 per cent replied that "both groups suffered about the same".

Poles took a largely positive view of Polish behaviour towards Jews in the context of the Holocaust. Thus, in response to the question, "Did Poles do enough to help Jews during the Second World War, or not?", 75 per cent answered either "did enough" (49 per cent) or "did as much as they could under the circumstances" (26 per cent), while 15 per cent responded "did not do enough".

A substantial majority of Poles acknowledged the reality of antisemitism in present-day Poland. Thus, when asked, "Do you think that antisemitism in Poland is currently a very serious problem, somewhat of a problem, or not a problem at all?", 18 per cent answered "very serious problem", 49 per cent "somewhat of a problem", and 23 per cent "not a problem at all".

In the survey carried out for the AJC in 1991, the corresponding figures were 10 per cent, 29 per cent and 24 per cent, showing a clear rise in the number of those who saw antisemitism as a major problem in Polish society.

At the same time, on "look[ing] ahead over the next several years" 26 per cent of Poles saw

antisemitism increasing ("increase greatly"—5 per cent; "increase somewhat"—21 per cent) and 42 per cent "remaining the same", while only 13 per cent saw it decreasing ("decrease somewhat"—10 per cent; "decrease greatly"—3 per cent).

In this respect, there was little difference from the 1991 survey, in which 4 per cent of Poles believed antisemitism would "increase greatly", 13 per cent that it would "increase somewhat", 35 per cent that it would "remain the same", 11 per cent that it would "decrease somewhat", and 5 per cent that it would "decrease greatly".

Thirty per cent of Poles "prefer not" to have Jews as neighbours. In the 1991 survey, the corresponding figure was 40 per cent.

Sixteen per cent of Poles saw Jews as having "too much influence" in Polish society. In 1991, the figure was 26 per cent.

Thirteen per cent of Poles thought that Jews "behave in a manner which provokes hostility towards them in our country". In 1991, the figure was 19 per cent.

Replies to these three questions all showed a positive trend in Poland.

While, taken as a whole, the results of the survey pertaining to the Holocaust were fairly positive, the finding that almost half the survey's respondents believed antisemitism was likely to increase in Poland was disturbing.

COUNTERING ANTISEMITISM

Reporting in February to the Council for Polish-Jewish relations, Andrzej Zakrzewski, secretary of President Wałęsa's chancellery, said that the commemoration in 1993 of the fiftieth anniversary of the Warsaw ghetto uprising had done much to improve Poland's image in the eyes of world Jewry.

The biennial "March of the Living" pilgrimage from Auschwitz to Birkenau was seen to have both positive and negative aspects. The march was said by the organizers to have been "inspired by the renewed wave of antisemitism, neo-fascism, racism and Holocaust denial". But members of the Polish Jewish community expressed concern that the 6,500 teenage participants had little chance to shed their negative preconceptions of Poland or to make meaningful contact with the Polish Jewish community. Stanisław Krajewski, the co-chairman of the Polish Council of Christians and Jews, said that the march could, without careful guidance, reinforce chauvinistic attitudes.

A major new initiative was an interchange of lecturers conceived by Archbishop Henryk Muszyński of Gniezno and Rabbi A. James Rudin, Director of Inter-religious Affairs of the

AJC. Under this scheme Professor Robert Cohn from Lafayette College (Easton, Pennsylvania) spent several weeks lecturing in Polish Catholic seminaries on "Jewish interpretations of the Hebrew Bible", while the Polish Catholic scholar Professor Waldemar Chrostowski made a lecture tour of universities and synagogues in the USA.

In May the joint Polish-Israeli textbook commision completed its formulation of guidelines. Issues discussed included the rise in antisemitism in Poland during the 1930s, the Holocaust and the establishment of the state of Israel.

In May President Wałęsa conferred the Polish Order of Merit on Roman Kent of the Jewish Foundation for Christian Rescuers/ Anti-Defamation League for his efforts on behalf of Polish-Jewish and Christian-Jewish relations.

On 29 September-2 October the Second Festival of Poland's National Minorities took place in Gdańsk. In addition to Jewish ensembles from Poland, Jewish groups from Ukraine participated. The festival was accompanied by a conference on minority cultures in Central and Eastern Europe hosted by the Institute of History of Gdańsk University.

In October President Wałęsa conferred on Simon Wiesenthal the Commander's Cross of the Order of Polonia Restituta. Wiesenthal also received an honorary doctorate from the Jagiellonian University of Kraków. A programme on his life and work was shown on Polish television.

ASSESSMENT

Ethnic strife was not a serious issue in Poland and antisemitism remained a relatively minor problem. The Polish authorities, with President Wałęsa and government leaders setting the example, continued their policy of opposing as actively as possible all manifestations of antisemitism, in particular through educational means. But there clearly remains a legacy of antisemitism in Poland. A number of extremist groups in whose ideology antisemitism plays at least some role were still active on the fringe of Polish politics: in recent years a pattern has been discerned in which anti-Jewish sentiments tend to come to the fore primarily during election periods. Moreover, the fact that almost half of the respondents questioned in a public opinion survey carried out at the turn of 1994-5 believed antisemitism was likely to increase in Poland was disturbing. Finally, there remained a considerable amount to be done regarding implementation, especially on the parish level, of the episcopal letter issued on the twenty-fifth anniversary of *Nostra Aetate*.

Romania

General population: 23.4 million
Jewish population: 9-14,000 (mainly in Bucharest)

GENERAL BACKGROUND

Since autumn 1992 Prime Minister Nicolae Văcăroiu has headed an executive based on the Partidul Social Democrat din România (PSDR, Party of Social Democracy in Romania). The cabinet was enlarged in August 1994, when the extreme-nationalist Partidul Unități Naționale Românesti (PUNR, Party of Romanian National Unity) formally entered into a coalition with the PSDR. Earlier, the PUNR, as well as the extreme-nationalist and openly antisemitic Partidul România Máre (PRM, Greater Romania Party) and the Partidul Socialist al Muncii (PSM, Socialist Labour Party) had backed the PSDR government in parliament without formally being members of the coalition. By the end of 1994 talks were underway with the PRM and the PSM to join the coalition as well, with the PRM threatening to withdraw support from the cabinet unless offered ministerial posts. The PUNR had similarly forced its way into the cabinet.

Economic conditions, which were bad in 1990-3, improved in 1994. Inflation dropped from around 300 per cent in 1993 to an estimated 65-70 per cent and the annual rate of growth, while modest, was expected to be 2.5 per cent, nearly doubling that of the previous year (1.3 per cent). This improvement in economic performance was achieved at the cost of tight economic policies, which led to a sharp drop in the government's popularity. Almost 11 per cent of the population was unemployed.

HISTORICAL LEGACY

In the nineteenth and early twentieth centuries Romania was generally considered one of the most antisemitic countries in Europe. Following foreign pressure, citizenship was granted to Jews on a collective basis only after 1923, but this step was resented by many political parties as well as large segments of the general population. Antisemitism emerged as a powerful factor in the country's political life in the 1920s, with the establishment of the Legion of Archangel Saint Michael by Corneliu Zelea Codreanu in June 1927. Many points included in the antisemitic programme of the Legion (also known as the Iron Guard and the All for the Country Party) were legislated by the Goga-Cuza government, which lasted only

from 27 December 1937 to 11 February 1938. On 14 September 1940 General (later Marshal) Ion Antonescu set up, together with the Iron Guard, the National Legionary State. In January 1941, following an abortive rebellion against Antonescu's rule, the Guard was banned. A part of the Jewish population was deported to the Transdniestr region which Romania occupied after the outbreak of the Second World War, and many of those deported died. Atrocities were also committed by the Romanian army against the Jewish population living in the occupied territories. A total of 25,000 Jews (some sources say 19,000) were burned alive by the Romanian army in Odessa on 23 October 1941 on orders from Antonescu, as a retaliatory measure against an attack by partisans on the army's headquarters in the town. There were also pogroms against the Jews in Romania proper.

The number of Romanian Jews exterminated in the Holocaust is subject to dispute. According to Jewish historians, between 250,000 and 300,000 Romanian Jews perished in the territories that were under Romanian jurisdiction during the Second World War. This figure does not include the approximately 150,000 Jews from Northern Transylvania who were exterminated in 1944 either by the Hungarian authorities or by the Germans, who deported them to concentration camps with the collaboration of the Hungarian government.

After the war several Jews were prominent in the leadership of the Romanian Communist Party. Of these, the best known are Ana Pauker and Iosif Chisinevschi. At no point after the Communist takeover, however, did the party's leadership contain a majority, or even a plurality, of Jews. Pauker was a victim of Stalin's antisemitic campaign, which was shrewdly exploited by the party's first secretary, Gheorghe Gheorghiu-Dej (who was no less a Stalinist than Pauker), in order to remove a political adversary. Chisinevschi survived politically until 1958, when he was caught attempting to strike an "unholy alliance" with some Stalinist-turned-liberal elements in the party in an effort to emulate the Khrushchev line in the USSR.

In 1964 Dej adopted a neo-nationalist policy, which reached a new peak under Nicolae Ceauşescu, who succeeded him as party leader in March 1965. Although under Ceauşescu antisemitism was never officially endorsed, it was condoned and occasionally appeared in the press and in literary works by authors closely associated with the presidential couple. The most prominent of these authors, the Ceauşescu hagiographers Eugen Barbu and Corneliu Vadim Tudor (who eventually became the leader of the PRM), re-emerged in prominent positions in Romania's antisemitic circles in 1990-1.

RACISM AND XENOPHOBIA

There were three main targets of racist and xenophobic attitudes in 1994. The first was the large (1.6 million according to the 1992 census) Hungarian minority. The second was the Roma community (according to some sources about 2 million). Although in 1994 only one violent incident against the Roma was registered—there have been some twenty such incidents since 1990—a report by Helsinki Watch in New York in November 1994 concluded that "there had been a consistent pattern by Romanian police, investigatory bodies and the judicial system of ignoring and downplaying the significance of violent attacks" against the Roma. The third target was foreigners residing in Romania. Romanian legislation on the status of foreigners in the country has not yet been approved by parliament. There are three main categories of foreigners residing in Romania—those with a valid residence permit (mostly students and businessmen); those who stayed after their residence permit expired; and those who officially requested the status of refugees. But the largest category are actually those who illegally cross the borders in an attempt to reach the West. The number of foreigners who are legally resident in Romania was put by Interior Minister Doru Ioan Taracila in November 1994 at 85,000, of which 32,000 were business people and 20,600 were students. Some 18,300 were said to be in the country after their residence permit had expired. Also in November it was announced by the ministry of labour and social security that 2,300 foreigners (mostly from Asian and Afri-

can states) had requested refugee status. Only in a few cases is such status granted and already in 1992 Romania began to forcefully deport refugees to their country of origin.

PARTIES, ORGANIZATIONS, MOVEMENTS

No political party in Romania openly admits to being antisemitic. However, two broad categories of parties in which antisemitism plays a role can be differentiated. The first category comprises the parties of "radical continuity", which advocate a continuation of the Ceauşescu line in foreign and internal policy but with a stronger emphasis on the xenophobia of the former regime. This category includes the PRM and the PUNR. The second category, which may be labeled "radical return", advocates a revival of the nationalist ethos based on interwar political and social values.

In the general election of 1992 the PRM obtained 3.89 per cent of the vote for the chamber of deputies and 3.85 per cent of the vote for the senate, as a result of which it gained twenty-two deputies and senators.

After a clash with Tudor, one deputy was expelled from the PRM in 1993. Two other PRM deputies left the party in early 1994 following a conflict with the PSDR. The conflict erupted when Tudor attacked Defence Minister Nicolae Spiroiu, whom he accused of corruption. One of the accusations was that he had concluded deals with Israel that were undermining Romania's defence industry. Tudor also attacked other prominent personalities close to President Iliescu in early 1994, accusing them of crimes ranging from spying to promiscuous sexual behaviour. The attacks led to the severing of discussions initiated with the purpose of enabling the PRM to formally join the coalition. However, the conflict was short-lived and, moreover, to Tudor's satisfaction, Spiroiu was replaced in March by Gheorghe Tinca.

In March 1993, when the PRM national congress was held, the party's weekly, *Politica*, estimated 20,000 card-carrying members and "an exceptionally high number of sympathizers". This represented a significant drop from 1992, when card-carrying membership was said to have been 28,000. The PRM was set up in May 1991, with Tudor as president and Barbu as vice-president and, from its foundation, has had a clear anti-Jewish orientation. At the 1993 congress Barbu became honorary vice-president (he died later in the year) and Mircea Musat, a historian who had been in charge of Communist-supervised historiography, replaced him as vice-president. Musat died in November 1994. In January 1994 PRM spokesman Mircea Hamza was promoted to vice-chairman. The basis on which the PRM was established was laid down by *România máre*, a weekly published by Tudor since May 1990 which regularly contains antisemitic material.

The PRM is close to both the former secret police and the PSM, which was set up in November 1990 and was registered with the Bucharest tribunal in January 1992. After the 1992 election the PRM and the PSM founded the national bloc in the senate. The most prominent member of the PSM in the senate is Adrian Păunescu who, like Tudor, is a former "court poet" of the Ceauşescu family. Păunescu owns both the weekly *Totusi iubirea* and the daily *Vremea*, both of which frequently carry antisemitic articles. No official figures for membership of the PSM are available. In the 1992 election the PSM obtained 3.03 per cent of the votes for the chamber of deputies and 3.18 per cent of those for the senate. It has thirteen deputies and five senators.

Both PRM and PSM are close to Vatra Românească (VR, Romanian Cradle), an anti-Hungarian organization founded in early 1990 whose political arm is the PUNR. VR's honorary president, Iosif Constantin Dragan, is known for his close links with the former regime. Dragan now heads the Europa Nova publishing trust, which is suspected of supporting *Europa*, a weekly even more antisemitic than *România máre* and *Politica*.

Although the Iron Guard was quashed by Antonescu, in the 1980s Dragan became a leading proponent of the campaign to rehabilitate the wartime dictator, a campaign tacitly backed by the Ceauşescu regime. Now Dragan heads the Pro-Liga "Maresalul Antonescu" (PLMA, Marshal Antonescu League) and the Marshal Antonescu foundation.

VR claims a membership of 6 million, but this figure is not credible. Total membership of the PUNR is unknown, but the party emerged as relatively strong in the 1992 elections. It obtained 7.7 per cent of the votes for the chamber of deputies and 8.1 per cent of the votes for the senate, gaining thirty deputies and fourteen senators. Senator Radu Ceontea (former leader of the PUNR) and deputy Petru Burca left the party after the elections, following conflicts with Georghe Funar. The PUNR officially joined the cabinet in August 1994. One of the ministers representing it, Valeriu Tabara, who is in charge of the agriculture portfolio, is a member of the PLMA. Minister of Justice Iosif Gavril Chiuzbaian, who also represents the PUNR, is known to be close to both Dragan and Tudor. On 22 September, two PUNR deputies initiated a letter of protest to the US Senate against the appointment of Alfred Moses, the president of the American Jewish Committee, as the next US ambassador to Bucharest. The move was backed by the entire PUNR leadership and was widely regarded as a display of antisemitic attitudes. It was, however, joined by five other parliamentarians, three of whom represented the democratic opposition. As a result of their having signed the protest letter against Moses's appointment, two of the democratic parliamentarians were expelled from their parties, but the third, a member of the Partidul Naţional fiărănesc Creştin şi Democrat (PNT-CD, National Peasant Party-Christian Democratic), was supported by his party. The PSDR forced its representative who had backed the PUNR initiative to withdraw his signature.

None of the "radical return" parties has been able to obtain parliamentary representation. The Noua Românie Creştina (NRC, New Christian Romania) did not run in the elections, having been set up in November 1992, on Codreanu's birth date. Its leader was Serban Suru, a thirty-one-year-old teacher, although the party includes mostly older members of the former Iron Guard. The NRC openly called for Codreanu's rehabilitation. It ceased to exist in 1994 but in October Suru announced he had set up the first "Legionary nest" in Bucharest. The "nests" were the basic organizational cells of Codreanu's movement. Suru said he had also set up a library providing documentation on the Iron Guard. The new "nest" is named after Codreanu's successor as leader of the Iron Guard, Horia Sima. So far, however, it has only five members.

Puncte cardinale is the monthly publication of another party formed by former Iron Guardists, the Uniunea Creştin-Democrata-Conventia Sibiu (UCD-CS, Christian Democratic Union-Sibiu Convention). Its members were expelled from the Uniunea Creştin-Democrata (UCD, Christian Democratic Union) in 1990 on account of pro-Iron Guard sympathies. Membership of the UCD-CS is unknown, but it sometimes overlaps with the membership of successor Iron Guardist organizations.

The Mişcarea pentru România (MPR, Movement for Romania), headed by Marian Munteanu, has an organizational structure resembling that of Codreanu's organization. Although it claims to be democratic, it openly expresses admiration for many aspects of Iron Guard ideology. In 1994 Munteanu published in *Mişcarea*, his party's monthly, a long series praising the Iron Guard. The MPR obtained only 13,000 votes in the 1992 election but the party's popularity is reported to be growing among the younger generation. Munteanu has opted for a "long-term strategy" aimed at attracting nationalist-minded young people who are members of other formations to his own organization. The MPR advocates "Romanianism" and the establishment of a corporatist state. In practice, this often translates into antisemitic attacks on those considered partisans of "cosmopolitanism" and hence of communism, and of proponents of human rights and the rights of the national minorities. In 1994 the MPR took the lead—soon to be followed by the PRM—in attacking the government for having agreed to discuss with Jewish representatives the restitution of Jewish property. Both parties claimed that Jews should, if anything, pay compensation to Romania for having plundered its wealth and having brought the "Red Holocaust" to the country.

The "radical return" category also includes the Partidul de Dreapta (PD, Party of the National Right), established by Radu Sorescu in April 1992. Estimated membership of the party is 7,000-8,000. The party's monthly changed its name from *Noua dreapta* to *Dreapta naţionala* in June. Its circulation is estimated at 5,000, but in 1994 there were indications that it was encountering difficulties (see **Publications and Media**). The PD has made efforts to establish links with movements in Western Europe. In his report to parliament Virgil Magureanu said the PD was "preoccupied with establishing contacts with like-minded formations from abroad with the purpose of obtaining moral and material support". He added that the leader of an exiled Iron Guardist organization based in New York had offered assistance to the PD conditional on its undertaking violent actions, which included the burning of synagogues, the profanation of Jewish cemeteries and attacks on Roma communities. According to Magureanu, the PD did not accept the offer. In October Sorescu announced he was resigning from the presidency of the PD. He was replaced by Aurelian Pavelescu, reportedly a teaching assistant at the Bucharest academy of theatre and film and a student at the Bucharest law faculty.

In June 1993 the political formation Pro-Patria (PP, For the Fatherland) was registered with the Bucharest tribunal. The formation had originally requested to be registered under the name "Everything for the Country", the name of the Legionary Movement's political arm in 1935-8. Precisely for this reason the request was turned down, but the court objected only to the name and not to the party's statutes. The party's leader is Nistor Chioreanu, an Iron Guardist who for some time after Codreanu's death was considered third in the movement's hierarchy.

Chioreanu's formation seems to be linked with that branch of the Iron Guard movement in exile which backed Codreanu's successor, Horia Sima, who died in exile in 1993. Apparently the UCD-CS and Suru's party have similar links and the "Simists" are certainly behind the most overtly pro-Iron Guard publication of Romania, *Gazeta de vest,* which is printed in Timişoara. Munteanu, on the other hand, seems to enjoy the backing of the branch of exiled Iron Guardists, the "Codreanists", who claim that Sima "deviated" from "genuine Legionism".

Also in the category of "radical return" formations are three "non-political" organizations linked by their Iron Guardist past—the Asociatia Fostilor Presedinti ai Organizatiilor Studentilor Creştini din Epoca Autonomiei Universitare (AFPOSCEAU, Association of Former Presidents of Romanian Christian Student Organizations from the Period of University Autonomy), the Liga pentru Apararea Adevarului Istoric (LAAI, League for the Defence of Historical Truth) and the Asociatia 10 decembrie (AD, 10 December Association). All three are active in rehabilitating the Guard.

MAINSTREAM POLITICS

As in 1993, members of parties and individuals not identified with antisemitic postures found themselves, deliberately or not, on the same side of the barricades as the antisemites. The case of the co-sponsors (with the PUNR) of the protest letter against Moses's appointment as US ambassador to Romania was mentioned above. In several instances, officials identified with the PSDR appeared not to object to an association with antisemitic publications and parties. Foreign Minister Teodor Melescanu, in an interview with the antisemitic monthly *Europa* in July, seemed to partly agree with his interviewer when she attacked Aurel Dragos Munteanu, Romania's former ambassador to the United States, who is of Jewish origin and had just resigned his position.

When the PRM weekly *Politica* celebrated the publication of its 200th issue, in May, it printed messages of congratulation from Prime Minister Văcăroiu and Education Minister Liviu Maior. Also among well-wishers was the priest Simeon Tatu, whose extreme nationalist views are well known and who was forced by the PSDR to remove his signature from the anti-Moses protest. Another PSDR parliamentarian, Senator Gheorghe Dumitrascu, is a regular contributor to the PRM's other weekly, *România máre,* along with the independent senator Petre Turlea, who was the first to initiate, in 1990, the marking of the anniversary of Antonescu's execution by the Romanian parliament (see **Publications and Media**).

Members of the democratic opposition and/or intellectuals identified with the cause of democratization did not always dissociate themselves from the antisemites. In May, for instance, at a symposium on the Romanian exile and its historical identity held in Paris, the list of participants included several prominent Iron Guardists from Romania and the exile (for example, Aurelio Rauta, Marcel Petrisor and Ion Halmaghi) alongside PNT-CD president Corneliu Coposu and the president of the Democratic Convention (the umbrella organization of centrist opposition parties and associations), Emil Constantinescu. Prominent intellectuals opposed to Iliescu's party, such as the poet Ana Blandiana, the writer Octavian Paler and the journalist Petre Mihai Bacanu, participated in August in Los Angeles in the Romanian Festival, an event traditionally linked with the Iron Guard.

MANIFESTATIONS

In his report to parliament, Magureanu said that, according to Romanian intelligence, 1994 witnessed an "intensification" of activities aimed at the unification of legally registered parties representing the former Iron Guard. He added that the former Legionary Movement was also attempting to recreate some of its organizational structures underground. Unlike in previous years, when such activities had been restricted to a handful of Romania's forty-one counties, in 1994 they had "spread nearly all over the country's territory". Magureanu added that Iron Guard organizations in exile were financing this campaign and participating in it through envoys sent to Romania.

CULTURAL LIFE

The independent weekly *Expres* claimed in May that "violent antisemitism" was taking over the Bucharest academic environment. As an example, it said that the group around sociologist Ilie Badescu (who is closely associated with the MPR) was becoming predominant in the faculty of sociology, while respectable professors were leaving the faculty's staff. Another example (also reported by other publications) was that of the philosopher Alexandru Surdu, who had recently become a member of the Romanian Academy and whose lectures were reportedly "viciously antisemitic". Speaking on the occasion of his reception by the Academy, Surdu eulogized a number of interwar far-right philosophers and launched an antisemitic attack on "import models". In a further example of antisemitism among academic staff, the MPR

weekly *Miṣcarea* published in May an "open letter" from a Cluj university lecturer in philosophy to Corneliu Coposu. The letter took Coposu to task for having attended the ceremonies marking the International Day of the Holocaust at the Choral Temple in Bucharest, and expressed dismay that Coposu, himself a "victim of the communist holocaust", should agree to play the game of the Jews.

EDUCATION

In his report to parliament, Magureanu illustrated the danger of Legionary propaganda being spread among the youth: he claimed a teacher at one of Bucharest's most prestigious high schools was proselytizing among his pupils. It turned out that the teacher was none other than Serban Suru (see **Parties, Organizations, Movements**).

PUBLICATIONS AND MEDIA

The main disseminators of antisemitism in the press in 1994 were those who had excelled in it since 1990. Among them, not only *Noua dreapta* (see **Parties, Organizations, Movements**) but also *Europa* appeared to encounter difficulties with publication and distribution. In March Ilie Neacṣu's weekly did not appear at all and in April it was announced that *Europa* was to become a monthly. After September it appeared twice a month.

Apart from the by-now "established" antisemitic publications (*România máre, Politica, Europa, Totusi iubirea, Vremea, Miṣcarea, Noua dreapta, Gazeta de vest, Puncte cardinale*), two additional periodicals deserve mention. The first, launched in 1993, is *Invierea*, which appears three times a year. Its sponsors are the above-mentioned "non-political" organizations, the AFPOSCEAU and the LAAI, and the journal is wholly dedicated to praising the Iron Guard. The other journal, *Arhivele totalitarianismului*, was launched in 1994 and is printed by the National Institute for the Study of Totalitarianism, which was set up in 1994 and is sponsored by the Romanian Academy.

On 24 January a round-table discussion on Antonescu was screened on Romanian television. Two of the historians participating in the discussion claimed that the dictator's antisemitism had been triggered by the fact that Jews had killed, molested and otherwise humiliated members of the Romanian armed forces as they were forced to leave Bessarabia in the wake of the Soviet ultimatum of 1940. Rabbi Rosen, the head of the Jewish community, protested the allegations.

Following the death of Rabbi Rosen in May the independent weekly *Baricada* noted that the number of victims among members of the Iron Guard during the 1941 rebellion against Antonescu had been larger than the number of Jews killed in the rebellion. Attacking President Iliescu's funeral speech at the Choral Temple, *Baricada* said he was playing into the hands of the Jews, who had invented the figure of 400,000 Holocaust victims in Romania in order to be able to claim compensation from an impoverished country.

Theodor Codreanu (no relation to the "Captain" of the Iron Guard) published a long article in *Totusi iubirea* under the title *"Mein Kampf* and Europe's destiny" in which he portrayed Hitler as a courageous man confronting Jewish-influenced, Western democratic imperialism. Hitler, according to Codreanu, had, however, also made mistakes, the foremost of which had been to abandon Christianity. And this, the reader was left to understand, was precisely what differentiated the Nazis from the Legionary Movement.

In his report to parliament, Magureanu singled out the Timişoara publishers Gordian and Marineasa for disseminating Iron Guardist literature. Although Marineasa had indeed published several volumes of Iron Guardist "productions", it is hardly the most important publisher to do so. A new publishing house specializing in Legionary literature was set up in 1994 in Bucharest. It is called Majadahonda, after the place in Spain where Iron Guard "martyrs" Vasile Marin and Ion Mota were killed in the Spanish Civil War. Also in 1994 the publishing house Fronde, said to operate both in Paris and in the Transylvanian town of Alba Iulia, printed the memoirs of the former foreign minister of the Legionary Movement, Mihai Sturdza, which had originally been published in the West in 1966.

Another editorial event during the year was the publication (at the Roza vanturilor publishing house, run by Dan Zamfirescu, a Ceauşescu hagiographer) of Radu Lecca's volume, "I Have Saved the Jews of Romania". Under Antonescu Lecca had been in charge of "Romanianizing" Jewish property while being at the same time a known German agent.

A volume originally published in the interwar period, Dumitru Murarasu's "Eminescu's Nationalism", was reprinted by the Pacifica publishing house, the publisher which a year earlier had brought out Hitler's *Mein Kampf.* The book is full of antisemitic remarks.

Meanwhile, books and articles presenting Antonescu as a hero saturated the market. If 1994 began with a scandal caused by the docu-

mentary on the former dictator's execution aired on television in December 1993, it ended with the announcement that another documentary presenting Antonescu in a positive light was about to have its première in late December in a Bucharest cinema.

DENIAL OF THE HOLOCAUST

In an article on the massacre of Muslims in a mosque in Hebron by a Jewish settler in February Tudor claimed that he himself had long been a victim of Jewish propaganda on the Holocaust. Little by little, however, he had learned that the Germans could not possibly have gassed 6 million Jews. It later became clear to him that "international Zionism" had invented the figure, just as now it was striving to inflate the number of Jewish victims in Romania during the war from "about 1,200" to the "fabulous figure of 400,000" in order to squeeze Romania out of its assets. In fact, as the PRM weekly *Politica* wrote in June, it was "not Romania, which defended its Jews and saved them, that must pay compensation, but the Jews should pay us moral and material compensation, taking into consideration the huge fortunes acquired here through profiteering, theft, the ruthless exploitation of the Romanian peasants . . . ". In turn, the PRM said in a statement by its leader, Marian Munteanu, published in *Mişcarea* in June, that "the Romanian state had never been a 'fascist' state and no Jewish Holocaust had ever taken place in Romania".

Similarly, PSM vice-chairman Senator Adrian Păunescu wrote in *Totusi iubirea* in April that Antonescu had never exterminated innocent Jews. Those who had suffered were Jews who had attacked the Romanian army as Soviet partisans. In October *Mişcarea* began a series of articles denying the Holocaust. In an introductory article, *Mişcarea* wrote that "nobody had been able to offer a reply that can refute the point of view of the revisionist historians".

OPINION POLLS

In early 1994 the Romanian media reported a survey conducted by the Centre of Studies and Research on the "problems of youth" which surveyed the attitudes of young people in 1990-3. Among other things, the pollsters sought to analyse attitudes towards ethnic minorities. There were only few references to Jews in the reported results. The survey revealed that young people on a low income rejected the idea of having Jews as neighbours and that young women thought Jews should "only occasionally visit Romania". On the whole, the survey showed that one-third of the respondents held that Roma, Hungarians and Turks should not be allowed to live at all on Romanian territory.

Another opinion poll was conducted by the Bucharest Institute for Marketing and Surveys (IMAS) in 1994. The survey, based on a representative sample of 1,022 persons, with a margin of error of 3 per cent and sponsored by the "Korunk" Hungarian-Romanian friendship association, sought to measure "social distances" among persons belonging to different ethnic groups. In this case, Romanians were compared with members of the Hungarian minority; attitudes were measured in both groups towards Romanians (respectively, Hungarians), Germans, Roma and Jews. "Social distance" was measured by asking respondents to react to four potential situations: having a Hungarian (respectively Romanian), a German, a Jew or a member of the Roma minority as spouse; being visited by a member of that ethnic group; having a member of that group as a colleague or neighbour; and having him or her visit the locality where the respondent lived. The respondents were also given the possibility of rejecting all four possibilities. The poll showed that in both groups "social distance" was smallest towards German ethnics and largest towards the Roma. In both groups Jews were second lowest (after the Roma).

A survey conducted in January by IMAS and Gallup UK jointly, based on a representative sample of 1,900 respondents and with a margin of error of 3 per cent, showed that 51 per cent of Romanians wished to impose limits on the number of foreigners from poor countries permitted to enter Romania. Twenty-two per cent of the respondents held that ethnic and national minorities presented a danger for Romania, 57 per cent were of the opposite opinion and 21 per cent did not reply to the question or said they did not know. The sample was equally divided (39 per cent) in evaluating the tensions existing between ethnic or religious minorities and the majority population as "serious" or "not serious", with 22 per cent replying that they did not know or not answering the question. Over a quarter (26 per cent) evaluated tensions between Romania's ultra-nationalists and the rest of the population as "serious", but 38 per cent said they were not of this opinion and 36 per cent did not reply or said they did not know.

In related polls carried out by IMAS and the Romanian Institute for Surveys and Opinion Polls (IRSOP) alternatively in March, June and September the evolution of attitudes was surveyed by asking identical questions. The March survey, based on a representative sample of 1,101 persons and with a margin of error of

3 per cent, showed that the ultra-nationalist leaders came low on the popularity scale. Gheorghe Funar, president of the PUNR, was ranked eleventh out of 14, PRM leader Corneliu Vadim Tudor was twelfth, and PSM leader Ilie Verdet was last. The June survey, based on a representative sample of 1,095 people and with a margin of error of 3 per cent, returned similar results. The September survey, based on a sample of 1,164 people and with a margin of error of 3 per cent, however, had Tudor in twelfth place, with Funar and Verdet closing the list.

LEGAL MATTERS

Both chambers of the Romanian parliament debated a new version of the country's penal code which was to replace the Ceauşescu version. The version adopted by the chamber of deputies stirred up negative reactions both in Romania and abroad. A mediation commission of the two chambers is yet to work out a compromise. According to the version adopted by the chamber of deputies, which approved an amendment proposed by a PUNR deputy on 10 November, the unauthorized hoisting of foreign flags and the singing of foreign national anthems is to be punished by prison sentences ranging from six months to three years. This article was perceived by representatives of the Uniunea Democrată Maghiară din România (Hungarian Democratic Union of Romania) as being directed against the Magyar minority in particular, and they hastened to announce that if the mediation commission did not strike the article out, they would ask the constitutional court to do so. Another controversial provision in the penal code's version passed by the chamber makes public defamation of the Romanian nation punishable by sentences ranging from one to five years in jail. It was pointed out that the text of the law lacked precision and was opening the door to abusive interpretations that could affect freedom of expression. On the other hand, disagreement between left and right prevented the adoption of an article that would have prohibited fascist and communist propaganda. PSDR deputies and their allies argued that the proposed article would introduce extremism through the back door by banning communist propaganda. The version of the article finally adopted merely prohibits "propaganda promoting the setting up of a totalitarian state".

COUNTERING ANTISEMITISM

As in the previous year, President Iliescu and the PSDR distanced themselves from attempts to rehabilitate Antonescu and the Iron Guard and spoke out against the revival of antisemitism. At the same time, as allies of the parties of "radical continuity", they strove to overlook the antisemitic pronouncements of their partners and present the rehabilitation attempts as if they were limited only to the parties of "radical return". By the end of the year, when dependency on the ultra-nationalists in parliament was becoming more critical, Iliescu sought to explain to foreign audiences that the campaign to rehabilitate Antonescu was not antisemitic.

Responding in January to a letter from the national director of the US Anti-Defamation League, Abraham Foxman, dated 9 December 1993, Iliescu agreed that the antisemitic manifestations in post-revolutionary Romania were a worrisome phenomenon. On attempts to rehabilitate Antonescu, he wrote that those who did so saw in him "an anti-communist symbol, because he joined the war against the Soviet Union in 1941 in order to regain the lost Romanian territories". The promoters of the rehabilitation, Iliescu wrote, were not taking into consideration the "anti-Jewish acts committed by the Iron Guard" in the early period of the Antonescu regime. But regardless of "historical circumstances and even of Antonescu's merits in liquidating the fascist movement in 1941," he emphasized, "he must be judged taking all his decisions into consideration". In early November, during a visit to Great Britain, Iliescu told a group of British Jewish parliamentarians that the attempts to rehabilitate Romania's wartime leader bore "no antisemitic connotation" and were due only to the Marshal's anti-communist postures. The difference between the comments of January and November was obvious to anyone who had followed Iliescu's pronouncements; earlier in the year (for instance, at the ceremony for Rosen at the Choral Temple or in his message to the Jewish community on the Day of the Holocaust), he had distanced himself from those who would not acknowledge the antisemitic measures of the Antonescu regime.

Warning in May against the "setting up and proliferation of organizations of the extreme right", several PSDR officials mentioned the publications of the "radical return" stream but were silent on the manifestations of their political allies. This seemed to confirm the diagnosis of Adrian Severin, vice-chairman of the opposition Democratic Party-National Salvation Front, who in April accused the PSDR of "political bigamy" with "extremist, xenophobic

and nostalgic-restoration parties".

But these parties (as demonstrated by the "Moses affair") had no intention of changing line. In March the Romania-Israel Cultural Friendship Association protested against the increasing proliferation of antisemitic and xenophobic attacks in the press. Although the publications that took this line were losing readers, the association said, the "attitude of passivity and indulgence" displayed by public authorities and those legally in charge of "taking measures for curbing" such manifestations "must be condemned". Yet not only was this not done, but when in May Hungarian Reformed Bishop Laszlo Toekes spoke out against the drive to rehabilitate Antonescu and the "antisemitic manifestations that had recently reappeared in Romanian society", he was attacked in parliament by Petre Turlea.

In line with the recommendations adopted at the October 1993 Vienna conference of European Council members, in March 1994 a National Committee for the Co-ordination of Activities for Combating Racism, Xenophobia and Antisemitism was set up in Bucharest. The committee is to co-ordinate at national level the activities of the European Campaign of the Youth for Combating Racism, Xenophobia, Antisemitism and Intolerance, which began in December 1994 and will end on 1 January 1997. It comprises both government and non-government organizations as well as youth organizations.

ASSESSMENT

The death of Rabbi Rosen and his replacement by Nicolae Cajal as president of the Jewish community marked an end to the open condemnation of antisemitism. The change to non-confrontationist tactics rendered antisemitic pronouncements less overt though by no means brought about their disappearance. The campaigns to rehabilitate wartime dictator Ion Antonescu and the Iron Guard continued.

Objectively, the threat to Jews was not serious, at least as far as Jewish lives and properties were concerned. The threat posed by anti-Roma sentiment was much greater, as was the threat of Romanian-Hungarian violent confrontation. However, the threat to Romania's Jewry was by no means marginal. In the case of a further deterioration of the economic situation (a not unlikely possibility), Jews could easily return to their traditional role of scapegoat, and antisemitism could become more than mere rhetoric.

Russia

General population: 149 million
Jewish population: 600,000 (mainly in Moscow and St Petersburg)

GENERAL BACKGROUND

The constitutional referendum of December 1993, which was concurrent with parliamentary elections, strengthened President Boris Yeltsin's position *vis-à-vis* the legislature. He continued to proclaim his commitment to political reform and the transition to a modern market economy. Nevertheless, the process of institutionalizing democracy and a modern market economy lagged due, in part, to the slow enactment of laws and development of regulatory institutions, widespread unfamiliarity with democratic and market principles, and a reaction against "democrats" and free market advocates because of social dislocation.

On 31 December official statistics revealed a 21 per cent decline for the year in industrial output, which thus stood at only 45 per cent of its 1991 level. The annual inflation rate was 300 per cent.

Organized crime was an increasingly serious problem (see **Racism and Xenophobia**).

President Yeltsin established late in 1993 a special commission on human rights headed by Sergey Kovalev, a former dissident and political prisoner widely respected in human rights circles. By the end of June the commission had drafted an unprecedented, highly critical report on human rights practices in Russia in 1993 which was leaked to the press and then published in full by an official government newspaper.

On 11 December Russian troops launched an offensive against rebel forces in the breakaway republic of Chechnya.

HISTORICAL LEGACY

The Bolshevik Revolution brought to an end a long history of institutionalized antisemitism in Russia and the tsarist empire and accorded the Jewish minority equal rights.

Jewish victims of the Nazi occupation of the Soviet Union numbered approximately 2 million.

In Stalin's last years, an institutionalized anti-Jewish campaign culminated in the so-called doctors' plot, an alleged assassination attempt on the Soviet dictator by a group of Jewish doctors.

Despite Khrushchev's policy of de-Stalinization, his rule was not devoid of anti-Jewish elements, in particular the so-called economic trials, in which a disproportionate number of the defendants appeared to be Jews.

In 1963 Trofim Kichko's book "Judaism without Embellishment" evoked a world-wide protest, in particular over its Nazi-style cartoons, leading to its withdrawal by the Soviet authorities.

In the Brezhnev era, an anti-Zionist and anti-Israeli ideological and political campaign aimed at countering the emigration sentiment of Soviet Jews was substantially influenced by a number of anti-Jewish propagandists who claimed that "international Zionism" (in effect the Jewish Diaspora using Israel as a pawn) was conspiring both to subvert the Soviet Bloc and to attain world supremacy.

In the Gorbachev period and following the collapse of the Communist regime, antisemitism was a common feature of the numerous ultra-nationalist and neo-Stalinist groups which emerged on the fringe of Russian politics.

The Gorbachev and Yeltsin administrations, deeply opposed to antisemitism in principle, combated it to the extent that political circumstances permitted.

RACISM AND XENOPHOBIA

Discrimination against people from the Caucasus and Central Asia increased in mid-1994 concurrently with new measures to combat crime. With wide public support, law enforcement authorities targeted dark-complexioned people for harassment, arrest and deportation from urban centres. Human rights groups in Moscow criticized the discriminatory procedures under which thousands of people were forced to leave the capital after the June crime decrees. However, the crackdown was generally welcomed by Muscovites, who blamed much of the crime in the city on people from the southern republics of the former USSR.

PARTIES, ORGANIZATIONS, MOVEMENTS

Consolidating his success in the December 1993 parliamentary elections, Vladimir Zhirinovsky, leader of the Liberalno-demokraticheskaya partiya Rossii (LDPR, Liberal Democratic Party of Russia), continued to conduct himself in a calculatedly provocative manner, in particular making unbridled threats against foreign powers and Russia's national minorities. Zhirinovsky's party was one of the few factions in the Duma (parliament) to support the government's increasingly unpopular conduct of the war in Chechnya.

Zhirinovsky maintained his party's particularly close relationship with the far-right Deutsche Volksunion led by Gerhard Frey, who apparently remained one of his major financial backers (see **Germany**). He invited to his party's congress in April France's Jean-Marie Le Pen and President Saddam Hussein of Iraq (neither of whom attended). A "sister party" of the LDPR was founded in Estonia (see **Estonia**).

While it cannot be said that Jews occupied a special place among his targets, Zhirinovsky made repeated anti-Jewish statements, some of them in a characteristically anti-Zionist guise.

For example, on 17 February Zhirinovsky told the Russian ultra-nationalist publication *Kubansky kuryer*: "Judge for yourself whose interests our parliament represents—American, Jewish or any others."

On 4 March he told *Die Zeit*: "Why are the Zionists so bad? . . . Because they weaken Russia. The American Jews make America strong but the Russian Jews make Russia weak. They do this so that they can leave for Israel. They should stay here. . . . Our greatest problems are the Americans and the Zionists."

In November, during a visit to the United States, Zhirinovsky told the UN Correspondents' Association that "the majority of journalists who welcomed the [collapse of the Soviet Union] joyously are of Jewish nationality"; that people in Russia blamed journalists "who represent the Jewish minority" for welcoming the destruction of the Soviet state; and that new businesses in Russia were "headed by Jews and a lot of the population understand that most of the money in these banks or structures is dirty money".

Zhirinovsky did not refrain from making anti-Jewish statements in the Russian parliament. On 21 October he said in a speech to the Duma: "I tell the whole world: It is you from Tel Aviv and Washington who are doing everything bad that is happening to us."

Similarly, in a Duma session on 18 November, he accused the Russian Federal Counter-Intelligence Service and its director, Sergey Stepashin, of working for the CIA and he described Stepashin as a "Mossad agent".

Whatever their effect on the Russian masses, these and other anti-Jewish utterances made little impression on many of Zhirinovsky's extremist rivals, who pointed to the Jewish origins of his father (which Zhirinovsky continued to deny).

Before the December 1993 parliamentary elections Zhirinovsky was regarded by many as a "political clown". This assessment was made notwithstanding the fact that in 1991 he had obtained several million votes in the presidential election in which Yeltsin had triumphed. Following the December 1993 election result many people began to write Zhirinovsky off once again. But given that a presidential election was due to be held as early as June 1996 (provided it was not cancelled) and that Yeltsin's position had been substantially weakened by, *inter alia*, obstacles to the reform drive and the incompetence surrounding the war in Chechnya, it could not be excluded that Zhirinovsky, with his refusal "to play by the rules of the game", would not reap the rewards.

There remained on the fringe of Russian politics eighty or more extremist groups— members of the ultra-nationalist/hardline communist "national-patriotic opposition" or the "red-brown alliance". These implacable opponents of the Yeltsin regime were by no means a monolithic entity but comprised fractious and overlapping groups, riven as much by personal rivalries as by doctrinal matters. In terms of ideology they ranged from neo-Nazism to neo-fascism, neo-Stalinism, Russian Orthodoxy, monarchism, paganism and the like. Anti-semitism was a common element in most of the groups.

The Russkoe natsionalnoe edinstvo (RNE, Russian National Unity) was, in some respects, the highest-profile far-right fringe group in Russia in 1994. The RNE's leader, Aleksandr Barkashev, first sprang to prominence following the rout of the October 1993 "White House" rising: having gone into hiding, he was arrested several weeks later. The RNE is a paramilitary neo-Nazi group. Barkashev has frequently voiced his admiration of Hitler. Wearing black uniforms with the swastika emblem, RNE members were sighted during the bloody attack on the Ostankino (television) tower and the office of the Moscow mayor on 3 October. In a letter which appeared in the liberal newspaper *Izvestiya* on 18 August, Andrey Khudokormov (pseudonym) claimed, no doubt with considerable exaggeration, that the RNE had over 10,000 full members, 500 of them in

Moscow alone; that it had the support of numerous sympathizers, many of whom belonged to the top layers of military, police and governmental circles; that RNE paramilitary troupers were well-trained and highly disciplined youths who were rewarded for their services with free food, free training in wrestling, free uniforms and free travel throughout Russia; and that he himself belonged to the party's formidable clandestine counter-intelligence service.

The ultra-nationalist and monarchist Natsionalno-patriotichesky front "Pamyat" (National Patriotic Front Remembrance), the oldest (dating from the mid-1980s) and most influential of the virulently antisemitic "Pamyat" groups, remained visibly active. It continued to be led by the former photographic journalist Dmitry Vasilev. Its number of active adherents was probably in the hundreds rather than in the thousands claimed by Vasilev.

Also prominent on the fringe of Russian politics were the Russky natsionalny sobor (Russian National Council), an ultra-nationalist coalition group set up in early 1992 by former KGB major-general Aleksandr Sterligov, a militant antisemite, and the Obshchestvenny klub "Soyuz ofitserov" (Public Club "Union of Officers"), a "red-brown" organization led by Lieutenant Colonel Stanislav Terekhov, also a virulent antisemite. The active adherents of these groups could probably be measured in dozens rather than in the thousands they claimed.

The most extensive foreign links maintained by Russia's far-right groups were with Serbian nationalists—among whom Radovan Karadzić was regarded as a particular hero—and Bolesław Tejkowski and the Polska Wspólnota Narodowa-Polskie Stronnictwo Narodowe (see **Poland**). Close ties were also maintained with elements of the Russian diaspora: many far-right activists displayed special reverence for Grigory Klimov, a man with intelligence connections and author of a number of antisemitic books (see **Publications and Media**).

Notable activities of the Russian far right in 1994 included:

On 16 February *Izvestiya* reported that the far-right newspaper *Chernaya sotnya* had held a readers' evening at the Novorossiysk cinema in Moscow. *Izvestiya* remarked that the newspaper's editor, Aleksandr Shtilmark, had worn a black uniform; that members of various extremist groups had been present, some carrying swastikas; that antisemitic literature had been on sale in the foyer; and that the event had been organized by "about a dozen monarchist and

Russian Orthodox movements".

On 4-5 June the "Days of Palestine in Moscow", a celebration of the second anniversary of the extremist and antisemitic weekly newspaper *Al-Quds* (see **Publications and Media**) took place in Moscow's Central House of the Tourist. Among the speakers were well known figures of the right and hardline opposition including Aleksandr Rutskoi, Sergey Baburin, Gennady Zyuganov, Viktor Anpilov, Aleksandr Nevzorov, Aleksandr Prokhanov and Vladimir Zhirinovsky. Unexpectedly, Ruslan Khasbulatov, the former parliamentary speaker, was also present. The event was reportedly attended by about 1,000 people.

On 6-7 October an All-Russian Monarchist Conference opened in the Columns Hall of Unions' House in Moscow. Among many monarchist and Orthodox publications, far-right newspapers such as *Pamyat* and *Shturmovik* were on sale.

On 22 October Ilya Konstantinov, a leader of the far-right umbrella group the Front natsionalnogo spaseniya (National Salvation Front), told the Front's third congress in Moscow, which was attended by about 400 delegates from forty-six areas of Russia, that the organization no longer existed as a union between the left and right oppositions. He said there was "internal dissent in its ranks and discord in its slogans".

In November in a local election in the Moscow suburb of Mitishi, Aleksandr Fydorov, the thirty-six-year-old candidate of the far-right RNE, fared badly. Fydorov and his supporters, wearing black armbands including swastikas, staged a number of rallies and public meetings during the campaign.

MAINSTREAM POLITICS

At the end of January Mikhail Poltoranin, former Russian minister of information and a member of the Vybor Rossii (Russia's Choice) party, said in a television interview that "while newspapers in other countries come out in that state's language—in France in French, in England in English etc—in Russia the means of mass communication are published in 'camp Hebrew', which could provoke a wave of antisemitism from below". He added that Russian journalists were guilty of "Russophobia, hatred of traditions, and lies".

These expressions were understood by some to mean that too many Jews appeared in the Russian media—an echo of statements by, among others, Vladimir Zhirinovsky—and that they used a clumsy Russian style to promote anti-Russian ideas.

On 1 February Vybor Rossii issued a

statement saying that Poltoranin apologized for his words but insisted that they had been taken out of context and distorted.

MANIFESTATIONS

There were throughout the year numerous demonstrations and rallies by hard-line anti-Yeltsin forces. In what appears to have been the largest of these, on 7 November, the seventy-seventh anniversary of the Russian Revolution, a 15,000-strong rally of communists was held in Moscow's Lubyanka Square, location of the former KGB headquarters. About a dozen of the numerous pro-Stalin and anti-government banners contained slogans attacking Jews, "Zionists" and the "Kike-Masonic conspiracy". Agitators in small informal groups made anti-semitic remarks. A striking array of anti-Jewish publications—books, brochures, journals, newspapers, leaflets and cartoons (see **Publications and Media**)—was on sale.

A group of thirty or forty hard-line opponents of the Yeltsin regime, including anti-Jewish agitators, met regularly at the Revolution Square underground station in central Moscow. At these meetings numerous antisemitic publications were on sale. Among such publications were hardcover and paperback issues of *The Protocols of the Elders of Zion* and a selection of lurid pamphlets, leaflets and crude cartoons on the "Jewish question". *Zavtra* and *Al-Quds* (see **Publications and Media**) were generally the most prominently displayed publications.

Near Gorky Park underground station antisemitic literature, including the ubiquitous *Protocols of the Elders of Zion*, *Zavtra* and *Al-Quds*, was on sale.

In July brisk sales of antisemitic literature were witnessed on the main streets of the Siberian cities of Novosibirsk and Tomsk, and in other cities in the area. Some of the books on sale, including *Mein Kampf*, were said to be recent reprints.

Opposite the "White House", scene of the anti-Yeltsin insurrection of October 1993, anti-semitic graffiti were to be found on the wall of a symbolic graveyard dedicated to the around 150 "patriots" who fell on that occasion.

Reported activities of ultra-nationalist and antisemitic groups were as follows:

On 9 March the RNE (see **Parties, Organizations, Movements**) held a march in Moscow. Participants wore uniforms decorated with swastikas.

On 24 April about fifteen members of the RNE marked Hitler's date of birth by marching in military uniforms through central Moscow chanting antisemitic slogans. In St Petersburg ten members of the Smerch (Tornado) group

marked the day with a meeting in front of the cathedral.

In early July Russian television showed scenes of the arrest of a gang of a dozen neo-Nazis (in their late teens or twenties) who were said to be planning to burn down any cinema in Russia that screened *Schindler's List*. The gang, which called itself "Werewolf", was also said to be planning acts of terror against "those who subscribe to other ideologies—democrats, communists and Jews". The gang members were accused of murdering three small traders from the Caucasus in April and May and a group member who had apparently deviated from their ideology. An official said government security agents had confiscated a large number of arms from the commercial firm (a private security agency) under whose cover the gang members acted. He added that the gang's leader, who oversaw security for the firm, had an office decorated with portraits of Hitler and various Nazi emblems.

On 3 October at a demonstration in St Petersburg marking the anniversary of the events of October 1993, anti-Jewish banners were displayed by members of ultra-nationalist and monarchist parties.

Incidents in which Jews were attacked were as follows:

On 14 July a Jewish woman and her son were murdered in their home in Makhachkala, Daghestan. It was not clear whether the murders were racially motivated.

On 7 September in St Petersburg Grigory Levin, a manager of Ulpan Chalom, was attacked in his car by hooligans who shouted antisemitic remarks.

In mid-September in Moscow several neo-Nazi youths dressed in black shirts assaulted two religious Jews.

Premises belonging to Jews were attacked or threats of attack were received in the following instances:

On 16 January a firebomb was thrown into the office of the Committee for Repatriation to Israel in Novosibirsk. The office and adjoining library were badly damaged in the ensuing fire. Following the incident, the head of the office received phone calls threatening that this would be the first of a number of terrorist acts if his organization did not bring its activities to an end. Several weeks after the firebombing, tombstones in the local Jewish cemetery were desecrated.

In February, following the massacre of Muslims by a Jewish settler in a Hebron mosque, threats were made against the Jewish community, including against Derbent's synagogue, in Daghestan. Also, there was street violence in Makhachkala, and on local television the sheikh of Daghestan called for a *jihad* against all Jews.

On 30 June the synagogue in the city of Irkutsk was broken into and six of the eight Torah scrolls were stolen.

On 27 July Moscow police received a bomb threat against the Choral Synagogue. No explosives were found.

On 12 October shots were fired at the Choral Synagogue in Moscow. Four bullets smashed windows but no other damage was caused. The attack came four days after an attempt to cause an explosion at the synagogue. These acts coincided with the opening and concluding dates of a conference of rabbis from Europe and the CIS in Moscow.

There were also instances of desecrations of Jewish cemeteries:

On 4 April 160 gravestones in the Jewish section of a cemetery in St Petersburg were desecrated in the worst attack of its kind in twenty years. The desecration followed the defacement in early March of the St Petersburg Jewish centre's entrance hall with swastikas and the words "Jude kaput!". Although, it was noted, similar attacks had taken place at the cemetery in 1992 and 1993, the police had failed to track down the culprits on each occasion.

In April a Jewish cemetery in Krasnoyarsk was desecrated. The city's Jewish community repeatedly requested that the authorities investigate the activities of a local newsaper which had been publishing antisemitic articles since 1992.

In May it was reported that tombstones in the Jewish cemetery in Smolensk had been desecrated for the seventh time since the previous autumn.

On 8 August thirty-eight Jewish tombstones in the Jewish section of a Kazan cemetery were desecrated. The Tatarstan procurator general said he would take personal responsibility for the investigation of the crime.

In early September the Jewish cemetery in the small town of Klintsi, near Bryansk, had reportedly been desecrated with many tombstones destroyed.

On 25 October it was announced that eleven tombstones in the Jewish section of a cemetery in Nizhny Novgorod had been smashed by vandals.

Among other extremist and antisemitic manifestations, on 25 February the Israeli newspaper *Ma'ariv* reported that Jews living in St Petersburg had found an antisemitic "help wanted" advertisement posted on notice boards and electricity poles in the city. The advertisement was for "strong young men aged 20 to 35 for carrying out pogroms against Jews and rich merchants". Also, on 2 November a swastika was daubed on the entrance to the Hermitage theatre in Moscow.

Owing to lack of consistency in the monitoring and reporting of extremist and anti-Jewish manifestations, it is not possible to say with any degree of certainty whether there was an increase in such phenomena over the preceding year. Certainly, there appeared to be no diminution.

PUBLICATIONS AND MEDIA

In 1994 the most prominent organs of the hard-line opposition press remained the newly established papers, *Zavtra* (formerly *Dyen*) and *Al-Quds*, as well as the literary monthlies *Nash sovremennik* and *Molodaya gvardiya*, the daily newspaper *Sovetskaya Rossiya* and the literary weekly *Literaturnaya Rossiya*—all established publications from the Soviet era.

Zavtra, a weekly newspaper whose masthead includes the desription "newspaper of the spiritual opposition", was founded in 1992 under the title *Dyen*. It was renamed following a temporary banning for what the Yeltsin administration saw as repeated calls for violent, unconstitutional actions. The most popular organ of the "national-patriotic" opposition, *Zavtra* provides a regular platform for hard-line communist and ultra-nationalist views, not excluding those of Zhirinovsky. It is edited by the polemicist and novelist Aleksandr Prokhanov. At the end of the year *Zavtra* was being investigated for possible closure.

The weekly *Al-Quds* was founded by Shabaan Khafez Shaaban, who first appeared in Moscow as a student in 1977. In 1992 Shaaban, who had apparently made a fortune out of currency speculation in Russia, founded *Al-Quds*, which was officially registered as a newspaper in May of that year. Shaaban proclaimed himself head of the "Palestinian Government in Exile" and described the paper as the "Voice of Russia and Palestine". *Al-Quds* specializes in publishing material alleging a Zionist/Jewish conspiracy against Russia and the Palestinian people and regularly contains lurid anti-Jewish cartoons. The paper claims an absurdly inflated circulation of 3 million. It also claims that it appears not only in Russian but also in Arabic and English and that it is on sale in Russia, the USA, Great Britain, France and the Arab countries. After repeated warnings for inciting ethnic and racial strife, the paper was closed down by the Russian authorities in late 1994 (see **Legal Matters**). An appeal was in progress.

Among the major themes of the hard-line opposition press—new and Soviet-era alike—were allegations of Zionist/Jewish/liberal/

Western conspiracies against Russia and the Russian people, in many cases attributing to Jews responsibility for Russia's present plight, the Bolshevik Revolution, the murder of the Russian imperial family, Stalin's purges and, in general, all the misfortunes which have befallen Russia during the last hundred years.

Accurate figures for the circulations of the numerous press organs of the far right, frequently inflated out of political considerations, were virtually impossible to obtain.

As previously, there was no difficulty in purchasing in Russian newspaper kiosks not only the above-mentioned publications but also numerous other forms of anti-Jewish printed material, including various editions of Hitler's *Mein Kampf* and such classics of world antisemitism as *The Protocols of the Elders of Zion* and Douglas Reed's *The Controversy of Zion*. *The Protocols* and *The Controversy of Zion* were also serialized by *Nash sovremennik*.

According to "A list of books of xenophobic, fascist and antisemitic content published in the last few years" which was prepared for an anti-fascist forum held in the Russian capital in February 1995, the following were among publications issued by Vityaz Publishing House, which specialized in "patriotic literature", in its series "A Russian Patriot's Small Library". Data have been added where available:

V. Stepin, *Sushchnost sionizma* (The Essence of Zionism, 1993, 5,000 copies)

V. Gladky, *Evrei* (The Jews)

Vasily Shulgin, *Shto nam v nikh ne nravitsya* (What We Dislike about Them, reprint of pre-revolutionary anti-Jewish work)

Grigory Klimov, *Krasnye protokoly* (The Red Protocols)

Yevgeny Yevseyev (Soviet anti-Zionist and antisemitic propagandist, died early 1990s), *Satrap*

A. Ivanov and I. Bogdanov, *Khristiantstvo* (Christianity, 1994)

B. Bashilov, *Istoriya russkogo masonstva* (History of Russian Freemasonry)

S. Melgunov, *Terror v Rossii* (The Terror in Russia, reprint)

B. Pinchukov, *Khazary* (The Khazars)

A. Melsky, *U istokov velikoy nenavisti* (At the Roots of the Great Hatred)

Conan Doyle protiv masonstva (Conan Doyle against Freemasonry)

L. N. Key, *Mirovoy zagovor* (The World Conspiracy)

Spiski palachey Rossii (1936-1939) (Lists of Executioners of Russia, 1936-1939)

S. Pechenev, *Rodnoy, dobry, silny* (A Kinsman Good and Strong)

V. Korchagin, *Russky vopros* (The Russian Question)

Sionskiye protokoly (The Protocols of the Elders of Zion, 1993, 5,000 copies)

Todor Dichev (as transliterated), *Adaptatsiya i zdorovie, vyzhivanie i ekologiya cheloveka* (Adaptation and Health, Survival and Ecology, 1994, 10,000 copies)

Todor Dichev (as transliterated), *Zloveshchy zagovor* (The Sinister Conspiracy).

Books and booklets put out by other publishing houses according to the above list were:

Adolf Hitler, *Moya borba* (*Mein Kampf*, 1992, 5,000 copies)

V. Ushkuynik, *Pamyatka russkomu cheloveku* (In Memory of a Russian, Moscow 1992, Library of [former KGB] General Aleksandr Sterligov, 100,000 copies)

S. Kravchenko, *Balagan na krovi* (Farce in Blood, Kiev 1994, 50,000 copies)

Stalin i masonstvo (Stalin and Freemasonry, Moscow 1994)

Tvortsy kataklizmov (The Creators of Cataclysms, Kiev 1994)

Yazychestvo (Paganism)/*U istokov velikoy tragedii* (At the Roots of a Great Tragedy)

Bitva za Rossiyu (The Struggle for Russia, Moscow 1992)

Shto sluchilos v TsDL (What Happened at the Central Writers' House)

*Alkogolny terror (*The Alcohol Terror, Irkutsk 1991, 10,000 copies)

N. Streshnev, *Zhidovskoye plenenie* (In Kike Captivity, St Petersburg 1905, reprint)

V. Kanashkin, *Stopami samosotvoreniya* (On the Way to Self-Creation)/*Natsionalno-istoricheskaya ideya i nasha sudba* (The National-Historical Idea and Our Destiny, Yekaterinodar 1992, 7,000 copies)

Nravstvennoe bogoslovie yevreyev-talmudistov (The Moral Theology of Talmudic Jews, St Petersburg 1898)

Yevreyskoe zertsalo (The Jewish Mirror)/*Nauchnoe issledovanie doktora Karla Marksa* (The Scholarly Research of Dr Karl Marks, New York 1922)

Umuchonnye ot zhidov: G. Zamyslovsky (Saratovsoe delo) (Persecuted by the Kikes: G. Zamyslovsky and the Saratov Affair, Kharkov 1911)

Tayna krovi u yevreyev (delo o ritualnom ubiystve Andryushi Yushchinskogo (The Blood Secret of the Jews: The Case of the Ritual Murder of Andryusha Yushchinsky, St Petersburg 1913)

Rene Genov (as transliterated), *Krizis sovremennogo mira* (The Crisis of the Modern World, Moscow 1911, 10,000 copies)

A. Selyaninov, *Taynaya sila masonstva* (The Secret Force of Freemasonry, St Petersburg 1911/N. Ierusalim 1993, 20,000 copies)

V. Prussakov, A. Shiropaev, *Slava Rossii!* (Glory to Russia!, Moscow 1993, a brief survey of the Russian fascist movement)

Aleksandr Barshakov, *Azbuka russkogo natsionalista* (A Russian Nationalist's Alphabet, Moscow 1994)

Aleksandr Barkashov, *Era Rossii* (The Era of Russia, Moscow 1993, 50,000 copies)

P. Peresvet, *Vragi* (The Enemies, Moscow 1993, 10,000 copies)

B. I. Pinchukov, *Khazary (Istoricheskaya poema, Pamyati zhertv Genotsida v Rossii v 617-1993 gg. posvyashchaetsya)* (The Khazars: A Historical Poem Dedicated to the Memory of the Victims of Genocide in Russia, 617-1993, Vladivostok 1993, 50,000 copies)

Vlast v litsakh (1917-1993) (Power in [Jewish Russian] Hands, 1917-93, Moscow 1993)

Zaveshchanie Gitlera (Hitler's Testament, Moscow 1991)

V. Khatyushin, *Urok na veka* (A Lesson for the Ages, Moscow 1992)

V. Khatyushin, *Parol presidentskoy vlasti* (Password of Presidential Power, Moscow 1992)

Henry Ford, *Mezhdurarodnoe yevreystvo* (*The International Jew*, Moscow 1993, 50,000 copies, translation of American work)

Igor Shafarevich, *Rusofobiya. Dve dorogi k odnomu obrivu* (Russophobia: Two Roads to One Precipice, Moscow, 100,000 copies)

V. Fomichev, *Sud nad russkimi* (Russians on Trial, Moscow 1993, 5,000 copies)

Metropolitan Ioann of St Petersburg and Ladoga, *Bitva za Rossiyu* (The Battle for Russia, Saratov 1993, 30,000 copies)

Metropolitan Ioann of St Petersburg and Ladoga, *Puti russkogo vozrozhdeniya* (Paths of Russian Revival, Moscow 1993, 1 million copies)

Metropolitan Ioann of St Petersburg and Ladoga, *Tvoreniem dobry i pravdy* (Through Goodness and Truth, Russian National Council, 100,000 copies)

Zhidy (The Kikes, Moscow 1993, 5,000 copies)

Douglas Reed, *Spor o sione* (*The Controversy of Zion*, Moscow 1993, translation of British work)

M. Nazarov, *Zagovor protiv Rossii (o zhidomasonstve)* (The Kike-Masonic Conspiracy against Russia, Potsdam 1993, 2,000 copies)

The Priest Rodion, *Russkoe pravoslavie i masonstvo* (Russian Orthodoxy and Freemasonry, St Petersburg 1993)

I. Khromov, *Kuda idut russkiye* (Where the Russians Are Going, St Petersburg 1993)

A. Klimov, *Yadovitye ryby (Sionisty i masony v Yaponii)* (Poisoned Fish: Zionists and Freemasons in Japan, Moscow 1992)

Zov pravoslaviya: taynaya kovarnaya voyna s Rossiyei podkhodit k zaversheniyu (The Call of Russian Orthodoxy: The Secret Perfidious War against Russia Is Reaching Its Conclusion, Moscow and St Petersburg, 100,000 copies)

Aleksandr Sterligov, *Nam nuzhny chisto russkiye resheniya* (We Need Purely Russian Solutions, Moscow 1993)

Russkoe delo segodnya (The Russian Cause Today)

Germansky natsional-sotsializm (German National Socialism, Moscow 1994)

A. Dugin, *Giperboreyskaya teoriya* (Moscow 1993)

A. Dugin, *Konspirologiya* (Moscow 1993, 10,000 copies)

S. Gorodnikov, *Istoricheskoe prednaznachenie russkogo natsionalizma* (The Historical Destiny of Russian Nationalism, Moscow 1994, 2,500 copies)

A. Liprandy, *Ravnopravie i yevreysky vopros* (Equality and the Jewish Question, Moscow 1994)

Meller Zakomelsky, *Strashny vopros (o Rossii i yevreystve)* (The Terrible Question: Russia and the Jews, Moscow 1994)

A. Shmakov, *Taynoe mezhdunarodnoe pravitelstvo* (The Secret International Government, Moscow 1994, reprint of pre-revolutionary work)

Metropolitan Ioann of St Petersburg and Ladoga, *Bud veren do smerti* (Be Faithful until Death, Moscow 1993, 100,000 copies)

Giperboreya N1 (Vilnius 1991)

Rech Patriarkha Alekseya II k ravvinam Niu-Yorka 13 noyabrya 1991 i eres zhidovstvuyushchikh (Speech by Patriarkh Aleksey II to New York Rabbis on 13 November 1991 and the Heresy of the Kikes)

Congress of Russian Communities, *Manifest* (Manifesto, 1994)

Na zastave bogatyrskoy (At the Gate of Hercules, Moscow 1993, 10,000 copies)

Khristofagiya (borba talmudicheskogo iudaizma s Tserkovyu Khristovoy (Khristofagiya[?]: Talmudic Judaism's Battle against the Church of Christ, Kiev 1993)

Julius Evola (as transliterated), *Yazychesky imperializm* (Pagan Imperialism, 1992)

V. Ivanov, *Pravoslavny mir i masonstvo* (The World of Russian Orthodoxy and Freemasonry, Moscow 1993)

Grigory Klimov, *Protokoly sovetskikh mudretsov* (*The Protocols of the Soviet Elders*, San Francisco 1981)

Grigory Klimov, *Imya moyo Legion* (My Name Is Legion, New York 1975)

Viktor Anpilov, Sergey Baburin, Dmitry Dudko, Gennady Zyuganov, V. Isakov, Eduard Limonov, Albert Makashov, Aleksandr Nevzorov, Aleksandr Prokhanov, Sazhi Umalatova, V. Ostretsov, *Chernaya sotnya i krasnaya sotnya* (Black Hundreds and Red Hundreds, Moscow 1991, 1 million copies, The Life of Outstanding Russians series, Moscow 1992)

Grigory Klimov, *Delo N 69 (publitsistika i satanistika* (Case 69: Pamphleteering and Satanism, 1974)

Miguel Serrano , *Voskreshenie geroya* (Resurrection of the Hero, 1994)

Magomed Pravoslavny, *Molniya posvyashcheniya nad satanizmom, ili religioznaya pravda* (Initiation into Satanism, or Religious Truth, St Petersburg 1993)

A. Krylov, *Pesni russkogo soprotovleniya (lirika smutnogo vremeni)* (Songs of Russian Resistance: Lyrics of a Time of Troubles, Moscow 1993)

The Moscow-based Anti-Fascist Centre was reported to have calculated that there existed in May 1994 a total of 157 "extremist publications"; this was, of course, a continually fluctuating figure. According to a list compiled by the Centre on 17 August and published in the newspaper *Novoe vremya* (no. 35, September), the following newspapers and periodicals, as well as the publishing houses Vityaz and Palya, were said to "regularly contain calls for social, national and religious discord, violence and totalitarianism in breach of the Russian Federation Law on the Means of Mass Information". In respect of the print-runs, no reliable figures are available: publishers and editors tend as a matter of course to inflate such figures.

Newspapers
Moscow
Al-Quds, Borba, Bumbarash—2017, Golos vseleyonnoy, Dubinushka, Zavtra, Zemshchina, Istoki, Molniya, Moskovsky literator, Narodny stroy (formerly *Nash marsh*), *Russky vestnik, Russky poryadok, Russky sobor, Russkoe voskresenie, Sovetskaya Rossiya, Sokol Zhirinovskogo, Trety put, Chornaya sotnya, Yusmalos*
St Petersburg
Golos Rossii, Za russkoe delo, Istoricheskaya pamyat, Narodnaya pravda, Nashe vremya
Other cities
Krasnoyarskaya gazeta (Krasnoyarsk), *Kulikovskaya bitva* (Vologda), *Pamyat* (Novosibirsk), *Russky vostok* (Irkutsk), *Ekho* (Vologda)

Journals
Moscow
Ataka, Liberal, Nashe Otechestvo, Primorskiye novosti, Rech, Rodnye prostory, Rossiyanin, Stranitsy rossiyskoy istorii
St Petersburg
Volkhv, Sobesednik pravoslavnykh, Khristianin
Other cities
Bolshevik (Murmansk), *Bolshevik* (Saransk), *Kolokol* (Volgograd), *Sergiev Posad* (Sergiev Posad), *Kuban* (Krasnodar)

RELIGION

Metropolitan Ioann of St Petersburg and Ladoga continued regularly to give lengthy and detailed interviews to, and write articles for, the "national-patriotic" press. One of his typical themes was the supposed authenticity of *The Protocols of the Elders of Zion*.

In December it was reported that the US-based Anti-Defamation League had written to the Russian Orthodox church expressing concern about antisemitic statements attributed to Metropolitan Ioann. Ioann had, among other things, ascribed responsibility for the recent devaluation of the Russian rouble to the Jews, claiming: "This rise of the dollar slaps Russians in their faces and beats them on the spine. We must stop the Zionists from taking over the world. It is their single goal." The church replied that the statements reflected the cleric's "personal opinions and not those of the church" and: "The loss of previous ideals, the growth of social tension and criminal debauchery have created . . . the emergence and the dissemination of 'ideological hate' in Russia."

On 24 January, at a press conference in Moscow, Duma deputy Gleb Yakunin said, regarding an open letter he had written to Patriarch Aleksey of Moscow and All-Russia, that he was motivated by a desire to warn the Russian Orthodox church leadership of the growing influence of the "red-browns". Yakunin said he believed that Metropolitan Ioann embodied the Black Hundred (pre-revolutionary extreme right) pro-fascist forces in the church. He added: "In the two years in which state security's control of the church has collapsed, effectively no reforms, either profound or even cosmetic, have taken place in the Russian church. I fear that eventually there will be a reorientation of the leadership of the Russian Orthodox church towards an alliance with the communists and the Zhirinovites."

According to materials prepared for the Anti-Fascist Forum which took place in Moscow in February 1995, some members of the clergy collaborated with the far right to one degree or another but only on the initiative of those groups. Also, some clerics who had a reputation for being on the right of the political spectrum were said to be attempting to influence the extremist groups to adopt a more moderate approach.

OPINION POLLS

While no major public opinion polls on antisemitism were conducted in Russia or the other states of the former Soviet Union in 1994, a noteworthy debate on the subject took place in the American journal *Slavic Review* (vol. 53, no. 3, summer 1994). Participants in the debate presented previously unanalysed poll data and re-interpreted previously analysed poll data relating to the period 1991-3.

James Gibson argued on the basis of his 1992 survey of over 2,300 adult citizens of Russia that the level of antisemitism was no higher in Russia than in the USA and represented no political danger to the Jewish population. He took issue with 1992 survey results analysed by Robert Brym in *Slavic Review* and elsewhere which seemed to show that Russian antisemitism was much more widespread and dangerous. Gibson did find, however, that Russian antisemites tended to have relatively little formal education, to be anti-democratic, to be relatively old and not to be acquainted with Jews.

Vicki Hesli and colleagues analysed the results of polls conducted in Russia and Ukraine in 1991 and 1992; 2,700 adult citizens of Russia and 1,900 adult citizens of Ukraine were interviewed in the two polls. Hesli *et al.* also concluded that Brym had exaggerated the level of antisemitism in Russia. Moreover, they showed that there was no cohesive ideology in Russia or Ukraine which linked antisemitism, illiberalism and authoritarianism.

Robert Brym took issue with both Gibson and Hesli *et al.*, defending his earlier analysis and presenting new 1993 Moscow data (based on a poll of nearly 2,300 adult respondents) to buttress his position. He sought to demonstrate, *inter alia*, that Gibson had misinterpreted the meaning of some questionnaire items; miscalculated the level of antisemitism in Russia by ignoring the large number of respondents who hid their true feelings and replied "don't know" to questions about Jews; ignored the fact that many Jews in Russia regard antisemitism as sufficiently serious to cause them to emigrate; and underestimated the political significance of the fact that antisemitism was concentrated among the increasingly powerful communists and ultranationalists. (For example, in the 1993 parliamentary elections, a third of communist supporters and nearly 40 per cent of Zhirinovsky supporters held antisemitic views in Moscow; and the communists and ultranationalists won 145 seats in the 1993 parliamentary elections compared to only 116 for the reformers.) Brym also showed that a cohesive ideology combining antisemitism, illiberalism and authoritarianism was evident in Moscow.

LEGAL MATTERS

Under Article 74 of the criminal code, which deals with national and racial incitement, there have been many failed attempts to convict mainly antisemitic writers and publishers: no one has been convicted on this charge since the break-up of the Soviet Union. Cases often require over two years to come to trial. Judges state, for instance, that they are unable to obtain "expert findings" on the nature of the articles involved.

In mid-November the weekly *Al-Quds* (see **Publications and Media**) was closed down by the Russian State Press Committee. The committee cancelled its registration on a technicality: contrary to Russian law, the paper's publisher, Shabaan Khafez Shaaban, did not hold Russian citizenship. In a statement the authorities noted that Shabaan had concealed his origins, which were the factor that had motivated him to "fill his paper with materials of an antisemitic content that overstepped all boundaries of the permissible".

On 26 November 1993 Moscow district court judge Ludmilla Belikova (Cherimushkinsky district) had ruled against Pamyat in its suit against the Jewish newspaper *Yevreyskaya gazeta*. The judge ordered Pamyat to pay court costs totalling about $250. In mid-December 1993 Judge Belikova handed down a written decision announcing that the court had heard the testimony of the experts and witnesses and had decided that it was not within its competence to determine the authenticity of the *Protocols*. *Yevreyskaya gazeta*, she said, had used its right of self-expression in describing the Pamyat newspaper as antisemitic and the court did not see any affront in this. Therefore Pamyat's suit was dismissed and that organization was ordered to pay the court costs. Both sides appealed against this decision. On 12 January 1994 both appeals were dismissed.

At the end of 1994 in St Petersburg a prosecution under Article 74 was launched against Viktor Bezverkhy in connection with his having published two articles of a racist nature in the journal *Volkhv*. In 1992-3 Bezverkhy, then a sixty-one-year-old former lecturer in Marxism-Leninism in St Petersburg and a man with a record of propagating neo-Nazi ideology, had been acquitted under the same article of publishing and distributing an abridged version of Hitler's *Mein Kampf*. On that occasion, the court had found that he had acted "without intent to incite national discord" and out of purely financial reasons.

COUNTERING ANTISEMITISM

On 18 December 1993 an "anti-fascist front" was set up in Moscow. The meeting, at the Russian Press Club, was addressed by Deputy Premier Anatoly Chubais, a leader of Vybor Rossii (Russia's Choice). A decision was taken to set up anti-fascist committees in Moscow, St Petersburg and in Russia's regions. The meeting rejected the possibility of compromise or co-operation with Zhirinovsky's LDPR.

Following a visit to Russia by President Clinton in January, a Joint American-Russian Statement on Human Rights said, among other things, that Clinton and Yeltsin had agreed that "aggressive nationalism and political extremism are the main threat to peace and democracy today. They therefore reaffirm their resolve to focus attention, through joint efforts where possible, on violations of human rights wherever they may occur and to continue to work for the elimination of discrimination, intolerance, racial and national prejudices, xenophobia and antisemitism."

On 26 April Russian prime minister Viktor Chernomyrdin vowed that the "judeophobia" in Russia's past would never be allowed to resurface, despite the recent rise of ultra-nationalism. Speaking after meeting visiting Israeli prime minister Rabin, he said that the rights of Jews would be protected against the "Zhirinovsky phenomenon" and that "no Zhirinovsky will be able to incite" a serious upsurge of antisemitism in Russia. "I can tell you unequivocally this will not happen."

On 2 September Boris Mironov was dismissed from his position as head of the Russian press committee in a joint action by President Yeltsin and Premier Chernomyrdin. He was replaced by his deputy, Sergey Gryzunov. Mironov had made no secret of his ultra-nationalist and antisemitic views. For instance, in an interview he gave to the liberal newspaper *Izvestiya* on 28 May, he justified a decision he had taken as a publisher to subsidize the publication of a reprint of "What We Dislike about Them", a well-known antisemitic work by the reactionary tsarist journalist and politician Vasily Shulgin. Echoing Shulgin's views, Mironov had replied: "There is a Jewish pogrom and a Russian pogrom. The Russian one is far more terrible." Mironov

had also insisted that the press committee must support "our national honour" as expressed in such newspapers as *Pravda* and *Sovetskaya Rossiya* and must subsidize "such publishing houses close to our way of thinking" as *Nash sovremennik*, *Voskresenye* and *Patriot*—all hard-line anti-Yeltsin opposition publications.

Following his dismissal, Mironov was quoted by the newspaper *Amurskaya pravda* (16 November) as having claimed that the liberal newspapers *Izvestiya*, *Moskovskiye novosti* and *Segodnya* were "of one nationality— Jewish. They get paid in dollars and they surround the president."

In September the human rights commission of the president's office reported its findings and made recommendations for a federal programme on human rights. The recommendations were adopted on 15 September and reported in parliament on 24 September. According to the report, the situation regarding human rights in the Russian army and prisons, the position of refugees, forced migrants, the freedom of movement and of choice of where to live was not improving but worsening. The recommendations said, among other things, that the existing judicial system failed to effectively protect the individual from departmental and bureacratic arbitrariness, and mass and systematic violations of human rights and freedoms.

In September the Russian "black book" on the Holocaust of Soviet Jewry, which was sponsored by Stalin and then suppressed, was published with help from US non-governmental organizations.

In early September Jewish organizations and individuals were among about 100 prominent human rights activists, lawyers, writers and trade union leaders who attended a session at the offices of the newspaper Mos*cow News* to discuss practical methods of countering the growth of fascist organizations and publications in Russia. One of the ideas discussed was that of organizing an international anti-fascist conference which would be held in Moscow in 1995.

On 6 October Sergey Filatov, head of the president's administration, told the Moscow-based Interfax news agency of his concern about growing financial support for pro-Nazi organizations and their media outlets. "This is a new problem for our country, but it is very grave. Large sums of money are being spent on this purpose. Such funds cannot be raised through party dues, which means they come from business groups and are meant for specific purposes."

ASSESSMENT

The continued existence of major obstacles to the government's reform programme, deep-rooted popular cynicism towards politicians, the increasingly serious problem of organized crime, the low state of morale in the armed forces as displayed in the disastrous Chechen campaign, the existence of a "diaspora" of some 25 million ethnic Russians facing varying degrees of hostility on the part of former Soviet minority peoples—all these were among factors which continued to contribute to the effective disintegration of Russian society.

While all the indications were that Jews were not the primary target of grassroots prejudice in Russia—ethnic and racial hostility was directed mainly against Chechens, Armenians and (as elsewhere in Central and Eastern Europe) Roma, who were often lumped together as "blacks" and held responsible for much of organized crime—Jews seemed likely to be caught up in any social or political convulsions that might arise in an inherently unstable situation.

It cannot be stated with any certainty that the position with regard to antisemitism in Russia in 1994 differed significantly from that which obtained in the previous year. There was, however, no doubt that the authorities lacked the degree of political will required to stem the rise of far-right extremism with its concomitant flood of racist and antisemitic publications.

It was by no means clear that President Yeltsin or other democratic forces would be victorious in the scheduled December 1995 parliamentary elections or the June 1996 presidential election, provided these elections took place, towards which Russia's political players were beginning to manoeuvre.

Slovakia

General population: 5.3 million
Jewish population: 3,000-6,000 (mainly in Bratislava and Košice)

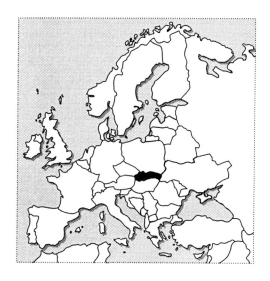

GENERAL BACKGROUND

The Slovak Republic became an independent state in 1993 following the dissolution of the Czech and Slovak Federal Republic. Its constitution provides for a multi-party, multi-ethnic parliamentary democracy.

In March President Michal Kováč dismissed the government headed by the populist Vladimir Mečiar, leader of the Hnutie za Demkraticke Slovensko (HDS, Movement for a Democratic Slovakia), following a parliamentary vote of no-confidence. In a general election held on 30 September-1 October the HDS won over one-third of the vote, a victory greater than opinion surveys had predicted. In December a new coalition government headed by Mečiar was sworn in (Mečiar thus becoming prime minister for the third time). The coalition included the ultra-nationalist Slovenská Národná Strana (SNS, Slovak National Party), which was given the key portfolios of defence and education.

Slovakia has made intermittent progress in developing a market economy. The 1994 inflation rate was around 15 per cent.

HISTORICAL LEGACY

For 1,000 years Slovakia was part of the Hungarian Kingdom; in 1918 it became part of Czechoslovakia. The mother tongue of most Jews was either Hungarian or German. Reference to this fact, together with the theme of the typically more favourable position of the Jews, developed into the principal slogans of Slovak antisemitism.

During the Second World War the pro-Nazi regime of President Tiso, a Catholic priest, not only acceded to the deportation of Jews but also paid Nazi Germany for every Jew deported. Of the 137,000 Jews in pre-war Slovakia, 72,000 perished in extermination camps and another 40,000 perished in the deportations from the southern part of the country, which was occupied by Hungary during the war. Most survivors of the Holocaust left the country before and after the communist takeover in 1948 or after the Soviet occupation in 1968.

RACISM AND XENOPHOBIA

Racist sentiment in Slovakia was directed mainly against the Roma community numbering 350,000-400,000.

PARTIES, ORGANIZATIONS, MOVEMENTS

In the general election of 30 September-1 October Mečiar's HDS gained 31 seats, the Association of Workers of Slovakia 13 seats, and Ján Slota's SNS 9 seats.

The SNS represents the most xenophobic elements of Slovak society. In its election propaganda it regularly made use of anti-Hungarian, anti-Roma and anti-Jewish slogans. Its leader, Ján Slota, repeatedly described the West as being in the grip of Freemasons and continued to attack a so-called Zionist conspiracy. He also charged Czechs and Hungarians with inciting anti-Slovak propaganda in the West and having invented antisemitism in order to discredit the Slovak people and the Slovak state.

While a host of far-right groupings—*inter alia*, the Slovenská Lidová Strana (Slovak People's Party) and Krestansko-Sociálná Uniá (Christian Social Union)—disappeared from the parliament, the extra-parliamentary far right was represented by the Jozef Tiso Society, the Andrej Hlinka Society, the cultural institution Matica Slovenská, several smaller political factions and the skinheads. Post-Second World War Slovak emigrés in Canada and the USA continued to provide the far right with material and moral support.

The campaign for the rehabilitation of the Slovak state and Tiso continued. Matica Slovenská stated its intention to publish a history of the Slovak post-war emigration, which comprises mainly pro-fascist exiles, on the initiative of Jozef Kirschbaum, former general secretary of the Hlinka People's Party. František Vnuk, an amateur historian and leading apologist for the war-time Slovak state, was elected to the Scientific Committee of the Slovak Academy of Sciences' Historical Institute.

SNS members "privately" attended a meeting of Vladimir Zhirinovsky's Liberal Democratic Party of Russia in Moscow in the summer and invited Zhirinovsky to Slovakia, although the visit did not materialize (see **Russia**).

MANIFESTATIONS

In the one reported case of the desecration of a Jewish cemetery, in which gravestones were overturned, local authorities apologized and the juvenile offenders were sentenced to community service.

On 14 March, the fifty-fourth anniversary of the establishment of the wartime Slovak state, pro-Slovak state demonstrations took place in a number of cities. In the largest demonstration (some 2,000 people), in a major square in Bratislava, several Radio Free Europe reporters were beaten up. Demonstrations also took place on 17 October, the anniversary of Tiso's birth. Extremist Slovak organizations in the West proclaimed their support for the demonstrators.

PUBLICATIONS AND MEDIA

Many of the smaller right-wing publications—including *Slovenská pravda, Nový Slovák, Hlas Slovenská*—disappeared from view.

Anti-Jewish writings appeared in the Slovak printed media, in particular in the semi-governmental *Republika* and *Zmena,* and on radio and television, charging Jews with, *inter alia*, having incited the foreign press to accuse Slovaks of antisemitism.

On 26 July the SNS placed in *Republika* a full-page ad headlined "It is hard to survive in our country if one is not Jewish" and reproduced a poem by the veteran pro-fascist poet Valentin Beniak entitled "A Year Later".

Towards the end of the year Prime Minister Mečiar visited the tabloid *Zmena* on the fifth anniversary of its founding. In October *Zmena's* editor, Maros Puchovský, was nominated to the council of the Slovak Broadcasting Service.

RELIGION

Spokespersons for the Catholic church frequently praised the Slovak state and described as martyrs Tiso and the antisemitic Bishop Ján Vojtaššak, a member of the Slovak wartime parliament who demanded the deportation of the Jews.

LEGAL MATTERS

Pavel Traubner, president of the Union of Jewish Communities of Slovakia, sued for slander by *Zmena*, counter-sued the tabloid on similar grounds. He won in both cases and was awarded damages.

There was little progress in the case of Martin Savel, the publisher of *The Protocols*. There have been twenty-one court hearings of this case in the last three years.

COUNTERING ANTISEMITISM

Government institutions condemned the occasional manifestations of antisemitism and repeatedly expressed a positive attitude towards individual Jews and Jewish institutions, local and foreign. Leading historians and intellectuals such as Jozef Jablonický, Lubomír Lipták and Du an KováÈ repeatedly condemned the wartime Slovak state and its deeds, including the Holocaust of Slovak Jewry.

Ethnic Hungarians in Slovakia marked 15 May as a "Day of Remembrance". On that day in 1942 János Eszterhazy, a Magyar nobleman, was the sole deputy to vote against the deportation of the Jews from Slovakia.

On 17-20 July a conference on tolerance in Central and Eastern Europe was held in Bratislava under the auspices of the Friedrich Naumann Foundation and in co-operation with the American Jewish Committee. It was attended by representatives from ten countries.

Among those who attended the commemoration of the fiftieth anniversary of the Slovak National Rising on 28-9 August was an Israeli delegation headed by the speaker of the Israeli parliament. For the first time, Jewish participation in the uprising was officially recognized.

The use of racism and antisemitism during the election campaign, in particular by the SNS, was condemned at a special meeting of the outgoing Moravčik cabinet on 4 October. The cabinet approved the establishment of a governmental agency to combat racism, xenophobia and antisemitism.

In the commemoration of the fiftieth anniversary of the Slovak national uprising many publications detailed Jewish participation in the uprising, thus countering allegations, frequent especially under the communist regime, of Jewish cowardice.

In December the incoming prime minister, Vladimir Mečiar, told the diplomatic corps, *inter alia*: "The Slovak government denounces all manifestations of intolerance, above all chauvinism, aggressive nationalism, racism, antisemitism and xenophobia . . . That is why we shall try to suppress and remove them."

ASSESSMENT

The major source of extremist and antisemitic influence in Slovak society was sympathizers of the wartime Slovak state. The participation of the extremist Slovak National Party in government—a worrying development—was more than counteracted by repeated condemnations of racism, xenophobia and antisemitism on the part of President Kováč, leading government figures and liberal intellectuals.

Spain

General population: 39.1 million
Jewish population: 20,000 (mainly in Madrid,
Barcelona and Malaga)

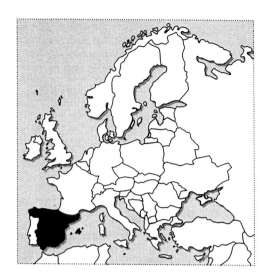

GENERAL BACKGROUND

Spain continued to be governed by the Partido
Socialista Obrero Español (PSOE, Spanish
Socialist Workers Party) in 1994, although the
PSOE lost its majority in the general election
of June 1993. Felipe Gonzalez was reconfirmed
as prime minister with the support of the
Convergència i Unió (CiU, Catalan Conver-
gence and Union) and the Partido Nacionalista
Vasco (PNV, Basque Nationalist Party), but
these two parties declined to join a coalition
government. The opposition conservative Partido Popular (PP, Popular Party) made large
gains in the elections to the European Parliament in June.

Politics was dominated by revelations of
corruption in public life and by the state of the
economy. Growth increased to 1.5 per cent in
1994 after shrinking by 1 per cent in 1993, and
inflation fell to 4.3 per cent from 4.8 per cent the
previous year. Spain's official unemployment
rate of 16.7 per cent was one of the highest in
the European Union.

HISTORICAL LEGACY

Following the Inquisition and the Edict of Expulsion of 1492, Spain remained officially
without Jews until 1869, when a new constitution, which implicitly revoked the edict, allowed private religious practice. Prior to
expulsion, Spanish Jewry had enjoyed a
"golden age" lasting several centuries and
played a prominent role in Spanish society. In
1992, Spain commemorated the quincentenary
of the expulsion of Jews who refused to convert to the Catholic faith.

The small Spanish Jewish community in
existence during the civil war of 1936-39 was
sometimes caught between the warring sides,
but most Jews fled the country during the
conflict.

Spain, under General Franco, remained officially neutral during the Second World War,
but sympathized with the German-Italian axis.
Spain's problems were often blamed on an
"Anglo-masonic-Jewish conspiracy". During
the war, however, the Spanish government issued passports to some 11,000 Sephardi Jews in
Nazi-occupied Europe. A further 35,000-
40,000 Jews were permitted to pass through
Spain *en route* to other destinations.

Franco also provided shelter to Nazis and
Nazi collaborators after the war. Those still
alive include the Dutch collaborator Auke
Pattist and Mauthausen concentration camp
doctor Aribert Heim. The Belgian Nazi collaborator Léon Degrelle, who subsequently
actively inspired and supported Spanish neo-
Nazi groups, died in March 1994. Other Nazis
went to South America via Spain with the
assistance of local bureaucrats.

Between the 1950s and 1970s, following
the independence of Morocco and adverse
political conditions in Argentina, Jews settled
in Spain in larger numbers.

In 1967, after the Six Day War in the Middle East, Jews in Egypt were issued with Spanish passports and thus were able to leave for the
country of their choice.

In 1992, Judaism, together with Islam and
Protestantism, was granted equal legal status
with Catholicism.

RACISM AND XENOPHOBIA

According to a report prepared for the ministry
of social affairs in July, the main target of popular racism in Spain was the 500,000-800,000-
strong Roma community. A programme for the
development and integration of the Roma has
been in practice since 1988.

There are over 393,000 foreigners with
residence permits in Spain. Non-European immigrants come from Morocco (54,000) or other
African countries (17,000), South America
(74,000) and Asia (34,000). There are approximately 5,000 people in Spain with asylum or
refugee status. It is difficult to estimate the
number of illegal immigrants.

Maria José Diaz Aguado, author of the
ministry report, listed three types of racism and

intolerance in Spain: violence against immigrants by gangs of youths; protests by local communities against the housing of Roma or immigrants; and racist and xenophobic attitudes. Between 5 and 7 per cent of people interviewed for an opinion poll showed a serious level of intolerance. Sixty-five per cent of those polled believed that foreigners "take jobs away from Spanish people". Nevertheless, only 1 per cent were opposed to the "promotion in schools of tolerance and mutual respect" (see **Opinion Polls**).

In June, a new asylum law came into force, intended to streamline applications for asylum in Spain. Officials now have to decide on the eligibility of a claimant's request within four days. However, the law also introduced new grounds of ineligibility in certain cases. Rejected asylum-seekers and those ineligible to apply must leave Spanish territory unless they satisfy the normal visa requirements. The United Nations High Commission for Refugees (UNHCR) can appeal for the suspension of deportation if it disagrees with a minister's decision.

PARTIES, ORGANIZATIONS, MOVEMENTS

There are at least 120 far-right organizations in Spain, although many have tiny memberships and minimal impact. The following are the most important ones:

The Barcelona-based Circulo Español de Amigos de Europa (CEDADE, Spanish Circle of Friends of Europe), led by the convicted neo-Nazi Pedro Varela, was the most prominent neo-Nazi organization in Spain, although it described itself as a "cultural association". Established in 1965, it has been one of the oldest, largest (with some 1,500 members) and most active neo-Nazi groups in Europe. Recently, CEDADE suffered internal divisions and a number of its supporters left to join the Movimento Social Español or the far-right activist Juan Peligro (see below). In a special general meeting held in Madrid on 12 October 1993, the leaders of CEDADE decided "to dissolve its organizational structure" (see also **Publications and Media**).

The Frente Nacional (FN, National Front), a far-right nationalist party led by the veteran fascist Blas Piñar López, was also dissolved in 1994. The FN was criticized by Spanish and other neo-Nazis for being too nostalgic for the Franco era and not promoting enough of a xenophobic and antisemitic message. A new party, the Frente de Alternativa Nacional (FAN, Alternative National Front), took its place. Led by Rafael Arroyo, FAN includes many of the younger members of the defunct

FN, and according to some sources has approximately 500 members.

One of Piñar López's former aides, Miguel Bernard, was prominent late in the year in promoting Derecha Española (Spanish Right) as a new democratic, conservative and nationalist party to occupy the political space between the mainstream PP and the far-right parties.

Movimento Social Español (MSE, Spanish Social Movement) was launched in 1993 by Ricardo Sáenz de Ynestrillas, and is modelled on the neo-Fascist Movimento Sociale Italiano (Italian Social Movement). Approximately 800 supporters attended the MSE's launch. The MSE defines itself as a "radical, nationalistic Spanish movement" and uses the flags and salutes associated with the Franco era. It opposes the established political and economic systems and calls for the Catalan and the Basque regional movements to be outlawed. Prior to forming the MSE, Ynestrillas was cleared of charges of murdering a representative of the political wing of the Basque separatist movement for which he had served thirty-one months in prison.

Ynestrillas has sought to strengthen his position since the disbandment of CEDADE and FN, which has left the Spanish far right without a solid base. He proposed a coalition of the MSE, the Movimento Catolico Español (MCE, Spanish Catholic Movement, see **Religion**), the FAN and Nación Joven (NJ, Young Nation), and put forward the possibility of fielding candidates in the local elections of spring 1995. Alianza Para la Unidad Nacional (Alliance for National Unity) was subsequently set up as a coalition of six organizations under Ynestrillas's leadership. As well as MSE, MCE, NJ and FAN, it comprises the far-right trade union, Fuerza Nacional del Trabajo (National Labour Force), and Colectivo Universitario DISPAR (DISPAR University Collective), led by José Maria Gonzalez.

The annual rally at Madrid's Plaza de Oriente to mark the anniversary of the death of Franco and fascist leader J. A. Primero de Rivera on 20 November was attended by an estimated 4,000 people. Whilst contemporary far-right parties previously tended to regard this event as excessively conservative, they now see it as useful for current political activities. Supporters of far-right organizations were seen at the 1994 rally carrying flags adorned with swastikas, and making Nazi salutes. In a speech to the rally, Ynestrillas condemned the mainstream right-wing PP, attacked abortion, immigrants, democratic institutions and regional governments, and announced the establishment of the far-right electoral pact. The event was attended by representatives of far-right organizations from abroad, including members of the German neo-Nazi Freiheitliche Deutsche Arbeiterpartei (see **Germany**). On sale was the Spanish edition of the bulletin of the Nationalsozialistische Deutsche Arbeiterpartei/Auslands- und Aufbauorganisation (NSDAP/AO, German National Socialist Workers' Party/Overseas Section), the international neo-Nazi organization based in Lincoln, Nebraska (see **United States**).

Democracia Española (Spanish Democracy) is a new party led by Juan Peligro, the head of Juntas Españolas (JE, Spanish Councils). JE was a far-right nationalist party which did not espouse antisemitism, but had a virulently xenophobic platform. It campaigned to "stop immigration" and proposed that blood, not residency, should be the only determining factor for Spanish citizenship. Democracia Española includes activists from JE, CEDADE and other far-right groups. It aims to imitate the political strategy of Gianfranco Fini, leader of Italy's neo-Fascist-led Alleanza Nazionale (see **Italy**).

Peligro formed an electoral alliance with other extreme right-wing groups, called Alternativa Democratica Nacional (National Democratic Alternative), for the June 1994 European elections, but failed to win any seats. The combined vote of far-right parties in the European elections was 18,334.

Juntas Jovenes (Young Councils) is the JE youth organization. Fuerza Nacional de Trabajo is a small labour movement linked to JE.

Nación Joven (NJ, Young Nation) was founded in February 1990 by Carlos Alberto Vazquez Sanjurjo after a disagreement with the FN. The NJ considers itself to be a "nationalist" grouping and not part of the far right. It is antisemitic but its main targets are immigrants and it calls for their total expulsion. NJ members are often responsible for disseminating racist, antisemitic, neo-Nazi and anti-PSOE graffiti and posters. At the beginning of 1994, NJ moved closer to the old FN.

Las Bases Autónomas (BB.AA., The Autonomous Bases) were established by the now defunct Coordinadora de Estudiantes Nacional-Revolucionaria (Co-ordination of National-Revolutionary Students) in 1987. The Bases, whose symbol is the Celtic cross, operate as autonomous "leaderless" cells and have a strong skinhead following. Their ideology is "anarconazi", a combination of anarchism and national socialism. The main activities of these groups included the dissemination of far-right propaganda, daubing racist and antisemitic graffiti, acts of violence and the selling of fascist insignia and clothes to skinheads through army surplus shops in Madrid. They are on the fringe of Spain's far-right groups but, according to some reports, have been considering a legitimate political strategy.

In April, antisemitic graffiti on the walls of Madrid synagogue was "signed" by BB.AA. (see **Manifestations**). On 24 May, a group of five skinheads with iron bars attacked and injured nine students who were holding a meeting at the Complutensis University of Madrid. Three weeks later, the police detained Ignacio Alonso Garcia in connection with the attack. Alonso Garcia is said to be one of the leaders of BB.AA., and has also been accused of involvement in the beating up of a number of leaders of the Centro Democrático y Social (CDS, Democratic and Social Centre Party) in 1990.

On 12 October (Hispanic Day), a rally of far-right groups took place in Madrid, under the slogan "Spain, One Nation". It was organized by the FAN, the MCE, NJ and the MSE and attended by Falangist veterans and nationalist sympathizers. Speakers at the rally urged all the fringe parties to unite. With the exception of the weekly newspaper La Nación, the Spanish media did not cover the event, apparently because a group of skinheads were hostile to the presence of journalists and photographers.

In the run-up to the June European elections, the far-right parties sought to distance themselves from the skinheads and their violent activities, although they have used them on a number of occasions for their own ends. In Barcelona, skinheads were closely associated with JE and, in Madrid, they were organized around BB.AA.. According to the police-run community relations monitoring office, there were just over 2,000 skinheads in Spain in 1993. Growing official concern over skinhead violence meant that in 1994 there was better police surveillance of skinhead activities and meeting places, and more arrests were planned.

Léon Degrelle, the veteran Nazi and former commander of the Belgian volunteer brigade, Wallonie, died in Malaga in March. He had been a Spanish citizen since 1954, and as recently as October 1993 had addressed a rally of neo-Nazis in Valencia. His organization, Nouvel Ordre Européen (NOE, New European Order) was one of the oldest international far-right networks, bringing together former SS officers and present-day neo-Nazis. Amongst the mourners at the mass for Degrelle were Nazi sympathizers and Jorge Mota, a former leader of CEDADE.

MANIFESTATIONS

There were several serious incidents of antisemitic daubings, harassment and violence in 1994. Antisemitic graffiti appeared on the walls of the Madrid synagogue and of a nearby kosher butcher's shop on the anniversary of Hitler's death in April. In June, a fourteen-year-old Jewish woman suffered concussion after being beaten by three skinheads on her way to school. The skinheads, who shouted "You are Jewish" as they attacked the young woman, could not be located by the police. In central Madrid, an American rabbi wearing a skullcap was pursued by a youth shouting antisemitic abuse. In July, a group of teenagers was involved in three antisemitic incidents at a Jewish children's summer camp outside Madrid.

EDUCATION

In March, at the Complutensis University in Madrid, a tutor insulted a student on discovering she was Jewish. The tutor went on to defend Nazism in front of fellow students.

GRASSROOTS

The Committee for the Prevention of Violence in Sport has estimated the number of violent supporters of Spanish football to be approximately 2,000. However, the problem is felt to have reached a peak and is being tackled by both the police and the football clubs. Hooligans still make use of Nazi symbols at matches played by Real Madrid, Atletico Madrid, Barcelona and Español. Skinheads, especially in Madrid and Barcelona, recruit amongst supporters.

PUBLICATIONS AND MEDIA

Among the more important of the far-right publications in Spain in 1994 were the following: *Fuerza Nueva*, published by the organization of the same name, continued to appear twice monthly in 1994, despite the disbanding of the associated political party; *La Nación*, a weekly espousing ideas close to the old Spanish fascist party, Falange Española; *El porvenir de la nación española*, a racist weekly which began to appear at the end of 1994; and *Covadonga*, an ultra-Catholic publication edited by H. F. Hernández Medina and produced by the Sociedad Española de Defensa de la Tradicion, Familia y Propiedad (Spanish Society for the Defence of Tradition, Family and Property).

CEDADE, through its four publishing houses, was one of the largest producers of antisemitic publications in Europe. After its dissolution in October 1993, Pedro Varela maintained control over the publishing houses and its book shop, Europa, in Barcelona. The publishing houses are used to print Nazi books, pamphlets and other material, some of which are exported to Latin America. In Barcelona, CEDADE publishes the Austrian monthly neo-Nazi magazine *Halt!* to circumvent Austrian laws which prohibit such publications.

Varela, who has been convicted in Austria for neo-Nazi activities but remains free, sent a letter to his followers and subscribers, promoting a new magazine *IDENTIDAD de los pueblos europeos* (IDENTITY of the European People) to replace the defunct *Cedade* magazine. It is intended to publish at least one issue every year, depending on financial constraints.

The well-known weekly magazine *Cambio 16*, which has a long record of defending freedom and democracy in Spain, published an article in October about cults, entitled "Gods who kill". The magazine's cover showed a montage of small photographs, each representing individuals of different cults, grouped around the enlarged face of an orthodox Jew. (The article itself did not describe orthodox Jews as a cult.) The magazine cover prompted a complaint from the Association of Spanish Jewish Youth and two critical articles by Herman Tertsch of the mainstream daily *El Pais*. Both pointed out that the cover pandered to the kind of prejudice that *Cambio 16* usually fought against.

La Vanguardia newspaper publicly acknowledged it had made a mistake when it published a sympathetic obituary notice from the family and friends of Léon Degrelle, the Nazi veteran who died in March. Readers complained that the notice presented Degrelle as a model of integrity and advertised the mass held in his honour, which was, in essence, a political event. The newspaper claimed the notice was only published because it was faxed to its offices at the last moment by a respected advertising agency.

In November, a Dutch television programme, "SS in Spain", interviewed Auke Pattist (also known as Elko Patist), a former SS lieutenant now resident in Spain who is accused of war crimes. Pattist, who was born in Utrecht but settled in Spain in 1951, denied that he tortured and murdered dozens of people while he was a member of the Black Tulip organization in the Dutch region of Veld in November 1944. Pattist stated: "I have never participated in any hunts of Jews. I have nothing against these people. There are good ones and there are bad ones, like any social or ethnic group. What I do not agree with is their desire for separation, to be different, marrying only each other and not integrating with others whom they live with. They feel national pride because they consider themselves to be the chosen people, and have maintained this for 2,000 years. But I think they as individuals should integrate with the societies in which they live. Not to do this provokes rejections as has happened with the Gypsies in Spain." The Dutch government sought Pattist's extradition ten years ago, but the Spanish authorities turned down the request.

RELIGION

La Voz de España, a monthly news-sheet circulated by the MCE continued its criticisms of Spanish society, including Jews. The MCE, which was founded by José Luis Corral, was cited by activists as one of the possible partners in a coalition of far-right parties. In October, *La Voz de España* published a special addition to accompany the "Spain, One Nation" rally in Madrid (see **Parties, Organizations, Movements**).

The French translation of the *Bible des communautés chrétiennes*, an edition of the Bible published in 1994 by the Madrid-based International Catholic Bible Society, was criticized in France for including antisemitic references. The Bishop of Versailles called for the "popular language" French edition to be withdrawn (see **France**).

DENIAL OF THE HOLOCAUST

In 1994, a number of Holocaust-denial associations and groups continued to operate in Spain.

In January, Bright-Rainbow Limited, a Spanish neo-Nazi publishing house, sent 3,000 Spanish intellectuals and politicians copies of the Holocaust-denial text, *¿Absolución para Hitler?* (Absolution for Hitler?), by Austrian neo-Nazi Gerd Honsik. Honsik, the publisher of *Halt!* magazine, has been resident in Spain since fleeing an eighteen-month prison sentence for denial of the Holocaust in Austria in 1992. Austria has applied for his extradition (see **Austria**).

Honsik had been helped in the publication of neo-Nazi literature by eighty-one-year-old Otto Ernst Remer, the former commander of Hitler's war-time headquarters and a leading activist in post-war German neo-Nazi organizations. He has been a public promoter of the idea that Auschwitz is a "lie". Remer sought political asylum in Spain, having fled Germany in March 1994 before he was due to begin a twenty-two-month prison sentence for Holocaust denial. He was arrested on a German extradition order and then put under house arrest at his villa in Marbella in June, before being conditionally released. Critics blame sympathizers of Franco in the judiciary for Remer's relatively lenient treatment. He was still awaiting his extradition to Germany or deportation

from Spain at the end of 1994 (see **Germany**).

Both Honsik and Remer appeared with Pedro Varela on the weekly television programme *Linea 900* (Line 900) on TVE-2, Spain's second state channel, in May. In an edition of the programme entitled *La semilla del odio* (Seed of Hatred) which examined Nazi activities in Spain, Remer and others repeated their Holocaust-denying views which were answered and commented upon as part of the programme.

In March 1994, young far-right activists distributed Holocaust-denial leaflets at the entrance of cinemas showing Steven Spielberg's film *Schindler's List*.

EFFECTS OF ANTI-ZIONISM

According to the French newspaper *Le Figaro*, in July, six Algerian Islamist terrorists were detained in Perpignan, in south-west France. The paper reported that they were planning to travel to Barcelona to organize an attack on the Jewish community in Spain (see **France**).

OPINION POLLS

Increasing racism among young Spaniards was revealed in an opinion poll of 5,168 school and university students aged between fourteen and nineteen from all areas of Spain, 47.3 per cent of whom were male and 52.7 per cent female. The survey results were published in *El Pais* in January. It was conducted in 1993 by Tomas Calvo Buezas, a professor of social anthropology, whose similar study in 1986 earned him a national prize for research.

Questioned about racism, 31 per cent agreed with the statement "if it was up to me, I would expel the Gypsies from Spain"; a point of view shared by only 11 per cent in 1986. Twenty-six per cent said they would expel North Africans and Arabs, compared to 11 per cent in favour in 1986, and 14 per cent would expel black Africans (4 per cent in 1986).

Thirteen per cent said they would expel the Jews from Spain (10 per cent in 1986), a figure which Calvo Buezas considered "significant", since it showed that Jews continued "to play a negative role in the collective imagination".

LEGAL MATTERS

Attempts to reform Spain's penal code to include prohibitions on racist and neo-Nazi activities, Nazi insignia and denial of the Holocaust, progressed in 1994. In July, the government approved and submitted to parliament a bill to reform the entire penal code. According to the bill, offences motivated by racism, antisemitism or the victim's national or ethnic origin, or religious beliefs, would be classified as an "aggravating circumstance".

The Spanish parliament also considered a bill submitted previously by the PP, the main opposition party, which would modify the basic penal code in relation to the legal classification of Holocaust denial. The PP proposed the addition of articles concerning the punishment of any behaviour which could be seen as defending or disseminating ideologies which promote or support racism, or justify genocide. Jewish organizations created an *ad hoc* commission on reform of the penal code to support these measures and submitted joint proposals to the main parliamentary groups. Two of these proposals were accepted. The PP bill was approved, with amendments taken from the government bill, by all parliamentary groups on the justice and interior commission in December. It awaited approval by the chamber of deputies and the senate, which was expected in 1995.

Spanish courts passed long sentences on skinheads found guilty of violent crimes. A twenty-six-year-old civil guard who, in November 1992, killed a Dominican immigrant woman for being black, was condemned by a Madrid court to fifty-four years' imprisonment. Three right-wing teenagers who were accomplices in the crime were sentenced to twenty-four years each. This was the first ever conviction in Spain for a recognized racist crime. The lawyers for the defence appealed to the supreme court.

A Madrid court refused political asylum to Austrian neo-Nazi Gerd Honsik in 1993. Austria has applied for his extradition and he was still facing deportation at the end of 1994 (see **Denial of the Holocaust**).

COUNTERING ANTISEMITISM

In 1994, for the first time, neo-Nazi booksellers were denied access to the main book fairs of Spain in Madrid and Barcelona. The organization of the Barcelona book fair added a new clause to its statutes which prohibited stands which "incite violence" or "fail to respect the spirit of democracy and freedom". The Europa book shop of Barcelona, which was linked to CEDADE, appealed against the decision.

A protocol of co-operation between the bar association of Madrid and the Anti-Defamation League (ADL) Commission of B'nai B'rith España was signed on 8 November. Both parties agreed to study and propose legal measures to fight racism, xenophobia and antisemitism, to raise the awareness of lawyers on these issues, and to develop further programmes. A committee of experts from both parties was appointed to draw up the protocol. Similar protocols were signed on the same occasion between the bar association, the Spanish Red Cross and the Spanish representative of UNHCR. In attendance at the agreement were senior officials of the Spanish ministry of social affairs, a representative of the mayor of Madrid, and the presidents of the bar associations of Buenos Aires and Mexico City.

The minister of social affairs appointed representatives from two Jewish organizations, the ADL Commission of B'nai B'rith España and Jóvenes Judios Españoles/Dor Hemshech (Young Spanish Jews), as members of the national committee for the 1995 European Youth Campaign against Racism, Xenophobia, Antisemitism and Intolerance. The campaign was co-ordinated by the Council of Europe.

In the aftermath of Steven Spielberg's film, *Schindler's List*, much media coverage was given to the story of Angel Sanz-Briz, a Spanish diplomat, and his colleague, Giorgio Perlasca, who helped 5,200 Jews to escape from Hungary during the Second World War. In 1990, in an official ceremony held at the Israeli embassy, Sanz-Briz was honoured by B'nai B'rith España in the presence of his widow, family and senior representatives of the Spanish foreign ministry. He was posthumously named a "Righteous Gentile" in Israel. At the time, the only magazine to report the event was *Hola!*.

King Carlos inaugurated the renovated Sephardi Museum of Toledo on 1 June.

ASSESSMENT

In 1994, the main sources of concern for the Jewish community were the increase in verbal abuse and physical assaults on Jews and the detention by French police of Islamist terrorists who were apparently planning an attack on a Jewish institution in Spain. Whilst an opinion poll showed that a small minority of young people viewed Jews in a negative light, the main victims of racism, as in recent years, were Roma and non-white immigrants.

Attempts to prohibit racist and neo-Nazi activities by law progressed in 1994, although the case of Otto Ernst Remer suggested that Spain still offered a legal refuge for those convicted of antisemitic or racist acts elsewhere in Europe.

Sweden

General population: 8.7 million
Jewish population: 16,000-20,000 (mainly in
Stockholm, Göteborg and Malmö)

GENERAL BACKGROUND

The liberal-conservative coalition government
was voted out of office in September. The
Sveriges Socialdemokratiska Arbetareparti
(Swedish Social Democratic Labour Party)
formed a minority government, relying initially
on the assistance of the former communist
Vänsterpartiet (Left Party) but retaining the
option of attracting support from the non-
socialist parties.

Although it lost all of its seats, the rightist-
populist Ny Demokrati (ND, New Democracy) received around 75,000 votes (1.2 per
cent). Combined with the votes for the smaller
far-right parties, approximately 100,000 people
voted for parties whose main priority was opposition to immigration policies.

The principal electoral issues were unemployment and the rapidly rising state budget
deficit. The unemployment rate fell from 8.2
per cent in 1993 to 7.4 per cent in 1994; inflation
fell from 4.1 per cent to 2.6 per cent. Growth
was 1.8 per cent.

In a referendum in November 52.2 per cent
of voters approved Sweden's membership of the
European Union.

HISTORICAL LEGACY

In the 1930s anti-Jewish attitudes influenced
Sweden's policy towards Jewish refugees from
Nazi persecution. In 1938 widespread fear of
mass Jewish immigration led Sweden virtually
to close its borders to Jewish refugees while, in
response to Swedish and Swiss demands, the
German authorities began stamping a red "J" in
the passports of Jews. Also in 1938, following
the German example, a law was introduced prohibiting *shekhita* (Jewish religious slaughter of
animals). (The law remains in effect to this day:
shekhita is regarded as incompatible with Swedish legislation for the protection of animals.)

In the late 1940s and 1950s Einar Åberg, a
founder/leader of the wartime organization
Sveriges Antijudiska Kampförbund (Swedish
Anti-Jewish Action League), became a leading
European antisemitic propagandist.

In the late 1970s material denying the
Holocaust was circulated on a larger scale than
hitherto by the neo-Nazi Ditlieb Felderer—
who in 1983 was sentenced to ten months' imprisonment for incitement of hatred against an

ethnic group—and his Bible Researcher publishing house. During the 1982 Israeli military
campaign in Lebanon, antisemitic expressions
surfaced in the mainstream Swedish press.

RACISM AND XENOPHOBIA

Scattered attacks against minorities, some of
them violent, continued. Most involved clashes
between Swedish and non-Swedish youths. At
least a dozen immigrants were physically assaulted and several homes and businesses were
burned or otherwise damaged. The authorities
investigated and prosecuted such crimes,
although in many clashes between youth gangs
both sides appeared to be at fault. Most cases
resulted in conviction and prison terms unless
the offender was a minor.

There are around 17,000 Samis (Lapps) in
Sweden. In 1994 Samis protested againt a 1993
law permitting others to hunt on designated
reindeer pastures and a 1994 law permitting
others to fish in lakes previously reserved for
Samis. Samis also complain that they encounter
discrimination in housing and employment.

PARTIES, ORGANIZATIONS, MOVEMENTS

There are a number of neo-Nazi groups in Sweden. Together, they comprise the so-called
Storm Network, an informal gathering of the
most militant neo-Nazi activists in Sweden,
many of them skinheads. The Network derives
its name from the racist and antisemitic magazine *Storm*. *Storm* has become the focal point
for several far-right organizations, of which Vitt
Ariskt Motstånd (VAM, White Aryan Resistance) is the best known. The number of
hardcore activists belonging to the Network is
60-100, with an additional 500-600 active sympathizers nationwide. The number of passive

sympathizers and/or consumers of propaganda material produced by various elements in the Network is certainly much larger.

The main groups associated with the Storm Network include the following:

VAM, modelled on the now probably defunct US neo-Nazi organization The Order (see **United States**), is promoted as the nucleus of an "Aryan Revolution". Activists have been sentenced for a number of violent crimes, including three cases of murder (in 1985, 1986 and 1990), armed robberies, burglaries in military arms depots and violent assaults. VAM has no formal structure but leading members include Göran Gullvang, Donald Hansson, Jonas Ledin, Klas Lund, Peter Melander (also known as Rindell), Christopher Rangne, Erik Rundqvist and David Tällfors (also known as Twaland and Emilsson). In 1994 Ledin, Lund and Rangne were serving prison sentences for armed robberies.

The Riksfronten (RF, National Front, formerly Föreningen Sveriges Framtid) is a racist and antisemitic organization with an estimated 500 members. Members of the RF acted as bodyguards for the Holocaust-denier Robert Faurisson (see **France**) during his three visits to Stockholm in 1992-3. The RF is led by Thorulf Magnusson from his hometown of Linköping.

The Kreativistens Kyrka (KK, Church of the Creator) is the Swedish branch of the North American neo-Nazi organization of the same name (see **Canada**). KK, which is virulently racist and antisemitic, has an estimated 100 members, most of whom also belong to the Storm Network. Tommy Rydén is the leader of the KK. Another important figure is VAM activist David Tällfors, leader of the KK's military arm, the White Berets.

Many Storm Network activists belong to more than one organization within the Network. Members of the Network maintain regular contact with similar groups in other countries. Several members have made extended visits to South Africa since the 1980s, spending their time there mostly with groups and persons connected with Eugene Terre-Blanche (see **South Africa**).

The Nordiska Rikspartiet (NRP, Nordic National Party), an old-style national-socialist party, is headed by Assar and Vera Oredsson. Vera Oredsson is a former Hitler Jugend (Hitler Youth) member. The NRP, in particular its "storm troops", National Action Group, has often been linked with neo-Nazi violence. In 1994 it was not very active. Membership is estimated at a maximum of 300.

The Nysvenska Rörelsen (New Swedish Movement) was previously led by the veteran fascist Per Engdahl. Following Engdahl's death in May, the future of this movement, with its estimated 300 members, is unclear.

Radio Islam/Svensk-Islamiska Föreningen (Radio Islam/Swedish-Islamic Association), a group centred around the (now closed) radio station Radio Islam, includes Radio Islam editor-in-chief Ahmed Rami and David Janzon, who is legally responsible for material published by the organization (see **Publications and Media**). Ahmed Rami has ties with neo-Nazi groups in Sweden, including the Storm Network, and elsewhere.

Sverigedemokraterna (SD, Swedish Democrats) is a far-right political party. Its overt political programme comprises mainly opposition to non-European immigration but its internal propaganda is racist and antisemitic. This situation has led to conflict over policy issues, with one faction moving towards hard-core neo-Nazism and another wishing to continue the parliamentary "Le Pen approach", although internal differences were played down during the election campaign. Many SD activists have close ties with the Storm Network. SD leader Anders Klarström began his career as a member of the NRP.

The SD's present membership is unknown. Although it adopted a neo-Nazi approach at public rallies, with uniforms, drummers and the like, its general election campaign was relatively low-key. It won 12,500 votes in the election, over twice the figure in the 1991 election. It also more than doubled its representation on local councils. It now has 5 representatives in the local councils of Dals-Ed (2), Höör (2) and Ekerö (1). The SD came close to gaining a seat in Trollhättan, a town where an arson attack on a mosque occurred in 1993.

The SD maintains contact with extremist organizations elsewhere in Europe, including the Republikaner and the Front national, especially its youth movement (see **France** and **Germany**).

The Sveriges Nationella Förbund (SNF, Swedish National League) is a racist and antisemitic movement which dates from before the Second World War. It has an estimated 200 members, many of whom are elderly. Several members of the SNF's Stockholm branch have maintained contact for several years with Ahmed Rami.

Virtus, a newly formed group of university students based in Uppsala and Stockholm, is led by Johan Rinderheim, a graduate student in political science. So far the group has not been overtly antisemitic, but there are strong reasons to believe that this is for tactical reasons only.

MANIFESTATIONS

The number of threatening letters and telephone calls to Jews or Jewish institutions, as well as material damage to the latter, decreased in relation to 1993.

There were two desecrations of Jewish cemeteries. In March sixteen tombstones in the central cemetery in Malmö were overturned. No arrests have been made. The incident may have been part of a larger wave of cemetery desecrations which swept the Malmö region at the time. In May three stones in the old Jewish cemetery in Göteborg were daubed with swastikas. No arrests were made by the end of 1994.

In 1994 Ditlieb Felderer (see **Historical Legacy**) returned to Sweden after spending several years in the Canary Islands. Shortly after his return he began sending hate material to Jews and non-Jews as well as Jewish and non-Jewish institutions in and outside Sweden.

Antisemitism was a common element at concerts and other activities organized by neo-Nazi groups. One notable example was a rally by members and sympathizers of the Storm Network on 30 April in the town of Alingsås: about 500 people marched in military fashion through the town centre, the largest Nazi march since the Second World War. The police, taken by surprise, did not intervene. The march was followed by a concert by Swedish neo-Nazi bands. The event was viewed as a huge success by the participants and the organizer, Thorulf Magnusson, spoke to the concert audience about the victory against the "Jew state".

PUBLICATIONS AND MEDIA

In 1994 the propaganda activities of the Storm Network developed in two directions. First, two new magazines were founded. *Gryning* (Dawn) is produced by VAM activists Christopher Rangne, Jonas Ledin and Bo Lindgren, who are currently serving prison terms. *Gryning*, for which the American Gary Yarbrough has been assigned legal responsibility, is well produced and printed on quality paper; it concentrates on the survival of the "white race" and the struggle against Jews. The magazine *Blod och Ära* (Blood and Honour) promotes skinhead music and is closely linked with the second major development, the swift growth of neo-Nazi bands and the extensive distribution of their music on compact discs.

The Riksfronten publishes the semi-annual magazine *Rikslarm* (National Alarm), which has a circulation of some 2,000 copies.

The KK distributes the Church of the Creator's English-language publication *Racial Loyalty* and irregularly publishes its own magazine *Rahowa* (Racial Holy War).

The Nordiska Rikspartiet publishes the quarterlies *Nordisk Kamp* (Nordic Struggle) and *Nordiska Rikspartiet* (Nordic National Party) as well as *Solhjulet* (The Sunwheel), which appears irregularly.

In March 1987 Radio Islam began broadcasting antisemitic propaganda in the Stockholm area. In November 1989 the Stockholm district court sentenced Rami to six months' imprisonment for incitement of hatred against an ethnic group; Radio Islam was forbidden to broadcast for one year. In October 1990 the appeal court upheld the conviction (with minor changes) and reaffirmed the prison sentence.

In October 1992 Radio Islam was again convicted by the Stockholm district court, a conviction upheld by the appeal court. David Janzon, formally responsible for the broadcasts, was sentenced to four months' imprisonment. Radio Islam has not been on the air since that time.

Ahmed Rami has published several antisemitic books, including *Vad är Israel?* (What Is Israel?), *Israels makt i Sverige* (Israel's Power in Sweden) and *Judisk häxprocess i Sverige* (Jewish Witch-hunt in Sweden).

In 1994 the SD's previously bi-monthly magazine *SD-Kuriren* (SD Courier) appeared irregularly.

In recent years, the Malmö branch of the SNF has established contacts with Gary Lauck's Nationalsozialistische Deutsche Arbeiterpartei/Auslands- und Aufbauorganisation (NSDAP/AO, German National Socialist Workers' Party/Overseas Section) (see **United States**), publishing the paper *Sveriges Nationella Förbund*, which is based on Lauck's magazine *The New Order*.

Virtus publishes a magazine by the same name which is critical of Sweden's immigration policies.

Expressions of antisemitism were standard features of neo-Nazi publications as well as of messages in the computer FidoNet discussion meeting "Racism". On computer bulletin board systems (BBS), expressions of antisemitism were common in the approximately fifteen neo-Nazi BBSs active in Sweden. During the year, these BBSs maintained a lower profile than previously. Most of them have no direct connection with the Storm Network but at least several members of one BBS seem to have been accepted by the Network under the name Kampgrupp Väst (Combat Group West). The best known are Henrik Bertilsson and Johan Alexandersson. Alexandersson also leads a new group named Antisionistisk aktion (Anti-Zionist Action) and writes for the circular *Wärendsbladet* (see also **Denial of the Holocaust**).

Antisemitic sentiment in the mainstream media was, as in 1993, relatively rare and was mostly evident in readers' letters. The public debate in 1994 over the Jewish religious slaughter of animals provoked many readers' letters. In some cases connections were made with the "primitiveness" of Judaism and Islam generally.

Also, in some cases the disclosure by Sweden's largest paper *Expressen* that Ingvar Kamprad, owner of the international furniture company IKEA, was a sympathizer in his early years of Per Engdahl's fascist movement prompted comments about the Jewish background of *Expressen's* owner family (Bonnier) and the chief editor, Olle Wästberg.

UFO activist Sune Hjorth during the year wrote antisemitic letters which were in mainstream papers. In one instance in December his review of a new book by the notorious antisemite Jüri Lina was published in the social democratic paper *Piteåtidningen*. The review, replete with antisemitic conspiracy theories, had not disturbed the editors. They claimed that they "did not know so much about these things", promised to be "more careful with Hjorth" in the future, and declared that they had "always sided with the Jews in these matters".

RELIGION

Antisemitic sentiments were again expressed by Sister Marianne, who is well known for her work with refugees. In 1988 she gained prominence by telling Radio Islam listeners that "the Jews have got the Holocaust on the brain".

In August *Expressen* printed a lengthy interview with Sister Marianne. Asked if she had been misquoted in 1988, she replied that she had not, but that she had made an "ill-considered statement". She continued, however: "I still hold that they have got the Holocaust on the brain. . . . More people than the Jews have had a bad time. It seems to me that they exaggerate their misfortune and believe they are the only people on earth that have had to suffer. It irritates me when they dwell on the Holocaust over and over again. As soon as Israel has committed an outrage they bring up the Shoah. The Holocaust was not about racial discrimination but about fear of the power of Jews in society. The fact is that like all Orientals they were clever businessmen."

These comments prompted a strong reaction in several quarters, especially on the part of liberal newspapers, and one government minister, Christian Democrat Alf Svensson, condemned Sister Marianne's statements forcefully. The church's reaction was subdued. The archbishop said that he would bring up the matter

with Sister Marianne in the course of pastoral care.

The controversy surrounding Professor Jan Bergman, who was a witness for the defence in the trial of Ahmed Rami in 1989, took a new turn in 1994. Bergman, a priest in the Swedish church, is head of the faculty of theology at Uppsala University and a professor of the history of religions. In the trial Bergman, among other things, supported Radio Islam's claim that it was a divinely ordained commandment for a Jew to kill a non-Jew.

Bergman's testimony was severely criticized by a number of scholars and intellectuals. Two of Sweden's rabbis, Chief Rabbi Morton Narrowe and Rabbi Robert Wolkoff, wrote in March 1990 to the board of the theology faculty demanding that Bergman be relieved of his duties with regard to the teaching of Judaism at the faculty. The vice-chancellor of Uppsala University, Professor Stig Strömholm, asked the then dean, Professor Ragnar Holte, to investigate the accusations against Bergman. Holte subsequently produced a document which exonerated Bergman and attacked his critics. Strömholm decided not to intervene.

But the criticism continued and in August 1991 the vice-chancellor wrote to the administrative head of the theology department, Dr Sigbert Axelson, stating that "possible doctrinal errors should not be corrected by disciplinary or administrative matters but through debate and criticism".

Dr Axelson has played a major role in the faculty's defence of Bergman. In an internal memorandum in 1992 he claimed that an "international Israeli/Zionist conspiracy" was seeking, through criticism of Bergman, to prepare the ground for the expulsion of a million Palestinians from Israel and was part of an "international Israeli campaign against the judicial system of the Western world". For Axelson, this campaign aimed not only at criminalizing antisemitism but also at "religious criticism of Judaism, historical research into Nazism [that is, denial of the Holocaust], political, humanistic and legal criticism of the state of Israel and its policies". In a radio interview in 1993 Strömholm described Axelson's memorandum as "statements critical of actions by the Jewish party to the Bergman controversy".

In December 1992 Zwi Werblowsky, professor of comparative religion at the Hebrew University, wrote a letter critical of Bergman to Professor Strömholm. Strömholm asked the dean, Professor Hallencreutz, to investigate the charges. In March 1993 the theology faculty claimed that "Jewish criticism" of Professor Bergman had been refuted. It then asked

Professor Inge Lønning, the former vice-chancellor of Oslo University, to give his evaluation of the affair and especially the faculty's handling of it.

In February 1994, in a report entitled "Antisemitism as a Legal, Intellectual and Moral Challenge", Lønning was extremely critical of Bergman and his testimony as well as of the faculty's and the university's handling of the case. His criticism of Axelson was equally scathing.

The first faculty reactions to the report, revealed in a press release and a separate statement by the dean in mid-March, were evasive and/or misrepresented Lønning's findings. Following renewed protests by leading Swedish intellectuals and academics, in April the board of the theology faculty accepted Lønning's conclusions and formed a committee with the intention of examining, among other things, how to deal with the teaching of Judaism in the faculty in the future.

In May the committee presented the results of its deliberations and proposed a statement to be adopted by the board, which was unanimously accepted. In the statement, the board accepted the criticism of Bergman as justified and said that the faculty had "consistently ignored and belittled the criticism that has been made". The faculty's most serious mistake, according to the board, was that it had been influenced by a conspiracy theory of "an organized Jewish campaign against Jan Bergman".

At the fifth conference of the European Association of Jewish Studies in Copenhagen in August, another Uppsala scholar, Tryggve Kronholm, professor of Semitic languages at the Institute of Afro-Asian Languages and a board member of the Association of Scandinavian Jewish Studies, delivered a lecture in which he reiterated claims central to Hallencreutz's and Axelson's response in March 1993 to Werblowsky's criticism and gave the impression that he supported the claim that it was a divinely-ordained commandment for a Jew to kill a non-Jew. The executive committee of the conference concluded that Kronholm's "scholarly misconduct is unacceptable".

DENIAL OF THE HOLOCAUST

Material denying the Holocaust was prominent in publications produced and distributed by a number of groups and individuals belonging to the far right. In particular, *Rikslarm* (the magazine produced by Riksfronten), Radio Islam's membership bulletin and *Wärendsbladet* emphasized Holocaust denial. *Wärendsbladet* is a small circular published by Nils Rydström, a former member of the NRP. Rydström has published material produced by Ernst Zündel

(see **Canada**), and Åke Lutner from Göteborg (apparently an associate of Rami) has contributed several Holocaust-denial pieces to *Wärendsbladet*.

The intense antisemitic and Holocaust-denial activity in the FidoNet discussion meetings begun in March 1993, especially by the two aliases "Fritz Goldman" and "Oskar Andersson", diminished in spring 1994 and ceased in June. Subsequently it was rumoured that Holocaust-denial activities continued on only one BBS, which, however, had no Nazi connections.

In May Robert Engström, a first-year history student active in ND, presented a paper in a seminar at the department of history at Uppsala University entitled "Revisionism in Holocaust research". The paper, which echoed the most common Holocaust-denial theses, evoked severe criticism from the chair as well as from students.

LEGAL MATTERS

On account of his resumed antisemitic activities (see **Historical Legacy**), Ditlieb Felderer was indicted and later tried for violating the law against "incitement against an ethnic group". The trial took place in December and Felderer was sentenced to one year's imprisonment. He has appealed the sentence and is now out of prison awaiting the next trial.

COUNTERING ANTISEMITISM

The première of Steven Spielberg's film *Schindler's List* in Sweden in February was a major success. The cinema was filled to capacity with 500 guests, including four government ministers and celebrities from cultural life and the media.

The work of the Holocaust survivors' organization, established in 1992, continued during the year. Members of this organization regularly visited schools and delivered lectures on their experiences under Nazism. The lecturers are much sought after by teachers and pupils.

The Swedish Committee against Antisemitism also intensified its efforts to reach teachers and pupils throughout Sweden, and members of the committee regularly gave lectures both in schools and in teachers' seminars. The committee began working on education programmes for teachers to be implemented in 1995. Per Ahlmark, a former vice-premier of Sweden and the founder of the Swedish Committee against Antisemitism, addressed many international gatherings urging a strong stand against antisemitism.

ASSESSMENT

There was in 1994 a decrease in reported anti-semitic incidents but not in the distribution of anti-Jewish propaganda which, following the pattern of recent years, is maintaining its dominant position in far-right propaganda. It is too early to tell whether the decrease in racist and antisemitic violence represents a new trend. Experts tend to see 1994 as a year of re-organization, stabilization and continued re-cruitment on the part of the far right. In many parts of the country, not only the larger cities and towns, there are now groups of young peo-ple, mostly males, between the ages of fifteen and twenty-five, who, though not part of the Storm Network, identify with it. This pheno-menon is especially marked in the west of Sweden.

Switzerland

General population: 6.9 million
Jewish population: 18,300 (mainly in Zürich, Geneva and Basel)

GENERAL BACKGROUND

Switzerland has a federal constitution under which the twenty cantons and six half-cantons retain considerable autonomy. The ruling coalition of the Christlichdemokratische Volkspartei der Schweiz/Parti démocrate-chrétien suisse (CVP/PDC, Christian Democratic People's Party), the Sozialdemo-kratische Partei der Schweiz/Parti socialiste suisse (SPS/PSS, Social Democratic Party), the Freisinnig-Demokratische Partei/Parti radical-démocratique suisse (FDP/PRD, Radical Democratic Party) and the Schweizerische Volkspartei/Parti suisse de l'Union démocratique du centre (SVP/UDC, Swiss People's Party), which has been in power since 1959, was last re-elected in 1991.

Political parties, such as the far-right Schweizer Demokraten/Démocrates suisses (SD/DS, Swiss Democrats, formerly Nationale Aktion) and the Zürich branch of the traditionally centre-right SVP, have capitalized on and fed the xenophobic climate, competing for right-wing voters. Even the liberal-moderate FDP has adopted some of the campaign terminology of the right, especially in the city of Zürich, where a rise in crime and drug-dealing has been blamed on asylum-seekers. Rolf Mauch, FDP member for the Aargau canton in the Nationalrat (national council), played a role in one of the smaller committees, led by Herbert Meier, which opposed the anti-racism law (see **Legal Matters**).

Despite some evidence of economic growth—gross domestic product rose by 2.1 per cent—there was a slight increase in unemployment, up from 4.5 per cent in 1993 to approximately 5 per cent in 1994.

HISTORICAL LEGACY

Switzerland's Jews were the last in Western Europe to acquire complete emancipation when the 1848 Swiss constitution was amended in 1866 to give them civic and legal equality and in 1874 to allow them freedom of religious expression.

In 1933 and 1935, the Swiss federation of Jewish communities took legal action against the distribution of *The Protocols of the Elders of Zion* and Henry Ford's *The International Jew*. During the Second World War, almost 40,000 Jewish refugees were refused asylum by the Swiss authorities and were forced to return to Germany, France or Italy. This information came to light in 1994, when the Swiss government finally granted four Israeli historians access to wartime files on Jewish immigration.

The period from 1945 to the end of the 1970s saw only isolated incidents of public antisemitism. Christian and Jewish organizations united to fight all forms of xenophobia.

In 1978-9, the screening of the American television series, *Holocaust,* led to the desecration of cemeteries, the daubing of graffiti and arson attacks on synagogues in Basel and Zürich. The 1982 Lebanon war brought about a renewed wave of anti-Jewish manifestations which subsided shortly afterwards. Apart from the activities of some small neo-Nazi groups, antisemitic incidents occur in Switzerland mainly as a reaction to events in the Middle East. In autumn 1992, however, following the events in the German town of Rostock there was a marked increase in incidents.

RACISM AND XENOPHOBIA

Continuing unemployment and public concern over levels of crime, especially drug-related violence, which were blamed on immigrants and asylum-seekers, contributed to an increasingly xenophobic climate. There were reports, in particular, of an increase in attacks on Kosova Albanian and Sri Lankan refugees.

In March the Nationalrat approved legislation to restrict the rights of asylum-seekers and illegal immigrants. In a referendum on the proposed law, held on 4 December, 72.9 per cent voted for, and 27.1 per cent voted against its implementation. Under the new law, which will come into effect during 1995, judges will be able to imprison asylum-seekers and illegal immigrants for up to a year without trial and authorize the jailing of asylum-seekers who stray out of their designated canton. Arnold Koller, the CVP minister of justice, claimed that the measures would allow judges to combat the country's growing drugs problem. Anti-racism campaigners attacked the proposal on the grounds that the government was making foreigners the scapegoats for the failure of its anti-drugs policies and pandering to those exacerbating the xenophobic climate.

PARTIES, ORGANIZATIONS, MOVEMENTS

Most far-right organizations in Switzerland are small and locally-based, with rarely more than a handful of members. Many are short-lived, but there has been a worrying tendency for new, more radical groups to replace their predecessors.

The Schweizer Democraten/Démocrates suisses (SD/DS, Swiss Democrats) is an established far-right party based in the Aargau canton. It was affiliated to a party in Geneva called Vigilance, and linked to Jean-Marie Le Pen of the French Front national, who has attended several of its rallies (see **France**).

Nationale Koordination (National Co-ordination), led by the veteran antisemite Gaston-Armand Amaudruz of Nouvel Ordre Européen (New European Order), remained the main umbrella organization for far-right groups. Amaudruz's best known writing is *Ist Rassebewusstsein verwerflich?* (Is Race Consciousness Objectionable?). He also publishes *Courrier du Continent* which carries racist and antisemitic articles and distributes *Die Auschwitz-Lüge* (The Auschwitz Lie) by Thies Christophersen, the former SS overseer in Auschwitz who runs a centre in Denmark for the distribution of antisemitic and Nazi propaganda (see **Denmark**). In April Amaudruz attended a meeting of Emil Rahm's referendum committee on the anti-racism law. Also active in Nationale Koordination was Roger Wüthrich, leader of the Avalon-Gemeinschaft (Avalon Society), which cultivates the "Celtic-Germanic heritage of Europe".

The number of skinheads and other potentially violent far-right activists has been estimated at around 250 in the north-eastern part of Switzerland alone. Members of the skinhead group Nationale Jugend Schweiz (National Youth of Switzerland) have claimed that there is a far-right weapons arsenal in central Switzerland.

In April, a meeting was held outside Bern by a previously unknown skinhead group, the Neo-Faschisten Front (NFF, Neo-Fascist Front). After a football match at the Wankdorf stadium, about twenty NFF activists caused a disturbance and fought with members of the left-wing Antifaschistische Aktion Bern (Bern Anti-Fascist Action). Four skinheads from Germany were taken into temporary custody.

In April, a Genevan neo-Nazi book shop, Excalibur, closed down after media reports and protests. The book shop had sold *The Protocols of the Elders of Zion,* the works of Léon Degrelle (leader of the Belgian Nazi movement during the Second World War), audio-cassettes of Nazi songs and other Nazi paraphernalia.

MAINSTREAM POLITICS

All established political parties disavow antisemitism, but two parties, the SD and the Autopartei (Auto Party), which began as a movement to protect the rights of car drivers, are openly hostile to Switzerland's hitherto relatively liberal policy towards asylum-seekers. In 1994 the Autopartei changed its name to the Freiheitspartei (Freedom Party) and most of its eight Nationalrat members were active in the campaign against the anti-racism law (see **Legal Matters**). Roger Wüthrich, leader of the Avalon-Gemeinschaft, reportedly joined the Autopartei/Freiheitspartei in 1994.

During the anti-racism law referendum campaign, a group of young politicians from mainstream parties formed a group called Jungbürgerliche (Young Citizens) which opposed the law. The group stated that it was not racist or antisemitic, but two leading members, Gregor Rutz of the FDP and Philip Rhomberg of the SVP, made thinly-veiled Holocaust-denial remarks in editorials and policy statements. The group was disavowed by all of the political parties of its members and disbanded after only six weeks.

MANIFESTATIONS

In February, sixty gravestones were overturned in the Friesenberg cemetery in Zürich. This was followed by a rise in the number of racist graffiti and incidents of harassment of Jews between February and June. In June, more than 100 gravestones were desecrated at the Friesenberg cemetery. Two eleven-year-old boys confessed to the desecration and were found guilty, but the police investigation concluded that their actions were was not motivated by antisemitism.

In July, eleven gravestones were overturned and four more were damaged in a Jewish cemetery in Baden. In the same month, several gravestones and crosses were overturned in a Roman Catholic cemetery in the north-western town of Appenzell.

Swastikas and antisemitic slogans also

appeared in the railway station and in large shopping centres in Geneva in April.

EDUCATION

A dozen cases of orthodox Jewish school-children having suffered abuse from older teenagers were reported during May and June.

PUBLICATIONS AND MEDIA

Eidgenoss (Swiss Citizen), hitherto the most notorious far-right, antisemitic and Holocaust-denial publication in Switzerland, ceased publication at the end of 1994 in anticipation of the introduction of the new anti-racist legislation in January 1995 (see **Legal Matters**). The eight-page monthly, established in 1977, was written entirely by Max Wahl, who was found guilty in Munich in 1991 of incitement to racial hatred. *Eidgenoss* frequently referred to the domination of Swiss political institutions by "organized Jewish circles".

Emil Rahm's bi-monthly newsletter, *Memopress*, which was founded in 1966, contained antisemitic articles and promoted the antisemitic German magazine *CODE*. Rahm, an entrepreneur who lives near Schaffhausen, was the prime mover in the petition campaign against the anti-racism law (see **Legal Matters**).

The *Courrier du Continent*, published by Gaston-Armand Amaudruz in Lausanne, carried racist articles and a catalogue of Nazi publications, films and audio-cassettes. The *Courrier* began as an information sheet for the Nouvel Ordre Européen, the international fascist movement founded shortly after the end of the Second World War.

DENIAL OF THE HOLOCAUST

Until the anti-racism law was adopted in the September referendum, Switzerland was a safe-haven for Holocaust-deniers, who could openly promote their ideas at public meetings and in print. Prior to the referendum, Bernard Schaub, Jürgen Graf, Andreas Studer and Walter Fischbacher formed a group called Aktionsgemeinschaft für die Enttabuisierung der Zeitgeschichte (Action Committee for the Removal of Taboos from Contemporary History). They sent Holocaust-denial propaganda to thousands of academics and university teachers, urging them to vote against the anti-racism law. The propaganda included a glossy brochure portraying German war criminals as victims of a Jewish propaganda lie.

Arthur Vogt has written Holocaust-denial articles in neo-Nazi publications, such as *Sieg* which was published by the Austrian Walter Ochensberger until his imprisonment in 1993.

Vogt regularly wrote Holocaust-denial letters to daily newspapers and spoke at meetings held by far-right groups. He helped to finance the publication of Jürgen Graf's book, *Der Holocaust Schwindel* (The Holocaust Swindle).

L' Holocauste au scanner (The Holocaust under the Scanner), the French-language edition of Jürgen Graf's Holocaust-denial book which was produced originally in German in 1993 by the Basel-based Guideon Burg Verlag publishing house, was distributed in Belgium and France during 1994 (see **Belgium** and **France**)

LEGAL MATTERS

A referendum was held on 25 September 1994 to decide on the introduction of an anti-racism law, which had been passed by large majorities in both houses of the Swiss parliament in June 1993. The legislation, which brings Switzerland into line with the United Nations' Convention on the Elimination of All Forms of Racial Discrimination, outlaws racial and religious discrimination in the public sphere, as well as Holocaust-denying and racist utterances in public.

Two committees submitted petitions containing the 50,000 signatures required to challenge legislation by referendum. Action for Free Speech, the main committee centred around *Memopress* publisher Emil Rahm, collected 47,000 signatures. Rahm's committee condemned the law as a "crude attack against freedom of speech", arguing that it would also lead to increased immigration into Switzerland. Rahm also claimed that the law would force minorities to intermingle with the Swiss and thereby lose their own identities.

The Committee for Freedom of Speech and Thought, led by Herbert Meier, collected 8,000 signatures. This committee, which ostensibly sought to distance itself from Rahm's, featured FDP member Rolf Mauch as a speaker at public meetings. Mauch, who modelled his arguments on the United States' constitutional protection of the freedom of the individual, was the only FDP Nationalrat member to vote against the anti-racism law.

Only 45 per cent of the electorate voted in the referendum, with 54.6 per cent approving the law and 45.4 per cent voting against. The major cities (Zürich, Bern, Basel and Geneva) recorded between 58.4 per cent and 65.8 per cent in favour. Rural voters tended to reject the legislation. While the passing of this law reflected the tolerant attitude of the majority of mainstream party politicians, the success of the campaign to force a referendum against the law indicated resistance to anti-discriminatory measures at the grassroots level.

In a 1994 decision, a Swiss court declared that Holocaust-denier Andreas Studer could be characterized as a Nazi-sympathizer.

COUNTERING ANTISEMITISM

The parliamentary group against racism and xenophobia, formed in 1992, continued to mobilize public opinion in favour of the anti-racism law in the run-up to the referendum in September. The government, major political parties, churches and the Jewish community all advised people to support the legislation.

ASSESSMENT

Antisemitism was publicly condemned by all mainstream political parties and was largely absent from Swiss daily life. However, there was concern about cemetery desecrations and the appearance of racist graffiti during 1994. Concern was also expressed at the continuing rightward move of the SVP in Zürich and the possibility of the national SVP and the moderate FDP following this trend. Furthermore, the referendum campaign against the anti-racism law raised fears of a surfacing of latent antisemitism.

Turkey

General population: 60 million
Jewish population: 25,000 (mainly in Istanbul)

GENERAL BACKGROUND

In 1994, Turkey was governed by a coalition
of the centre-right Dogru Yol Partisi (DYP,
True Path Party), led by Prime Minister Tansu
Çiller, and Murat Karayalçin's centre-left
Sosyal Demokrat Halkci Parti (SHP, Social
Democratic Populist Party). The conservative
Anavatan Partisi (ANAP, Motherland Party),
led by Mesut Yilmaz, was the main opposition
party although, after the municipal elections in
March, the pro-Islamic Refah Partisi (Welfare
Party) emerged as a significant political force.
During the year, Tansu Çiller's pro-Western
government pushed through legislation for fur-
ther democratization and privatization.

The country remained the scene of rising
political violence in 1994. During the year,
attacks by the separatist, Marxist-inclined PKK
(Kurdish Workers' Party), which have so far resulted in 4,000 deaths, spread from the country's south-eastern provinces, where there is a
large concentration of ethnic Kurds, to other
regions, including the major cities of Istanbul,
Izmir and Ankara. Militant Islamic groups were
also a source of violence. One notable case was
the arson attack by Islamists on a hotel in the
city of Sivas, where secular poets, writers and
intellectuals were staying, causing the deaths of
thirty-six people.

Turkey's economy deteriorated in 1994, in
spite of a package of measures announced in
April, after a 13 per cent devaluation of the
Turkish lira. The rate of growth (which was
nearly 7 per cent in 1993) was 6 per cent in 1994,
while inflation soared to an unprecedented 150
per cent, compared to 62 per cent in 1993.
Unemployment was approximately 9 per cent,
compared to 8.6 per cent in 1993. The spread of
political violence, the deterioration of the
economy and the failure to resolve these problems eroded the popularity of the governing
parties to the advantage of Refah, which conducted a disciplined and well-organized political campaign throughout the country.

HISTORICAL LEGACY

The ancestors of the present-day Turkish Jewish community came to the Ottoman Empire
after their expulsion from Spain in 1492,
although there were Jewish settlements in various parts of Anatolia under Roman and Byzan-
tine rule.

Sephardic Jews formed the bulk of the
community, which enjoyed a comfortable life
under the protection of the Ottoman administration. However, the police had to intervene to
quell outbreaks of violence against Jews which
occurred in Smyrna in 1872 and in Constanti-
nople in 1874. In 1872, a synagogue on the island of Marmara was destroyed. During this
period, Jews also became victims of blood libel
accusations. In one reported case in Constanti-
nople in 1870, Jewish merchants were forced to
open their sacks, which supposedly contained
Christian children.

After the establishment of the Turkish
republic in 1923, the constitution provided for
equal rights for Jews and other religious minorities. There has been little antisemitism since
then, except during the Second World War,
when neutral Turkey imposed discriminatory
measures against the non-Muslim minorities,
including the Jewish community.

In recent years, there have been few cases
of antisemitism, none of which emanated from
official quarters. Since the 1960s, antisemitic
articles have appeared in the Turkish press,
particularly in the pro-Islamic publications.
Turkey's first antisemitic political party
emerged in the early 1970s, known originally as
the National Salvation Party, and now called
the Welfare Party.

In September 1986, twenty-two worshippers were killed in an attack by the Abu Nidal
terrorist group on the Neve Shalom synagogue
in Istanbul. In March 1992, Neve Shalom was
again the target of a violent attack, when terrorists with links to the Turkish Hizbullah group
threw two grenades at the synagogue, injuring a
Jewish passer-by.

RACISM AND XENOPHOBIA

The 1923 Treaty of Lausanne recognizes the status of only three religious minorities—Armenians, Jews and Greeks. Official attitudes towards the Greek Orthodox and Armenian churches, however, can be affected by Turkey's political relations with Greece and Armenia.

The Alawi Muslim minority is estimated to number at least 12 million. Alawis allege informal discrimination concerning the teaching of Islam in religious instruction classes and complain of a Sunni Muslim bias in the religious affairs ministry and its tendency to view Alawis as a cultural, rather than a religious, group.

The government's campaign against the PKK has affected the treatment of the Kurdish community, which is concentrated in the south-eastern provinces and is not recognized as a national, racial or ethnic minority. The US state department's report on human rights practices in 1994 noted that, in many human rights cases, the targets of abuse were ethnic Kurds or their supporters.

PARTIES, ORGANIZATIONS, MOVEMENTS

Refah is the main political organization with antisemitic tendencies. The party, which has 40 seats in the 450-seat parliament, argues that secularism is a "foreign" concept and that Turkey should return to its Islamic roots. Therefore, Refah opposes Turkey's membership of the North Atlantic Treaty Organization (NATO) and its ambitions for membership of the European Union (EU), advocating participation in an Islamic common market instead. In the past, Necmettin Erbakan, Refah's chairman, and other leading party representatives made strongly anti-Jewish and anti-Israeli statements in parliament and to the media. However, at the start of the year, Refah played down its Islamist and antisemitic views in order to attract mass support in the March local elections. Nevertheless, in its pre-election manifesto, entitled *Adil Düzen* (Just Order), Refah advocated an Islamic economic system and reference was made to the alleged Jewish control of Wall Street and the world economy.

During the campaign, Necmettin Erbakan and other senior party members refrained from making any antisemitic, or even anti-Israeli, remarks. On the eve of the elections, Erbakan told a television interviewer that he would pursue a policy of friendship with all countries, including Israel, if he came to power. He said Israel was part of the region and that it was in Turkey's interests "to trade with Israel".

Some Refah representatives even made positive gestures towards Jews, such as in Izmir, where Dr Süleyman Akdemir, Refah's mayoral candidate, and a group of party officials visited a local synagogue and met with Jewish communal leaders. Dr Akdemir praised Jews and promised to solve any problem the Jewish community in Izmir might encounter. (In the event, Akdemir was not elected.)

In the elections, Refah scored a considerable victory, doubling its share of the vote to 18 per cent, compared with the previous local elections in 1989. It did even better, in terms of mayoral posts and local councils, in Turkey's largest cities, including Istanbul and Ankara, and in the sensitive south-eastern provinces, where there is a large concentration of ethnic Kurds.

Tayyip Erdogan, a leading figure in Refah, announced shortly after his election as the new mayor of Istanbul that "it was my ancestors who opened the doors to the Jews. All the citizens of Turkey are equal in our eyes." Erdogan welcomed Chief Rabbi David Asseo and a Jewish community delegation when they visited him in July and promised to attend to their concerns, although he said that neither he nor his party could control the antisemitic campaigns in the pro-Islamist newspapers (see **Publications and Media**).

Prime Minister Çiller's visit to Israel in October, the first such visit by a Turkish premier to the Jewish state, provoked renewed antisemitic and anti-Israeli attacks by Refah. Refah representatives took particular exception to the prime minister's favourable comments about Jews and Israel during her visit, including her reference to Israel as the "promised land". Erbakan made several statements on television accusing Israel of seeking to bring Turkey under its domain and attacking world Jewry. In one statement, he claimed that "the Holocaust was nothing but a pretext used by Zionists to seize Palestine and settle the Jews there".

Refah's electoral successes brought to the surface the tensions in Turkish society between the secularists or Kemalists (named after Kemal Atatürk, the founder of modern Turkey) and the Islamists. The results also encouraged Refah and its supporters to press for the national elections to be brought forward from 1996 in the expectation that the party would come to power. Public opinion polls carried out at the end of the year showed that Refah could win as much as 25 per cent of the vote in a national election. Although this percentage would not enable Refah to form a majority government, it would be sufficient for it to emerge as the largest single party and possibly become a coalition partner in a new government.

The Bilim Arastirma Vakfi (Foundation for Research of Knowledge), led by Adnan Oktar (also known as Adnan Hodja, a name which confers upon him the status of an Islamic religious teacher), continued to be active in 1994. This organization, which draws its support from educated and wealthy young men and women, follows a nationalistic and Islamic line (although its attitude towards Islam is very different from Refah, since most of its supporters do not adopt Muslim dress and are not regular mosque-goers). Oktar is notorious for his virulent attacks on Israel, Jews and freemasons, having published several books and magazines expressing such views (see **Publications and Media**).

The Milli Hareket Partisi (MHP, Nationalist Action Party), led by former Colonel Alparslan Türkeş, had an ultra-nationalist, pan-Turkish programme and Türkeş was known in the past as having pro-fascist tendencies. However, recently he has adopted a strongly pro-Israeli, pro-Western and pro-Jewish stance, maintaining close contacts with the Jewish community and Israeli representatives. He has repeatedly declared that it is in Turkey's regional interests to co-operate with Israel and has attended several Jewish communal events. While the MHP's leadership is not antisemitic, some question-marks remain concerning grass-roots elements in the party. Youth groups, including the ultra-nationalist Ulkücüler (Idealists), have been unhappy with attitudes of Türkeş (who they call *Basbug*, meaning *führer* or leader) and some pro-MHP publications have criticized his involvement with the Jewish community.

MANIFESTATIONS

On 5 April, seventy-five tombstones were vandalized in the Jewish cemetery of Istanbul. Coming immediately after Refah's election victory, the desecration horrified the Jewish community. Although the authorities launched an investigation, no one claimed responsibility for the attack and the perpetrators had not been found by the end of the year.

BUSINESS AND COMMERCE

In February and early March, prior to the municipal elections on 27 March, anonymous letters, calling for a boycott of Jewish firms and shops, were faxed to the Istanbul and Ankara chambers of commerce as well as to many businesses throughout Turkey. Lists of Jewish firms in Turkey accompanied some of these letters. The letters claimed that Jews were preparing to leave Turkey or to smuggle their capital to Israel and other foreign countries (the implication being that they were worried about the possibility of Refah's success in the municipal elec-

tions). The chambers of commerce were told that it was their "duty to warn all firms and shops to end dealings with the Jewish firms and collect all money owing to them before 27 March".

While this caused considerable unease among Jewish entrepreneurs, the threats had no economic impact on Jewish businesses. The mainstream press reacted angrily to the letters. The mass circulation daily *Hürriyet* reported the story under the headline "A Nazi-style fax". Another leading daily, *Sabah*, published a strongly-worded editorial against the letters, stating that this kind of racism would be counter-productive for the economy and was unfair towards the Jewish community which had always been loyal to Turkey.

Alarko, which is one of the largest construction companies in Turkey and is owned by two Jews, Izak Alaton and Uzeyir Garih, faced an anti-Jewish campaign by an Islamist daily, *Vakit*, which tried to block the contract the company had won to build the new Iranian embassy in Moscow. *Vakit* alleged that the Iranians were planning to cancel the contract after discovering that Alarko had Jewish (and "Zionist") owners. The Iranian ambassador in Ankara denied the story and Alarko completed the construction of the embassy. The pro-Islamic publications and television stations usually highlight the Jewish ownership of Alarko and other companies owned by Jews, referring to them as "Jewish firms".

PUBLICATIONS AND MEDIA

The pro-Islamic media flourished in 1994 with the launch of new publications and the establishment of privately-owned radio and television stations, following the ending of the state monopoly on electronic media in 1992. Their circulations and ratings have been rising, while the circulations of the mainstream, secular newspapers and magazines have been falling. The dailies—*Türkiye*, *Zaman*, *Milli Gazete* and *Vakit*—frequently publish anti-Israeli, and sometimes antisemitic, articles. Three pro-Islamic television channels—TGRT, Samanyolu and Kanal-7—have followed suit.

During the year, the pro-Islamic media published a number of attacks on Israel combining antisemitic undertones (see **Effects of anti-Zionism**). There was also a marked increase in the number of negative articles about Turkish Jews, as well as Jews in general.

Zaman, which is considered the most moderate of the pro-Islamic publications, occasionally featured attacks on Turkish Jews, including entrepreneurs Jak Kamhi and Izak Alaton. For instance, when Professor Yuda Yurum, a Jewish university professor in Ankara, was awarded the annual chemistry award for his research, *Zaman* claimed that Albert Bilen, the chair of the association of chemical industries and an active member of the Jewish community, was instrumental in giving this award to another Jew. *Zaman* also attacked Yusuf Azuz, a Jewish model, for "immoral" behaviour, stressing his Jewishness. Similar attacks were made repeatedly against Nedim Saban, a producer of a popular television chat show, for his programmes on various subjects, including sex, women's rights and secularism, again emphasizing his Jewishness.

In 1994, anti-Israeli and anti-Jewish remarks started to appear in the pro-Kurdish press for the first time. In August, *Ozgur Ulke*, a Kurdish nationalist paper which opposes the government's campaign against the PKK, ran a series of anti-Jewish articles. The articles alleged that the Turkish government was acting in concert with "Jewish imperialists" (used interchangeably with "Zionist imperialists") and freemasons in Turkey's "special war" against the Kurds (the paper uses the term "special war" when referring to the campaign against the PKK). It also referred to a "holy alliance" between "Turkish politicians and Zionists". A. Inanc, the author of these articles, further claimed that it was a known "fact" that President Süleyman Demirel was a former freemason and therefore took orders from the "masonic organization" which the Jews "control".

The publication of antisemitic notions in a Kurdish newspaper, which had not previously shown hostility towards Jews or Israel, was of some concern to Turkey's Jews. The change in attitude was attributed to statements made by Israeli politicians and officials (including President Weizman) who, when visiting Turkey, condemned the PKK's activities and promised to help the Turkish government with security and intelligence in its campaign against PKK terrorism. An agreement to facilitate the exchange of information and co-operation in this regard was signed during the prime minister's visit to Israel in October, provoking anger in Turkey's Kurdish nationalist circles.

In 1994, Adnan Oktar of the Bilim Arastirma Vakfi launched a newsletter called *Siyasi Çizgi* (Political Line) and claimed to have sent over 11,000 copies to senior figures in the establishment. This newsletter appeared irregularly throughout the year and featured slanderous attacks on various (non-Jewish) individuals, such as journalists, artists and entrepreneurs. In December, a three-page edition of *Siyasi Çizgi* was devoted to the prime minis-

ter's visit to Israel and claimed that Jews and freemasons had, with the help of Mossad, established contacts with the entrepreneurs and officials in the large delegation accompanying Tansu Çiller. *Siyasi Çizgi* alleged that some of the Jews amongst the delegation were intent on strengthening the "Zionist-masonic" lobby in Turkey in order to counter Muslim anti-Zionist activities and to try to influence public opinion against Muslims.

RELIGION

On several occasions, imams in mosques used the terms "Jew" or "Jewish" when denouncing Israeli actions against Palestinian Muslims. The Jewish community reported such statements but the authorities did not act on its objections. In December, Ali Bozkurt, one of the imams at the Fatih mosque in Istanbul, called for the annihilation of "the Jewish nation, the Israeli government, the Greeks, the Armenians, the Bulgarians, the terrorists, the anarchists, the communists and all our secret enemies". Bozkurt's sermon was part of a service commemorating the ascent of the Prophet Muhammad to heaven, which was televised by the commercial Channel 6. In another speech during the same service, Professor Ihsan S. Sirma, a theologian, attacked journalists and the secular press. While the newspapers and press associations protested Professor Sirma's words, there was no mention of Ali Bozkurt's curse on the Jewish nation. The Jewish community reported the incident to the authorities and demanded that they take some action, since imams are appointed by the department of religious affairs, which is attached to the prime minister's office.

EFFECTS OF ANTI-ZIONISM

During the year, after Friday prayer services, young, mostly Islamist, protesters frequently marched in the streets waving green flags with inscriptions calling for *Sharia* (Islamic law), despite such actions constituting a legal offence. While such demonstrations may have been prompted by a domestic event, such as opposition to a proposed anti-terrorism law, or by a foreign issue, such as solidarity with Bosnian Muslims or opposition to the United Nations (UN) and the West, they usually resulted in the chanting of slogans against Israel and Jews and the burning of Israeli flags. Similar demonstrations were also sparked off by the massacre of Muslims by a Jewish settler in a Hebron mosque in February.

In March, the Islamic Avengers of the Great East, a previously unknown organization, distributed leaflets calling on Muslims in

Turkey to kill Jews in retaliation for the Hebron massacre. It also provided a list of prominent Jews to target, promising to pay DM500 for every Jew murdered. The authorities launched an investigation into the incident, and strict security measures were introduced in synagogues and other Jewish communal institutions.

On a number of occasions, particularly surrounding Tansu Çiller's visit to Israel in October, the pro-Islamic media ran stories implying Israeli ambitions for global or regional domination and also drew analogies between Turkish Jews and the actions of the Israeli government. For example, Abdullah Altay, a commentator for *Milli Gazete*, alleged that Israel was seeking to establish a "Greater Israel" which would include parts of Turkey. Regarding the proposed co-operation over water between the two countries, he claimed that Israel's interest in Turkey's water was part of this expansionist policy to subjugate Turkey. On the water issue, *Vakit* referred to a Jewish conspiracy in which, it claimed, Alarko was involved (see also **Business and Commerce**). *Vakit* attacked a group of Jews who purchased some land in an Istanbul suburb to build villas, claiming that they intended to construct a Jewish settlement to which non-Jews would not be admitted. It also claimed that the Jews in that area were destroying the trees and polluting the environment, and that they were "applying exactly the same methods of acquiring land as the Jewish settlers did in Palestine".

LEGAL MATTERS

In November, Can Ozbilen, Osman Erdemir and Ali Riza Bayramçavus were sentenced to fifteen years' imprisonment by the state security court in Istanbul for the attempted murder of Jewish entrepreneur Jak Kamhi in January 1993. The prosecutor had sought death sentences, but only one of the three judges agreed, arguing that the assassination attempt should be considered a challenge to Turkey's secular constitution. The three men were members of a radical Islamist organization called the Islamic Action Period, which was found to have connections with Iran.

COUNTERING ANTISEMITISM

Turkish officials took a number of opportunities during the year to praise the Jewish community and condemn antisemitism. Tansu Çiller's October visit to Israel highlighted the friendship not only between the two countries but also between Jews and Turks. The prime minister visited Bat-Yam near Tel Aviv, where many emigrants from Turkey live and, at a dinner that evening, praised Turkish Jews for their

services and loyalty to the country, highlighting as an example the attachment displayed by the Israelis of Turkish descent to their native land. This was widely reported in the mainstream Turkish media and was hailed in editorial comments.

Earlier in the year, during Israeli President Ezer Weizman's January visit to Ankara, President Süleyman Demirel also praised Turkey's Jews and said that Turkish Jews in Turkey and in Israel were becoming a natural bridge between the two countries. He also recalled that Turkey, which has had a Jewish community for the last five centuries, had always displayed affection to the Jews and was one of the few countries in the world where antisemitism and ethnic oppression has not existed.

In December, Hayri Kozakçioglu, the governor of Istanbul, took the opportunity to make similar favourable comments at a reception held to celebrate the centenary of the Maccabi.

In March, Turkey sponsored the resolution passed by the UN Human Rights Commission in Geneva, condemning antisemitism, racism and xenophobia—the first explicit resolution against antisemitism by a UN body for some decades. Turkey worked closely with the US to have the fifty-three-nation body adopt this document after several Western countries refused to act as sponsor. When the resolution was adopted, a Turkish government spokesman welcomed the "acceptance of the draft we have worked on".

Antisemitic remarks made by pro-Islamists either in speeches or publications in many cases provoked sharp reactions from some newspapers. Columnist Hadi Uluengin in *Hürriyet* and Güngor Mengi in *Sabah* reacted strongly against such attacks on Jews as well as the sending of the letters to Turkish entrepreneurs calling for a boycott of Jewish businesses. "We are hand in glove with the Jews", noted Uluengin, "antisemitism goes against our traditions. To provoke such feelings is sheer racism and is contrary to our national interests." Mengi wrote, "antisemitism is not compatible with Turkey's policy, nor with Islam. Our Jews are part of this nation. They are loyal and useful citizens of Turkey. No one has the right to provoke the masses against them."

In contrast to the antisemitic content of programmes broadcast on the pro-Islamic television channels, the main commercial channels screened a number of pro-Jewish programmes. For instance, the channel HBB broadcast a half-hour programme presenting the Jewish community, past and present, in a favourable light and the English-language *Turkish Daily News* devoted a full page in its features section to the Jews of Turkey.

ASSESSMENT

The increased number of antisemitic publications and media outlets, together with the growing popularity of the pro-Islamic Refah Partisi, continued to be a source of concern for Turkish Jews during 1994. Following Refah's success in the March municipal elections, the possibility, indicated by opinion polls, that it could emerge as the largest single party in a national election was a worrying prospect for many Jews, who fear for their future under a pro-Islamist regime.

Ukraine

General population: 52.2 million
Jewish population: 446,000 (mainly in Kiev,
Lvov and Kharkov)

GENERAL BACKGROUND

The parliamentary elections in March-April resulted in a legislature dominated by communists and independent candidates. The results
also confirmed a political split between western
Ukraine, which favoured moderate nationalist
candidates, and the more populous eastern
Ukraine, which supported pro-Russian candidates of the left. In July, following his unexpected victory in a run-off election, Leonid
Kuchma, who had campaigned on a platform of
gradual economic reform and closer links with
Russia, was sworn in as president.

There was continuing tension between
Ukraine and Russia over the Black Sea fleet,
based mainly in the Crimean port of Sevastopol.

The economy of this former Soviet republic remains dependent on state-owned industry
and state and collectivized agriculture. Little
privatization has occurred. There has been a
serious decline in gross domestic product, a
high level of hidden unemployment and
hyperinflation.

HISTORICAL LEGACY

Jews have inhabited the territory known as
Ukraine for almost 1,000 years. Intolerance towards the Jewish population in this area is
traceable to the establishment of the early Russian church. During the period of Polish-
Lithuanian rule Jews, used by the nobility as
lessees of their estates and collectors of taxes
levied on the peasantry, were regarded by
the impoverished masses as allies of their
oppressors.

In 1648 thousands of Jews were massacred
in an uprising led by Bohdan Khmelnitsky
against the Polish-Lithuanian overlords.

In the eighteenth and nineteenth centuries,
when the territory had become part of the tsarist Russian empire, attacks on Jews by groups of
peasants known as Haidamaki were more limited in scope than the 1648 massacre but in some
respects more vicious. The perpetrators of these
massacres were regarded by the Ukrainians as
national heroes and this gave rise to a popular
tradition of antisemitism in which the Jews
were identified with aliens and the hated Mus-
covite government.

In the civil war that followed the Bolshevik
Revolution, Jews were widely regarded as allies
of the Bolsheviks. Thousands of Jews were
murdered in pogroms.

By 1939 the Jewish population of Ukraine
totaled over 1.5 million.

Ukrainian nationalist forces welcomed the
Nazi invaders of the former Soviet Union (see
Russia) as liberators and joined them, forming
the Galician SS divisions. Many Ukrainians actively participated in the rounding up and murder of Ukrainian Jews.

The publication in 1963 of the book
Iudaizm bez prikras (Judaism without Embellishment) by Trofim Kichko, an anti-Zionist
work which contained Nazi-style anti-Jewish
caricatures, was met by a world-wide storm of
protest leading to the Soviet authorities' with-
drawing it from circulation.

RACISM AND XENOPHOBIA

There were only isolated instances of ethnic
discrimination in Ukraine. Contrary to the
situation in 1993, there were no known instances of anti-Roma violence in 1994.

PARTIES, ORGANIZATIONS, MOVEMENTS

Four far-right parties contested the March-
April parliamentary elections—the Derzhavna
samostiinist Ukrainy (DSU, State Independence of Ukraine), the Ukrainska natsionalna
konservativna partiya (UNKP, Ukrainian
National Conservative Party), the Ukrainska
konservativna respublikanska partiya (UKRP,
Ukrainian Conservative Republican Party) and
the Ukrainska natsionalna asambleya and its
paramilitary wing, the Ukrainska samo-
oborona (UNA-UNSO, Ukrainian National
Assembly-Ukrainian Self-Defence).

Yury Tima, an UNSO candidate, won a seat in Ternopol. In Lviv, the focus of far-right campaigning, two UNSO candidates, Oleh Vitovich and Yaroslav Illiasevich, joined Stepan Khmara, the antisemitic demagogue representing the UKRP. Ten further UNSO candidates, including four in Kiev, failed to win seats but polled sufficient votes to take them to the run-off stage of the election. A total of 394 seats were filled.

Among the over 100 parties which failed to qualify for registration were a number of ultra-nationalist bodies, notably the Organizatsya idealistiv Ukrainy (OIU, Organization of Ukrainian Idealists), which regularly attracted large audiences at meetings in Lviv's Independence Square where it displayed anti-Jewish banners.

MANIFESTATIONS

On 5 February shots were fired from a hunting rifle through the window of the Israeli Centre in Kiev causing damage to property.

In March antisemitic leaflets were distributed in Odessa during the parliamentary election campaign. Also in March antisemitic slogans were painted on the walls of the university building in Kharkov.

In April, following threatening phone calls to Solomon Gulkin, the head of the city's Jewish religious association, the synagogue in Kremenchug was burned down. The authorities launched a fruitless investigation.

On 10 April Jewish gravestones were broken or defaced in the cemetery in Tulchin, in the Vinnitsa region.

On 23 April the door of the home of Rabbi Shmuel Kamensky in Dnepropetrosk was defaced.

In June in Dnepropetrovsk a swastika was daubed on a wall of the Israeli Centre and leaders of the local Jewish community received threatening letters.

In July windows of the building housing the Israeli Centre in Dnepropetrovsk were broken.

In August leaflets distributed in Odessa by a group known as Slavic Alliance claimed that Jewish members of parliament were pressing for privatization of public property and acquiring the property for themselves. The Jewish organization Memorial reported that organization's activities to the local procurator.

On 17 August anti-Russian and antisemitic leaflets were found in the centre of Lviv.

In September the election of Eduard Gurvits as mayor of Odessa was accompanied by an antisemitic campaign.

On 30 October the Israeli Centre in Kiev received an anonymous phone call threatening Ukrainian Jews.

On 31 October antisemitic slogans appeared in Kiev's Independence Square.

On 14 November a Jewish student and a representative of the Jewish Agency in Dnepropetrovsk were attacked by five men who shouted antisemitic slogans.

PUBLICATIONS AND MEDIA

Antisemitic material continued to appear regularly in the far-right press.

A recurrent theme of this material was that the Bolshevik punishment gangs sent by Stalin to Ukraine in the 1930s and responsible for mass atrocities against the population were led mainly by Jews. In a television broadcast in January the far-right activist Ivan Kandyba claimed that in Kiev alone 300 Ukrainian intellectuals had been slaughtered by Bolshevik gangsters under the leadership of the Jew, Isaak Shvarts.

On 23 October the US television programme *60 Minutes*, broadcast on Ukrainian television, showed Ukraine's chief rabbi, Yaakov Bleich, citing a newspaper article calling for the destruction of the Jews if they did not leave forthwith, reporting that his home had been set on fire, and claiming that Jews had been murdered. In a subsequent statement Rabbi Bleich said that his remarks had been taken out of context and he stressed that Ukraine had an excellent record on human rights. The US television programme also reported a meeting in Lviv's council building of Ukrainians who had served in the SS and claimed that the meeting had the blessing of Catholic Cardinal Lubchinsky, who denied that the Ukrainian policemen had murdered Jews. The programme provoked a number of antisemitic articles in the ultra-nationalist press.

Oleksey Boyko wrote in *Neskorena natsiya* in November: "It is difficult to find a people who have done Ukraine more harm than the Kikes. Before their crimes, all the misdemeanours of Moscow, Warsaw and Berlin combined pale into insignificance."

Jewish business-owners and elected officials were vilified as criminals. For example, in August *Neskorena natsiya* wrote: "For generations Vinnitsa was a Ukrainian town. Now we are ruled by the Dvorkises ... and the Hurvitses [the mayors of Vinnitsa and Odessa respectively]. ... For them a motherland is a place to grab dollars and steal with impunity."

Articles denying that the Holocaust happened appeared in some newspapers. *Za vilnu Ukrainu* called on its readers in a June issue: "Help us prove once and for all that the 50,000 [Jews] destroyed by Ukrainians in the capital of

Galitsia is a total myth."

Calls for retribution and the removal of Jews from the media and positions of authority in Ukraine appeared regularly in the extremist press, particularly during the run-up to the March-April parliamentary elections.

In an analysis of the western Ukrainian press in 1994 a Ukrainian Jewish journalist found that nineteen papers had carried "blatant" or "implied" antisemitic material; the journalist defined "implied" antisemitic material as the use of negative synonyms for the Jews such as "transnational forces", "Christ-sellers" and "prophets of the market economy". He listed *Za vilnu Ukrainu, Golos natsii* and *Neskorena natsiya* as the worst offenders.

The other newspapers which published "implied" or "blatant" antisemitic articles during 1994 were: *Prosvita, Poklik Sumliniya, Shlyakh peremogi, Ratusha, Post-Postup, Zemlya i volya, Lvivsky noviny, Molodaya Galichina, Osnova, Zakhidna Ukraina, Frankova Krinitsa, Visoky zamok, Derzhavnist, Viche, Sotsial natsionalist, Zorya galitska.*

In June, in a reference to the Donetsk monthly *Vitchizna otechestva* (reported circulation 10,000), the first issue of which carried an article entitled "Kike conspiracy against Ukraine", the Moscow-based mainstream newspaper *Novaya ezhednevnaya gazeta* reported: "The antisemites of Donbass finally have their own newspaper." One of the contributors to *Vitchizna otechestva* was the anti-Jewish activist Anatoly Shcherbatiuk.

OPINION POLLS

See **Russia.**

COUNTERING ANTISEMITISM

On 13 July Ukrainian nationalities minister Mykola Shulha was reported as stating that his ministry's "main task" was "to create an efficient legal mechanism to protect ethnic minorities" .

In August Aleksandr Moroz, chairman of the Ukrainian parliament, attacked papers which condoned antisemitism and condemned Ukrainians who had aided the Nazi occupiers.

On 19 November, on a visit to the Holocaust Museum in Washington DC, President Kuchma repeated the condemnation by his predecessor Leonid Kravchuk of Ukrainians who had committed war crimes as well as the latter's assurances that Jews were free to leave Ukraine or to remain and develop their own religious and cultural institutions.

Prominent journalists, authors and intellectuals made statements condemning antisemitism.

ASSESSMENT

There has been over the last two or three years a perceptible growth in Ukrainian ultra-nationalist activities. At the present time, these activities remain on the fringe of Ukrainian politics and do not present a threat to Ukrainian democracy or the Jewish population. The degree of political polarization, revealed starkly by the March-April parliamentary election results, between the western and eastern regions of the country, together with an unstable economic situation, was not, however, reassuring.

United Kingdom

General population: 57.2 million
Jewish population: 300,000 (two-thirds in London; other main centres: Manchester, Leeds, Glasgow)

GENERAL BACKGROUND

The popularity of Prime Minister John Major's Conservative government waned to a point unprecedented for any post-war government, as it faced repeated scandals affecting senior politicians, continuing internal opposition to closer European political and economic union, and a loss of confidence.

The election of Tony Blair as leader of the main opposition Labour Party, following the sudden death of its former leader John Smith, and his attempts to portray his party as the next government-in-waiting, also affected the Conservatives' standing.

The government's unpopularity was reflected in its widespread losses in the May municipal elections, when the Conservatives lost control of 18 city councils and gained just 1, losing 429 seats overall. These losses were repeated in the elections to the European Parliament in June, when the number of Conservative MEPs was reduced from 32 to 18, out of a total of 87.

The fragile economic recovery recorded last year continued in 1994, with gross domestic product up by 4.2 per cent at the end of the third quarter of the year and the balance of payments current account in surplus for the first time since the early 1980s. Unemployment continued its slow downward trend, falling to 8.8 per cent of the work force, compared to 9.8 per cent the previous year. Business failures declined by 16.3 per cent, the biggest reduction since 1988, although they fuelled a continuing economic pessimism, as did the rise in inflation from 1.9 per cent in 1993 to 2.6 per cent for the twelve months to the end of November.

HISTORICAL LEGACY

Individual Jews were present in the British Isles in Roman times but organized settlement began after the Norman conquest of 1066.

Massacres of Jews occurred in many cities in 1190, most notably in York. The medieval settlement of Jews came to an end with their expulsion by King Edward I in 1290. After that date, only a few converts to Christianity or secret adherents to Judaism remained. Following the expulsion of the Jews from Spain in 1492, a

covert Jewish community became established in London, but the present community dates from 1656.

During the following three centuries, there were few serious outbreaks of antisemitic violence. By the early nineteenth century, Jews had achieved virtual economic and social emancipation. In the next eighty years, all barriers to political emancipation were removed.

The influx of Jewish refugees from Russia between 1881 and 1914 (when the British Jewish community grew from 60,000 to 300,000) led to antisemitic agitation on the streets and in parliament, although these activities were less organized than in France or Germany.

The rise of fascism and Nazism encouraged the growth in Britain of the British Union of Fascists and National Socialists, and the Imperial Fascist League. Antisemitic rallies and marches in the mid-1930s led to street battles between right-wingers on the one hand, and Jews and left-wingers on the other. At no time was there any likelihood of far-right electoral success. The government, while sometimes unsympathetic to those who resisted antisemitism, was ultimately concerned with the threat to public order and Britain's legislation banning overt paramilitary activity dates from this time.

Sir Oswald Mosley, the leader of the British Union of Fascists and National Socialists, was interned during the Second World War, together with other fascist and Nazi sympathizers, but despite protests was released in 1943.

In the post-war years, Jews were faced with attempts by antisemitic groups to re-establish themselves. In the 1960s, a younger generation of neo-Nazis agitated against the Jewish community. While there were several arson attacks on synagogues and physical assaults on Jews,

anti-fascist disclosures prompted the authorities to take action (if somewhat belatedly),
and several leading neo-Nazi activists were
imprisoned.

During the late 1970s and early 1980s, the
forerunners of the groups now active achieved
their widest support, but they were ultimately
undermined by the changing political climate
and their own internal divisions.

RACISM AND XENOPHOBIA

According to the 1991 census (the first to include a question on ethnic origin), non-white
ethnic minority groups constituted 5.5 per cent
(approximately 3 million people) of the population of Great Britain (that is, excluding Northern Ireland) and 20.2 per cent of the Greater
London area. Some 2.6 per cent identified
themselves as "South Asian" (of Indian, Paki-
stani and Bangladeshi origin); 1.6 per cent identified themselves as "black" (of African,
Caribbean and other origin); and people of Chinese origin constituted 0.3 per cent of the remainder. Members of the Irish, Greek and
Turkish communities were included in the
"white" category.

Although British laws prohibit discrimination on the basis of race, colour, nationality or
national or ethnic origin, and outlaws incitement to racial hatred, studies have found that
various minority groups, and members of the
black and Asian communities in particular, continue to suffer levels of inequality and disadvantage in differing degrees in the areas of
employment, education, housing, health and
criminal justice. Despite the evidence of such
discrimination, it is less overt than it was prior
to the introduction of legislation to counter it,
and of more pressing concern is the rise in
racially-motivated crime.

According to government and police
sources, available statistics of recorded racist
crimes do not present an accurate picture as the
majority of such crimes are not reported. The
police recorded 9,762 racial incidents between
April 1993 and April 1994, a 25 per cent increase over the previous twelve months, with
approximately 40 per cent occurring in the
Greater London area.

The British Crime Survey indicates that
racially-motivated crime has increased substantially although, as a proportion of all other
crimes, it only began to grow after 1992. The
survey also estimates an under-reporting rate of
one in ten. The home office (Britain's interior
ministry) analysis of the survey estimated that
there were approximately 130,000 racially-
inspired criminal incidents in 1994, double the
1992 figure.

Rising public concern over the issue was
addressed by the House of Commons home
affairs select committee, which began an investigation into racial attacks and harassment in
1993. The committee's report, published in May
1994, recognized that the problem of racial attacks and harassment was growing but, because
of the deficiencies in the collection of statistics,
recommended that the government improve its
performance in this area by commissioning a
specific and regular survey of racist crimes.
Among its many other recommendations, it
urged the police to establish racial incident
units to monitor and investigate such incidents.
These recommendations were accepted by the
home office, although many other recommendations were rejected (see also **Legal Matters**).

The government makes provision for political refugees but passed legislation in 1993 to
speed the processing of unsubstantiated requests after an exponential rise in the number of
asylum applications. Human rights groups have
claimed that the new legislation undermines the
UK's commitment to provide a haven for legitimate refugees. In 1994, there were 32,830 applications for asylum, compared to 22,370 in 1993;
825 applications were granted (1,590 in 1993)
and 3,660 applicants were given exceptional
leave to remain (11,125 in 1993).

In October, two reports were published
which criticized the detention of large numbers
of asylum-seekers for long periods without
proper explanation or opportunity to challenge
the decision. Amnesty International carried out
a study of fifty asylum cases. In the other report, the Medical Foundation for the Care of
Victims of Torture found that asylum-seekers
who had experienced torture in their own
countries were being detained in the UK for
periods ranging from two to seventeen months.
It was reported that the number of asylum-
seekers held in British prisons and immigration
detention centres had doubled over the previous eighteen months to more than 600. Amnesty claimed that "in most cases detention is
neither necessary nor for reasons recognized as
legitimate under international standards".

PARTIES, ORGANIZATIONS, MOVEMENTS

Antisemitism is central to the ideology of most
far-right groups, including the British National
Party (BNP), Combat 18 (C18), Blood and
Honour (B&H) and the International Third
Position.

Islamist groups (generally known as Islamic fundamentalists) also regularly display a
hatred of Jews of a kind which goes well beyond political anti-Zionism or anti-Israel activity, and which must legitimately be described as

antisemitism (see **Religion**). Much of this antisemitism employs typical European antisemitic motifs, including Holocaust denial and racial stereotyping.

Antisemitism from other sources, including the far left, the establishment and the churches, is limited and declining.

The British National Party is Britain's largest far-right movement, whose position was consolidated by its unique council by-election victory in Millwall, east London, in September 1993. However, by the end of 1994, the BNP was apparently losing members to the National Socialist Alliance (see below) and its membership is now estimated at around 800.

Although it lost its sole council seat in the May 1994 local elections, the BNP polled substantially more votes around the country in that election then it had ever achieved previously. Twenty-nine candidates were fielded (against 11 in 1990, and 6 in 1986); each won an average of 603 votes (7.86 per cent of the total poll) in those seats which it contested (2.29 per cent in 1990, and 1.96 per cent in 1986 respectively). In the Beckton ward of the east London borough of Newham, two BNP candidates achieved 16.49 per cent and 16.42 per cent respectively. In two local by-elections in Tower Hamlets, east London, later in the year, the BNP polled 12.3 per cent and 19.5 per cent. In a parliamentary by-election in June in Dagenham, east London, John Tyndall, the BNP leader, polled 1,511 votes, 7 per cent of the total, only 300 votes behind the Liberal Democrat candidate, and the first time a BNP candidate had retained his deposit in a parliamentary election.

While the fact that the BNP lost Millwall is in itself important, the scale of support for the BNP throughout the swathe of London's East End, which borders the River Thames, is of longer-term significance. It is now the main opposition party to Labour in a number of wards and, if it is able to sustain its momentum, may pose an increasingly difficult electoral challenge throughout the area. Most BNP voters do not share the more radical and neo-Nazi aspects of BNP ideology, including Jewish conspiracy theories and Holocaust denial. However, many who vote for the BNP do genuinely feel that they have been abandoned by the mainstream political parties.

BNP ideology is a crude mix of national socialism and British nationalism. It is fundamentally antisemitic and makes regular thinly-veiled accusations of Jewish/Zionist conspiracies to destroy the "white race". It also disseminates a considerable amount of Holocaust-denial propaganda.

After winning its council seat in September

1993, the BNP changed its tactics. Where previously the party was dedicated to provocative and publicity-seeking street demonstrations and marches, it now attempts to appear as a normal, respectable political party. This has led to internal dissent, and a number of BNP street activists have sought to follow the more radical, violent and overtly neo-Nazi approach of Combat 18.

The BNP leadership's conflict with Combat 18 intensified during the autumn following demands that C18 activists be expelled from BNP branches. However, a number of BNP branches remain dominated by C18 and some BNP leaders have been brutally assaulted by their C18 rivals. This internecine conflict has helped prevent the BNP from fully capitalizing on widespread voter dissatisfaction in London and other regions.

Combat 18 (a numerical representation of Adolf Hitler's initials) evolved in 1991 as a stewarding body for far-right, primarily BNP, events. Initially, it worked in co-operation with the BNP, and was composed mainly of hardened BNP street activists. Other members were recruited from the Blood and Honour skinhead movement and various football hooligan gangs. The group's influence on the far right is now significant. C18's leadership was (and remains) drawn mainly from former British Movement activists, several of whom have extensive links with Ulster Loyalist terrorists and violent North American and European neo-Nazis. It is also reputed to be involved in criminal conspiracies, particularly drug smuggling.

During 1994, C18 spawned a political wing, the National Socialist Alliance (NSA), which has become an umbrella movement for British neo-Nazis. Unlike the BNP, the NSA is overtly neo-Nazi and is modelled on the American racist group, the National Alliance (see **United States**). By the end of the year, some estimated the combined membership of C18 and the NSA to be over 1,000, higher than that of the BNP.

C18's commitment to violence and harassment continued in 1994, encouraged by the lack of police action against the group. In December 1993, C18 published the first issue of a glossy magazine entitled *Combat 18*. This was perhaps the most violent, racist and antisemitic publication published in Britain for many years. By January 1995, C18 had published the next issue of *Combat 18*, misleadingly numbered "issue 3". This included bomb-making instructions and was even more offensive than the previous publication. Police raids on two C18 leaders followed, and the magazine's publishers currently are being considered for prosecution.

The Blood and Honour movement is an umbrella organization of bands, supporting and supported by young racist skinheads. B&H developed in Britain during the 1970s and 1980s and is highly regarded by its counterparts elsewhere in Europe and in North America. B&H's importance to the far right is its use as a recruiting ground for other organizations and a source of funding raised by music and merchandising sales.

Since the death of its inspirational leader, Ian Stuart Donaldson, in September 1993, B&H has become increasingly dominated by the C18 leadership, which now controls much of its activities and finances. Donaldson handed control of the organization to C18 in June 1993 before his death. C18's domination of B&H has led to internal disputes between some senior B&H activists and the C18 leadership, which has largely served to limit the scope of B&H's concerts in 1994. The anniversary of Donaldson's death may become the focus for annual international skinhead gatherings in years to come.

The National Front (NF), led by Ian Anderson, currently has no more than 200 active members. It is now reduced in size and activity, having lost members to the more active BNP. However, it continued to publish its journals regularly and to field candidates in local and national elections.

In the May local elections, the NF candidate in Dudley, West Midlands, polled 10.3 per cent of the vote, and two candidates in Sandwell, Birmingham, received over 9 per cent each. The NF fielded five candidates in the European elections in June, winning less than 1 per cent of the vote in those constituencies.

Former NF members were believed to be responsible for the widespread distribution of antisemitic letters, some of them sophisticated hoaxes, which continue to bedevil the Jewish community.

The British Movement continued some independent activity but many of its members were also active in either C18/NSA, B&H or the BNP. There was some activity in the UK by supporters of the North American-based white-supremacist groups, Ku Klux Klan and Church of the Creator, but again, for the most part, activists are also members of other groups, such as the BNP or C18 (see **Canada** and **United States**). During the course of the year, the British far right's links with similar groups abroad, particularly in France, Scandinavia and the US, were further strengthened by mutual visits and the distribution of literature. Claude Cornilleau, leader of the French neo-Nazi Parti nationaliste français et européen (PNFE, French and European Nationalist Party), has

spoken at the past three BNP annual rallies (see **France**). C18's magazine, *The Order,* endorsed the campaign to free Gottfried Küssel, the Austrian neo-Nazi imprisoned in December 1993, and Vitt Ariskt Motstånd (VAM, White Aryan Resistance), the Swedish neo-Nazi group, has been linked to C18 (see **Austria** and **Sweden**).

The International Third Position and Third Way both contain no more than a few dozen members, but their continuing links with violent third-positionist groups abroad, as well as with Islamists, make them a potential threat to Jews. Five Third Way candidates stood in the May local election, winning 782 votes in Havering, west London. A Third Way candidate in the East London Euro-constituency in the June European elections attracted 3,484 votes, just over 2 per cent of the poll.

The Revolutionary Conservative Caucus (RCC), run by Stuart Millson and Jonathan Bowden, both former BNP members, aims to infiltrate the Conservative Party with far-right activists. In February 1994, the infiltration of the Mistley branch of Colchester Conservative Association by a group including Bowden and Millson was exposed. The branch chair at the time, David Moon, was a former member of the NF.

The Nation of Islam (NOI), the US-based Afrocentrist organization, is represented in Britain by the so-called People's Trust (PT). NOI activists regularly sell literature, videos, and cassettes at London markets and underground stations in Brixton, Tottenham and Shepherds Bush, all of which have large Afro-Caribbean populations. NOI is profoundly antisemitic and its British activists follow the antisemitic lead given by their American counterparts (see **United States**).

The NOI/PT organized a public meeting to celebrate the birthday of the late founder of the NOI, Elijah Muhammad, at London's Wembley Conference Centre in October 1994, to be addressed via satellite by NOI leader Louis Farrakhan, who was banned from entering Britain in 1986. Wembley cancelled the event, which eventually took place at a London night-club, where speakers made viciously antisemitic statements. NOI official Derek Hunt declared, for example, that "Jews are the most powerful financial force on the planet". Minister Wayne X, Farrakhan's UK representative, added that "Jews were involved in the slave trade and we therefore must warn other people about the snake that has bitten us".

MAINSTREAM POLITICS

Antisemitism rarely surfaces in mainstream political life. Stories occasionally circulate about antisemitic attitudes expressed in higher political circles but none achieved any prominence in 1994. When such incidents do get reported, they tend to demonstrate residual antisemitic sentiment rather than anything more wide-spread and influential.

The scale of success achieved by the BNP in east London has influenced some local branches of mainstream parties to echo the par-ty's message, which legitimizes the BNP and re-inforces its propaganda. This effect was most visible in the Newham wards of Beckton and Custom House in Silvertown, where the New-ham South Conservative Party campaigned as "Conservatives against Labour's unfair ethnic policies".

MANIFESTATIONS

The Board of Deputies of British Jews (BoD) reported that there were 327 reported antise-mitic incidents during 1994 (328 in 1993).

As in previous years, abusive behaviour constituted the largest category, with 44.3 per cent of the total (38.1 per cent in 1993). This cat-egory regularly provides the highest number of incidents, but it is likely that only a very small proportion are actually reported.

Verbal or written threats directed against Jewish individuals, organizations or properties, constituted 15.6 per cent of the total (11.3 per cent in 1993). Threats are often directly fuelled by national or international events; there were six hoax bomb threats made against Jewish buildings in the week following the car bomb attacks in London in July (see below and **Effects of anti-Zionism**). The most common type of threat is by telephone, sometimes in the form of a message left on an answering machine. Threats of violence are seldom, if ever, carried out.

Unsolicited mailings of antisemitic litera-ture, to Jews and non-Jews, individuals and or-ganizations, constituted 13.2 per cent of the total (16 per cent in 1993). Mass mailings of a particular leaflet are recorded as a single inci-dent and, during 1994, there were forty-three different examples of antisemitic literature re-ceived by members of the Jewish community.

Damage and desecration of communal property constituted 12.8 per cent of the total (23.3 per cent in 1993). Many of these incidents, particularly those against synagogues—the most common target—took place in the after-math of the massacre of Muslims by a Jewish settler at a Hebron mosque in February, dem-onstrating the link between world events and domestic antisemitism (see also **Effects of anti-Zionism**). The most worrying of these "revenge attacks" involved two petrol bombs, which were thrown at the synagogue in Luton. Seven

Jewish cemeteries were desecrated during 1994: in East Ham (London), Grimsby, Southport, Hull, Birmingham, north London and Southend.

Physical assaults against members of the Jewish community constituted 12.2 per cent of the total (11.6 per cent in 1993), the majority of them against Jewish school children in north-west London. A growing number of assaults were also perpetrated against members of the strictly Orthodox community in Gateshead, north-east England.

Extreme violence, defined as a potentially life-threatening attack, constituted 1.8 per cent of the total, the first time since 1991 that any incidents of extreme violence have been re-corded. They included two car bombs in Lon-don, at the Israeli embassy and the offices of the Joint Israel Appeal (JIA), a petrol bomb attack on the home of a rabbi and an explosive device planted at a Jewish butchers in north-east Lon-don (see **Effects of Anti-Zionism**).

GRASSROOTS

There has been organized far-right activity amongst British football hooligan gangs since the late 1970s. The typical football hooligan, a young, white male with a taste for violence, is an obvious potential recruit for the far right. This was first recognized by the NF, whose concerted effort to recruit football fans led ulti-mately to the BNP's involvement in the Heysel stadium disaster in the Netherlands in 1985. Neo-Nazi influence amongst football gangs is now firmly established and is in evidence amongst the supporters of certain football clubs, and particularly amongst the hooligans who follow England's national team.

The nominal leader of C18, Charlie Sargent, is a leading member of the Chelsea Headhunter hooligan gang, and many other members of C18 are also football hooligans. The first issue of *Combat 18* contained a section called "Hooligans rule OK", which claimed that the reason that the authorities hate "hoolies" so much was because 99 per cent of football thugs are white, 99 per cent of whom are nationalistic and patriotic. The magazine also contained a section entitled "C18 on tour" concerning the rioting which accompanied England's game in the Netherlands in October 1993, which stated that C18 had sent a fifty-strong "expeditionary force" to Holland. *Combat 18* "issue 3", published in January 1995, contained features on the hooligans who follow Glasgow Rangers, referred to as "100 per cent racist, 100 per cent Loyalist, 100 per cent Hoolie"; on the rioting of the first division playoff game between Millwall and Derby in

May 1994; an account of an attack by Chelsea-supporting C18 members on anti-racist Chelsea fans; and a report on C18's activities on a trip to Czechoslovakia to see Chelsea play in the European Cup Winners' Cup in 1994. An England-Germany match to be played in Berlin on the anniversary of Hitler's birth was eventually cancelled by the British and German football associations to allay fears of violence by far-right hooligans after protests in both countries (see **Germany**).

PUBLICATIONS AND MEDIA

The main far-right publications include: *Spearhead*, produced monthly by the BNP with an estimated circulation of 2,000; *British Nationalist*, also produced monthly by the BNP, with an estimated circulation of up to 4,000; *Flag*, up to 2,000 copies of which are circulated monthly by the NF; and *Candour*, with a monthly circulation of 500.

The first issue of *Combat 18* appeared in December 1993. Amongst its virulently racist and antisemitic contents is a list of C18's proclaimed "aims". These include: "to weed out all Jews in the government, the media, the arts, the professions. To execute all Jews who have actively helped to damage the white race and to put into camps the rest until we find a final solution for the eternal Jew", and "to re-educate and reintroduce decent white values and promote a healthy white community free from Jewish poison and phoney ideas of 'freedom' and 'democracy'". Other C18 publications include the monthlies *Putsch* and *The Order*.

Tony Hancock, the Brighton-based printer of material for neo-Nazis in the UK, Germany and Scandinavia, including the pseudo-scientific Holocaust-denying "Rudolf Expertise" (see **Germany**), was the subject of a police raid in 1994. The attorney-general is considering whether his case merits prosecution under part 3 of the Public Order Act.

In October, there was widespread public anger at an article by William Cash in the respected right-of-centre political weekly, the *Spectator*, in which he claimed that Hollywood was run by a "Jewish cabal", which he described as the "white-sock mediocracy". Cash subsequently said that he had been misunderstood because he is "rude and impolite about everyone". A second article in the same month in the same journal by William Dalrymple, which alleged Israeli complicity in the destruction of the ancient Christian communities of Palestine, was later shown to contain significant factual flaws.

The Muslim media also portray Israel, and frequently the Jewish community by implica-tion, in a negative manner, and in December the Arabic language programme of Spectrum Radio, a London-based multicultural radio station, was fined £1,000 by the radio authority for broadcasting material considered offensive to the Jewish community. This followed previous warnings earlier in the year.

Among literature circulated in 1994 was *Tales of the Holohoax*, a crude piece of Holocaust-denial propaganda presented in the form of a comic. The cover, which carried the subtitle *A Journal of Satire*, featured a frightened young man on his knees, surrounded by a religious Jewish teacher with a cane, a *New York Times* reporter, a Christian cleric, three security men or policemen, admitting that: "The extermination gas chambers *did* exist." In his trouser pocket is a copy of *The Hoax of the Twentieth Century* by Arthur Butz, a classic Holocaust-denial text.

Leaflets sent to Jewish and other targets included an "Auschwitz" letter sent to Jewish and non-Jewish homes; "Church of the Creator" hoax letters sent to Jewish and non-Jewish homes in east London; "Mad Jews Disease" leaflets sent to Jewish homes; "Avoid Orthodox Jews" leaflets sent to schools throughout Britain; and "Happy Chanukah from Yidneyland" cards sent to Jewish homes.

Concern grew during the year at the increasing use of the Internet (the international computer network) by antisemitic groups. Most of the racist material on the Internet does not originate in Britain, but in the US. Antisemitic and Holocaust-denial material now appears regularly on certain bulletin boards and newsgroups.

RELIGION

Jewish-Christian dialogue groups, and well-publicized meetings between Jewish and Christian religious leaders, indicate a strong determination to overcome any Christian antisemitism in the mid-1990s. The one area of Christian religious activity which does still cause concern, however, is that of missionaries and church support for such groups as Jews for Jesus. Some view this activity as antisemitic in effect if not necessarily in intention.

Concern was expressed in October when it emerged that a new religious local radio station, London Christian Radio (LCR), would give Christian missionary groups a platform from which to spread their message. The chief executive of LCR, Peter Meadows, told the *Jewish Chronicle* that the regular Sunday service slot would, from time to time, come from a "completed synagogue"—the term used by some missionary groups to describe their meeting place.

Tensions between Jews and Muslims were exacerbated by the activities of Islamist groups, a small minority within the British Muslim population whose aggressive propagation of their religious message involves the dissemination of some virulent antisemitic statements.

The most vocal and visible of these groups is Hizb al-Tahrir (HT, Liberation Party), an Islamist movement, dedicated to the creation of a *Khilafah* (unified Islamic state) throughout "Muslim lands". It was founded in Jerusalem in 1953 and operates openly in Britain, North America and Western Europe. It is banned throughout the Middle East due to its subversive attempts at fomenting Islamic revolution. In 1994, this was most notably in evidence in Jordan, where HT members stood trial for the attempted assassination of King Hussein (see **Jordan**).

HT is implacably hostile to all other modes of thought and practice, particularly Judaism. The group is openly antisemitic, but describes itself as anti-Zionist, a claim belied by the fact that HT speakers have denied the Holocaust at student meetings.

In 1994, HT consolidated its position as Britain's most active Islamist group, especially on campus, where it now dominates Islamic student activity. It claims that its speakers collectively give over 700 lectures per week. While this figure is probably an exaggeration, HT's activities are certainly extensive.

The group publishes a small monthly magazine, *Khilafah*, and distributes dozens of different leaflets, pamphlets and posters. Many of these are deliberately provocative, typically attacking Jews, Hindus, homosexuals and student union authorities. During 1994, there was regular distribution of a HT leaflet which stated the "only place is the battlefield between the Muslim and the Jews" and which quoted the Qur'anic hadith: "Oh Muslim! A Jew is here behind me, kill him." A flyer advertising a HT meeting at the Central mosque in Birmingham in January 1994 showed a bomb dropping on the Star of David, and repeated the Qur'anic hadith: "The last hour will not come until the Muslim fight the Jews and kill them."

HT's biggest event of 1994 was the Khilafah Conference at London's Wembley Arena. The meeting occurred two weeks after the car bomb attacks in London, and attracted widespread publicity and protests. The scale of the meeting, attended by 8,000 British Muslims and Islamist speakers from other countries, showed HT's strength and financial backing.

By the end of 1994, HT's vitriol had led to its being banned on a number of campuses, and its censure by the National Union of Students.

This was a welcome recognition of the intimidation felt by many Jewish students as a result of HT's activities, but was also spurred by HT's hostile attitude to all non-Muslims, particularly Hindus and homosexuals.

There are a number of groups who appear to comprise a support network for Hamas, the Islamic Resistance Movement which uses antisemitism and anti-Zionism interchangeably, in Britain. Its main Arabic magazine, *Philistina al-Muslima*, is published in Britain, and London is reported to be the centre for Hamas fundraising around the world.

British groups that support Hamas include the Islamic Association of Palestinian Youth (IAPY), which kept a relatively low public profile in 1994. IAPY's antisemitism (as distinct from anti-Zionism) was apparent at a meeting in Bristol, where Jews were viciously attacked by the main speaker. IAPY not only has links with Hamas; its meetings have also been addressed by representatives of the Algerian Front islamique du salut (FIS, Islamic Salvation Front, see **Algeria**) and Hizb al-Tahrir.

The Palestine Relief and Development Fund/Interpal is a fundraising group backed by IAPY, and appears to be part of Hamas's international funding network. It is ostensibly a welfare charity and has not engaged in antisemitic activity. *Palestine Times* is an English-language newspaper which regularly contains official Hamas communiqués and is a mouth-piece for Hamas in Britain, as is *Philistin al-Yawm*, an occasional Arabic-language paper.

The Muslim Parliament and the Muslim Institute in London have close links with Iran and with many of the world's violent Islamist groups. *Crescent International*, their publication, is consistently hostile towards Israel and supportive of such groups. The Muslim Parliament appeared relatively inactive in 1994, amid reports of financial collapse, and only one session was held, attended by approximately 100 people. Of more interest is the connection between the founder of both the parliament and the institute, Kalim Siddiqui, and the Islamic Culture and Information Bureau, which jointly sponsored the Al-Hussein World Conference in London in July. Speakers at this conference included Islamic clerics from Iran, Saudi Arabia, Yemen, the US, France and Sweden, and antisemitism formed a substantial part of some of the speeches made. The Islamic Culture and Information Bureau also organized the Yawm al-Zahra World Conference, held in London in December, addressed again by speakers from around the Islamic world. The Muslim Parliament organizes the Iranian-inspired annual Al-Quds Day (Jerusalem Day) march, at the end of

Ramadan (the Muslim holy month of fasting), where anti-Israeli and anti-Jewish slogans are regularly featured.

The Islamic community has many youth movements, the most prominent of which are Young Muslims (UK) and the Young Muslims' Organization. Their meetings and publications regularly feature anti-Zionist propaganda which is couched in antisemitic terms.

DENIAL OF THE HOLOCAUST

Denial of the Holocaust in Britain tends to be centred around the activities of David Irving and the Clarendon Club, his organizational pseudonym. Additionally, Holocaust denial began to appear regularly within Islamist organizations, particularly Hizb al-Tahrir. During 1994, attempts to hold Clarendon Club meetings failed or were cancelled, and David Irving spent much of the year abroad, most publicly at the Institute for Historical Review's international seminar in California in September, and on a prolonged speaking tour of American universities. In the US, he is regarded as one of Holocaust denial's leading intellects and promoters. Despite his ban from Germany, Irving continued to visit the country, where he is fêted by both Nazi veterans and skinheads alike. In February, Irving was sentenced *in absentia* to three months' imprisonment for contempt of court in a row with a German publisher (see **Germany**).

EFFECTS OF ANTI-ZIONISM

The clearest connection between anti-Zionist sentiment and domestic antisemitism was demonstrated in a spate of antisemitic incidents following the massacre of Muslims by a Jewish settler at a Hebron mosque in February. A total of 30 incidents were reported in February, compared with 17 in February 1993. The two car bombings in London in July 1994, which occurred shortly after the car bomb attack on a Jewish centre in Buenos Aires (see **Argentina**), suggested further evidence of this connection: there were six hoax bomb threats made against Jewish buildings in the week following the car bombs. Suspects apprehended for the car bombings are from a secular Palestinian group which opposes the Middle East peace process.

Since anti-Zionism in general has diminished over the last few years, the degree to which its antisemitic aspects have an impact in the UK has also been reduced. However, anti-Zionism remains the staple of those Muslim and Palestinian organizations which are implacably opposed to the Middle East peace process, and their increasing desperation has been reflected in the more blatantly antisemitic nature of their

anti-Zionism. This is linked to the preponderantly Islamist nature of that anti-Zionism which draws on Qur'anic anti-Jewish themes and is more ready to adopt aspects of classic European antisemitism. For example, a Hizb al-Tahrir meeting held at London University's School of Oriental and African Studies in January was entitled "Peace with Israel: A Crime against Islam", and was advertised by a poster which showed a gun pointing at the Star of David.

LEGAL MATTERS

British laws prohibit discrimination on the basis of race, colour, nationality, or national or ethnic origin, and outlaw incitement to racial hatred. During 1994, significant efforts were made by various organizations to persuade the government to make British legislation more effective against race hatred and racial attacks. These efforts were largely prompted by mounting concern at the number of racial attacks taking place and by the increased dissemination of racist literature and propaganda, especially antisemitic material. A noteworthy aspect of this campaign was the creation of a broad alliance ranging from Conservative MPs to left-wing anti-racist groups. The BoD both advocated and supported a much tougher approach to racial violence—even though Jews suffer little in this respect—and church and other groups proposed and supported measures to tighten the legal provisions against racial incitement, with antisemitic material uppermost in their minds.

Early in the year, the groups advocating change and the government both staked out their positions. The BoD, together with the Commission for Racial Equality (CRE), the Law Society, the Bar Council, the Churches Commission for Racial Justice, the Anti-Racist Alliance, the Inter-Parliamentary Council against Antisemitism and the Metropolitan Police, supported a private member's bill tabled by the Conservative MP Hartley Booth which contained a clause introducing the offence of group defamation, making it illegal to "vilify, threaten or expose to racial hatred or discrimination" ethnic groups. It also introduced penalty enhancement, proposing the imposition of up to "twice the normal maximum prescribed penalty" when an act of violence is found to have been inspired by racism. The bill was debated in March but failed to win the backing of the government. The home secretary (interior minister), Michael Howard, had already indicated his unwillingness to accept the Booth proposals when he appeared before the home affairs select committee in January which was enquiring into the problem of racial attacks and harassment.

A further effort was made to change the law in April when a series of amendments to the then Criminal Justice and Public Order Bill was introduced demanding a new offence of racially-motivated assault, an offence of racial harassment and provision for the police to be given wider powers of arrest against individuals inflaming racial hatred. These amendments were defeated, much to the dismay of both Conservative and Labour MPs. The passing of the government's own amendment, which makes the production and distribution of racist publications an arrestable offence, did little to satisfy them.

Further pressure was brought to bear on the government when the home affairs select committee produced a report on *Racial Attacks and Harassment* in June, which recommended that two new criminal offences be created to make it easier to prove a racial motive in court, and suggested that additional sentences of up to five years should be available for race crimes. Many organizations submitted evidence and proposals to the committee, but the government proved no more willing to accept the committee's views than it had been earlier in the year.

The Criminal Justice and Public Order Act was passed in December. Members of the House of Lords (the upper chamber of parliament) had tried unsuccessfully to reintroduce the amendments that had failed when the bill was being read in the House of Commons (the lower chamber of parliament). In addition, the Bishop of Oxford moved an amendment to protect religious minorities from incitement to religious hatred, but this too was unsuccessful. In addition to the power of arrest given to the police for the distribution of racist and antisemitic literature, the act also made harassment, or causing personal alarm or distress, an arrestable offence, and it is intended that this may be used in cases where racism or antisemitism is the motive.

Convictions obtained in recent criminal court cases involving racial harassment were also the subject of penalty enhancement. At Sunderland crown court, the judge referred to the racist motivation behind the violent crimes of Gary Mitchell, Craig Bond and Steven Thacker, and increased their sentences. Mitchell and Bond, both BNP members, received three years, and Thacker, eighteen months.

During the course of 1994, there was only one conviction under the Public Order Act for distributing racist and antisemitic literature, but three other cases were initiated.

On 24 March, the veteran antisemite, eighty-year-old Lady Birdwood, was convicted of possessing and distributing a booklet likely to stir up racial hatred. The booklet, *The Longest Hatred*, claimed that the Holocaust was a lie and that there was a Jewish conspiracy to undermine society through control of financial institutions. Lady Birdwood was found with the book while she was subject to a two-year conditional discharge imposed for similar offences. In April she was given a three-month prison sentence suspended for two years. The judge stated that a non-custodial sentence was appropriate because of her age and poor health.

The Norwich industrial tribunal heard a claim by a Jewish artisan alleging that he had been the subject of antisemitic taunts over a number of years by his colleagues. The case was adjourned at the end of the year and has still to be resolved.

Paul Thomas, a constable in the Metropolitan police, brought an action against his employers, initially supported by the CRE, on the grounds that he had been victimized and denied promotion by his superiors after his conversion to orthodox Judaism. The case remained unresolved at the end of the year.

In June, two elderly brothers and their widowed sister were convicted of threatening behaviour towards a Jewish neighbour in the latest clash of a long-running feud. The court was told that the four had confronted the neighbour, hurled antisemitic abuse at him and spat at him. The conviction was not made under race hatred legislation and the defending lawyer claimed that there was no racial motive in the defendants' minds.

In the same month, the national organizer of the BNP, Richard Edmonds, and two party activists, Simon Biggs and Steven O'Shea, were convicted of a brutal attack on a black man which took place in September 1993. Biggs and O'Shea were imprisoned for four-and-a-half years and one year respectively, but Edmonds had already served his three-month sentence while awaiting trial and was released.

Perpetrators of Nazi war crimes can be prosecuted under the 1991 War Crimes Act, although no prosecutions have yet been brought. In February, a decision was made not to prosecute Anton Gecas, a former Lithuanian living in Scotland, who had been the subject of a lengthy war-crimes investigation. The Scottish war-crimes unit attached to Strathclyde police was subsequently closed.

In July, the Metropolitan police war-crimes unit announced that it was investigating twenty-eight cases against alleged Nazi war criminals and had submitted interim reports to the Crown Prosecution Service (CPS, the public prosecution service) with respect to ten of them. In October, it was reported that the CPS was considering action in seven cases. The apparent delay in bringing any prosecutions was welcomed by those who opposed the process from the start. Supporters of this process, however, did their best to stiffen the resolve of the war-crimes unit and the CPS.

COUNTERING ANTISEMITISM

A wide variety of organizations work to counter antisemitism in the UK, but the BoD, the representative body of British Jewry, is the most active. Interfaith organizations, especially the Council of Christians and Jews, are particularly industrious among religious groups. The Institute of Jewish Affairs disseminates up-to-date information on antisemitism throughout the world. A great deal of work is done indirectly by educationalists and academics. The British branch of the Inter-Parliamentary Council against Antisemitism, a world-wide body co-ordinated from the UK, is active in parliament. Anti-racist organizations naturally tend to focus on the wider problems of racism, but in recent years they have been giving greater recognition to the problem of antisemitism.

In January, the Commission on Antisemitism of the Runnymede Trust, the UK's leading race relations research body, issued a report and recommendations entitled *A Very Light Sleeper: The Persistence and Dangers of Antisemitism*. This was the first time that the trust had addressed the question of antisemitism directly.

In May, the Archbishop of Canterbury (the leading cleric of the Church of England) organized the publication of a statement on racism by European church leaders, in which the rise in racism, xenophobia and antisemitism throughout Europe was viewed with the very gravest concern. The statement rejected any suggestion of superiority, or movement towards exclusiveness, which would deprive non-Christians of a place in the new Europe and called upon all Christians, and those of other faiths, to work to eradicate racism. The statement was co-signed by leading Catholic, Protestant, Orthodox and Free Church leaders in all European countries, and was supported by the Conference of European Churches, the World Council of Churches Programme to Combat Racism, the European Catholic Episcopal Conference, the European Evangelical Alliance, the Church Commission for Migrants in Europe and the Catholic Pontifical Commission for Justice and Peace.

Relations between the Jewish and Christian communities continued to strengthen, through the work of national bodies, such as the Council of Christians and Jews, the Inter Faith Network and the Inner Cities Religious Council, and partly through many local contacts and initiatives. Contacts exist with senior British Muslim religious leaders at both national and local level and close working links have been developed with the Hindu community.

The BoD was instrumental in founding the United Campaign against Racism (UCAR) which brought together leaders of all faiths prior to the May municipal elections. This initiative came about in reaction to the success of the BNP in the Tower Hamlets by-election in 1993. The UCAR sponsored a public meeting at which the home secretary, Michael Howard, the then shadow home secretary, Tony Blair, the Liberal Democrat home affairs spokeswoman Baroness Seear, members of parliament, Christian, Muslim, Hindu and Jewish leaders, pledged to fight racism and to keep it out of the electoral process. The UCAR was also responsible for publishing anti-BNP leaflets and for assisting the main parties in those wards where extremists stood as candidates.

Major anti-racist demonstrations took place during the course of the year at which the rise in antisemitism was noted and condemned. The Trades Union Congress, the umbrella body for most British trades unions, organized a rally against racism, which was attended by 40,000 people. The Week against Racism, organized by United against Racism, a Council of Europe-sponsored body, and *Searchlight* magazine, "the international anti-fascist monthly", held a rally in November on the anniversary of Kristallnacht addressed by Jewish and Gypsy leaders.

ASSESSMENT

During 1994, antisemitism emanated from two main sources: the activities of Islamist groups and the activities of nationalist and neo-Nazi organizations. The security of the Jewish community was directly threatened by secular Palestinian terrorist activity, with the bombing in July of the Israel embassy in central London and the building housing the JIA and other major Jewish charities in north London.

The bomb attack on the offices of the JIA was the first direct terrorist attack against an Anglo-Jewish institution and came in the wake of a series of threats made by Hizbullah, Hamas and other Middle East-based terrorist organizations. The bombings resulted in the implementation of an unprecedented security operation within the Jewish community, carried out jointly by the police and the Community Security Organization of the BoD. Applications were subsequently made to the home office for funding to enhance the security of the community's institutions.

Jews in Britain do not experience the same levels of racial harassment, violence and common prejudice suffered by the visible ethnic minorities. But the rising level of racist violence has an impact on Jews, whether they are specifically targeted or not. Much political activity by concerned groups during the course of the year was devoted to lobbying for the strengthening of legislation dealing with the prosecution of racial attacks and the outlawing of incitement to race hatred.

The police take very seriously the likelihood of further significant terrorist action, but the threat posed by antisemitic activity in general is small. However, Islamist organizations are increasingly adopting anti-Jewish themes and have the potential to undermine Jewish-Muslim relations. Such organizations can claim the allegiance of only very small sectors of Britain's Muslim community, which itself is more likely to be affected adversely by Islamism— because it is principally directed at revolution within Islam—than is the Jewish community.

Yugoslavia
(Serbia and Montenegro)

General population: 10.6 million
Jewish population: 2,500-3,000 (mainly in Belgrade)

GENERAL BACKGROUND

Yugoslavia is dominated by Slobodan Milošević, leader of the Socijalistička Partija Srbije (Socialist Party of Serbia), who is serving his second five-year term as president. Until August Milošević's government actively fostered violence in Bosnia-Hercegovina by providing military, economic, political and moral support to ethnic Serbs responsible for massive human rights violations including "ethnic cleansing". In September the UN Security Council approved a selective suspension of international sanctions against Serbia and Montenegro for 100 days.

An economic stabilization programme introduced in January succeeded in bringing hyperinflation under control but by the end of the year the programme was beginning to show serious cracks. Unemployment continued at a level in excess of 50 per cent.

HISTORICAL LEGACY OF ANTISEMITISM

There is no significant tradition of antisemitism in the former Yugoslav federation (see **Croatia**).

RACISM AND XENOPHOBIA

The government continued to inflict abuses on the one-third of the population who were not ethnic Serbs and repressed voices of opposition in the ethnic Serb community as well. The ethnic Albanians of Kosovo and the Muslims of Sandžak suffered the heaviest abuses. Traditional societal discrimination against the substantial Roma population remained widespread.

PARTIES, GROUPS, MOVEMENTS

On 28 April the ultra-nationalist Srpska Radikalna Stranka (SRS, Serbian Radical Party) abolished its paramilitary wing, the Serbian Chetnik Movement. The Chetnik Movement, which had revived the Second World War nationalist army of the same name when it was established in July 1990, had been widely accused of committing war crimes during fighting in Croatia in 1991-2.

On 19 September Vojislav Seselj, president of the SRS and a suspected war criminal, re-ceived a suspended eight-month prison sentence for his part in scuffles in the Serbian assembly on 18 May. On 29 September, following a further altercation in the assembly two days earlier, Seselj was given a thirty-day prison sentence.

PUBLICATIONS AND MEDIA

At the beginning of the year Velvet, an obscure private Belgrade publisher, brought out a reprint of *The Protocols of the Elders of Zion*. The book went on sale in some bookshops and on the streets. The small-circulation newspapers *Kruna* and *Velika Srbija*, a publication of the SRS, printed sections of it. The Jewish community pressed charges against both publisher and editor on the basis of a court order prohibiting the printing and circulation of *The Protocols*. All remaining copies of *Velika Srbija* were confiscated by police. The reprint was condemned by, among others, various parliamentary parties, several newspapers and the Serbian Academy of Science and Art.

On 17 July the "Information Bulletin" of the nationalist non-parliamentary Srpska Narodna Obnova (SNO, Serbian National Renewal) in Bijelo Polje (Montenegro) published an antisemitic article entitled "The Jewish vampire ball". Following a protest by the Jewish community to government authorities and the Orthodox church, the general secretary of the Montenegro branch of the SNO wrote a letter of apology to the Jewish community and the party's head of public relations resigned. A letter by Patriarch Pavle, the head of the Serbian Orthodox church, to Jewish leaders condemning the article was published in full in the church's publication, *Pravoslavlje*.

Logos, a quarterly publication of students

at the Orthodox seminary in Belgrade, included in its January issue, which appeared belatedly, an anti-Jewish article entitled "Jewish games behind the global scenes". The article was critical of Patriarch Pavle for "apologizing" to the Jewish community. The article was condemned by, among others, some members of the Serbian Academy of Science and Art representing various political standpoints and several newspapers.

There were in 1994 a number of reprints of anti-Jewish books published during the Second World War. The publisher was again Velvet.

COUNTERING ANTISEMITISM

At an international seminar on minorities in Yugoslavia organized by the Serbian Academy of Science and Art, Aca Singer, the president of the Jewish community, submitted a paper partly devoted to antisemitism in Serbia and Montenegro. He argued that, despite the fact that there was little antisemitism in the country, it should not be taken lightly and individuals, intellectuals and relevant government institutions should take a stand against it in every instance. He praised the prompt response of the Serbian Orthodox church and pointed out that the Jewish community in Yugoslavia had no special problems.

ASSESSMENT

Still deeply involved in the vicious warfare which followed the disintegration of the Yugoslav federal republic and experiencing severe international sanctions, the country continued to undergo major political and economic upheaval. Xenophobia and ethnic discrimination remained an important feature of the Belgrade regime. As confirmed by the Jewish community president, antisemitism was not a serious problem in Serbia and Montenegro.

Middle East and North Africa

THE INSTITUTE OF JEWISH AFFAIRS AND THE AMERICAN JEWISH COMMITTEE

Algeria

General population: 27.1 million
Jewish population: 100

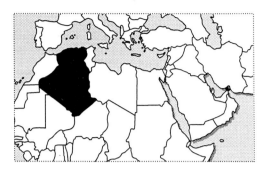

GENERAL BACKGROUND

Although a multi-party system was established by constitutional amendment in 1989, the electoral process was suspended in January 1992 to prevent a probable victory by the militant Front islamique du salut (FIS, Islamic Salvation Front). A nation-wide state of emergency was declared, and following the assassination of President Mohammed Boudiaf by Islamic activists in June 1992, a five-member high council of state (HCS), was appointed. Suspected FIS activists and other militants were rounded up and the FIS was officially dissolved. Algeria has subsequently witnessed increasing conflict between Islamist groups and government forces.

In 1994 former minister of defence, Brigadier-General Liamine Zeroual, was appointed as president and the HCS was disbanded. Further attempts to restore stability through political dialogue met with little success.

Throughout the year violence escalated in Algeria. Islamists moved beyond attacking military targets to the kidnapping and assassination of local and foreign civilians, including academics, journalists and other professionals. Also targeted were feminists and women accused of failing to observe the strict Islamic dress code. Among the most serious incidents in 1994 was the hijacking of an Air France airplane in December by the Groupe islamique armé (GIA, Armed Islamic Group). In October 1994 Amnesty International estimated that at least 30,000 people had been killed in Algeria since January 1992.

HISTORICAL LEGACY

During the nineteenth century, traditional Christian antisemitism was introduced into parts of the Muslim world, including Algeria, by European clerics and missionaries. At the same time, Jews received favoured treatment from the French colonists and, despite Muslim resentment, soon seized the new economic opportunities.

Following the 1894 "Dreyfus affair", leading French antisemite Edouard Drumont was elected as the representative for Algiers. Although the antisemitic movement of the time was short-lived in Algeria, Nazi propaganda in the 1940s brought about its resurgence. Under the Vichy regime, Jews were treated with contempt by the French authorities, who applied the antisemitic Vichy laws in all their severity.

After Algeria gained independence from France in 1962, most of the country's 140,000 Jews emigrated. Algerian Jews, almost universally gallicized, were viewed by Muslims not only as Zionists, and therefore as enemies of Arab national aspirations, but also as Europeans. Jews were also resented for their economic success and the privileges they enjoyed under French rule. In 1960, during anti-French riots, the Great Synagogue of Algiers was destroyed. Jewish areas were attacked repeatedly and synagogues and cemeteries were desecrated. Large-scale emigration followed. The 1967 Six Day War provided an occasion for further looting, attacks and desecrations.

In recent years, Islamist opposition forces have frequently combined antisemitic, anti-Zionist and anti-Western rhetoric. During the 1991-2 Gulf War, the use of antisemitic slogans was particularly evident. In January 1991, for example, Ali Belhadj, a leader of the FIS, led a demonstration in support of Iraq, proclaiming: "We are here to drink the blood of the Jews."

RACISM AND XENOPHOBIA

Islamist groups have repeatedly warned foreign workers and business-owners to leave the country. In 1994 the abduction and killing of foreign tourists and workers prompted many international companies to evacuate staff and dependents. Among the most serious incidents were the killings of seven Italian sailors on board a cargo ship in Algiers in July and three French security officers and two consular staff at the French embassy housing complex in August, and the murder of two Spanish nuns in October (see **Parties, Organizations, Movements**).

PARTIES, ORGANIZATIONS, MOVEMENTS

Following the foiled hijacking in December by the GIA, the armed wing of the FIS, known as Armé islamique du salut (AIS, Islamic Salvation Army) warned that further attacks would take place in France, and that Jews and Christians would be targeted. In the December edition of its newsletter, *al-Fath al-Moubine*, AIS leaders asserted: "The Algerian nation is directly in conflict with France and all those who support it including the Jews and Christians of the world."

The GIA, which rivals the FIS, issued statements that attacks on foreigners within Algeria were intended to rid the country of Jews and Christians. The GIA claimed, for example, that the May killing of a French nun and priest was part of "a policy of liquidation of Jews and Christians". The GIA described the murder of two Spanish nuns in October as a "campaign of purification of Jews and Christians and unbelievers from the land of Islam".

MANIFESTATIONS

A sixty-two-year-old Tunisian-born Jew named Raymond Louzoum was killed in January by Islamist attackers. Louzoum was an actor who regularly played the part of a French officer in popular Algerian films.

PUBLICATIONS AND MEDIA

Press articles continued to blame Jewish journalists in France for Algeria's poor image on the international stage.

Copies of *The Protocols of the Elders of Zion*, including a new translation which was published by the Jeune Indépendant, continued to circulate in Algeria.

ASSESSMENT

With only a tiny Jewish population, Algeria is an example of a country with "antisemitism without Jews". World Jewry, and French Jews in particular, are used as scapegoats in a society which is facing severe economic and political problems. Increasing levels of violence raise concern over the likely impact of an Islamist victory in Algeria and its possible repercussions for other North African and Middle Eastern regimes, as well as its potential ramifictions for the nearby continent of Europe.

Egypt

General population: 56.1 million
Jewish population: 200 (mainly in Cairo)

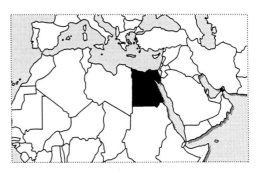

GENERAL BACKGROUND

In 1994 the security situation in Egypt deteriorated as clashes between government forces and Islamist opposition groups intensified. Prominent among Islamic splinter groups was the Gama'a al-Islamiya (GI, Islamic Group), led by Sheikh Omar Abd al-Rahman, who was awaiting trial in the United States for his alleged role in the February 1993 bombing of the World Trade Centre. Illegal opposition groups in Egypt also include: al-Jihad (Holy Struggle), which was accused of the 1981 assassination of President Anwar Sadat; Thawrat Misr (Egypt's Revolution); al-Najoun Min al-Nar (Survivors from Hell); and Takfir w'al-Hajra (Denunciation and Holy Flight). Islamist violence was directed not only against security forces but also against foreigners and tourists (see **Racism and Xenophobia**).

The 1981 emergency law promulgated after President Sadat's assassination was extended for a further three years. Hundreds of suspected militants were arrested leading to swift trials in military courts and an unprecedented number of hangings. The Egyptian organization for human rights and the UN human rights commission also documented the increasing use of torture. Local elections in the provinces were banned and government control in rural areas was tightened. Efforts to return wanted militants from Yemen and Pakistan were stepped up, and pressure was placed on the Gulf states to block funds to militant groups in Egypt.

The government also tightened control over the press, evicted suspects from student housing and waged legal battles against the boards of professional syndicates dominated by the illegal but publicly tolerated al-Ikhwan al-Islamiya (Muslim Brotherhood). Most significantly, prominent members were arrested. In an obvious appeal to public opinion, papers allegedly seized in 1992 from the organization, which revealed plans to take over the government, were released for publication.

In response to condemnation by Islamist parliamentarians of "moral transgressions", the minister of culture allowed al-Azhar, the leading Islamic institution, to review and reject books scheduled for publication.

On the international front, Eygpt acted as mediator in the Middle East peace process. Israeli and Palestine Liberation Organization (PLO) negotiators met regularly in Cairo and Taba, Egyptian Foreign Minister Amr Moussa visited Israel, and Egyptian diplomats shuttled to and from Arab capitals. Following the massacre of Muslims by a Jewish settler in a Hebron mosque in February, angry demonstrations revealed the extent of opposition to Egypt's role in the peace process. Amr Moussa and his assistant, Nabil Fahmi, led the Egyptian effort to disarm Israel of its alleged nuclear capacity. The Alexandria summit in December demonstrated Egypt's commitment to Arab solidarity.

HISTORICAL LEGACY

Following the establishment of Ottoman rule over Egypt in 1517, the position of the Jews deteriorated, but Western influences throughout the nineteenth and early twentieth centuries led to better conditions. Prior to 1948, the Jewish community in Egypt numbered 65-70,000. During the 1948-9 Arab-Israeli war, hundreds of Jews were arrested, Jewish-owned property and businesses were confiscated, and there were bombings in Jewish areas which killed or maimed hundreds of Jews. Between 1948 and 1950, about 25,000 Jews left, many for Israel.

In 1952, attacks were made on Jewish establishments causing millions of pounds worth of damage. After the 1956 war, 3,000 Jews were interned and thousands of others were given a few days to leave the country while their property was confiscated by the state. By 1957, there were only 8,000 Jews left. After the 1967 war, hundreds of Jews were arrested and tortured, and Jews still in public employment were dismissed. Further emigration ensued, so that, by the mid-1970s, only 350 Jews remained.

RACISM AND XENOPHOBIA

Throughout 1994, the GI issued frequent warnings to foreigners to leave the country and carried out violent attacks against foreign investors, business-owners and tourists. Buses, trains and tourist boats, especially those in Upper Egypt, were targeted on several occasions. Among the most serious incidents were the 23 February bombing of a train in Assyut, which injured two German, two Australian and two New Zealand tourists and five Egyptians, and the 26 August shooting at a tour bus that killed a Spanish youth and injured several other foreigners.

Islamist groups claimed responsibility for several attacks on churches and other property, such as shops and nightclubs, belonging to members of Christian minorities, especially Copts. The GI also threatened to carry out attacks on American targets world-wide in retaliation for the arrest of Sheikh Abd al-Rahman.

PARTIES, ORGANIZATIONS, MOVEMENTS

The effort to resist normalization with Israel by the Islamist movement was imbued with antisemitic arguments. As Hamid Abu al-Nasr, a leader of the Muslim Brotherhood, asserted in an interview in *al-Safir* on 28 June: "We have prior experience of dealing with the Jews. We saw how they were planning to control our trade and economy, how they had a monopoly over several basic commodities, and how they manipulated prices to serve their interests at the public's expense. The Jews have not changed. Shall we now give them another opportunity to control the Arab economies as a prelude to their political and eventually military hegemony over us?" He also explained why the Muslim Brotherhood identified with Hamas, the Palestinian rejectionist group: "The alien Jewish entity is a usurper entity, and *Jihad* is the only way to liberate the land from this entity."

Such allegations were enhanced by Islamic references. Muhammad Sayyid Tantawi, mufti of the republic, declared on 4 April: "As to the reference in the Qur'an that they [the Jews] were given preference over all other people, the context relates to a specific time and place when the Jews were committed to heavenly laws. Later on, no people were so strongly vilified in the Qur'an as the Jews."

CULTURAL LIFE

In July, Steven Spielberg's film *Schindler's List* was banned by the board of censors on the grounds that scenes of torture, nudity and violence would offend public morality. The ban was upheld by the appeals committee of the Higher Arts and Culture Council.

PUBLICATIONS AND MEDIA

Antisemitism in the media was triggered by specific incidents, such as the Hebron massacre on 25 February. Negative images of Jews, which had receded somewhat in the wake of the Israeli-Palestinian Declaration of Principles, assumed exaggerated dimensions both in the government newspaper *al-Ahram* and the opposition press, such as *al-Wafd*. On 1 March, the Islamist newspaper *al-Sha'ab* warned the Jews of a recurrence of the historic conquest by Muhammad's army in 628. The article invoked quotations from the Qu'ran to suggest that "this ugly incident indicates the aggressive nature of the Zionist enemy, who has gathered the [Jews who were] scattered all over the world, and usurped the land".

Antisemitic articles were also published in the government press. Mustafa Mahmud, a Marxist-turned-Islamist, for example, wrote in *al-Ahram* on 26 November that "Jews are forgerers, murderers of the prophets, guilty of all evil and malice". Antisemitism also featured regularly in the columns of Mahmud al-Sa'dani in the weekly magazine *al-Musawwar* and Mohammed al-Hayawn in the daily newspaper *al-Jumhuriyya*.

There was an increase in the number of anti-Zionist books as opposed to purely antisemitic ones, but many still used classical antisemitic images. Antisemitic texts such as *The Protocols of the Elders of Zion*, Hitler's *Mein Kampf*, Henry Ford's *The International Jew* and the more recent "World Zionism", translated from Russian and printed in Damascus, continued to circulate. More recent antisemitic publications by Egyptian authors were also available such as "The Wall and the Tears" by the popular writer, Anis Mansur, and "The Water Conflict between Arabs and Israel" by Dr Rifa'at Sayyid Ahmad, the cover of which shows an observant Jew wearing a skullcap drowning.

As in previous years, a number of academic books featuring antisemitic themes were on sale in Egypt. "The Jewish Personality" by Dr Muhammad Jala Idris of Tanta University states that Jews "are not human, but something in the form of humans" and concludes that "the Jewish personality, as presented in the course of [literary] analysis and based on findings by psychologists, is abnormal and totally irregular, marked by considerable deviation and derangement".

Also on sale was a book published by a professor of Islamic philosophy and comparative religions at Cairo University, Dr Muhammad Abd Allah al-Sharqawi, in 1990, entitled "A Treasury of Talmud Infamies", which was republished in 1993 by Cairo University. The covers of both books include detailed illustrations of Jews using Christian blood during rituals such as wedding ceremonies.

In a prologue to "Studies on Arab

Influence on Hebrew and Religious Thought and Hebrew Culture through the Ages", Dr Rashid al-Shami noted that "Jews did not create arts or sciences or industry or ideas or anything which constitutes a civilization, and did not achieve any significant accomplishment in the world of human knowledge. Jews . . . keep repeating the maxim of the 'Jewish Genius', a false maxim which they strive to instil in the souls of the non-Jews."

Ahmad al-Tuhami Sultan's 1993 book was entitled "The Biggest Deception: The Schemes of the Evil Men of Zion and the Misleading of the World by Political Myths". It includes such statements as: "We do not intend here to count the defects in the Jewish personality, nor the maxims planted by the *Protocols of the Elders of Zion* in the hearts of all Jews; we'll make do in mentioning the causes for the hatred felt by blacks in New York to Jews."

EFFECTS OF ANTI-ZIONISM

Antisemitic rhetoric featured in various anti-Zionist speeches, particularly among Islamist leaders. For example, in an article in *al-Sha'ab* on 8 February, Mustafa Mashhur of the Muslim Brotherhood invoked classical antisemitic themes to argue against the lifting of the Arab boycott against Israel: "Some Jews have been involved in narcotics and counterfeit currency cases and have attempted to spread AIDS or sow sedition between Muslims and Christians. Our Arab countries must protect themselves from this evil which will corrupt our young people, ruin our economy and spoil all spheres of life."

Egyptian sources were quoted on 25 April in the Lebanese publication, *al-Safir*, alleging that Israeli criminals were engaged in an exhaustive process to inflict harm on Egypt, including "forgery, drug-smuggling by persons in the Israeli academic centre and the Israeli embassy and spreading AIDS".

ASSESSMENT

The increasing influence of radical Islam, among opposition forces as well as the establishment, lends increasing legitimization to antisemitism. Antisemitic maxims and imagery have become entrenched in public discourse and are bound to surface in interactions with Jews or with Israel.

Gulf States

General population:
Bahrain: 500,000
Kuwait: 1.2 million
Oman: 1.7 million
Qatar: 400,000
Saudi Arabia: 16.5 million
United Arab Emirates: 1.7 million
Jewish population: 20 (in Bahrain)

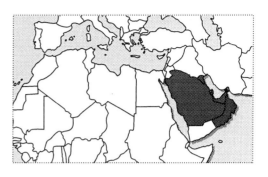

GENERAL BACKGROUND

Saudi Arabia is an absolute monarchy, ruled by King Fahd. The Gulf states, with the exception of Oman, are tribal sheikhdoms, governed by emirs who rule by decree and are advised by cabinets appointed largely from their respective family members. Oman is a sultanate whose ruler appoints a council of advisors chosen from tribal dignitaries.

Throughout the Gulf, the Iraqi invasion of Kuwait in 1991 helped to foster the development of loosely-organized opposition groups demanding political change. Pressure for liberalization also emanated from the USA and its Western allies. There has been some evidence of limited democratization: in 1992 King Fahd of Saudi Arabia appointed a consultative council; Oman convened a fifty-nine-member consultative council; and Kuwait held elections for a reconstituted national assembly. Among the opposition forces emerging within Saudi Arabia and the other Gulf states are radical Islamic groups which reject the conservatism of the current regimes and may seek to exploit consitutional changes to promote a more militant form of Islamic rule. The London-based Islamic Liberation Front and the Bahrain Liberation Movement, for example, represent a threat to the Bahrain regime and to stability in the entire region.

The leaders of Saudi Arabia and other Gulf states met in Bahrain in December at the fifteenth summit of the Gulf Co-Operation Council (GCC). Among other issues of mutual concern, the GCC noted the rise in Islamist violence.

In 1994 violations of human rights were reported in Saudi Arabia and Kuwait in particular. Amnesty International accused Kuwait in February of serious human rights violations, including the unlawful detention of some 120 people accused of collaborating with Iraqi occupation forces during the 1991 Gulf crisis.

Economic recovery continued after the devastating effects of the recent Gulf War.

Saudi Arabia and the other Gulf states remained keen to support the Middle East peace process and to benefit from regional development. In September the six members of the GCC agreed to lift the secondary and tertiary aspects of the economic boycott of Israel.

In 1994 Israeli delegates visited Qatar and Oman for the first time in order to participate in the multilateral peace talks. However, it remains unlikely that the Gulf states, and Saudi Arabia in particular, would fully normalize relations before Israel made further progress in its negotiations with the Palestinians and reached a peace agreement with Syria.

HISTORICAL LEGACY

The influence of European antisemitism is deeply-rooted in the Gulf states. With the exception of Bahrain, Gulf societies evolved without Jewish communities. Western travellers and businessmen imported classical images of greedy, plotting and monstrous-looking Jews. Gulf societies often accepted as facts such fabrications as *The Protocols of the Elders of Zion*. Due to state control of the media, many Gulf Arabs still do so. Moreover, the continuous and unconditional identification of the Gulf societies with Arab and Palestinian issues has encouraged the persistence of a belief in a demonic image of Jews.

However, Israel's role in the 1991 Gulf War led Gulf societies to develop a more positive image of Jews. They were able to identify with Israeli society's position, which, like their own, had been attacked and victimized by Saddam Hussein's ventures. They appreciated Israel's restraint in avoiding retaliation against Iraq, which helped facilitate the anti-Iraq coalition's victory. The Gulf states therefore started viewing Israel as a factor of stability in the Middle East and supported the US-initiated Arab-Israeli peace process. Israel's earlier image as the "Zionist enemy" was definitely undermined. In addition, the Palestinians' support for Saddam Hussein earned them the animosity of many Gulf Arabs, who resented their disregard for the hospitality and financial and material support which the Gulf states had always offered them.

PUBLICATIONS AND MEDIA

A book published in 1993 by Mohammed Qasim Mohammed of Qatar University, entitled "The Contradiction in the Annals and Events of the Torah from Adam to Babel", continued to circulate throughout the Gulf and the rest of the Arab world. The book was a lengthy attempt to discredit "historical" aspects of the Jewish scriptures and, thereby, Jewish history and historical experience itself. Arabic translations of classical antisemitic texts such as *The Protocols of the Elders of Zion* were also available.

English-language programmes broadcast on state-controlled television in Saudi Arabia frequently invoked religious rhetoric to promote antisemitism. An English-language programme, entitled *Issues and Answers*, which aims to promote Islam among foreign workers in Saudi Arabia, regularly sought to discredit both Judaism and Christianity. On 6 August,

for example, the programme claimed that "Allah has cursed Jews and Christians". Particular hostility, however, was aimed at Jews. For example, on 16 September, a Muslim cleric broadcast the following speech: "Aren't they, the Jews, the killers of the prophets? Didn't they try to kill Jesus Christ? Didn't they destroy the scriptures and the revelation of Allah? Aren't they trying to spread corruption on the earth?" On 26 October a Muslim broadcaster on the English-language television channel asserted: "Jews say they believe in the Torah. But they misinterpret it . . . Islam is the truth."

ASSESSMENT

In 1994, the attitudes of Saudi Arabia and the other Gulf states towards Jews continued to reflect an interplay between traditional antisemitic stereotypes and more positive images developed in the wake of the Gulf War and the Middle East peace process. The threat of Islamic extremism continued to give concern in the region.

Iran

General population 63.2 million
Jewish population 20,000-25,000

GENERAL BACKGROUND

The year 1994, which marked the fifteenth anniversary of the Islamic Republic of Iran, witnessed severe political and economic turmoil. President Hojat-al-Eslam Hashemi Rafsanjani failed to win support for constitutional changes and may therefore have to step down in 1997 after two terms. He was criticized by the Majlis-e Shura-ye Melli (consultative council) for introducing economic liberalization and attempting to improve relations with Egypt, Saudi Arabia and the West.

Despite the introduction of new monetary policies in April, inflation soared and the economy was adversely affected by a sharp decrease in oil prices. Economic problems and political restrictions led to many public protests and rioting.

Iranian Sunni Muslims clashed with security forces after the demolition of a Sunni mosque in the Shi'ite holy city of Mashhad. A bomb which exploded in June in the city, causing tens of deaths and injuries, was regarded as an act of revenge by Sunni extremists.

As for foreign policy, Iran strengthened economic ties with Europe but relations with the United States, which regards Iran as the principal sponsor of international terrorism, remained strained. Iran also refused to lift the death sentence, dating from 14 February 1989, on the British author Salman Rushdie.

Iran continued to call for the destruction of the state of Israel and to oppose the Middle East peace process, providing financial and political support for Palestinian rejectionist groups, such as Hamas and Islamic Jihad, as well as for the militant Islamic movement Hizbullah in South Lebanon. The bombings of Jewish targets in Buenos Aires and London (see **Argentina** and **United Kingdom**) fuelled speculation over Iran's financial links, political support and military training of militant Islamist groups world-wide.

The UN human rights commission reported that Iran was holding 19,000 political prisoners.

HISTORICAL LEGACY

Throughout their long history in the region, Iranian Jews have experienced several periods of persecution and discrimination.

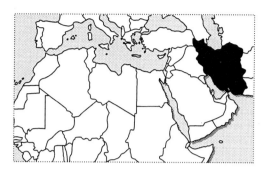

Persecution was intensified under the Safavid Dynasty (1501-1736), once Shi'ite Islam became the official religion. Between 1613 and 1662, many Jews were forced to convert, property was looted and those who resisted were murdered. Further restrictions were enforced in the eighteenth century.

Under the Qajar Dynasty (1796-1925) various atrocities were perpetrated against Jews. Hundreds were murdered at the end of the eighteenth century in Tabriz after a Jewish merchant was accused of killing a Muslim boy to use his blood at Passover. In 1839, thirty Jews were killed in Mashhad following allegations of blasphemy. In order to save the remainder of the community, the Jews agreed to convert to Islam. These forced converts practised their faith in secret until 1925, when religious persecution was eased and freedom of worship was granted. The Jewish quarter of Tehran was besieged in 1897 and Jews were forced to wear red patches on their clothes.

The 1907 constitution granted civil and judicial rights to religious minorities, including one representative to the Jews in the Majlis. The more institutionalized forms of religious discrimination were eased, especially under the Pahlavi dynasty. They did, however, continue in sporadic fashion at a local level, especially during the years of close relations with Nazi Germany.

Zionism and the establishment of the state of Israel played a key role in the status of Iranian Jewry. As co-operation between the Shah and the state of Israel intensified, the Jewish community became increasingly identified with the regime.

The 1979 revolution and the antisemitism of Shi'ite leaders, and of Khomeini in particular, left the Jewish community with two choices—either to leave the country or to express vigorous support for the revolution, including its animosity towards Israel and Zionism. In the first decade after the revolution, more than 50,000 Jews fled the country.

The regime has emphasized its implacable enmity to the state of Israel and Zionism, and uses the words "Jew", "Zionist" and "Israel" interchangeably. Community leaders were forced publicly to condemn Israel and Zionism. A number of Jewish communal leaders and some dozens of other Jews were arrested and imprisoned for espousing "Zionism", having connections with Israel and collaborating with the Shah. The regime also confiscated Jewish property, including factories, hotels, cinemas, houses and other assets and made it increasingly difficult for Jews to obtain business licences.

RACISM AND XENOPHOBIA

In 1994 the UN human rights commission documented severe human rights violations and denounced Iran's treatment of Christian, Kurd and Arab minorities. Of particular concern was the abduction and murder of three prominent Christian leaders, including Haik Hovsepian Mehr, the chair of the Council of Pastors of the Iranian Protestant Churches, and Mehdi Dibaj, an evangelist who was sentenced to death for converting to Christianity from Islam.

MAINSTREAM POLITICS

Since religion and politics are virtually synonymous in Iran, political statements are often expressed in religious terms. Likewise, the religious and political leadership is inextricably linked. Speeches by leading clerics frequently referred to antisemitic themes, such as the notion that Jewish control of the media was responsible for the misrepresentation of Iranian policies in the West and that "international Zionism" and American Jews manipulated US policy in the Middle East. In a sermon at Tehran University on 4 March, Ayatollah Khamenei accused "American Jews, those big capitalists" of using their money and political influence to support Israel which was referred to as "that malignant cell which was created in the heart of the Islamic nations".

MANIFESTATIONS

On 24 February Feyzollah Mechubad, an elderly member of the Jewish Council of Synagogues in Tehran, was hanged. He was arrested on 19 May 1992, on his way to the Tehran synagogue, and charged with "associating with Zionism" (apparently after trying to contact his two sons in Israel). During his two years of detention, much of which was spent in solitary confinement, Mechubad was denied any legal defence, permitted only short and infrequent visits, and subjected to severe physical and mental torture. In the aftermath of the 1979 revolution, approximately twelve Iranian Jews were hung but Mechubad's hanging—which may have been an act of vengeance after the massacre of Muslims by a Jewish settler in a Hebron mosque—marked the first known summary killing of a Jew since the early 1980s.

CULTURAL LIFE

The Iranian media responded to the international acclaim of Steven Spielberg's *Schindler's List* by claiming that "Zionism exploits the Holocaust for propaganda in different areas including the cinema". Many articles appeared in Iranian newspapers claiming that "Zionists" controlled the film industry. Similarly, following the opening of the Holocaust Museum in Washington DC, the official daily *Keyhan* referred on 10 March to "the movie-making power of international Zionism, Auschwitz and the Holocaust".

The only Jewish newspaper *Tammuz*, a monthly published by the Jewish Intellectual Organization, which included several anti-Israeli and anti-Zionist articles, ceased to appear after protesting against the increasing number of antisemitic articles in Iranian newspapers. The publication of Jewish calendars was also banned.

BUSINESS AND COMMERCE

Although the 1979 constitution grants some civil rights to religious minorities, including Jews, Zoroastrians and Christians (primarily Armenians and Assyrians), they are not accepted as employees in government offices or in any organization run by the regime. Business permits and economic advantages are granted only to Muslims, especially those loyal to the regime. Since the beginning of 1994 premises belonging to religious minorities, especially those serving food, were ordered to hang a sign at the entrance saying "run by a religious minority". This order, derived from the distinctive Shi'ite Muslim notion of the ritual impurity of unbelievers, caused much concern within Jewish and Christian business circles for fear of violent attacks.

EDUCATION

School books in Iran often include antisemitic remarks relating to Middle Eastern history or religion. Jewish schools virtually ceased to exist when they were forced to accept non-Jewish pupils and to hold classes on the sabbath. Teaching of Torah (Jewish law) is permitted only in Farsi translations of the Bible, to prevent any "Zionist manipulations".

PUBLICATIONS AND MEDIA

Antisemitic articles accusing Jews of a range of offences, from undermining the revolution to offending Islam, were published in various journals. The Iranian media frequently included antisemitic statements when criticizing Israel and Zionism (see **Effects of Anti-Zionism**).

Anger was also expressed over the Vatican's decision to establish diplomatic relations with Israel at the end of 1993. On 13 January, for example, *Salam* claimed that the Pope had made a pact with the "crucifiers of Jesus Christ" and that "till now Christians hated Jews because of the betrayal of Jewish ancestors. In spite of diplomatic relations between the Vatican and Zionism, the demand for blood revenge from Jewish deviators who crucified his holiness The Christ still exists." The state-controlled Iranian news agency, IRNA, also reported that "for centuries the church hated Jews because of their betrayal Christ but Pope Paul VI has pardoned them".

The Hebron massacre provoked not only anti-Zionist but also antisemitic responses in the Iranian media. On 15 March, for example, *Keyhan* asserted: "In Deuteronomy and Numbers, Jews are ordered to kill; and it reminds me that they cut into pieces the bodies of Palestinians who have been murdered by racist Zionists, and according to orders of the falsified Bible."

The external service of the Voice of the Islamic Republic of Iran, the official radio station, invoked fears of Jewish domination when it asserted, for example, on 26 February that the "attack on Muslim worshippers in a sacred place reflects the depth of Jewish hatred. The Talmudic mentality is consistent with the logic of force used by Jews against the Palestinians and other Muslim peoples." The broadcast subsequently called for "a single *jihad* action" to be conducted from southern Lebanon or the "occupied territories" in order "to teach the Jews many lessons".

In the aftermath of the Hebron massacre, media reports also sought to delegitimize Judaism by invoking Qur'anic verses. *Jomhuri-e Eslami*, for example, asserted on 2 March: "In spite of the fact that Jews have falsified the Bible, we still can read in the Book of Samuel: Go to Amaleq and kill them, take whatever belongs to them, murder all men, women, children and even animals."

The Iranian media occasionally mentioned the victories of the Prophet in wars against Jews during the early days of Islam. *Andiseh*, a monthly review, described the extermination of the Jewish tribe of Bani-Ghoreiza by order of Muhammad as "the conquest of the last bastion of the enemy".

Many different translations, mostly from Arabic, of *The Protocols of the Elders of Zion* were widely distributed in Iran. The last edition was published in 1994 by Astan-e Ghods-e Razavi publications which belongs to the Islamic Foundation of Emam-Reza Shrine in Mashhad. The Arabic version was written by Ajjaj Nowbahz and translated into Persian by Hamid-Reza Sheikhi. In March, the daily newspaper *Jomhuri-e Eslami* serialized an abridged version of *The Protocols*.

RELIGION

Antisemitic themes frequently figured in sermons delivered by leading clerics in mosques as well as the political sphere (see also **Mainstream Politics**). The religious leader of Shiraz, for example, called on Muslims to go out and do battle with the Jew.

EFFECTS OF ANTI-ZIONISM

Iranian authorities consistently deny the legitimacy of the Jewish state, referring to Israel as "the usurper Zionist regime" or as a "cancerous growth within the Islamic body". In a radio broadcast on 20 October, Ayatollah Khamenei characterized Israel as a "false nation" and accused the West of having "gathered wicked people from all over the world and made something called the Israeli nation . . . all the malevolent and evil Jews have gathered there."

Responding to allegations that Iran was implicated in terrorist attacks on Jewish and Israeli targets in Buenos Aires and London in July (see **United Kingdom** and **Argentina**), Khamenei condemned Israel as "a baseless, false and untrue Zionist regime who gathered a bunch of Jewish criminals with records of viciousness, malevolence, thievery and murders [in this land] and called it the Nation of Israel, ruled only by the logic of terror and crime". IRNA criticized "Zionist-orchestrated propaganda" and several newspaper articles accused "International Zionism" of involvement in the bombings. The weekly *Keyhan-e Havaii* (an airmail edition of *Keyhan*), for example, published a series of articles by Hussein al-Tariki, former director of the Arab League in Argentina, referring to "the extensive net of Zionist terror and military activities in Argentina".

Reporting on the visit of Israeli Foreign Minister Shimon Peres to Germany in August, *Keyhan International*, the English-language daily, suggested that German Foreign Minister Klaus Kinkel had other priorities "besides kowtowing to Tel Aviv for some Jewish suffering during Nazi rule".

Antisemitism also featured in media

responses to the report of the UN human rights commission. Criticizing the rapporteur, Galindo Pohl, of using biased reports linked to "international Zionism", the state-controlled radio, VIRI, announced on 9 March that "if anyone, of whatever status, were to attribute something to a Jewish personality or comment on a historical issue which did not please the Jews, they would raise their hue and cry".

Iranian officials and clerics continued to condemn the Arab or Muslim states seeking normalization of relations with Israel and maintained financial and material support for Palestinian rejectionist groups, such as Hamas and Islamic Jihad.

LEGAL MATTERS

Jews are banned from having any connection with Zionist or Jewish organizations abroad. They are banned from travelling to Israel and there have been many cases of imprisonment or fines for those suspected of visiting Israel in secret.

ASSESSMENT

Continual verbal attacks by the regime on Israel, Zionism and the role of Jews in world affairs continued to create a threatening atmosphere for Iranian Jews. An increase in antisemitic publications and propaganda in Iran may have been linked to heightened opposition to the Middle East peace process.

Iraq

General population: 19.9 million
Jewish population: 200-300 (in Baghdad)

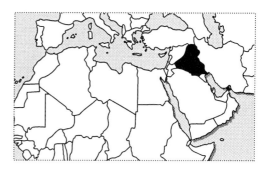

GENERAL BACKGROUND

Political power in the Republic of Iraq remained concentrated exclusively in the hands of President Saddam Hussein and his family, under the guise of the rule of a single party, the Ba'ath Arab Socialist Party. The supreme political decision-making, law-making and judicial body was the Revolutionary Command Council, a small and tightly-knit group. Among Saddam Hussein's foremost supporters are the tribal federation of albu-Naşir, which hails from the area of Tikrit, and the Sunni Arab population of Iraq, residing in a triangle between Baghdad, Mosul and the Syrian border. Iraq's eight-year war with Iran (1980-88), its invasion of Kuwait and the subsequent war (1991), and the massive Shi'ite and Kurdish uprisings that followed, caused severe economic hardship which has been exacerbated by the UN sanctions. Hussein has taken draconian measures to prevent the economic collapse of Iraq, such as introducing the amputation of hands as a punishment for theft. He has attempted to eliminate opposition by ordering mass arrests, torture and executions, mainly of Shi'ites and Kurds, but also of dissidents in the Sunni Arab community, including army officers. In order to strengthen his control in the face of worsening food shortages in May, Hussein assumed the position of prime minister himself and appointed two new deputy prime ministers in addition to Tariq Aziz.

HISTORICAL LEGACY

During the 1930s and up to the anti-British and pro-Nazi Rashid Ali revolt of May 1941, anti-Jewish sentiments among Iraqi intellectuals, army officers and politicians were heightened by Nazi influence in Baghdad. In June 1941, a wide-scale pogrom was carried out: 129 Jews were murdered, many hundreds were wounded and much Jewish property was looted and destroyed.

In August 1948 many Jews were imprisoned on charges of "Zionism" and a few were executed for "espionage". In early 1950 Jews were allowed to leave for Israel, but were required to relinquish their Iraqi citizenship and forfeit their assets. The virulent anti-Jewish atmosphere in Baghdad and the introduction of anti-Jewish laws encouraged approximately 120,000 Jews to emigrate to Israel in 1950-51.

Under the Republican rule of General 'Abd al-Karim Qasim (1958-63), many Jews were released from prison and deported. The situation of the Jews deteriorated during the period of Ba'ath rule, and that of the Arif brothers (1963-68).

Following the 1967 Six Day War, Jews were subject to severe restrictions and were forbidden, for example, to leave their home towns. Some 300 Jewish business-owners and community leaders were arrested and tortured for "espionage" or for "economic support for Israel". All the property of the Jewish religious endowment (*waqf*) was placed under government control.

When the Ba'ath Party came to power, it conducted a mock espionage trial and public hanging of thirteen young Jews. By 1971, about forty Jews had either been executed or had died under torture, and many more were jailed. Due to rising international pressure, most of Iraq's remaining Jews were eventually allowed to leave the country between 1971 and 1973.

During the war against Iran and the Kuwait crisis, antisemitic themes were quite widespread in the regime's war propaganda. Most conspicuous were claims that the Persian enemy had an ancient alignment with the Jews, dating back to the era of the Persian empire of Cyrus and his successors.

RACISM AND XENOPHOBIA

Sunni Arabs, who dominate the ruling élite, comprise only some 20 per cent of the total population of Iraq; most of the rest—some 18 per cent Kurds and 55 per cent Shi'ite Arabs—are hostile to the regime, or at least alienated from it.

In 1994, the United Nations and human rights organizations, such as Amnesty International, condemned Iraq for its continuing persecution of the Kurdish minority in the north and the Shi'ites in the marshlands in the south.

MAINSTREAM POLITICS

Iraq's objection to the Middle East peace process was justified by moral, historical, cultural and religious considerations. Iraqi leaders described the conflict between Muslim Arabs and Jews as a clash between two civilizations that could not be reconciled. The political links between Israel, the Jews and the United States were also emphasized in speeches and articles. On 7 September Deputy Prime Minister Tariq Aziz, for example, referred to the "Jewish lobby" active on behalf of Israel in the United States, warning that "the United States and Israel have a common objective of seeing a politically, militarily and economically weak and fragmented Arab homeland".

SOCIAL ANTISEMITISM

There is a widespread belief in the authenticity of *The Protocols of the Elders of Zion* and, more generally, in a Jewish conspiracy to dominate, and even destroy, the world. It has been frequently claimed that the USA and Europe are controlled by "Jewish finance" and that the Allied attack on Iraq following the invasion of Kuwait was a Jewish-Zionist "plot". Occasionally, there have been claims that Jews belong to a different race from all other human beings.

PUBLICATIONS AND MEDIA

The strong stand taken by the USA against lifting the embargo on Iraq was attributed to the manipulation of world Zionism and the Jewish lobby active in the USA, who were referred to in the government daily *al-Jumhuriyya* on 12 February as the "secret decision makers". This notion was most vividly expressed in cartoons, one of which showed an American gangster wearing a hat with a Star of David shooting at, and blackmailing, the United Nations.

Iraqi cartoons continued to portray Jews as monstrous creatures who are the source of all Iraqi and Arab troubles; several examples appeared in *Babil* in September and October.

Criticism of American support for Israel also provided a pretext for antisemitism. *Al-Thawra*, for example, asserted on 21 January: "To the Jew who is skilled in blackmail, the US presence in the Golan is a gain for Washington, and Israeli military power, which was created through US support, is also a gain for Washington and its Middle East Policy."

Iraqi newspapers refer to Israel in quotation marks or call it "the enemy state". According to Baghdad, the most serious clash was during the second Gulf War, when the guns of "the mother of battles" (the Iraqi name for the second Gulf War) clashed with the "guns of the Torah". *Al-Jumhuriyya* stated on 12 February: "As the guns of the Torah continue to menace the Ka'bah, Jerusalem, Baghdad and Algiers, Iraq called on 1 billion Muslims to stand against them, until Islam becomes victorious."

Attacking Arab countries for their apparent willingness to sign peace agreements with Israel, Iraq sought to raise the spectre of Israel and "world Zionism" using these agreements to control and enslave the Arabs. *Babil* thus warned on 1 August that Israel's aim was to take revenge on the Arabs and Muslims by turning them into slaves in "Greater Israel from the Euphrates to the Nile". This revenge, *Babil* contended, was prompted by the Jews' bad memories of the ancient past, "the memory of Jewish Babylonian captivity and the fate of [the Jewish] Bani qaynuqa' and Khaybar tribes in Yathrib". This is a reference to the clash between Muhammad and the Jews in early Islam, when Muhammad expelled two Jewish tribes from Medina and massacred a third.

EFFECTS OF ANTI-ZIONISM

The massacre of Muslims by a Jewish settler in a Hebron mosque on 25 February was seized upon by the Iraqi media to inflame antisemitic sentiment and to incite Iraqis, Arabs and Muslims against the peace process. The daily bulletin of the ministry of defence, *al-Qadisiyya*, claimed that the "Zionists are thirsty for the blood of Muslims and Arabs and that they have always been seeking to kill and persecute them and to confiscate their rights in Palestine". Other critics spoke of the "fascist" and racist nature of the Zionist movement, and the "impossibility of co-existence between it and the Palestinian Arab people".

ASSESSMENT

Anti-Zionist, antisemitic and anti-American motifs were intermingled by Iraqi authorities and media, with the political aims of mobilizing support for the regime, deflecting attention from serious internal problems and inciting Arab and Muslim masses against their governments. The specific pretexts for antisemitism in 1994 were the continuing sanctions against Iraq, the Hebron massacre and the Middle East peace process.

Jordan

General population: 3.9 million
Jewish population: none

GENERAL BACKGROUND

The Hashemite Kingdom of Jordan, which became independent in 1946, is a constitutional monarchy ruled by King Hussein ibn Talal, who succeeded his father in 1953. In 1992 King Hussein lifted the ban on political parties, imposed during the 1967 Six Day War. The first multi-party elections since 1956 were held in November 1993 and the largest bloc of seats was won by the Hizb Jabha al-Amal al-Islami (IAF, Islamic Action Front) backed by the Muslim Brotherhood. In August 1993, however, a change in the electoral law to a one-person-one-vote system produced a parliament with significantly reduced Islamist influence, compared to the house elected on a non-party basis in November 1989. Although Islamists have gained parliamentary representation, the Jordanian regime took strong measures in 1994 to restrict Islamic extremists. In December, for example, eleven Islamists were sentenced to death for plotting to bomb two cinemas and to assassinate leading officials including Jordan's former peace negotiator with Israel.

Following the Declaration of Principles between Israel and the Palestine Liberation Organization (PLO), Israel and Jordan signed a "common agenda" on 14 September 1993. Local opposition to the peace process was mobilized by the Jordanian branch of the Muslim Brotherhood. On 26 July 1994 King Hussein met with Israeli Prime Minister Yitzhak Rabin in Washington DC to sign the Washington Declaration, thereby formally ending forty-six years of hostilities. Shortly afterwards King Hussein made an unprecedented flight over Israel with an Israeli military escort, telephone lines between Israel and Jordan were opened and the border crossing between Aqaba and Eilat was opened for third-country nationals. An historic peace treaty between Israel and Jordan was finally signed on 26 October and the Israeli embassy in Jordan was opened on 10 December.

HISTORICAL LEGACY

Unlike almost all other Arab countries, Jordan did not have a sizeable Jewish population. Antisemitism in Jordan has invariably been linked to anti-Zionism. It is important to stress that while Islamist rejectionism is often antisemitic, secular opponents to the normalization

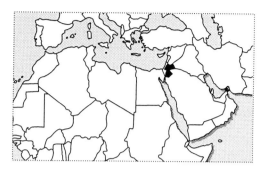

of Arab relations with Israel are primarily anti-Zionist.

RACISM AND XENOPHOBIA

Jordan absorbed several waves of Palestinian refugees—in 1948 from Israel, in 1967 from the West Bank, and in 1990 from the Gulf—and unlike other Arab countries, Jordan has granted citizenship to Palestinians. More than half of the Jordanian population is currently estimated to be of Palestinian origin. Palestinians are largely excluded from high-ranking positions in the armed forces, security services and government.

Jordan also accepted many Iraqi refugees during and after the 1991 Gulf War. As a result of a rescue mission in June 1993, over 400 Bosnian Muslims were brought to the kingdom.

As Islamist views become increasingly popular, anti-Christian sentiments have become more widespread. Christians account for approximately 6 per cent of the population, but Christian migration to Western countries is increasing. When Marwan Muasher, a prominent Christian, was named as Jordan's first ambassador to Israel, many Christians feared that their community would be closely associated with the peace treaty and that there would be an Islamist backlash against Christian businesses. By law only Christians can sell alcohol; in October, one such shop was bombed.

Other minorities in predominantly Sunni Muslim Jordan include Circassians, Chechens, Druze and Armenians.

PARTIES, ORGANIZATIONS, MOVEMENTS

Islamist groups, which are combating all forms of normalization with Israel, especially in the cultural sphere, draw on antisemitic ideas from Islamic and European sources alleging Jewish conspiracies.

The Anti-Zionism Anti-Racism Centre, which was opened in March 1993 by Leith Shubeilat, a popular Islamist leader, was outlawed by the government but continued to operate. Its stated aim is "to unveil the motives of Zionism around the world, its expansionist plans and its power in manipulating the world's public opinion". The Committee against Normalization and Submission, whose objective is to fight the normalization of relations with Israel in all spheres, was also banned. It provides a network for various professional organizations, including the Islamist-dominated Jordanian Writers' Union and the Jordanian Engineers' Association which recently announced their own boycott against Israel. Since the Anti-Zionism Anti-Racism Centre and the Committee against Normalization and Submission were banned, newspapers were not allowed, under the press and publication law, to report on their activities or publish their statements. At the time of the signing of the peace treaty, several newspaper editors were given warnings after articles which made reference to one or other of these opposition groups were published.

The Palestinian Islamist organization, Hamas (Islamic Resistance Movement), maintains an office in Amman, from which press statements regarding policies and activities within Israel and the West Bank were issued in 1994 by representatives, including Ibrahim Ghawshah and Muhammad Nazzal. In April Israeli Prime Minister Yitzhak Rabin criticized Jordan for allowing Hamas to operate from Jordanian territory. In response, the Jordanian government issued warnings to Hamas and a few suspected activists were questioned.

MAINSTREAM POLITICS

The militant Islamic party, the Hizb Jabha al-Amal al-Islami (Islamic Action Front), led by Ishaq al-Farhan, represents the Muslim Brotherhood in parliament. It rejects the Middle East peace process and has combined antisemitic and anti-Zionist rhetoric. A statement issued, for example, on the opening of the Israeli embassy in Amman, said: "We are sure that the Israeli embassy here will serve as a centre for hatching conspiracies against our culture, our mosques, our Koran, our schools, our morals and our national economy." The statement also called upon Jordanians to follow the Egyptian example and "reject the presence of the Jews".

MANIFESTATIONS

A Jewish American tourist in Amman was stabbed by a Jordanian four days before the signing of the peace treaty, ostensibly because the tourist said he was from Israel. The perpetrator of the attack subsequently commented that he "did not want to see a Jewish tourist in Jordan".

CULTURAL LIFE

In 1994 the ministry of information banned all public screenings of Steven Spielberg's *Schindler's List*, on the grounds that it was pornographic, but the film was available for hire from many video shops. According to the Jordanian information minister, Jawad al-Anani, the ban was due to popular anger over the massacre of Muslims by a Jewish settler in a mosque in Hebron, following which it would not be opportune to show a film sympathetic to Jewish suffering.

EDUCATION

In the wake of the Israel-Jordan peace treaty, opposition groups on campus invoked antisemitic themes. A joint statement issued on 27 July by the student unions at Jordan's principal universities to the weekly newpaper *The Star* asserted: "The Jordanian government has rushed to negotiate and meet with the killers of the prophets and innocents. [Israel] has never felt anything for Jordan and its people other than hate and contempt."

PUBLICATIONS AND MEDIA

Book vendors in Amman, Aqaba, Zarqa and other towns continued to sell a range of antisemitic works in Arabic; translations of Western texts such as *The Protocols of the Elders of Zion*, and Arabic works continued to circulate in Jordan, particularly in Islamic bookshops. The covers of such books often feature antisemitic images, such as a Star of David combined with a dagger and pool of blood. An example of antisemitic iconography was found in *al-Masieh al-Dajal* (The Antichrist) which alleges an Israeli-American conspiracy against Islam and includes images of Jews as hook-nosed and militaristic.

The mainstream press, in which the government holds considerable shares, focused its coverage of negotiations with Israel on the political issues, although occasional negative stereotypes of Jews appeared in cartoons. This was less true for Jordan's privately owned weekly tabloids, where antisemitic themes were more common. On 26 October, the day of the signing of the peace treaty, the Islamic weekly *al-Sabil* reported that the residents of Aqaba were alarmed about the possible influx of Israeli tourists "whose penny-pinching ways and immodest behaviour on the beaches are part of a concerted and premeditated plan to undermine the values of local youth".

RELIGION

The visit to Jordan by eighty rabbis from the Association of Reform Zionists of America on

20 January was fiercely condemned by the Muslim Brotherhood, which opposes the Middle East peace process. Sheikh Abd al-Rahman Khalifa, the deputy spiritual leader of the organization, asserted: "Jews have proved their deception throughout history and God has punished them by exiling them."

DENIAL OF THE HOLOCAUST

While public statements denying the Holocaust are virtually non-existent, there is popular support for the view that the mass destruction of European Jewry during the Second World War either did not take place or, as is widely held in the Arab world, that the Holocaust has been exaggerated for political purposes. A few bookshops sell works in Arabic translation which claim that the Holocaust is a hoax. Books which document the Holocaust continue to be banned in Jordan and the topic is not taught in schools.

EFFECTS OF ANTI-ZIONISM

While newspapers have long made a distinction between Israelis and Jews, no such distinction is made in common discourse, irrespective of socio-economic class or education. Therefore the antisemitic effects of anti-Zionism in Jordan are relatively widespread.

As noted above (see **Mainstream Politics** and **Parties, Organizations, Movements**) opposition to the Israel-Jordan peace treaty in 1994 combined both anti-Zionist and antisemitic reactions. References to Zionist conspiracies against Islam may also reflect antisemitic views.

The weekly newspaper *Shihan*, asserted on 11 August for example, that "Zionist secret agents" had carried out the terrorist attacks against Jewish and Israeli targets in London and Buenos Aires in order to discredit the Islamist movement which was opposed to the peace process.

COUNTERING ANTISEMITISM

Since the signing of the Washington Declaration, King Hussein repeatedly referred in public to the links between the "children of Abraham" and to the three great faiths of Islam, Judaism and Christianity, thereby emphasizing the legitimacy to the Jewish religion. During his

visit to Washington DC, King Hussein held a meeting with American Jewish community leaders which was broadcast on state-controlled Jordanian television. Crown Prince Hassan also addressed an interfaith conference in Vienna in February, calling for greater understanding between the three faiths through dialogue and education. Speaking in London in May to mark his joining the Inter-Parliamentary Council against Antisemitism, the crown prince drew attention to the "vital similarities" between antisemitism and anti-Muslim sentiment: "Both Jews and Muslims are felt by those antagonistic towards them to be misplaced in European societies . . . both forms of racism demand similar responses."

The ministry of education announced its intention to reform the social studies curriculum in the light of the peace treaty with Israel. The aim is to minimize the "emotionally charged" content of schoolbooks, much of which is antisemitic. Officials state that facts will not be altered and the Arab claim to Palestine will remain. Derogatory statements about Jews, such as the following, which appears in *al-Kadiat al-Filistiniya* (The Palestinian Cause), will be removed: "Their usury and love of money was the reason that people hated them and this caused them to hate the societies they lived in."

ASSESSMENT

There was a significant improvement in the official attitudes towards Jews in 1994. After the signing of the peace treaty in July the Jordanian government seemed more committed to normalizing economic and political relations with Israel. However, growing co-operation is likely between militant Islamic groups, which are antisemitic, anti-Zionist and anti-Western, and secular Arab nationalists, who are less inclined to express antisemitic sentiments.

Since the signing of the Israel-Jordan peace treaty and the regional economic summit in Casablanca, fear of Israeli economic domination has increased. High profile Israeli business schemes coupled with low levels of financial rewards to middle-and lower-income Jordanians could shift the focus of criticism from anti-Israeli to antisemitic rhetoric.

Lebanon

General population: 2.9 million
Jewish population: 270

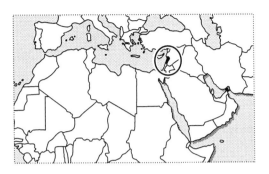

GENERAL BACKGROUND

After fifteen years of civil war between Muslim and Christian factions from 1975 to 1990, the political situation in Lebanon has become more stable in the 1990s. The first parliamentary elections to the national assembly since 1972 were held in 1992 but were boycotted by leading Maronite Christian parties in opposition to the continuing Syrian military presence in Lebanon. The Shi'ite Muslim parties, Amal and Hizbullah, emerged as the largest bloc of deputies in the new national assembly. Rafiq al-Hariri was appointed prime minister in October 1992. The equal distribution of parliamentary seats between Muslims and Christians is determined by law. The cabinet too must reflect the principal religious divisions.

In 1994 the Syrian government continued to exert political influence on Lebanese domestic and foreign policy. Palestinian groups operated autonomously in refugee camps throughout the country. In southern Lebanon, the Iranian-backed Islamist movement, Hizbullah, continued to launch attacks against Israel and Israeli-backed militia, resulting in retaliatory air attacks by Israeli forces.

Sporadic violence between supporters of different political forces continued to erupt, but political killings declined as the government consolidated its authority over the country. In one of the most serious incidents, ten Christians were killed and forty were wounded when a Maronite church in Jounieh was bombed on 27 February.

During 1994 Lebanon proceeded with plans for the economic reconstruction of areas affected by the civil war, including the large-scale redevelopment of Beirut.

HISTORICAL LEGACY

The Jewish community in Lebanon is one of many religious minorities in a multi-denominational state. In 1952 there were approximately 100,000 Jews but emigration occurred in two major waves, after the Six Day War in 1967 and following the civil war of 1976. The presence of Hizbullah and the Syrian military have severely restricted Jewish cultural and religious life in Lebanon.

Between 1984 and 1986 eleven Lebanese Jews, including the president and secretary-general of the community and a local paediatrician, were taken hostage by the Organization of the Oppressed of the Earth which has links with Hizbullah. It claims to have executed nine of these hostages, ostensibly because Israel failed to release all Lebanese and Palestinian prisoners in South Lebanon, but only the bodies of four have been recovered. On 28 December 1985, the group threatened that unless its demands were met it would not only kill the remaining hostages but also any other Jews "upon whom we can lay our hands".

The Lebanese law protecting religious minorities has ceased to apply under *de facto* Syrian military control. Jews are thus forced to keep a low profile and cannot practise their religion openly. This situation is unlikely to change until a breakthrough is achieved in the Israeli-Syrian peace talks.

PARTIES, ORGANIZATIONS, MOVEMENTS

Militant Islamists based in Lebanon continued to invoke antisemitic themes, such as that of an international Jewish conspiracy to discredit Islam. The spiritual leader of Hizbullah, Sayyid Muhammed Husayn Fadlallah, for example, regards opposition to Israel as part of the "old struggle of the Muslims against the Jewish conspiracy against Islam".

Invoking religious rhetoric, in a statement issued after the murder of an Israeli taxi driver by Palestinian Islamists, Hizbullah warned that "every Jew in Jerusalem is an usurpist enemy and a target for the *mujahidin*. Tourism in Jerusalem will only lead to *jihad* and fighting against God's enemies." On 2 November, Hizbullah issued a statement condeming the Casablanca conference on economic development, which it accused of ensuring "American and Zionist economic domination of the region" and warned that "no Jews will be safe, either in their tourism or trade".

A number of other Islamist groups linked to Hizbullah are also active in Lebanon. The Movement of the Oppressed was among the groups which claimed to have bombed Israeli and Jewish targets in London on 26 and 27 July (see **United Kingdom**). A statement issued from Beirut on 6 August warned that the group would hit Jewish targets around the world creating "rivers of blood" if Israel continued to attack Lebanon. It also claimed responsibility for firing Katyusha rockets on "Jewish settlements in northern Palestine".

Ansar Allah (Followers of God) is a Hizbullah splinter group reportedly led by Jamal Suleiman.

MAINSTREAM POLITICS

In 1994, some Muslim politicians reportedly attempted to discredit Christian opposition party members and other public figures by terming them "Jews inside".

CULTURAL LIFE

Universal Pictures, the distributors of Steven Spielberg's *Schindler's List*, withdrew the film in Lebanon after pre-release advertisements were prohibited in Lebanese cinemas. The authorities gave no explanation for the ban but threatened to confiscate any copies of the film in Lebanon. Nonetheless pirated videotapes of *Schindler's List* were widely available.

PUBLICATIONS AND MEDIA

The hostility of Islamist movements and of Syrian forces towards the Jewish community in Lebanon is reflected in the press. In 1994 the Islamist daily newspaper *al-Liwa* invoked antisemitic themes, such as a Jewish conspiracy against Islam. The daily newspaper published by the Syrian Socialist Nationalist Party in Lebanon, *al-Diyar*, also used antisemitic slogans as part of its regular campaign against Israel. No distinction was made between Jews, Zionists and Israel. Antisemitic editorials also appeared in the mainstream Muslim daily, *al-Safir.*

Antisemitic cartoons which portrayed Jews as ugly, hook-nosed and money-grabbing appeared regularly in the Lebanese press.

Arabic translations of classical antisemitic texts such as *The Protocols of the Elders of Zion* continued to circulate in Lebanon.

ASSESSMENT

Militant Islamic groups in Lebanon continued to combine antisemitic rhetoric with vehement opposition to Israel. International efforts to discover the fate of the remaining seven Jewish hostages in Lebanon continued to prove fruitless.

Libya

General population: 5.5 million
Jewish population: none

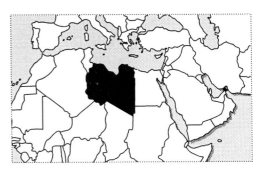

GENERAL BACKGROUND

The year 1994 marked the twenty-fifth anniversary of the September Revolution, which brought Colonel Muammar Qaddafi to power and led to the establishment of his dictatorship.

United Nations sanctions were imposed in 1992 over Qaddafi's refusal to extradite two Libyan citizens believed to be responsible for the 1988 bombing of an American airplane over Scotland. In 1994 Libya remained in diplomatic isolation because of its alleged support of international terrorism. Although sanctions were believed to have had an adverse effect on various industries much of the economy remained highly centralized and under state control.

In an effort to eliminate potential opposition, the Sanusiyya Islamic sect was banned in 1992 and suspected members of Islamist groups such as al-Jama'mat al-Islamiyya (Islamic Group) were arrested. Following an attempted coup in October 1993, security forces tightened political control in 1994, entailing systematic violations of human rights.

Qaddafi has indicated support for Palestinian rejectionists who oppose the Middle East peace process. In 1994 he hosted a meeting of the ten groups which comprise the Alliance of Palestinian Forces including Hamas, Islamic Jihad, the Democratic Front for the Liberation of Palestine and the Palestine Liberation Front.

HISTORICAL LEGACY

From the fifteenth century onwards, Jews in Libya experienced many periods of persecution. Libyan Jews were subjected to Italian racial laws in 1936. During the Second World War, the Jewish quarter of Benghazi was sacked and 2,000 Jews were deported. In November 1945, more than 100 Jews were murdered in anti-Jewish riots in Tripoli.

Prior to Libya's independence in 1951, most of the 38,000 Libyan Jews emigrated to Israel. Those who stayed were disenfranchised in 1963 and forbidden to hold office. During the 1967 Six Day War about 118 Jews were killed and there was widespread destruction of Jewish property.

When Qaddafi came to power in 1971, all Jewish property was seized without compensation. In 1993, Qaddafi announced that he was willing to compensate Jewish and Italian emigrés for property left in Libya and that Jews of Libyan origin, including the 100,000 living in Israel, would be welcome to visit the country. These conciliatory statements were possibly intended to soften Western attitudes towards Libya.

RACISM AND XENOPHOBIA

Libya is a relatively homogenous society— approximately 97 per cent of the population are Sunni Muslim Arabs or Muslims of Berber descent. The Berber minority are subject to some discrimination, as are other tribal groups, such as the Tuarags in the south. Since 1990, thousands of black African workers from Nigeria, Mali and Ghana, for example, have been detained or expelled from Libya on the grounds that they were illegal immigrants.

MAINSTREAM POLITICS

In 1994, Qaddafi's hostility to the United States and Britain was frequently combined with allegations of a Christian-Jewish conspiracy. In a response to a British media report that Libya was developing nuclear weapons, Qaddafi broadcast a speech on 19 February in which he referred to the "Jewish and Christian alliance against all non-Jewish religions such as Islam, Buddhism and Confucianism, in order to establish the Jewish and Christian control over the whole world" (see also **Effects of Anti-Zionism**).

EFFECTS OF ANTI-ZIONISM

In many statements condemning Israel, Qaddafi used the terms "Israeli" and "Jew" interchangeably, and repeatedly suggested that Jews were attempting to destabilize the Middle East not only by military means, but also by spreading drugs. In a speech broadcast on state-controlled television on 23 January, Qaddafi claimed: "Israel runs drugs farms. Hashish is planted in Palestine and directed against the Arab countries . . . Who grows it? The Jews grow it."

In response to the massacre of Muslims by a Jewish settler in a Hebron mosque in February,

Qaddafi not only condemned Jewish settlers and the state of Israel but also alleged that a "Jewish-Christian alliance" was waging a "Crusader war". In an address broadcast on the state-controlled radio on 13 March, Qaddafi asserted: "The new world order means that Jews and Christians control Muslims, and if they can, they will dominate Confucianism, and other religions in India, China and Japan." He also identified a "Zionist-Jewish-Christian plot to Balkanize Egypt" (see also **Mainstream Politics**).

ASSESSMENT

The Libyan leader Qaddafi has played a major part in financing the spread of negative perceptions of Jews throughout the Islamic world and has often used antisemitic imagery to express his anti-Zionism. In 1994 Qaddafi made little attempt to distinguish between hostility to Jews and opposition to the Zionist movement and the state of Israel. He also expressed antipathy to the West by repeatedly alleging a Jewish-Christian conspiracy against Islam.

Morocco

General population: 27 million
Jewish population: 7,000 (mainly in Casablanca)

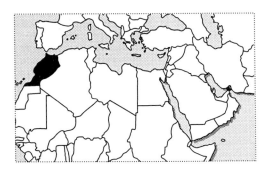

GENERAL BACKGROUND

King Hassan II, Morocco's constitutional monarch since 1962, belongs to the Alawi dynasty which has ruled the country since the seventeenth century. In 1992 King Hassan held a referendum to endorse constitutional reforms in order to establish a better balance between legislative and executive bodies. Direct elections —the first since 1984—to the chamber of representatives were held in 1993. The ruling centre-right coalition won the largest number of seats but the Democractic Bloc, a coalition of the legal opposition parties—the nationalist Istiqlal (Independence Party), the Union socialiste des forces populaires (Socialist Union of Popular Forces), the Organization pour l'action populaire démocratique (Organization for Democratic Popular Action) and the centre-left Union nationale des forces populaires (National Union of Popular Forces)—performed well, gaining ninety-nine seats.

Despite the releases and pardons of a number of political prisoners, there were continued reports in 1994 of human rights abuses.

The effects of drought, currency fluctuations and world recession contributed to Morocco's continuing economic difficulties.

The Middle East peace process has strengthened relations between King Hassan and Israel. In June following Israeli Foreign Minister Shimon Peres's visit to Morocco, the two countries agreed to establish telephone and postal links. Moroccan officials participated in several international meetings within the framework of the multilateral peace talks. In September Israel and Morocco announced the opening of economic interest sections in their respective capitals. The regional development conference hosted in Casablanca in November indicated Morocco's eagerness to capitalize on the economic benefits of peace in the region.

HISTORICAL LEGACY

The Jewish community of Morocco, which dates back more than 2,000 years, has experienced various waves of both tolerance and discrimination. The worst outbreaks of antisemitic violence occurred during the Middle Ages when Jews were massacred in Fez in 1033 and in Marrakesh in 1232. Following the establishment of the French protectorate in 1912, Jews began to enjoy equality. Under the Vichy regime, Jews suffered discrimination but King Muhammed V did much to ensure that they were not deported.

By 1948, there were some 270,000 Jews in Morocco but, thereafter, the population decreased rapidly. Following the establishment of the state of Israel, there were numerous attacks on Jewish individuals and premises. In June 1953, forty-three Jews were murdered, and violence persisted until Morocco gained independence in 1956. Following independence, Jews were granted full suffrage and complete freedom of movement but emigration was restricted (although thousands of Jews continued to leave for Israel clandestinely). After the 1967 Six Day War, a worsening of conditions, including a virulent press campaign against the Jewish community as well as against Israel, led many middle-class Jews to emigrate.

In recent years, the Jewish community has maintained good relations with the monarch. The positive climate was reinforced by King Hassan's appointment of a Jew, André Azoulay, as his advisor on economic affairs and, more significantly, by the appointment of the president of Morocco's Jewish Communities Council, Serge Berdugo, as minister of tourism. Berdugo, who was awarded the prestigious medal of the order of the throne in July, became only the second Jewish minister in Moroccan history (the first was Leon Ben Zeken in the 1950s).

PUBLICATIONS AND MEDIA

L'Opinion, the daily newspaper of the opposition party, Istiqlal, published a vehemently antisemitic article on 27 December, invoking *The Protocols of the Elders of the Zion* and alleging: "Jewish evil knows no limits." The article blamed Israel for forcing the resignation of President Chadli in Algeria and for assassinating his successor, Mohamed Boudiaf. The author, a high-ranking official in the ministry of tourism, concluded: "An important step in the building of North Africa was sabotaged by

Jews working on behalf of Israel through the use of false religious Muslim guides."

RELIGION

Although good relations generally exist between the Jewish and Muslim communities, antisemitic themes have emerged in sermons by Islamist clerics. Since the regime seeks to quell the spread of militant Islamic ideas, particularly in view of the situation in neighbouring Algeria, all statements, antisemitic or otherwise, by these circles tend to be made clandestinely.

COUNTERING ANTISEMITISM

King Hassan met with an American delegation of United Jewish Appeal leaders in August and the event was widely reported in the Moroccan media. In his televised speech, the king appealed to American Jews to support the Middle East peace process and declared: "It is our duty to live together in peace and understanding. There were clouds lately in the horizons of Jews, Muslims and Arabs. But now we note that these horizons are beginning to clear and are brightened by the light of hope."

Plans were announced in December for a Jewish museum to be opened in Casablanca in 1995, the first to be built in an Arab country.

ASSESSMENT

Moroccan Jewry currently enjoys the tolerance of King Hassan's regime and antisemitic sentiment has not been evident in the government or in the media. Concern has been expressed over the possibility of change when his rule comes to an end.

Syria

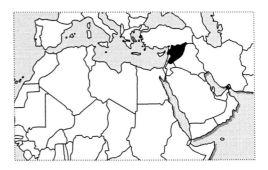

General population: 13.8 million
Jewish population: 230 (mainly in Damascus)

GENERAL BACKGROUND

President Asad's autocratic regime, which has dominated Syrian politics for over two decades, continued to rule with the support of the military and the secret services. Economic liberalization has led to some improvement in the economy; gross domestic product rose slightly to 5.5 per cent in 1994 and inflation increased to 20 per cent.

Since the end of the Cold War, Syria has attempted to improve relations with the West, particularly with the USA. Diplomatic relations with the UK were restored in 1990. Syria supported the anti-Iraq coalition during the 1991 Gulf War and, since attending the Madrid talks, has also shown some readiness to participate in the peace process with Israel. In March 1994 a delegation of Israeli Arabs paid an unprecedented visit to Syria, ostensibly to offer President Asad condolences on the death of his eldest son, Basil. Towards the end of 1994 reports indicated the likelihood of a breakthrough in negotiations between Syria and Israel.

Syria has endeavoured, with some success, to improve its image in the West. Indeed, in October, US President Clinton visited Damascus. In November the European Union lifted its arms embargo, imposed in 1986, after Syria was implicated in an attempt to plant a bomb on an Israeli plane in London. Nonetheless, Syria remained on the US state department's list of countries sponsoring terrorism.

Despite the recent release of many political prisoners, Syria was still condemned for violating civil rights. In 1994, Amnesty International reiterated its concern about the number of executions, the lack of fair trials and the detention of more than a thousand political prisoners.

HISTORICAL LEGACY

Following the Ottoman conquest in 1516, the Jewish community, which dates back to the third century BCE, prospered in cultural, political and economic terms. In 1840, however, the Jews were accused of murdering a Capuchin friar and using his blood for the manufacture of Passover bread; this so-called "Damascus affair" may represent the first use of doctrinaire Christian European antisemitism in the Muslim Arab world. A series of late nineteenth-century reforms, known as the Tanzimat, granted legal

equality to Jews; nonetheless many started to emigrate for economic reasons.

In 1947, there were about 30,000 Jews in Syria. Hostility towards Israel led to officially orchestrated riots in Aleppo and Damascus, which destroyed hundreds of Jewish homes and several synagogues. Many Jews were killed and 15,000 fled the country. A further 10,000 subsequently left during periods when emigration restrictions were temporarily lifted.

During the 1960s, the Ba'ath regime subjected Syrian Jews to strict supervision by the security services. Jews were denied most civil rights, economically harassed and often threatened with violence. Their situation gradually improved after Asad assumed power in 1970. Nevertheless, Jews were still prevented from emigrating and their mobility within the country was restricted. Among those attempting to leave Syria illegally were several Jewish women, some of whom were detained and killed. The issue of emigration was raised in discussions between Syria and US officials, and by the Israeli delegation to the Madrid peace talks in 1991.

In 1992, the regime announced that Jews could leave Syria provided their destination was not Israel and that the purpose of their trip was study, tourism or business. By early 1993, some 2,400 Jews had emigrated, mostly to the USA. Towards the end of 1992, however, the Syrians temporarily halted Jewish emigration, apparently in order to express dissatisfaction with what it saw as the slow pace of the development of Syrian-US relations and the Middle East peace process. In December 1993, when the US secretary of state, Warren Christopher, visited Damascus, Syria issued 200 exit visas to Jews and agreed to allow further emigration in 1994.

Towards the end of 1994 only 230 Jews had chosen to remain. A few Jewish families reportedly returned to Syria, hoping to benefit from the increasing economic prosperity. Of a total of 3,800 Jews who left Syria since 1992, 1,300 have emigrated to Israel.

MANIFESTATIONS

After the massacre of Muslims by a Jewish settler in a Hebron mosque in February, an antisemitic manifesto was distributed in Damascus by a little-known group called the Syrian Muslim Party of Justice. The leaflet warned Jews that "Hitler was weak in comparison to what we will do to you" and asserted that "the blood of all Jews living in Syria will be spilled". Although the Syrian authorities attempted to deny its existence—an article in the daily, *Tishreen,* on 5 March, for example, claimed that allegations about a threat to the Jewish community in Syria were fabrications and that Syrian Jews enjoyed the same rights as any other citizens—security measures were reportedly increased outside Jewish businesses, homes and synagogues.

PUBLICATIONS AND MEDIA

A series of antisemitic texts published in Damascus from the late 1980s accused Jews of using blood for ceremonial purposes and of promoting hatred towards other religions. Among the most prominent antisemitic publications are "The Matza of Zion" by Syrian Minister of Defence Mustafa Tlass, published by his Dar al-Tlass publishing company, which attempted to prove the 1840 blood libel against the Jews of Damascus.

Changes in Syria's foreign policy are perceived by the government-controlled media as a necessary evil, and therefore there has been no accompanying change in the regime's attitude towards Israel (which is implicitly identified with the Jews). Antisemitic cartoons continued to appear frequently in the media. Those published in *al-Thawra* on 9 and 14 August, for example, showed Jews as deformed, and those in *al-Thawra*

on 6 September portrayed Jews as aggressive.

An article in the English-language *Syria Times,* which is published by the official government daily *Tishreen,* alleged that Jews manipulate American foreign policy, control the majority of American newspapers and are disproportionately represented in the White House and state department. It also asserted that "the secret of Jewish influence on the American arena lies in their understanding of the nature of American society" and continued: "Jews used all forms of falsification of historical facts in order to mislead the public."

In his interview on Israeli television in October, Foreign Minister Farouq al-Shar'a stated that Israel had benefited from its influence over the Western media to project an image of itself as a victim in its struggle with the Arabs, thereby implying Jewish control over the media.

LEGAL MATTERS

During the last two years, most of the restrictions imposed on Syrian Jews have been lifted. In 1994, for example, the special stamp of *musawi* in the identity card was changed to a small blue sign. Nevertheless, Jews remained subject to the supervision of the security services.

ASSESSMENT

The gradual progress achieved in the peace negotiations has also contributed to the disappearance of an ancient Jewish community, due to the emigration of most of its members. Changes in foreign policy did not alter Syria's perception of Israel and Jews, which remained deeply hostile, as evidenced by antisemitic representations in the media.

Tunisia

General population: 8.7 million
Jewish population: 2,500 (mainly in Tunis and
Djerba)

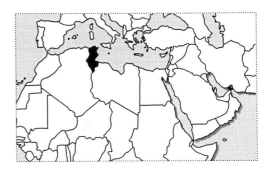

GENERAL BACKGROUND

The Tunisian constitution provides for a parliamentary democracy with separation of powers,
but decision-making at all levels is dominated
by the president, General Zine el-Abidine Ben
Ali, and his party, the Rassemblement consti-
tutionel démocratique (RCD, Constitutional
Democratic Rally). Ben Ali replaced President
Habib Bourguiba in a bloodless coup in 1987,
and, as sole candidate, was elected president in
1989.

On 20 March Ben Ali was re-elected unop-
posed with 99.9 per cent of the vote and the
RCD won 144 of the 163 seats in the national
assembly. Electoral reforms introduced in 1993
enabled six legal opposition parties to gain representation for the first time with nineteen seats
amongst them. The outlawed Islamist party, al-
Nahda (Renaissance), was not permitted to
contest the elections.

Tunisia was criticized by Amnesty International for systematic human rights violations
including the detention of 8,000 political prisoners. Concern over the escalation of political
violence in neighbouring Algeria led to a crackdown on potential opposition forces. The regime arrested suspected members of al-Nahda
and restricted the activities of trade unionists
and members of the banned Communist Workers' Party.

Despite a severe drought, Tunisia benefited
from a substantial increase in tourism, resulting
in economic growth of 6 per cent.

Following the signing of the Israeli-
Palestinian Declaration of Principles in September 1993, relations between Israel and Tunisia
have also improved. The Tunisian-born
general-secretary of the Israeli Labour Party,
Nissim Zvilli, led an official delegation to
Tunisia which resulted in the opening in October of interest offices in the Belgian embassies
in Tel Aviv and Tunis. Yossi Beilin, Israel's
deputy foreign minister, met with Tunisian
authorities to discuss in particular the issue of
tourism.

HISTORICAL LEGACY

In the early years of Islam, at least in certain
periods, Jews were tolerated and even respected. By the nineteenth century, most Jews
lived in squalor in the sprawling ghettos of

Tunisian cities. The conditions of the Jews of
southern Tunisia and those on the island of
Djerba were considerably better.

Tunisia was occupied by France in 1830
and a French protectorate was established in
1881. By and large, the Jews benefited from the
French presence. The so-called "fundamental
pact" of 1857 gave equality under the law to
non-Muslims, and other liberal measures were
introduced even before the protectorate. During the Second World War, the brief German
occupation of Tunisia led to the establishment
of forced labour camps for thousands of Jews.

Following independence in 1956, the situation of Tunisian Jewry was tolerable but anti-
Jewish rioting broke out during the Six Day
War in 1967, resulting in the destruction of several Jewish shops and damage to the Great
Synagogue in Tunis. Despite the authorities'
concern to allay the fears of the Jewish community, occasional attacks on Jews and Jewish
property have recurred, among them the
destruction in 1979 of a synagogue on the island
of Djerba and, in 1983, of a synagogue in Zaris,
near the Libyan border.

Since 1982, the presence of the Palestine
Liberation Organization's headquarters in
Tunis (tolerated by the Tunisian government
not least for economic reasons) deterred Jewish
visitors to Tunisia. Nonetheless, the Tunisian
authorities have recently encouraged tourism
from Tunisian-born Jews, including many rabbis who emigrated to France or Israel, and have
sought to promote business links through these
visits.

PARTIES, ORGANIZATIONS, MOVEMENTS

The founder and leader of al-Nahda, Rashid al-
Ghannouchi, who was granted political asylum
in the United Kingdom in 1993 after receiving a
life sentence *in absentia* for plotting to assassinate the president, continued to exercise influence over the movement in Tunisia. Al-
Ghannouchi has invoked antisemitic themes
such as the claim that Jews and Zionists are

responsible for a world-wide campaign against Islam.

In August a new Islamist group with the same name as the Algerian Islamist party, Front islamique du salut (FIS, Islamic Salvation Front), was reportedly established in Tunisia. Led by Mohamed Ali El-Horani, the group advocated armed revolt in Tunisia and criticized al-Ghannouchi for denouncing violence in interviews with the Western press. It published a newsletter from Vienna called *El-Rajna*.

EFFECTS OF ANTI-ZIONISM

Ahmed Khalaoui, a teacher and trade unionist, was arrested on 4 March for distributing illegal leaflets after the massacre of Muslims by a Jewish settler in a Hebron mosque. The leaflets called for confrontation with all Jews, both in Tunisia and other countries, and a boycott of all conferences and scientific meetings attended by Jews. It also condemned all economic and political dealings with Jews and called for the Tunisian people to harass the Jewish community in Djerba.

LEGAL MATTERS

On 27 June Ahmed Khalaoui was sentenced to two years' imprisonment and a fine of 1,000 dinars for incitement of hatred between races, religions and peoples, and to eight months' imprisonment for publication of leaflets liable to disturb public order (see **Effects of Anti-Zionism**). Khalaoui's case was brought to the attention of the United Nations Working Group on Arbitrary Detention which decided on 28 September that the restrictions placed by Tunisian law on freedom of opinion in order to combat the dissemination of racist ideas were compatible with international law.

COUNTERING ANTISEMITISM

The Tunisian ambassador to the United Nations Economic, Social and Cultural Organization held a series of seminars in Paris which aimed to bring together Jewish and Arab intellectuals of Tunisian origin.

ASSESSMENT

Despite their liberal treatment by the Bourguiba and Ben Ali regimes, Tunisian Jews have always felt vulnerable. Strong elements in Tunisia have supported Arab nationalism and a potential threat is posed by the Islamic fundamentalist movement. Although the current regime has attempted to limit the influence of Islamic radicals, the latter have a substantial infrastructure which may result in violence against foreigners and Jews should the domestic situation worsen.

Southern Africa

THE INSTITUTE OF JEWISH AFFAIRS AND THE AMERICAN JEWISH COMMITTEE

Namibia

General population: 1.6 million
Jewish population: 60 (mainly in Windhoek)

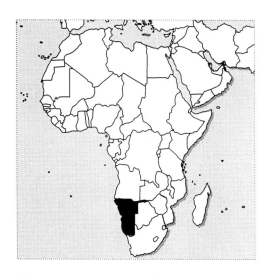

GENERAL BACKGROUND

Namibia gained independence from South Africa in 1990 and is now a democracy led by President Sam Nujoma. The first elections were held in December 1994. The South West Africa People's Organization (SWAPO) maintained a majority in parliament and the main opposition party is the Democratic Turnhalle Alliance (DTA).

Relations between Namibia and Israel have warmed since the advent of the Middle East peace process, leading to the establishment of diplomatic relations on 11 February.

PARTIES, ORGANIZATIONS AND MOVEMENTS

A small number of German neo-Nazis operate covertly in Namibia but little is known about their activities.

PUBLICATIONS AND MEDIA

A full page advertisement was placed in the English-language daily, *Windhoek Advertiser*, on the seventh anniversary of the death of the Rudolf Hess. The advertisement evoked sympathy for Hess, describing him as a "martyr for peace", comparing him with Christ and glorifying the Third Reich and its leaders. It stated that Hess "and his fellow accused repented of nothing because there was nothing to repent". German and Afrikaans newspapers refrained from publishing the advertisement at the request of their publishers.

DENIAL OF THE HOLOCAUST

Following the release of the film *Schindler's List*, the German newspaper, *Allgemeine Zeitung,* published a number of letters, some of which denounced the film as a mere display of film director Steven Spielberg's imagination while others acknowledged its historical authenticity (see **Countering Antisemitism**).

COUNTERING ANTISEMITISM

The German ambassador in Namibia, Dr Hans Schumacher, invited a few hundred schoolchildren, including those from German schools, to screenings of *Schindler's List*. Although the initiative was welcomed by the Jewish community, it also exacerbated controversy over the film (see **Denial of the Holocaust**).

Dr Schumacher also condemned the advertisement in the *Windhoek Advertiser* which glorified Rudolf Hess, on the grounds that it was blasphemous and that in Germany it would have violated laws against discrimination (see **Publications and Media**).

ASSESSMENT

The Jewish community enjoys good relations with President Nujoma, (who has indicated his interest in encouraging Jewish immigration), with the current regime, and with other religious and ethnic communities in Namibia. There is little evidence of antisemitism in Namibia.

South Africa

General population: 41.8 million
Jewish population: 100,000 (mainly in Johannesburg and Capetown)

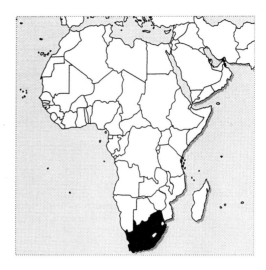

GENERAL BACKGROUND

South Africa's first democratic elections on 27-8 April demonstrated overwhelming support for the African National Congress (ANC), in alliance with the South African Communist Party (SACP). In addition to winning 62.6 per cent of the national vote, the ANC gained control of seven of the nine provincial legislatures. The National Party (NP) attained 20.4 per cent of the national vote and won control of the Western Cape provincial legislature, while the Inkatha Freedom Party (IFP) gained 10.5 per cent of the national vote and won control of the Kwazulu-Natal provincial legislature. The left-wing Pan Africanist Congress (PAC) won only 1.25 per cent of the national vote, and the far-right Freedom Front (FF) only 2.2 per cent. The Democratic Party (DP), which historically represented liberal, white opposition, obtained 1.4 per cent of the national vote.

On 10 May Nelson Mandela was inaugurated as South Africa's first democratically-elected president, who will preside over a national unity government. Thabo Mbeki of the ANC was appointed first deputy president and F. W. De Klerk second deputy president. A constituent assembly began to draft a new constitution. The Reconstruction and Development Programme (RDP) was launched.

The successfully conducted election engendered great optimism, although political violence, confined largely to Kwazulu-Natal province, continued. Labour disputes and criminal violence dampened optimism and lowered investor confidence but the year ended with the country broadly united behind the RDP.

HISTORICAL LEGACY

The ban on Jewish settlement at the Cape, introduced during the rule of the Dutch East India Company (1652-1795) was abrogated by the Batavian administration (1803-1806) and the British. In the South African Republic (Transvaal), established by the Voortrekkers in the mid-nineteenth century, non-Protestants (including Jews) remained disenfranchised until the British occupation in 1902.

Jewish immigration, mainly from Lithuania, following the discovery of diamonds and gold in the late nineteenth century, generated considerable antisemitism. During the First World War antisemites accused Jews of shirking military responsibilities and, in the post-war years, tried to associate Jews with Bolshevik subversion. Antisemitism in the 1920s culminated in the 1930 Quota Act, which virtually ended Jewish immigration from Eastern Europe.

Popular antisemitism during the 1930s and 1940s, was evident among the "Shirt" movements (most notably Louis T. Weichardt's Greyshirts, the Ossewabrandwag (Oxwagon Sentinel) and Oswald Pirow's New Order). The Afrikaner nationalist movement was also influenced by Nazi ideology. Antisemitism prompted the governing United Party to introduce the 1937 Aliens Act curtailing German-Jewish immigration. National Party publications during the Second World War were also influenced by European fascism.

Antisemitism declined rapidly after 1945, although Prime Minister Jan Smuts opposed large-scale Jewish immigration. The Greyshirts and New Order disbanded and, in 1951, the ban on Jewish membership of the Transvaal National Party was lifted. Nonetheless, the NP, in power since 1948, resented disproportionate Jewish involvement in liberal and communist activities and Israel's support for the African bloc at the United Nations in the early 1960s.

Close ties between South Africa and Israel developed in the 1970s, engendering favourable attitudes towards the Jews on the part of the white population, although antisemitic outbursts, including expressions of Holocaust denial, were prevalent among elements of the white far right.

The majority black population felt betrayed by Israel's close relations with South Africa and sympathized with the Palestinian cause. Although black leaders clearly distinguished between anti-Zionism and antisemitism, there are indications of some anti-Jewish attitudes among black élites. Since the "normalization" of South African politics, antisemitic incidents have been relatively isolated and largely confined to the far right.

RACISM AND XENOPHOBIA
The 1994 Interim Constitution and Bill of Fundamental Rights explicitly prohibited discrimination on the grounds of race, gender, ethnic or social origin, colour, sexual orientation, age, disability, religion, conscience, belief, culture or language. Despite the dramatic political and legal changes witnessed in 1994, *de facto* racial discrimination remained widespread.

PARTIES, ORGANIZATIONS, MOVEMENTS
In 1969 the Herstigte Nasionale Party (HNP, Reconstituted National Party) was formed to counter deviation from apartheid philosophy and to uphold the idea of Christian Afrikaner nationalism. Although not avowedly antisemitic, the party's official organ, *Die Afrikaner* (circulation 8,000), has featured numerous anti-Jewish articles including Holocaust-denial material. The party has, however, remained a marginal political influence.

In 1981 the Afrikaner Weerstandsbeweging (AWB, Afrikaner Resistance Movement) became active. Its leader, Eugene Terre'Blanche, pursues exclusivist, racist and antisemitic policies. The movement includes a paramilitary outfit, the Storm Falcons, and a crack guerrilla unit, the Ystergarde (Iron Guard). Although the organization claims more than 40,000 members, the commandos have no more than 5,000 members. Several bombings during the period leading up to the April election were initiated by the AWB and a number of key members were arrested. Since the election the AWB has limited its operations and shifted its focus towards defensive activities.

Antisemitic views are also expounded in approximately 120 small white supremacist groups and neo-Nazi cells, including the Israelites, the Church of the Creator (COTC), the Kultuur Studie Groep (Culture Study Group), the Blanke Bevrydingsbeweging (White Liberation Movement), the World Preservatist Movement (formerly the World Apartheid Movement), the Afrikaner Nationalist Socialist Movement, the Kerk van die Verbondsvolk (Church of the People of the Covenant) and the Boere Republican Army. In terms of membership and influence, these groups are of little consequence.

Many right-wing groups have toned down

their rhetoric and some activists have left South Africa. Dr Jan Smith, former head of the COTC, reportedly had his immigration application to New Zealand delayed (see **New Zealand**). Many right-wing groups may adapt to the new circumstances in South Africa without resorting to violence but the Afrikaner Volksfront, an umbrella Afrikaner body, is strongly divided.

MANIFESTATIONS
Antisemitic Hanukkah cards, similar to those distributed in Britain, were sent to a member of the Cape Town Jewish community as well as Nobel prize-winning author, Nadine Gordimer, and Chief Rabbi Cyril Harris (see **United Kingdom**).

Bomb scares occurred at two Jewish schools in Johannesburg in March but no bombs were found.

A number of incidents were reported in 1994 involving verbal attacks against Jews. In May, for example, antisemitic abuse was hurled at guests at a Jewish wedding in a Johannesburg hotel by the Bavarian Rugby Supporters from Bloemfontein. A security guard outside a synagogue in Johannesburg was insulted by people in a passing car. In November, the chair of a tenants' association condemned "Jewish landlords" in an interview with the *Johannesburg City Vision* newspaper about the inner city housing crisis in Johannesburg. His remarks were criticized by an alliance of the ANC Youth League, the SACP and other organizations.

A Jewish employee of a hospital in Johannesburg consulted the Industrial Relations Training and Consultancy Service over a sustained antisemitic campaign by another member of staff. The consultancy service advised the hospital that discrimination on the grounds of religious conviction was a serious violation of the individual's constitutional rights.

Of particular concern was the increase in the level of industrial disputes which involved protests against Jewish "capitalists" and "exploiters of the workers". Antisemitic placards were displayed at six strikes around the country between mid-May and early August and at some of them slogans were chanted. A pamphlet accusing Jews of controlling the country and calling for the killing of the "capitalist Jew pigs" was distributed at a strike by Volkswagen car workers in Port Elizabeth in August. Some of the placards read "Away with the Jewish settlers", "Jews dismiss innocent workers" and "Jews are union bashers".

The Congress of South African Trades

Unions (COSATU), the largest trade union federation in South Africa, unanimously agreed that anti-Jewish slogans were racist and contrary to their policy of non-racialism.

In Johannesburg a shop steward was found guilty of racially abusing a Jewish store manager. The shop steward's dismissal was challenged by the union but when an arbitrator was appointed the dismissal was upheld.

In another case, strikers chanted antisemitic slogans at Highlands House, a Jewish old-age home in Cape Town. The dispute arose following the dismissal of a number of employees affiliated to the National Education Health and Allied Workers Union (NEHAWU), who had participated in an illegal strike in April. The union's president, Vusi Nhlapo, condemned the antisemitic slogans and said the march was supported by people from organizations over which NEHAWU had no control.

EDUCATION

In September a letter alleging a Jewish conspiracy and threatening to "finish what Hitler started" was sent to the principal of the King David High School in Johannesburg.

PUBLICATIONS AND MEDIA

Die Afrikaner, the official newspaper of the HNP, featured numerous antisemitic articles as well as Holocaust-denial material (see **Parties, Organizations, Movements**). An antisemitic cartoon of a Nazi concentration camp was published in an article on Holocaust denial in the October issue of *Hustler*, a pornographic monthly. This issue was declared "undesirable" under the Publications Act due to its pornographic content. Another antisemitic joke appeared in the November issue of *Hustler*.

An advertisement which appeared for four days in August in Johannesburg's daily newspaper, *The Star*, challenged the facts of the Holocaust and raised other canards such as Zionist collaboration with the SS during the Second World War. The advert, entitled "Jews against Zionism", was allegedly placed by Rabbi Schwartz from the "American Neturei Karta" but this was denied by Neturei Karta.

RELIGION

Antisemitism is prevalent among certain Muslim groups in South Africa, but was not highly visible in 1994.

A militant Islamic group called al-Qibla, which is closely allied to the Pan Africanist Congress (PAC), propagates extreme anti-Zionist and often antisemitic views. The PAC, however, has taken some pains to show that it is not antisemitic and has condemned terrorist incidents in Israel.

There was, however, evidence of Christian theological antisemitism in sermons broadcast on the radio. Father Desmond Nair, for example, speaking on a religious programme on Radio SA on 12 December, blamed the Jews at the time of Jesus for not accepting him as their saviour.

DENIAL OF THE HOLOCAUST

In March, Dr Milton Shain, a historian at the University of Cape Town, faced a barrage of Holocaust-denial questions following a lecture to the Cape Town Military History Society. Numerous members of the audience referred to the *Leuchter Report* (see **United States**).

Examples of Holocaust denial in the media are relatively rare in South Africa and are invariably countered by members of the public. The "Anne Frank in the World" exhibition, which toured South Africa during most of 1994, was condemned in many letters and phone calls. In March, for example, a Dr Migeod wrote to the *Cape Times* questioning the authenticity of Anne Frank's diary, and in October, Jaap Marais, leader of the HNP, wrote to the director of the Pretoria Art Museum (where the exhibition was mounted in October) alleging that Anne Frank's diary was known to be a forgery. The HNP published a letter in *Die Afrikaner* by G. T. Robertson of Cape Town supporting Holocaust denial. Following the banning of the October issue of *Hustler* (see **Publications and Media**), a letter from C. Za Verdinos of Pietermaritzburg was published in a Johannesburg daily, *The Citizen*, entitled "Holocaust denial ban is unfair". The writer claimed that "in none of the post-war trials has material evidence been produced to prove mass-killings took place by means of gas-chambers".

EFFECTS OF ANTI-ZIONISM

Anti-Zionist literature which featured antisemitic themes was distributed on university campuses on al-Quds Day during the Muslim holy month of Ramadan.

LEGAL MATTERS

In February a twenty-year-old Cape Town man and a fourteen-year-old youth who had made antisemitic remarks and obscene gestures at a Jewish neighbour were ordered by the supreme court to stop harassing or threatening the neighbour.

The Johannesburg supreme court heard the case of M. Levitas, a Jewish town councillor in Springs, who had called an emergency meeting in 1992 to discuss a boycott. In response to Levitas's remark that some accommodation for black aspirations needed to be made, Dr R. D. L. Gous, a Conservative Party member, said: "Spoken like a true Jew, no wonder they killed six million of them." Dr Gous refused to apologize and was fined R30,000.

COUNTERING ANTISEMITISM

The South African Jewish Board of Deputies monitored antisemitism and responded to incidents and offensive statements where appropriate. The Board also promoted dialogue with opinion-makers in the wider community.

During an address in a Cape Town synagogue, shortly before his inauguration, President-elect Nelson Mandela thanked Jews for their contribution to South Africa and assured the congregation that they had nothing to fear from a government of national unity. He also affirmed his recognition of the state of Israel along with the right of Palestinians to their own homeland.

In 1994, the "Anne Frank in the World" exhibition toured South Africa, promoting tolerance and understanding. The exhibition was accompanied by an exhibit on "Apartheid and Resistance" compiled by the Mayibuye Centre of the University of the Western Cape. The exhibition, which was seen by almost 100,000 people, was opened by President Mandela in Johannesburg and by Archbishop Desmond Tutu in Cape Town. Although the exhibition provoked some criticism, it created opportunities for members of the Jewish community to meet with other groups to promote tolerance and to counter discrimination (see also **Denial of the Holocaust**).

ASSESSMENT

1994 was a historic year for South Africa, with democratic elections in April and the beginning of a transformation of the political and social structures. Antisemitism was of marginal significance in South African public life and was generally not more prevalent than in 1993. Ultimately the fate of South African Jews is tied up with that of the white population as a whole. Given the ANC's opposition to racism, the climate for opposing antisemitism in South Africa publicly is more favourable than it has been in the past. The quick repudiation of occasional and individual expressions of antisemitism by various organizations and institutions bears testimony to this. The acceptance of South Africa as a multi-faith society, shown by the participation of the chief rabbi and Hindu and Muslim representatives at the inauguration of President Mandela, has also helped to create a new climate.